Genetic Disorders

SOURCEBOOK

SEVENTH EDITION

Genetic Disorders
SOURCEBOOK

SEVENTH EDITION

Basic Consumer Health Information about Heritable Disorders, Including Disorders Resulting from Abnormalities in Specific Genes, Such as Hemophilia, Sickle Cell Disease, and Cystic Fibrosis, Chromosomal Disorders, Such as Down Syndrome, Fragile X Syndrome, and Klinefelter Syndrome, and Complex Disorders with Environmental and Genetic Components, Such as Alzheimer Disease, Cancer, Heart Disease, and Obesity

Along with Information about the Human Genome Project, Genetic Testing and Newborn Screening, Gene Therapy and Other Current Research Initiatives, the Special Needs of Children with Genetic Disorders, a Glossary of Terms, and a Directory of Resources for Further Help and Information

OMNIGRAPHICS

615 Griswold, Ste. 520, Detroit, MI 48226

Bibliographic Note
Because this page cannot legibly accommodate all the copyright notices, the Bibliographic Note portion of the Preface constitutes an extension of the copyright notice.

* * *

OMNIGRAPHICS
Angela L. Williams, *Managing Editor*
* * *

Copyright © 2019 Omnigraphics

ISBN 978-0-7808-1694-7
E-ISBN 978-0-7808-1696-1

Library of Congress Cataloging-in-Publication Data

Names: Omnigraphics, Inc., issuing body.

Title: Genetic disorders sourcebook: basic consumer health information about heritable disorders, including disorders resulting from abnormalities in specific genes, such as hemophilia, sickle cell disease, and cystic fibrosis, chromosomal disorders, such as down syndrome, fragile X syndrome, and klinefelter syndrome, and complex disorders with environmental and genetic components, such as alzheimer disease, cancer, heart disease, and obesity; along with information about the human genome project, genetic testing and newborn screening, gene therapy and other current research initiatives, the special needs of children with genetic disorders, a glossary of terms, and a directory of resources for further help and information.

Description: Seventh edition. | Detroit, MI: Omnigraphics, [2019] | Series: Health reference series | Includes index.

Identifiers: LCCN 2018061623 (print) | LCCN 2019000434 (ebook) | ISBN 9780780816961 (ebook) | ISBN 9780780816947 (hard cover: alk. paper)

Subjects: LCSH: Human chromosome abnormalities--Popular works.

Classification: LCC RB155.5 (ebook) | LCC RB155.5.G455 2019 (print) | DDC 616/.042--dc23

LC record available at https://lccn.loc.gov/2018061623

Table of Contents

Part III: Chromosome Abnormalities

Part IV: Complex Disorders with Genetic and Environmental Components

Part V: Genetic Research

Part VI: Information for Parents of Children with Genetic Disorders

Part VII: Additional Help and Information

Preface

About This Book

Genes provide the information that directs the human body's basic cellular activities. Research on the human genome has shown that the DNA sequences of any two individuals are 99.9 percent identical. That 0.1 percent variation, however, is profoundly important. It contributes to visible differences, such as height and hair color, and also to invisible differences, such as increased risk for—or protection from—a myriad of diseases and disorders.

As medical researchers unlock the secrets of the human genome, they are learning that nearly all diseases have a genetic component. Some are caused by a mutation in a gene or group of genes. Such mutations can occur randomly or as the result of exposure to hazardous conditions or substances. Other disorders are hereditary. These can be passed down from generation to generation within a family. Finally, many—perhaps most—genetic disorders are caused by a combination of small variations in genes operating in concert with environmental factors.

Genetic Disorders Sourcebook, Seventh Edition offers updated information on how genes work and how genetic mutations affect health. It provides facts about the most common genetic disorders, including those that arise from mutations in specific genes—for example, muscular dystrophy, sickle cell anemia, and cystic fibrosis—as well as those arising from chromosomal abnormalities—such as Down syndrome and fragile X syndrome. A section on disorders with genetic and environmental components explains the hereditary components of Alzheimer disease, cancer, diabetes, mental illness, obesity, addiction, and others.

Reports on current research initiatives provide detailed information on the newest breakthroughs in the causes and treatments of genetic disorders, including strategies—such as gene therapy, nutrigenomics, and pharmacogenetics—that could radically change how these disorders are treated in the future. A section for parents of children with genetic disorders offers information about assistive technologies, educational options, transition to adulthood, and estate planning. Information about genetic counseling, prenatal testing, newborn screening, and preventing genetic discrimination is also provided. The book concludes with a glossary of genetic terms and a list of resources for additional help and information.

How to Use This Book

This book is divided into parts and chapters. Parts focus on broad areas of interest. Chapters are devoted to single topics within a part.

Part I: Introduction to Genetics describes how genes work and explains what is known about how genetic mutations affect health. It details how genetic inheritance works, explains when genetic counseling might be advisable, and describes how genetic testing works and the type of information it can provide. The part concludes with a discussion of the legal framework currently in place to prevent discrimination on the basis of genetic background.

Part II: Disorders Resulting from Abnormalities in Specific Genes provides basic information about the types of disorders that are caused by changes in one or more genes. These include blood and clotting disorders, connective tissue disorders, heart rhythm disorders, muscular dystrophy and other neuromuscular disorders, cystic fibrosis, and hearing and vision disorders. Individual chapters include information about the inheritance, symptoms, diagnosis, and treatment of each disorder.

Part III: Chromosome Abnormalities offers detailed information about the types of disorders caused by changes in chromosomes. It explains how Down syndrome, fragile X syndrome, Turner syndrome, and other chromosomal disorders are inherited and describes the diagnostic tests and treatment techniques used.

Part IV: Complex Disorders with Genetic and Environmental Components explains what is known about the causes of addiction, obesity, mental-health disorders, heart disease, diabetes, cancer, and other disorders with both genetic and environmental components. It describes the genetic associations related to each disorder and discusses the research advances that may lead to improved prevention efforts and treatment outcomes.

Part V: Genetic Research describes recent advances in the field of genetics as doctors seek ways to use knowledge of an individual's genetic background to target disease prevention and treatment techniques. It includes a discussion of what has been discovered during the course of the Human Genome Project and describes promising new avenues of research, including pharmacogenomics and gene therapy.

Part VI: Information for Parents of Children with Genetic Disorders addresses the challenges of raising special needs children. It discusses early interventions, assistive technologies, educational concerns, and the transition into adulthood. The part also explains government benefits available to children and adults with disabilities and offers estate planning information for families of children with special needs.

Part VII: Additional Help and Information includes a glossary of terms related to human genetics and a directory of resources offering additional help and support.

Bibliographic Note

This volume contains documents and excerpts from publications issued by the following U.S. government agencies: Center for Parent Information and Resources (CPIR); Centers for Disease Control and Prevention (CDC); Child Welfare Information Gateway; *Eunice Kennedy Shriver* National Institute of Child Health and Human Development (NICHD); Genetic and Rare Diseases Information Center (GARD); Genetics Home Reference (GHR); MedlinePlus; National Cancer Institute (NCI); National Eye Institute (NEI); National Heart, Lung, and Blood Institute (NHLBI); National Human Genome Research Institute (NHGRI); National Institute of Arthritis and Musculoskeletal and Skin Diseases (NIAMS); National Institute of Diabetes and Digestive and Kidney Diseases (NIDDK); National Institute of Environmental Health Sciences (NIEHS); National Institute of General Medical Sciences (NIGMS); National Institute of Mental Health (NIMH); National Institute of Neurological Disorders and Stroke (NINDS); National Institute on Aging (NIA); National Institute on Deafness and Other Communication Disorders (NIDCD); National Institute on Drug Abuse

(NIDA); National Institutes of Health (NIH); Office on Women's Health (OWH); Research Portfolio Online Reporting Tools (RePORT); U.S. Department of Education (ED); and U.S. Drug Enforcement Administration (DEA).

About the Health Reference Series

The *Health Reference Series* is designed to provide basic medical information for patients, families, caregivers, and the general public. Each volume takes a particular topic and provides comprehensive coverage. This is especially important for people who may be dealing with a newly diagnosed disease or a chronic disorder in themselves or in a family member. People looking for preventive guidance, information about disease warning signs, medical statistics, and risk factors for health problems will also find answers to their questions in the *Health Reference Series*. The *Series*, however, is not intended to serve as a tool for diagnosing illness, in prescribing treatments, or as a substitute for the physician/patient relationship. All people concerned about medical symptoms or the possibility of disease are encouraged to seek professional care from an appropriate healthcare provider.

A Note about Spelling and Style

Health Reference Series editors use *Stedman's Medical Dictionary* as an authority for questions related to the spelling of medical terms and the *Chicago Manual of Style* for questions related to grammatical structures, punctuation, and other editorial concerns. Consistent adherence is not always possible, however, because the individual volumes within the *Series* include many documents from a wide variety of different producers, and the editor's primary goal is to present material from each source as accurately as is possible. This sometimes means that information in different chapters or sections may follow other guidelines and alternate spelling authorities. For example, occasionally a copyright holder may require that eponymous terms be shown in possessive forms (Crohn's disease vs. Crohn disease) or that British spelling norms be retained (leukaemia vs. leukemia).

Medical Review

Omnigraphics contracts with a team of qualified, senior medical professionals who serve as medical consultants for the *Health*

Reference Series. As necessary, medical consultants review reprinted material for currency and accuracy. Citations including the phrase "Reviewed (month, year)" indicate material reviewed by this team. Medical consultation services are provided to the *Health Reference Series* editors by:

Dr. Vijayalakshmi, MBBS, DGO, MD
Dr. Senthil Selvan, MBBS, DCH, MD
Dr. K. Sivanandham, MBBS, DCH, MS (Research), PhD

Our Advisory Board

We would like to thank the following board members for providing initial guidance on the development of this series:

- Dr. Lynda Baker, Associate Professor of Library and Information Science, Wayne State University, Detroit, MI

- Nancy Bulgarelli, William Beaumont Hospital Library, Royal Oak, MI

- Karen Imarisio, Bloomfield Township Public Library, Bloomfield Township, MI

- Karen Morgan, Mardigian Library, University of Michigan-Dearborn, Dearborn, MI

- Rosemary Orlando, St. Clair Shores Public Library, St. Clair Shores, MI

Health Reference Series *Update Policy*

The inaugural book in the *Health Reference Series* was the first edition of *Cancer Sourcebook* published in 1989. Since then, the *Series* has been enthusiastically received by librarians and in the medical community. In order to maintain the standard of providing high-quality health information for the layperson the editorial staff at Omnigraphics felt it was necessary to implement a policy of updating volumes when warranted.

Medical researchers have been making tremendous strides, and it is the purpose of the *Health Reference Series* to stay current with the most recent advances. Each decision to update a volume is made on an individual basis. Some of the considerations include how much new information is available and the feedback we receive from people who use the books. If there is a topic you would like to see added to the update list, or an area of medical concern you feel has not been adequately addressed, please write to:

Managing Editor
Health Reference Series
Omnigraphics
615 Griswold, Ste. 520
Detroit, MI 48226

Part One

Introduction to Genetics

Chapter 1

Cells and DNA: The Basics

What Is a Cell?

Cells are the basic building blocks of all living things. The human body is composed of trillions of cells. They provide structure for the body, take in nutrients from food, convert those nutrients into energy, and carry out specialized functions. Cells also contain the body's hereditary material and can make copies of themselves.

Cells have many parts, each with a different function. Some of these parts, called "organelles," are specialized structures that perform certain tasks within the cell. Human cells contain the following major parts, listed in alphabetical order:

- **Cytoplasm.** Within cells, the cytoplasm is made up of a jelly-like fluid (called "the cytosol") and other structures that surround the nucleus.

- **Cytoskeleton.** The cytoskeleton is a network of long fibers that make up the cell's structural framework. The cytoskeleton has several critical functions, including determining cell shape, participating in cell division, and allowing cells to move. It also provides a track-like system that directs the movement of organelles and other substances within cells.

This chapter includes text excerpted from "Help Me Understand Genetics— Cells and DNA," Genetics Home Reference (GHR), National Institutes of Health (NIH), February 19, 2019.

- **Endoplasmic reticulum (ER).** This organelle helps process molecules created by the cell. The endoplasmic reticulum (ER) also transports these molecules to their specific destinations either inside or outside the cell.

- **Golgi apparatus.** The Golgi apparatus packages molecules processed by the endoplasmic reticulum to be transported out of the cell.

- **Lysosomes and peroxisomes.** These organelles are the recycling center of the cell. They digest foreign bacteria that invade the cell, rid the cell of toxic substances, and recycle worn-out cell components.

- **Mitochondria.** Mitochondria are complex organelles that convert energy from food into a form that the cell can use. They have their own genetic material, separate from the deoxyribonucleic acid (DNA) in the nucleus, and can make copies of themselves.

- **Nucleus.** The nucleus serves as the cell's command center, sending directions to the cell to grow, mature, divide, or die. It also houses DNA, the cell's hereditary material. The nucleus is surrounded by a membrane called the "nuclear envelope," which protects the DNA and separates the nucleus from the rest of the cell.

- **Plasma membrane.** The plasma membrane is the outer lining of the cell. It separates the cell from its environment and allows materials to enter and leave the cell.

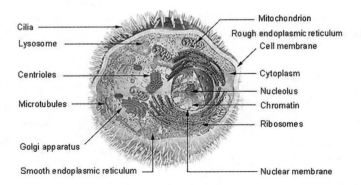

Figure 1.1. *Cell Structure* (Source: "Cell Structure," Surveillance, Epidemiology and End Results Program (SEER), National Cancer Institute (NCI).)

4

- **Ribosomes.** Ribosomes are organelles that process the cell's genetic instructions to create proteins. These organelles can float freely in the cytoplasm or be connected to the endoplasmic reticulum.

What Is Deoxyribonucleic Acid?

DNA is the hereditary material in humans and almost all other organisms. Nearly every cell in a person's body has the same DNA. Most DNA is located in the cell nucleus (where it is called "nuclear DNA"), but a small amount of DNA can also be found in the mitochondria (where it is called "mitochondrial DNA" or "mtDNA"). Mitochondria are structures within cells that convert the energy from food into a form that cells can use.

The information in DNA is stored as a code made up of four chemical bases: adenine (A), guanine (G), cytosine (C), and thymine (T). Human DNA consists of about three billion bases, and more than 99 percent of those bases are the same in all people. The order, or sequence, of these bases determines the information available for building and

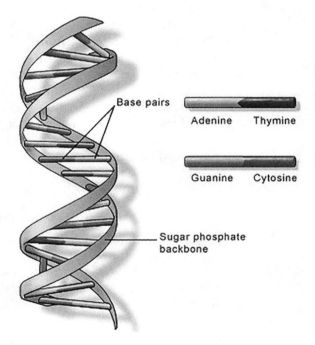

Figure 1.2. *Structure of DNA*

maintaining an organism, similar to the way in which letters of the alphabet appear in a certain order to form words and sentences.

DNA bases pair up with each other, A with T and C with G, to form units called "base pairs." Each base is also attached to a sugar molecule and a phosphate molecule. Together, a base, sugar, and phosphate are called a "nucleotide." Nucleotides are arranged in two long strands that form a spiral called a "double helix." The structure of the double helix is somewhat like a ladder, with the base pairs forming the ladder's rungs and the sugar and phosphate molecules forming the vertical side pieces of the ladder.

An important property of DNA is that it can replicate, or make copies of itself. Each strand of DNA in the double helix can serve as a pattern for duplicating the sequence of bases. This is critical when cells divide because each new cell needs to have an exact copy of the DNA present in the old cell.

What Is a Gene?

A gene is the basic physical and functional unit of heredity. Genes are made up of DNA. Some genes act as instructions to make molecules called "proteins." However, many genes do not code for proteins. In humans, genes vary in size from a few hundred DNA bases to more than 2 million bases. The Human Genome Project (HGP) estimated that humans have between 20,000 and 25,000 genes.

Every person has two copies of each gene, one inherited from each parent. Most genes are the same in all people, but a small number of genes (less than 1 percent of the total) are slightly different between people. Alleles are forms of the same gene with small differences in their sequence of DNA bases. These small differences contribute to each person's unique physical features.

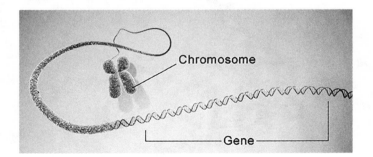

Figure 1.3. *Structure of a Gene*

Scientists keep track of genes by giving them unique names. Because gene names can be long, genes are also assigned symbols, which are short combinations of letters (and sometimes numbers) that represent an abbreviated version of the gene name. For example, a gene on chromosome seven that has been associated with cystic fibrosis is called the "cystic fibrosis transmembrane conductance regulator;" its symbol is CFTR.

What Is a Chromosome?

In the nucleus of each cell, the DNA molecule is packaged into threadlike structures called "chromosomes." Each chromosome is made up of DNA tightly coiled many times around proteins called "histones" that support its structure.

Chromosomes are not visible in the cell's nucleus—not even under a microscope—when the cell is not dividing. However, the DNA that makes up chromosomes becomes more tightly packed during cell division and is then visible under a microscope. Most of what researchers know about chromosomes was learned by observing chromosomes during cell division.

Each chromosome has a constriction point called the "centromere," which divides the chromosome into two sections, or "arms." The short

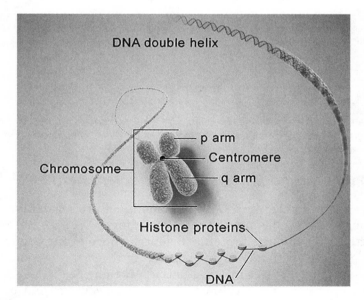

Figure 1.4. *Structure of a Chromosome*

7

arm of the chromosome is labeled the "p arm." The long arm of the chromosome is labeled the "q arm." The location of the centromere on each chromosome gives the chromosome its characteristic shape, and can be used to help describe the location of specific genes.

How Many Chromosomes Do People Have?

In humans, each cell normally contains 23 pairs of chromosomes, for a total of 46. Twenty-two of these pairs, called "autosomes," look the same in both males and females. The 23rd pair, the sex chromosomes, differ between males and females. Females have two copies of the X chromosome, while males have one X and one Y chromosome.

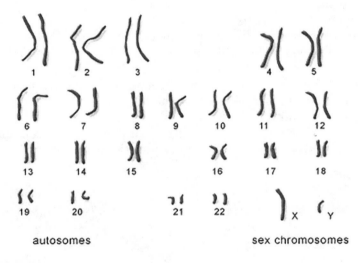

Figure 1.5. *Karyotype*

The 22 autosomes are numbered by size. The other two chromosomes, X and Y, are the sex chromosomes. This picture of the human chromosomes lined up in pairs is called a "karyotype."

What Is Noncoding Deoxyribonucleic Acid?

Only about 1 percent of DNA is made up of protein-coding genes; the other 99 percent is noncoding. Noncoding DNA does not provide instructions for making proteins. Scientists once thought noncoding DNA was "junk," with no known purpose. However, it is becoming clear that at least some of it is integral to the function of cells, particularly the control of gene activity. For example, noncoding DNA contains sequences that act as regulatory elements, determining when and where genes are turned on and off. Such elements provide sites for specialized proteins (called "transcription factors") to attach (bind) and either activate or repress the process by which the information from genes is turned into proteins (transcription). Noncoding DNA contains many types of regulatory elements:

- **Promoters** provide binding sites for the protein machinery that carries out transcription. Promoters are typically found just ahead of the gene on the DNA strand.

- **Enhancers** provide binding sites for proteins that help activate transcription. Enhancers can be found on the DNA strand before or after the gene they control, which are sometimes far away on the DNA strand.

- **Silencers** provide binding sites for proteins that repress transcription. Like enhancers, silencers can be found before or after the gene they control and can be some distance away on the DNA strand.

- **Insulators** provide binding sites for proteins that control transcription in a number of ways. Some prevent enhancers from aiding in transcription (enhancer-blocker insulators). Others prevent structural changes in the DNA that repress gene activity (barrier insulators). Some insulators can function as both an enhancer blocker and a barrier.

Other regions of noncoding DNA provide instructions for the formation of certain kinds of ribonucleic acid (RNA) molecules. RNA is a chemical cousin of DNA. Examples of specialized RNA molecules produced from noncoding DNA include transfer RNAs (tRNAs) and ribosomal RNAs (rRNAs), which help assemble protein building blocks (amino acids) into a chain that forms a protein; microRNAs (miRNAs), which are short lengths of RNA that block the process of protein production; and long noncoding RNAs (lncRNAs), which are longer lengths of RNA that have diverse roles in regulating gene activity.

Some structural elements of chromosomes are also part of noncoding DNA. For example, repeated noncoding DNA sequences at the ends of chromosomes form telomeres. Telomeres protect the ends of chromosomes from being degraded during the copying of genetic material. Repetitive noncoding DNA sequences also form satellite DNA, which is a part of other structural elements. Satellite DNA is the basis of the centromere, which is the constriction point of the X-shaped chromosome pair. Satellite DNA also forms heterochromatin, which is densely packed DNA that is important for controlling gene activity and maintaining the structure of chromosomes.

Some noncoding DNA regions, called "introns," are located within protein-coding genes but are removed before a protein is made. Regulatory elements, such as enhancers, can be located in introns. Other noncoding regions are found between genes and are known as "intergenic regions."

The identity of regulatory elements and other functional regions in noncoding DNA is not completely understood. Researchers are working to understand the location and role of these genetic components.

Chapter 2

How Genes Work

What Are Proteins and What Do They Do?

Proteins are large, complex molecules that play many critical roles in the body. They do most of the work in cells and are required for the structure, function, and regulation of the body's tissues and organs.

Proteins are made up of hundreds or thousands of smaller units called "amino acids," which are attached to one another in long chains.

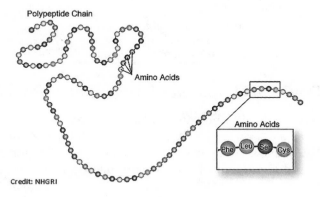

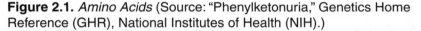

Figure 2.1. *Amino Acids* (Source: "Phenylketonuria," Genetics Home Reference (GHR), National Institutes of Health (NIH).)

This chapter includes text excerpted from "Help Me Understand Genetics—How Genes Work," Genetics Home Reference (GHR), National Institutes of Health (NIH), February 19, 2019.

There are 20 different types of amino acids that can be combined to make a protein. The sequence of amino acids determines each protein's unique three-dimensional structure and its specific function.

Proteins are described according to their large range of functions in the body, and are listed in alphabetical order:

Table 2.1. Examples of Protein Functions

Function	Description	Example
Antibody	Antibodies bind to specific foreign particles, such as viruses and bacteria, to help protect the body.	Immunoglobulin G (IgG)
Enzyme	Enzymes carry out almost all of the thousands of chemical reactions that take place in cells. They also assist with the formation of new molecules by reading the genetic information stored in DNA.	Phenylalanine hydroxylase
Messenger	Messenger proteins, such as some types of hormones, transmit signals to coordinate biological processes between different cells, tissues, and organs	Growth hormone
Structural component	These proteins provide structure and support for cells. On a larger scale, they also allow the body to move.	Actin
Transport/storage	These proteins bind and carry atoms and small molecules within cells and throughout the body.	Ferritin

How Do Genes Direct the Production of Proteins?

Most genes contain the information needed to make functional molecules called "proteins." (A few genes produce other molecules that help the cell assemble proteins.) The journey from gene to protein is complex and tightly controlled within each cell. It consists of two major steps:

- Transcription

- Translation

Together, transcription and translation are known as "gene expression."

During the process of transcription, the information stored in a gene's deoxyribonucleic acid (DNA) is transferred to a similar molecule called "ribonucleic acid (RNA)" in the cell nucleus. Both RNA and DNA are made up of a chain of nucleotide bases, but they have slightly different chemical properties. The type of RNA that contains the information for making a protein is called "messenger RNA (mRNA)" because it carries the information, or message, from the DNA out of the nucleus into the cytoplasm.

Translation, the second step in the journey from a gene to a protein, takes place in the cytoplasm. The messenger RNA (mRNA) interacts with a specialized complex called a "ribosome," which "reads" the sequence of mRNA bases. Each sequence of three bases, called a "codon," usually codes for one particular amino acid. (Amino acids are the building blocks of proteins.) A type of RNA called "transfer RNA (tRNA)" assembles the protein, one amino acid at a time. Protein assembly continues until the ribosome encounters a "stop" codon (a sequence of three bases that does not code for an amino acid).

The flow of information from DNA to RNA to proteins is one of the fundamental principles of molecular biology. It is so important that it is sometimes called the "central dogma."

Can Genes Be Turned On and Off in Cells?

Each cell expresses, or turns on, only a fraction of its genes. The rest of the genes are repressed or turned off. The process of turning genes on and off is known as "gene regulation." Gene regulation is an important part of normal development. Genes are turned on and off in different patterns during development to make a brain cell look and act differently from a liver cell or a muscle cell, for example.

Gene regulation also allows cells to react quickly to changes in their environments. Although we know that the regulation of genes is critical for life, this complex process is not yet fully understood. Gene regulation can occur at any point during gene expression, but most commonly occurs at the level of transcription (when the information in a gene's DNA is transferred to mRNA). Signals from the environment or from other cells activate proteins called "transcription factors." These proteins bind to regulatory regions of a gene and increase or decrease the level of transcription. By controlling the level of transcription, this process can determine the amount of protein product that is made by a gene at any given time.

What Is Epigenetics?

DNA modifications that do not change the DNA sequence can affect gene activity. Chemical compounds that are added to single genes can regulate their activity; these modifications are known as "epigenetic changes." The epigenome comprises all of the chemical compounds that have been added to the entirety of one's DNA (genome) as a way to regulate the activity (expression) of all the genes within the genome. The chemical compounds of the epigenome are not part of the DNA sequence, but are on or attached to DNA ("epi-" means "above" in Greek).

Epigenetic modifications remain as cells divide and in some cases can be inherited through multiple generations. Environmental influences, such as a person's diet and exposure to pollutants, can also impact the epigenome.

Epigenetic changes can help determine whether genes are turned on or off and can influence the production of proteins in certain cells, ensuring that only necessary proteins are produced. For example, proteins that promote bone growth are not produced in muscle cells. Patterns of epigenetic modification vary among individuals, different tissues within an individual, and even different cells.

A common type of epigenetic modification is called "methylation." Methylation involves attaching small molecules called "methyl groups," each consisting of one carbon atom and three hydrogen atoms, to segments of DNA. When methyl groups are added to a particular gene, that gene is turned off or silenced, and no protein is produced from that gene.

Because errors in the epigenetic process, such as modifying the wrong gene or failing to add a compound to a gene, can lead to abnormal gene activity or inactivity, they can cause genetic disorders. Conditions including cancers, metabolic disorders, and degenerative disorders have all been found to be related to epigenetic errors.

Scientists continue to explore the relationship between the genome and the chemical compounds that modify it. In particular, they are studying what effect the modifications have on gene function, protein production, and human health.

How Do Cells Divide?

There are two types of cell division: mitosis and meiosis. Most of the time when people refer to "cell division," they mean mitosis, the process of making new body cells. Meiosis is the type of cell division that creates egg and sperm cells.

14

Mitosis is a fundamental process of life. During mitosis, a cell duplicates all of its contents, including its chromosomes, and splits to form two identical daughter cells. Because this process is so critical, the steps of mitosis are carefully controlled by a number of genes. When mitosis is not regulated correctly, health problems, such as cancer, can result.

The other type of cell division, meiosis, ensures that humans have the same number of chromosomes in each generation. Meiosis is a two-step process that reduces the chromosome number by half—from 46 to 23—to form sperm and egg cells. When the sperm and egg cells unite at conception, each contributes 23 chromosomes so that the resulting embryo will have the usual 46. Meiosis also allows genetic variation through a process of DNA shuffling while the cells are dividing.

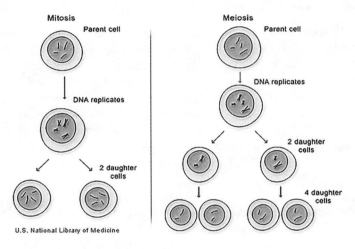

Figure 2.2. *Two Types of Cell Division*

How Do Genes Control the Growth and Division of Cells?

A variety of genes are involved in the control of cell growth and division. The cell cycle is the cell's way of replicating itself in an organized, step-by-step fashion. Tight regulation of this process ensures that a dividing cell's DNA is copied properly, any errors in the DNA are repaired, and each daughter cell receives a full set of chromosomes. The cycle has checkpoints (also called "restriction points"), which allow certain genes to check for problems and halt the cycle for repairs if something goes wrong.

If a cell has an error in its DNA that cannot be repaired, it may undergo programmed cell death (apoptosis). Apoptosis is a common process throughout life that helps the body get rid of cells it doesn't need. Cells that undergo apoptosis break apart and are recycled by a type of white blood cell (WBC) called a "macrophage." Apoptosis protects the body by removing genetically damaged cells that could lead to cancer, and it plays an important role in the development of the embryo and the maintenance of adult tissues.

Cancer results from a disruption of the normal regulation of the cell cycle. When the cycle proceeds without control, cells can divide without order and accumulate genetic defects that can lead to a cancerous tumor.

How Do Geneticists Indicate the Location of a Gene?

Geneticists use maps to describe the location of a particular gene on a chromosome. One type of map uses the cytogenetic location to describe a gene's position. The cytogenetic location is based on a distinctive pattern of bands created when chromosomes are stained with certain chemicals. Another type of map uses the molecular location, a precise description of a gene's position on a chromosome. The molecular location is based on the sequence of DNA building blocks (base pairs) that make up the chromosome.

Cytogenetic Location

Geneticists use a standardized method to describe a gene's cytogenetic location. In most cases, the location describes the position of a particular band on a stained chromosome: 17q12

It can also be written as a range of bands if less is known about the exact location: 17q12-q21

The combination of numbers and letters provide a gene's "address" on a chromosome. This address is made up of several parts:

- **The chromosome on which the gene can be found.**
  The first number or letter used to describe a gene's location represents the chromosome. Chromosomes 1 through 22 (the autosomes) are designated by their chromosome number. The sex chromosomes are designated by X or Y.

- **The arm of the chromosome.** Each chromosome is divided into two sections (arms) based on the location of a narrowing (constriction) called the "centromere." By convention, the shorter arm is called "p," and the longer arm is called "q." The chromosome arm is the second part of the gene's address. For example, 5q is the long arm of chromosome 5, and Xp is the short arm of the X chromosome.

- **The position of the gene on the p or q arm.** The position of a gene is based on a distinctive pattern of light and dark bands that appear when the chromosome is stained in a certain way. The position is usually designated by two digits (representing a region and a band), which are sometimes followed by a decimal point and one or more additional digits (representing sub-bands within a light or dark area). The number indicating the gene position increases with distance from the centromere. For example: 14q21 represents position 21 on the long arm of chromosome 14. 14q21 is closer to the centromere than 14q22.

Sometimes, the abbreviations "cen" or "ter" are also used to describe a gene's cytogenetic location. "Cen" indicates that the gene is very close to the centromere. For example, 16pcen refers to the short arm of chromosome 16 near the centromere. "Ter" stands for the terminus, which indicates that the gene is very close to the end of the p or q arm. For example, 14qter refers to the tip of the long arm of chromosome 14. ("Tel" is also sometimes used to describe a gene's location. "Tel" stands for telomeres, which are at the ends of each chromosome. The abbreviations "tel" and "ter" refer to the same location.)

Molecular Location

The Human Genome Project (HGP), an international research effort completed in 2003, determined the sequence of base pairs for each human chromosome. This sequence information allows researchers to provide a more specific address than the cytogenetic location for many genes. A gene's molecular address pinpoints the location of that gene in terms of base pairs. It describes the gene's precise position on a chromosome and indicates the size of the gene. Knowing the molecular location also allows researchers to determine exactly how far a gene is from other genes on the same chromosome. Different groups of researchers often present slightly different values for a gene's molecular location. Researchers interpret the sequence of the human genome using a variety of methods, which can result in small differences in a gene's molecular address.

Chapter 3

Genetic Mutations and Health

What Is a Gene Mutation and How Do Mutations Occur?

A gene mutation is a permanent alteration in the deoxyribonucleic acid (DNA) sequence that makes up a gene, such that the sequence differs from what is found in most people. Mutations range in size; they can affect anywhere from a single DNA building block (base pair) to a large segment of a chromosome that includes multiple genes.

Gene mutations can be classified in two major ways:

- **Hereditary mutations** are inherited from a parent and are present throughout a person's life in virtually every cell in the body. These mutations are also called "germline mutations" because they are present in the parent's egg or sperm cells, which are also called "germ cells." When an egg and a sperm cell unite, the resulting fertilized egg cell receives DNA from both parents. If this DNA has a mutation, the child that grows from the fertilized egg will have the mutation in each of his or her cells.

This chapter includes text excerpted from "What Is a Gene Mutation and How Do Mutations Occur?" Genetics Home Reference (GHR), National Institutes of Health (NIH), February 19, 2019.

- **Acquired (or somatic) mutations** occur at some time during a person's life and are present only in certain cells, but not in every cell in the body. These changes can be caused by environmental factors, such as ultraviolet (UV) radiation from the sun, or can occur if an error is made as DNA copies itself during cell division. Acquired mutations in somatic cells (cells other than sperm and egg cells) cannot be passed to the next generation.

Genetic changes that are described as de novo (new) mutations can be either hereditary or somatic. In some cases, the mutation occurs in a person's egg or sperm cell but is not present in any of the person's other cells. In other cases, the mutation occurs in the fertilized egg shortly after the egg and sperm cells unite. (It is often impossible to tell exactly when a de novo mutation happened.) As the fertilized egg divides, each resulting cell in the growing embryo will have the mutation. De novo mutations may explain genetic disorders in which an affected child has a mutation in every cell in the body but the parents do not, and there is no family history of the disorder.

Somatic mutations that happen in a single cell early in embryonic development can lead to a situation called "mosaicism." These genetic changes are not present in a parent's egg or sperm cells, or in the fertilized egg, but happen a bit later when the embryo includes several cells. As all the cells divide during growth and development, cells that arise from the cell with the altered gene will have the mutation, while other cells will not. Depending on the mutation and how many cells are affected, mosaicism may or may not cause health problems.

Most disease-causing gene mutations are uncommon in the general population. However, other genetic changes occur more frequently. Genetic alterations that occur in more than one percent of the population are called "polymorphisms." They are common enough to be considered a normal variation in the DNA. Polymorphisms are responsible for many of the normal differences between people, such as eye color, hair color, and blood type. Although many polymorphisms have no negative effects on a person's health, some of these variations may influence the risk of developing certain disorders.

How Can Gene Mutations Affect Health and Development?

To function correctly, each cell depends on thousands of proteins to do their jobs in the right places at the right times. Sometimes, gene mutations prevent one or more of these proteins from working properly. By changing a gene's instructions for making a protein, a mutation can cause the protein to malfunction or to be missing entirely. When a mutation alters a protein that plays a critical role in the body, it can disrupt normal development or cause a medical condition. A condition caused by mutations in one or more genes is called a "genetic disorder."

In some cases, gene mutations are so severe that they prevent an embryo from surviving until birth. These changes occur in genes that are essential for development, and often disrupt the development of an embryo in its earliest stages. Because these mutations have very serious effects, they are incompatible with life.

It is important to note that genes themselves do not cause disease— genetic disorders are caused by mutations that make a gene function improperly. For example, when people say that someone has "the cystic fibrosis (*CF*) gene," they are usually referring to a mutated version of the cystic fibrosis transmembrane conductance regulator (*CFTR*) gene, which causes the disease. All people, including those without cystic fibrosis, have a version of the *CFTR* gene.

Do All Gene Mutations Affect Health and Development?

No; only a small percentage of mutations cause genetic disorders— most have no impact on health or development. For example, some mutations alter a gene's DNA sequence but do not change the function of the protein made by the gene.

Often, gene mutations that could cause a genetic disorder are repaired by certain enzymes before the gene is expressed and an altered protein is produced. Each cell has a number of pathways through which enzymes recognize and repair errors in DNA. Because DNA can be damaged or mutated in many ways, DNA repair is an important process by which the body protects itself from disease.

A very small percentage of all mutations actually have a positive effect. These mutations lead to new versions of proteins that help an individual better adapt to changes in her or his environment. For example, a beneficial mutation could result in a protein that protects an individual and future generations from a new strain of bacteria.

Because a person's genetic code can have a large number of mutations with no effect on health, diagnosing genetic conditions can be difficult. Sometimes, genes thought to be related to a particular genetic condition have mutations, but whether these changes are involved in development of the condition has not been determined; these genetic changes are known as "variants of unknown significance (VOUS)" or "(VUS)." Sometimes, no mutations are found in suspected disease-related genes, but mutations are found in other genes whose relationship to a particular genetic condition is unknown. It is difficult to know whether these variants are involved in the disease.

What Kinds of Gene Mutations Are Possible?

The DNA sequence of a gene can be altered in a number of ways. Gene mutations have varying effects on health, depending on where they occur and whether they alter the function of essential proteins. The types of mutations include:

Missense Mutation

This type of mutation is a change in one DNA base pair that results in the substitution of one amino acid for another in the protein made by a gene.

Nonsense Mutation

A nonsense mutation is also a change in one DNA base pair. Instead of substituting one amino acid for another, however, the altered DNA sequence prematurely signals the cell to stop building a protein. This type of mutation results in a shortened protein that may function improperly or not at all.

Insertion

An insertion changes the number of DNA bases in a gene by adding a piece of DNA. As a result, the protein made by the gene may not function properly.

Deletion

A deletion changes the number of DNA bases by removing a piece of DNA. Small deletions may remove one or a few base pairs within a gene, while larger deletions can remove an entire gene or several neighboring genes. The deleted DNA may alter the function of the resulting protein(s).

Duplication

A duplication consists of a piece of DNA that is abnormally copied one or more times. This type of mutation may alter the function of the resulting protein.

Frameshift Mutation

This type of mutation occurs when the addition or loss of DNA bases changes a gene's reading frame. A reading frame consists of groups of three bases that each code for one amino acid. A frameshift mutation shifts the grouping of these bases and changes the code for amino acids. The resulting protein is usually nonfunctional. Insertions, deletions, and duplications can all be frameshift mutations.

Repeat Expansion

Nucleotide repeats are short DNA sequences that are repeated a number of times in a row. For example, a trinucleotide repeat is made up of 3-base-pair sequences, and a tetranucleotide repeat is made up of four-base-pair sequences. A repeat expansion is a mutation that increases the number of times that the short DNA sequence is repeated. This type of mutation can cause the resulting protein to function improperly.

Can a Change in the Number of Genes Affect Health and Development?

People have two copies of most genes, one copy inherited from each parent. In some cases, however, the number of copies varies—meaning that a person can be born with one, three, or more copies of particular genes. Less commonly, one or more genes may be entirely missing. This type of genetic difference is known as copy number variation (CNV).

Copy number variation results from insertions, deletions, and duplications of large segments of DNA. These segments are big enough to include whole genes. Variation in gene copy number can influence the activity of genes and ultimately affect many body functions.

Researchers were surprised to learn that CNV accounts for a significant amount of genetic difference between people. More than ten percent of human DNA appears to contain these differences in gene copy number. While much of this variation does not affect health or development, some differences likely influence a person's risk of disease and response to certain drugs. Future research will focus on the consequences of CNV in different parts of the genome and study the contribution of these variations to many types of disease.

Can Changes in the Number of Chromosomes Affect Health and Development?

Human cells normally contain 23 pairs of chromosomes, for a total of 46 chromosomes in each cell. A change in the number of chromosomes can cause problems with growth, development, and function of the body's systems. These changes can occur during the formation of reproductive cells (eggs and sperm), in early fetal development, or in any cell after birth. A gain or loss of chromosomes from the normal 46 is called "aneuploidy."

A common form of aneuploidy is trisomy, or the presence of an extra chromosome in cells. "Tri-" is Greek for "three"; people with trisomy have three copies of a particular chromosome in cells instead of the normal two copies. Down syndrome (DS) is an example of a condition caused by trisomy. People with DS typically have three copies of chromosome 21 in each cell, for a total of 47 chromosomes per cell.

Monosomy, or the loss of one chromosome in cells, is another kind of aneuploidy. "Mono-" is Greek for "one"; people with monosomy have one copy of a particular chromosome in cells instead of the normal two copies. Turner syndrome (TS) is a condition caused by monosomy. Women with TS usually have only one copy of the X chromosome in every cell, for a total of 45 chromosomes per cell.

Rarely, some cells end up with complete extra sets of chromosomes. Cells with one additional set of chromosomes, for a total of 69 chromosomes, are called "triploid." Cells with two additional sets of chromosomes, for a total of 92 chromosomes, are called "tetraploid." A condition in which every cell in the body has an extra set of chromosomes is not compatible with life.

In some cases, a change in the number of chromosomes occurs only in certain cells. When an individual has two or more cell populations with a different chromosomal makeup, this situation is called "chromosomal mosaicism." Chromosomal mosaicism occurs from an error in cell division in cells other than eggs and sperm. Most commonly, some cells end up with one extra or missing chromosome (for a total of 45 or 47 chromosomes per cell), while other cells have the usual 46 chromosomes. Mosaic TS is one example of chromosomal mosaicism. In females with this condition, some cells have 45 chromosomes because they are missing one copy of the X chromosome, while other cells have the usual number of chromosomes.

Many cancer cells also have changes in their number of chromosomes. These changes are not inherited; they occur in somatic cells (cells other than eggs or sperm) during the formation or progression of a cancerous tumor.

Can Changes in the Structure of Chromosomes Affect Health and Development?

Changes that affect the structure of chromosomes can cause problems with growth, development, and function of the body's systems. These changes can affect many genes along the chromosome and disrupt the proteins made from those genes.

Structural changes can occur during the formation of egg or sperm cells, in early fetal development, or in any cell after birth. Pieces of DNA can be rearranged within one chromosome or transferred between two or more chromosomes. The effects of structural changes depend on their size and location, and whether any genetic material is gained or lost. Some changes cause medical problems, while others may have no effect on a person's health.

Changes in chromosome structure include:

Translocations

A translocation occurs when a piece of one chromosome breaks off and attaches to another chromosome. This type of rearrangement is described as balanced if no genetic material is gained or lost in the cell. If there is a gain or loss of genetic material, the translocation is described as unbalanced.

Deletions

Deletions occur when a chromosome breaks and some genetic material is lost. Deletions can be large or small and can occur anywhere along a chromosome.

Duplications

Duplications occur when part of a chromosome is copied (duplicated) too many times. This type of chromosomal change results in extra copies of genetic material from the duplicated segment.

Inversions

An inversion involves the breakage of a chromosome in two places; the resulting piece of DNA is reversed and re-inserted into the chromosome. Genetic material may or may not be lost as a result of the chromosome breaks. An inversion that involves the chromosomes' constriction point (centromere) is called a "pericentric inversion." An inversion that occurs in the long (q) arm or short (p) arm and does not involve the centromere is called a "paracentric inversion."

Isochromosomes

An isochromosome is a chromosome with two identical arms. Instead of one long (q) arm and one short (p) arm, an isochromosome has two long arms or two short arms. As a result, these abnormal chromosomes have an extra copy of some genes and are missing copies of other genes.

Dicentric Chromosomes

Unlike normal chromosomes, which have a single constriction point (centromere), a dicentric chromosome contains two centromeres. Dicentric chromosomes result from the abnormal fusion of two chromosome pieces, each of which includes a centromere. These structures are unstable and often involve a loss of some genetic material.

Ring Chromosomes

Ring chromosomes usually occur when a chromosome breaks in two places and the ends of the chromosome arms fuse together to form a circular structure. The ring may or may not include the chromosomes' constriction point (centromere). In many cases, genetic material near the ends of the chromosome is lost.

Many cancer cells also have changes in their chromosome structure. These changes are not inherited; they occur in somatic cells (cells other than eggs or sperm) during the formation or progression of a cancerous tumor.

Can Changes in Noncoding Deoxyribonucleic Acid Affect Health and Development?

It is well established that changes in genes can alter a protein's function in the body, potentially causing health problems. It is becoming clear that changes in regions of DNA that do not contain genes (noncoding DNA) can also lead to disease.

Many regions of noncoding DNA play a role in the control of gene activity, determining when and where certain genes are turned on or off. By altering these sequences, a mutation in noncoding DNA can cause a protein to be expressed in the wrong place or at the wrong time or can reduce or eliminate expression of an important protein when it is needed. Not all changes in noncoding DNA have an impact on health, but those that alter the expression pattern of a protein that plays a critical role in the body can disrupt normal development or cause a health problem.

Mutations in noncoding DNA have been linked to developmental disorders, such as isolated Pierre Robin sequence (PRS), which is caused by changes in enhancer elements that control the activity of the SOX9 gene. Noncoding DNA mutations have also been associated with several types of cancer. In addition to enhancer elements, these mutations can disrupt other regulatory elements, including promoters, insulators, and silencers. Mutations in regions that provide instructions for making functional RNA molecules, such as transfer RNAs, microRNAs, or long noncoding RNAs, have also been implicated in disease.

The same types of genetic changes that occur in genes or that alter the structure of chromosomes can affect health and development when they occur in noncoding DNA. These mutations include changes in single DNA building blocks (point mutations), insertions, deletions, duplications, and translocations. Noncoding DNA mutations can be inherited from a parent or acquired during a person's life.

Much is still unknown about how to identify functional regions of noncoding DNA and the role such regions play. As a result, linking genetic changes in noncoding DNA to their effects on certain genes and to health conditions is difficult. The roles of noncoding DNA and the effects of genetic changes in it are growing areas of research.

Can Changes in Mitochondrial Deoxyribonucleic Acid Affect Health and Development?

Mitochondria are structures within cells that convert the energy from food into a form that cells can use. Although most DNA is packaged in chromosomes within the nucleus, mitochondria also have a small amount of their own DNA (known as "mitochondrial DNA" or "mtDNA"). In some cases, inherited changes in mitochondrial DNA can cause problems with growth, development, and function of the body's systems. These mutations disrupt the mitochondria's ability to generate energy efficiently for the cell.

Conditions caused by mutations in mitochondrial DNA often involve multiple organ systems. The effects of these conditions are most pronounced in organs and tissues that require a lot of energy, such as the heart, brain, and muscles. Although the health consequences of inherited mitochondrial DNA mutations vary widely, frequently observed features include muscle weakness and wasting, problems with movement, diabetes, kidney failure, heart disease, loss of intellectual functions (dementia), hearing loss, and abnormalities involving the eyes and vision.

Mitochondrial DNA is also prone to somatic mutations, which are not inherited. Somatic mutations occur in the DNA of certain cells during a person's lifetime and typically are not passed to future generations. Because mitochondrial DNA has a limited ability to repair itself when it is damaged, these mutations tend to build up over time. A buildup of somatic mutations in mitochondrial DNA has been associated with some forms of cancer and an increased risk of certain age-related disorders, such as heart disease, Alzheimer disease (AD), and Parkinson disease (PD). Additionally, research suggests that the progressive accumulation of these mutations over a person's lifetime may play a role in the normal process of aging.

What Are Complex or Multifactorial Disorders?

Researchers are learning that nearly all conditions and diseases have a genetic component. Some disorders, such as sickle cell disease (SCD) and cystic fibrosis (CF), are caused by mutations in a single gene. The causes of many other disorders, however, are much more complex. Common medical problems, such as heart disease, type 2 diabetes, and obesity do not have a single genetic cause—they are likely associated with the effects of multiple genes (polygenic) in combination with lifestyle and environmental factors. Conditions caused by many contributing factors are called "complex" or "multifactorial disorders."

Although complex disorders often cluster in families, they do not have a clear-cut pattern of inheritance. This makes it difficult to determine a person's risk of inheriting or passing on these disorders. Complex disorders are also difficult to study and treat because the specific factors that cause most of these disorders have not yet been identified. Researchers continue to look for major contributing genes for many common complex disorders.

What Does It Mean to Have a Genetic Predisposition to a Disease?

A genetic predisposition (sometimes called "genetic susceptibility") is an increased likelihood of developing a particular disease based on a person's genetic makeup. A genetic predisposition results from specific genetic variations that are often inherited from a parent. These genetic changes contribute to the development of a disease but do not directly cause it. Some people with a predisposing genetic variation will never get the disease while others will, even within the same family.

Genetic variations can have large or small effects on the likelihood of developing a particular disease. For example, certain mutations in the *BRCA1* or *BRCA2* genes greatly increase a person's risk of developing breast cancer and ovarian cancer. Variations in other genes, such as *BARD1* and *BRIP1*, also increase breast cancer risk, but the contribution of these genetic changes to a person's overall risk appears to be much smaller.

Current research is focused on identifying genetic changes that have a small effect on disease risk but are common in the general population. Although each of these variations only slightly increases a person's risk, having changes in several different genes may combine to increase disease risk significantly. Changes in many genes, each with a small effect, may underlie susceptibility to many common diseases, including cancer, obesity, diabetes, heart disease, and mental illness.

In people with a genetic predisposition, the risk of disease can depend on multiple factors in addition to an identified genetic change. These include other genetic factors (sometimes called "modifiers") as well as lifestyle and environmental factors. Diseases that are caused by a combination of factors are described as "multifactorial." Although a person's genetic makeup cannot be altered, some lifestyle and environmental modifications, such as having more frequent disease screenings and maintaining a healthy weight may be able to reduce disease risk in people with a genetic predisposition.

Chapter 4

What Causes Genetic Disorders

Genetics research studies how individual genes or groups of genes are involved in health and disease. Understanding genetic factors and genetic disorders is important in learning more about preventing birth defects, developmental disabilities, and other unique conditions among children.

Some genetic changes have been associated with an increased risk of having a child with a birth defect or developmental disability. Genetics also can help us understand how birth defects and developmental disabilities happen.

Causes of Genetic Disorders

Genetic disorders can happen for many reasons.

Genetic disorders often are described in terms of the chromosome that contains the gene. If the gene is on one of the first 22 pairs of chromosomes, called the "autosomes," the genetic disorder is called an "autosomal condition." If the gene is on the X chromosome, the disorder is called "X-linked."

Genetic disorders also are grouped by how they run in families. Disorders can be dominant or recessive, depending on how they cause conditions and how they run in families.

This chapter includes text excerpted from "Genetics Basics," Centers for Disease Control and Prevention (CDC), November 14, 2018.

Dominant. Dominant diseases can be caused by only one copy of a gene with a deoxyribonucleic acid (DNA) mutation. If one parent has the disease, each child has a 50 percent chance of inheriting the mutated gene.

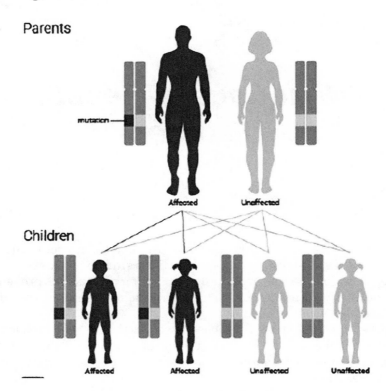

Figure 4.1. *Autosomal Dominant* (Source: "Help Me Understand Genetics—Inheriting Genetic Conditions," Genetics Home Reference (GHR), National Institutes of Health (NIH).)

In this example, a man with an autosomal dominant disorder has two affected children and two unaffected children.

Recessive. For recessive diseases, both copies of a gene must have a DNA mutation in order to get one of these diseases. If both parents have one copy of the mutated gene, each child has a 25 percent chance of having the disease, even though neither parent has it. In such cases, each parent is called a "carrier" of the disease. They can pass the disease on to their children, but do not have the disease themselves.

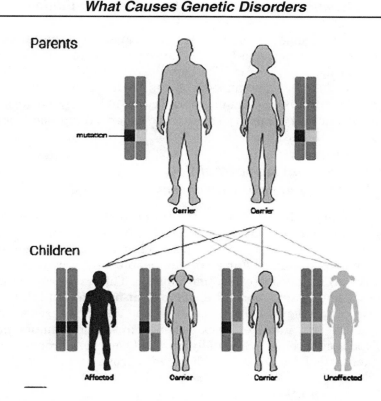

Figure 4.2. *Autosomal Recessive* (Source: "Help Me Understand Genetics—Inheriting Genetic Conditions," Genetics Home Reference (GHR), National Institutes of Health (NIH).)

In this example, two unaffected parents each carry one copy of a gene mutation for an autosomal recessive disorder. They have one affected child and three unaffected children, two of which carry one copy of the gene mutation.

Single-Gene Disorders

Some genetic diseases are caused by a DNA mutation in one of a person's genes. For example, suppose part of a gene usually has the sequence TAC. A mutation can change the sequence to TTC in some people. This change in sequence can change the way that the gene works, for example by changing the protein that is made. Mutations can be passed down to a child from her or his parents. Or, they can happen for the first time in the sperm or egg, so that the child will have the mutation but the parents will not. Single-gene disorders can be autosomal or X-linked. For example, sickle cell disease (SCD) is an autosomal single-gene disorder. It is caused by a mutation in a gene found on chromosome 11. SCD causes anemia and other complications. Fragile X syndrome (FXS), on the other hand, is an X-linked single-gene disorder. It is caused by a change in a gene on the X chromosome. It is the most commonly known cause of intellectual disability and developmental disability that can be inherited (passed from one generation to the next).

Chromosomal Abnormalities
Different Number of Chromosomes

People usually have 23 pairs of chromosomes. But, sometimes a person is born with a different number. If a person has an extra chromosome it is called "trisomy." If a person has a missing chromosome it is called "monosomy." For example, people with Down syndrome (DS) have an extra copy of chromosome 21. This extra copy changes the body's and brain's normal development and causes intellectual and physical problems for the person. Some disorders are caused by having a different number of sex chromosomes. For example, people with Turner syndrome (TS) usually have only one sex chromosome, an X. Women with TS can have problems with growth and heart defects.

Changes in Chromosomes

Sometimes chromosomes are incomplete or shaped differently than usual. When a small part of a chromosome is missing, it is called a "deletion." If it has moved to another chromosome, it is called a "translocation." If it has been flipped over, it is called an "inversion." For example, people with Williams syndrome (WS) are missing a small part of chromosome 7. This deletion can result in intellectual disability and a distinctive facial appearance and personality.

Complex Conditions

A complex disease is caused by both genes and environmental factors. Complex diseases also are called "multifactorial." Many birth defects and developmental disabilities are complex conditions. For example, while some orofacial clefts are associated with single gene disorders, the majority most likely are caused by changes in several genes acting together with environmental exposures.

Chapter 5

Genetic Inheritance

What Does It Mean If a Disorder Seems to Run in Your Family?

A particular disorder might be described as "running in a family" if more than one person in the family has the condition. Some disorders that affect multiple family members are caused by gene mutations, which can be inherited (passed down from parent to child). Other conditions that appear to run in families are not caused by mutations in single genes. Instead, environmental factors, such as dietary habits or a combination of genetic and environmental factors, are responsible for these disorders.

It is not always easy to determine whether a condition in a family is inherited. A genetics professional can use a person's family history (a record of health information about a person's immediate and extended family) to help determine whether a disorder has a genetic component. She or he will ask about the health of people from several generations of the family, usually, first-, second-, and third-degree relatives.

This chapter includes text excerpted from "Help Me Understand Genetics," Get Smart About Drugs, U.S. Drug Enforcement Administration (DEA), January 22, 2019.

Table 5.1. Degrees of Relationship

Degrees of Relationship	Examples
First-degree relatives	Parents, children, brothers, and sisters
Second-degree relatives	Grandparents, aunts and uncles, nieces and nephews, and grandchildren
Third-degree relatives	First cousins

Why Is It Important to Know Your Family Medical History?

A family medical history is a record of health information about a person and his or her close relatives. A complete record includes information from three generations of relatives, including children, brothers and sisters, parents, aunts and uncles, nieces and nephews, grandparents, and cousins.

Families have many factors in common, including their genes, environment, and lifestyle. Together, these factors can give clues to medical conditions that may run in a family. By noticing patterns of disorders among relatives, healthcare professionals can determine whether an individual, other family members, or future generations may be at an increased risk of developing a particular condition.

A family medical history can identify people with a higher-than-usual chance of having common disorders, such as heart disease, high blood pressure, stroke, certain cancers, and diabetes. These complex disorders are influenced by a combination of genetic factors, environmental conditions, and lifestyle choices. A family history also can provide information about the risk of rarer conditions caused by mutations in a single gene, such as cystic fibrosis (CF) and sickle cell disease (SCD).

While a family medical history provides information about the risk of specific health concerns, having relatives with a medical condition does not mean that an individual will definitely develop that condition. On the other hand, a person with no family history of a disorder may still be at risk of developing that disorder.

Knowing one's family medical history allows a person to take steps to reduce his or her risk. For people at an increased risk of certain cancers, healthcare professionals may recommend more frequent screening, such as mammography or colonoscopy, starting at an earlier age. Healthcare providers may also encourage regular checkups or testing for people with a medical condition that runs in their family. Additionally, lifestyle changes, such as adopting a healthier diet, getting regular exercise, and quitting smoking, help many people lower their chances of developing heart disease and other common illnesses.

The easiest way to get information about family medical history is to talk to relatives about their health. Have they had any medical problems, and when did they occur? A family gathering could be a good time to discuss these issues. Additionally, obtaining medical records and other documents, such as obituaries and death certificates, can help complete a family medical history. It is important to keep this information up-to-date and to share it with a healthcare professional regularly.

What Are the Different Ways in Which a Genetic Condition Can Be Inherited?

Some genetic conditions are caused by mutations in a single gene. These conditions are usually inherited in one of several patterns, depending on the gene involved.

Many health conditions are caused by the combined effects of multiple genes (described as polygenic) or by interactions between genes and the environment. Such disorders usually do not follow the patterns of inheritance listed above. Examples of conditions caused by multiple genes or gene/environment interactions include heart disease, type 2 diabetes, schizophrenia, and certain types of cancer.

Disorders caused by changes in the number or structure of chromosomes also. Other genetic factors sometimes influence how a disorder is inherited.

If a Genetic Disorder Runs in Your Family, What Are the Chances That Your Children Will Have the Condition?

When a genetic disorder is diagnosed in a family, family members often want to know the likelihood that they or their children will develop the condition. This can be difficult to predict in some cases because many factors influence a person's chances of developing a genetic condition. One important factor is how the condition is inherited. For example:

- **Autosomal dominant inheritance.** A person affected by an autosomal dominant disorder has a 50 percent chance of

37

passing the mutated gene to each child. The chance that a child will not inherit the mutated gene is also 50 percent. However, in some cases an autosomal dominant disorder results from a new (de novo) mutation that occurs during the formation of egg or sperm cells or early in embryonic development. In these cases, the child's parents are unaffected, but the child may pass on the condition to his or her own children.

- **Autosomal recessive inheritance.** Two unaffected people who each carry one copy of the mutated gene for an autosomal recessive disorder (carriers) have a 25 percent chance with each pregnancy of having a child affected by the disorder. The chance with each pregnancy of having an unaffected child who is a carrier of the disorder is 50 percent, and the chance that a child will not have the disorder and will not be a carrier is 25 percent.

- **X-linked dominant inheritance.** The chance of passing on an X-linked dominant condition differs between men and women because men have one X chromosome and one Y chromosome, while women have two X chromosomes. A man passes on his Y chromosome to all of his sons and his X chromosome to all of his daughters. Therefore, the sons of a

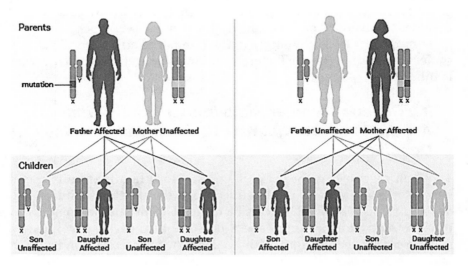

Figure 5.1. *X-Linked Dominant* (Source: U.S. National Library of Medicine (NLM).)

man with an X-linked dominant disorder will not be affected, but all of his daughters will inherit the condition. A woman passes on one or the other of her X chromosomes to each child. Therefore, a woman with an X-linked dominant disorder has a 50 percent chance of having an affected daughter or son with each pregnancy.

- **X-linked recessive inheritance.** Because of the difference in sex chromosomes, the probability of passing on an X-linked recessive disorder also differs between men and women. The sons of a man with an X-linked recessive disorder will not be affected, and his daughters will carry one copy of the mutated gene. With each pregnancy, a woman who carries an X-linked recessive disorder has a 50 percent chance of having sons who are affected and a 50 percent chance of having daughters who carry one copy of the mutated gene.

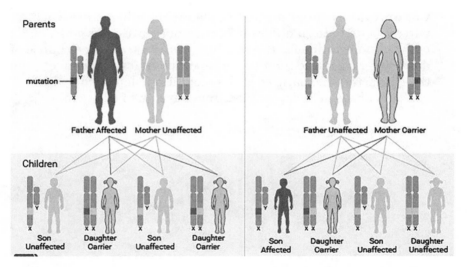

Figure 5.2. *X-Linked Recessive* (Source: U.S. National Library of Medicine (NLM).)

- **Y-linked inheritance.** Because only males have a Y chromosome, only males can be affected by and pass on Y-linked disorders. All sons of a man with a Y-linked disorder will inherit the condition from their father.

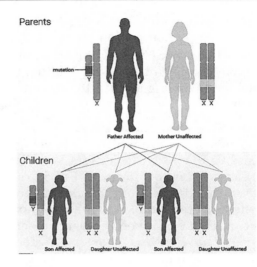

Figure 5.3. *Y-Linked* (Source: U.S. National Library of Medicine (NLM).)

- **Codominant inheritance.** In codominant inheritance, each parent contributes a different version of a particular gene, and both versions influence the resulting genetic trait. The chance of developing a genetic condition with codominant inheritance, and the characteristic features of that condition, depend on which versions of the gene are passed from parents to their child.

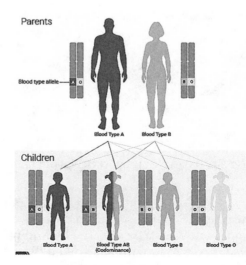

Figure 5.4. *Codominant—Example Blood Type* (Source: U.S. National Library of Medicine (NLM).)

- **Mitochondrial inheritance.** Mitochondria, which are the energy-producing centers inside cells, each contain a small amount of deoxyribonucleic acid (DNA). Disorders with mitochondrial inheritance result from mutations in mitochondrial DNA. Although these disorders can affect both males and females, only females can pass mutations in mitochondrial DNA to their children. A woman with a disorder caused by changes in mitochondrial DNA will pass the mutation to all of her daughters and sons, but the children of a man with such a disorder will not inherit the mutation.

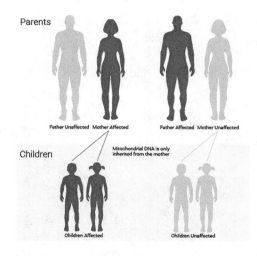

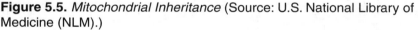

Figure 5.5. *Mitochondrial Inheritance* (Source: U.S. National Library of Medicine (NLM).)

It is important to note that the chance of passing on a genetic condition applies equally to each pregnancy. For example, if a couple has a child with an autosomal recessive disorder, the chance of having another child with the disorder is still 25 percent (or 1 in 4). Having one child with a disorder does not "protect" future children from inheriting the condition. Conversely, having a child without the condition does not mean that future children will definitely be affected.

Although the chances of inheriting a genetic condition appear straightforward, factors, such as a person's family history and the results of genetic testing, can sometimes modify those chances. In addition, some people with a disease-causing mutation never develop any health problems or may experience only mild symptoms of the disorder. Estimating the chances of developing or passing on a genetic disorder can be complex. Genetics professionals can help people understand these chances and help them make informed decisions about their health.

41

Table 5.2. Patterns of Inheritance

Inheritance Pattern	Description	Examples
Autosomal dominant	One mutated copy of the gene in each cell is sufficient for a person to be affected by an autosomal dominant disorder. In some cases, an affected person inherits the condition from an affected parent. In others, the condition may result from a new mutation in the gene and occur in people with no history of the disorder in their family.	Huntington disease (HD), Marfan syndrome (MFS)
Autosomal recessive	In autosomal recessive inheritance, both copies of the gene in each cell have mutations. The parents of an individual with an autosomal recessive condition each carry one copy of the mutated gene, but they typically do not show signs and symptoms of the condition. Autosomal recessive disorders are typically not seen in every generation of an affected family.	Cystic fibrosis (CF), sickle cell disease (SCD)
X-linked dominant	X-linked dominant disorders are caused by mutations in genes on the X chromosome, one of the two sex chromosomes in each cell. In females (who have two X chromosomes), a mutation in one of the two copies of the gene in each cell is sufficient to cause the disorder. In males (who have only one X chromosome), a mutation in the only copy of the gene in each cell causes the disorder. In most cases, males experience more severe symptoms of the disorder than females. A characteristic of X-linked inheritance is that fathers cannot pass X-linked traits to their sons (no male-to-male transmission).	Fragile X syndrome (FXS)
X-linked recessive	X-linked recessive disorders are also caused by mutations in genes on the X chromosome. In males (who have only one X chromosome), one altered copy of the gene in each cell is sufficient to cause the condition. In females (who have two X chromosomes), a mutation would have to occur in both copies of the gene to cause the disorder. Because it is unlikely that females will have two altered copies of this gene, males are affected by X-linked recessive disorders much more frequently than females. A characteristic of X-linked inheritance is that fathers cannot pass X-linked traits to their sons (no male-to-male transmission).	Hemophilia, Fabry disease (FD)

Table 5.2. Continued

Inheritance Pattern	Description	Examples
Y-linked	A condition is considered Y-linked if the mutated gene that causes the disorder is located on the Y chromosome, one of the two sex chromosomes in each of a male's cells. Because only males have a Y chromosome, in Y-linked inheritance, a mutation can only be passed from father to son.	Y chromosome infertility, some cases of Swyer syndrome
Codominant	In codominant inheritance, two different versions (alleles) of a gene are expressed, and each version makes a slightly different protein. Both alleles influence the genetic trait or determine the characteristics of the genetic condition.	*ABO* blood group, alpha-1 antitrypsin deficiency (AAT)
Mitochondrial	Mitochondrial inheritance, also known as maternal inheritance, applies to genes in mitochondrial DNA (mtDNA). Mitochondria, which are structures in each cell that convert molecules into energy, each contain a small amount of DNA. Because only egg cells contribute mitochondria to the developing embryo, only females can pass on mitochondrial mutations to their children. Conditions resulting from mutations in mitochondrial DNA can appear in every generation of a family and can affect both males and females, but fathers do not pass these disorders to their daughters or sons.	Leber hereditary optic neuropathy (LHON)

What Are Reduced Penetrance and Variable Expressivity?

Reduced penetrance and variable expressivity are factors that influence the effects of particular genetic changes. These factors usually affect disorders that have an autosomal dominant pattern of inheritance, although they are occasionally seen in disorders with an autosomal recessive inheritance pattern.

Reduced Penetrance

Penetrance refers to the proportion of people with a particular genetic change, such as a mutation in a specific gene, who exhibit signs and symptoms of a genetic disorder. If some people with the mutation do not develop features of the disorder, the condition is said to have reduced (or incomplete) penetrance. Reduced penetrance often occurs with familial cancer syndromes. For example, many people with a mutation in the *BRCA1* or *BRCA2* gene will develop cancer during their lifetime, but some people will not. Doctors cannot predict which people with these mutations will develop cancer or when the tumors will develop.

Reduced penetrance probably results from a combination of genetic, environmental, and lifestyle factors, many of which are unknown. This phenomenon can make it challenging for genetics professionals to interpret a person's family medical history and predict the risk of passing a genetic condition to future generations.

Variable Expressivity

Although some genetic disorders exhibit little variation, most have signs and symptoms that differ among affected individuals. Variable expressivity refers to the range of signs and symptoms that can occur in different people with the same genetic condition. For example, the features of Marfan syndrome (MFS) vary widely—some people have only mild symptoms, such as being tall and thin with long, slender fingers, while others also experience life-threatening complications involving the heart and blood vessels. Although the features are highly variable, most people with this disorder have a mutation in the same gene (*FBN1*).

As with reduced penetrance, variable expressivity is probably caused by a combination of genetic, environmental, and lifestyle factors, most of which have not been identified. If a genetic condition has highly variable signs and symptoms, it may be challenging to diagnose.

What Do Geneticists Mean by Anticipation?

The signs and symptoms of some genetic conditions tend to become more severe and appear at an earlier age as the disorder is passed from one generation to the next. This phenomenon is called "anticipation." Anticipation is most often seen with certain genetic disorders of the nervous system, such as Huntington disease (HD), myotonic dystrophy (DM), and fragile X syndrome (FXS).

Anticipation typically occurs with disorders that are caused by an unusual type of mutation called a "trinucleotide repeat expansion." A trinucleotide repeat is a sequence of three DNA building blocks (nucleotides) that is repeated a number of times in a row. DNA segments with an abnormal number of these repeats are unstable and prone to errors during cell division. The number of repeats can change as the gene is passed from parent to child. If the number of repeats increases, it is known as a "trinucleotide repeat expansion." In some cases, the trinucleotide repeat may expand until the gene stops functioning normally. This expansion causes the features of some disorders to become more severe with each successive generation.

Most genetic disorders have signs and symptoms that differ among affected individuals, including affected people in the same family. Not all of these differences can be explained by anticipation. A combination of genetic, environmental, and lifestyle factors is probably responsible for the variability, although many of these factors have not been identified. Researchers study multiple generations of affected family members and consider the genetic cause of a disorder before determining that it shows anticipation.

What Are Genomic Imprinting and Uniparental Disomy?

Genomic imprinting and uniparental disomy (UPD) are factors that influence how some genetic conditions are inherited.

Genomic Imprinting

People inherit two copies of their genes—one from their mother and one from their father. Usually, both copies of each gene are active, or "turned on," in cells. In some cases, however, only one of the two copies is normally turned on. Which copy is active depends on the parent of origin: some genes are normally active only when they are inherited from a person's father; others are active only when inherited from a person's mother. This phenomenon is known as "genomic imprinting."

In genes that undergo genomic imprinting, the parent of origin is often marked, or "stamped," on the gene during the formation of egg and sperm cells. This stamping process, called "methylation," is a chemical reaction that attaches small molecules called "methyl groups" to certain segments of DNA. These molecules identify which copy of a gene was inherited from the mother and which was inherited from the father. The addition and removal of methyl groups can be used to control the activity of genes.

Only a small percentage of all human genes undergo genomic imprinting. Researchers are not yet certain why some genes are imprinted and others are not. They do know that imprinted genes tend to cluster together in the same regions of chromosomes. Two major clusters of imprinted genes have been identified in humans, one on the short (p) arm of chromosome 11 (at position 11p15) and another on the long (q) arm of chromosome 15 (in the region 15q11 to 15q13).

Uniparental Disomy

Uniparental disomy occurs when a person receives two copies of a chromosome, or part of a chromosome, from one parent and no copies from the other parent. UPD can occur as a random event during the formation of egg or sperm cells or may happen in early fetal development.

In many cases, UPD likely has no effect on health or development. Because most genes are not imprinted, it doesn't matter if a person inherits both copies from one parent instead of one copy from each parent. In some cases, however, it does make a difference whether a gene is inherited from a person's mother or father. A person with UPD may lack any active copies of essential genes that undergo genomic imprinting. This loss of gene function can lead to delayed development, intellectual disability, or other health problems.

Several genetic disorders can result from UPD or a disruption of normal genomic imprinting. The most well-known conditions include Prader-Willi syndrome (PWS), which is characterized by uncontrolled eating and obesity, and Angelman syndrome (AS), which causes intellectual disability and impaired speech. Both of these disorders can be caused by UPD or other errors in imprinting involving genes on the long arm of chromosome 15. Other conditions, such as

Beckwith-Wiedemann syndrome (BWS) (a disorder characterized by accelerated growth and an increased risk of cancerous tumors), are associated with abnormalities of imprinted genes on the short arm of chromosome 11.

Are Chromosomal Disorders Inherited?

Although it is possible to inherit some types of chromosomal abnormalities, most chromosomal disorders, such as Down syndrome (DS) and Turner syndrome (TS) are not passed from one generation to the next.

Some chromosomal conditions are caused by changes in the number of chromosomes. These changes are not inherited but occur as random events during the formation of reproductive cells (eggs and sperm). An error in cell division is called "nondisjunction results" in reproductive cells with an abnormal number of chromosomes. For example, a reproductive cell may accidentally gain or lose one copy of a chromosome. If one of these atypical reproductive cells contributes to the genetic makeup of a child, the child will have an extra or missing chromosome in each of the body's cells.

Changes in chromosome structure can also cause chromosomal disorders. Some changes in chromosome structure can be inherited, while others occur as random accidents during the formation of reproductive cells or in early fetal development. Because the inheritance of these changes can be complex, people concerned about this type of chromosomal abnormality may want to talk with a genetics professional.

Some cancer cells also have changes in the number or structure of their chromosomes. Because these changes occur in somatic cells (cells other than eggs and sperm), they cannot be passed from one generation to the next.

Why Are Some Genetic Conditions More Common in Particular Ethnic Groups?

Some genetic disorders are more likely to occur among people who trace their ancestry to a particular geographic area. People in an ethnic group often share certain versions of their genes, which have been passed down from common ancestors. If one of these shared genes contains a disease-causing mutation, a particular genetic disorder may be more frequently seen in the group.

Examples of genetic conditions that are more common in particular ethnic groups are SCD, which is more common in people of African,

African American, or Mediterranean heritage; and Tay-Sachs disease (TSD), which is more likely to occur among people of Ashkenazi (eastern and central European) Jewish (AJ) or French Canadian ancestry. It is important to note, however, that these disorders can occur in any ethnic group.

Chapter 6

Genetic Counseling

What Is Genetic Counseling?

Genetic counseling gives you information about how genetic conditions might affect you or your family. The genetic counselor or other healthcare professional will collect your personal and family health history. They can use this information to determine how likely it is that you or your family member has a genetic condition. Based on this information, the genetic counselor can help you decide whether a genetic test might be right for you or your relative.

Reasons for Genetic Counseling

Based on your personal and family health history, your doctor can refer you for genetic counseling. There are different stages in your life when you might be referred for genetic counseling:

- **Planning for pregnancy.** Genetic counseling before you become pregnant can address concerns about factors that might

---

This chapter contains text excerpted from the following sources: Text beginning with the heading "What Is Genetic Counseling?" is excerpted from "Genetic Counseling," Centers for Disease Control and Prevention (CDC), October 4, 2018; Text beginning with the heading "Finding a Genetic Professional" is excerpted from "Frequently Asked Questions about Genetic Counseling," National Human Genome Research Institute (NHGRI), November 20, 2013. Reviewed March 2019.

affect your baby during infancy or childhood or your ability to become pregnant, including:

- Genetic conditions that run in your family or your partner's family

- History of infertility, multiple miscarriages, or stillbirth

- Previous pregnancy or child affected by a birth defect or genetic condition

- Assisted reproductive technology (ART) options

- **During pregnancy.** Genetic counseling while you are pregnant can address certain tests that may be done during your pregnancy, any detected problems, or conditions that might affect your baby during infancy or childhood, including:

  - History of infertility, multiple miscarriages, or stillbirth

  - Previous pregnancy or child affected by a birth defect or genetic condition

  - Abnormal test results, such as a blood test, ultrasound, chorionic villus sampling (CVS), or amniocentesis

  - Maternal infections, such as cytomegalovirus (CMV), and other exposures, such as medications, drugs, chemicals, and X-rays

  - Genetic screening that is recommended for all pregnant women, which includes cystic fibrosis (CF), sickle cell disease (SCD), and any conditions that run in your family or your partner's family

- **Caring for children.** Genetic counseling can address concerns if your child is showing signs and symptoms of a disorder that might be genetic, including:

  - Abnormal newborn screening results

  - Birth defects

  - Intellectual disability or developmental disabilities (IDDs)

  - Autism spectrum disorders (ASD)

  - Vision or hearing problems

- **Managing your health.** Genetic counseling for adults includes specialty areas, such as cardiovascular, psychiatric, and cancer.

Genetic counseling can be helpful if you have symptoms of a condition or have a family history of a condition that makes you more likely to be affected with that condition, including:

- Hereditary breast and ovarian cancer (HBOC) syndrome

- Lynch syndrome (hereditary colorectal and other cancers)

- Familial hypercholesterolemia (FH)

- Muscular dystrophy (MD) and other muscle diseases

- Inherited movement disorders, such as Huntington disease (HD)

- Inherited blood disorders, such as SCD

Following your genetic counseling session, you might decide to have genetic testing. Genetic counseling after testing can help you better understand your test results and treatment options, help you deal with emotional concerns, and refer you to other healthcare providers and advocacy and support groups.

Finding a Genetic Professional

Your healthcare provider may refer you to a genetic professional. Universities and medical centers also often have affiliated genetic professionals, or can provide referrals to a genetic professional or genetics clinic.

As more has been learned about genetics, genetic professionals have grown more specialized. For example, they may specialize in a particular disease, such as cancer genetics, an age group, such as adolescents, or a type of counseling, such as prenatal.

How Do You Decide Whether You Need to See a Geneticist or Other Specialist?

Your healthcare provider may refer you to a geneticist—a medical doctor or medical researcher—who specializes in your disease or disorder. A medical geneticist has completed a fellowship or has other advanced training in medical genetics. While a genetic counselor or genetic nurse may help you with testing decisions and support issues, a medical geneticist will make the actual diagnosis of a disease or condition. Many genetic diseases are so rare that only a geneticist can provide the most complete and current information about your condition. Along with a medical geneticist, you may also be referred to a physician who is a specialist in the type of disorder you have. For example, if a genetic test is positive for colon cancer, you might be referred to an oncologist. For a diagnosis of HD, you may be referred to a neurologist.

Chapter 7

Genetic Testing

Chapter Contents

Section 7.1

What You Need to Know about Genetic Testing

This section includes text excerpted from "What Is Genetic Testing?" Genetics Home Reference (GHR), National Institutes of Health (NIH), January 29, 2019.

Genetic testing is a type of medical test that identifies changes in chromosomes, genes, or proteins. The results of a genetic test can confirm or rule out a suspected genetic condition or help determine a person's chances of developing or passing on a genetic disorder. More than 1,000 genetic tests are currently in use, and more are being developed.

Several methods can be used for genetic testing:

- Molecular genetic tests (or gene tests) study single genes or short lengths of deoxyribonucleic acid (DNA) to identify variations or mutations that lead to a genetic disorder.

- Chromosomal genetic tests analyze whole chromosomes or long lengths of DNA to see if there are large genetic changes, such as an extra copy of a chromosome, that cause a genetic condition.

- Biochemical genetic tests study the amount or activity level of proteins; abnormalities in either can indicate changes to the DNA that result in a genetic disorder.

Genetic testing is voluntary. Because testing has benefits as well as limitations and risks, the decision about whether to be tested is a personal and complex one. A geneticist or genetic counselor can help by providing information about the pros and cons of the test and discussing the social and emotional aspects of testing.

What Are the Types of Genetic Tests?

Genetic testing can provide information about a person's genes and chromosomes. Available types of testing include:

Newborn Screening

Newborn screening is used just after birth to identify genetic disorders that can be treated early in life. Millions of babies are tested each year in the United States. All states currently test infants for phenylketonuria (PKU) (a genetic disorder that causes intellectual disability if left untreated) and congenital hypothyroidism (CH) (a disorder of the thyroid gland). Most states also test for other genetic disorders.

Diagnostic Testing

Diagnostic testing is used to identify or rule out a specific genetic or chromosomal condition. In many cases, genetic testing is used to confirm a diagnosis when a particular condition is suspected based on physical signs and symptoms. Diagnostic testing can be performed before birth or at any time during a person's life, but is not available for all genes or all genetic conditions. The results of a diagnostic test can influence a person's choices about healthcare and the management of the disorder.

Carrier Testing

Carrier testing is used to identify people who carry one copy of a gene mutation that, when present in two copies, causes a genetic disorder. This type of testing is offered to individuals who have a family history of a genetic disorder and to people in certain ethnic groups with an increased risk of specific genetic conditions. If both parents are tested, the test can provide information about a couple's risk of having a child with a genetic condition.

Prenatal Testing

Prenatal testing is used to detect changes in a fetus's genes or chromosomes before birth. This type of testing is offered during pregnancy if there is an increased risk that the baby will have a genetic or chromosomal disorder. In some cases, prenatal testing can lessen a couple's uncertainty or help them make decisions about a pregnancy. It cannot identify all possible inherited disorders and birth defects, however.

Preimplantation Testing

Preimplantation testing, also called "preimplantation genetic diagnosis (PGD)," is a specialized technique that can reduce the risk of having a child with a particular genetic or chromosomal disorder. It is used to detect genetic changes in embryos that were created using assisted reproductive techniques such as in-vitro fertilization (IVF).

In-vitro fertilization involves removing egg cells from a woman's ovaries and fertilizing them with sperm cells outside the body. To perform preimplantation testing, a small number of cells are taken from these embryos and tested for certain genetic changes. Only embryos without these changes are implanted in the uterus to initiate a pregnancy.

Predictive and Presymptomatic Testing

Predictive and presymptomatic types of testing are used to detect gene mutations associated with disorders that appear after birth, often later in life. These tests can be helpful to people who have a family member with a genetic disorder, but who have no features of the disorder themselves at the time of testing. Predictive testing can identify mutations that increase a person's risk of developing disorders with a genetic basis, such as certain types of cancer. Presymptomatic testing can determine whether a person will develop a genetic disorder, such as hereditary hemochromatosis (an iron overload disorder) before any signs or symptoms appear. The results of predictive and presymptomatic testing can provide information about a person's risk of developing a specific disorder and help with making decisions about medical care.

Forensic Testing

Forensic testing uses DNA sequences to identify an individual for legal purposes. Unlike the tests described above, forensic testing is not used to detect gene mutations associated with the disease. This type of testing can identify crime or catastrophe victims, rule out or implicate a crime suspect, or establish biological relationships between people (for example, paternity).

How Is Genetic Testing Done?

Once a person decides to proceed with genetic testing, a medical geneticist, primary-care doctor, specialist, or nurse practitioner can order the test. Genetic testing is often done as part of a genetic consultation.

Genetic tests are performed on a sample of blood, hair, skin, amniotic fluid (the fluid that surrounds a fetus during pregnancy), or other tissue. For example, a procedure called a "buccal smear" uses a small brush or cotton swab to collect a sample of cells from the inside surface of the cheek. The sample is sent to a laboratory where technicians look for specific changes in chromosomes, DNA, or proteins, depending on the suspected disorder. The laboratory reports the test results in writing to a person's doctor or genetic counselor, or directly to the patient if requested.

Newborn screening tests are done on a small blood sample, which is taken by pricking the baby's heel. Unlike other types of genetic testing, a parent will usually only receive the result if it is positive. If the test result is positive, additional testing is needed to determine whether the baby has a genetic disorder.

Before a person has a genetic test, it is important that she or he understand the testing procedure, the benefits, and limitations of the test, and the possible consequences of the test results. The process of educating a person about the test and obtaining permission is called "informed consent."

How Can Consumers Be Sure a Genetic Test Is Valid and Useful?

Before undergoing genetic testing, it is important to be sure that the test is valid and useful. A genetic test is valid if it provides an accurate result. Two main measures of accuracy apply to genetic tests: analytical validity and clinical validity. Another measure of the quality of a genetic test is its usefulness or clinical utility.

- Analytical validity refers to how well the test predicts the presence or absence of a particular gene or genetic change. In other words, can the test accurately detect whether a specific genetic variant is present or absent?

- Clinical validity refers to how well the genetic variant being analyzed is related to the presence, absence, or risk of a specific disease.

- Clinical utility refers to whether the test can provide information about diagnosis, treatment, management, or prevention of a disease that will be helpful to a consumer.

All laboratories that perform health-related testing, including genetic testing, are subject to federal regulatory standards called the "Clinical Laboratory Improvement Amendments" (CLIA) or even stricter state requirements. CLIA standards cover how tests are performed, the qualifications of laboratory personnel, and quality-control and testing procedures for each laboratory. By controlling the quality of laboratory practices, CLIA standards are designed to ensure the analytical validity of genetic tests.

CLIA standards do not address the clinical validity or clinical utility of genetic tests. The U.S. Food and Drug Administration (FDA) requires information about clinical validity for some genetic tests. Additionally, the state of New York requires information on clinical validity for all laboratory tests performed for people living in that state. Consumers, health providers, and health insurance companies are often the ones who determine the clinical utility of a genetic test.

It can be difficult to determine the quality of a genetic test sold directly to the public. Some providers of direct-to-consumer genetic tests are not CLIA-certified, so it can be difficult to tell whether their tests are valid. If providers of direct-to-consumer genetic tests offer easy-to-understand information about the scientific basis of their tests, it can help consumers make more informed decisions. It may also be helpful to discuss any concerns with a health professional before ordering a direct-to-consumer genetic test.

What Do the Results of Genetic Tests Mean?

The results of genetic tests are not always straightforward, which often makes them challenging to interpret and explain. Therefore, it is important for patients and their families to ask questions about the potential meaning of genetic test results both before and after the test is performed. When interpreting test results, healthcare professionals consider a person's medical history, family history, and the type of genetic test that was done.

A positive test result means that the laboratory found a change in a particular gene, chromosome, or protein of interest. Depending on the purpose of the test, this result may confirm a diagnosis, indicate that a person is a carrier of a particular genetic mutation, identify an increased risk of developing a disease (such as cancer) in the future or suggest a need for further testing. Because family members have some genetic material in common, a positive test result may also have implications for certain blood relatives of the person undergoing testing. It is important to note that a positive result of a predictive or presymptomatic genetic test (PST) usually cannot establish the exact risk of developing a disorder. Also, health professionals typically cannot use a positive test result to predict the course or severity of a condition.

A negative test result means that the laboratory did not find a change in the gene, chromosome, or protein under consideration. This result can indicate that a person is not affected by a particular disorder, is not a carrier of a specific genetic mutation, or does not have an increased risk of developing a certain disease. It is possible, however, that the test missed a disease-causing genetic alteration because many tests cannot detect all genetic changes that can cause a particular disorder. Further testing may be required to confirm a negative result.

In some cases, a test result might not give any useful information. This type of result is called "uninformative," "indeterminate," "inconclusive," or "ambiguous." Uninformative test results sometimes occur because everyone has common, natural variations in their DNA, called "polymorphisms," that do not affect health. If a genetic test finds a change in DNA that has not been associated with a disorder in other people, it can be difficult to tell whether it is a natural polymorphism or a disease-causing mutation. An uninformative result cannot confirm or rule out a specific diagnosis, and it cannot indicate whether a person has an increased risk of developing a disorder. In some cases, testing other affected and unaffected family members can help clarify this type of result.

What Is the Cost of Genetic Testing, and How Long Does It Take to Get the Results?

The cost of genetic testing can range from under $100 to more than $2,000, depending on the nature and complexity of the test. The cost increases if more than one test is necessary or if multiple family members must be tested to obtain a meaningful result. For newborn screening, costs vary by state. Some states cover part of the total cost, but most charge a fee of $15 to $60 per infant.

From the date that a sample is taken, it may take a few weeks to several months to receive the test results. Results for prenatal testing are usually available more quickly because time is an important consideration in making decisions about a pregnancy. The doctor or genetic counselor who orders a particular test can provide specific information about the cost and time frame associated with that test.

Will Health Insurance Cover the Costs of Genetic Testing?

In many cases, health insurance plans will cover the costs of genetic testing when it is recommended by a person's doctor. Health insurance providers have different policies about which tests are covered, however. A person interested in submitting the costs of testing may wish to contact his or her insurance company beforehand to ask about coverage.

Some people may choose not to use their insurance to pay for testing because the results of a genetic test can affect a person's insurance coverage. Instead, they may opt to pay out-of-pocket for the test. People considering genetic testing may want to find out more about their state's privacy protection laws before they ask their insurance company to cover the costs.

What Are the Benefits of Genetic Testing?

Genetic testing has potential benefits whether the results are positive or negative for a gene mutation. Test results can provide a sense of relief from uncertainty and help people make informed decisions about managing their healthcare. For example, a negative result can eliminate the need for unnecessary checkups and screening tests in some cases. A positive result can direct a person toward available prevention, monitoring, and treatment options. Some test results can also help people make decisions about having children. Newborn screening can identify genetic disorders early in life so treatment can be started as early as possible.

What Are the Risks and Limitations of Genetic Testing?

The physical risks associated with most genetic tests are very small, particularly for those tests that require only a blood sample or buccal smear (a method that samples cells from the inside surface of the cheek). The procedures used for prenatal testing carry a small but real risk of losing the pregnancy (miscarriage) because they require a sample of amniotic fluid or tissue from around the fetus.

Many of the risks associated with genetic testing involve the emotional, social, or financial consequences of the test results. People may feel angry, depressed, anxious, or guilty about their results. In some cases, genetic testing creates tension within a family because the results can reveal information about other family members in addition to the person who is tested. The possibility of genetic discrimination in employment or insurance is also a concern.

Genetic testing can provide only limited information about an inherited condition. The test often can't determine if a person will show symptoms of a disorder, how severe the symptoms will be, or whether the disorder will progress over time. Another major limitation is the lack of treatment strategies for many genetic disorders once they are diagnosed.

A genetics professional can explain in detail the benefits, risks, and limitations of a particular test. It is important that any person who is considering genetic testing understand and weigh these factors before making a decision.

How Does Genetic Testing in a Research Setting Differ from Clinical Genetic Testing?

The main differences between clinical genetic testing and research testing are the purpose of the test and who receives the results. The goals of research testing include finding unknown genes, learning how genes work, developing tests for future clinical use, and advancing our understanding of genetic conditions. The results of testing done as part of a research study are usually not available to patients or their healthcare providers. Clinical testing, on the other hand, is done to find out about an inherited disorder in an individual patient or family. People receive the results of a clinical test and can use them to help them make decisions about medical care or reproductive issues.

It is important for people considering genetic testing to know whether the test is available on a clinical or research basis. Clinical and research testing both involve a process of informed consent in which patients learn about the testing procedure, the risks and benefits of the test, and the potential consequences of testing.

Section 7.2

Noninvasive Prenatal Testing (NIPT)

This section includes text excerpted from "What Is
Noninvasive Prenatal Testing (NIPT) and What Disorders Can It
Screen For?" Genetics Home Reference (GHR), National
Institutes of Health (NIH), March 5, 2019.

Noninvasive prenatal testing (NIPT), sometimes called "noninvasive prenatal screening" (NIPS), is a method of determining the risk that the fetus will be born with certain genetic abnormalities. This testing analyzes small fragments of DNA that are circulating in a pregnant woman's blood. Unlike most DNA, which is found inside a cell's nucleus, these fragments are free-floating and not within cells, and so are called "cell-free DNA" (cfDNA). These small fragments usually contain fewer than 200 DNA building blocks (base pairs) and arise when cells die off and get broken down and their contents, including DNA, are released into the bloodstream.

During pregnancy, the mother's bloodstream contains a mix of cfDNA that comes from her cells and cells from the placenta. The placenta is tissue in the uterus that links the fetus and the mother's blood supply. These cells are shed into the mother's bloodstream throughout pregnancy. The DNA in placental cells is usually identical to the DNA of the fetus. Analyzing cfDNA from the placenta provides an opportunity for early detection of certain genetic abnormalities without harming the fetus.

NIPT is most often used to look for chromosomal disorders that are caused by the presence of an extra or missing copy (aneuploidy) of a chromosome. NIPT primarily looks for Down syndrome (trisomy 21, caused by an extra chromosome 21), trisomy 18 (caused by an extra chromosome 18), trisomy 13 (caused by an extra chromosome 13), and extra or missing copies of the X chromosome and Y chromosome (the sex chromosomes). The accuracy of the test varies by disorder.

NIPT may include screening for additional chromosomal disorders that are caused by missing (deleted) or copied (duplicated) sections of a chromosome. NIPT is beginning to be used to test for genetic disorders that are caused by changes (variants) in single genes. As technology improves and the cost of genetic testing decreases, researchers expect that NIPT will become available for many more genetic conditions.

NIPT is considered noninvasive because it requires drawing blood only from the pregnant woman and does not pose any risk to the fetus. NIPT is a screening test, which means that it will not give a definitive answer about whether or not a fetus has a genetic condition. The test can only estimate whether the risk of having certain conditions is increased or decreased. In some cases, NIPT results indicate an increased risk for a genetic abnormality when the fetus is actually unaffected (false positive), or the results indicate a decreased risk for a genetic abnormality when the fetus is actually affected (false negative). Because NIPT analyzes both fetal and maternal cfDNA, the test may detect a genetic condition in the mother.

There must be enough fetal cfDNA in the mother's bloodstream to be able to identify fetal chromosome abnormalities. The proportion of cfDNA in maternal blood that comes from the placenta is known as the fetal fraction. Generally, the fetal fraction must be above 4 percent, which typically occurs around the tenth week of pregnancy. Low fetal fractions can lead to an inability to perform the test or a false negative result. Reasons for low fetal fractions include testing too early in the pregnancy, sampling errors, maternal obesity, and fetal abnormality.

There are multiple NIPT methods to analyze fetal cfDNA. To determine chromosomal aneuploidy, the most common method is to count all cfDNA fragments (both fetal and maternal). If the percentage of cfDNA fragments from each chromosome is as expected, then the fetus has a decreased risk of having a chromosomal condition (negative test result). If the percentage of cfDNA fragments from a particular chromosome is more than expected, then the fetus has an increased likelihood of having a trisomy condition (positive test result). A positive screening result indicates that further testing (called "diagnostic testing," because it is used to diagnose a disease) should be performed to confirm the result.

Section 7.3

Newborn Screening

This section includes text excerpted from "Help Me Understand Genetics," Genetics Home Reference (GHR), National Institutes of Health (NIH), January 29, 2019.

Newborn screening is the practice of testing all babies in their first days of life for certain disorders and conditions that can hinder their normal development. This testing is required in every state and is typically performed before the baby leaves the hospital. The conditions included in newborn screening can cause serious health problems starting in infancy or childhood. Early detection and treatment can help prevent intellectual and physical disabilities and life-threatening illnesses.

How Is Newborn Screening Done?

Newborn screening usually begins with a blood test 24 to 48 hours after a baby is born, while she or he is still in the hospital. In some states, a second blood test is performed at a check-up appointment with the baby's pediatrician when the baby is 1 to 2 weeks old. Newborn screening is part of standard care; parents do not need to request to have the test done.

The test is performed by pricking the baby's heel to collect a few drops of blood. There are very few risks associated with this procedure, and it involves minimal discomfort to the baby. The blood is placed on a special type of paper and sent to a laboratory for analysis. Within two to three weeks, the test results are sent to the baby's doctor's office or clinic.

If a baby is born outside a hospital (for example, at home or in a birthing center), a doula or midwife may collect the blood sample needed for the newborn screening test. Otherwise, the required testing can be performed at the baby's doctor's office or at a hospital.

In addition to the blood test, most states also screen newborns for hearing loss and critical congenital heart disease (CCHD). These tests are also done shortly after birth. The hearing test uses earphones and sensors to determine whether the baby's inner ear or brain respond to sound. The test for CCHD, called "pulse oximetry," uses a sensor on the skin to measure how much oxygen is in the blood. Low oxygen levels suggest that an infant may have heart problems. The hearing and pulse oximetry tests are painless and can be done while the baby is sleeping.

What Disorders Are Included in Newborn Screening?

The disorders included in newborn screening vary from state to state. Most states test for all of the conditions specified by the Health Resources and Services Administration (HRSA) in their Recommended Uniform Screening Panel (RUSC). These conditions include phenylketonuria (PKU), cystic fibrosis (CF), sickle cell disease (SCD), CCHD, hearing loss, and others. Some states test for additional disorders that are not part of the HRSA panel.

Most of the conditions included in newborn screening can cause serious health problems if treatment is not started shortly after birth. Prompt identification and management of these conditions may be able to prevent life-threatening complications.

Parents can ask their baby's healthcare provider about expanded (supplemental) screening if they live in a state that screens for a smaller number of disorders. Supplemental screening is typically done by commercial laboratories. It is separate from the testing done by the state, although it often uses a blood sample drawn at the same time.

Who Pays for Newborn Screening?

Newborn screening is performed on every infant regardless of the parents' health insurance status or ability to pay. The fees for newborn screening vary by state, from less than $15 to about $150. Some states do not charge a fee for this testing. When there is a fee, it is often covered by private health insurance plans. This testing is also covered under the Children's Health Insurance Program (CHIP) and Medicaid for those who are eligible.

If a parent chooses to have supplemental screening done through a private laboratory, that testing is not covered under the fees charged by each state for newborn screening. The costs of supplemental testing are charged by the laboratory that performs the tests. Parents should check with their health insurer to find out whether supplemental newborn screening is a covered service.

If a newborn screening test comes back positive (abnormal), further testing needs to be done to determine whether the baby has a particular condition. This additional testing involves separate costs that may be covered by health insurance plans.

What Happens If a Newborn Screening Test Comes Back Negative?

Within two to three weeks after newborn screening tests are performed, results are sent to the baby's doctor's office or clinic. A negative result means that all of the tests are in the normal range, and they do not indicate any increased risk. Other words for a negative test result are "passing," "in-range," or "normal."

In most cases, families are not notified of negative results. Parents can contact their baby's healthcare provider if they wish to confirm that the results were negative. Usually, no follow-up testing is necessary.

Rarely, the results of a newborn screening test can be a false negative. "False negative" means that a disease was missed by the screen; the test results came back negative, but the child actually has the disease. Possible reasons for a false negative result include laboratory errors, such as mixing up samples, and doing the test too early. Because false negatives are possible, further testing should be done if a baby has a family history of a particular disease or shows signs and symptoms, regardless of the newborn screening result.

What Happens If a Newborn Screening Test Comes Back Positive?

Within two to three weeks after newborn screening tests are performed, results are sent to the baby's doctor's office or clinic. A positive result means that at least one of the tests came back outside the normal range. Other words for a positive result are "failing," "out-of-range," or "abnormal."

The healthcare provider will notify parents of a positive test result. A positive result does not mean that a baby definitely has a disease, but it indicates that further testing (called "diagnostic testing," because it is used to diagnose disease) should be performed as soon as possible. If the baby does have the disease, quick follow-up testing can allow treatment or management, such as a special diet, to begin very soon after birth.

Often when there is a positive screening test result, follow-up diagnostic testing shows that the baby does not have the disease. In these cases, the results of the newborn screening test are described as "false positive," meaning that the test suggested an increased risk of the disease when the baby does not actually have the disease. False positive test results occur because screening tests are designed to identify as many babies affected by treatable diseases as possible. Because it is critical not to miss affected babies, some babies who are unaffected also have a positive screening result.

Occasionally, the results of a newborn screening test are reported as "borderline." These results are not quite normal, but they are not clearly abnormal, either. In these cases, the baby's healthcare provider may repeat the test.

What Is Newborn Genomic Sequencing?

Newborn genomic sequencing is an approach currently under study to collect and analyze large amounts of DNA sequence data in the newborn period. Genomic sequencing, a technology used to determine the order of DNA building blocks (nucleotides) in an individual's genetic code, is already available to test for genetic disorders in children and adults. Researchers have proposed using this technology to screen all newborns for health conditions they may have or be at risk of developing in childhood.

Newborn genomic sequencing would not replace standard newborn screening, which tests for a recommended 34 health conditions (although the exact number varies by state). Like current newborn screening, newborn genomic sequencing would allow doctors to identify health conditions very early in life. This technique would significantly expand the number and scope of health conditions that could be diagnosed soon after birth, potentially allowing doctors to start treatment and other follow-up as soon as possible.

As interest in newborn genomic sequencing grows, researchers and ethicists have identified possible ethical, social, and legal issues that need to be considered before the technology is widely adopted. These include the following considerations:

- Some genetic changes will have implications for the health of not only the infant, but of his or her parents and other family members.

- The interpretation of genomic data is constantly evolving, and right now it is unclear whether some changes in the genome are relevant to a person's health or not.

- While some genetic changes have immediate significance for an infant's health, other changes only influence the risk of developing health problems later in life. Infants are unable to provide informed consent, which is generally required when testing for adult-onset diseases.

- Newborn genomic screening raises issues of privacy and potential genetic discrimination if genomic data becomes part of a baby's medical record.

Section 7.4

Whole Exome Sequencing and Whole Genome Sequencing

This section includes text excerpted from "What Is Genetic Testing?" Genetics Home Reference (GHR), National Institutes of Health (NIH), January 29, 2019.

Determining the order of DNA building blocks (nucleotides) in an individual's genetic code, called "DNA sequencing," has advanced the study of genetics and is one technique used to test for genetic disorders. Two methods, whole exome sequencing and whole genome sequencing, are increasingly used in healthcare and research to identify genetic variations; both methods rely on new technologies that allow rapid sequencing of large amounts of DNA. These approaches are known as "next-generation sequencing" (or "next-gen sequencing").

The original sequencing technology, called "Sanger sequencing" (named after the scientist who developed it, Frederick Sanger), was a breakthrough that helped scientists determine the human genetic code, but it is time-consuming and expensive. The Sanger method has been automated to make it faster and is still used in laboratories nowadays to sequence short pieces of DNA, but it would take years to sequence all of a person's DNA (known as the person's genome).

Next-generation sequencing has sped up the process (taking only days to weeks to sequence a human genome) while reducing the cost. With next-generation sequencing, it is now feasible to sequence large amounts of DNA, for instance, all the pieces of an individual's DNA that provide instructions for making proteins. These pieces, called exons, are thought to make up one percent of a person's genome.

Together, all the exons in a genome are known as the exome, and the method of sequencing them is known as whole exome sequencing (WES). This method allows variations in the protein-coding region of any gene to be identified, rather than in only a select few genes.

Because most known mutations that cause disease occur in exons, whole exome sequencing is thought to be an efficient method to identify possible disease-causing mutations.

However, researchers have found that DNA variations outside the exons can affect gene activity and protein production and lead to genetic disorders—variations that whole exome sequencing would miss. Another method, called "whole genome sequencing," determines the order of all the nucleotides in an individual's DNA and can determine variations in any part of the genome.

While many more genetic changes can be identified with whole exome and whole genome sequencing than with select gene sequencing, the significance of much of this information is unknown. Because not all genetic changes affect health, it is difficult to know whether identified variants are involved in the condition of interest. Sometimes, an identified variant is associated with a different genetic disorder that has not yet been diagnosed (these are called "incidental or secondary findings").

In addition to being used in the clinic, whole exome and whole genome sequencing are valuable methods for researchers. Continued study of exome and genome sequences can help determine whether new genetic variations are associated with health conditions, which will aid disease diagnosis in the future.

Section 7.5

What Are Secondary Findings from Genetic Testing?

This section includes text excerpted from "What Is Genetic Testing?" Genetics Home Reference (GHR), National Institutes of Health (NIH), January 29, 2019.

Secondary findings are genetic test results that provide information about changes (variants) in a gene unrelated to the primary purpose for the testing.

When a clinician orders a genetic test to discover the genetic cause of a particular condition, the test will often sequence one or a few genes that seem most likely to be associated with that individual's set of signs and symptoms. However, if the individual's signs and symptoms do not have an obvious genetic cause, a clinician might order a test that sequences all of the pieces of an individual's DNA that provide instructions for making proteins (called an "exome") or a test that sequences all of an individual's DNA building blocks (nucleotides), called a "genome." These tests are called "whole exome sequencing" and "whole genome sequencing" (WGS), respectively.

Many more genetic changes can be identified with whole exome and whole genome sequencing than by sequencing just one or a few genes. Sometimes, testing finds a variant that is associated with a condition other than the one for which testing was originally indicated. This is called a "secondary finding." Some individuals with a secondary finding may not yet have any of the symptoms associated with the condition, but may be at risk of developing it later in life. For example, a person with a variant in the *BRCA1* gene, which is associated with an increased risk of breast and ovarian cancer, may not have developed cancer. Other individuals with secondary findings may have a known medical condition, such as extremely high cholesterol, but receive results that indicate a genetic cause for that condition, such as a variant in the *LDLR* gene.

In 2013 (and again in 2017), the American College of Medical Genetics and Genomics (ACMG) recommended that all labs performing whole exome and whole genome sequencing tests include the reporting of secondary findings, in addition to any variants that are found related to the primary purpose of the testing. The ACMG proposed a list of 59 genes that are associated with a variety of conditions, from cancer to heart disease. The 59 genes for which secondary findings are reported were chosen because they are associated with conditions that have a definable set of clinical features, the possibility of early diagnosis, a reliable clinical genetic test, and effective intervention or treatment. The goal of reporting these secondary findings to an individual is to provide medical benefit by preventing or better managing health conditions. The variants that are reported are known to cause disease. Variants of unknown significance, whose involvement in disease at the current time is unclear, are not reported.

The information provided by secondary findings can be very important because it may help prevent a disease from occurring or guide the management of signs and symptoms if the disease develops or is already present. However, as with any type of medical diagnosis, the news of an unexpected potential health problem may lead to additional health costs and stress for individuals and their families. On the basis of secondary findings, additional testing to confirm results, ongoing screening tests, or preventive care may be advised. Individuals receiving whole exome or whole genome sequencing can choose to "opt out" of analysis of the 59 secondary finding genes and not receive variant results. As whole exome and whole genome sequencing become more common, it is important for individuals to understand what type of information they may learn and how it can impact their medical care.

Chapter 8

Preventing Genetic Discrimination

What Is Genetic Discrimination?

Genetic discrimination occurs if people are treated unfairly because of differences in their deoxyribonucleic acid (DNA) that increase their chances of getting a certain disease. For example, a health insurer might refuse to give coverage to a woman who has a DNA difference that raises her odds of getting breast cancer. Employers also could use DNA information to decide whether to hire or fire workers.

Who Needs Protection from Genetic Discrimination

Everyone should care about the potential for genetic discrimination. Every person has dozens of DNA differences that could increase or decrease his or her chances of getting a disease, such as diabetes, heart disease, cancer, or Alzheimer disease (AD). It's important to remember that these DNA differences don't always mean someone will develop a disease, just that the risk to get the disease may be greater.

More and more tests are being developed to find DNA differences that affect our health. Called "genetic tests," these tests will become a

This chapter includes text excerpted from "Genetic Information Nondiscrimination Act of 2008," National Human Genome Research Institute (NHGRI), April 6, 2015. Reviewed March 2019.

routine part of healthcare in the future. Healthcare providers will use information about each person's DNA to develop more individualized ways of detecting, treating, and preventing disease. But unless this DNA information is protected, it could be used to discriminate against people.

What Is the Genetic Information Nondiscrimination Act?

The Genetic Information Nondiscrimination Act of 2008, also referred to as "GINA," protects Americans from being treated unfairly because of differences in their DNA that may affect their health. The law prevents discrimination from health insurers and employers. The act was signed into federal law on May 21, 2008. The parts of the law relating to health insurers took effect in May 2009, and those relating to employers took effect in November 2009.

Why Was the Law Needed?

The law was needed to help ease concerns about discrimination that might keep some people from getting genetic tests that could benefit their health. The law also enables people to take part in research studies without fear that their DNA information might be used against them in health insurance or the workplace.

What Is Included and What's Not in the Law?

The law protects people from discrimination by health insurers and employers on the basis of DNA information.

The law does not cover life insurance, disability insurance, and long-term care insurance.

How Does the Federal Law Affect State Laws?

Before the federal law was passed, many states had passed laws against genetic discrimination. The degree of protection from these laws varies widely among the different states. The federal law sets a minimum standard of protection that must be met in all states. It does not weaken the protections provided by any state law.

Part Two

Disorders Resulting from Abnormalities in Specific Genes

Chapter 9

Albinism

Albinism is a group of inherited disorders that result in little or no production of the pigment melanin, which determines the color of the skin, hair, and eyes. Melanin also plays a role in the development of certain optical nerves; therefore, all forms of albinism cause problems with the development and function of the eyes. Other symptoms can include:

- Light skin or changes in skin color

- Very white to brown hair

- Very light blue to brown eye color that may appear red in some light and may change with age

- Sensitivity to sun exposure

- Increased risk of developing skin cancer

Albinism is caused by mutations in one of several genes, and most types are inherited in an autosomal recessive manner. Although there's no cure, people with the disorder can take steps to improve vision and avoid too much sun exposure.

This chapter includes text excerpted from "Albinism," Genetic and Rare Diseases Information Center (GARD), National Center for Advancing Translational Sciences (NCATS), May 24, 2016.

Albinism: Inheritance

Different types of albinism can have different patterns of inheritance, depending on the genetic cause of the condition. Oculocutaneous albinism (OCA) involves the eyes, hair, and skin. Ocular albinism (OA), which is much less common, involves primarily the eyes, while skin and hair may appear similar or slightly lighter than that of other family members. Mutations in several different genes, on different chromosomes, can cause different types of albinism.

OCA is inherited in an autosomal recessive manner. This means that two mutations are necessary for an individual to have OCA. Individuals normally have two copies of each numbered chromosome and the genes on them—one inherited from the father, the other inherited from the mother. Neither of these gene copies is functional in people with albinism. Each unaffected parent of an individual with an autosomal recessive condition carries one functional copy of the causative gene and one nonfunctional copy. They are referred to as carriers, and do not typically show signs or symptoms of the condition. Both parents must carry a defective *OCA* gene to have a child with albinism. When 2 individuals who are carriers for the same autosomal recessive condition have children, there is a 25 percent (1 in 4) risk for the child to have the condition, a 50 percent (1 in 2) risk for the child to be an unaffected carrier like each of the parents, and a 25 percent chance for the child to not have the condition and not be a carrier.

OA type 1 is inherited in an X-linked pattern. A condition is considered X-linked if the mutated gene that causes the disorder is located on the X chromosome, one of the two sex chromosomes. In males (who have only one X chromosome and one Y), one altered copy of the causative gene in each cell is sufficient to cause the characteristic features of OA, because males do not have another X chromosome with a working copy of the gene. Because females have two copies of the X chromosome, women with only one copy of a mutation in each cell usually do not experience vision loss or other significant eye abnormalities. They may have mild changes in retinal pigmentation that can be detected during an eye examination.

Researchers have also identified several other genes in which mutations can result in albinism with other features. One group of these includes at least nine genes (on different chromosomes) leading to Hermansky-Pudlak syndrome (HPS). In addition to albinism, HPS is associated with bleeding problems and bruising. Some forms are also associated with lung and bowel disease. Like OCA, HPS is inherited in an autosomal recessive manner.

Treatment of Albinism

The goal of treatment is to address the symptoms present in each individual. People with albinism should protect their skin and eyes from the sun. This can be done by:

- Avoiding prolonged exposure to the sun
- Using sunscreen with a high sun protection factor (SPF) rating (20 or higher)
- Covering up completely with clothing when exposed to the sun
- Wearing sunglasses with ultraviolet (UV) protection

Individuals with vision problems may need corrective lenses. They should also have regular follow-up exams with an ophthalmologist. In rare cases, surgery may be needed. Individuals with albinism should also have regular skin assessments to screen for skin cancer or lesions that can lead to cancer.

Prognosis for People with Albinism

Most people with albinism live a normal life span and have the same types of medical problems as the rest of the population. Although the risk of developing skin cancer is increased, with careful surveillance and prompt treatment, this is usually curable.

Chapter 10

Alpha-1 Antitrypsin Deficiency

Alpha-1 antitrypsin deficiency (AATD) is an inherited disease that causes an increased risk of having chronic obstructive pulmonary disease (COPD), liver disease, skin problems (panniculitis), and inflammation of the blood vessels (vasculitis). Lung (pulmonary) problems almost always occur in adults, whereas liver and skin problems may occur in adults and children. The age when symptoms begin and the severity of symptoms can vary depending on how much working alpha-1 antitrypsin protein (AAT) a person has. Symptoms may include:

- Shortness of breath and wheezing
- Repeated infections of the lungs and liver
- Yellow skin
- Feeling overly tired (fatigue)
- Rapid heartbeat when standing
- Vision problems
- Weight loss

However, some people with AATD do not have any problems.

This chapter includes text excerpted from "Alpha-1 Antitrypsin Deficiency," Genetic and Rare Diseases Information Center (GARD), National Center for Advancing Translational Sciences (NCATS), September 26, 2018.

Cause of Alpha-1 Antitrypsin Deficiency

AATD is caused by mutations in the *SERPINA1* gene and it is inherited in a codominant manner. The genetic changes cause too little or no working AAT to be made. AAT is made in the liver cells and sent through the bloodstream to the lungs where it helps protect the lungs from damage. Having low levels of AAT (or no AAT) may allow the lungs to become damaged. A buildup of abnormal AAT can cause liver damage. Diagnosis may be suspected by finding low levels of AAT in the blood and confirmed by genetic testing. Treatment may include infusions of AAT. Other treatment depends on the type and severity of the person's medical problems but may include bronchodilators to open airways, antibiotics for upper respiratory tract infections (URTI), and in severe cases, lung transplantation or liver transplantation.

AATD is caused by changes (pathogenic variants, also known as "mutations") in the *SERPINA1* gene. This gene gives the body instructions to make a protein called "AAT." One of the jobs of AAT is to protect the body from another protein called "neutrophil elastase (NE)." Neutrophil elastase is an enzyme that helps the body fight infections, but it can also attack healthy tissues (especially the lungs), if not controlled by AAT.

Genetic changes that cause AAT may mean that the body's liver cells make too little or no AAT, or make a form (variant) of AAT that does not work well (abnormal AAT). This allows neutrophil elastase to destroy lung tissue, causing lung disease.

In addition, abnormal AAT can build up in the liver and cause damage to the liver, especially in people who have two copies of the specific genetic variant called "allele Z." Liver problems do not occur in people who do not make any detectable AAT, such as when a person has two null alleles of the *SERPINA1* gene.

The severity of AATD may also be worsened by environmental factors, such as exposure to tobacco smoke, dust, and chemicals.

Diagnosis of Alpha-1 Antitrypsin Deficiency

AATD may first be suspected in people who have symptoms of liver disease at any age, or who have symptoms of lung disease (such as emphysema), especially when there is no obvious cause or it is diagnosed at a younger age.

Confirming the diagnosis involves a blood test showing a low level of AAT in the blood, and either:

- Detecting an AAT protein variant that does not work properly (functionally deficient) using a special test called "isoelectric focusing."

  or

- Finding a disease-causing change (pathogenic variant, also called "mutation") in both copies of the *SERPINA1* gene by genetic testing. (This confirms the diagnosis when the above-mentioned tests are not performed or their results are not in agreement.)

Specialists involved in the diagnosis may include primary care doctors, lung specialists (pulmonologists), and/or liver specialists (hepatologists).

Treatment of Alpha-1 Antitrypsin Deficiency

In general, the treatment of medical problems associated with AATD includes the standard medical therapies (SMT) and supportive care for the specific medical problem. However, there is one special therapy called "augmentation therapy" available to some people with AATD who have lung problems.

Augmentation therapy aims to increase the blood level of AAT by adding purified, human AAT directly into the person's blood through intravenous (IV) infusion. The goal is to prevent the progression of lung disease. Skin problems usually get better as well. Augmentation therapy does not affect liver disease associated with AATD.

Augmentation therapy is indicated only when people with AATD:

- Are older than 18 years of age

- Have levels of alpha-1 antitrypsin in their blood that are less than 11 micromoles/liter

- Have pulmonary function tests (spirometer) that show airway obstruction

- Do not smoke or have stopped smoking for at least the last 6 months

- Are willing to get the infusions weekly at the hospital

- Do not have immunoglobulin A deficiency, because the therapy with alpha-1 may contain traces of immunoglobulin type A (IgA), and patients with IgA deficiency may have antibodies against IgA

In some cases, it is also done in people who have normal airflow, but who have a computed tomography (CT) scan that shows emphysema in the lung.

Other treatments depend on symptoms but may include:

- Antibiotics to treat infections
- Bronchodilators and inhaled steroids to help open the airways and make breathing easier
- Exercise program
- Oxygen
- Lung volume reduction surgery
- Lung transplantation for patients with advanced emphysema due to severe AAT deficiency
- Liver transplantation for patients with severe liver disease. After a liver transplant, the AAT deficiency is corrected, because the normal donor liver produces and secretes normal AAT.

Routine recommendations to avoid medical complications include:

- Vaccination against hepatitis A and B
- Preventive vaccines against influenza and pneumococcal vaccines
- Avoid using tobacco
- Avoid or minimize drinking alcohol (for those at risk for liver disease)
- Avoid other environmental risk factors, such as chemical exposures
- Liver function tests periodically for people with two copies of the Z allele (PI*ZZ)
- Lung function test every 6 to 12 months people with severe AATD
- Liver ultrasound, in cases of liver disease, every 6 to 12 months to monitor for fibrotic changes (cirrhosis) and liver cancer (hepatocellular carcinoma (HCC))

Chapter 11

Blood Disorders (Hemoglobinopathies)

Chapter Contents

Section 11.1

Hemochromatosis

This section contains text excerpted from the following sources:
Text beginning with the heading "What Is Hemochromatosis?" is
excerpted from "Hereditary Hemochromatosis," Centers for Disease
Control and Prevention (CDC), July 17, 2018; Text beginning
with heading "What Are the Complications of Hemochromatosis?"
is excerpted from "Hemochromatosis," National Institute of
Diabetes and Digestive and Kidney Diseases (NIDDK),
March 2014. Reviewed March 2019.

What Is Hemochromatosis?

Hemochromatosis is a disorder in which the body can build up too
much iron in the skin, heart, liver, pancreas, pituitary gland, and
joints. Too much iron is toxic to the body and, over time, the high levels
of iron can damage tissues and organs and lead to:

- Cirrhosis (liver damage)

- Hepatocellular carcinoma (HCC) (liver cancer)

- Heart problems

- Arthritis (joint pain)

- Diabetes

In the United States, about 1 in 300 non-Hispanic Whites has
hereditary hemochromatosis, with lower rates among other races and
ethnicities. Many people with hereditary hemochromatosis (HH) don't
know they have it. Early symptoms, such as feeling tired or weak, are
common and can cause hemochromatosis to be confused with a variety
of other diseases. Most people with hereditary hemochromatosis never
develop symptoms or complications. Men are more likely to develop
complications and often at an earlier age. An estimated 9 percent
(about 1 in 10) of men with hereditary hemochromatosis will develop
severe liver disease.

How Do You Know If You Have Hereditary Hemochromatosis?

A blood test can be used to screen people who may have hemochromatosis by measuring how much iron is in their blood. Affected people with

or without a known family history of hemochromatosis can be diagnosed through blood tests for iron, followed by genetic testing if they are symptomatic or have complications. Symptoms of hemochromatosis include:

- Feeling of tiredness or weakness
- Weight loss
- Joint pain
- Bronze or grey skin color
- Abdominal pain
- Loss of sex drive

Hereditary hemochromatosis is most commonly caused by certain variants in the *HFE* gene. If you inherit two of these variants, one from each parent, you have hereditary hemochromatosis and are at risk for developing high iron levels. If you have a family member, especially a sibling, who is known to have hereditary hemochromatosis, talk to your doctor about genetic testing.

How Can You Prevent Complications from Hereditary Hemochromatosis?

If you or your family members have hereditary hemochromatosis, your doctor may suggest ways to lower the amount of iron in your body. The earlier hemochromatosis is diagnosed, the less likely you are to develop serious complications—many of which can cause permanent problems. If you are diagnosed with hemochromatosis, regularly scheduled blood removal is the most effective way to lower the amount of iron in your body. Your doctor may also recommend:

- Annual blood tests to check your iron levels
- Liver biopsy to check for cirrhosis
- Iron chelation therapy, if you cannot have blood removed, which involves medicine taken either orally or injected to lower the amount of iron in your body
- Dietary changes, such as avoiding multivitamins, vitamin C supplements, and iron supplements, which can increase iron throughout your body
- No alcohol use (because alcohol increases the risk of liver damage)

- Steps to prevent infections, including not eating uncooked fish and shellfish and getting recommended vaccinations, including those against hepatitis A and B

What Are the Complications of Hemochromatosis?

Without treatment, iron may build up in the organs and cause complications, including:

- Cirrhosis, or scarring of liver tissue

- Diabetes

- Irregular heart rhythms or weakening of the heart muscle

- Arthritis

- Erectile dysfunction (ED)

The complication most often associated with hemochromatosis is liver damage. Iron buildup in the liver causes cirrhosis, which increases the chance of developing liver cancer.

For some people, complications may be the first sign of hemochromatosis. However, not everyone with hemochromatosis will develop complications.

How Is Hemochromatosis Diagnosed?

Healthcare providers use medical and family history, a physical exam, and routine blood tests to diagnose hemochromatosis or other conditions that could cause the same symptoms or complications.

- **Medical and family history.** Taking a medical and family history is one of the first things a healthcare provider may do to help diagnose hemochromatosis. The healthcare provider will look for clues that may indicate hemochromatoses, such as a family history of arthritis or unexplained liver disease.

- **Physical exam.** After taking a medical history, a healthcare provider will perform a physical exam, which may help diagnose hemochromatosis. During a physical exam, a healthcare provider usually:

  - Examines a patient's body

  - Uses a stethoscope to listen to bodily sounds

  - Taps on specific areas of the patient's body

- **Blood tests.** A blood test involves drawing blood at a healthcare provider's office or a commercial facility and sending the sample to a lab for analysis. Blood tests can determine whether the amount of iron stored in the body is higher than normal:

  - The transferrin saturation test shows how much iron is bound to the protein that carries iron in the blood. Transferrin saturation values above or equal to 45 percent are considered abnormal.

  - The serum ferritin test detects the amount of ferritin—a protein that stores iron—in the blood. Levels above 300 μg/L in men and 200 μg/L in women are considered abnormal. Levels above 1,000 μg/L in men or women indicate a high chance of iron overload and organ damage.

  If either test shows higher-than-average levels of iron in the body, healthcare providers can order a special blood test that can detect two copies of the C282Y mutation to confirm the diagnosis. If the mutation is not present, healthcare providers will look for other causes.

- **Liver biopsy.** Healthcare providers may perform a liver biopsy, a procedure that involves taking a piece of liver tissue for examination with a microscope for signs of damage or disease. The healthcare provider may ask the patient to temporarily stop taking certain medications before the liver biopsy. The healthcare provider may ask the patient to fast for eight hours before the procedure.

During the procedure, the patient lies on a table, right hand resting above the head. The healthcare provider applies a local anesthetic to the area where she or he will insert the biopsy needle. If needed, a healthcare provider will also give sedatives and pain medication. The healthcare provider uses a needle to take a small piece of liver tissue. He or she may use ultrasound, computerized tomography (CT) scans, or other imaging techniques to guide the needle. After the biopsy, the patient must lie on the right side for up to two hours and is monitored an additional two to four hours before being sent home.

A healthcare provider performs a liver biopsy at a hospital or an outpatient center. The healthcare provider sends the liver sample to a pathology lab where the pathologist—a doctor who specializes in diagnosing disease—looks at the tissue with a microscope and sends a report to the patient's healthcare provider. The biopsy shows how much iron has accumulated in the liver and whether the patient has liver damage.

Hemochromatosis is rare, and healthcare providers may not think to test for this disease. Thus, the disease is often not diagnosed or treated. The initial symptoms can be diverse, vague, and similar to the symptoms of many other diseases. Healthcare providers may focus on the symptoms and complications caused by hemochromatosis rather than on the underlying iron overload. However, if a healthcare provider diagnoses and treats the iron overload caused by hemochromatosis before organ damage has occurred, a person can live a normal, healthy life.

Who Should Be Tested for Hemochromatosis?

Experts recommend testing for hemochromatosis in people who have symptoms, complications, or a family history of the disease.

Some researchers have suggested widespread screening for the C282Y mutation in the general population. However, screening is not cost-effective. Although the C282Y mutation occurs quite frequently, the disease caused by the mutation is rare, and many people with two copies of the mutation never develop iron overload or organ damage.

Researchers and public health officials suggest the following:

- Siblings of people who have hemochromatosis should have their blood tested to see if they have the C282Y mutation.

- Parents, children, and other close relatives of people who have hemochromatosis should consider being tested.

- Healthcare providers should consider testing people who have severe and continuing fatigue, unexplained cirrhosis, joint pain or arthritis, heart problems, erectile dysfunction, or diabetes because these health issues may result from hemochromatosis.

How Is Hemochromatosis Treated?

Healthcare providers treat hemochromatosis by drawing blood. This process is called "phlebotomy." Phlebotomy rids the body of extra iron. This treatment is simple, inexpensive, and safe.

Based on the severity of the iron overload, a patient will have phlebotomy to remove a pint of blood once or twice a week for several months to a year, and occasionally longer. Healthcare providers will test serum ferritin levels periodically to monitor iron levels. The goal is to bring serum ferritin levels to the low end of the average range and keep them there. Depending on the lab, the level is 25 to 50 μg/L.

After phlebotomy reduces serum ferritin levels to the desired level, patients may need maintenance phlebotomy treatment every few months. Some patients may need phlebotomies more often. Serum ferritin tests every six months or once a year will help determine how often a patient should have blood drawn. Many blood donation centers provide free phlebotomy treatment for people with hemochromatosis.

Treating hemochromatosis before organs are damaged can prevent complications, such as cirrhosis, heart problems, arthritis, and diabetes. Treatment cannot cure these conditions in patients who already have them at diagnosis. However, treatment will help most of these conditions improve. The treatments' effectiveness depends on the degree of organ damage. For example, treating hemochromatosis can stop the progression of liver damage in its early stages and lead to a normal life expectancy. However, if a patient develops cirrhosis, his or her chance of developing liver cancer increases, even with phlebotomy treatment. Arthritis usually does not improve even after phlebotomy removes extra iron.

Eating, Diet, and Nutrition

Iron is an essential nutrient found in many foods. People with hemochromatosis absorb much more iron from the food they eat compared with healthy people. People with hemochromatosis can help prevent iron overload by:

- Eating only moderate amounts of iron-rich foods, such as red meat and organ meat

- Avoiding supplements that contain iron

- Avoiding supplements that contain vitamin C, which increases iron absorption

People with hemochromatosis can take steps to help prevent liver damage, including:

- Limiting the amount of alcoholic beverages they drink because alcohol increases their chance of cirrhosis and liver cancer

- Avoiding alcoholic beverages entirely if they already have cirrhosis

Section 11.2

Sickle Cell Disease

This section includes text excerpted from "Sickle Cell Disease," Office on Women's Health (OWH), U.S. Department of Health and Human Services (HHS), September 14, 2018.

What Is Sickle Cell Disease?

Sickle cell disease (SCD) is a group of red blood cell (RBC) disorders that are passed down from your parents. This means that it is a genetic disease, and you are born with it.

People with SCD have some RBCs that are shaped like a "sickle" or crescent, instead of round. Normal, round RBCs are flexible enough to move through blood vessels to carry oxygen to the body. Sickle-shaped RBCs can stick to each other inside blood vessels, blocking blood flow and causing pain and problems in many different parts of the body. People with SCD also have fewer RBCs, because sickle cells die sooner than normal RBCs. Over time, blocked blood flow and lack of oxygen can cause serious health problems and organ damage.

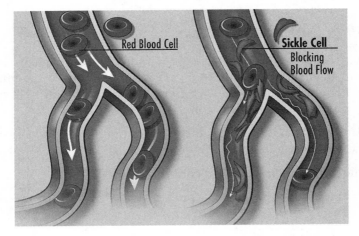

Figure 11.1. *Sickle Cell Disease* (Source: "Sickle Cell Disease," National Human Genome Research Institute (NHGRI).)

What Causes Sickle Cell Disease

All RBCs have hemoglobin, which makes the cell red and helps carry oxygen to different parts of the body. RBCs with normal hemoglobin are round and flexible. If you have SCD, your RBCs have abnormal hemoglobin and are crescent- or sickle-shaped.

Abnormal hemoglobin genes (sickle cell genes) run in families. Having two sickle cell genes causes SCD. If you get one sickle cell gene from each of your parents, then you have SCD. If you get one sickle cell gene and one normal gene from your parents, you have sickle cell trait.

Why Does Sickle Cell Disease Cause Health Problems?

RBCs that are crescent- or sickle-shaped cannot slide smoothly through small blood vessels like normal, round RBCs. Sickle cells can get stuck in small blood vessels and block blood flow to organs and tissues in the body. When organs do not get enough blood, they do not get enough oxygen. This can cause organ damage and pain. When organs are damaged, they do not work properly. Many of the complications or health problems caused by SCD are caused by organ damage or inflammation.

Sickle cells also die sooner than normal RBCs. Not having enough healthy RBCs causes anemia, which can make you feel tired or weak because there is less oxygen in your body.

What Are Common Types of Sickle Cell Disease?

There are different types of SCD because there are different types of sickle cell genes. You can inherit different types of abnormal hemoglobin genes that cause different types of SCD. Hemoglobin is what gives RBCs their red color and is the part of the cell that helps carry oxygen to different parts of the body. In SCD, the type of disease you have is named after the type of abnormal hemoglobin genes you have. The most common types of SCD are:

- **Hemoglobin (Hb) SS or sickle cell anemia.** This is usually the most severe type of SCD, when you inherit two *HbS* genes, one from each parent. Sickle cells break apart or die more easily than normal RBCs, causing severe anemia. Severe means that problems can happen more often and be more serious. Anemia happens when you have low numbers of RBCs, which can make you feel tired and weak and cause other serious health problems.

- **Hemoglobin (Hb) SC disease.** People with HbSC sickle cell have inherited one hemoglobin *S* gene and one hemoglobin *C* gene. Both genes are abnormal, but HbSC is usually a less severe or serious type of SCD compared with HbSS. Less severe means that it may lead to fewer problems or that problem may show up later in life compared with more severe types of the disease.

- **Hemoglobin (Hb) S beta thalassemia.** People with HbS beta thalassemia (β thalassemias), inherit one hemoglobin *S* gene and one gene for beta thalassemia, another type of anemia. Anemia is when you have low numbers of RBCs. There are two types of beta thalassemia, called "zero" and "plus," written as "0" or "+." People with HbS beta 0 thalassemias usually have a more severe or serious type of SCD. People with HbS beta + thalassemia usually have a less severe type of SCD.

What Is the Difference between Sickle Cell Trait and Sickle Cell Disease?

People who have sickle cell trait have one gene that causes SCD and one normal gene. Because they have only one sickle cell gene, they do not have the disease. Most people who have sickle cell trait, or just one sickle cell gene, do not have any symptoms of the disease and can live a normal, active life.

People who have sickle cell trait may be at a slightly higher risk of:

- Kidney disease

- Blood clots, especially in the lungs (called "pulmonary embolism")

- Sudden death from very intense exercise

People with sickle cell trait can pass the gene that causes SCD on to their children. If a mother and a father both have sickle cell trait, there is a one in four chance that both sickle cell genes will be passed on and their child will have SCD.

Who Gets Sickle Cell Disease

Researchers are not sure how many people are living with SCD. In the United States, researchers think as many as 100,000 people may have the disease.

SCD happens more often in people whose families came from Africa, India, the Middle East, and Southeast Asia. In the United States, it is most common among people who are Black or African American.

About 1 out of every 365 Black or African American newborns has SCD. Hispanic Americans are also at higher risk. SCD happens in about 1 out of every 16,300 Hispanic American newborns.

Researchers estimate that more than 2 million Americans have sickle cell trait.

What Are the Symptoms of Sickle Cell Disease?

Symptoms can be different for each person with SCD. People who have mild types of SCD may start having symptoms and complications at older ages than those with severe SCD.

The most common symptom is pain caused by sickle cells blocking blood flow in blood vessels. When blood vessels are blocked, organs and tissue do not get oxygen, which causes pain. Having fewer red blood cells (RBCs) than normal causes anemia or not enough oxygen in the blood, making you feel tired and weak. You may also have symptoms of other health problems if the disease causes damage to a part of the body, such as the spleen, heart, lungs, eyes, kidneys, liver, or other organs.

When Should You Go to the Hospital for Your Sickle Cell Disease Symptoms?

You may have to go to the hospital for treatment you cannot get at home or at a doctor's office. Anyone having a medical emergency should call 911. Everyone with SCD should make a pain management plan with their doctor. The pain management plan helps you know when to go to the hospital for a pain crisis. You may need to go to the hospital for other health problems caused by SCD.

People with SCD should go to the hospital for:

- A pain crisis (also called a "pain episode") that cannot be treated with over-the-counter (OTC) pain medicines or your own prescription pain medicine

- A fever over 101°F

- Stroke symptoms, such as:

  - Numbness or weakness in the face, arm, or leg, especially on only one side of the body

  - Confusion or trouble speaking or understanding

  - Trouble seeing in one or both eyes

- Trouble walking, dizziness, or loss of balance or coordination

- Severe headache with no known cause

- Problems breathing

- Signs that the spleen, an organ near the stomach, is getting bigger (when sickle cells get trapped in the spleen). This is a medical emergency if it causes anemia or not enough RBCs in your body. A spleen that is larger than normal can cause pain in the left side of your stomach.

- Sudden loss of vision

- Symptoms of severe anemia, such as shortness of breath, feeling very tired or dizzy, or having very pale skin compared with normal

How Is Sickle Cell Disease Diagnosed?

In the United States, all newborn babies are tested for SCD.

Your doctor or nurse may do tests to diagnose SCD if you were not diagnosed as a baby but have symptoms as an adult. These tests may include:

- **Blood tests.** Your doctor may do a complete blood test to screen for anemia. To identify the type of hemoglobin that is in your blood, your doctor will do a high-performance liquid chromatography (HPLC) or hemoglobin electrophoresis test.

- **Genetic testing.** The genetic test confirms the results of the HPLC or hemoglobin electrophoresis test. With this information, your doctor will be able to tell whether you have the two genes for SCD or a different abnormal hemoglobin gene.

If you are pregnant, you may choose to have a test called "amniocentesis" to see if the fetus has SCD. The doctor uses a needle to take a small amount of fluid from around the fetus inside your uterus (womb). Health risks for the fetus during amniocentesis are very rare but can be serious. Talk to your doctor, nurse, or midwife about the risks and benefits of testing.

What Medicines Treat Sickle Cell Disease

Medicines for SCD include:

- **Hydroxyurea.** The most commonly used medicine for SCD is a prescription medicine you take every day, called "hydroxyurea."

Hydroxyurea may help prevent problems from SCD, such as pain crises, stroke, and acute chest syndrome (ACS). Hydroxyurea may also make these problems less serious when they happen. Experts recommend that children with SCD over nine months old and all adults who have severe SCD take hydroxyurea unless there is a medical reason they should not take it. Most people do not have any serious side effects from the medicine. Hydroxyurea may lower the number of white blood cells (WBC) and platelets in your body, which is usually higher in people with SCD and may cause pain crises. Lowering the number of WBCs and platelets may put you at higher risk of infection and bleeding. WBCs, help you fight infections. Platelets help your blood clot when you get a cut or other injury. The long-term effects of this medicine are still unknown. Pregnant women, or women trying to become pregnant, should not take hydroxyurea.

- **L-glutamine.** In 2017, the U.S. Food and Drug Administration (FDA) approved a prescription medicine called "L-glutamine" for anyone over age five with SCD. It may help prevent sickle cell crises, which include pain crises and acute chest syndrome. Your doctor may prescribe this medicine if hydroxyurea does not work for you.

- **Pain medicines.** Most people with SCD use OTC pain medicine to relieve pain along with other at-home pain treatments, such as warm baths, relaxation training, or distracting activities. Sometimes these treatments are not strong enough. You may need a stronger opioid pain medicine from your doctor or a hospital. Talk to your doctor or nurse about a pain management plan so that you know how best to treat pain when a pain crisis happens.

- **Medicines for infections.** People with SCD are more likely to get infections, and the infections are more likely to be serious. A doctor or nurse will usually treat an infection with antibiotics. Children younger than five with SCD should take penicillin every day to prevent serious infections. Many children five and older and adults with SCD do not need to take penicillin every day. Talk to your SCD doctor about your medical history and if you need to take penicillin every day.

What Medical Procedures Treat Sickle Cell Disease

Some medical procedures can treat problems caused by SCD or cure SCD.

- **Blood transfusions.** You may get a RBC transfusion if you have SCD complications or health problems caused by SCD, such as anemia, ACS, or stroke. Some people with SCD who had a stroke in the past may need regular blood transfusions to help prevent another stroke. Regular blood transfusions are also used to prevent crises in people who can't take hydroxyurea. But blood transfusions can lead to dangerously high iron levels in the blood that can damage the heart and lungs. If this happens, you may need a medicine called "iron chelation therapy (ICT)" to lower the iron levels in your blood.

- **Bone marrow transplant (BMT).** As of now, bone marrow transplant, or hematopoietic stem cell transplant (HSCT), is the only cure for SCD. But a bone marrow transplant is not an option for many people with SCD because there is no matched bone marrow donor available. Also, a bone marrow transplant is a risky medical procedure that can cause serious health problems.

During a bone marrow transplant, a person's bone marrow stem cells are replaced with bone marrow stem cells from a healthy, matched donor. The bone marrow (the tissue inside of bones) makes new RBCs for the body. The healthy new bone marrow stem cells make healthy RBCs instead of sickle cells.

Finding a matched donor can be difficult. The bone marrow has to come from a donor who has matching proteins on their cells, usually a brother or sister. More than 90 percent of transplants are successful when the bone marrow comes from a matched sister or brother.

Severe complications can happen if the cells are not matched. Complications can include severe infections, seizures, or possibly death. Graft versus host disease, where the transplanted cells attack the recipient's organs, can happen if the donor is not well-matched. Sometimes these complications happen with a well-matched donor. Having a stem cell transplant may mean that you cannot get pregnant in the future.

Researchers are looking for ways to make bone marrow transplants safer for more people.

What Are the Major Complications of Sickle Cell Disease?

Complications of SCD depend on your age, your medical history, and the type of disease you have. SCD complications are not always the same in different people and can happen at any time in life. People with mild types of SCD usually have complications at an older age compared with people who have severe types of the disease.

Serious complications include:

- Pain

- Acute chest syndrome

- Lung problems

- Anemia

- Stroke

Some specialists do not recommend combination hormonal birth control (containing a combination of two different hormones) for women with SCD, because it adds to your higher risk of stroke.

Other complications include:

- Kidney problems

- Gallstones

- Bone and joint problems

- Heart failure and abnormal heart rhythms

- Eye problems

- Liver damage

- Leg ulcers

- Mental-health conditions, such as anxiety disorder or depression

- Problems with pregnancy

How Can You Stay Well with Sickle Cell Disease?

SCD is a chronic (long-term) disease, but you can live a full and active life by learning how to stay as healthy as possible. Follow these tips to manage your SCD:

- **Find a doctor who specializes in SCD.** You will probably need to see a hematologist, a doctor who specializes in blood diseases. You may have other types of doctors who treat certain complications from organ damage, such as a nephrologist for kidney problems. Some places in the United States have special centers at hospitals or doctors' offices for people with SCD. At a special center, you might be able to see different types of doctors in one location, or the center might be open later, to help treat a pain crisis.

- **Get an annual checkup.** Your doctor or nurse can help you coordinate healthcare among different specialists or locations. An annual checkup can help you keep track of other health conditions or concerns.

- **Prevent infections.** Infections can cause complications from SCD, so it is important to get all of the vaccines your doctor or nurse recommends.

- **Try to have healthy habits**. Staying hydrated is very important. Try to drink 8 to 10 glasses of water a day. Choose healthy foods and get regular physical activity, while being careful not to overdo it. Take care not to get too hot or too cold. Get enough sleep. Do not smoke.

- **Get support**. Your mental and emotional health are important. Find a support system. Support can come from friends and family or patient groups and community organizations. Talk to a professional counselor or therapist if you are feeling overwhelmed or depressed.

What Should You Know about the Transition from Childhood to Adult Care for Sickle Cell Disease?

Adults with SCD are likely to experience chronic or long-term pain and health problems that happen because of organ damage.

Moving from pediatric (childhood) to adult medical care is a high-risk period for people with SCD. This might be because damage from SCD builds up over time and might not cause health problems until you are an adult. Or, it may be difficult to find a doctor who specializes in SCD in adults.

Teens and young adults should prepare ahead of time for living on their own with SCD. Some doctors and nurses begin talking about the transition to adult care with patients as young as 13. Discussions between doctors, nurses, social workers, the patient, and family members about the transition should start at least 1 year before the transition to adult care. Healthy eating, regular exercise (not intense exercise), getting enough sleep, and dealing with stress in healthy ways can help prevent sickle cell crises. Find a specialist as soon as possible if you move to a new area. Figure out which hospital or center is closest if you have a medical emergency. Tell friends or loved ones who are nearby about the type of support you might need if you have a sickle cell crisis.

Section 11.3

Thalassemia

This section includes text excerpted from "Thalassemias," National Heart, Lung, and Blood Institute (NHLBI), September 9, 2016.

Thalassemias are inherited blood disorders. "Inherited" means that the disorder is passed from parents to children through genes.

Thalassemias cause the body to make fewer healthy red blood cells (RBCs) and less hemoglobin than normal. Hemoglobin is an iron-rich protein in RBCs. It carries oxygen to all parts of the body. Hemoglobin also carries carbon dioxide from the body to the lungs, where it's exhaled.

People who have thalassemias can have mild or severe anemia. Anemia is caused by a lower than normal number of RBCs or not enough hemoglobin in the RBCs.

Causes of Thalassemia

Your body makes three types of blood cells: RBCs, white blood cells (WBC), and platelets. Hemoglobin has two kinds of protein chains: alpha globin and beta globin. If your body doesn't make enough of these protein chains or they're abnormal, RBCs won't form correctly or carry enough oxygen. Your body won't work well if your RBCs don't make enough healthy hemoglobin.

Genes control how the body makes hemoglobin protein chains. When these genes are missing or altered, thalassemias occur.

Thalassemias are inherited disorders—that is, they're passed from parents to children through genes. People who inherit faulty hemoglobin genes from one parent but normal genes from the other are called "carriers." Carriers often have no signs of illness other than

99

mild anemia. However, they can pass the faulty genes on to their children.

People who have moderate to severe forms of thalassemia have inherited faulty genes from both parents.

Alpha Thalassemias

You need four genes (two from each parent) to make enough alpha globin protein chains. If one or more of the genes is missing, you'll have alpha thalassemia (α-thalassemia) trait or disease. This means that your body doesn't make enough alpha globin protein.

- If you're only missing one gene, you're a "silent" carrier. This means you won't have any signs of illness.

- If you're missing two genes, you have alpha thalassemia trait (also called "alpha thalassemia minor"). You may have mild anemia.

- If you're missing three genes, you likely have hemoglobin H disease (which a blood test can detect). This form of thalassemia causes moderate to severe anemia.

Very rarely, a baby is missing all four genes. This condition is called "alpha thalassemia major" or "hydrops fetalis." Babies who have hydrops fetalis usually die before or shortly after birth.

Beta Thalassemias

You need two genes (one from each parent) to make enough beta globin protein chains. If one or both of these genes are altered, you'll have beta thalassemia. This means that your body won't make enough beta globin protein.

- If you have one altered gene, you're a carrier. This condition is called "beta thalassemia trait" or "beta thalassemia minor." It causes mild anemia.

- If both genes are altered, you'll have beta thalassemia intermedia or beta thalassemia major (also called "Cooley's anemia"). The intermedia form of the disorder causes moderate anemia. The major form causes severe anemia.

Risk Factors for Thalassemia

Family history and ancestry are the two risk factors for thalassemias.

Family History

Thalassemias are inherited—that is, the genes for the disorders are passed from parents to their children. If your parents have missing or altered hemoglobin-making genes, you may have thalassemia.

Ancestry

Thalassemias occur most often among people of Italian, Greek, Middle Eastern, Southern Asian, and African descent.

Screening and Prevention of Thalassemia

You can't prevent thalassemias because they're inherited (passed from parents to children through genes). However, prenatal tests can detect these blood disorders before birth.

Family genetic studies may help find out whether people have missing or altered hemoglobin genes that cause thalassemias.

If you know of family members who have thalassemias and you're thinking of having children, consider talking with your doctor and a genetic counselor. They can help determine your risk for passing the disorder to your children.

Signs, Symptoms, and Complications of Thalassemia

A lack of oxygen in the bloodstream causes the signs and symptoms of thalassemias. The lack of oxygen occurs because the body doesn't make enough healthy RBCs and hemoglobin. The severity of symptoms depends on the severity of the disorder.

No Symptoms

Alpha thalassemia silent carriers generally have no signs or symptoms of the disorder. The lack of the alpha globin protein is so minor that the body's hemoglobin works normally.

Mild Anemia

People who have alpha or beta thalassemia trait can have mild anemia. However, many people who have these types of thalassemia have no signs or symptoms.

Mild anemia can make you feel tired. Mild anemia caused by alpha thalassemia trait might be mistaken for iron-deficiency anemia.

Mild to Moderate Anemia and Other Signs and Symptoms

People who have beta thalassemia intermedia have mild to moderate anemia. They also may have other health problems, such as:

- **Slowed growth and delayed puberty.** Anemia can slow down a child's growth and development.

- **Bone problems**. Thalassemia may cause bone marrow to expand. Bone marrow is the spongy substance inside bones that makes blood cells. When bone marrow expands, the bones become wider than normal. They may become brittle and break easily.

- **An enlarged spleen.** The spleen is an organ that helps your body fight infection and remove unwanted material. When a person has thalassemia, the spleen has to work very hard. As a result, the spleen becomes larger than normal. This makes anemia worse. If the spleen becomes too large, it must be removed.

Severe Anemia and Other Signs and Symptoms

People who have hemoglobin H disease or beta thalassemia major have severe thalassemia. Signs and symptoms usually occur within the first two years of life. They may include severe anemia and other health problems, such as:

- A pale and listless appearance

- Poor appetite

- Dark urine (a sign that RBCs are breaking down)

- Slowed growth and delayed puberty

- Jaundice (a yellowish color of the skin or whites of the eyes)

- An enlarged spleen, liver, or heart

- Bone problems (especially with bones in the face)

Complications of Thalassemias

Better treatments now allow people who have moderate and severe thalassemias to live much longer. As a result, these people must cope with complications of these disorders that occur over time.

Heart and Liver Diseases

Regular blood transfusions are a standard treatment for thalassemias. Transfusions can cause iron to build up in the blood (iron overload). This can damage organs and tissues, especially the heart and liver.

Heart disease caused by iron overload is the main cause of death in people who have thalassemias. Heart disease includes heart failure, arrhythmias (irregular heartbeats), and heart attack.

Infection

Among people who have thalassemias, infections are a key cause of illness and the second most common cause of death. People who have had their spleens removed are at an even higher risk because they no longer have this infection-fighting organ.

Osteoporosis

Many people who have thalassemias have bone problems, including osteoporosis. This is a condition in which bones are weak and brittle and break easily.

Diagnosis of Thalassemia

Doctors diagnose thalassemias using blood tests, including a complete blood count (CBC) and special hemoglobin tests.

- A CBC measures the amount of hemoglobin and the different kinds of blood cells, such as RBCs, in a sample of blood. People who have thalassemias have fewer healthy RBCs and less hemoglobin than normal in their blood. People who have alpha or beta thalassemia trait may have RBCs that are smaller than normal.

- Hemoglobin tests measure the types of hemoglobin in a blood sample. People who have thalassemias have problems with the alpha or beta globin protein chains of hemoglobin.

Moderate and severe thalassemias usually are diagnosed in early childhood. This is because signs and symptoms, including severe anemia, often occur within the first two years of life.

People who have milder forms of thalassemia might be diagnosed after a routine blood test shows they have anemia. Doctors might suspect thalassemia if a person has anemia and is a member of an ethnic group that's at increased risk for thalassemias.

Doctors also test the amount of iron in the blood to find out whether the anemia is due to iron deficiency or thalassemia. Iron-deficiency anemia occurs if the body doesn't have enough iron to make hemoglobin. The anemia in thalassemia occurs because of a problem with either the alpha globin or beta globin chains of hemoglobin, not because of a lack of iron.

Because thalassemias are passed from parents to children through genes, family genetic studies also can help diagnose the disorder. These studies involve taking a family medical history and doing blood tests on family members. The tests will show whether any family members have missing or altered hemoglobin genes.

If you know of family members who have thalassemias and you're thinking of having children, consider talking with your doctor and a genetic counselor. They can help determine your risk for passing the disorder to your children.

If you're expecting a baby and you and your partner are thalassemia carriers, you may want to consider prenatal testing.

Prenatal testing involves taking a sample of amniotic fluid or tissue from the placenta. (Amniotic fluid is the fluid in the sac surrounding a growing embryo. The placenta is the organ that attaches the umbilical cord to the mother's womb.) Tests done on the fluid or tissue can show whether your baby has thalassemia and how severe it might be.

Treatment of Thalassemia

Treatments for thalassemias depend on the type and severity of the disorder. People who are carriers or who have alpha or beta thalassemia trait have mild or no symptoms. They'll likely need little or no treatment.

Doctors use three standard treatments for moderate and severe forms of thalassemia. These treatments include blood transfusions, iron chelation therapy, and folic acid supplements. Other treatments have been developed or are being tested, but they're used much less often.

Standard Treatments
Blood Transfusions

Transfusions of RBCs are the main treatment for people who have moderate or severe thalassemias. This treatment gives you healthy RBCs with normal hemoglobin.

During a blood transfusion, a needle is used to insert an intravenous (IV) line into one of your blood vessels. Through this line, you receive healthy blood. The procedure usually takes one to four hours.

RBCs live only for about 120 days. So, you may need repeated transfusions to maintain a healthy supply of RBCs.

If you have hemoglobin H disease or beta thalassemia intermedia, you may need blood transfusions on occasion. For example, you may have transfusions when you have an infection or other illness, or when your anemia is severe enough to cause tiredness.

If you have beta thalassemia major, you'll likely need regular blood transfusions (often every 2 to 4 weeks). These transfusions will help you maintain normal hemoglobin and red blood cell levels.

Blood transfusions allow you to feel better, enjoy normal activities, and live into adulthood. This treatment is lifesaving, but it's expensive and carries a risk of transmitting infections and viruses (for example, hepatitis). However, the risk is very low in the United States because of careful blood screening.

Iron Chelation Therapy

The hemoglobin in RBCs is an iron-rich protein. Thus, regular blood transfusions can lead to a buildup of iron in the blood. This condition is called "iron overload." It damages the liver, heart, and other parts of the body.

To prevent this damage, doctors use iron chelation therapy to remove excess iron from the body. Two medicines are used for iron chelation therapy (ICT).

- Deferoxamine is a liquid medicine that's given slowly under the skin, usually with a small portable pump used overnight. This therapy takes time and can be mildly painful. Side effects include problems with vision and hearing.

- Deferasirox is a pill taken once daily. Side effects include headache, nausea (feeling sick to the stomach), vomiting, diarrhea, joint pain, and tiredness.

Folic Acid Supplements

Folic acid is a B vitamin that helps build healthy RBCs. Your doctor may recommend folic acid supplements in addition to treatment with blood transfusions and/or iron chelation therapy.

Other Treatments

Other treatments for thalassemias have been developed or are being tested, but they're used much less often.

Blood and Marrow Stem Cell Transplant

A blood and marrow stem cell transplant replaces faulty stem cells with healthy ones from another person (a donor). Stem cells are the cells inside of bone marrow that make RBCs and other types of blood cells.

A stem cell transplant is the only treatment that can cure thalassemia. But only a small number of people who have severe thalassemias are able to find a good donor match and have the risky procedure.

Possible Future Treatments

Researchers are working to find new treatments for thalassemias. For example, it might be possible someday to insert a normal hemoglobin gene into stem cells in bone marrow. This will allow people who have thalassemias to make their own healthy RBCs and hemoglobin.

Researchers also are studying ways to trigger a person's ability to make fetal hemoglobin after birth. This type of hemoglobin is found in fetuses and newborns. After birth, the body switches to making adult hemoglobin. Making more fetal hemoglobin might make up for the lack of healthy adult hemoglobin.

Treating Complications

Better treatments now allow people who have moderate and severe thalassemias to live longer. As a result, these people must cope with complications that occur over time.

An important part of managing thalassemias is treating complications. Treatment might be needed for heart or liver diseases, infections, osteoporosis, and other health problems.

Living with Thalassemia

Survival and quality of life (QOL) have improved for people who have moderate or severe thalassemias. This is because:

- More people are able to get blood transfusions now

- Blood screening has reduced the number of infections from blood transfusions. Also, treatments for other kinds of infections have improved.

- Iron chelation treatments are available and are easier for some people to take

- Some people have been cured through blood and marrow stem cell transplants

Living with thalassemia can be challenging, but several approaches can help you cope.

Follow Your Treatment Plan

Following the treatment plan your doctor gives you is important. For example, get blood transfusions as your doctor recommends, and take your iron chelation medicine as prescribed.

Iron chelation treatment can take time and be mildly painful. However, don't stop taking your medicine. The leading cause of death among people who have thalassemias is heart disease caused by iron overload. Iron buildup can damage your heart, liver, and other organs.

Several chelation treatments are now available, including injections and pills. Your doctor will talk with you about which treatment is best for you.

Take folic acid supplements if your doctor prescribes them. Folic acid is a B vitamin that helps build healthy RBCs. Also, talk with your doctor about whether you need other vitamin or mineral supplements, such as vitamins A, C, or D, or selenium.

Get Ongoing Medical Care

Keep your scheduled medical appointments, and get any tests that your doctor recommends.

These tests may include:

- Monthly complete blood counts and tests for blood iron levels every three months

- Yearly tests for heart function, liver function, and viral infections (for example, hepatitis B and C and human immunodeficiency virus (HIV))

- Yearly tests to check for iron buildup in your liver

- Yearly vision and hearing tests

- Regular checkups to make sure blood transfusions are working

- Other tests as needed (such as lung function tests, genetic tests, and tests to match your tissues with a possible donor if a stem cell transplant is being considered)

Children who have thalassemias should receive yearly checkups to monitor their growth and development. The checkups include a physical exam, including height and weight check, and any necessary tests.

Take Steps to Stay Healthy

Take steps to stay as healthy as possible. Follow a healthy eating plan and your doctor's instructions for taking iron supplements.

Get vaccinations as needed, especially if you've had your spleen removed. You may need vaccines for the flu, pneumonia, hepatitis B, and meningitis. Your doctor will advise you about which vaccines you need.

Watch for signs of infection (such as a fever) and take steps to lower your risk for infection (especially if you've had your spleen removed). For example:

- Wash your hands often.

- Avoid crowds during cold and flu season.

- Keep the skin around the site where you get blood transfusions as clean as possible.

- Call your doctor if a fever develops.

Emotional Issues and Support

If you or your child has thalassemia, you may have fear, anxiety, depression, or stress. Talk about how you feel with your healthcare team. Talking to a professional counselor also can help. If you're very depressed, your doctor may recommend medicines or other treatments that can improve your QOL.

Joining a patient support group may help you adjust to living with thalassemia. You can see how other people who have the same symptoms have coped with them. Talk with your doctor about local support groups or check with an area medical center.

Support from family and friends also can help relieve stress and anxiety. Let your loved ones know how you feel and what they can do to help you.

Some teens and young adults who have thalassemias may have a hard time moving from pediatric care to adult care. Doctors and other health professionals who care for these children might not be familiar with adult issues related to the disorder, such as certain complications.

Also, it might be hard for adults who have thalassemias to find doctors who specialize in treating the disorder. Ask your child's doctor to help you find a doctor who can care for your child when the time comes to make the switch. Planning and good communication can help this move go smoothly.

Chapter 12

Blood-Clotting Disorders

Chapter Contents

Section 12.1

Factor V Leiden Thrombophilia

This section includes text excerpted from "Factor V Leiden
Thrombophilia," Genetic and Rare Diseases Information
Center (GARD), National Center for Advancing Translational
Sciences (NCATS), August 23, 2017.

Factor V Leiden thrombophilia is a genetic disorder that makes it more likely for you to develop a blood clot sometime during your life. Still, it is estimated that 95 percent of people with factor V Leiden never develop a clot. When a clot does form, the clot most often occurs in your leg (deep venous thrombosis or DVT) or lungs (pulmonary embolism or PE). Factor V Leiden is the name of a specific gene mutation in the *F5* gene. This gene plays a role in how your body forms blood clots after an injury. People can inherit one or two copies of the *factor V Leiden* gene mutation.

People with factor V Leiden thrombophilia have a higher risk for blood clots. However, the severity of factor V Leiden thrombophilia varies greatly from person to person. Only 5 percent of people with 1 factor V Leiden mutation develop a clot by age 65.

The chance a person with a *factor V Leiden* gene mutation develops a blood clot is affected by a number of factors, such as having a family history of clots, a second *factor V Leiden* gene mutation, a second genetic or acquired blood-clotting disorder, and other nongenetic risk factors. Nongenetic risk factors include surgery, long periods of not moving (such as sitting on a long airplane ride), birth control pills and other female hormones, childbirth within the last 6 months, non-O blood group, cancer, and injuries (such as bone fractures).

The most common type of blood clots associated with factor V Leiden thrombophilia, are deep venous thrombosis or DVT and pulmonary embolism or PE. Signs and symptoms of DVT include leg pain, tenderness, swelling, and increased warmth or redness in one leg. Signs and symptoms of pulmonary embolism usually include cough, chest pain, shortness of breath, and rapid heartbeat or breathing.

While less common, other possible sites of blood clots, include superficial veins of the leg, veins carrying blood from the digestive organs and spleen to the liver, veins carrying blood away from the liver, and veins supplying the brain. Factor V Leiden thrombophilia may contribute a small amount of risk toward a heart attack, stroke, or pregnancy complication.

Factor V Leiden thrombophilia is caused by a specific mutation in the *F5* or *Factor V* gene. *F5* plays a critical role in the formation of blood clots in response to injury. Genes are our body's instructions for making proteins. *F5* instructs the body how to make a protein called "coagulation factor V." Coagulation factor V is involved in a series of chemical reactions that hold blood clots together. A molecule called "activated protein C" (APC) prevents blood clots from growing too large by inactivating factor V. *Factor V Leiden* gene mutations cause factor V to be inactivated more slowly than normal. This leaves more time for blood clots to form.

We all inherit two copies of the *F5 (factor V)* gene. We inherit one copy from our mother and the other from our father. As a result, our risk for having factor V Leiden thrombophilia depends on the genetic status of each of our parents.

Most people with factor V Leiden thrombophilia have one "normal" *F5* gene and one with the *factor V Leiden* gene mutation. People with one copy of the mutation are called "heterozygotes." Assuming this person and a person without the mutation have a child, this couple would have a 50 percent, or 1 in 2 chance, of having a child with a single F5 mutation.

Factor V Leiden thrombophilia is a relatively common condition. In some families, both parents have the F5 mutation. In this scenario, each child of the couple would have a 25 percent or 1 in 4 chance of having 2 mutations, a 25 percent chance of having no mutation, and a 50 percent chance of having a 1 mutation.

People with two copies of the F5 mutation are said to be "homozygotes." They will always pass one copy of the mutated gene to their children. A child's risk for a second mutation will depend on whether or not her or his other parent has the F5 mutation.

A diagnosis of factor V Leiden thrombophilia may be considered in people with a notable personal or family history of venous thromboembolism (VTE), such as having a VTE at an atypically young age, in an unusual location, or having multiple VTEs. A doctor may confirm the diagnosis by ordering a genetic or a PC resistance test. Alternatively, it is becoming more common for people to learn they have a *factor V Leiden* gene mutation from an advertised genetic test they purchased directly.

Treatment of factor V Leiden thrombophilia varies depending on the patient's medical history and current circumstances.

People with factor V Leiden thrombophilia who've had a deep venous thrombosis (DVT) or pulmonary embolism (PE) are usually treated with blood thinners, or anticoagulants (such as heparin and warfarin).

Anticoagulants are given for varying amounts of time depending on the person's situation. It is not usually recommended that people with factor V Leiden be treated lifelong with anticoagulants if they have had only one DVT or PE, unless they have additional blood clot risk factors.

People who have factor V Leiden but have never had a blood clot are not routinely treated with an anticoagulant. Instead, they are counseled about reducing or eliminating other factors that add to their risk for clots. They may require temporary treatment with an anticoagulant during periods of particularly high risk, such as major surgery.

Women with factor V Leiden thrombophilia most often have normal pregnancies. Treatment with an anticoagulant during pregnancy and/or following delivery is often not needed, but may be recommended depending on the woman's personal and family health history, method of delivery, and other risk factors.

The factor V Leiden mutation is the most common inherited risk factor for abnormal blood clotting in the United States. Factor V Leiden mutations are estimated to be carried by:

- 5 percent of Caucasians

- 2 percent of Hispanic Americans

- 1 percent of Native Americans

- 1 percent of African Americans

- 0.5 percent of Asian Americans

In addition, up to 14 percent of people in populations from Greece, Sweden, and Lebanon are thought to carry factor V Leiden.

Having 2 factor V Leiden mutations is much rarer, affecting around 1 in 1,600 people.

Section 12.2

Hemophilia

This section includes text excerpted from
"Hemophilia," National Heart, Lung, and Blood
Institute (NHLBI), February 28, 2018.

Hemophilia is a rare bleeding disorder in which the blood doesn't clot normally. If you have hemophilia, you may bleed for a longer time than others after an injury. You also may bleed inside your body (internally), especially in your knees, ankles, and elbows. This bleeding can damage your organs and tissues and may be life-threatening.

Causes of Hemophilia

A defect in one of the genes that determines how the body makes blood clotting factor VIII or IX causes hemophilia. These genes are located on the X chromosomes.

Chromosomes come in pairs. Females have two X chromosomes, while males have one X and one Y chromosome. Only the X chromosome carries the genes related to clotting factors.

A male who has a hemophilia gene on his X chromosome will have hemophilia. When a female has a hemophilia gene on only one of her X chromosomes, she is a "hemophilia carrier" and can pass the gene to her children. Sometimes carriers have low levels of clotting factor and have symptoms of hemophilia, including bleeding. Clotting factors are proteins in the blood that work together with platelets to stop or control bleeding.

Very rarely, a girl may be born with a very low clotting factor level and have a greater risk for bleeding, similar to boys who have hemophilia and very low levels of clotting factor. There are several hereditary and genetic causes of this much rarer form of hemophilia in females.

Some males who have the disorder are born to mothers who aren't carriers. In these cases, a mutation (random change) occurs in the gene as it is passed to the child.

Below are two examples of how the hemophilia gene is inherited.

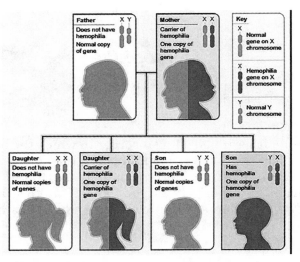

Figure 12.1. *Inheritance Pattern for Hemophilia—Example 1*

The image shows one example of how the hemophilia gene is inherited. In this example, the father doesn't have hemophilia (that is, he has two normal chromosomes—X and Y). The mother is a carrier of hemophilia (that is, she has one hemophilia gene on one X chromosome and one normal X chromosome)

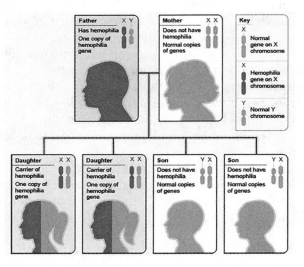

Figure 12.2. *Inheritance Pattern for Hemophilia—Example 2*

The image shows one example of how the hemophilia gene is inherited. In this example, the father has hemophilia (that is, he has the hemophilia gene on the X chromosome). The mother isn't a hemophilia carrier (that is, she has two normal X chromosomes)

Signs, Symptoms, and Complications of Hemophilia

The major signs and symptoms of hemophilia are excessive bleeding and easy bruising.

Excessive Bleeding

The extent of bleeding depends on how severe the hemophilia is. Children who have mild hemophilia may not have signs unless they have excessive bleeding from a dental procedure, an accident, or surgery. Males who have severe hemophilia may bleed heavily after circumcision.

Bleeding can occur on the body's surface (external bleeding) or inside the body (internal bleeding).

Signs of external bleeding may include:

- Bleeding in the mouth from a cut or bite or from cutting or losing a tooth
- Nosebleeds for no obvious reason
- Heavy bleeding from a minor cut
- Bleeding from a cut that resumes after stopping for a short time

Signs of internal bleeding may include:

- Blood in the urine (from bleeding in the kidneys or bladder)
- Blood in the stool (from bleeding in the intestines or stomach)
- Large bruises (from bleeding into the large muscles of the body)

Bleeding in the Joints

Bleeding in the knees, elbows, or other joints is another common form of internal bleeding in people who have hemophilia. This bleeding can occur without obvious injury.

At first, the bleeding causes tightness in the joint with no real pain or any visible signs of bleeding. The joint then becomes swollen, hot to touch, and painful to bend.

Swelling continues as bleeding continues. Eventually, movement in the joint is temporarily lost. Pain can be severe. Joint bleeding that isn't treated quickly can damage the joint.

Bleeding in the Brain

Internal bleeding in the brain is a very serious complication of hemophilia. It can happen after a simple bump on the head or a more serious injury. The signs and symptoms of bleeding in the brain include:

- Long-lasting, painful headaches or neck pain or stiffness
- Repeated vomiting
- Sleepiness or changes in behavior
- Sudden weakness or clumsiness of the arms or legs or problems walking
- Double vision
- Convulsions or seizures

Diagnosis of Hemophilia

If you or your child appears to have a bleeding problem, your doctor will ask about your personal and family medical histories. This will reveal whether you or your family members have bleeding problems. However, some people who have hemophilia have no recent family history of the disease.

You or your child also will likely have a physical exam and blood tests to diagnose hemophilia. Blood tests are used to find out:

- How long it takes for your blood to clot
- Whether your blood has low levels of any clotting factors
- Whether any clotting factors are completely missing from your blood

The test results will show whether you have hemophilia, what type of hemophilia you have, and how severe it is.

Hemophilia A and B are classified as mild, moderate, or severe, depending on the amount of clotting factor VIII or IX in the blood.

Classification	The Amount of Clotting Factor VIII or IX in the Blood
Mild hemophilia	5 to 40 percent of normal clotting factor
Moderate hemophilia	1 to 5 percent of normal clotting factor
Severe hemophilia	Less than 1 percent of normal clotting factor

The severity of symptoms can overlap between the categories. For example, some people who have mild hemophilia may have bleeding problems almost as often or as severe as some people who have moderate hemophilia.

Severe hemophilia can cause serious bleeding problems in babies. Thus, children who have severe hemophilia usually are diagnosed during the first year of life. People who have milder forms of hemophilia may not be diagnosed until they are adults.

The bleeding problems of hemophilia A and hemophilia B are the same. Only special blood tests can tell which type of disorder you or your child has. Knowing which type is important because the treatments are different.

Pregnant women who are known hemophilia carriers can have the disorder diagnosed in the fetuses as early as 12 weeks into their pregnancies.

Women who are hemophilia carriers also can have "preimplantation diagnosis" to have children who don't have hemophilia.

For this process, women have their eggs removed and fertilized by sperm in a laboratory. The embryos are then tested for hemophilia. Only embryos without the disorder are implanted in the womb.

Treatment for Hemophilia
Treatment with Replacement Therapy

The main treatment for hemophilia is called "replacement therapy." Concentrates of clotting factor VIII (for hemophilia A) or clotting factor IX (for hemophilia B) are slowly dripped or injected into a vein. These infusions help replace the clotting factor that's missing or low.

Clotting factor concentrates can be made from human blood. The blood is treated to prevent the spread of diseases, such as hepatitis. With the current methods of screening and treating donated blood, the risk of getting an infectious disease from human clotting factors is very small.

To further reduce the risk, you or your child can take clotting factor concentrates that aren't made from human blood. These are called "recombinant clotting factors." Clotting factors are easy to store, mix, and use at home—it only takes about 15 minutes to receive the factor.

You may have replacement therapy on a regular basis to prevent bleeding. This is called "preventive" or "prophylactic therapy." Or, you may only need replacement therapy to stop bleeding when it occurs. This use of the treatment, on an as-needed basis, is called "demand therapy."

Demand therapy is less intensive and expensive than preventive therapy. However, there's a risk that bleeding will cause damage before you receive the demand therapy.

Complications of Replacement Therapy

Complications of replacement therapy include:

- Developing antibodies (proteins) that attack the clotting factor
- Developing viral infections from human clotting factors
- Damage to joints, muscles, or other parts of the body resulting from delays in treatment

Antibodies to the clotting factor. Antibodies can destroy the clotting factor before it has a chance to work. This is a very serious problem. It prevents the main treatment for hemophilia (replacement therapy) from working.

These antibodies, also called "inhibitors," develop in about 20 to 30 percent of people who have severe hemophilia A. Inhibitors develop in 2 to 5 percent of people who have hemophilia B.

When antibodies develop, doctors may use larger doses of clotting factor or try different clotting factor sources. Sometimes the antibodies go away.

Researchers are studying new ways to deal with antibodies to clotting factors.

Viruses from human clotting factors. Clotting factors made from human blood can carry viruses that cause human immunodeficiency virus (HIV)/acquired immunodeficiency syndrome (AIDS) and hepatitis. However, the risk of getting an infectious disease from human clotting factors is very small due to:

- Careful screening of blood donors
- Testing of donated blood products
- Treating donated blood products with a detergent and heat to destroy viruses
- Vaccinating people who have hemophilia for hepatitis A and B

Damage to joints, muscles, and other parts of the body. Delays in treatment can cause damage, such as:

- Bleeding into a joint. If this happens many times, it can lead to changes in the shape of the joint and impair the joint's function
- Swelling of the membrane around a joint
- Pain, swelling, and redness of a joint
- Pressure on a joint from swelling, which can destroy the joint

Home Treatment with Replacement Therapy

You can do both preventive (ongoing) and demand (as-needed) replacement therapy at home. Many people learn to do the infusions at home for their child or for themselves. Home treatment has several advantages:

- You or your child can get quicker treatment when bleeding happens. Early treatment lowers the risk of complications.

- Fewer visits to the doctor or emergency room are needed.

- Home treatment costs less than treatment in a medical care setting.

- Home treatment helps children accept treatment and take responsibility for their own health.

Discuss options for home treatment with your doctor or your child's doctor. A doctor or other healthcare provider can teach you the steps and safety procedures for home treatment. Hemophilia treatment centers are another good resource for learning about home treatment.

Doctors can surgically implant vein access devices to make it easier for you to access a vein for treatment with replacement therapy. These devices can be helpful if treatment occurs often. However, infections can be a problem with these devices. Your doctor can help you decide whether this type of device is right for you or your child.

Other Types of Treatment
Desmopressin

Desmopressin (DDAVP) is a human-made hormone used to treat people who have mild hemophilia A. DDAVP isn't used to treat hemophilia B or severe hemophilia A.

DDAVP stimulates the release of stored factor VIII and von Willebrand factor (vWF); it also increases the level of these proteins in your blood. vWF carries and binds factor VIII, which can then stay in the bloodstream longer.

DDAVP, usually, is given by injection or as nasal spray. Because the effect of this medicine wears off if it's used often, the medicine is given only in certain situations. For example, you may take this medicine prior to dental work or before playing certain sports to prevent or reduce bleeding.

Antifibrinolytic Medicines

Antifibrinolytic medicines (including tranexamic acid (TXA) and epsilon-aminocaproic acid (EACA)) may be used with replacement therapy. They're usually given as a pill, and they help keep blood clots from breaking down.

These medicines most often are used before dental work or to treat bleeding from the mouth or nose or mild intestinal bleeding.

Gene Therapy

Researchers are trying to find ways to correct the faulty genes that cause hemophilia. Gene therapy hasn't yet developed to the point that it's an accepted treatment for hemophilia. However, researchers continue to test gene therapy in clinical trials.

Treatment of a Specific Bleeding Site

Pain medicines, steroids, and physical therapy may be used to reduce pain and swelling in an affected joint. Talk with your doctor or pharmacist about which medicines are safe for you to take.

Which Treatment Is Best for You?

The type of treatment you or your child receives depends on several things, including how severe the hemophilia is, the activities you'll be doing, and the dental or medical procedures you'll be having.

- Mild hemophilia. Replacement therapy usually isn't needed for mild hemophilia. Sometimes, though, DDAVP is given to raise the body's level of factor VIII.

- Moderate hemophilia. You may need replacement therapy only when bleeding occurs or to prevent bleeding that could occur when doing certain activities. Your doctor also may recommend DDAVP prior to having a procedure or doing an activity that increases the risk of bleeding.

- Severe hemophilia. You usually need replacement therapy to prevent bleeding that could damage your joints, muscles, or other parts of your body. Typically, replacement therapy is given at home two or three times a week. This preventive therapy usually is started in patients at a young age and may need to continue for life.

For both types of hemophilia, getting quick treatment for bleeding is important. Quick treatment can limit damage to your body. If you or your child has hemophilia, learn to recognize signs of bleeding.

Other family members also should learn to watch for signs of bleeding in a child who has hemophilia. Children sometimes ignore signs of bleeding because they want to avoid the discomfort of treatment.

Living with Hemophilia

If you or your child has hemophilia, you can take steps to prevent bleeding problems. Thanks to improvements in treatment, a child who has hemophilia nowadays are likely to live a normal lifespan.

Hemophilia Treatment Centers

The federal government funds a nationwide network of hemophilia treatment centers (HTCs). These centers are an important resource for people who have hemophilia and their families.

The medical experts at HTCs provide treatment, education, and support. They can teach you or your family members how to do home treatments. The center staff also can provide your doctor with information.

People who get care at HTCs are less likely than those who get care elsewhere to have bleeding complications and hospitalizations. They're also more likely to have a better quality of life (QOL). This may be due to the centers' emphasis on bleeding prevention and the education and support provided to patients and their caregivers.

More than 100 federally funded HTCs are located throughout the United States. Many HTCs are located at major university medical and research centers. The hemophilia teams at these centers include:

- Nurse coordinators
- Pediatricians (doctors who treat children) and adult and pediatric hematologists (doctors who specialize in blood disorders)
- Social workers (who can help with financial issues, transportation, mental health, and other issues)
- Physical therapists and orthopedists (doctors who specialize in disorders of the bones and joints)
- Dentists

Many people who have hemophilia go to HTCs for annual checkups, even if it means traveling some distance to do so.

At an HTC, you or your child may be able to take part in clinical research and benefit from the latest hemophilia research findings. The HTC team also will work with your local healthcare providers to help meet your needs or your child's needs.

Ongoing Care

If you have hemophilia, you can take steps to avoid complications. For example:

- Follow your treatment plan exactly as your doctor prescribes.

- Have regular checkups and vaccinations as recommended.

- Tell all of your healthcare providers—such as your doctor, dentist, and pharmacist—that you have hemophilia. You also may want to tell people like your employee health nurse, gym trainer, and sports coach about your condition.

- Have regular dental care. Dentists at the HTCs are experts in providing dental care for people who have hemophilia. If you see another dentist, tell her or him that you have hemophilia. The dentist can provide medicine that will reduce bleeding during dental work.

- Know the signs and symptoms of bleeding in joints and other parts of the body. Know when to call your doctor or go to the emergency room. For example, you'll need care if you have:

  - Heavy bleeding that can't be stopped or a wound that continues to ooze blood.

  - Any signs or symptoms of bleeding in the brain. Such bleeding is life-threatening and requires emergency care.

  - Limited motion, pain, or swelling of any joint.

  - It's a good idea to keep a record of all previous treatments. Be sure to take this information with you to medical appointments and to the hospital or emergency room.

It's a good idea to keep a record of all previous treatments. Be sure to take this information with you to medical appointments and to the hospital or emergency room.

If Your Child Is Diagnosed with Hemophilia

You may have emotional, financial, social, or other strains as you adjust to having a child who has hemophilia. Learn all you can about the disorder and get the support you need. Talk with doctors and other healthcare providers about treatment, prevention of bleeding, and what to do during an emergency.

The care teams at HTCs can provide your child with treatment and help educate and support you. The social worker on the team can help with emotional issues, financial and transportation problems, and other concerns.

Look into support groups that offer a variety of activities for children who have hemophilia and for family members. Some groups offer summer camps for children who have hemophilia. Ask your doctor, nurse coordinator, or social worker about these groups and camps.

Challenges will occur as your child grows and becomes more active. In addition to treatment and regular health and dental care, your child needs information about hemophilia that she or he can understand.

Children who have hemophilia also need ongoing support, and they need to be reassured that the condition isn't their fault.

Young children who have hemophilia need extra protection from things in the home and elsewhere that could cause injuries and bleeding:

- Protect toddlers with knee pads, elbow pads, and protective helmets. All children should wear safety helmets when riding tricycles or bicycles.

- Be sure to use the safety belts and straps in highchairs, car seats, and strollers to protect your child from falls.

- Remove furniture with sharp corners or pad them while your child is a toddler.

- Keep out of reach or lock away small and sharp objects and other items that could cause bleeding or harm.

- Check play equipment and outdoor play areas for possible hazards.

You also should learn how to examine your child for and recognize signs of bleeding. Learn to prepare for bleeding episodes when they occur. Keep a cold pack in the freezer ready to use as directed or to take along with you to treat bumps and bruises.

Popsicles work fine when there is minor bleeding in the mouth. You also might want to keep a bag ready to go with items you'll need if you must take your child to the emergency room or elsewhere.

Be sure that anyone who is responsible for your child knows that she or he has hemophilia. Talk with your child's babysitters, day-care providers, teachers, other school staff, and coaches or leaders of afterschool activities about when to contact you or to call 911 for emergency care.

Your child should wear a medical ID bracelet or necklace. If your child is injured, the ID will alert anyone caring for your child about her or his hemophilia.

Physical Activity and Hemophilia

Physical activity helps keep muscles flexible, strengthens joints, and helps maintain a healthy weight. Children and adults who have hemophilia should be physically active, but they may have limits on what they can do safely.

People who have mild hemophilia can take part in many activities. Those who have severe hemophilia should avoid contact sports and other activities that are likely to lead to injuries that could cause bleeding. Examples of these activities include football, hockey, and wrestling.

Physical therapists at HTCs can develop exercise programs tailored to your needs and teach you how to exercise safely.

Talk with your doctor or physical therapist about recommended types of physical activity and sports. In general, some safe physical activities are swimming, biking (wearing a helmet), walking, and golf.

To prevent bleeding, you also may be able to take clotting factors prior to exercise or a sporting event.

Medicine Precautions

Some medicines increase the risk of bleeding, such as:

- Aspirin and other medicines that contain salicylates

- Ibuprofen, naproxen, and some other nonsteroidal anti-inflammatory medicines

Talk with your doctor or pharmacist about which medicines are safe for you to take.

Treatment at Home and When Traveling

Home treatment with replacement therapy has many benefits. It lets you treat bleeding early, before complications are likely to develop. Home treatment also can prevent frequent trips to the doctor's office or hospital. This can give you more independence and control over your hemophilia.

However, if you're treating yourself or your child with clotting factors at home, you should take some steps for safety:

- Follow instructions for storage, preparation, and use of clotting factors and treatment materials.

- Keep a record of all medical treatment

- Know the signs and symptoms of bleeding, infection, or an allergic reaction, and know the correct way to respond.

- Have someone with you when you treat yourself

- Know when to call the doctor or 911

When you're traveling, be sure to take enough treatment supplies along. You also should carry a letter from your doctor describing your hemophilia and treatment. It's a good idea to find out in advance where to go for care when out of town.

Cost Issues

Clotting factors are very costly. Many health insurance companies will only pay for clotting factors on a case-by-case basis. It's important to know:

- What your insurance covers

- Whether your insurance has a limit on the dollar amount it will cover and what that amount is

- Whether restrictions or waiting periods apply

As children grow, it's important to learn about available options for insurance. Look into what kinds of health insurance are offered when seeking a job.

Section 12.3

von Willebrand Disease

This section includes text excerpted from "What Is von
Willebrand Disease?" Centers for Disease Control and
Prevention (CDC), October 23, 2018.

von Willebrand disease (vWD) is a blood disorder in which the blood
does not clot properly. Blood contains many proteins that help the body
stop bleeding. One of these proteins is called "von Willebrand factor"
(vWF). People with vWD either have a low level of vWF in their blood
or the vWF protein doesn't work the way it should.

Normally, when a person is injured and starts to bleed, the vWF
in the blood attaches to small blood cells called "platelets." This helps
the platelets stick together, such as glue, to form a clot at the site of
injury and stop the bleeding. When a person has vWD, the clot might
take longer to form or not form the way it should, and bleeding might
take longer to stop. This can lead to heavy, hard-to-stop bleeding.
Although rare, the bleeding can be severe enough to damage joints or
internal organs, or even be life-threatening.

Who Is Affected by von Willebrand Disease?

vWD is the most common bleeding disorder, found in up to 1 percent of the U.S. population. This means that 3.2 million (or about 1
in every 100) people in the United States have the disease. Although
vWD occurs among men and women equally, women are more likely
to notice the symptoms because of heavy or abnormal bleeding during
their menstrual periods and after childbirth.

Types of von Willebrand Disease
Type 1

This is the most common and mildest form of vWD, in which a
person has lower than normal levels of vWF. A person with Type
1 vWD also might have low levels of factor VIII, another type of
blood-clotting protein. This should not be confused with hemophilia,
in which there are low levels or a complete lack of factor VIII but
normal levels of vWF. About 85 percent of people treated for vWD
have Type 1.

Type 2

With this type of vWD, although the body makes normal amounts of the vWF, the factor does not work the way it should. Type 2 is further broken down into four subtypes: 2A, 2B, 2M, and 2N, depending on the specific problem with the person's vWF. Because the treatment is different for each type, it is important that a person know which subtype she or he has.

Type 3

This is the most severe form of vWD, in which a person has very little or no vWF and low levels of factor VIII. This is the rarest type of vWD. Only 3 percent of people with vWD have Type 3.

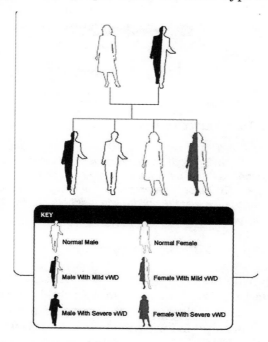

Figure 12.3. *Type 1 and 2 vWD Inheritance*

vWD Inheritance of Type 1 and Type 2 (except Type 2N)
The inheritance of both Type 1 and Type 2 vWD occurs in a dominant pattern. A person can have vWD because they inherited the gene from either parent who has the same changed gene or they could have a new change in the vWD gene which has occurred for the first time in the family. Someone with Type 1 or Type 2 vWD has a 50-50 chance to pass on the changed gene to a child.

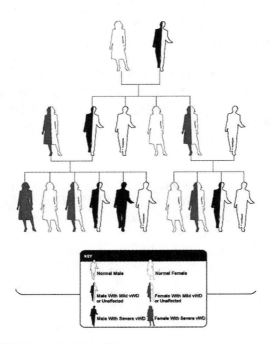

Figure 12.4. *vWD Inheritance of Type 3*

Inheritance of Type 3 vWD and Type 2N vWD Type 3 is the least common type of vWD and is caused by having both changed genes. This is a recessive inheritance pattern. Recessive means that a person must inherit two changed copies of the gene in order to have Type 3 vWD. If both parents have mild vWD and have a child together there is a 25 percent chance that the child will inherit both changed genes (one from each parent) and have Type 3 vWD.

Causes of von Willebrand Disease

Most people who have vWD are born with it. It almost always is inherited, or passed down, from a parent to a child. vWD can be passed down from either the mother or the father, or both, to the child.

While rare, it is possible for a person to get vWD without a family history of the disease. This happens when a "spontaneous mutation" occurs. That means there has been a change in the person's gene. Whether the child received the affected gene from a parent or as a result of a mutation, once the child has it, the child can later pass it along to her or his children. Rarely, a person who is not born with vWD can acquire it or have it first occur later in life. This can happen when a person's own immune system destroys her or his vWF, often as a result of the use of a medication or as a result of another disease.

If vWD is acquired, meaning it was not inherited from a parent, it cannot be passed along to any children.

How von Willebrand Disease is Inherited

Most people who have vWD are born with it. It almost always is inherited, or passed down, from a parent to a child. vWD can be passed down from either the mother or the father, or both, to the child.

The child of a parent with vWD has a 50 percent chance of getting the gene for the condition and, therefore, of having vWD. In types 1 and 2, if even one parent has the gene for the disease and passes it to a child, the child will have the disease. In type 3, the child usually gets the gene for the disease from both parents. If both parents have vWD, the child could get either a mild (50% chance) or severe (25% chance) form of the disease. If neither parent shows the disease (recessive vWD), the child could get the severe form (25%). vWD Type 2N is also inherited as a recessive trait.

Signs and Symptoms of von Willebrand Disease

The major signs of vWD are:

Frequent or hard-to-stop nosebleeds. People with vWD might have nosebleeds that:

- Start without injury (spontaneous)

- Occur often, usually five times or more in a year

- Last more than ten minutes

- Need packing or cautery to stop the bleeding

Easy bruising. People with vWD might experience easy bruising that:

- Occurs with very little or no trauma or injury

- Occurs often (one to four times per month)

- Is larger than the size of a quarter

- Is not flat and has a raised lump

Heavy menstrual bleeding. Women with vWD might have heavy menstrual periods during which:

- Clots larger than the size of a quarter are passed

- More than one pad is soaked through every two hours

- A diagnosis of anemia (not having enough red blood cells (RBCs)) is made as a result of bleeding from heavy periods

Longer than normal bleeding after injury, surgery, childbirth, or dental work. People with vWD might have longer than normal bleeding after injury, surgery, or childbirth, for example:

- After a cut to the skin, the bleeding lasts for longer than five minutes

- Heavy or longer bleeding occurs after surgery. Bleeding sometimes stops but starts up again hours or days later.

- Heavy bleeding occurs during or after childbirth

People with vWD might have longer than normal bleeding during or after dental work, for example:

- Heavy bleeding occurs during or after dental surgery

- The surgery site oozes blood longer than three hours after the surgery

- The surgery site needs packing or cautery to stop the bleeding

The amount of bleeding depends on the type and severity of vWD. Other common bleeding events include:

- Blood in the stool (feces) from bleeding into the stomach or intestines

- Blood in the urine from bleeding into the kidneys or bladder

- Bleeding into joints or internal organs in severe cases (Type 3)

Diagnosis of von Willebrand Disease

To find out if a person has vWD, the doctor will ask questions about personal and family histories of bleeding. The doctor also will check for unusual bruising or other signs of recent bleeding and order some blood tests that will measure how the blood clots. The tests will provide information about the amount of clotting proteins present in the blood and if the clotting proteins are working properly. Because certain medications can cause bleeding, even among people without a bleeding disorder, the doctor will ask about recent or routine medications taken that could cause bleeding or make bleeding symptoms worse.

Treatments of von Willebrand Disease

The type of treatment prescribed for vWD depends on the type and severity of the disease. For minor bleeds, treatment might not be needed.

The most commonly used types of treatment are:

- **Desmopressin acetate injection.** This medicine (DDAVP®) is injected into a vein to treat people with milder forms of vWD (mainly type 1). It works by making the body release more vWF into the blood. It helps increase the level of factor VIII in the blood as well.

- **Desmopressin acetate nasal spray.** This high-strength nasal spray (Stimate®) is used to treat people with milder forms of vWD. It works by making the body release more vWF into the blood.

- **Factor replacement therapy.** Recombinant vWF (such as Vonvendi®) and medicines rich in vWF and factor VIII (for example, Humate P®, Wilate®, Alphanate®, or Koate DVI®) are used to treat people with more severe forms of vWD or people with milder forms of vWD who do not respond well to the nasal spray. These medicines are injected into a vein in the arm to replace the missing factor in the blood.

- **Antifibrinolytic drugs.** These drugs (for example, Amicar®, Lysteda®) are either injected or taken orally to help slow or prevent the breakdown of blood clots.

- **Birth control pills.** Birth control pills can increase the levels of vWF and factor VIII in the blood and reduce menstrual blood loss. A doctor can prescribe these pills for women who have heavy menstrual bleeding.

Chapter 13

CHARGE Syndrome

What Is CHARGE Syndrome?

CHARGE syndrome is a disorder that affects many areas of the body. CHARGE is an abbreviation for several of the features common in the disorder: coloboma, heart defects, atresia choanae (also known as "choanal atresia"), growth retardation, genital abnormalities, and ear abnormalities. The pattern of malformations varies among individuals with this disorder, and the multiple health problems can be life-threatening in infancy. Affected individuals usually have several major characteristics or a combination of major and minor characteristics.

The major characteristics of CHARGE syndrome are common and occur less frequently in other disorders. Most individuals with CHARGE syndrome have a gap or hole in one of the structures of the eye (coloboma), which forms during early development. A coloboma may be present in one or both eyes and may impair a person's vision, depending on its size and location. Some affected individuals also have abnormally small or underdeveloped eyes (microphthalmia). In many people with CHARGE syndrome, one or both nasal passages are

This chapter contains text excerpted from the following sources: Text beginning with the heading "What Is CHARGE Syndrome?" is excerpted from "CHARGE Syndrome," Genetics Home Reference (GHR), National Institutes of Health (NIH), January 29, 2019; Text under the heading "Is Genetic Testing Available for CHARGE Syndrome?" is excerpted from "CHARGE Syndrome," Genetic and Rare Diseases Information Center (GARD), National Center for Advancing Translational Sciences (NCATS), November 3, 2013. Reviewed March 2019.

narrowed (choanal stenosis) or completely blocked (choanal atresia), which can cause difficulty breathing. Affected individuals frequently have cranial nerve abnormalities. The cranial nerves emerge directly from the brain and extend to various areas of the head and neck, controlling muscle movement and transmitting sensory information. Abnormal function of certain cranial nerves can cause swallowing problems, facial paralysis, a sense of smell that is diminished (hyposmia) or completely absent (anosmia), and mild to profound hearing loss. People with CHARGE syndrome also typically have middle and inner ear abnormalities, which can contribute to hearing problems, and unusually shaped external ears.

While the minor characteristics of CHARGE syndrome are common, they are also frequently present in people without the disorder. The minor characteristics include heart defects; slow growth starting in late infancy; delayed development of motor skills, such as sitting unsupported and walking; and an opening in the lip (cleft lip) with or without an opening in the roof of the mouth (cleft palate). Affected individuals frequently have hypogonadotropic hypogonadism (HH), which affects the production of hormones that direct sexual development. As a result, males with CHARGE syndrome are often born with an unusually small penis (micropenis) and undescended testes (cryptorchidism). Abnormalities of external genitalia are seen less often in affected females. Puberty can be incomplete or delayed in affected males and females. Another minor feature of CHARGE syndrome is the tracheoesophageal fistula (TEF), which is an abnormal connection (fistula) between the esophagus and the trachea. Most people with CHARGE syndrome also have distinctive facial features, including a square-shaped face and differences in appearance between the right and left sides of the face (facial asymmetry). Affected individuals have a wide range of cognitive function, from normal intelligence to major learning disabilities with absent speech and poor communication.

Less common features of CHARGE syndrome include kidney abnormalities; immune system problems; abnormal curvature of the spine (scoliosis or kyphosis); and limb abnormalities, such as extra fingers or toes (polydactyly), missing fingers or toes (oligodactyly), an inward and upward-turning foot (club foot), and abnormalities of the long bones of the arms and legs.

Frequency and Causes of CHARGE Syndrome

CHARGE syndrome occurs in approximately 1 in 8,500 to 10,000 newborns.

Mutations in the *CHD7* gene cause most cases of CHARGE syndrome. The *CHD7* gene provides instructions for making a protein that regulates gene activity (expression) by a process known as "chromatin remodeling." Chromatin is the complex of deoxyribonucleic acid (DNA) and protein that packages DNA into chromosomes. The structure of chromatin can be changed (remodeled) to alter how tightly DNA is packaged. When DNA is tightly packed, gene expression is lower than when DNA is loosely packed. Chromatin remodeling is one-way gene expression is regulated during development.

Most mutations in the *CHD7* gene lead to the production of an abnormal CHD7 protein that is broken down prematurely. Shortage of this protein is thought to disrupt chromatin remodeling and the regulation of gene expression. Changes in gene expression during embryonic development likely cause the signs and symptoms of CHARGE syndrome.

A small percentage of individuals with CHARGE syndrome do not have an identified mutation in the *CHD7* gene. Some of them may have a genetic change affecting the *CHD7* gene that has not been found, and others may have a change in a different gene, although additional genes associated with CHARGE syndrome have not been identified.

Is Genetic Testing Available for Charge Syndrome?

Genetic testing is available for CHARGE syndrome. The *CHD7* gene is the only gene in which mutations are known to cause CHARGE syndrome. The CHD7 mutation detection rate when sequence analysis is performed is estimated to be 65 to 70 percent for all typical and suspected cases combined.

GeneTests lists the names of laboratories that are performing clinical genetic testing for CHARGE syndrome. Please note that most of the laboratories listed through GeneTests do not accept direct contact from patients and their families. Therefore, if you are interested in learning more, you will need to work with a healthcare provider or a genetics professional.

Chapter 14

Connective Tissue Disorders

Chapter Contents

Section 14.1

What Are Heritable Disorders of Connective Tissue?

This section includes text excerpted from "Heritable Disorders of Connective Tissue," National Institute of Arthritis and Musculoskeletal and Skin Diseases (NIAMS), August 30, 2016.

Heritable disorders of connective tissue are a family of more than 200 conditions that affect tissues between cells that give tissues form and strength. All of these diseases are directly related to problems in genes that are responsible for building connective tissues.

Some other connective tissue problems are not directly linked to changes in tissue-building genes. Many, but not all, of the disorders are rare.

What Happens in Heritable Disorders of Connective Tissue

Some gene defects alter the proteins that make up connective tissue. This can alter normal function of connective tissue, which usually supports many parts of the body by:

- Bringing nutrients to the tissue

- Giving tissue form and strength

- Helping some of the tissues do their work

Who Gets Heritable Disorders of Connective Tissue

If you have a heritable disorder of connective tissue, you inherited an altered gene either from one or from both parents. This defective gene affects functioning of connective tissues.

Heritable disorders of connective tissue can affect people of all racial and ethnic groups. All ages and both sexes are affected. Many of these disorders are rare. Some may not be seen at birth, but only appear after a certain age or after exposure to a particular environmental stress.

You are more likely to have the disease if someone in your family has had the disease, or if one of your parents have the gene for the disorder.

Types of Heritable Disorders of Connective Tissue

Some common heritable disorders of connective tissue include:

- **Ehlers-Danlos syndrome** can be caused by defects in several genes. In most cases, the gene defect involves collagen, the major protein-building material of bone. People with this syndrome have loose joints; fragile, small blood vessels; abnormal scar formation and wound healing; and soft skin that stretches excessively but returns to normal after being pulled. Some forms can cause problems with the eyes, spine, and internal organs.

- **Epidermolysis bullosa** affects the skin, causing it to blister easily. Some people may have just a few blisters on the skin, whereas others may have many blisters. In some forms, blisters may form in the mouth, stomach, esophagus, bladder, and other parts of the body.

- **Marfan syndrome (MFS)** is caused by a defect in the gene that produces a protein important to connective tissue. People with MFS tend to have a tall, thin build with long arms and legs and "spider-like" fingers. Other problems include a sideways curve of the spine; crowded teeth; flat feet; an abnormal position of the eye's lens; and enlargement of the beginning part of the aorta, the major vessel carrying blood away from the heart.

- **Osteogenesis imperfecta (OI)** is caused by a defect in the gene that makes collagen. People with this disorder have fragile bones, low muscle mass, and loose joints and ligaments. Some people may have a blue or gray tint to the whites of the eyes, thin skin, growth deficiencies, and fragile teeth. A curved spine, breathing problems, and hearing loss may also develop.

Symptoms of Heritable Disorders of Connective Tissue

Symptoms of heritable disorders of connective tissue can include:

- **Bone growth problems.** Bones can be brittle, too long, or too short.

- **Joint issues.** Joints can be too loose or too tight.

- **Skin problems.** Skin may be loose, hang in folds, or easily blister.

- **Blood vessel damage.** Blood vessels may be weak or become blocked.

- **Height issues.** You may be unusually tall or short.

- **Head and facial structural problems.** The head and face may look different from others.

Diagnosis of Heritable Disorders of Connective Tissue

Your doctor may do the following to diagnose you with heritable disorders of connective tissue:

- Use your medical history to determine system and ask about family history of the disease

- Physical examination

- Laboratory tests to confirm the disease

You may wish to seek genetic counseling if you wish to have a child. A genetic counselor can help you estimate the risk of having a child with the disease. The genetic counselor can also tell you about certain tests that:

- Determine if you have certain altered genes that could be passed to your children

- Screen your newborn for the disease

- Test your fetus early in pregnancy to look for an altered form of a gene

Treatment of Heritable Disorders of Connective Tissue

Heritable disorders of connective tissue are a wide range of disorders, each requiring a specific program for management and treatment. Treatments can include:

- **Regular monitoring** to assess tissue changes

- **Metabolic treatments** such as:

  - Vitamin B_6 to correct a liver enzyme problem

  - Drugs to slow the widening of the aorta

  - Drugs to strengthen brittle bones

142

Living with Heritable Disorders of Connective Tissue

Maintaining general health is important if you have a heritable disorder of connective tissue. You should talk to your doctor about a plan that includes:

- A nutritious diet

- Exercise

- Healthy lifestyle habits

Section 14.2

Beals Syndrome (Congenital Contractural Arachnodactyly)

This section includes text excerpted from "Congenital Contractural Arachnodactyly," Genetics Home Reference (GHR), National Institutes of Health (NIH), January 29, 2019.

Congenital contractural arachnodactyly (CCA) is a disorder that affects many parts of the body. People with this condition typically are tall with long limbs (dolichostenomelia) and have long, slender fingers and toes (arachnodactyly). They often have permanently bent joints (contractures) that can restrict movement in their hips, knees, ankles, or elbows. Additional features of CCA include underdeveloped muscles, a rounded upper back that also curves to the side (kyphoscoliosis), permanently bent fingers and toes (camptodactyly), ears that look "crumpled," and a protruding chest (pectus carinatum). Rarely, people with CCA have heart defects, such as an enlargement of the blood vessel that distributes blood from the heart to the rest of the body (aortic root dilatation) or a leak in one of the valves that control blood flow through the heart (mitral valve prolapse). The life expectancy of individuals with CCA varies depending on the severity of symptoms but is typically not shortened.

A rare, severe form of CCA involves both heart and digestive system abnormalities in addition to the skeletal features described above;

individuals with this severe form of the condition usually do not live past infancy.

Frequency and Causes of Beats Syndrome

The prevalence of CCA is estimated to be less than 1 in 10,000 worldwide.

Mutations in the *FBN2* gene cause CCA. The *FBN2* gene provides instructions for producing the fibrillin-2 protein. Fibrillin-2 binds to other proteins and molecules to form threadlike filaments called "microfibrils." Microfibrils become part of the fibers that provide strength and flexibility to connective tissue that supports the body's joints and organs. Additionally, microfibrils regulate the activity of molecules called "growth factors." Growth factors enable the growth and repair of tissues throughout the body.

Mutations in the *FBN2* gene can decrease fibrillin-2 production or result in the production of a protein with impaired function. As a result, microfibril formation is reduced, which probably weakens the structure of connective tissue and disrupts regulation of growth factor activity. The resulting abnormalities of connective tissue underlie the signs and symptoms of CCA.

Section 14.3

Ehlers-Danlos Syndrome

This section includes text excerpted from "Ehlers-Danlos Syndromes," Genetic and Rare Diseases Information Center (GARD), National Center for Advancing Translational Sciences (NCATS), April 20, 2017.

Ehlers-Danlos syndromes (EDS) are a group of inherited connective tissue disorders caused by abnormalities in the structure, production, and/or processing of collagen. The new classification, from 2017, includes 13 subtypes of EDS. Although other forms of the condition may exist, they are extremely rare and are not well-characterized. The signs and symptoms of EDS vary by type and range from mildly loose joints to life-threatening complications. Features shared by many types include joint hypermobility and soft, velvety skin that is highly elastic (stretchy) and bruises easily. Mutations in a variety of genes may lead to EDS; however, the underlying genetic cause in some families is unknown. Depending on the subtype, EDS may be inherited in an autosomal dominant or an autosomal recessive manner. There is no specific cure for EDS. The treatment and management is focused on preventing serious complications and relieving associated signs and symptoms.

Symptoms of Ehlers-Danlos Syndrome

There are 13 types of EDS, with a significant overlap in features:

- **Hypermobile EDS** is characterized primarily by joint hypermobility affecting both large and small joints, which may lead to recurrent joint dislocations and subluxations (partial dislocation). In general, people with this type have soft, smooth, and velvety skin with easy bruising and chronic pain of the muscles and/or bones.

- **Classical EDS** is associated with extremely elastic (stretchy), smooth skin that is fragile and bruises easily; wide, atrophic scars (flat or depressed scars); and joint hypermobility. Molluscoid pseudotumors (calcified hematomas over pressure points, such as the elbow) and spheroids (fat-containing cysts on forearms and shins) are also frequently seen. Hypotonia and delayed motor development may occur.

- **Vascular EDS** is characterized by thin, translucent skin that is extremely fragile and bruises easily. Arteries and certain organs, such as the intestines and uterus, are also fragile and prone to rupture. People with this type of EDS typically have short stature; thin scalp hair; and characteristic facial features including large eyes, a thin nose, and lobeless ears. Joint hypermobility is present but generally confined to the small joints (fingers, toes). Other common features include club foot; tendon and/or muscle rupture; acrogeria (premature aging of the skin of the hands and feet); early onset varicose veins; pneumothorax (collapse of a lung); recession of the gums; and a decreased amount of fat under the skin.

- **Kyphoscoliosis EDS** is associated with severe hypotonia at birth, delayed motor development, progressive scoliosis (present from birth), and scleral fragility. Affected people may also have easy bruising; fragile arteries that are prone to rupture; unusually small corneas; and osteopenia (low bone density). Other common features include a "marfanoid habitus" which is characterized by long, slender fingers (arachnodactyly); unusually long limbs; and a sunken chest (pectus excavatum) or protruding chest (pectus carinatum).

- **Arthrochalasia EDS** is characterized by severe joint hypermobility and congenital hip dislocation. Other common features include fragile, elastic skin with easy bruising; hypotonia; kyphoscoliosis (kyphosis and scoliosis); and mild osteopenia.

- **Dermatosparaxis EDS** is associated with extremely fragile skin leading to severe bruising and scarring; saggy, redundant skin, especially on the face; and hernias.

- **Brittle cornea syndrome (BCS).** It is characterized by a thin cornea, early onset progressive keratoglobus; and blue sclerae.

- **Classical-like EDS (clEDS)** is characterized by skin hyperextensibility with velvety skin texture and absence of atrophic scarring, generalized joint hypermobility (GJH) with or without recurrent dislocations (most often shoulder and ankle), and easily bruised skin or spontaneous ecchymoses (discolorations of the skin resulting from bleeding underneath).

- **Spondylodysplastic EDS (spEDS)** is characterized by short stature (progressive in childhood), muscle hypotonia (ranging from severe congenital, to mild later-onset), and bowing of limbs.

- **Musculocontractural EDS (mcEDS)** is characterized by congenital multiple contractures, characteristically adduction-flexion contractures and/or talipes equinovarus (clubfoot), characteristic craniofacial features, which are evident at birth or in early infancy, and skin features such as skin hyperextensibility, easy bruisability, skin fragility with atrophic scars, and increased palmar wrinkling.

- **Myopathic EDS (mEDS)** is characterized by congenital muscle hypotonia, and/or muscle atrophy, that worsens with age, proximal joint contractures (joints of the knee, hip and elbow); and hypermobility of distal joints (joints of the ankles, wrists, feet and hands).

- **Periodontal EDS (pEDS)** is characterized by severe and intractable periodontitis of early onset (childhood or adolescence), lack of attached gingiva, pretibial plaques; and family history of a first-degree relative who meets clinical criteria.

- **Cardiac-valvular EDS (cvEDS)** is characterized by severe progressive cardiac-valvular problems (aortic valve, mitral valve), skin problems (hyperextensibility, atrophic scars, thin skin, easy bruising) and joint hypermobility (generalized or restricted to small joints).

Other forms of the condition may exist but are extremely rare and are not well-characterized.

Causes of Ehlers-Danlos Syndrome

EDS are genetic disorders that can be caused by mutations in several different genes, including *COL5A1, COL5A2, COL1A1, COL3A1, TNXB, PLOD1, COL1A2, FKBP14* and *ADAMTS2*. However, the underlying genetic cause is unknown in some families.

Mutations in these genes usually change the structure, production, and/or processing of collagen, or proteins that interact with collagen. Collagen provides structure and strength to connective tissues throughout the body. A defect in collagen can weaken connective tissues in the skin, bones, blood vessels, and organs, resulting in the signs and symptoms of EDS.

Inheritance of Ehlers-Danlos Syndrome

The inheritance pattern of EDS varies by subtype. The arthrochalasia EDS, classical EDS, hypermobile EDS, periodontal EDS, some cases of myopathic EDS, and vascular forms of EDS usually have an autosomal dominant pattern of inheritance. This means that to be affected, a person needs to have a change (mutation) in only one copy of the disease-causing gene in each cell. In some cases, a person with these forms of EDS inherits the mutation from an affected parent. Other cases may result from new (de novo) mutations in the gene; these cases occur in people with no family history of EDS. Each child of a person with autosomal dominant EDS has a 50 percent chance of inheriting the mutation.

The dermatosparaxis EDS, kyphoscoliosis EDS, classical-like EDS, cardiac-vascular EDS, brittle cornea syndrome, spondylodysplastic

EDS, musculocontractural EDS, and some cases of myopathic EDS are inherited in an autosomal recessive pattern. This means that, with any of these types of EDS, a person must have a mutation in both copies of the disease-causing gene in each cell. The parents of an affected person usually each carry one mutated copy of the gene and are referred to as carriers. Carriers typically do not show signs or symptoms of the condition. When 2 carriers of an autosomal recessive condition have children, each child has a 25 percent (1 in 4) risk to have the condition, a 50 percent (1 in 2) risk to be a carrier like each of the parents, and a 25 percent chance to not have the condition and not be a carrier.

Diagnosis of Ehlers-Danlos Syndrome

A diagnosis of the EDS is typically based on the presence of characteristic signs and symptoms. Depending on the subtype suspected, some of the following tests may be ordered to support the diagnosis:

- **Collagen typing**, performed on a skin biopsy, may aid in the diagnosis of vascular type, arthrochalasia type, and dermatosparaxis type. People with EDS often have abnormalities of certain types of collagen.

- **Genetic testing** is available for many subtypes of EDS; however, it is not an option for most families with the hypermobility type.

- **Imaging studies** such as computed tomography (CT) scan, magnetic resonance imaging (MRI), ultrasound, and angiography may be useful in identifying certain features of the condition.

- **Urine tests** to detect deficiencies in certain enzymes that are important for collagen formation may be helpful in diagnosing the kyphoscoliosis type.

Treatment of Ehlers-Danlos Syndrome

The treatment and management of EDS is focused on preventing serious complications and relieving signs and symptoms. The features of EDS vary by subtype, so management strategies differ slightly. Because several body systems may be affected, different medical specialists may need to be involved. The main aspects of management include cardiovascular (heart) work-up, physical therapy, pain management, and psychological follow-up as needed. Surgery is sometimes recommended for various reasons in people with EDS. However, depending on the type of EDS and severity, there may be an increased risk of various surgical complications, such as wound healing problems, excessive bleeding, dissection, and hernias. Surgery for non-life threatening conditions particularly should be carefully considered.

Please speak to your healthcare provider if you have any questions about your personal medical management plan.

Prognosis for Ehlers-Danlos Syndrome

The long-term outlook (prognosis) for people with EDS varies by subtype. The vascular type is typically the most severe form of EDS and is often associated with a shortened lifespan. People affected by vascular EDS have a median life expectancy of 48 years, and many will have a major event by age 40. The lifespan of people with the kyphoscoliosis form is also decreased, largely due to the vascular involvement and the potential for restrictive lung disease.

Other forms of EDS are typically not as dangerous and can be associated with normal lifespans. Affected people can often live healthy, if somewhat restricted, lives.

Section 14.4

Marfan Syndrome

This section includes text excerpted from "Learning about Marfan Syndrome," National Human Genome Research Institute (NHGRI), May 30, 2017.

Marfan syndrome (MFS) is one of the most common inherited disorders of connective tissue. It is an autosomal dominant condition occurring once in every 10,000 to 20,000 individuals. There is wide variability in clinical symptoms in MFS with the most notable occurring in the eye, skeleton, connective tissue, and cardiovascular systems.

MFS is caused by mutations in the *FBN1* gene. *FBN1* mutations are associated with a broad continuum of physical features ranging from isolated features of MFS to a severe and rapidly progressive form in newborns.

What Are the Symptoms of Marfan Syndrome?

The most common symptom of MFS is myopia (nearsightedness from the increased curve of the retina due to connective tissue changes in the globe of the eye). About 60 percent of individuals who have MFS have lens displacement from the center of the pupil (ectopia lentis). Individuals who have MFS also have an increased risk for retinal detachment, glaucoma, and early cataract formation.

Other common symptoms of MFS involve the skeleton and connective tissue systems. These include bone overgrowth and loose joints (joint laxity). Individuals who have MFS have long thin arms and legs (dolichostenomelia). Overgrowth of the ribs can cause the chest bone (sternum) to bend inward (pectus excavatum or funnel chest) or push outward (pectus carinatum or pigeon breast). The curvature of the spine (scoliosis) is another common skeletal symptom that can be mild or severe and progressively worsen with age. Scoliosis shortens the trunk and also contributes to the arms and legs appearing too long.

Cardiovascular malformations are the most life-threatening symptom of MFS. They include a dilated aorta just as it leaves the heart (at the level of the sinuses of valsalva), mitral valve prolapse, tricuspid valve prolapse, enlargement of the proximal pulmonary artery, and a high risk for aortic tear and rupture (aortic dissection).

How Is Marfan Syndrome Diagnosed?

The diagnosis of MFS is a clinical diagnosis that is based on family history and the presence of characteristic clinical findings in ocular, skeletal, and cardiovascular systems. There are four major clinical diagnostic features:

1. Dilatation or dissection of the aorta at the level of the sinuses of valsalva

2. Ectopia lentis (dislocated lens of the eye)

3. Lumbosacral dural ectasia determined by CT scan or magnetic resonance imaging (MRI)

4. Four of the eight typical skeletal features

Major criteria for establishing the diagnosis in a family member also includes having a parent, child, or sibling who meets major criteria independently, the presence of an *FBN-1* mutation known to cause the syndrome, or a haplotype around *FBN-1* inherited by descent and identified in a familial Marfan patient (also known as "genetic linkage to the gene").

The *FBN1* gene is the gene associated with true MFS. Genetic testing of the *FBN1* gene identifies 70 to 93 percent of the mutations and is available in clinical laboratories. However, patients negative for the test for gene mutation should be considered for evaluation for other conditions that have similar features of MFS, such as Dietz syndrome, Ehlers Danlos syndrome (EDS), and homocystinuria. To unequivocally establish the diagnosis in the absence of a family history requires a major manifestation from two systems and involvement of a third system. If a mutation known to cause MFS is identified, the diagnosis requires one major criterion and involvement of a second organ system.

To establish the diagnosis in a relative of a patient known to have MFS (index case), it requires the presence of a major criterion in the family history and one major criterion in an organ system with involvement of a second organ system.

What Is the Treatment for Marfan Syndrome?

Individuals who have MFS are treated by a multidisciplinary medical team that includes a geneticist, cardiologist, ophthalmologist, orthopedist, and cardiothoracic surgeon.

Eye problems are generally treated with eyeglasses. When lens dislocation interferes with vision or causes glaucoma, surgery can be performed and an artificial lens implanted.

Skeletal problems, such as scoliosis and pectus excavatum, may require surgery. For those individuals who have pes planus (flat feet), arch supports and orthotics can be used to decrease leg fatigue and muscle cramps.

Medication, such as beta-blockers, is used to decrease the stress on the aorta at the time of diagnosis or when there is progressive aortic dilatation. Surgery to repair the aorta is done when the aortic diameter is greater than 5 cm in adults and older children, when the aortic diameter increases by 1.0 cm per year, or when there is progressive aortic regurgitation.

Cardiovascular surveillance includes yearly echocardiograms to monitor the status of the aorta. As of now, the use of beta-blocker medications has delayed but not prevented the need to eventually perform aortic surgery.

The work on Angiotensin II receptor blockers, another blood pressure medication, has shown additional promise to protect the aorta from dilatation. Clinical trials will be starting soon to see if this drug can prevent the need for surgery better than beta-blockers have.

Individuals who have Marfan syndrome are advised to avoid contact and competitive sports and isometric exercises, such as weight lifting and other static forms of exercise. They can participate in aerobic exercises, such as swimming. They are also advised to avoid medications, such as decongestants and foods that contain caffeine, which can lead to chronic increases in blood pressure and stretch the connective tissue in the cardiovascular system.

Is Marfan Syndrome Inherited?

Marfan syndrome is inherited in families in an autosomal dominant manner. Approximately 75 percent of individuals who have MFS have a parent who also has the condition (inherited). Approximately 25 percent of individuals who have MFS, have the condition as a result of a new (de novo) mutation. When a parent has MFS, each of his or her children has a 50 percent chance (1 chance in 2) to inherit the *FBN1* gene. While MFS is not always inherited, it is always heritable.

When a child with MFS is born to parents who do not show features of the MFS, it is likely the child has a new mutation. In this family situation, the chance for future siblings (brothers and sisters of the child with MFS) to be born with MFS is less than 50 percent. But the risk is still greater than the general population risk of 1 in 10,000. The risk is higher for siblings because there are rare families where a Marfan gene mutation is in some percentage of the germline cells of one of the parents (testes or ovaries).

Prenatal testing for MFS is available when the gene mutation is known, as well as a technique called "linkage analysis" (tracking the gene for MFS in a family using genetic markers).

Section 14.5

Osteogenesis Imperfecta

This section includes text excerpted from "Learning about
Osteogenesis Imperfecta," National Human Genome Research
Institute (NHGRI), July 5, 2017.

What Is Osteogenesis Imperfecta?

Osteogenesis imperfecta (OI) is a genetic disorder that causes
a person's bones to break easily, often from little or no apparent
trauma. OI is also called "brittle bone disease." OI varies in severity
from person to person, ranging from a mild type to a severe type
that causes death before or shortly after birth. In addition to having
fractures, people with OI also have teeth problems (dentinogenesis
imperfecta) and hearing loss when they are adults. People who have
OI may also have muscle weakness, loose joints (joint laxity) and
skeletal malformations.

OI occurs in approximately 1 in 20,000 individuals, including people
diagnosed after birth. OI occurs with equal frequency among males and
females and among racial and ethnic groups. Life expectancy varies
depending on how severe the OI is, ranging from very brief (lethal
form, OI type II) to average.

There are four well-known types of OI. These types are distinguished mostly by fracture frequency and severity and by characteristic features. Three additional types of OI (type V, VI, and VII) have
also been identified.

The vast majority (90%) of OI is caused by a single dominant mutation in one of two type I collagen genes: *COL1A1* or *COL1A2*. The
COL1A1 and *COL1A2* genes provide instructions for making proteins
that are used to create a larger molecule called "type I collagen." This
type of collagen is the most common protein in bone, skin, and other
tissues that provide structure and strength to the body (connective
tissues). OI type VII is caused by recessive mutations in the CRTAP
gene.

What Are the Symptoms of Osteogenesis Imperfecta?

Osteogenesis imperfecta (OI) causes bones to be fragile and easily
broken and is also responsible for other health problems.

Type I OI is the mildest form of the condition. People who have type I OI have bone fractures during childhood and adolescence often due to minor trauma When these individuals reach adulthood they have fewer fractures.

Type II OI is the most severe form of OI. Infants with type II have bones that appear bent or crumpled and fractured before birth. Their chest is narrow and they have fractured and misshapen ribs and underdeveloped lungs. These infants have short, bowed arms and legs; hips that turn outward; and unusually soft skull bones. Most infants with type II OI are stillborn or die shortly after birth, usually from breathing failure.

Type III OI also has relatively severe signs and symptoms. Infants with OI type III have very soft and fragile bones that may begin to fracture before birth or in early infancy. Some infants have rib fractures that can cause life-threatening problems with breathing. Bone abnormalities tend to get worse over time and often interfere with the ability to walk.

Type IV OI is the most variable form of OI. Symptoms of OI type IV can range from mild to severe. About 25 percent of infants with OI type IV are born with bone fractures. Others may not have broken bones until later in childhood or adulthood. Infants with OI type IV have leg bones that are bowed at birth, but bowing usually lessens as they get older.

Some types of OI are also associated with progressive hearing loss, a blue or grey tint to the part of the eye that is usually white (the sclera), teeth problems (dentinogenesis imperfecta), abnormal curvature of the spine and loose joints. People with this condition may have other bone abnormalities and are often shorter in stature than average.

How Is Osteogenesis Imperfecta Diagnosed?

OI is often inherited from an affected parent. The diagnosis of OI is made on the basis of family history and/or clinical presentation. Frequent fractures, short stature, a blue hue to the white part of the eye (blue sclera), teeth problems (dentinogenesis imperfecta), and hearing loss that progresses after puberty may be present.

X-rays are also used to diagnose OI. X-ray findings include fractures that are at different stages of healing; an unexpected skull bone pattern called "Wormian bones;" and bones in the spine called "codfish vertebrae."

Laboratory testing for OI may include either biochemical testing or deoxyribonucleic acid (DNA)-based sequencing of *COL1A1* and

COL1A2. Biochemical testing involves studying collagens taken from a small skin biopsy. Changes in type I collagen are an indication of OI.

DNA sequencing of *COL1A1* and *COL1A2* is used to identify the type I collagen gene mutation responsible for the altered collagen protein. DNA testing requires a blood sample for DNA extraction. Both tests are relatively sensitive, detecting approximately 90 percent and 95 percent, respectively, of individuals with the clinical diagnosis of OI. Normal biochemical and molecular testing in a child with OI warrants additional testing of less common collagen genes (*CRTAP* and *P3H (LEPRE1)*) responsible for some of the rare recessive forms of OI.

What Is the Treatment for Osteogenesis Imperfecta?

There is no cure for OI. Treatment involves supportive therapy to decrease the number of fractures and disabilities, and help with independent living and maintain overall health. OI is best managed by a medical team including the child's own doctor, and genetic, orthopedic, and rehabilitation medicine. Supportive therapy is unique to each individual depending on the severity of their condition and their age.

Physical and occupational therapies to help improve their ability to move, to prevent fractures, and to increase muscle strength are often useful.

Fractures are treated as they would be in children and adults who do not have OI. An orthopedic treatment called "intramedullary rodding" (placing rods in the bones) is used to help with the positioning of legs that helps with more normal functioning when necessary.

A newer treatment with a medication called "bisphosphonates" is being used to help with bone formation and to decrease the need for surgery.

Is Osteogenesis Imperfecta Inherited?

Most types of OI are inherited in an autosomal dominant pattern. Almost all infants with the severe type II OI are born into families without a family history of the condition. Usually, the cause in these families is a new mutation in the egg or sperm or very early embryo in the *COL1A1* or *COL1A2* gene. In the milder forms of OI, 25 to 30 percent of cases occur as a result of new mutations. The other cases are inherited from a parent who has the condition. Whether a person has OI due to a new mutation or an inherited genetic change, an adult with the disorder can pass the condition down to future generations.

In autosomal dominant inherited OI, a parent who has OI has one copy of a gene mutation that causes OI. With each of his/her pregnancies, there is a 1 in 2 (50%) chance to pass on the *OI* gene mutation to a child who would have OI, and a one in two (50%) chance to pass on the normal version of the gene to a child who would not have OI.

Rarely, OI can be inherited in an autosomal recessive pattern. Most often, the parents of a child with an autosomal recessive disorder are not affected but are carriers of one copy of the altered gene. Autosomal recessive inheritance means two copies of the gene must be altered for a person to be affected by the disorder. The autosomal recessive form of type III OI usually results from mutations in genes other than *COL1A1* and *COL1A2*.

Section 14.6

Stickler Syndrome

This section includes text excerpted from "Stickler Syndrome," Genetic and Rare Diseases Information Center (GARD), National Center for Advancing Translational Sciences (NCATS), January 1, 2018.

Stickler syndrome is a group of hereditary connective tissue disorders characterized by distinctive facial features, eye abnormalities, hearing loss, and joint problems. The symptoms of Stickler syndrome may vary but include nearsightedness (myopia), retinal detachment, underdevelopment of the middle of the face, and the development of arthritis at a young age.

Stickler syndrome is caused by genetic changes (mutations or pathogenic variants) in one of six genes: *COL2A1, COL11A1, COL11A2, COL9A1, COL9A2,* or *COL9A3*. The syndrome can be inherited in an autosomal dominant or autosomal recessive manner. Stickler syndrome can be diagnosed when a doctor observes many symptoms consistent with the syndrome. Genetic testing can be used to confirm the diagnosis. Treatment for Stickler syndrome may include surgeries, medications to reduce joint pain, and hearing aids.

Stickler syndrome can be divided into subtypes based on the pathogenic variant that is causing the syndrome.

Symptoms of Stickler Syndrome

The signs and symptoms of Stickler syndrome may include distinctive facial features, eye abnormalities, hearing loss, and symptoms affecting the joints. Facial features common to people who have Stickler syndrome may include being born with a cleft palate, having a small chin (micrognathia), and having a tongue that is placed further back in the mouth (glossoptosis). These features together are known as "Pierre-Robin sequence." In some cases, these facial features may make it difficult for babies with Stickler syndrome to breathe or eat. People with Stickler syndrome may also have underdevelopment of the middle of the face (midface hypoplasia).

Eye abnormalities associated with Stickler syndrome may include extreme nearsightedness (myopia). This can cause an increased risk for retinal detachment or the development of clouding of the lens (cataracts). These problems can lead to vision loss in some cases. People with Stickler syndrome may also have some hearing loss.

Stickler syndrome can cause people to have joint problems. Children with this syndrome may experience loose joints (joint laxity) or may be very flexible. Some people may develop arthritis at a young age, typically before 40-years-old. Other signs may include a curvature of the spine (scoliosis) or having flat vertebrae (platyspondyly). These features can cause back pain for some people. People with Stickler syndrome may also have weakened bones (osteoporosis), which can cause an increased risk for bone fractures.

Other signs of Stickler syndrome may include an increased risk for the valves in the heart to close improperly (mitral valve prolapse).

Causes of Stickler Syndrome

Stickler syndrome is caused by genetic changes (mutations or pathogenic variants) in one of six genes: *COL2A1, COL11A1, COL11A2, COL9A1, COL9A2,* or *COL9A3.* These genes are all responsible for providing instructions to the body to produce collagen. Collagen is involved in providing length and structure to tissues in the body known as "connective tissues." Connective tissues are present in many parts of the body including the eyes, skin, and joints. When there are pathogenic variants in any of the genes associated with Stickler syndrome, it causes the collagen in the body to not be made or processed properly. This causes the signs and symptoms associated with Stickler syndrome.

In some cases, people who have symptoms of Stickler syndrome have genetic testing that does not identify the pathogenic variant that is causing the syndrome. Therefore, researchers think that there might be other genes in which pathogenic variants cause Stickler syndrome, but these genes have not yet been identified.

Inheritance of Stickler Syndrome

Stickler syndrome can be inherited in an autosomal dominant manner or in an autosomal recessive manner, depending on the gene that has a change (mutation or pathogenic variant).

When Stickler syndrome is caused by pathogenic variants in *COL2A1, COL11A1, or COL11A2*, it is inherited in an autosomal dominant manner. This means that only one copy of one of the genes causing Stickler syndrome has a pathogenic variant. We inherit one copy of every gene from our mother and the other from our father. When a person who has Stickler syndrome has children, for each child there is a:

- 50 percent chance that the child will inherit the gene with a pathogenic variant, meaning she or he will have Stickler syndrome

- 50 percent chance that the child will inherit the working copy of the gene, meaning he or she will not have Stickler syndrome

In some cases, people who have an autosomal dominant form of Stickler syndrome are the first people to be diagnosed in the family. This may be because they inherited the genetic change from a parent, but the parent has mild symptoms of the syndrome and was never diagnosed. Most people who have an autosomal dominant form of Stickler syndrome inherited the genetic change from a parent. In other cases, the genetic change may be new in the person who was diagnosed with Stickler syndrome. Genetic changes that are new in a person are called "de novo."

Pathogenic variants in the other genes that cause Stickler syndrome (*COL9A1, COL9A2,* or *COL9A3)* are inherited in an autosomal recessive manner. This means that both copies of one of these genes must have a pathogenic variant for a person to have signs of Stickler syndrome. People who only have one changed copy of a gene that causes an autosomal recessive form of Stickler syndrome are known as "carriers." Carriers do not have signs or symptoms of the syndrome. When two carriers of Stickler syndrome have children together, for each child there is a:

- 25 percent chance that the child will inherit both changed copies of the gene, so she or he has Stickler syndrome

- 50 percent chance that the child will inherit only one changed copy of the gene, so he or she is a carrier of the syndrome like each of the parents

- 25 percent chance that the child will inherit both working copies of the gene, so she or he does not have Stickler syndrome and is not a carrier of the syndrome

Stickler syndrome shows a characteristic known as "variable expressivity." This means that people with Stickler syndrome can have different signs and symptoms of the syndrome, even among members of the same family. However, anyone with a pathogenic variant that causes Stickler syndrome is expected to have some symptoms of the syndrome. This is called "full penetrance."

Diagnosis of Stickler Syndrome

Stickler syndrome is suspected when a doctor observes signs or symptoms such as distinctive facial features, symptoms affecting the eyes, hearing loss, joint problems, and other people in the family with similar symptoms. The diagnosis can be confirmed by comparing the features seen in the person to the features seen in people who have Stickler syndrome. A set of criteria has been published to help doctors determine if a person should be diagnosed with Stickler syndrome based on his or her signs and symptoms.

Some people with Stickler syndrome may decide to have genetic testing to confirm the diagnosis. This can allow other family members to have testing for Stickler syndrome. It can also provide information about the inheritance pattern so that the chances for future children to have Stickler syndrome can be better understood.

Treatment of Stickler Syndrome

After a person is diagnosed with Stickler syndrome, some evaluations may be recommended to determine if there are other signs of the syndrome that have not been previously noticed. These evaluations may include an eye exam, exam by a doctor who can check for facial differences such as cleft palate (craniofacial specialist), a hearing (audiometry) exam, and evaluation for any possible heart problems.

Treatment for Stickler syndrome is aimed at treating the specific symptoms each person has. For some, this may involve surgeries to correct a cleft palate or retinal detachment. Other treatments may include hearing aids for hearing loss or medications for joint pain.

Prognosis of Stickler Syndrome

Because the symptoms of Stickler syndrome are variable, it can be difficult to predict what the long-term outlook is for people who have the syndrome. There is an increased risk for eye problems associated with Stickler syndrome, including retinal detachment and cataracts. These symptoms can lead to vision loss. People with Stickler syndrome may also experience arthritis before 40 years of age. In general, people with Stickler syndrome have typical intelligence and can function well in society. Some people do not know they have Stickler syndrome until another family member is diagnosed because the symptoms can be relatively mild.

Chapter 15

Cornelia de Lange Syndrome

Cornelia de Lange syndrome (CdLS) is a developmental disorder that affects many parts of the body. The severity of the condition and the associated signs and symptoms can vary widely but may include distinctive facial characteristics, growth delays, intellectual disability, and limb defects. Approximately 60 percent of people affected by CdLS have a disease-causing variation (mutation) in the *NIPBL* gene, and about 10 percent of cases are caused by mutations in 1 of 4 known genes: *SMC1A, SMC3, HDAC8*, and *RAD21*. In the remaining 30 percent of cases, the underlying genetic cause of the condition is unknown. CdLS can be inherited in an autosomal dominant (*NIPBL, SMC2*, or *RAD21*) or X-linked (*SMC1A* or *HDAC8*) manner. However, most cases result from new (de novo) mutations and occur in people with no family history of the condition. Treatment is based on the signs and symptoms present in each person.

Symptoms of Cornelia de Lange Syndrome

The signs and symptoms of CdLS vary widely among affected people and can range from relatively mild to severe. Affected people may experience:

- Slowed growth before and after birth

This chapter includes text excerpted from "Cornelia de Lange Syndrome," Genetic and Rare Diseases Information Center (GARD), National Center for Advancing Translational Sciences (NCATS), May 5, 2018.

- Intellectual disability (ID)

- Developmental delay

- Autistic and/or self-destructive behaviors

- Skeletal abnormalities of the arms and hands

- Gastrointestinal (GI) problems

- Hirsutism (excess hair growth)

- Hearing loss

- Myopia

- Congenital heart defects (CHDs)

- Genital abnormalities (i.e., cryptorchidism)

- Seizures

Affected people typically have distinctive craniofacial features, as well, which may include microcephaly; arched eyebrows that often grow together in the middle (synophrys); long eyelashes; low-set ears; small, widely spaced teeth; and a small, upturned nose.

Cause of Cornelia de Lange Syndrome

Most cases (approximately 60 percent) of CdLS are caused by changes (mutations) in the *NIPBL* gene. About 10 percent of people affected by the condition have mutations in 1 of 4 known genes (*SMC1A, SMC3, HDAC8*, and *RAD21*). Many of the genes associated with CdLS encode proteins that play an important role in human development before birth. Mutations in these genes may result in an abnormal protein that is not able to carry out its normal function. This is thought to interfere with early development leading to the many signs and symptoms of CdLS.

In the remaining 30 percent of people with CdLS, the underlying genetic cause of the condition is unknown.

Inheritance of Cornelia de Lange Syndrome

Depending on the mutated gene, CdLS can be inherited in an autosomal dominant manner, when it is caused by variations in the *NIPBL, SMC2*, or *RAD21* genes, or it can have an X-linked inheritance when it is caused by variations in the *SMC1A* or *HDAC8* genes. However, most cases (more than 99%) result from new mutations, which means that they are not inherited from the parents and occur in people with no family history of the condition.

Diagnosis of Cornelia de Lange Syndrome

The diagnosis is suspected when the following signs and symptoms are present:

- Head and face appearance (greater than 95%). Very small and flat head (microbrachycephaly), unibrow (synophrys) and highly arched eyebrows (in 98% of the cases), long and thick eyelashes, low-set abnormally placed ears with a thick helix (curve of the outer ear), short nose with upturned tip with nares that are easily seeing from the front (anteverted nares), long space between the nose and the superior lip, thin downturned lips, high and arched palate with clefts (30% of the cases), very small jaw (micrognathia) in 80 percent of the cases, with spurs (42% of the cases), and short neck.

- Growth failure (greater than 95%). Growth failure that starts while the fetus is growing inside the womb, resulting in a very low height and weight throughout life, and failure to thrive secondary to gastroesophageal reflux (GER) and other issues with feeding.

- Intellectual disability (greater than 95%). Severe-to-profound developmental delay.

- Limb abnormalities (greater than 95%). Small or absent forearms and missing fingers in about 30 percent of the cases. Some people do not have limb deficiencies but have micromelia (small hands), abnormal placed thumbs, and abnormal curvature of the fifth finger (clinodactyly). A fusion of the bones of the forearm (radioulnar synostosis) is common and may result in a defect of the elbows. Small feet and joined toes (syndactyly) in more than 80 percent of the cases.

- Excess of hair in the face, back and arms (hirsutism) in more than 80 percent of the cases.

People with milder syndrome usually have many of the characteristic facial features but with less severe cognitive and upper extremities defects, and mild intellectual disability (intelligence is normal in some cases). A milder syndrome is more common in people with variants in the *SMC3, RAD21, HDAC8*, or *SMC1A* genes.

The diagnosis of CdLS is established with the presence of the clinical features and/or by the genetic test showing a variation in any of the genes associated with the syndrome. However, about 30 percent of the people affected by the syndrome do not have any known cause.

Testing Resources

The Genetic Testing Registry (GTR) provides information about the genetic tests for this condition. The intended audience for the GTR is healthcare providers and researchers. Patients and consumers with specific questions about a genetic test should contact a healthcare provider or a genetics professional.

Treatment of Cornelia de Lange Syndrome

Because CdLS affects many different systems of the body, medical management is often provided by a team of doctors and other healthcare professionals. Treatment for this condition varies based on the signs and symptoms present in each person. It may include:

- Supplemental formulas and/or gastrostomy tube (G-tube) placement to meet nutritional needs and improve the growth delay

- Ongoing physical, occupational, and speech therapies

- Surgery to treat skeletal abnormalities, gastrointestinal problems, congenital heart defects, and other health problems

- Medications to prevent or control seizures

Prognosis for Cornelia de Lange Syndrome

Life expectancy is relatively normal for people with CdLS and most affected children live well into adulthood. For example, one article mentioned a woman with CdLS who lived to age 61 and an affected man who lived to age 54. However, certain features of this condition, particularly severe malformations of the heart or throat, may decrease life expectancy in some affected people.

Chapter 16

Cystic Fibrosis

Cystic fibrosis, or CF, is an inherited disease of the secretory glands. Secretory glands include glands that make mucus and sweat.

"Inherited" means the disease is passed from parents to children through genes. People who have CF inherit two faulty genes for the disease—one from each parent. The parents likely don't have the disease themselves.

CF mainly affects the lungs, pancreas, liver, intestines, sinuses, and sex organs.

Causes of Cystic Fibrosis

A defect in the *CFTR* gene causes CF. This gene makes a protein that controls the movement of salt and water in and out of your body's cells. In people who have CF, the gene makes a protein that doesn't work well. This causes thick, sticky mucus and very salty sweat.

Research suggests that the CFTR protein also affects the body in other ways. This may help explain other symptoms and complications of CF.

More than a thousand known defects can affect the *CFTR* gene. The type of defect you or your child has may affect the severity of CF. Other genes also may play a role in the severity of the disease.

This chapter includes text excerpted from "Cystic Fibrosis," National Heart, Lung, and Blood Institute (NHLBI), May 22, 2018.

How Is Cystic Fibrosis Inherited?

Every person inherits two *CFTR* genes—one from each parent. Children who inherit a faulty *CFTR* gene from each parent will have CF.

Children who inherit one faulty *CFTR* gene and one normal *CFTR* gene are "CF carriers." CF carriers usually have no symptoms of CF and live normal lives. However, they can pass the faulty *CFTR* gene to their children.

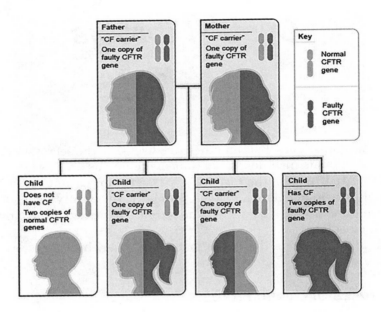

Figure 16.1. *Example of an Inheritance Pattern for Cystic Fibrosis*

The image shows how CFTR genes are inherited. A person inherits two copies of the CFTR gene—one from each parent. If each parent has a normal CFTR gene and a faulty CFTR gene, each child has a 25 percent chance of inheriting two normal genes; a 50 percent chance of inheriting one normal gene and one faulty gene; and a 25 percent chance of inheriting two faulty genes.

Risk Factors for Cystic Fibrosis

CF affects both males and females and people from all racial and ethnic groups. However, the disease is most common among Caucasians of Northern European descent.

CF also is common among Latinos and American Indians, especially the Pueblo and Zuni. The disease is less common among African Americans and Asian Americans.

More than 10 million Americans are carriers of a faulty *CF* gene. Many of them don't know that they're CF carriers.

Cystic Fibrosis: Signs, Symptoms, and Complications

The signs and symptoms of CF vary from person to person and change over time. Sometimes you'll have a few symptoms. Other times, your symptoms may become more severe.

One of the first signs of CF that parents may notice is that their baby's skin tastes salty when kissed, or the baby doesn't pass stool when first born.

Most of the other signs and symptoms of CF happen later. They're related to how CF affects the respiratory, digestive, or reproductive systems of the body.

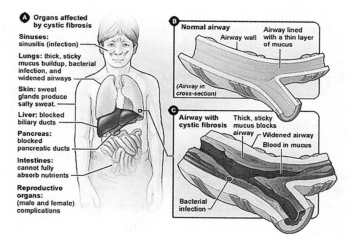

Figure 16.2. *Cystic Fibrosis*

Figure A shows the organs that cystic fibrosis (CF) can affect. Figure B shows a cross-section of a normal airway. Figure C shows an airway with CF. The widened airway is blocked by thick, sticky mucus that contains blood and bacteria.

Respiratory System Signs and Symptoms

People who have CF have thick, sticky mucus that builds up in their airways. This buildup of mucus makes it easier for bacteria to grow and cause infections. Infections can block the airways and cause frequent coughing that brings up thick sputum (spit) or mucus that's sometimes bloody.

People who have CF tend to have lung infections caused by unusual germs that don't respond to standard antibiotics. For example, lung infections caused by bacteria called "mucoid Pseudomonas" are much more common in people who have CF than in those who don't. An infection caused by these bacteria may be a sign of CF.

People who have CF have frequent bouts of sinusitis, an infection of the sinuses. The sinuses are hollow air spaces around the eyes, nose, and forehead. Frequent bouts of bronchitis and pneumonia also can occur. These infections can cause long-term lung damage.

As CF gets worse, you may have more serious problems, such as pneumothorax or bronchiectasis.

Some people who have CF also develop nasal polyps (growths in the nose) that may require surgery.

Digestive System Signs and Symptoms

In CF, mucus can block tubes, or ducts, in your pancreas (an organ in your abdomen). These blockages prevent enzymes from reaching your intestines.

As a result, your intestines can't fully absorb fats and proteins. This can cause ongoing diarrhea or bulky, foul-smelling, greasy stools. Intestinal blockages also may occur, especially in newborns. Too much gas or severe constipation in the intestines may cause stomach pain and discomfort.

A hallmark of CF in children is poor weight gain and growth. These children are unable to get enough nutrients from their food because of the lack of enzymes to help absorb fats and proteins.

As CF gets worse, other problems may occur, such as:

- Pancreatitis. This is a condition in which the pancreas becomes inflamed, which causes pain.

- Rectal Prolapse. Frequent coughing or problems passing stools may cause rectal tissue from inside you to move out of your rectum.

- Liver disease due to inflamed or blocked bile ducts.

- Diabetes

- Gallstones

Reproductive System Signs and Symptoms

Men who have CF are infertile because they're born without a vas deferens. The vas deferens is a tube that delivers sperm from the testes to the penis.

Women who have CF may have a hard time getting pregnant because of mucus blocking the cervix or other CF complications.

Other Signs, Symptoms, and Complications

Other signs and symptoms of CF are related to an upset of the balance of minerals in your blood.

CF causes your sweat to become very salty. As a result, your body loses large amounts of salt when you sweat. This can cause dehydration (a lack of fluid in your body), increased heart rate, fatigue (tiredness), weakness, decreased blood pressure, heat stroke, and, rarely, death.

CF also can cause clubbing and low bone density. Clubbing is the widening and rounding of the tips of your fingers and toes. This sign develops late in CF because your lungs aren't moving enough oxygen into your bloodstream.

Low bone density also tends to occur late in CF. It can lead to bone-thinning disorders called "osteoporosis" and "osteopenia."

Diagnosis of Cystic Fibrosis

Doctors diagnose CF based on the results from various tests.

Newborn Screening

All states screen newborns for CF using a genetic test or a blood test. The genetic test shows whether a newborn has faulty *CFTR* genes. The blood test shows whether a newborn's pancreas is working properly.

Sweat Test

If a genetic test or blood test suggests CF, a doctor will confirm the diagnosis using a sweat test. This test is the most useful test for diagnosing CF. A sweat test measures the amount of salt in sweat.

For this test, the doctor triggers sweating on a small patch of skin on an arm or leg. she or he rubs the skin with a sweat-producing chemical and then uses an electrode to provide a mild electrical current. This may cause a tingling or warm feeling.

Sweat is collected on a pad or paper and then analyzed. The sweat test usually is done twice. High salt levels confirm a diagnosis of CF.

Other Tests

If you or your child has CF, your doctor may recommend other tests, such as:

- Genetic tests to find out what type of CFTR defect is causing your CF.

- A chest X-ray. This test creates pictures of the structures in your chest, such as your heart, lungs, and blood vessels. A chest X-ray can show whether your lungs are inflamed or scarred, or whether they trap air.

- A sinus X-ray. This test may show signs of sinusitis, a complication of CF.

- Lung function tests. These tests measure how much air you can breathe in and out, how fast you can breathe air out, and how well your lungs deliver oxygen to your blood.

- A sputum culture. For this test, your doctor will take a sample of your sputum (spit) to see whether bacteria are growing in it. If you have bacteria called "mucoid Pseudomonas," you may have more advanced CF that needs aggressive treatment.

Prenatal Screening

If you're pregnant, prenatal genetic tests can show whether your fetus has CF. These tests include amniocentesis and chorionic villus sampling (CVS).

In amniocentesis, your doctor inserts a hollow needle through your abdominal wall into your uterus. She or he removes a small amount of fluid from the sac around the fetus. The fluid is tested to see whether both of the fetus's *CFTR* genes are normal.

In CVS, your doctor threads a thin tube through the vagina and cervix to the placenta. The doctor removes a tissue sample from the placenta using gentle suction. The sample is tested to see whether the fetus has CF.

Cystic Fibrosis Carrier Testing

People who have one normal *CFTR* gene and one faulty *CFTR* gene are CF carriers. CF carriers usually have no symptoms of CF and live normal lives. However, carriers can pass faulty *CFTR* genes on to their children.

If you have a family history of CF or a partner who has CF (or a family history of it) and you're planning a pregnancy, you may want to find out whether you're a CF carrier.

A genetics counselor can test a blood or saliva sample to find out whether you have a faulty *CF* gene. This type of testing can detect faulty *CF* genes in 9 out of 10 cases.

Treatment of Cystic Fibrosis

CF has no cure. However, treatments have greatly improved in recent years. Depending on the severity of CF, you or your child may be treated in a hospital.

Specialists Involved

If you or your child has CF, you may be treated by a CF specialist. This is a doctor who is familiar with the complex nature of CF.

Often, a CF specialist works with a medical team of nurses, physical therapists, dietitians, and social workers. CF specialists often are located at major medical centers.

The United States also has more than 100 CF Care Centers. These centers have teams of doctors, nurses, dietitians, respiratory therapists, physical therapists, and social workers who have special training related to CF care. Most CF Care Centers have pediatric and adult programs or clinics.

Treatment for Lung Problems

The main treatments for lung problems in people who have CF are chest physical therapy (CPT), exercise, and medicines. Your doctor also may recommend a pulmonary rehabilitation (PR) program.

Chest Physical Therapy

CPT also is called "chest clapping" or "percussion." It involves pounding your chest and back over and over with your hands or a device to loosen the mucus from your lungs so that you can cough it up.

You might sit down or lie on your stomach with your head down while you do CPT. Gravity and force help drain the mucus from your lungs.

Some people find CPT hard or uncomfortable to do. Several devices have been developed that may help with CPT, such as:

- An electric chest clapper, known as a "mechanical percussor"

- An inflatable therapy vest that uses high-frequency airwaves to force the mucus that's deep in your lungs toward your upper airways so you can cough it up

- A small, handheld device that you exhale through. The device causes vibrations that dislodge the mucus.

- A mask that creates vibrations that help break the mucus loose from your airway walls

Breathing techniques also may help dislodge mucus so you can cough it up. These techniques include forcing out a couple of short breaths or deeper breaths and then doing relaxed breathing. This may help loosen the mucus in your lungs and open your airways.

Exercise

Aerobic exercise that makes you breathe harder can help loosen the mucus in your airways so you can cough it up. Exercise also helps improve your overall physical condition.

However, CF causes your sweat to become very salty. As a result, your body loses large amounts of salt when you sweat. Thus, your doctor may recommend a high-salt diet or salt supplements to maintain the balance of minerals in your blood.

If you exercise regularly, you may be able to cut back on your CPT. However, you should check with your doctor first.

Medicines

If you have CF, your doctor may prescribe antibiotics, anti-inflammatory medicines, bronchodilators, or medicines to help clear the mucus. These medicines help treat or prevent lung infections, reduce swelling and open up the airways, and thin mucus. If you have mutations in a gene called "*G551D*," which occurs in about five percent of people who have CF, your doctor may prescribe the oral medicine ivacaftor (approved for people with CF who are six years of age and older).

Antibiotics are the main treatment to prevent or treat lung infections. Your doctor may prescribe oral, inhaled, or intravenous (IV) antibiotics.

Oral antibiotics often are used to treat mild lung infections. Inhaled antibiotics may be used to prevent or control infections caused by the bacteria mucoid Pseudomonas. For severe or hard-to-treat infections, you may be given antibiotics through an IV tube (a tube inserted into a vein). This type of treatment may require you to stay in a hospital.

Anti-inflammatory medicines can help reduce swelling in your airways due to ongoing infections. These medicines may be inhaled or oral.

Bronchodilators help open the airways by relaxing the muscles around them. These medicines are inhaled. They're often taken just before CPT to help clear mucus out of your airways. You also may take bronchodilators before inhaling other medicines into your lungs.

Your doctor may prescribe medicines to reduce the stickiness of your mucus and loosen it up. These medicines can help clear out mucus, improve lung function, and prevent worsening lung symptoms.

Treatment for Advanced Lung Disease

If you have advanced lung disease, you may need oxygen therapy. Oxygen usually is given through nasal prongs or a mask.

If other treatments haven't worked, a lung transplant may be an option if you have severe lung disease. A lung transplant is a surgery to remove a person's diseased lung and replace it with a healthy lung from a deceased donor.

Pulmonary Rehabilitation

Your doctor may recommend pulmonary rehabilitation (PR) as part of your treatment plan. PR is a broad program that helps improve the well-being of people who have chronic (ongoing) breathing problems.

PR doesn't replace medical therapy. Instead, it's used with medical therapy and may include:

- Exercise training

- Nutritional counseling

- Education on your lung disease or condition and how to manage it

- Energy-conserving techniques

- Breathing strategies

- Psychological counseling and/or group support

PR has many benefits. It can improve your ability to function and your quality of life (QOL). The program also may help relieve your breathing problems. Even if you have advanced lung disease, you can still benefit from PR.

Treatment for Digestive Problems

CF can cause many digestive problems, such as bulky stools, intestinal gas, a swollen abdomen, severe constipation, and pain or discomfort. Digestive problems also can lead to poor growth and development in children.

Nutritional therapy can improve your strength and ability to stay active. It also can improve growth and development in children. Nutritional therapy also may make you strong enough to resist some lung infections. A nutritionist can help you create a nutritional plan that meets your needs.

In addition to having a well-balanced diet that's rich in calories, fat, and protein, your nutritional therapy may include:

- Oral pancreatic enzymes to help you digest fats and proteins and absorb more vitamins

- Supplements of vitamins A, D, E, and K to replace the fat-soluble vitamins that your intestines can't absorb

- High-calorie shakes to provide you with extra nutrients

- A high-salt diet or salt supplements that you take before exercising

- A feeding tube to give you more calories at night while you're sleeping. The tube may be threaded through your nose and throat and into your stomach. Or, the tube may be placed directly into your stomach through a surgically made hole. Before you go to bed each night, you'll attach a bag with a nutritional solution to the entrance of the tube. It will feed you while you sleep.

Other treatments for digestive problems may include enemas and mucus-thinning medicines to treat intestinal blockages. Sometimes surgery is needed to remove an intestinal blockage.

Your doctor also may prescribe medicines to reduce your stomach acid and help oral pancreatic enzymes work better.

Treatments for Cystic Fibrosis Complications

A common complication of CF is diabetes. The type of diabetes associated with CF often requires different treatment than other types of diabetes.

Another common CF complication is the bone-thinning disorder osteoporosis. Your doctor may prescribe medicines that prevent your bones from losing their density.

Living with Cystic Fibrosis

If you or your child has CF, you should learn as much as you can about the disease. Work closely with your doctors to learn how to manage CF.

Ongoing Care

Having ongoing medical care by a team of doctors, nurses, and respiratory therapists who specialize in CF is important. These specialists often are located at major medical centers or CF Care Centers.

The United States has more than 100 CF Care Centers. Most of these centers have pediatric and adult programs or clinics.

It's standard to have CF checkups every three months. Talk with your doctor about whether you should get an annual flu shot and other vaccines. Take all of your medicines as your doctor prescribes. In between checkups, be sure to contact your doctor if you have:

- Blood in your mucus, increased amounts of mucus, or a change in the color or consistency of your mucus

- Decreased energy or appetite

- Severe constipation or diarrhea, severe abdominal pain, or vomit that's dark green

- A fever, which is a sign of infection. (However, you may still have a serious infection that needs treatment even if you don't have a fever.)

Transition of Care

Better treatments for CF allow people who have the disease to live longer now than in the past. Thus, the move from pediatric care to adult care is an important step in treatment.

If your child has CF, encourage him or her to learn about the disease and take an active role in treatment. This will help prepare your child for the transition to adult care.

CF Care Centers can help provide age-appropriate treatment throughout the transition period and into adulthood. They also will support the transition to adult care by balancing medical needs with other developmental factors, such as increased independence, relationships, and employment.

Lifestyle Changes

In between medical checkups, you can practice good self-care and follow a healthy lifestyle.

For example, follow a healthy diet. A healthy diet includes a variety of fruits, vegetables, and whole grains. Talk to your doctor about what types and amounts of foods you should include in your diet.

Other lifestyle changes include:

- Not smoking and avoiding tobacco smoke

- Washing your hands often to lower your risk of infection

- Exercising regularly and drinking lots of fluids

- Doing chest physical therapy (as your doctor recommends)

Other Concerns

Although CF requires daily care, most people who have the disease are able to attend school and work.

Adults who have CF can expect to have normal sex lives. Most men who have the disease are infertile (unable to have children). However, modern fertility treatments may help them.

Women who have CF may find it hard to get pregnant, but they usually can have children. If you have CF, you should talk to your doctor if you're planning a pregnancy.

Although CF can cause fertility problems, men and women who have the disease should still have protected sex to avoid sexually transmitted diseases (STD).

Emotional Issues

Living with CF may cause fear, anxiety, depression, and stress. Talk about how you feel with your healthcare team. Talking to a professional counselor also can help. If you're very depressed, your doctor may recommend medicines or other treatments that can improve your quality of life.

Joining a patient support group may help you adjust to living with CF. You can see how other people who have the same symptoms have coped with them. Talk with your doctor about local support groups or check with an area medical center.

Support from family and friends also can help relieve stress and anxiety. Let your loved ones know how you feel and what they can do to help you.

Chapter 17

Endocrine Disorders

Chapter Contents

Section 17.1

Congenital Adrenal Hyperplasia (21-Hydroxylase Deficiency)

This section includes text excerpted from "Facts about CAH (Congenital Adrenal Hyperplasia)," Clinical Center, National Institutes of Health (NIH), March 2, 2016.

What Is Congenital Adrenal Hyperplasia?

Congenital adrenal hyperplasia (CAH) is a genetic disorder of the adrenal glands that affects the body's general health, growth, and development.

The Adrenal Glands

The adrenal glands are a pair of walnut-sized organs above the kidneys. They make hormones, which act like chemical messengers that affect other organs in the body. An organ at the base of the brain, called the "pituitary gland," helps regulate the adrenal glands. Each adrenal gland has two parts: the medulla (the inner part), and the cortex (the outer part). The medulla makes the hormone adrenaline. The cortex makes the hormones cortisol, aldosterone, and androgens. CAH affects how the adrenal cortex works. In severe cases, the adrenal medulla also may not function normally.

What Do Adrenal Hormones Do?

Hormones made by the adrenal glands are important for the body's normal functioning. Cortisol affects energy levels, sugar levels, blood pressure, and the body's response to illness or injury. Aldosterone helps maintain the proper salt level and blood pressure. Androgens are hormones needed for normal growth and development in both boys and girls. Adrenaline affects blood sugar levels, blood pressure, and the body's response to physical stress. The adrenal glands help keep the body in balance by making the right amounts of these hormones. In patients with CAH, there is an abnormal production of adrenal hormones.

Symptoms of Congenital Adrenal Hyperplasia

Too little cortisol may cause tiredness, nausea, and weight loss. During illness or injury, low cortisol levels can lead to low blood pressure and even death. Also, treating a cortisol imbalance with too much cortisol can cause abnormal development in children, obesity, short stature, and decreased bone density (osteoporosis). Lack of aldosterone, which occurs in three out of four patients with classic (severe) CAH, upsets salt levels. This imbalance may cause dehydration, and possibly death. Chronic salt imbalance may cause abnormal growth.

Too much androgen causes abnormal physical development in children. Boys and girls with CAH may either grow too fast, develop pubic hair and acne early, and/or stop growing too soon, causing short stature. Girls exposed to high levels of androgens before birth may have abnormal external genitalia at birth, and genital surgery is usually performed in infancy. Although their internal female organs are normal, excess androgens may affect puberty and cause irregular menstrual periods.

Classic Congenital Adrenal Hyperplasia

The severe form of CAH is called "classic CAH," and it occurs in 1 in 16,000 births. The most common is 21-hydroxylase deficiency, which makes up about 95 percent of cases. A child with this type of CAH has adrenal glands that cannot make enough cortisol and may or may not make aldosterone. As a result, the glands overwork trying to make these hormones and end up making too many androgens.

The second most common form of classic CAH is 11-hydroxylase deficiency. A child with this type of classic CAH has adrenal glands that make too much androgen and not enough cortisol. Children with this type of CAH may have high blood pressure. These patients do not have aldosterone deficiency.

Other rare types of classic CAH include 3-beta-hydroxysteroid dehydrogenase deficiency, lipoid CAH, and 17-hydroxylase deficiency.

Nonclassic (Late-Onset) Congenital Adrenal Hyperplasia

The mild form of CAH is called "non-classic CAH." This type of CAH is almost always due to 21-hydroxylase deficiency. Only a handful of people have been described as having non-classic CAH due to other causes. People with non-classic 21-hydroxylase deficiency usually make enough cortisol and aldosterone, but make excess androgens. Symptoms may come and go, beginning at any time, but typically develop in late childhood or early adulthood. Boys often do not need treatment, but girls often need treatment to suppress their excess androgens.

Non-classic CAH is common. 1 in every 1,000 people has non-classic 21-hydroxylase deficiency. Incidence is higher in certain ethnic groups including Ashkenazi Jews, Hispanics, Yugoslavs, and Italians.

How Is Congenital Adrenal Hyperplasia Inherited?

An inherited disorder is one that can be passed from the parents to their children. CAH is a type of inherited disorder called "autosomal recessive." For a child to have CAH, each parent must either have CAH or carry an abnormal gene. This means that if 2 parents are CAH carriers (have the gene for CAH but not the disorder), then their children have a 25 percent chance (1 in 4) of being born with CAH. Each sibling without CAH has 2 chances in 3 of being a carrier. Tests can be done to find out if someone is a carrier.

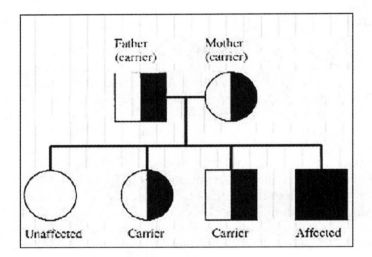

Figure 17.1. *Genetic Pedigree*

How Is Congenital Adrenal Hyperplasia Treated?

People with CAH have a normal life expectancy, but CAH cannot be outgrown. Classic CAH requires treatment for life. Some patients with non-classic CAH may not require treatment as adults. Treatment is tailored for each patient and adjusted during childhood for growth. The standard treatment for children with classic CAH 21-hydroxylase deficiency is hydrocortisone, which replaces cortisol and fludrocortisone which replaces aldosterone. For classic CAH 11-hydroxylase deficiency, the treatment is only hydrocortisone. Patients can be started on longer-acting forms of hydrocortisone-like medication (i.e., prednisone or dexamethasone) when they are done growing.

Patients with the non-classic form of CAH need only hydrocortisone (or a longer-acting form of hydrocortisone-like medication). Some patients with non-classic CAH are able to come off of medication as adults, but patients with classic CAH need lifelong treatment.

Experimental prenatal treatment is available for fetuses at risk for classic CAH. For this treatment, mothers take dexamethasone, a potent form of hydrocortisone-like medication. This medication suppresses androgens in the fetus and allows female genitalia to develop more normally. This treatment lessens or eliminates the need for surgery in girls. It does not, however, treat other aspects of the disorder. Children with CAH still need to take hydrocortisone and fludrocortisone for life.

What If a Child or an Adult with Congenital Adrenal Hyperplasia Has an Illness, Surgery, or a Major Injury?

During these times, a patient with CAH needs closer medical attention and should be under a doctor's care. More cortisol is needed to meet the body's increased needs for this hormone. Higher doses of hydrocortisone are given by mouth or sometimes by intramuscular injection (into the muscle). Intravenous (IV) medication is needed before surgery.

Medical Alert Identification

In an emergency, it is important to alert medical personnel about the diagnosis of adrenal insufficiency, so wearing a medical alert identification bracelet or necklace is recommended. The information on the medic alert should include, "Adrenal Insufficiency Requires Hydrocortisone." It is important for the adult patient or parent of a child patient to learn how to administer an intramuscular injection of hydrocortisone in the case of an emergency.

Can a Woman with Congenital Adrenal Hyperplasia Become Pregnant and Have a Baby?

Increased androgens may cause irregular menstrual periods and make it harder for a woman with CAH to conceive a child. But if she takes her medications as directed, then she can become pregnant and have a baby.

Do Men with Congenital Adrenal Hyperplasia Have Fertility Problems?

Men who take medications as directed usually have normal fertility. Rarely, however, they may develop "adrenal rest tissue" in their testes. This is when adrenal tissue grows in other parts of the body, such as the testes. The tissue does not turn into cancer, but it can grow enough to cause discomfort or infertility. Large growths are rare, and surgery is usually not needed.

Can Congenital Adrenal Hyperplasia Be Diagnosed Prenatally?

CAH can be diagnosed before birth. Amniocentesis or chorionic villus sampling during pregnancy can check for the disorder. Testing for classic CAH is part of the routine newborn screening done in all states in the United States.

Section 17.2

Congenital Hypothyroidism

This section includes text excerpted from "Congenital Hypothyroidism," Genetics Home Reference (GHR), National Institutes of Health (NIH), January 29, 2019.

Congenital hypothyroidism is a partial or complete loss of function of the thyroid gland (hypothyroidism) that affects infants from birth (congenital). The thyroid gland is a butterfly-shaped tissue in the lower neck. It makes iodine-containing hormones that play an important role in regulating growth, brain development, and the rate of chemical reactions in the body (metabolism). People with congenital hypothyroidism have lower-than-normal levels of these important hormones.

Congenital hypothyroidism occurs when the thyroid gland fails to develop or function properly. In 80 to 85 percent of cases, the thyroid gland is absent, severely reduced in size (hypoplastic), or abnormally located. These cases are classified as thyroid dysgenesis. In the remainder of cases, a normal-sized or enlarged thyroid gland (goiter) is present, but production of thyroid hormones is decreased or absent. Most of these cases occur when one of several steps in the hormone synthesis process is impaired; these cases are classified as thyroid dyshormonogenesis. Less commonly, reduction or absence of thyroid hormone production is caused by impaired stimulation of the production process (which is normally done by a structure at the base of the brain called "the pituitary gland"), even though the process itself is unimpaired. These cases are classified as central (or pituitary) hypothyroidism.

Signs and symptoms of congenital hypothyroidism result from the shortage of thyroid hormones. Affected babies may show no features of the condition, although some babies with congenital hypothyroidism are less active and sleep more than normal. They may have difficulty feeding and experience constipation. If untreated, congenital hypothyroidism can lead to intellectual disability and slow growth. In the United States and many other countries, all hospitals test newborns for congenital hypothyroidism. If treatment begins in the first two weeks after birth, infants usually develop normally.

Congenital hypothyroidism can also occur as part of syndromes that affect other organs and tissues in the body. These forms of the condition are described as syndromic. Some common forms of syndromic hypothyroidism include Pendred syndrome, Bamforth-Lazarus syndrome, and brain-lung-thyroid syndrome.

Frequency and Causes

Congenital hypothyroidism affects an estimated 1 in 2,000 to 4,000 newborns. For reasons that remain unclear, congenital hypothyroidism affects more than twice as many females as males.

Congenital hypothyroidism can be caused by a variety of factors, only some of which are genetic. The most common cause worldwide is a shortage of iodine in the diet of the mother and the affected infant. Iodine is essential for the production of thyroid hormones. Genetic causes account for about 15 to 20 percent of cases of congenital hypothyroidism.

The cause of the most common type of congenital hypothyroidism, thyroid dysgenesis, is usually unknown. Studies suggest that two to five percent of cases are inherited. Two of the genes involved in this form of the condition are *PAX8* and *TSHR*. These genes play roles in the proper growth and development of the thyroid gland. Mutations in these genes prevent or disrupt the normal development of the gland.

The abnormal or missing gland cannot produce normal amounts of thyroid hormones.

Thyroid dyshormonogenesis results from mutations in one of several genes involved in the production of thyroid hormones. These genes include *DUOX2, SLC5A5, TG,* and *TPO*. Mutations in each of these genes disrupt a step in thyroid hormone synthesis, leading to abnormally low levels of these hormones. Mutations in the *TSHB* gene disrupt the synthesis of thyroid hormones by impairing the stimulation of hormone production. Changes in this gene are the primary cause of central hypothyroidism. The resulting shortage of thyroid hormones disrupts normal growth, brain development, and metabolism, leading to the features of congenital hypothyroidism.

Mutations in other genes that have not been as well characterized can also cause congenital hypothyroidism. Still, other genes are involved in syndromic forms of the disorder.

Section 17.3

Kallmann Syndrome

This section includes text excerpted from "Kallmann syndrome," Genetic and Rare Diseases Information Center (GARD), National Center for Advancing Translational Sciences (NCATS), June 22, 2016.

Kallmann syndrome (KS) is a condition that causes hypogonadotropic hypogonadism (HH) and an impaired sense of smell. HH affects the production of the hormones needed for sexual development. It is present from birth and is due to deficiency of gonadotropin-releasing hormone (GnRH). KS is often diagnosed at puberty, due to lack of sexual development. It may first be suspected in infancy in males with undescended testicles or a small penis. Symptoms in untreated, adult males may include decreased bone density and muscle mass; small testicles; erectile dysfunction; low sex drive; and infertility. Untreated adult females with KS usually do not have menstrual periods (amenorrhea) and normal, little, or no breast development. Rarely, a person with KS will have failure of kidney development (renal agenesis);

hearing impairment; cleft lip or palate; and/or dental abnormalities. Most cases of KS are sporadic (not inherited) but some cases are inherited. The mode of inheritance depends on the gene involved. Treatment includes hormone replacement therapy for sexual development. Fertility can be achieved in most cases.

When the features of Kallmann syndrome are not accompanied by an impaired sense of smell, the condition is referred to as idiopathic or isolated hypogonadotropic hypogonadism, or normosmic isolated GnRH deficiency (IGD).

Symptoms of Kallmann Syndrome

Kallmann syndrome (KS) is not a life-threatening condition. The main features are delayed or absent signs of puberty, and an absent or diminished sense of smell (anosmia or hyposmia, respectively).

Males with KS may have signs of the condition at birth, such as undescended testes or a smaller than average penis. However, most cases are diagnosed at the time of puberty due to lack of sexual development. Males usually have no growth of facial or body hair and a decreased growth of pubic hair and genitals. They also have a delayed pubertal growth spurt in comparison to their peers. If not treated, adult males may have decreased bone density and muscle mass; decreased testicular volume; erectile dysfunction; low sex drive; and infertility.

Females with KS usually have absent breast development, an attenuated growth spurt, decreased pubic hair growth, and no initiation of menses (primary amenorrhea). However, some females partially undergo puberty with the beginning of breast development that fails to progress. Very occasionally, affected females have an onset of menses at an appropriate age, but it stops after a few cycles.

In both males and females, development of pubic hair can be normal because it is controlled by secretion of androgens from the adrenal glands, which are not affected by the condition. Almost all untreated people with KS are infertile, but fertility can be restored in those that respond to certain treatments.

Some people with KS have any of various non-reproductive features. These may include:

- Cleft lip and palate

- Renal agenesis (one kidney does not develop)

- Hearing impairment

- Dental abnormalities

- Eye movement abnormalities

- Poor balance

- Scoliosis (curvature of the spine)

- Synkinesis of the hands, in which the movements of one hand are mirrored by the other hand

Inheritance of Kallmann Syndrome

KS may be inherited in an X-linked recessive, autosomal dominant, or autosomal recessive manner depending on the responsible gene. For example:

KS due to mutations in the *KAL1* gene (also called "the *ANOS1*" gene), causing KS 1, is inherited in an X-linked recessive manner.

KS due to mutations in the *FGFR1, PROKR2, PROK2, CHD7* or *FGF8* genes (causing KS types 2, 3, 4, 5, and 6, respectively) is usually inherited in an autosomal dominant manner.

KS due to mutations in *PROKR2* and *PROK2* can also be inherited in an autosomal recessive manner.

The majority of people with KS have a negative family history (the condition occurs sporadically). However, affected people are still at risk to pass the responsible mutation(s) on to their children, or to have an affected child. The risk for each child to be affected depends on the genetic cause in each case and may be up to 50 percent.

People with personal questions about the genetic cause and inheritance of KS are encouraged to speak with a genetic counselor or other genetics professionals. The genetic cause in many cases remains unknown, and a thorough family history should be obtained to understand the mode of inheritance in each family and to aid in genetic testing and counseling. Information about whether specific features are present in all family members can help determine the mode of inheritance.

Diagnosis of Kallmann Syndrome

The diagnosis of KS may be suspected with evidence of lack of sexual maturation or hypogonadism, and evidence of incomplete sexual maturity by Tanner staging. Tanner staging is an established method used by endocrinologists worldwide to evaluate the maturation of primary and secondary sexual characteristics.

The diagnosis of KS additionally relies on hormone evaluation, as well as evaluation of the sense of smell (olfactory function testing).

Analysis of the olfactory bulbs by magnetic resonance imaging (MRI) can be useful, especially in young children. Genetic testing can also be used to diagnose the condition by identifying a disease-causing mutation in one of the genes responsible for KS.

Chapter 18

Growth Disorders

Chapter Contents

Section 18.1

What Is Growth Disorder?

This section includes text excerpted from "Growth Disorders," MedlinePlus, National Institutes of Health (NIH), November 13, 2018.

Does your child seem much shorter—or much taller—than other kids her or his age? It could be normal. Some children may be small for their age but still be developing normally. Some children are short or tall because their parents are.

But some children have growth disorders. Growth disorders are problems that prevent children from developing a normal height, weight, sexual maturity, or other features.

What Causes Growth Disorder

Very slow or very fast growth can sometimes signal a gland problem or disease.

The pituitary gland makes growth hormone, which stimulates the growth of bone and other tissues. Children who have too little of it may be very short.

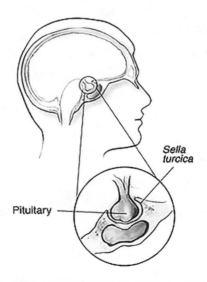

Sella
turcica

Pituitary

Figure 18.1. *Pituitary Gland* (Source: "Prolactinoma," National Institute of Diabetes and Digestive and Kidney Diseases (NIDDK).)

People can also have too much growth hormone. Usually, the cause is a pituitary gland tumor, which is not cancer. Too much growth hormone can cause gigantism in children, where their bones and their body grow too much. In adults, it can cause acromegaly, which makes the hands, feet, and face larger than normal.

Can Growth Disorder Be Treated?

Possible treatments include surgery to remove the tumor, medicines, and radiation therapy. Treatment with growth hormone can stimulate growth.

Section 18.2

Achondroplasia

This section contains text excerpted from the following sources: Text beginning with the heading "What Is Achondroplasia?" is excerpted from "Learning about Achondroplasia," National Human Genome Research Institute (NHGRI), July 15, 2016; Text under the heading "Treatment for Achondroplasia" is excerpted from "Achondroplasia," Genetic and Rare Diseases Information Center (GARD), National Center for Advancing Translational Sciences (NCATS), December 20, 2017.

What Is Achondroplasia?

Achondroplasia is a disorder of bone growth. It is the most common form of disproportionate short stature. It occurs in 1 in every 15,000 to 1 in 40,000 live births. Achondroplasia is caused by a gene alteration (mutation) in the *FGFR3* gene. The *FGFR3* gene makes a protein called "fibroblast growth factor receptor 3" that is involved in converting cartilage to bone. *FGFR3* is the only gene known to be associated with achondroplasia. All people who have only a single copy of the normal *FGFR3* gene and a single copy of the *FGFR3* gene mutation have achondroplasia.

Most people who have achondroplasia have average-size parents. In this situation, the *FGFR3* gene mutation occurs in one parent's egg or sperm cell before conception. Other people with achondroplasia inherit the condition from a parent who has achondroplasia.

What Are the Symptoms of Achondroplasia?

People who have achondroplasia have abnormal bone growth that causes the following clinical symptoms: short stature with disproportionately short arms and legs, short fingers, a large head (macrocephaly), and specific facial features with a prominent forehead (frontal bossing) and midface hypoplasia.

The intelligence and life span in individuals with achondroplasia is usually normal.

Infants born with achondroplasia typically have weak muscle tone (hypotonia). Because of the hypotonia, there may be delays in walking and other motor skills. Compression of the spinal cord and/or upper airway obstruction increases the risk of death in infancy.

People with achondroplasia commonly have breathing problems in which breathing stops or slows down for short periods (apnea). Other health issues include obesity and recurrent ear infections. Adults with achondroplasia may develop a pronounced and permanent sway of the lower back (lordosis) and bowed legs. The problems with the lower back can cause back pain, leading to difficulty with walking.

How Is Achondroplasia Diagnosed?

Achondroplasia is diagnosed by characteristic clinical and X-ray findings in most affected individuals. In individuals who may be too young to diagnose with certainty or in individuals who do not have the typical symptoms, genetic testing can be used to identify a mutation in the *FGFR3* gene.

Genetic testing can identify mutations in 99 percent of individuals who have achondroplasia. Testing for the *FGFR3* gene mutation is available in clinical laboratories.

Treatment for Achondroplasia

Recommendations for management of children with achondroplasia were outlined by the American Academy of Pediatrics (AAP) Committee on Genetics in the article, Health Supervision for Children with Achondroplasia. You can review this article with your child's healthcare provider(s). These recommendations include:

- Monitoring of height, weight, and head circumference using growth curves standardized for achondroplasia

- Measures to avoid obesity starting in early childhood
- Careful neurologic examinations, with referral to a pediatric neurologist as necessary
- Magnetic resonance imaging (MRI) or computed tomography (CT) of the foramen magnum region for evaluation of severe hypotonia or signs of spinal cord compression
- Obtaining history for possible sleep apnea, with sleep studies as necessary
- Evaluation for low thoracic or high lumbar gibbus if truncal weakness is present
- Referral to a pediatric orthopedist if bowing of the legs interferes with walking
- Management of frequent middle-ear infections
- Speech evaluation, once the individual has reached two years of age
- Careful monitoring of social adjustment

Section 18.3

Dwarfism

This section contains text excerpted from the following sources: Text in this section begins with excerpts from "Dwarfism" MedlinePlus, National Institutes of Health (NIH), April 4, 2016; Text under the heading "How Is Dwarfism Diagnosed?" is excerpted from "Dwarfism," Genetic and Rare Diseases Information Center (GARD), National Center for Advancing Translational Sciences (NCATS), May 19, 2011. Reviewed March 2019.

People with dwarfism have short stature. This means that their height is under 4' 10" as an adult. They are usually of normal intelligence. Dwarfism most often occurs in families where both parents are of average height.

More than 300 different conditions can cause dwarfism. Achondroplasia is the most common type of dwarfism. Achondroplasia is a genetic condition that affects about 1 in 15,000 to 1 in 40,000 people. It makes your arms and legs short in comparison to your head and trunk. You may also have a larger head and weak muscle tone. Other genetic conditions, kidney disease, and problems with metabolism or hormones can also cause dwarfism.

The conditions that cause dwarfism can also cause other health problems. Most of them are treatable. It is important to have regular checkups throughout your life. With proper medical care, most people with dwarfism have active lives and live as long as other people.

How Is Dwarfism Diagnosed?

Some types of dwarfism can be identified through prenatal testing if a doctor suspects a particular condition and tests for it. However, most cases are not identified until after the child is born. In those instances, the doctor makes a diagnosis based on the child's appearance, failure to grow, and X-rays of the bones. Depending on the type of dwarfism the child has, diagnosis often can be made almost immediately after birth. Once a diagnosis is made, there is no "treatment" for most of the conditions that lead to short stature. Hormonal or metabolic problems may be treated with hormone injections or special diets to spark a child's growth, but skeletal dysplasias cannot be "cured." Individuals who are interested in learning whether they or family members have, or are at risk for, dwarfism should speak with their healthcare provider or a genetics professional.

Section 18.4

Multiple Epiphyseal Dysplasia

This section includes text excerpted from "Multiple Epiphyseal Dysplasia," Genetics Home Reference (GHR), National Institutes of Health (NIH), January 29, 2019.

Multiple epiphyseal dysplasia (MED) is a disorder of cartilage and bone development, primarily affecting the ends of the long bones in the arms and legs (epiphyses). There are two types of MED, which can be distinguished by their pattern of inheritance. Both the dominant and recessive types have relatively mild signs and symptoms, including joint pain that most commonly affects the hips and knees, early-onset arthritis, and a waddling walk. Although some people with MED have mild short stature as adults, most are of normal height. The majority of individuals are diagnosed during childhood; however, some mild cases may not be diagnosed until adulthood.

Recessive MED is distinguished from the dominant type by malformations of the hands, feet, and knees and abnormal curvature of the spine (scoliosis). About 50 percent of individuals with recessive MED are born with at least 1 abnormal feature, including an inward- and upward-turning foot (clubfoot), an opening in the roof of the mouth (cleft palate), an unusual curving of the fingers or toes (clinodactyly), or ear swelling. An abnormality of the kneecap called a "double-layered patella" is also relatively common.

Frequency and Causes

The incidence of dominant MED is estimated to be at least 1 in 10,000 newborns. The incidence of recessive MED is unknown. Both forms of this disorder may actually be more common because some people with mild symptoms are never diagnosed.

Mutations in the *COMP, COL9A1, COL9A2, COL9A3*, or *MATN3* gene can cause dominant MED. These genes provide instructions for making proteins that are found in the spaces between cartilage-forming cells (chondrocytes). These proteins interact with each other and play an important role in cartilage and bone formation. Cartilage is a tough, flexible tissue that makes up much of the skeleton during early development. Most cartilage is later converted to bone, except for the cartilage that continues to cover and protect the ends of bones and is present in the nose and external ears.

The majority of individuals with dominant MED have mutations in the *COMP* gene. About 10 percent of affected individuals have mutations in the *MATN3* gene. Mutations in the *COMP* or *MATN3* gene prevent the release of the proteins produced from these genes into the spaces between the chondrocytes. The absence of these proteins leads to the formation of abnormal cartilage, which can cause the skeletal problems characteristic of dominant MED.

The *COL9A1, COL9A2*, and *COL9A3* genes provide instructions for making a protein called "type IX collagen." Collagens are a family of proteins that strengthen and support connective tissues, such as skin, bone, cartilage, tendons, and ligaments. Mutations in the

COL9A1, COL9A2, or *COL9A3* gene are found in less than five percent of individuals with dominant MED. It is not known how mutations in these genes cause the signs and symptoms of this disorder. Research suggests that mutations in these genes may cause type IX collagen to accumulate inside the cell or interact abnormally with other cartilage components.

Some people with dominant MED do not have a mutation in the *COMP, COL9A1, COL9A2, COL9A3,* or *MATN3* gene. In these cases, the cause of the condition is unknown.

Mutations in the *SLC26A2* gene cause recessive MED. This gene provides instructions for making a protein that is essential for the normal development of cartilage and for its conversion to bone. Mutations in the *SLC26A2* gene alter the structure of developing cartilage, preventing bones from forming properly and result in the skeletal problems characteristic of recessive MED.

Section 18.5

Russell-Silver Syndrome

This section includes text excerpted from "Russell-Silver Syndrome," Genetic and Rare Diseases Information Center (GARD), National Center for Advancing Translational Sciences (NCATS), June 29, 2017.

Russell-Silver syndrome (RSS) is a rare condition associated with poor growth both before and after birth. Signs and symptoms vary and may include low birth weight, short stature, characteristic facial features, large head in relation to body size, body asymmetry, and feeding difficulties. Other features may include poor appetite, clinodactyly (curved finger), digestive system abnormalities, delayed development, and/or learning disabilities.

The genetic causes of RSS are complex and relate to certain genes that control growth. Sometimes, the genetic cause cannot be identified. Most cases are not inherited from a parent and occur sporadically. In rare cases, RSS may be inherited in an autosomal dominant or autosomal recessive manner. Because RSS can lead to a wide variety of physical abnormalities and health problems, treatment ideally should be managed by a team of specialists with knowledge of RSS. Early intervention is recommended to help children with RSS reach their full potential.

Symptoms of Russell-Silver Syndrome

Features of RSS can vary. Some people with RSS have many features, while others have very few features. Signs and symptoms may include:

- Intrauterine growth restriction (IUGR) (poor growth before birth)
- Low birth weight
- Head that appears large in relation to body size (relative macrocephaly)
- Poor appetite and feeding difficulties
- Hypoglycemia
- Poor growth after birth, leading to short stature
- Scoliosis
- Curving of the pinky finger (clinodactyly)
- Characteristic facial features (prominent forehead; small, triangular-shaped face; a small jaw; a narrow chin; and downturned corners of the mouth)
- Arms and legs of different lengths (body asymmetry)
- Delayed bone age
- Gastroesophageal reflux disease (GERD) or other digestive problems
- Kidney problems
- Developmental delay and/or learning disabilities
- Psychosocial challenges

Causes of Russell-Silver Syndrome

RSS is a genetic disorder that usually results from the abnormal regulation of certain genes that control growth. 2 genetic causes have been found to result in about 60 percent of the cases:

- Abnormalities at an imprinted region on chromosome 11p15—for some genes, only the copy inherited from a person's father (paternal copy) or mother (maternal copy) is "turned on," or expressed. These parent-specific differences in gene expression are caused by a phenomenon called "genomic imprinting." Abnormalities involving genes that undergo imprinting are responsible for many cases of RSS.

- Maternal disomy of chromosome 7 (written as matUPD7)—this occurs when a child inherits both copies of chromosome 7 from the mother, instead of one copy from the mother and one copy from the father.

Other chromosome abnormalities have also been described as causing RSS, or RSS-like syndromes.

In many people with RSS, the cause of the condition is unknown. Researchers are working to identify additional genetic changes that cause RSS.

Inheritance of Russell-Silver Syndrome

Most cases of RSS are sporadic (not inherited), occurring in people with no family history of RSS.

Rarely, RSS may be inherited. In some families, it appears to be inherited in an autosomal dominant manner. This means that having a genetic change in only one copy of the responsible gene in each cell is enough to cause the disorder. In other families, RSS is inherited in an autosomal recessive manner. This means that to have RSS, a person must have a change in both copies of the responsible gene in each cell. Affected people inherit one copy from each parent, who is referred to as a carrier. Carriers of autosomal recessive conditions typically do not have any signs or symptoms (they are unaffected).

Diagnosis of Russell-Silver Syndrome

RSS is currently a clinical diagnosis, based on a combination of characteristic features. Because the condition varies widely in severity and many of its features are nonspecific, making a diagnosis can be difficult.

Molecular genetic testing can confirm the diagnosis in around 60 percent of patients and may be useful in guiding management. However, genetic testing results are negative ("normal") in a notable

proportion of patients with the characteristic features of RSS. Therefore, a negative genetic test result does not exclude the diagnosis
of RSS.

Prognosis for Russell-Silver Syndrome

The long-term outlook associated with RSS is generally good, but
may depend on how severely affected a person is and whether complications arise. People with RSS may face challenges from birth to
adulthood. While some people with RSS believe that they are not at
risk for associated health issues once they reach their adult height,
recent research has shown there may be increased risks for certain
health issues in adulthood. These possible risks include:

- Metabolic syndrome

- Uterine and vaginal dysgenesis (in females with 11p15-related
  RSS)

- Gonadal hypofunction or testicular cancer in males

- Low muscle mass or low bone-mineral density

- Myoclonus-dystonia (M-D) (in people with chromosome 7-related
  RSS)

Section 18.6

Thanatophoric Dysplasia

This section contains text excerpted from the following sources: Text beginning with the heading "What Is Thanatophoric Dysplasia?" is excerpted from "Thanatophoric Dysplasia," Genetics Home Reference (GHR), National Institutes of Health (NIH), January 29, 2019; Text beginning with the heading "What Causes Thanatophoric Dysplasia?" is excerpted from "Thanatophoric Dysplasia," Genetic and Rare Diseases Information Center (GARD), National Center for Advancing Translational Sciences (NCATS), May 6, 2014. Reviewed March 2019.

What Is Thanatophoric Dysplasia?

Thanatophoric dysplasia (TD) is a severe skeletal disorder characterized by extremely short limbs and folds of extra (redundant) skin on the arms and legs. Other features of this condition include a narrow chest, short ribs, underdeveloped lungs, and an enlarged head with a large forehead and prominent, wide-spaced eyes.

Researchers have described two major forms of TD, type I and type II. Type I TD is distinguished by the presence of curved thigh bones and flattened bones of the spine (platyspondyly). Type II TD is characterized by straight thigh bones and a moderate to severe skull abnormality called a "cloverleaf skull."

The term thanatophoric is a Greek word which means "death bearing." Infants with TD are usually stillborn or die shortly after birth from respiratory failure; however, a few affected individuals have survived into childhood with extensive medical help.

Frequency and Causes of Thanatophoric Dysplasia

This condition occurs in 1 in 20,000 to 50,000 newborns. Type I TD is more common than type II.

TD is caused by mutations in the *FGFR3* gene. This gene provides instructions for making a protein that is involved in the development and maintenance of bone and brain tissue. Mutations in this gene cause the FGFR3 protein to be overly active, which leads to the severe problems with bone growth that are seen in TD. It is not known how FGFR3 mutations cause the brain and skin abnormalities associated with this disorder.

Is Thanatophoric Dysplasia Inherited?

TD is considered an autosomal dominant disorder because one mutated copy of the *FGFR3* gene in each cell causes the condition. However, almost all cases of TD are caused by new mutations in the *FGFR3* gene and occur in people with no history of the disorder in their family. No affected individuals are known to have had children, so the disorder has not been passed to the next generation.

What Are the Chances That You Will Have Another Child Affected by Thanatophoric Dysplasia?

Most parents who have had a child with TD are not at increased risk of having another child with the condition. The mutation that causes TD is almost always a new mutation that was not inherited from either parent. There is a very rare possibility that a healthy parent could have a mutation only in their reproductive cells (called "germline mosaicism"), but there have been no reports of this situation. Prenatal testing to diagnose TD is available through ultrasound examination and molecular genetic testing.

Chapter 19

Heart Rhythm Disorders

Chapter Contents

Section 19.1

Arrhythmia

This section contains text excerpted from the following
sources: Text under the heading "What Is Arrhythmia?" is
excerpted from "Arrhythmia," MedlinePlus, National Institutes of
Health (NIH), August 15, 2016; Text beginning with the
heading "Types" is excerpted from "Arrhythmia," National Heart,
Lung, and Blood Institute (NHLBI), March 29, 2012.
Reviewed March 2019.

What Is Arrhythmia?

An arrhythmia is a problem with the rate or rhythm of your heartbeat. It means that your heart beats too quickly, too slowly, or with an irregular pattern. When the heart beats faster than normal, it is called "tachycardia." When the heart beats too slowly, it is called "bradycardia." The most common type of arrhythmia is atrial fibrillation (AF), which causes an irregular and fast heartbeat.

Many factors can affect your heart's rhythm, such as having had a heart attack, smoking, congenital heart defects, and stress. Some substances or medicines may also cause arrhythmias.

Symptoms of arrhythmias include:

- Fast or slow heartbeat

- Skipping beats

- Lightheadedness or dizziness

- Chest pain

- Shortness of breath

- Sweating

Your doctor can run tests to find out if you have an arrhythmia. Treatment to restore a normal heart rhythm may include medicines, an implantable cardioverter-defibrillator (ICD) or pacemaker, or sometimes surgery.

Types of Arrhythmia

Arrhythmias differ from normal heartbeats in speed or rhythm. Arrhythmias are also grouped by where they occur—in the upper chambers of the heart, in its lower chambers, or between the chambers.

The main types of arrhythmia are bradyarrhythmias; premature, or extra, beats; supraventricular arrhythmias (SVT); and ventricular arrhythmias.

Bradyarrhythmia

Bradyarrhythmia is a slow arrhythmia in a heart that beats too slowly—a condition called "bradycardia." For adults, this means slower than 60 beats per minute. Some people, especially people who are young or physically fit, may normally have slow heart rates. For them, bradycardia is not dangerous and does not cause symptoms.

Premature or Extra Heartbeat

A premature heartbeat happens when the signal to beat comes early. It can feel like your heart skipped a beat. The premature, or extra, heartbeat creates a short pause, which is followed by a stronger beat when your heart returns to its regular rhythm. These extra heartbeats are the most common type of arrhythmia. They are called "ectopic heartbeats" and can trigger other arrhythmias.

Supraventricular Arrhythmia

Arrhythmias that start in the heart's upper chambers, called the "atrium," or at the gateway to the lower chambers are called "supraventricular arrhythmias." Supraventricular arrhythmias are known by their fast heart rates or tachycardia. Tachycardia occurs when the heart, at rest, goes above 100 beats per minute. The fast pace is sometimes paired with uneven heart rhythm. Sometimes the upper and lower chambers beat at different rates.

Types of supraventricular arrhythmias include:

- **Atrial fibrillation (AF).** This is one of the most common types of arrhythmia. The heart can race at more than 400 beats per minute.

- **Atrial flutter (AFL).** Atrial flutter can cause the upper chambers to beat 250 to 350 times per minute. The signal that tells the upper chambers to beat may be disrupted when it encounters damaged tissue, such as a scar. The signal may find an alternate path, creating a loop that causes the upper chamber to beat repeatedly. As with atrial fibrillation, some but not all of these signals travel to the lower chambers. As a result, the upper chambers and lower chambers beat at different rates.

- **Paroxysmal supraventricular tachycardia (PSVT).** In PSVT, electrical signals that begin in the upper chambers and travel to the lower chambers cause extra heartbeats. This arrhythmia begins and ends suddenly. It can happen during vigorous physical activity. It is usually not dangerous and tends to occur in young people.

Ventricular Arrhythmia

These arrhythmias start in the heart's lower chambers. They can be very dangerous and usually require medical care right away.

- Ventricular tachycardia (VT) is a fast, regular beating of the ventricles that may last for only a few seconds or for much longer. A few beats of VT often do not cause problems. However, episodes that last for more than a few seconds can be dangerous. VT can turn into other more serious arrhythmias, such as ventricular fibrillation (VF), or v-fib.

- VF occurs if disorganized electrical signals make the ventricles quiver instead of pumping normally. Without the ventricles pumping blood to the body, sudden cardiac arrest and death can occur within a few minutes. Torsades de pointes is a type of arrhythmia that causes a unique pattern on an electrocardiogram (ECG or EKG) and often leads to v-fib.

Causes of Arrhythmia

Arrhythmia is caused by changes to heart tissue. It can also occur suddenly as a result of exertion or stress, imbalances in the blood, medicines, or problems with electrical signals in the heart. Typically, an arrhythmia is set off by a trigger, and the irregular heartbeat can continue if there is a problem in the heart. Sometimes the cause of an arrhythmia is unknown.

Changes to the Heart

The following conditions may cause arrhythmia:

- Changes to the heart's anatomy
- Reduced blood flow to the heart or damage to the heart's electrical system

- Restoring blood flow as part of treating a heart attack
- Stiffening of the heart tissue, known as fibrosis, or scarring

Exertion or Strain

Strong emotional stress, anxiety, anger, pain, or a sudden surprise can make the heart work harder, raise blood pressure (BP), and release stress hormones. Sometimes these reactions can lead to arrhythmias. If you have heart disease, physical activity can trigger arrhythmia due to an excess of hormones, such as adrenaline. Sometimes vomiting or coughing can trigger arrhythmia.

Imbalances in the Blood

An excess or deficiency of electrolytes, hormones, or fluids can alter your heartbeat.

- An excess of thyroid hormone (TH) can cause the heart to beat faster, and thyroid deficiency can slow your heart rate.
- Dehydration can cause the heart to race.
- Low blood sugar, from an eating disorder or higher insulin levels in someone who has diabetes, can lead to slow or extra heartbeats.
- Low levels of potassium, magnesium, or calcium can trigger arrhythmia. These electrolyte disturbances can occur after a heart attack or surgery.

Medicines

Certain medicines can cause arrhythmia. These include medicines to treat high blood pressure (HBP) and other conditions, including arrhythmia, depression, and psychosis. Some people also need to be careful about taking certain antibiotics and over-the-counter (OTC) medicines, such as allergy and cold medicines.

Problems with the Electrical Signals in the Heart

An arrhythmia can occur if the electrical signals that control the heartbeat are delayed or blocked. This can happen when the nerve cells that produce electrical signals do not work properly or when the electrical signals do not travel normally through the heart. Another part of the heart could start to produce electrical signals, disrupting a normal heartbeat.

Disorders of electrical signaling in the heart are called "conduction disorders."

Risk Factors of Arrhythmia

You may have an increased risk of arrhythmia because of your age, environment, family history and genetics, habits in your daily life, certain medical conditions, race or ethnicity, sex, or a previous surgery.

Age

The chances of having arrhythmia grow as we age, in part because of changes in heart tissue and how the heart works over time. Older people are also more likely to have health conditions, including heart disease, that raise the risk of arrhythmia.

Some types of arrhythmia happen more often in children and young adults, including arrhythmias due to congenital heart defects or inherited conduction disorders.

Environment

Some research suggests that exposure to air pollutants, especially particulates and gases, is linked to a short-term risk of arrhythmia.

Family History and Genetics

You may have an increased risk of some types of arrhythmia if your parent or other close relative has had an arrhythmia too. Also, some inherited types of heart disease can raise your risk of arrhythmia. With some conduction disorders, gene mutations cause the ion channels that transmit signals through heart cells to work incorrectly or stop working.

Lifestyle Habits

Your risk for arrhythmia may be higher because of certain lifestyle habits, including:

- Drinking alcohol
- Smoking
- Using illegal drugs, such as cocaine or amphetamines

Other Medical Conditions

Arrhythmias are more common in people who have diseases or conditions that weaken the heart, but many conditions can raise the risk for arrhythmia. These include:

- Aneurysms

- Autoimmune disorders, such as rheumatoid arthritis (RA) and lupus

- Diabetes, which increases the risk of high blood pressure and coronary heart disease (CHD)

- Diseases of the heart and blood vessels, including a heart that is larger than normal and heart inflammation

- Eating disorders, such as bulimia and anorexia, which cause electrolyte imbalance and severe malnutrition

- Heart attack

- Heart failure, which weakens the heart and changes the way electrical signals move through the heart

- Heart tissue that is too thick or stiff or that has not formed normally. Arrhythmias can be more common among people who have had surgery to repair a congenital heart defect.

- High blood pressure

- Influenza, or flu

- Kidney disease

- Leaking or narrowed heart valves that make the heart work too hard and can lead to heart failure.

- Low blood sugar

- Lung diseases, such as chronic obstructive pulmonary disease (COPD)

- Musculoskeletal disorders (MSDs)

- Obesity

- Overactive or underactive thyroid gland, caused by too much or too little thyroid hormone in the body. The most common cause of excess thyroid hormone is Graves' disease.

- Sepsis, a toxic immune response to infection

- Sleep apnea, which can stress the heart by preventing it from getting enough oxygen

Race or Ethnicity

Studies suggest that White Americans may be more likely than African Americans to have some arrhythmias, such as atrial fibrillation, although African Americans have higher rates of high blood pressure and other arrhythmia risk factors.

Sex

Some studies suggest that men are more likely to have atrial fibrillation than women. However, women taking certain medicines appear to be at a higher risk of a certain type of arrhythmia. Certain times of the menstrual cycle also appear to increase women's risk of some arrhythmia events. If you are pregnant, you may notice that an existing arrhythmia occurs more often. Benign extra beats are also more common during pregnancy. In some cases, the complications that can develop with arrhythmia also differ by sex.

Surgery

You may be at a higher risk of developing atrial flutter in the early days and weeks after surgery involving the heart, lungs, or esophagus.

Screening and Prevention of Arrhythmia

If you or your child is at increased risk of arrhythmia, the doctor may want to do a screening to assess the risk of a life-threatening event. Sometimes screening is required to participate in competitive sports. If your child carries a genetic risk of arrhythmia, your child's doctor may recommend regular screening to monitor your child's heart or other family members' health. The doctor may also ask about risk factors and may suggest genetic testing if your child, parent, or other family member has a known or suspected arrhythmia or other heart condition. Heart-healthy lifestyle changes and other precautions can help decrease the risk of triggering arrhythmia.

Screening Tests

Your doctor may recommend screening tests based on your risk factors, such as age or family history.

- An **electrocardiogram (EKG)** is the main test for detecting arrhythmia. An EKG records the heart's electrical activity. Your doctor may do the test while you are at rest or may do a stress test, which records the heart's activity when it is working hard. Your doctor may also give you a portable monitor to wear for a day or several days if no arrhythmia was detected during testing in the clinic. If you have a child who is at risk of arrhythmia because of a genetic condition, the doctor may recommend regular testing for your child and her or his siblings.

- **Genetic testing** can help you understand your risk when a family member has been diagnosed with a genetic condition. Testing is especially important if your newborn or another close relative died suddenly and had a genetic risk. Your doctor may also suggest genetic testing if you have a history of fainting or have survived cardiac arrest or near drowning.

- **Imaging tests**, such as cardiac magnetic resonance imaging (MRI), can help detect scarring or other problems that can increase your risk of arrhythmia.

Prevention Strategies

Learn about prevention strategies that your doctor may recommend, including:

- Avoiding triggers, such as caffeine or stimulant medicines, that can cause arrhythmias or make them worse. Your doctor can also help if you are trying to avoid illegal drugs.

- Getting an implantable or wearable cardioverter defibrillator to prevent sudden cardiac arrest from arrhythmia if you have heart disease. Defibrillators can correct arrhythmias by sending an electric shock to the heart.

- Making heart-healthy lifestyle changes, such as heart-healthy eating, being physically active, aiming for a healthy weight, quitting smoking, and managing stress.

- Monitoring you after surgery, if you are having heart surgery. The surgical team may also use medicine and maintain or supplement electrolyte levels during or after the procedure to prevent arrhythmia.

If you are the parents of a child with an inherited condition that increases the risk of arrhythmia, discuss prevention strategies with your pediatrician as part of your child's care.

- If your child is a newborn, follow safe sleeping recommendations to help reduce the risk of sudden infant death syndrome (SIDS).

- Your doctor may recommend routine assessments of your child's heart activity to detect patterns or symptoms of arrhythmia that emerge over time.

Signs, Symptoms, and Complications of Arrhythmia

An arrhythmia may not cause any obvious signs or symptoms. You may notice something that occurs only occasionally, or your symptoms may become more frequent over time. Keep track of when and how often arrhythmia occurs, what you feel, and whether these things change over time. They are all important clues your doctor can use. If left untreated, arrhythmia can lead to life-threatening complications such as stroke, heart failure, or sudden cardiac arrest.

Signs and Symptoms

You may be able to feel a slow or irregular heartbeat or notice pauses between heartbeats. If you have palpitations, you may feel like your heart skipped a beat or may notice it pounding or racing. These are all symptoms of arrhythmia.

More serious signs and symptoms include:

- Anxiety

- Blurred vision

- Chest pain

- Difficulty breathing

- Fainting or nearly fainting

- Foggy thinking

- Fatigue

- Sweating

- Weakness, dizziness, and light-headedness

Complications

Arrhythmias that are unrecognized or left untreated can cause sometimes life-threatening complications affecting the heart and brain.

- **Cognitive impairment and dementia**. Alzheimer disease (AD) and vascular dementia (VD) are more common in people who have arrhythmia. This may be due to reduced blood flow to the brain over time.

- **Heart failure**. Repeat arrhythmias can lead to a rapid decline in the ability of the lower chambers to pump blood. Heart failure is especially likely to develop or grow worse as a result of arrhythmia when you already have heart disease.

- **Stroke**. This can occur in some patients who have atrial fibrillation. With an arrhythmia, blood can pool in the atria, causing blood clots to form. If a clot breaks off and travels to the brain, it can cause a stroke.

- **Sudden cardiac arrest (SCA)**. The heart may suddenly and unexpectedly stop beating as a result of ventricular fibrillation.

- **Sudden infant death syndrome (SIDS)**. SIDS can be attributed to an inherited conduction disorder that causes arrhythmia.

- **Worsening arrhythmia**. Some arrhythmias trigger another type of arrhythmia or get worse over time.

Diagnosis of Arrhythmia

To diagnose arrhythmia, your doctor will ask you about your symptoms, your medical history, and any signs of arrhythmia in your family. Your doctor may also do an EKG and a physical exam as part of your diagnosis. Additional tests may be necessary to rule out another cause or to help your doctor decide on treatment.

Medical history

To diagnose an arrhythmia, your doctor will ask about your eating and physical activity habits, family history, and other risk factors for arrhythmia. Your doctor may ask whether you have any other signs or symptoms. This information can help your doctor determine whether you have complications or other conditions that may be causing you to have an arrhythmia.

Physical Exam

During a physical exam, your doctor may take these steps:

- Check for swelling in your legs or feet, which could be a sign of an enlarged heart or heart failure
- Check your pulse to find out how fast your heart is beating
- Listen to the rate and rhythm of your heartbeat
- Listen to your heart for a heart murmur
- Look for signs of other diseases, such as thyroid disease, that could be causing the arrhythmia

Diagnostic Tests and Procedures

Your doctor may order some of the following tests to diagnose arrhythmia:

- Blood tests to check the level of certain substances in the blood, such as potassium and thyroid hormone, that can increase your risk of arrhythmia.
- Cardiac catheterization to see whether you have complications from heart disease.
- Chest X-ray to show whether your heart is larger than normal.
- Echocardiography (echo) to provide information about the size and shape of your heart and how well it is working. Echocardiography may also be used to diagnose fetal arrhythmia in the womb.
- EKG, or ECG, to see how fast the heart is beating and whether its rhythm is steady or irregular. This is the most common test used to diagnose arrhythmias.
- Electrophysiology study (EPS) to look at the electrical activity of the heart. The study uses a wire to electrically stimulate your heart and trigger an arrhythmia. If your doctor has already detected another condition that raises your risk, an EPS can help her or him assess the possibility that an arrhythmia will develop. An EPS also allows your doctor to see whether a treatment, such as medicine, will stop the problem.
- Holter or event monitor to record your heart's electrical activity over long periods of time while you do your normal activities.

- Implantable loop recorder (ILR) to detect abnormal heart rhythms. It is placed under the skin and continuously records your heart's electrical activity. The recorder can transmit data to the doctor's office to help with monitoring. An implantable loop recorder helps doctors figure out why a person may be having palpitations or fainting spells, especially if these symptoms do not happen very often.

- Sleep study to see whether sleep apnea is causing your arrhythmia.

- Stress test or exercise stress test to detect arrhythmias that happen while the heart is working hard and beating fast. If you cannot exercise, you may be given medicine to make your heart work hard and beat fast.

- Tilt table testing to help find the cause of fainting spells. You lie on a table that moves from a lying-down position to an upright position. The change in position may cause you to faint. Your doctor watches your symptoms, heart rate, EKG reading, and blood pressure throughout the test.

- Ultrasound to diagnose a suspected fetal arrhythmia in the womb.

Treatment of Arrhythmia

Common arrhythmia treatments include heart-healthy lifestyle changes, medicines, surgically- implanted devices that control the heartbeat, and other procedures that treat abnormal electrical signals in the heart.

Healthy Lifestyle Changes

Your doctor may recommend that you adopt the following lifelong heart-healthy lifestyle changes to help lower your risk for conditions such as high blood pressure and heart disease, which can lead to arrhythmia.

- Aiming for a healthy weight
- Being physically active
- Heart-healthy eating
- Managing stress
- Quitting smoking

Medicines

Your doctor may give you medicine for your arrhythmia. Some medicines are used in combination with each other or together with a procedure or a pacemaker. If the dose is too high, medicines to treat arrhythmia can cause an irregular rhythm. This happens more often in women.

- Adenosine to slow a racing heart. Adenosine acts quickly to slow electrical signals. It can cause some chest pain, flushing, and shortness of breath, but any discomfort typically passes soon.

- Atropine to treat a slow heart rate. This medicine may cause difficulty swallowing.

- Beta-blockers to treat high blood pressure or a fast heart rate or to prevent repeat episodes of arrhythmia. Beta-blockers can cause digestive trouble, sleep problems, and sexual dysfunction and can make some conduction disorders worse.

- Blood thinners to reduce the risk of blood clots forming. This helps prevent stroke. With blood-thinning medicines, there is a risk of bleeding.

- Calcium-channel blockers to slow a rapid heart rate or the speed at which signals travel. Typically, they are used to control arrhythmias of the upper chambers. In some cases, calcium-channel blockers can trigger ventricular fibrillation. They can also cause digestive trouble, swollen feet, or low blood pressure.

- Digitalis, or digoxin, to treat a fast heart rate. This medicine can cause nausea and may trigger arrhythmias.

- Potassium channel blockers to slow the heart rate. They work by lengthening the time it takes for heart cells to recover after firing so that they do not fire and squeeze as often. Potassium channel blockers can cause low blood pressure or another arrhythmia.

- Sodium-channel blockers to block transmission of electrical signals, lengthen cell recovery periods, and make cells less excitable. However, these drugs can increase risks of sudden cardiac arrest in people who have heart disease.

Procedures

If medicines do not treat your arrhythmia, your doctor may recommend one of these procedures or devices.

- Cardioversion

- Catheter ablation

- Implantable cardioverter defibrillators (ICDs)

- Pacemakers

Other Treatments

Treatment may also include managing any underlying condition, such as an electrolyte imbalance, high blood pressure, heart disease, sleep apnea, or thyroid disease.

Your doctor may use supplements to treat magnesium or electrolyte deficiencies. Electrolytes can also be an alternative to medicines that treat arrhythmia if your doctor is concerned that those medicines might trigger an arrhythmia.

Your doctor may also perform certain techniques to slow your heart rate. The exercises stimulate your body's natural relaxation processes. They do this by affecting the vagus nerve, which helps control the heart rate. Techniques can include:

- Having you cough or gag

- Having you hold your breath and bear down, which is called the "Valsalva maneuver"

- Having you lie down

- Putting a towel dipped in ice-cold water over your face

Living with Arrhythmia

If you have been diagnosed and treated for arrhythmia, make sure to follow your treatment plan. Your ongoing care may focus on reducing the chance that you will have another episode or a complication. Keep your regular appointments with your doctor. Ask about heart-healthy lifestyle changes that you can make to keep your arrhythmia from happening again or getting worse.

Receive Routine Follow-Up Care

How often you need to see your doctor for follow-up care will depend on your symptoms and treatment.

- Get regular vaccinations, including a flu shot every year.

- Follow your doctor's recommendations for adopting lifelong lifestyle changes, such as heart-healthy eating, being physically active, quitting smoking, managing stress, and aiming for a healthy weight. Your doctor may also recommend that you reduce or stop drinking alcohol and consuming coffee, tea, soda, chocolate, or other sources of caffeine, to avoid triggering arrhythmia.

- Keep all of your medical appointments. Bring a list of all the medicines you take to every doctor and emergency room (ER) visit. This will help your doctors know exactly what medicines you are taking, which can help prevent medicine errors.

- See your doctor for regular checkups if you are taking blood-thinning medicines. Your doctor may recommend blood thinners to prevent stroke, even if your heart rhythm has returned to normal. You may need routine blood tests to check how the medicines are working or the effect they are having on your organs.

- Take your medicines as prescribed. Your doctor may also ask you to check your pulse regularly to monitor the effectiveness of the medicines.

- Tell your doctor if you have side effects from your medicines, such as depression, light-headedness, or palpitations. Some of the medicines can cause low blood pressure or a slow heart rate or can make heart failure worse.

- Tell your doctor if your symptoms are getting worse or if you have new symptoms. Over time, arrhythmias can become more common, last longer, or get worse. This can sometimes make arrhythmia resistant to medicines. Some arrhythmias can also make it more likely for other types of arrhythmia to develop.

Monitor Your Condition

To monitor your condition, your doctor may recommend the following tests.

- Blood tests to check the effects of medicines you are taking

- Echocardiography (echo) to check your heart function, if you have underlying heart disease

- EKGs to monitor changes in heart rhythm

- Holter or event monitors to record your heart's electrical activity over several days

- Smartphone-based monitors to record heart rhythms and detect when atrial fibrillation occurs. A band that can record a 30-second EKG has been approved by the U.S. Food and Drug Administration (FDA).

Learn the Warning Signs of Serious Complications and Have a Plan

Arrhythmia can lead to serious complications, such as sudden cardiac arrest and severe bleeding in the brain. If you suspect any of the following in yourself or someone else, call 911 immediately:

- **Bleeding in the brain or digestive system.** If you take too high a dose of blood-thinning medicines, it may cause bleeding in the brain or digestive system. Signs and symptoms may include bright red vomit; bright red blood in your stool or black, tarry stools; severe pain in the abdomen or head; sudden, severe changes in your vision or ability to move your arms or legs; or memory loss. A lot of bleeding after a fall or injury or easy bruising or bleeding may mean that your blood is too thin. Excessive bleeding is bleeding that will not stop after you apply pressure to a wound for 10 minutes. Call your doctor right away if you have any of these signs.

- **Heart attack.** Signs of a heart attack include mild or severe chest pain or discomfort in the center of the chest or upper abdomen that lasts for more than a few minutes or goes away and comes back. It can feel like pressure, squeezing, fullness, heartburn, or indigestion. There may also be pain down the left arm. Women may also have chest pain and pain down the left arm, but they are more likely to have other symptoms, such as shortness of breath, nausea, vomiting, unusual tiredness, and pain in the back, shoulders, or jaw.

- **Stroke.** If you think someone may be having a stroke, act F.A.S.T. and do the following simple test.

F—Face: Ask the person to smile. Does one side of the face droop?

A—Arms: Ask the person to raise both arms. Does one arm drift downward?

S—Speech: Ask the person to repeat a simple phrase. Is their speech slurred or strange?

T—Time: If you observe any of these signs, call 911 immediately. Every minute matters.

- **Sudden cardiac arrest.** Usually, the first sign of sudden cardiac arrest is fainting. At the same time, no heartbeat can be felt. Some people may have a racing heartbeat or feel dizzy or lightheaded just before they faint. Within an hour before cardiac arrest, some people have chest pain, shortness of breath, nausea, or vomiting. Call 911 right away if someone has signs or symptoms of sudden cardiac arrest. Look for a defibrillator nearby and follow the instructions.

Learn about Other Precautions to Help You Stay Safe

If you have an arrhythmia, you will need to learn ways to care for your condition at home. You will also need to avoid activities that may trigger your arrhythmia.

- Ask your doctor whether you can continue your daily activities without any changes. Your doctor may recommend low or moderate activity; avoiding competitive sports; eliminating activities that might trigger an arrhythmia, such as swimming or diving; or participating in activities with a partner.

- Carry a medical-device ID card with information about your defibrillator or pacemaker and contact information for the healthcare provider who oversees your care. Medical bracelets with information about your condition can also be helpful in the event of an emergency.

- Check with your doctor before taking over-the-counter (OTC) medicines, nutritional supplements, or cold and allergy medicines. Some of these products can trigger rapid heart rhythms or interact poorly with heart rhythm medicines.

- Learn how to take your pulse. Discuss with your doctor what pulse rate is normal for you. Keep a record of changes in your pulse rate, and share this information with your doctor.

- Lie down if you feel dizzy or faint or if you feel palpitations. Do not try to walk or drive. Let your doctor know about these symptoms.

- Talk to your doctor about techniques that you can do at home if you notice your heart racing. These include breathing out without letting your breath escape or putting a cold, wet towel over your face.

Section 19.2

Brugada Syndrome

This section contains text excerpted from the following sources: Text beginning with the heading "What Is Brugada Syndrome?" is excerpted from "Brugada Syndrome," Genetics Home Reference (GHR), National Institutes of Health (NIH), March 2015. Reviewed March 2019; Text beginning with the heading "Symptoms of Brugada Syndrome" is excerpted from "Brugada Syndrome," Genetic and Rare Diseases Information Center (GARD), National Center for Advancing Translational Sciences (NCATS), March 16, 2016.

What Is Brugada Syndrome?

Brugada syndrome (BrS) is a condition that causes a disruption of the heart's normal rhythm. Specifically, this disorder can lead to irregular heartbeats in the heart's lower chambers (ventricles), which is an abnormality called "ventricular arrhythmia." If untreated, the irregular heartbeats can cause fainting (syncope), seizures, difficulty breathing, or sudden death. These complications typically occur when an affected person is resting or asleep.

BrS usually becomes apparent in adulthood, although it can develop any time throughout life. Signs and symptoms related to arrhythmias, including sudden death, can occur from early infancy to late adulthood. Sudden death typically occurs around the age of 40. This condition may explain some cases of sudden infant death syndrome (SIDS), which is a major cause of death in babies younger than one year. SIDS is characterized by sudden and unexplained death, usually during sleep.

Sudden unexplained nocturnal death syndrome (SUNDS) is a condition characterized by unexpected cardiac arrest in young adults, usually at night during sleep. This condition was originally described in South-East Asian populations, where it is a major cause of death. Researchers have determined that SUNDS and BrS are the same disorder.

Frequency and Causes

The exact prevalence of BrS is unknown, although it is estimated to affect 5 in 10,000 people worldwide. This condition occurs much more frequently in people of Asian ancestry, particularly in Japanese and South-East Asian populations.

Although BrS affects both men and women, the condition appears to be 8 to 10 times more common in men. Researchers suspect that testosterone, a sex hormone present at much higher levels in men, may account for this difference.

BrS can be caused by mutations in one of several genes. The most commonly mutated gene in this condition is *SCN5A*, which is altered in approximately 30 percent of affected individuals. This gene provides instructions for making a sodium channel, which normally transports positively charged sodium atoms (ions) into heart muscle cells. This type of ion channel plays a critical role in maintaining the heart's normal rhythm. Mutations in the *SCN5A* gene alter the structure or function of the channel, which reduces the flow of sodium ions into cells. A disruption in ion transport alters the way the heart beats, leading to the abnormal heart rhythm characteristic of BrS.

Mutations in other genes can also cause BrS. Together, these other genetic changes account for less than two percent of cases of the condition. Some of the additional genes involved in BrS provide instructions for making proteins that ensure the correct location or function of sodium channels in heart muscle cells. Proteins produced by other genes involved in the condition form or help regulate ion channels that transport calcium or potassium into or out of heart muscle cells. As with sodium channels, proper flow of ions through calcium and potassium channels in the heart muscle helps maintain a regular heartbeat. Mutations in these genes disrupt the flow of ions, impairing the heart's normal rhythm.

In affected people without an identified gene mutation, the cause of BrS is often unknown. In some cases, certain drugs may cause a nongenetic (acquired) form of the disorder. Drugs that can induce an altered heart rhythm include medications used to treat some forms of arrhythmia, a condition called "angina" (which causes chest pain), high blood pressure, depression, and other mental illnesses. Abnormally high blood levels of calcium (hypercalcemia) or potassium (hyper-kalemia), as well as unusually low potassium levels (hypokalemia), also have been associated with acquired BrS. In addition to causing a nongenetic form of this disorder, these factors may trigger symptoms in people with an underlying mutation in *SCN5A* or another gene.

Symptoms of Brugada Syndrome

While symptoms of BrS usually develop in adulthood, they can develop at any age. Symptoms associated with irregular heartbeat (arrhythmia) can cause fainting, seizures, difficulty breathing, or sud-den death. These symptoms and complications usually occur during rest or sleep. Sudden cardiac arrest may be the initial symptom of BrS in as many as one-third of affected people. The risk of cardiac arrest is much lower in people with no symptoms. After diagnosis, specific tests may provide an estimate of the risk of ventricular arrhythmias and sudden cardiac death in each person.

Prognosis for Brugada Syndrome

The long-term outlook (prognosis) for people with BrS varies because the condition is very unpredictable. The condition manifests primarily during adulthood, and causes a high risk of ventricular arrhythmias and sudden death. The average age of sudden death is approximately 40 years. Affected people with a history of sudden cardiac arrest and/ or fainting have an increased risk for subsequent episodes compared to people with no symptoms.

Section 19.3

Familial Atrial Fibrillation

> This section contains text excerpted from the following sources:
> Text in this section begins with excerpts from "Familial Atrial
> Fibrillation," Genetics Home Reference (GHR), National Institutes of
> Health (NIH), October 2017; Text beginning with the heading "How
> Might Familial Atrial Fibrillation Be Treated?" is excerpted from
> "Familial Atrial Fibrillation," Genetic and Rare Diseases Information
> Center (GARD), National Center for Advancing Translational
> Sciences (NCATS), November 9, 2015. Reviewed March 2019.

Familial atrial fibrillation is an inherited abnormality of the heart's normal rhythm. Atrial fibrillation is characterized by episodes of uncoordinated electrical activity (fibrillation) in the heart's upper chambers (the atria), which cause a fast and irregular heartbeat. If untreated, this abnormal heart rhythm (arrhythmia) can lead to dizziness, chest pain, a sensation of fluttering or pounding in the chest (palpitations), shortness of breath, or fainting (syncope). Atrial fibrillation also increases the risk of stroke and sudden death. Complications of atrial fibrillation can occur at any age, although some people with this heart condition never experience any health problems associated with the disorder.

Frequency and Causes

Atrial fibrillation is the most common type of recurrent arrhythmia, affecting more than 3 million people in the United States. The risk of developing this irregular heart rhythm increases with age. The incidence of the familial form of atrial fibrillation is unknown; however, studies suggest that up to 30 percent of all people who have atrial fibrillation without an identified cause have a history of the condition in their family.

Changes in some genes can cause atrial fibrillation on their own, while changes in other genes affect a person's risk of developing this condition in combination with a variety of environmental and lifestyle factors. Familial atrial fibrillation often results from rare mutations in single genes. However, these cases represent only a small fraction of all individuals with atrial fibrillation.

The first single gene found to be associated with familial atrial fibrillation was *KCNQ1*, which provides instructions for making a channel that is embedded in the outer membrane of heart (cardiac) muscle cells. This channel transports positively charged atoms (ions) of potassium out of cells. In cardiac muscle, this ion transport plays a critical role in maintaining the heart's normal rhythm. Since that discovery, rare genetic variants in other ion channel genes have been found to cause familial atrial fibrillation. Mutations in ion channel genes lead to the production of altered channels, which may either increase or decrease the flow of ions across the outer cell membrane and alter the way the heart beats.

Mutations in other types of genes have also been found to cause familial atrial fibrillation. Some of these genes provide instructions for making cardiac transcription factors, which regulate the activity of certain genes involved in the formation and development of the heart before birth. Other genes provide instructions for making parts of structural elements of cardiac muscle, such as sarcomeres. These structures are necessary for cardiac muscle to contract and produce the heart's pumping action. Mutations in these nonion channel genes have a variety of effects on the structure and function of cardiac muscle, all of which can lead to an abnormal heartbeat.

Most cases of atrial fibrillation are not caused by inherited mutations in single genes. However, relatively common variations (polymorphisms) in more than two dozen genes appear to influence the likelihood of developing the condition. Each of these polymorphisms on its own has a small effect on a person's overall risk, but an individual may have multiple polymorphisms that together have a significant effect. In addition to these common genetic variations, risk factors for atrial fibrillation include high blood pressure (hypertension), diabetes mellitus, a previous stroke, or an accumulation of fatty deposits and scar-like tissue in the lining of the arteries (atherosclerosis). Researchers are working to determine how a combination of genetic changes, environmental influences, and lifestyle factors contribute to a person's risk of developing atrial fibrillation.

How Might Familial Atrial Fibrillation Be Treated?

We are unaware of treatment recommendations specific to familial atrial fibrillation, but there is information available about treatment for atrial fibrillation in general.

Treatment for atrial fibrillation depends on the frequency and severity of symptoms and may involve medications, medical procedures, and lifestyle changes. People who don't have symptoms or related heart problems may not need treatment.

What Is the Long-Term Outlook for People with Familial Atrial Fibrillation?

The long-term outlook (prognosis) for a person with familial atrial fibrillation varies depending on the type of atrial fibrillation the person has, as well as whether another underlying heart condition or disease is present. Generally, affected people can live normal, active lives, but ongoing medical care is important. While a person does not die from AF itself, a person can die from complications that result from having AF. The main risks in affected people are stroke and heart failure. AF is also associated with an increased risk of a first myocardial infarction (heart attack).

Many people with familial AF are said to have "lone AF"—a term that describes AF in people younger than 60 years of age with no underlying heart disease. The prognosis is reportedly very good in people with lone AF. However, other cardiovascular risk factors, such as age, diabetes, hypertension, and prior stroke, can further increase the risk of stroke.

Other complications that may be associated with AF include adverse hemodynamics, reduced exercise tolerance, degraded quality of life (QOL), impaired cognition or dementia, and tachycardia-induced cardiomyopathy (TIC).

Generally, while there is conflicting evidence in younger people with no underlying heart abnormalities, AF is associated with reduced life expectancy in older affected people. In some cases, antiarrhythmic drugs appear to contribute to increased mortality.

Section 19.4

Long QT Syndrome

This section includes text excerpted from "Long QT
Syndrome," National Heart, Lung, and Blood
Institute (NHLBI), December 14, 2017.

What Is Long QT Syndrome?

Long QT syndrome (LQTS) is a disorder of the heart's electrical
activity. It can cause sudden, uncontrollable, and dangerous arrhythmias in response to exercise or stress. Arrhythmias are problems with
the rate or rhythm of the heartbeat.

People who have LQTS also can have arrhythmias for no known
reason. However, not everyone who has LQTS has dangerous heart
rhythms. When they do occur, though, they can be fatal.

What Does "Long QT" Mean?

The term "long QT" refers to an abnormal pattern seen on an electrocardiogram (EKG). An EKG is a test that detects and records the
heart's electrical activity.

With each heartbeat, an electrical signal spreads from the top of
your heart to the bottom. As it travels, the signal causes the heart to
contract and pump blood. An EKG records electrical signals as they
move through your heart.

Data from the EKG are mapped on a graph so your doctor can
study your heart's electrical activity. Each heartbeat is mapped as
five distinct electrical waves: P, Q, R, S, and T.

Electrocardiogram

The electrical activity that occurs between the Q and T waves is
called the "QT interval." This interval shows electrical activity in the
heart's lower chambers, the ventricles.

The timing of the heart's electrical activity is complex, and the body
carefully controls it. Normally the QT interval is about a third of each
heartbeat cycle. However, in people who have LQTS, the QT interval
lasts longer than normal.

A long QT interval can upset the careful timing of the heartbeat
and trigger dangerous heart rhythms.

LQTS is also known by names such as Jervell and Lange-Nielsen syndrome (JLNS) and Romano-Ward syndrome (RWS).

Causes of Long QT Syndrome

Long QT syndrome (LQTS) can be inherited or acquired. "Inherited" means you're born with the condition and have it your whole life. Inherited conditions are passed from parents to children through genes. "Acquired" means you aren't born with the condition, but you develop it during your lifetime.

Inherited Long QT Syndrome

Faulty genes cause inherited LQTS. These genes control the production of certain types of ion channels in your heart. Faulty genes may cause the body to make too few ion channels, ion channels that don't work well, or both.

There are seven known types of inherited LQTS (types 1 through 7). The most common types are LQTS 1, 2, and 3.

Some types of LQTS involve faulty or lacking potassium ion or sodium ion channels.

If you have LQTS 1 or LQTS 2, the flow of potassium ions through the ion channels in your heart cells isn't normal. This may cause problems when you exercise or when you have strong emotions.

You may develop a rapid, uncontrollable heart rhythm that prevents your heart from pumping blood. This type of heart rhythm can be fatal if it's not quickly brought under control.

If you have LQTS 3, the flow of sodium ions through ion channels in your heart cells isn't normal. This can trigger a rapid, uncontrollable heart rhythm that can be fatal. In LQTS 3, problems usually occur when your heart beats slower than normal, such as during sleep.

Acquired Long QT Syndrome

Some medicines and conditions can cause acquired LQTS.

Medication-Induced Long QT Syndrome

More than 50 medicines have been found to cause LQTS. Some common medicines that may cause the disorder include:

- Antihistamines and decongestants
- Diuretics (pills that remove excess water from your body)

- Antibiotics

- Antiarrhythmic medicines

- Antidepressant and antipsychotic medicines

- Cholesterol-lowering medicines and some diabetes medicines

Some people who have medication-induced LQTS also may have an inherited form of the disorder. They may not have symptoms unless they take medicines that lengthen the QT interval or lower potassium levels in the blood. When LQTS doesn't cause symptoms, it's called "silent LQTS."

Other Causes of Acquired Long Qt Syndrome

Severe diarrhea or vomiting that causes a major loss of potassium or sodium ions from the bloodstream may cause LQTS. The disorder lasts until these ion levels return to normal.

The eating disorders anorexia nervosa and bulimia and some thyroid disorders may cause a drop in potassium ion levels in the blood, causing LQTS.

Risk Factors of Long QT Syndrome

Long QT syndrome (LQTS) is a rare disorder. Experts think that about 1 in 7,000 people has LQTS. But no one knows for sure, because LQTS often goes undiagnosed.

LQTS causes about 3,000 to 4,000 sudden deaths in children and young adults each year in the United States. Unexplained sudden deaths in children are rare. When they do occur, LQTS often is the cause.

Inherited LQTS usually is first detected during childhood or young adulthood. Half of all people who have LQTS have their first abnormal heart rhythm by the time they're 12 years old, and 90 percent by the time they're 40 years old. The condition rarely is diagnosed after the age of 40.

In boys who have LQTS, the QT interval (which can be seen on an EKG test) often returns toward normal after puberty. If this happens, the risk of LQTS symptoms and complications goes down.

LQTS is more common in women than men. Women who have LQTS are more likely to faint or die suddenly from the disorder during menstruation and shortly after giving birth.

Children who are born deaf also are at increased risk for LQTS. This is because the same genetic problem that affects hearing also affects the function of ion channels in the heart.

Major Risk Factors

You're at risk of having LQTS if anyone in your family has ever had it. Unexplained fainting or seizures, drowning or near drowning, and unexplained sudden death are all possible signs of LQTS.

You're also at risk for LQTS if you take medicines that make the QT interval longer. Your doctor can tell you whether your prescription or over-the-counter (OTC) medicines might do this.

You also may develop LQTS if you have excessive vomiting or diarrhea or other conditions that cause low blood levels of potassium or sodium. These conditions include the eating disorders anorexia nervosa and bulimia, as well as some thyroid disorders.

Signs, Symptoms, and Complications of Long QT Syndrome

Major Signs and Symptoms

If you have LQTS, you can have sudden and dangerous arrhythmias (abnormal heart rhythms). Signs and symptoms of LQTS-related arrhythmias often first occur during childhood and include:

- Unexplained fainting. This happens because the heart isn't pumping enough blood to the brain. Fainting may occur during physical or emotional stress. Fluttering feelings in the chest may occur before fainting.

- Unexplained drowning or near drowning. This may be due to fainting while swimming.

- Unexplained sudden cardiac arrest (SCA) or death. SCA is a condition in which the heart suddenly stops beating for no obvious reason. People who have SCA die within minutes unless they receive treatment. In about 1 out of 10 people who have LQTS, SCA or sudden death is the first sign of the disorder.

Other Signs and Symptoms

Often, people who have LQTS 3 develop an abnormal heart rhythm during sleep. This may cause noisy gasping while sleeping.

Silent Long QT Syndrome

Sometimes long QT syndrome doesn't cause any signs or symptoms. This is called "silent LQTS." For this reason, doctors often advise family members of people who have LQTS to be tested for the disorder, even if they have no symptoms.

Medical and genetic tests may reveal whether these family members have LQTS and what type of the condition they have.

Diagnosis of Long QT Syndrome

Cardiologists diagnose and treat LQTS. Cardiologists are doctors who specialize in diagnosing and treating heart diseases and conditions. To diagnose LQTS, your cardiologist will consider your:

- EKG (electrocardiogram) results
- Medical history and the results from a physical exam
- Genetic test results

Electrocardiogram

An EKG is a simple test that detects and records the heart's electrical activity. This test may show a long QT interval and other signs that suggest LQTS. Often, doctors first discover a long QT interval when an EKG is done for another suspected heart problem.

Not all people who have LQTS will always have a long QT interval on an EKG. The QT interval may change from time to time; it may be long sometimes and normal at other times. Thus, your doctor may want you to have several EKG tests over a period of days or weeks. Or, your doctor may have you wear a device called a "Holter monitor."

A Holter monitor records the heart's electrical activity for a full 24 or 48 hour period. It can detect heart problems that occur for only a few minutes out of the day.

You wear small patches called "electrodes" on your chest. Wires connect the patches to a small, portable recorder. You can clip the recorder to a belt, keep it in a pocket, or hang it around your neck.

While you wear the monitor, you do your usual daily activities. You also keep a notebook, noting any symptoms you have and the time they occur. You then return both the recorder and the notebook to your doctor to read the results. Your doctor can see how your heart was beating at the time you had symptoms.

Some people have a long QT interval only while they exercise. For this reason, your doctor may recommend that you have a stress test.

During a stress test, you exercise to make your heart work hard and beat fast. An EKG is done while you exercise. If you can't exercise, you may be given medicine to increase your heart rate.

Medical History and Physical Exam

Your doctor will ask whether you've had any symptoms of an abnormal heart rhythm. Symptoms may include:

- Unexplained fainting

- A fluttering feeling in your chest, which is the result of your heart beating too fast

- Loud gasping during sleep

Your doctor may ask what OTC, prescription, or other drugs you take. She or he also may want to know whether anyone in your family has been diagnosed with or has had signs of LQTS. Signs of LQTS include unexplained fainting, drowning, sudden cardiac arrest, or sudden death.

Your doctor will check you for signs of conditions that may lower blood levels of potassium or sodium. These conditions include anorexia nervosa and bulimia, excessive vomiting or diarrhea, and certain thyroid disorders.

Genetic Tests

Genetic blood tests can detect some forms of inherited LQTS. If your doctor thinks that you have LQTS, he or she may suggest genetic testing. Genetic blood tests usually are suggested for family members of people who have LQTS as well.

However, genetic tests don't always detect LQTS. So, even if you have the disorder, the tests may not show it.

Also, some people who test positive for LQTS don't have any signs or symptoms of the disorder. These people may have silent LQTS. Less than 10 percent of these people will faint or suddenly die from an abnormal heart rhythm.

Even if you have silent LQTS, you may be at increased risk of having an abnormal heart rhythm while taking medicines that affect potassium ion channels or blood levels of potassium.

Types of Inherited Long QT Syndrome

If you have inherited LQTS, it may be helpful to know which type you have. This will help you and your doctor plan your treatment and decide which lifestyle changes you should make.

To find out what type of LQTS you have, your doctor will consider:

- Genetic test results

- The types of situations that trigger an abnormal heart rhythm

- How well you respond to medicine

Treatment of Long QT Syndrome

The goal of treating LQTS is to prevent life-threatening, abnormal heart rhythms and fainting spells.

Treatment isn't a cure for the disorder and may not restore a normal QT interval on an EKG. However, treatment greatly improves the chances of survival.

Specific Types of Treatment

Your doctor will recommend the best treatment for you based on:

- Whether you've had symptoms, such as fainting or sudden cardiac arrest (SCA)

- What type of LQTS you have

- How likely it is that you'll faint or have SCA

- What treatment you feel most comfortable with

People who have LQTS without symptoms may be advised to:

- Make lifestyle changes that reduce the risk of fainting or SCA. Lifestyle changes may include avoiding certain sports and strenuous exercise, such as swimming, which can cause abnormal heart rhythms.

- Avoid medicines that may trigger abnormal heart rhythms. This may include some medicines used to treat allergies, infections, high blood pressure, high blood cholesterol, depression, and arrhythmias.

- Take medicines, such as beta-blockers, which reduce the risk of symptoms by slowing the heart rate.

The type of medicine you take will depend on the type of LQTS you have. For example, doctors usually will prescribe sodium-channel blocker medicines only for people who have LQTS 3.

If your doctor thinks you're at increased risk for LQTS complications, she or he may suggest more aggressive treatments (in addition to medicines and lifestyle changes). These treatments may include:

- A surgically implanted device, such as a pacemaker or implantable cardioverter defibrillator (ICD). These devices help control abnormal heart rhythms.

- Surgery on the nerves that regulate your heartbeat.

People at increased risk are those who have fainted or who have had dangerous heart rhythms from their LQTS.

Lifestyle Changes

If possible, try to avoid things that can trigger abnormal heart rhythms. For example, people who have LQTS should avoid medicines that lengthen the QT interval or lower potassium blood levels.

Many people who have LQTS also benefit from adding more potassium to their diets. Check with your doctor about eating more potassium-rich foods (such as bananas) or taking potassium supplements daily.

Medicines

Beta-blockers are medicines that prevent the heart from beating faster in response to physical or emotional stress. Most people who have LQTS are treated with beta-blockers.

Doctors may suggest that people who have LQTS 3 take sodium-channel blockers, such as mexiletine. These medicines make sodium ion channels less active.

Medical Devices

Pacemakers and ICDs are small devices that help control abnormal heart rhythms. Both devices use electrical currents to prompt the heart to beat normally. Surgeons implant pacemakers and ICDs in the chest or stomach with a minor procedure.

The use of these devices is similar in children and adults. However, because children are still growing, other issues may arise. For example, as children grow, they may need to have their devices replaced.

Surgery

People who are at high risk of death from LQTS sometimes are treated with surgery. During surgery, the nerves that prompt the heart to beat faster in response to physical or emotional stress are cut.

This type of surgery keeps the heart beating at a steady pace and lowers the risk of dangerous heart rhythms in response to stress or exercise.

Living with Long QT Syndrome

LQTS usually is a lifelong condition. The risk of having an abnormal heart rhythm that leads to fainting or sudden cardiac arrest may lessen as you age. However, the risk never completely goes away.

You'll need to take certain steps for the rest of your life to prevent abnormal heart rhythms. You can:

- Avoid things that trigger abnormal heart rhythms

- Let others know you might faint or your heart might stop beating, and tell them what steps they can take

- Have a plan in place for how to handle abnormal heart rhythms

If an abnormal heart rhythm does occur, you'll need to seek treatment right away.

Avoid Triggers

If exercise triggers an abnormal heart rhythm, your doctor may tell you to avoid any strenuous exercise, especially swimming. Ask your doctor what types and amounts of exercise are safe for you.

If you have a pacemaker or implantable cardioverter defibrillator (ICD), avoid contact sports that may dislodge these devices. You may want to exercise in public or with a friend who can help you if you faint.

Avoid medicines that can trigger an abnormal heart rhythm. This includes some medicines used to treat allergies, infections, high blood pressure, high blood cholesterol, depression, and arrhythmias. Talk with your doctor before taking any prescription, over-the-counter (OTC), or other medicines or drugs.

Seek medical care right away for conditions that lower the sodium or potassium level in your blood. These conditions include anorexia nervosa and bulimia, excessive vomiting or diarrhea; and certain thyroid disorders.

If you have LQTS 2, try to avoid unexpected noises, such as loud or jarring alarm clock buzzers and telephone ringers.

Inform Others

You may want to wear a medical ID necklace or bracelet that states that you have LQTS. This will help alert medical personnel and others about your condition if you have an emergency.

Let your roommates, coworkers, or other people with whom you have regular contact know that you have a condition that might cause you to faint or go into cardiac arrest. Tell them to call 911 right away if you faint.

Consider asking a family member and/or coworker to learn cardio-pulmonary resuscitation (CPR) in case your heart stops beating.

You also may want to keep an automated external defibrillator (AED) with you at home or at work. This device uses electric shocks to restore a normal heart rhythm.

Someone at your home and/or workplace should be trained on how to use the AED, just in case your heart stops beating. If a trained person isn't available, an untrained person also can use the AED to help save your life.

If you have LQTS 3 and you sleep alone, you may want to have an intercom in your bedroom that's connected to someone else's bedroom. This will let others detect the noisy gasping that often occurs if you have an abnormal heart rhythm while lying down.

Ongoing Healthcare Needs

You should see your cardiologist (heart specialist) regularly. She or he will adjust your treatment as needed. For example, if you still faint often while using less aggressive treatments, your doctor may suggest other treatment options.

Emotional Issues and Support

Living with LQTS may cause fear, anxiety, depression, and stress. Talk about how you feel with your healthcare team. Talking to a professional counselor also can help. If you're very depressed, your doctor may recommend medicines or other treatments that can improve your quality of life (QOL).

Joining a patient support group may help you adjust to living with LQTS. You can see how other people have coped with the condition.

Talk with your doctor about local support groups or check with an area medical center.

Support from family and friends also can help relieve stress and anxiety. Let your loved ones know how you feel and what they can do to help you.

Some people learn they have LQTS because they're tested after a family member dies suddenly from LQTS. Grief counseling may help you cope if this has happened to you. Talk with your doctor about finding a grief counselor.

Chapter 20

Hereditary Deafness

Chapter Contents

Section 20.1

Nonsyndromic Hearing Loss

This section includes text excerpted from "Nonsyndromic Hearing Loss," Genetics Home Reference (GHR), National Institutes of Health (NIH), January 29, 2019.

What Is Nonsyndromic Hearing Loss?

Nonsyndromic hearing loss (NSHL) is a partial or total loss of hearing that is not associated with other signs and symptoms. In contrast, syndromic hearing loss occurs with signs and symptoms affecting other parts of the body.

NSHL can be classified in several different ways. One common way is by the condition's pattern of inheritance: autosomal dominant (DFNA), autosomal recessive (DFNB), X-linked (DFNX), or mitochondrial (which does not have a special designation). Each of these types of hearing loss includes multiple subtypes. DFNA, DFNB, and DFNX subtypes are numbered in the order in which they were first described. For example, DFNA1 was the first type of autosomal dominant NSHL to be identified.

The characteristics of NSHL vary among the different types. Hearing loss can affect one ear (unilateral) or both ears (bilateral). Degrees of hearing loss range from mild (difficulty understanding soft speech) to profound (inability to hear even very loud noises). The term "deafness" is often used to describe the severe-to-profound hearing loss. Hearing loss can be stable, or it may be progressive, becoming more severe as a person gets older. Particular types of nonsyndromic hearing loss show distinctive patterns of hearing loss. For example, the loss may be more pronounced at high, middle, or low tones.

Most forms of NSHL are described as sensorineural, which means they are associated with a permanent loss of hearing caused by damage to structures in the inner ear. The inner ear processes sound and send the information to the brain in the form of electrical nerve impulses. Less commonly, NSHL is described as conductive, meaning it results from changes in the middle ear. The middle ear contains three tiny bones that help transfer sound from the eardrum to the inner ear. Some forms of NSHL, particularly a type called "DFNX2," involve changes in both the inner ear and the middle ear. This combination is called "mixed hearing loss."

Depending on the type, NSHL can become apparent at any time from infancy to old age. Hearing loss that is present before a child learns to speak is classified as prelingual or congenital. Hearing loss that occurs after the development of speech is classified as postlingual.

Frequency and Causes of Nonsyndromic Hearing Loss

Between 2 and 3 per 1,000 children in the United States are born with detectable hearing loss in one or both ears. The prevalence of hearing loss increases with age; the condition affects 1 in 8 people in the United States age 12 and older, or about 30 million people. By age 85, more than half of all people experience hearing loss.

The causes of NSHL are complex. Researchers have identified more than 90 genes that, when altered, are associated with nonsyndromic hearing loss. Many of these genes are involved in the development and function of the inner ear. Mutations in these genes contribute to hearing loss by interfering with critical steps in processing sound. Different mutations in the same gene can be associated with different types of hearing loss, and some genes are associated with both syndromic and nonsyndromic forms. In many affected families, the factors contributing to hearing loss have not been identified.

Most cases of NSHL are inherited in an autosomal recessive pattern. About half of all severe-to-profound autosomal recessive NSHL results from mutations in the *GJB2* gene; these cases are designated DFNB1. The *GJB2* gene provides instructions for making a protein called "connexin 26," which is a member of the connexin protein family. Mutations in another connexin gene, *GJB6*, can also cause DFNB1. The *GJB6* gene provides instructions for making a protein called "connexin 30." Connexin proteins form channels called "gap junctions," which allow communication between neighboring cells, including cells in the inner ear. Mutations in the *GJB2* or *GJB6* gene alter their respective connexin proteins, which changes the structure of gap junctions and may affect the function or survival of cells that are needed for hearing.

The most common cause of moderate autosomal recessive nonsyndromic hearing loss is mutations in the *STRC* gene. These mutations cause a form of the condition known as "DFNB16." Mutations in more than 60 other genes can also cause autosomal recessive nonsyndromic hearing loss. Many of these gene mutations have been found in one or a few families.

NSHL can also be inherited in an autosomal dominant pattern. Mutations in at least 30 genes have been identified in people with autosomal dominant NSHL; mutations in some of these genes (including *GJB2* and *GJB6*) can also cause autosomal recessive forms of the condition. Although no single gene is associated with a majority of autosomal dominant NSHL cases, mutations in a few genes, such as *KCNQ4* and *TECTA*, are relatively common. Mutations in many of the other genes associated with autosomal dominant NSHL have been found in only one or a few families.

X-linked and mitochondrial forms of NSHL are rare. About half of all X-linked cases are caused by mutations in the *POU3F4* gene. This form of the condition is designated "DFNX2." Mutations in at least three other genes have also been identified in people with X-linked NSHL.

Mitochondrial forms of hearing loss resulting from changes in mitochondrial DNA (mtDNA). Mitochondria are structures within cells that convert the energy from food into a form that cells can use. Although most deoxyribonucleic acid (DNA) is packaged in chromosomes within the nucleus, mitochondria also have a small amount of their own DNA. Only a few mutations in mtDNA have been associated with hearing loss, and their role in the condition is still being studied.

Mutations in some of the genes associated with nonsyndromic hearing loss can also cause syndromic forms of hearing loss, such as Usher syndrome (CDH23 and MYO7A, among others), Pendred syndrome (SLC26A4), Wolfram syndrome (WFS1), and Stickler syndrome (COL11A2). It is often unclear how mutations in the same gene can cause isolated hearing loss in some individuals and hearing loss with additional signs and symptoms in others.

In addition to genetic changes, hearing loss can result from environmental factors or a combination of genetic risk and a person's environmental exposures. Environmental causes of hearing loss include certain medications, specific infections before or after birth, and exposure to loud noise over an extended period. Age is also a major risk factor for hearing loss. Age-related hearing loss (presbycusis) is thought to have both genetic and environmental influences.

Section 20.2

Usher Syndrome

This section includes text excerpted from "Usher Syndrome," National Institute on Deafness and Other Communication Disorders (NIDCD), March 16, 2017.

What Is Usher Syndrome?

Usher syndrome is the most common condition that affects both hearing and vision; sometimes it also affects balance. The major symptoms of Usher syndrome are deafness or hearing loss and an eye disease called "retinitis pigmentosa" (RP).

Deafness or hearing loss in Usher syndrome is caused by abnormal development of hair cells (sound receptor cells) in the inner ear. Most children with Usher syndrome are born with moderate to profound hearing loss, depending on the type. Less commonly, hearing loss from Usher syndrome appears during adolescence or later. Usher syndrome can also cause severe balance problems due to abnormal development of the vestibular hair cells, sensory cells that detect gravity and head movement.

RP initially causes night-blindness and a loss of peripheral (side) vision through the progressive degeneration of cells in the retina. The retina is the light-sensitive tissue at the back of the eye and is crucial for vision. As RP progresses, the field of vision narrows until only central vision remains, a condition called "tunnel vision." Cysts in the macula (the central part of the retina) and cataracts (clouding of the lens) can sometimes cause an early decline in central vision in people with Usher syndrome.

Who Is Affected by Usher Syndrome?

Usher syndrome affects approximately 4 to 17 per 100,000 people and accounts for about 50 percent of all hereditary deaf-blindness cases. The condition is thought to account for 3 to 6 percent of all children who are deaf, and another 3 to 6 percent of children who are hard-of-hearing.

What Causes Usher Syndrome

Usher syndrome is inherited, which means that it is passed from parents to a child through their genes. Each person inherits 2 copies of

245

a gene, 1 from each parent. Sometimes genes are altered, or mutated. Mutated genes may cause cells to develop or act abnormally.

Usher syndrome is inherited as an autosomal recessive disorder. "Autosomal" means that men and women are equally likely to have the disorder and equally likely to pass it on to a child of either sex. "Recessive" means that the condition occurs only when a child inherits 2 copies of the same faulty gene, one from each parent. A person with 1 abnormal Usher gene does not have the disorder but is a carrier who has a 50 percent chance of passing on the abnormal gene to each child. When 2 carriers with the same mutated Usher syndrome gene have a child together, each birth has a:

- One-in-four chance of having a child who neither has Usher syndrome nor is a carrier

- Two-in-four chance of having a child who is an unaffected carrier

- One-in-four chance of having a child who has Usher syndrome

What Are the Characteristics of the Three Types of Usher Syndrome?

There are 3 types of Usher syndrome. In the United States, types 1 and 2 are the most common. Together, they account for up to 95 percent of Usher syndrome cases.

Type 1. Children with type 1 Usher syndrome have profound hearing loss or deafness at birth and have severe balance problems. Many obtain little or no benefit from hearing aids but may be candidates for a cochlear implant—an electronic device that can provide a sense of sound to people with severe hearing loss or deafness. Parents should consult with their child's doctor and other hearing health professionals early to determine communication options for their child. Intervention should begin promptly, when the brain is most receptive to learning language, whether spoken or signed.

Balance problems associated with type 1 Usher syndrome delay sitting up without support. Walking rarely occurs prior to 18 months. Vision problems with type 1 Usher syndrome usually begin before 10 years of age, starting with difficulty seeing at night and progressing to severe vision loss over several decades.

Type 2. Children with type 2 Usher syndrome are born with moderate to severe hearing loss but normal balance. Although the severity of hearing loss varies, most children with type 2 Usher syndrome can communicate orally and benefit from hearing aids. RP is usually diagnosed during late adolescence in people with type 2 Usher syndrome.

Type 3. Children with type 3 Usher syndrome have normal hearing at birth. Most have normal to near-normal balance, but some develop balance problems with age. Decline in hearing and vision varies. Children with type 3 Usher syndrome often develop hearing loss by adolescence, requiring hearing aids by mid-to-late adulthood. Night blindness also usually begins during adolescence. Blind spots appear by the late teens to early twenties. Legal blindness often occurs by midlife.

How Is Usher Syndrome Diagnosed?

Diagnosis of Usher syndrome involves pertinent questions regarding the person's medical history and testing of hearing, balance, and vision. Early diagnosis is important, as it improves treatment success. An eye-care specialist can use dilating drops to examine the retina for signs of RP. Visual field testing measures peripheral vision. An electroretinogram (ERG) measures the electrical response of the eye's light-sensitive cells in the retina. Optical coherence tomography (OCT) may be helpful to assess for macular cystic changes. Videonystagmography (VNG) measures involuntary eye movements that could signify a balance problem. Audiology testing determines hearing sensitivity at a range of frequencies.

Genetic testing may help in diagnosing Usher syndrome. So far, researchers have found nine genes that cause Usher syndrome. Genetic testing is available for all of them:

- Type 1 Usher syndrome: *MY07A, USH1C, CDH23, PCHD15, USH1G*

- Type 2 Usher syndrome: *USH2A, GPR98, DFNB31*

- Type 3 Usher syndrome: *CLRN1*

Genetic testing for Usher syndrome may be available through clinical research studies.

How Is Usher Syndrome Treated?

Presently, there is no cure for Usher syndrome. Treatment involves managing hearing, vision, and balance problems. Early diagnosis helps tailor educational programs that consider the severity of hearing and vision loss and a child's age and ability. Treatment and communication services may include hearing aids, assistive listening devices (ALDs), cochlear implants (CI), auditory (hearing) training, and/or learning American Sign Language (ASL). Independent-living training may include orientation and mobility training for balance problems, Braille instruction, and low-vision services.

Vitamin A may slow the progression of RP, according to results from a long-term clinical trial supported by the National Eye Institute (NEI) and the Foundation Fighting Blindness (FFB). Based on the study, adults with a common form of RP may benefit from a daily supplement of 15,000 international units (IU) of the palmitate form of vitamin A. Patients should discuss this treatment option with their healthcare provider before proceeding. Because people with type 1 Usher syndrome did not take part in the study, high-dose vitamin A is not recommended for these patients.

General precautions for vitamin A supplementation:

- Do not substitute vitamin A palmitate with a beta-carotene supplement.

- Do not take vitamin A supplements greater than the recommended dose of 15,000 IU or modify your diet to select foods with high levels of vitamin A.

- Pregnant women should not take high-dose vitamin A supplements due to the increased risk of birth defects. Women considering pregnancy should stop taking high-dose vitamin A supplements for six months before trying to conceive.

Section 20.3

Waardenburg Syndrome

This section contains text excerpted from the following sources: Text beginning with the heading "What Is Waardenburg Syndrome?" is excerpted from "Waardenburg Syndrome," Genetics Home Reference (GHR), National Institutes of Health (NIH), January 29, 2019; Text beginning with the heading "Can People with Waardenburg Syndrome Have Two Brown Eyes?" is excerpted from "Waardenburg Syndrome," Genetic and Rare Diseases Information Center (GARD), National Center for Advancing Translational Sciences (NCATS), February 11, 2016.

What Is Waardenburg Syndrome?

Waardenburg syndrome (WS) is a group of genetic conditions that can cause hearing loss and changes in coloring (pigmentation) of the hair, skin, and eyes. Although most people with WS have normal hearing, moderate to profound hearing loss can occur in one or both ears. The hearing loss is present from birth (congenital). People with this condition often have very pale blue eyes or different colored eyes, such as one blue eye and one brown eye. Sometimes one eye has segments of two different colors. Distinctive hair coloring (such as a patch of white hair or hair that prematurely turns gray) is another common sign of the condition. The features of WS vary among affected individuals, even among people in the same family.

There are four recognized types of WS, which are distinguished by their physical characteristics and sometimes by their genetic cause. Types I and II have very similar features, although people with type I almost always have eyes that appear widely spaced and people with type II do not. In addition, hearing loss occurs more often in people with type II than in those with type I. Type III (sometimes called "Klein-Waardenburg syndrome") includes abnormalities of the arms and hands, in addition to hearing loss and changes in pigmentation. Type IV (also known as "Waardenburg-Shah syndrome") has signs and symptoms of both WS and Hirschsprung disease, an intestinal disorder that causes severe constipation or blockage of the intestine.

Frequency and Causes of Waardenburg Syndrome

WS affects an estimated 1 in 40,000 people. It accounts for 2 to 5 percent of all cases of congenital hearing loss. Types I and II are the most common forms of WS, while types III and IV are rare.

Mutations in the *EDN3*, *EDNRB*, *MITF*, *PAX3*, *SNAI2*, and *SOX10* genes can cause WS. These genes are involved in the formation and development of several types of cells, including pigment-producing cells called "melanocytes." Melanocytes make a pigment called "melanin," which contributes to skin, hair, and eye color and plays an essential role in the normal function of the inner ear. Mutations in any of these genes disrupt the normal development of melanocytes, leading to abnormal pigmentation of the skin, hair, and eyes and problems with hearing.

WS types I and III are caused by mutations in the *PAX3* gene. Mutations in the *MITF* or *SNAI2* gene can cause WS type II.

Mutations in the *SOX10*, *EDN3*, or *EDNRB* gene can cause WS type IV. In addition to melanocyte development, these genes are important for the development of nerve cells in the large intestine. Mutations in one of these genes result in hearing loss, changes in pigmentation, and intestinal problems related to Hirschsprung disease.

In some cases, the genetic cause of WS has not been identified.

Can People with Waardenburg Syndrome Have Two Brown Eyes?

Yes. People can have WS without having some type of heterochromia iridis. In general, heterochromia iridis is less common in affected people than the hair and skin features of WS.

In WS type I for example, heterochromia iridis is present in 15 to 31 percent of affected people, and hypoplastic blue irides is present in 15 to 18 percent of affected people. Ocular features are more common in WS type II than in type I.

Are People with Waardenburg Syndrome Born with a White Forelock or Can It Develop Later?

The white forelock may be present at birth, or it may appear later (typically in the teen years). It can also become normally pigmented over time. Red and black forelocks have also been described. The majority of people with WS type one have either a white forelock, or early graying of scalp hair (before age 30).

What Type of Digestive Problems Can Be Associated with Waardenburg Syndrome?

Type IV WS (also called "Waardenburg-Shah syndrome") is characterized by symptoms of Hirschsprung disease in addition to the classic features of hearing loss and pigmentation abnormalities. Hirschsprung disease is a digestive (gastrointestinal) disorder in which nerves are missing from part of the bowel, impairing the ability to move material through the bowel. This causes a blockage, which in turn causes contents of the intestine to build up behind the blockage. As a result, the bowel and abdomen swell. We are not aware of other gastrointestinal (GI) problems typically associated with WS.

How Is Waardenburg Syndrome Diagnosed?

A diagnosis of WS is made based on the presence of signs and symptoms. In 1992, the Waardenburg Consortium proposed diagnostic criteria, which includes both major and minor criteria. A diagnosis of WS type I (the most common type) needs two major, or one major and two minor of the following criteria:

Major Criteria

- Congenital sensorineural hearing loss (present from birth)
- Iris pigmentary (coloration) abnormality, such as heterochromia iridis (complete, partial, or segmental); pale blue eyes (isohypochromia iridis); or pigmentary abnormalities of the fundus (part of the eye opposite the pupil)
- Abnormalities of hair pigmentation, such as white forelock (lock of hair above the forehead), or loss of hair color
- Dystopia canthorum—lateral displacement of inner angles (canthi) of the eyes (in WS types I and III only)
- Having a first degree relative with Waardenburg syndrome

Minor Criteria

- Leukoderma (white patches of skin) present from birth
- Synophrys (connected eyebrows, or "unibrow") or medial eyebrow flare
- Broad or high nasal bridge (uppermost part of the nose)
- Hypoplasia (incomplete development) of the nostrils
- Premature gray hair (under the age of 30)

WS type II has features similar to type I, but the inner canthi of the eyes are normal (no dystopia canthorum present).

WS type III also has similar features to WS type I, but is additionally characterized by musculoskeletal abnormalities, such as muscle hypoplasia; flexion contractures (inability to straighten joints); or syndactyly (webbed or fused fingers or toes).

WS type IV has similar features to WS type II, but with Hirschsprung disease (a condition resulting from missing nerve cells in the muscles of part or all of the large intestine).

Chapter 21

Huntington Disease

What Is Huntington Disease?

Huntington disease (HD) is an inherited disease that causes the progressive dying off, or degeneration, of nerve cells in certain parts of the brain. American physician George Huntington wrote the first thorough description of Huntington disease in 1872, calling it "hereditary chorea" to underscore some of its key features. Chorea is derived from the Greek word for dance and describes the uncontrollable dance-like movements seen in people with HD. The hereditary nature of HD helps distinguish it from other types of chorea with infectious, metabolic, or hormonal causes. Understanding the hereditary nature of HD eventually enabled modern researchers to pinpoint the cause of the disease—a mutation or misspelling in a single gene.

More than 30,000 Americans have HD. Although the mutation is present from birth, symptoms of HD typically appear in middle age (adult HD), and in rare cases, they appear in children (juvenile HD). The disease, which gets progressively worse, attacks motor control regions of the brain, as well as other areas. Chorea, abnormal body

This chapter contains text excerpted from the following sources: Text beginning with the heading "What Is Huntington Disease?" is excerpted from "Huntington's Disease: Hope through Research," National Institute of Neurological Disorders and Stroke (NINDS), December 31, 2018; Text beginning with the heading "Treatment of Huntington Disease" is excerpted from "Huntington Disease," Genetic and Rare Diseases Information Center (GARD), National Center for Advancing Translational Sciences (NCATS), July 8, 2015. Reviewed March 2019.

postures, and impaired coordination are among the most visible symptoms. But HD also causes changes in emotion and cognition (thinking) that can be devastating for people with the disorder and for their families.

Although there is no cure for HD, treatments are available to help manage its symptoms and other potential treatments are under investigation to slow or stop its course. And there are now genetic tests available for HD, which gives people at risk for the disease the option to plan for their health and the health of future generations.

How Does Huntington Disease Affect the Brain?

The most severe loss of nerve cells (also called "neurons") occurs in deep brain structures called the "basal ganglia," especially in a part of the basal ganglia called the "striatum." The basal ganglia have a variety of functions, including helping to control voluntary (intentional) movement. Subsections of the basal ganglia called the "caudate nuclei" (CN) and putamen, are most severely affected. Another strongly affected area is the brain's outer surface, or cerebral cortex, which has important roles in the movement, as well as thought, perception, memory, and emotion. As HD progresses over time, neuronal degeneration becomes more widespread throughout the brain. In addition to metabolic changes, there is degeneration in areas of the brain that control hormones.

How Is Huntington Disease Inherited?

HD is passed from parent to child through a mutation in a gene. Genes contain the blueprint for who we are, from our outer appearance to the composition and workings of our internal organs, including the brain. The gene responsible for HD lies on chromosome 4.

When a parent has HD, each child has a 50 percent chance of inheriting the copy of chromosome 4 that carries the HD mutation. If a child does not inherit the HD mutation, she or he will not develop the disease and cannot pass it to subsequent generations. In some families, all the children may inherit the HD gene; in others, none do. Whether one child inherits the gene has no bearing on whether others will or will not share the same fate. A person who inherits the HD mutation and survives long enough will develop the disease.

To understand the HD gene mutation, it helps to know a little more about what genes are and what they do. Genes contain the instructions for making the approximately one million proteins that run everything in our bodies. The HD gene makes an essential protein called "huntingtin," whose function is largely unknown but may be necessary for early nerve cell development. Huntingtin is most active in the brain. Genes are composed of deoxyribonucleic acid (DNA), a long chain-like molecule. The links in a DNA chain are called "bases," or nucleotides, and there are four varieties — adenine, thymine, cytosine, and guanine — typically abbreviated as A, T, C, and G. Within each gene, a unique combination of these nucleotides serves as a code that determines the gene's function; changes in the code — such as through a mutation — can change a gene's function.

The disease-causing mutation inside the HD gene consists of a three-base sequence repeated many times. This type of mutation, called a "triplet" (or trinucleotide) repeat expansion, is responsible for dozens of other neurological diseases, but in each case, the triplet, resides within a different gene. The triplet sequences also vary; in HD, the triplet consists of the bases C-A-G. Most people have fewer than 27 CAG repeats in the HD gene and are not at risk for the disease. Individuals with the disease may have 36 or more repeats. People who have repeated in the intermediate range (27 to 35) are unlikely to develop the disease, but they could pass it on to future generations.

Table 21.1. Number of CAG Repeats

Number of CAG Repeats	Outcome
< 26	Normal range; individual will not develop HD
27 to 35	Individual will not develop HD but the next generation is at risk
35 to 39	Some, but not all, individuals in this range will develop HD; next generation is also at risk
> 40	Individual will develop HD

When HD occurs without a family history, it is called "sporadic HD." These cases can occur when one parent has an intermediate range of CAG repeats, sometimes called a "premutation." Prior to the conception of a child, the number of repeats may expand into the disease-causing range. Most often, these expansions occur in the father's sperm cells, rather than in the mother's egg cells. Each time the father's DNA is copied to make new sperm, there is a possibility for the number of CAG repeats to expand. This increase in disease severity from one generation to the next — with a younger onset and faster progression — is called "anticipation."

What Are the Major Effects of Huntington Disease?

Early signs of the disease vary greatly from person to person, but typically include cognitive or psychiatric symptoms, difficulties with movement, and behavioral changes. Symptoms of HD include:

- **Behavioral changes.** The individual experiences mood swings or becomes uncharacteristically irritable, apathetic, passive, depressed, or angry. These symptoms may lessen as the disease progresses or, in some individuals, may continue and include hostile outbursts, thoughts of suicide, deep bouts of depression, and, rarely, psychosis. Social withdrawal is common.

- **Cognitive/judgment changes.** HD may affect a person's judgment, attention, and other cognitive functions. Early signs might include having trouble with driving, problem-solving or decision making, prioritizing tasks, and difficulty organizing, learning new things, remembering a fact, putting thoughts into words, or answering a question. Familiar tasks that were simple to complete when the individual was healthy now take longer or cannot be done at all. As the disease progresses, these cognitive problems worsen and affected individuals are no longer able to work, drive, or care for themselves. When the level of cognitive impairment is significant enough to impair daily functioning, it is described as dementia. Many people, however, remain aware of their environment and are able to express emotions. Some individuals cannot recognize other family members.

- **Uncontrolled and difficult movement.** Movement problems may begin with uncontrolled movement in the fingers, feet, face, or trunk. These movements, which are signs of chorea, often intensify when the person is anxious or distracted and become larger and more apparent over time. HD can also begin with mild clumsiness or problems with balance. Some people develop chorea-related movements. Chorea often creates serious problems with walking, increasing the likelihood of falls. Some individuals with HD do not develop chorea; instead, they may become rigid and move very little, or not at all, a condition called "akinesia." Others may start out with chorea but become rigid as the disease progresses. In addition to chorea, some individuals have unusual fixed postures, called "dystonia." The two-movement disorders can blend or alternate. Other symptoms may include tremor (unintentional rhythmic muscle movement in a back-and-forth manner) and abnormal eye movements that often occur early.

- **Physical changes.** Speech becomes slurred and vital functions, such as swallowing, eating, speaking, and especially walking, continue to decline. Many people with HD lose weight as they encounter problems with feeding, swallowing, choking, and chest infections. Other symptoms may include insomnia, loss of energy, and fatigue. Some individuals with HD develop seizures. Eventually, the person will be confined to a bed or wheelchair.

In general, the duration of the illness ranges from 10 to 30 years. The most common causes of death are an infection (most often pneumonia) and injuries related to falls.

At What Age Does Huntington Disease Appear?

The rate of disease progression and the age at onset vary from person to person. As a general rule, having a higher number of CAG repeats is associated with an earlier onset and faster course of the disease. A common observation is that the earlier the symptoms appear, the faster the disease progresses.

Adult Huntington Disease

Adult-onset HD most often begins between ages 30 to 50. A few individuals develop HD after age 55. Diagnosis of these people can be very difficult. The symptoms of HD may be masked by or confused with other health problems, or the person may not display the severity of symptoms seen in individuals with HD of earlier onset. These individuals may also show symptoms of depression rather than anger or irritability, or they may retain sharp control over their intellectual functions, such as memory, reasoning, and problem-solving.

There is also a related disorder called "senile chorea." Some elderly individuals develop choreic movements, but do not become demented, have a normal HD gene, and lack a family history of the disorder. Some scientists believe that a different gene mutation may account for this small number of cases, but this has not been proven.

Juvenile Huntington Disease

Some individuals develop symptoms of HD before 20 years of age. This is called "early-onset" or "juvenile HD." A common early sign of juvenile HD is a rapid decline in school performance. Movement problems soon become apparent, but they differ from the chorea typically seen in adult-onset HD. One common motor symptom in juvenile HD is myoclonus, which involves rapid involuntary muscle twitches or jerks. Other motor symptoms typical in juvenile HD include slowness, rigidity (in which the muscles remain constantly tense), and tremor. This constellation of symptoms can resemble Parkinson disease (PD) and is sometimes called "akinetic-rigid" HD or the Westphal variant of HD. People with juvenile HD may also have seizures and mental disabilities. The earlier the onset, the faster the disease seems to progress. The disease progresses most rapidly in individuals with juvenile or early-onset HD, and death often follows within 10 years.

Individuals with juvenile HD usually inherit the disease from their fathers, who typically have a later onset form of HD themselves. To verify the link between the number of CAG repeats in the HD gene and the age at onset of symptoms, scientists studied a boy who developed HD symptoms at the age of two, one of the youngest and most severe cases ever recorded. They found that he had nearly 100 repeats. The boy's case was central to the identification of the HD gene and at the same time helped confirm that juveniles with HD have the longest segments of CAG repeats. This correlation has been confirmed in other studies.

How Is Huntington Disease Diagnosed?

A diagnosis of HD is generally based on findings from neurological, psychological, and genetic testing.

- **Neurological tests**. A neurologist will interview the individual intensively to obtain the medical history and rule out other conditions. Tests of neurological and physical functions may review reflexes, balance, movement, muscle tone, hearing, walking, and mental status. A number of laboratory tests may be ordered as well, and individuals with HD may be referred to other healthcare professionals, such as psychiatrists, genetic counselors, clinical neuropsychologists, or speech pathologists for specialized management and/or diagnostic clarification.

- A tool used by physicians to diagnose HD is to take the family history, sometimes called a "pedigree" or "genealogy." It is extremely important for family members to be candid and truthful with a professional who is taking a family history since another family member(s) may not have been accurately diagnosed with the disease but thought to have other issues.

- **Genetic tests**. The most effective and accurate method of testing for HD—called the "direct genetic test"—counts the number of CAG repeats in the HD gene, using DNA taken from a blood sample. The presence of 36 or more repeats supports a diagnosis of HD. A test result of 26 or fewer repeats rules out HD. A small percentage of individuals will have repeats in a borderline range. For such individuals, doctors may try to get a clearer picture of disease risk by asking other family members to come in for examination and genetic testing.

- Prior to the availability of the direct genetic test, clinics used a method called "linkage testing." This older method requires a sample of DNA from a closely related affected relative, preferably a parent, for the purpose of identifying markers close to the HD gene. A version of the linkage method is sometimes still used for prenatal testing.

- **Diagnostic imaging**. In some cases, especially if a person's family history and genetic testing are inconclusive, the physician may recommend brain imaging, such as computed tomography (CT) or, more likely, magnetic resonance imaging (MRI). As the disease progresses, these scans typically reveal shrinkage of the striatum and parts of the cortex, and enlargement of fluid-filled cavities within the brain called "ventricles." These changes do not necessarily indicate HD, however, because they can occur in other disorders. Conversely, a person can have early symptoms of HD and still have normal findings on a structural CT or magnetic resonance imaging scan.

What Is Predictive Testing and How Is It Done?

A predictive or presymptomatic genetic test is an option for someone who has a family history of HD but shows no symptoms. Genetic testing makes it possible to predict with a higher degree of certainty whether or not the person will develop HD.

The decision to undergo presymptomatic testing is highly personal and often difficult one to make. Common reasons that people choose to take the test include planning for marriage, children, education and career decisions, finances, stress, or simply to relieve uncertainty.

Centers across the United States offer genetic testing for HD, as well as pre- and post-test counseling. A list of such centers is available from the Huntington Disease Society of America (HDSA) at 800-345-4372 (hdsa.org). With the participation of families with HD, researchers and health professionals have developed guidelines for HD genetic testing. A team of specialists will help the at-risk person decide if testing is the right choice, and will carefully prepare the person for a negative, positive, or inconclusive test result. Whatever the results of genetic testing, the at-risk individual and family members can expect powerful and complex emotional responses. Because receiving test results may prove to be devastating, testing guidelines call for continued counseling even after the test is complete and the results are known.

In order to protect the interests of minors, including confidentiality, testing is not recommended for those under the age of 18 unless there is a compelling medical reason (for example, the child is exhibiting symptoms).

Treatment of Huntington Disease

Unfortunately, there is currently no cure for HD. The current goal of treatment is to slow down the course of the disease and help affected people function for as long and as comfortable as possible.

Current treatment strategies involve the use of various medications to treat specific symptoms, such as abnormal movements and behaviors. Depression and suicide are more common among affected people, so caregivers should monitor for associated symptoms and seek help if necessary. As symptoms of the disease worsen, affected people need more assistance, supervision, and care.

Prognosis for Huntington Disease

Huntington disease is progressive, eventually leading to disability and death (usually from a coexisting illness or infection). However, the disease affects everyone differently; the age of onset, specific symptoms, and the rate of progression varies for each person with HD.

While the symptoms of HD are well-characterized, their progression (especially in the early and middle stages) remains unpredictable. With the approach of late-stage HD, affected people have speech difficulty and weight loss. In the late stage, affected people lose bowel and bladder control.

The duration of the disease (from onset until death) varies considerably, with an average of approximately 19 years. Most people with HD survive for 10 to 25 years after the onset of symptoms. The average age at death ranges from 51 to 57 years, but the range may be broader. In a large study, pneumonia and cardiovascular (heart) disease (CVD) were the most common primary causes of death.

The length of the CAG repeat (the type of mutation in the *HTT* gene responsible for HD) is the most important factor that determines age of onset of HD. However, there is still a lot of variabilities. Both genetic and environmental factors are thought to play a role in the age of onset in people with a mutation. Inheritance through the father can lead to more repeat expansion and earlier onset through succeeding generations, a phenomenon called "anticipation."

People with HD, family members, and/or caregivers with specific questions about the prognosis should speak with their healthcare provider.

Chapter 22

Hypohidrotic Ectodermal Dysplasia

Hypohidrotic ectodermal dysplasia (HED) is one of more than 100 types of ectodermal dysplasia. Starting before birth, these disorders result in the abnormal development of ectodermal tissues, particularly the skin, hair, nails, teeth, and sweat glands.

Most people with HED have a reduced ability to sweat (hypohidrosis) because they have fewer sweat glands than normal or their sweat glands do not function properly. Sweating is a major way that the body controls its temperature; as sweat evaporates from the skin, it cools the body. Reduced sweating can lead to a dangerously high body temperature (hyperthermia), particularly in hot weather. In some cases, hyperthermia can cause life-threatening health problems.

Affected individuals tend to have sparse scalp and body hair (hypotrichosis). The hair is often light-colored, brittle, and slow-growing. HED is also characterized by several missing teeth (hypodontia) or teeth that are malformed. The teeth that are present erupt from the gums later than usual and are frequently small and pointed.

This chapter contains text excerpted from the following sources: Text in this chapter begins with excerpts from "Hypohidrotic Ectodermal Dysplasia," Genetics Home Reference (GHR), National Institutes of Health (NIH), November 2018; Text beginning with the heading "Diagnosis of Hypohidrotic Ectodermal Dysplasia" is excerpted from "Hypohidrotic Ectodermal Dysplasia," Genetic and Rare Diseases Information Center (GARD), National Center for Advancing Translational Sciences (NCATS), January 21, 2014. Reviewed March 2019.

Some people with HED have distinctive facial features, including a prominent forehead, thick lips, and a flattened bridge of the nose. Additional features of this condition can include thin, wrinkled, and dark-colored skin around the eyes; chronic skin problems, such as eczema; and a bad-smelling discharge from the nostrils (ozena).

Intellectual ability and growth are typically normal in people with HED.

Frequency and Causes

HED is the most common form of ectodermal dysplasia. It is estimated to occur in 1 in 20,000 newborns worldwide.

HED is a genetic condition that can result from mutations in one of several genes. These include ectodysplasin A (*EDA*), ectodysplasin A receptor (*EDAR*), *EDAR* associated death domain (*EDARADD*), and Wnt family member 10A (*WNT10A*). *EDA* gene mutations are the most common cause of the disorder, accounting for more than half of all cases. *EDAR, EDARADD*, and *WNT10A* gene mutations each account for a smaller percentage of cases. In about 10 percent of people with HED, the genetic cause is unknown.

The *EDA, EDAR,* and *EDARADD* genes provide instructions for making proteins that work together during embryonic development. These proteins form part of a signaling pathway that is critical for the interaction between two cell layers, the ectoderm, and the mesoderm. In the early embryo, these cell layers form the basis for many of the body's organs and tissues. Ectoderm-mesoderm interactions are essential for the formation of several structures that arise from the ectoderm, including the skin, hair, nails, teeth, and sweat glands.

Mutations in the *EDA, EDAR,* or *EDARADD* gene prevent normal interactions between the ectoderm and the mesoderm, which impairs the normal development of skin, hair, nails, teeth, and sweat glands. Mutations in any of these three genes lead to the major signs and symptoms of HDA described above.

The *WNT10A* gene provides instructions for making a protein that is part of a different signaling pathway known as "Wnt signaling." Wnt signaling controls the activity of certain genes and regulates the interactions between cells during embryonic development. Signaling involving the *WNT10A* protein is critical for the development of ectodermal structures, particularly the teeth. The *WNT10A* gene mutations that cause HDA impair the protein's function, which disrupts the development of teeth and other structures that arise from the ectodermal cell layer.

When HED results from *WNT10A* gene mutations, its features are more variable than when the condition is caused by mutations in the *EDA, EDAR*, or *EDARADD* gene. Signs and symptoms range from mild to severe, and mutations in the *WNT10A* gene are more likely to cause all of the permanent (adult) teeth to be missing.

Diagnosis of Hypohidrotic Ectodermal Dysplasia

Genetic testing for HED is available. In most cases, HED can be diagnosed after infancy based upon the physical features in the affected child. Genetic testing may be ordered to confirm the diagnosis. Other reasons for testing may include to identify carriers or for prenatal diagnosis.

Clinical testing is available for detection of disease-causing mutations in the *EDA, EDAR*, and *EDARADD* genes. You should speak with a healthcare provider or a genetics professional to learn more about your testing options.

The Genetic Testing Registry (GTR) provides information about the genetic tests for this condition. The intended audience for the GTR is healthcare providers and researchers. Patients and consumers with specific questions about a genetic test should contact a healthcare provider or a genetics professional.

Treatment of Hypohidrotic Ectodermal Dysplasia

There is no specific treatment for HED. The condition is managed by treating the various symptoms. For patients with abnormal or no sweat glands, it is recommended that they live in places with air conditioning at home, school, and work. In order to maintain normal body temperature, they should frequently drink cool liquids and wear cool clothing. Dental defects can be managed with dentures and implants. Artificial tears are used to prevent cornea damage for patients that do not produce enough tears. Surgery to repair a cleft palate is also helpful in improving speech and facial deformities.

Chapter 23

Inborn Errors of Metabolism

Chapter Contents

Section 23.1

General Information about Inborn Errors of Metabolism

This section includes text excerpted from "The NIH Mini Study: Metabolism, Infection and Immunity in Inborn Errors of Metabolism," National Human Genome Research Institute (NHGRI), February 22, 2013. Reviewed March 2019.

What Are Inborn Errors of Metabolism?

Metabolism is a sequence of chemical reactions that take place in cells in the body. These reactions are responsible for the breakdown of nutrients and the generation of energy in our bodies. Inborn errors of metabolism (IEM) are a group of disorders that causes a block in a metabolic pathway, leading to clinically significant consequences.

Specific chemical compounds, called "enzymes," are responsible for the reactions that make up metabolism. There are also co-factors, or compounds, that help enzymes carry out their reactions.

What Are the Different Forms of Inborn Errors of Metabolism?

The different IEM are usually named for the enzyme that is not working properly. For example, if the enzyme carbamoyl phosphate synthetase 1 (CPS1) is not working, the IEM is called "CPS1 deficiency."

Table 23.1. Inborn Errors of Metabolism

IEM	Examples
Urea cycle disorders	Ornithine transcarbamylase deficiency, citrullinemia, argininosuccinic aciduria, argininemia
Organic acidemias	Propionic acidemia, methylmalonic aciduria, isovaleric acidemia, glutaric acidemia, maple syrup urine disease
Fatty acid oxidation defects	Medium chain acyl-CoA dehydrogenase deficiency, carnitine palmitoyltransferase 1 deficiency, long chain hydroxyacyl-CoA dehydrogenase deficiency
Aminoacidopathies	Tyrosinemia, phenylketonuria, homocystinuria
Carbohydrate disorders	Galactosemia, fructosemia
Mitochondrial disorders	MELAS, MERFF, pyruvate dehydrogenase deficiency

What Causes the Inborn Errors of Metabolism, and How Are the Different Forms Inherited

The IEM are caused by mutations (or alterations) in the genes that tell our cells how to make the enzymes and the cofactors for metabolism. A mutation causes a gene to not function at all or not to function as well as it should. Most often these altered genes are inherited from parent(s), but they may also occur spontaneously.

When discussing how genetic conditions are passed on in a family, it is important to understand that we have two copies of most genes, with one copy inherited from our mother and one copy inherited from our father. This is not the case for the genes that are on our sex chromosomes (the "X" and "Y" chromosomes). These are different in men and women: men have only one X chromosome and, therefore, only one copy of the genes on that chromosome, while women have two X chromosomes and, therefore, have two copies of the genes on that chromosome. A father passes on his X chromosome to all of his daughters and his Y chromosome on to all of his sons. A mother passes on an X chromosome to each child.

What Is the Chance of Having an Inborn Errors of Metabolism If Someone Else in the Family Has It?

The chance that someone else in the family has the same IEM as their relative depends on the inheritance pattern of the IEM, whether the at-risk family member is male or female, and the rest of the family history (how many relatives have been diagnosed with the disorder already and whether genetic testing has been performed in other relatives). In some cases, the age of the at-risk family member and whether or not they have shown any signs or symptoms of the disorder is helpful in estimating the chances that they also have the disorder.

What Are the Symptoms of Inborn Errors of Metabolism and How Are They Diagnosed?

In general, the earlier someone develops symptoms of an IEM, the more severe their disorder. The severity of symptoms is generally based on:

- The position of the defective enzyme within the metabolic pathway
- Whether or not there is any functional enzyme or cofactor being produced

However, other environmental and genetic factors may play a role in determining the severity of symptoms for a given patient.

IEM are multisystemic diseases and, thus patients may present a variety of symptoms, many of which depend on the specific metabolic pathway(s) involved. Some findings in patients with IEM may include elevated acid levels in the blood, low blood sugar, high blood ammonia, abnormal liver function tests, and blood cell abnormalities. Certain patients may also have neurologic abnormalities, such as seizures and developmental delays. Growth may also be affected.

How Are Inborn Errors of Metabolism Treated?

Treatment of IEM is tailored to the specific disorder once a diagnosis is made. In general, the goals of treatment are to minimize or eliminate the buildup of toxic metabolites that result from the block in metabolism while maintaining growth and development. This may be accomplished by special modified diets, supplements, and medications.

Section 23.2

Biotinidase Deficiency

This section contains text excerpted from the following sources: Text in this section begins with excerpts from "Biotinidase Deficiency," Genetic and Rare Diseases Information Center (GARD), National Center for Advancing Translational Sciences (NCATS), August 4, 2015. Reviewed March 2019; Text beginning with the heading "Causes of Biotinidase Deficiency" is excerpted from "Biotinidase Deficiency," Genetics Home Reference (GHR), National Institutes of Health (NIH), December 2014. Reviewed March 2019.

Biotinidase deficiency (BTD) is an inherited disorder in which the body is unable to recycle the vitamin biotin. The disorder may become apparent in the first few months of life, or later in childhood. The more severe form of the disorder is called "profound biotinidase deficiency" and may cause delayed development, seizures, weak muscle tone (hypotonia), breathing problems, hearing and vision loss, problems with movement and balance (ataxia), skin rashes, hair loss (alopecia), and a fungal infection called "candidiasis." The milder form is called "partial biotinidase deficiency;" without treatment, affected children may experience hypotonia, skin rashes, and hair loss. In some cases, these symptoms only appear during illness, infection, or other times of stress on the body. BTD is caused by mutations in the *BTD* gene and is inherited in an autosomal recessive manner. Lifelong treatment with biotin can prevent symptoms and complications from occurring or improve them if they have already developed.

Symptoms of Biotinidase Deficiency

The signs and symptoms of BTD typically appear within the first few months of life, but the age of onset varies. Children with profound biotinidase deficiency, the more severe form of the condition, may have seizures, weak muscle tone (hypotonia), breathing problems, and delayed development. If left untreated, the disorder can lead to hearing loss, eye abnormalities and loss of vision, problems with movement and balance (ataxia), skin rashes, hair loss (alopecia), and candidiasis. Immediate treatment and lifelong management with biotin supplements can prevent many of these complications.

Partial biotinidase deficiency is a milder form of this condition. Affected children may experience hypotonia, skin rashes, and hair loss, but these problems may appear only during illness, infection, or other times of stress on the body.

Causes of Biotinidase Deficiency

Mutations in the *BTD* gene cause BTD. The *BTD* gene provides instructions for making an enzyme called "biotinidase." This enzyme recycles biotin, a vitamin B found in foods, such as liver, egg yolks, and milk. Biotinidase removes biotin that is bound to proteins in food, leaving the vitamin in its free (unbound) state. Free biotin is needed by enzymes called "biotin-dependent carboxylases" to break down fats, proteins, and carbohydrates. Because several of these enzymes are impaired in BTD, the condition is considered a form of multiple carboxylase deficiency.

Mutations in the *BTD* gene reduce or eliminate the activity of biotinidase. Profound biotinidase deficiency results when the activity of biotinidase is reduced to less than 10 percent of normal. Partial biotinidase deficiency occurs when biotinidase activity is reduced to between 10 percent and 30 percent of normal. Without enough of this enzyme, biotin cannot be recycled. The resulting shortage of free biotin impairs the activity of biotin-dependent carboxylases, leading to a buildup of potentially toxic compounds in the body. If the condition is not treated promptly, this buildup damages various cells and tissues, causing the signs and symptoms described above.

Frequency of Biotinidase Deficiency

Profound or partial biotinidase deficiency occurs in approximately 1 in 60,000 newborns.

Section 23.3

Galactosemia

This section includes text excerpted from "Galactosemia," Genetic and Rare Diseases Information Center (GARD), National Center for Advancing Translational Sciences (NCATS), October 11, 2018.

Galactosemia, which means "galactose in the blood," refers to a group of inherited disorders that impair the body's ability to process and produce energy from a sugar called "galactose." When people with galactosemia ingest foods or liquids containing galactose, undigested sugars build up in the blood.

Galactose is present in many foods, including all dairy products (milk and anything made from milk), many baby formulas, and some fruits and vegetables. The impaired ability to process galactose can be due to the deficiency of any of three enzymes, caused by mutations in different genes. There are three main types of galactosemia which are distinguished based on their genetic causes, signs and symptoms, and severity:

- **Classic galactosemia (type 1)** is the most common and severe type, caused by mutations in the *GALT* gene, and characterized by a complete deficiency of an enzyme called "galactose-1-phosphate uridyl transferase (GALT)." Early signs and symptoms include liver dysfunction, susceptibility to infections, failure to thrive, and cataracts. These can usually be prevented or improved by early diagnosis and treatment, but other progressive or long-term problems are common despite treatment. These include intellectual deficits, movement disorders, and premature ovarian failure (in females).

- **Galactokinase deficiency (type 2)** is caused by mutations in the *GALK1* gene and characterized by a deficiency of the enzyme galactokinase 1. This type typically causes only the development of cataracts, which may be prevented or resolved with treatment. Rarely, this type causes pseudotumor cerebri (PTC) (a condition which mimics the symptoms of a large brain tumor when no brain tumor is present).

- **Galactose epimerase deficiency (type 3)** is caused by mutations in the *GALE* gene and characterized by a deficiency of the enzyme UDP-galactose-4-epimerase. Symptoms and severity of this type depend on whether the deficiency is confined to certain types of blood cells or is present in all tissues. Some people with this type have no signs or symptoms, while others have symptoms similar to those with classic galactosemia. Like in classic galactosemia, many symptoms can be prevented or improved with treatment.

There is also a "variant" of classic galactosemia called "duarte variant galactosemia," in which a person has mutations in the *GALT* gene but has only partial deficiency of the enzyme. Infants with this form may have jaundice, which resolves when switched to a low-galactose formula. Some studies have found that people with this form are at increased risk for mild neurodevelopmental problems, but other studies have found there is no increased risk. The risk may depend on the extent of the deficiency.

Inheritance of all types of galactosemia is autosomal recessive. The diagnosis may be suspected based on symptoms or results of newborn screening tests, and can be confirmed by measuring enzyme activity and genetic testing. Depending on the type of galactosemia, treatment may involve removing galactose from the diet (as soon as the disorder is suspected), calcium supplementation, and individualized care for any additional symptoms. The long-term outlook for people with galactosemia varies depending on the type, symptoms present, and commitment to the diet.

Is Breast Enlargement in Teen Boys Normal?

Yes. Around the time of puberty, about 50 to 60 percent of boys experience breast enlargement. In these boys, breast enlargement typically goes away within 6 months to 2 years of onset.

What Are Other Causes of Male Breast Development?

In addition to puberty, male breast enlargement can also be caused by certain drugs (e.g., human growth hormone (HGH), 5-alpha-reductase inhibitors (such as finasteride/propecia), liver scarring, malnutrition, kidney disease, hyperthyroidism, hypogonadism, and testicular tumors.

Can Dietary Soy Cause Male Breast Development?

From review of the literature, it appears that this question remains incompletely resolved. The answer is likely complex and may depend on age and a variety of other factors. Reports of feminization in humans consuming large quantities of soy are rare. Large population studies have reported small/subtle effects on growth.

The Micronutrient Information Center (www.lpi.oregonstate.edu/mic) at the Linus Pauling Institute is a rich source for information on nutrients and diet.

Section 23.4

Hereditary Fructose Intolerance

This section contains text excerpted from the following sources: Text in this section begins with excerpts from "Hereditary Fructose Intolerance," Genetics Home Reference (GHR), National Institutes of Health (NIH), February 5, 2019; Text under the heading "How Is Hereditary Fructose Intolerance Treated?" is excerpted from "Hereditary Fructose Intolerance," Genetic and Rare Diseases Information Center (GARD), National Center for Advancing Translational Sciences (NCATS), August 21, 2015. Reviewed March 2019.

Hereditary fructose intolerance (HFI) is a condition that affects a person's ability to digest the sugar fructose. Fructose is a simple sugar found primarily in fruits. Affected individuals develop signs and symptoms of the disorder in infancy when fruits, juices, or other foods containing fructose are introduced into the diet. After ingesting fructose, individuals with HFI may experience nausea, bloating, abdominal pain, diarrhea, vomiting, and low blood sugar (hypoglycemia). Affected infants may fail to grow and gain weight at the expected rate (failure to thrive).

Repeated ingestion of fructose-containing foods can lead to liver and kidney damage. The liver damage can result in a yellowing of the skin and whites of the eyes (jaundice), an enlarged liver (hepatomegaly), and chronic liver disease (cirrhosis). Continued exposure to fructose may result in seizures, coma, and ultimately death from liver and kidney failure. Due to the severity of symptoms experienced when fructose is ingested, most people with HFI develop a dislike for fruits, juices, and other foods containing fructose.

HFI should not be confused with a condition called "fructose malabsorption." In people with fructose malabsorption, the cells of the intestine cannot absorb fructose normally, leading to bloating, diarrhea or constipation, flatulence, and stomach pain. Fructose malabsorption is thought to affect approximately 40 percent of individuals in the Western hemisphere; its cause is unknown.

Frequency and Causes of Hereditary Fructose Intolerance

The incidence of HFI is estimated to be 1 in 20,000 to 30,000 individuals each year worldwide.

Mutations in the Aldolase B (*ALDOB*) gene cause HFI. The *ALDOB* gene provides instructions for making the aldolase B enzyme. This enzyme is found primarily in the liver and is involved in the breakdown (metabolism) of fructose so this sugar can be used as energy. Aldolase B is responsible for the second step in the metabolism of fructose, which breaks down the molecule fructose-1-phosphate into other molecules called "glyceraldehyde" and "dihydroxyacetone phosphate."

ALDOB gene mutations reduce the function of the enzyme, impairing its ability to metabolize fructose. A lack of functional aldolase B results in an accumulation of fructose-1-phosphate in liver cells. This buildup is toxic, resulting in the death of liver cells over time. Additionally, the breakdown products of fructose-1-phosphate are needed in the body to produce energy and to maintain blood sugar levels. The combination of decreased cellular energy, low blood sugar, and liver cell death leads to the features of HFI.

How Is Hereditary Fructose Intolerance Treated?

Complete elimination of fructose and sucrose from the diet is an effective treatment for most patients with HFI. This involves exclusion of anything containing fructose, sucrose, or sorbitol. Implementation and adherence to this diet is challenging. People following this diet can live normal and healthy lives, although the danger of inadvertent fructose ingestion remain. In extreme cases of life-threatening liver damage, liver transplants have been performed.

Section 23.5

Homocystinuria

This section includes text excerpted from "Homocystinuria," Genetic and Rare Diseases Information Center (GARD), National Center for Advancing Translational Sciences (NCATS), December 28, 2018.

Homocystinuria refers to a group of inherited disorders in which the body is unable to process certain building blocks of proteins (amino acids) properly. This leads to increased amounts of homocysteine and other amino acids in the blood and urine. The most common type of genetic homocystinuria, called "CBS deficiency," is caused by the lack of an enzyme known as "cystathionine beta-synthase (CBS)." Most states in the United States test for homocystinuria due to CBS deficiency at birth by newborn screening. Other types are less common, and are caused by different missing or nonworking enzymes. Homocystinuria can affect the eyes, skeleton, central nervous system (CNS), and the blood clotting system. Mutations in the *MTHFR, MTR, MTRR,* and *MMADHC* genes can cause homocystinuria. All these forms of homocystinuria are inherited in an autosomal recessive manner. Treatment and long-term outlook varies depending upon the cause of the disorder.

Symptoms of Homocystinuria

Symptoms of the most severe form of homocystinuria will start in infancy or early childhood. The first of these symptoms may be poor growth and failure to gain weight. Other people with homocystinuria may not have any symptoms until adulthood. The most common symptom seen in adults with homocystinuria is an abnormal blood clot.

Other symptoms of untreated homocystinuria can include:

Eye:

- Dislocation of the lens of the eye
- Nearsightedness

Skeletal:

- Caved-in chest (pectus excavatum)
- Curvature of the spine (scoliosis)
- Long, thin bones
- Osteoporosis (weak, brittle bones)

Central nervous system (CNS):

- Learning and intellectual disabilities
- Psychiatric problems

Blood and heart:

- Cardiovascular disease (CVD)
- Abnormal blood clots

Causes of Homocystinuria

Homocystinuria can be caused by mutations in several different genes. All of these genes are responsible for making enzymes that are involved in the way our body uses and processes amino acids. The most common gene associated with homocystinuria is the *CBS* gene that causes a lack of the enzyme, cystathionine beta-synthase. Rarer causes of homocystinuria include mutations in the *MTHFR, MTR, MTRR,* and *MMADHC* genes. It is not clear why high levels of homocysteine cause the symptoms seen in homocystinuria.

There are other, nongenetic causes of high levels of homocysteine. Nongenetic homocystinuria is not a rare condition. Some of the nongenetic causes are listed here.

- Vitamin B_6 or vitamin B_{12} deficiency
- Folate deficiency

- Low thyroid hormones (hypothyroidism)

- Obesity

- Diabetes

- High cholesterol

- Physical inactivity

- High blood pressure (HBP)

- Certain medications (such as carbamazepine, atorvastatin, fenofibrate, methotrexate, phenytoin, and nicotinic acid)

- Smoking

- Advanced age

Inheritance of Homocystinuria

The genetic forms of homocystinuria are inherited in an autosomal recessive pattern, which means both copies of the gene in every cell have mutations. This means that to have the condition, a person must have a mutation in both copies of the responsible gene in each cell. There is nothing either parent can do, before or during pregnancy, to cause a child to have this.

People with homocystinuria inherit one mutation from each of their parents. The parents, who each have one mutation, are known as "carriers." Carriers of an autosomal recessive condition typically do not have any signs or symptoms (they are unaffected). When two carriers of an autosomal recessive condition have children, each child has a:

- 25 percent chance to have the condition

- 50 percent chance to be an unaffected carrier like each parent

- 25 percent chance to be unaffected and not a carrier

Diagnosis of Homocystinuria

Most states in the United States test for homocystinuria due to CBS deficiency at birth by newborn screening. A baby that has a positive newborn screening test needs to have additional blood testing to look for high levels of homocysteine and methionine in the blood. Genetic testing can also be helpful for diagnosis.

A child or an adult with dislocation of the lens of the eye may also get tested for homocystinuria using blood and urine testing. In addition, a child or adult who has a blood clot, especially at an early age, may also get tested for homocystinuria.

Treatment of Homocystinuria

People who have the most severe form of homocystinuria are put on a special protein-restricted diet to reduce the blood levels of homocysteine and methionine. In addition, they may be given supplements including vitamin B_6, vitamin B_{12}, folate, and betaine. The recommendation is that these people stay on the protein-restricted diet for life. People with milder forms may be treated with supplements depending on the level of homocysteine in their blood.

Prognosis for Homocystinuria

Lowering the level of homocysteine in the blood, either with diet or supplements or both, can prevent symptoms. With treatment, people with the most severe form of homocystinuria can have normal growth and development. Some may still have eye problems or blood clots and should be monitored. Blood clots can be serious and cause organ damage.

Treatment for milder forms of homocystinuria may depend on clinical symptoms and the level of homocysteine in the blood.

Frequency of Homocystinuria

Approximately 1 in 200,000 to 1 in 300,000 people in the U.S. has the most common type of homocystinuria (homocystinuria due to CBS deficiency). In other countries, the prevalence is higher. In Qatar, about 1 in 1,800 people has this disorder and in Norway, about 1 in 6,400 people has it. Worldwide, it is thought that about 1 in 150,000 people has homocystinuria due to either a CBS or an *MTHFR* gene mutation. It is unclear how many people have homocystinuria due to other gene mutations.

Homocystinuria and Pregnancy

Pregnancy increases the risk for blood clots, stroke, and heart disease in women with homocystinuria, especially in the postpartum period. Most pregnancies, however, are uncomplicated. Prophylactic anticoagulation (preventing blood clots) during the third trimester of pregnancy and postpartum in women with homocystinuria is recommended to reduce risk of thromboembolism. Women are often given blood-thinning medication (such as heparin) during the last few months of pregnancy until about six weeks after delivery. Aspirin in low doses has also been given throughout pregnancy. The usual treatments for homocystinuria are typically continued during pregnancy. In addition to blood clots, untreated women are at higher risk for miscarriage and stillbirth.

Maternal homocystinuria does not appear to have major teratogenic effects (effects that can harm the development of the embryo or fetus) requiring additional counseling or, with respect to the fetus, more stringent management. Nevertheless, treatment with pyridoxine or methionine-restricted diet or both should be continued during pregnancy. Betaine may also be continued and appears not to be teratogenic.

A study in the *Journal of Inherited Metabolic Disease* (JIMD) obtained information on 11 women with maternal homocystinuria, their pregnancies (15 total), and their offspring. 5 women were pyridoxine-nonresponsive and 6 were pyridoxine-responsive. The authors reported there was no relationship between the severity of the homocystinuria or the therapies during pregnancy to either the pregnancy complications or the offspring outcomes. They stated that the infrequent occurrences of pregnancy complications, offspring abnormalities, and maternal thromboembolic events in the series suggest that pregnancy and outcome in maternal homocystinuria are usually normal. Nevertheless, a cautious approach would include careful monitoring of these pregnancies with attention to metabolic therapy and possibly anticoagulation.

Section 23.6

Maple Syrup Urine Disease

This section includes text excerpted from "Maple Syrup
Urine Disease," Genetic and Rare Diseases Information
Center (GARD), National Center for Advancing Translational
Sciences (NCATS), May 10, 2012. Reviewed March 2019.

What Is Maple Syrup Urine Disease?

Maple syrup urine disease (MSUD) is an inherited disorder in which
the body is unable to process certain protein building blocks (amino
acids) properly. Beginning in early infancy, this condition is characterized by poor feeding, vomiting, lack of energy (lethargy), seizures, and
developmental delay. The urine of affected infants has a distinctive
sweet odor, much like burned caramel, that gives the condition its
name. MSUD can be life-threatening if untreated.

Are There Different Types of Maple Syrup Urine Disease?

There are four general types of MSUD. The different types are
classified based on the amount and type of enzyme activity present in
the affected individual.

- **Classic maple syrup urine disease** is the most common type.
  Individuals with classic maple syrup urine disease have little
  or no enzyme activity (usually less than two percent of normal).
  Infants with this type of MSUD will show symptoms within the
  first several days of life. It is managed through diet with severe
  protein restriction.

- **Intermediate maple syrup urine disease** is a variant of the
  classic type. Individuals with intermediate maple syrup urine
  disease have a higher level of enzyme activity (approximately
  three to eight percent of normal) and can tolerate a greater
  amount of leucine. However, in periods of illness or fasting,
  these individuals may react like a child with the classic type of
  MSUD. Management is similar to that used for the classic type.

- **Intermittent maple syrup urine disease** is a milder form
  of the disease. Individuals with this type have a greater level
  of enzyme activity (approximately 8 to 15 percent of normal)

and often do not have symptoms until 12 to 24 months of age, usually as a result of an illness or surge in protein intake. During an illness, an individual with intermittent maple syrup urine disease may exhibit a strong maple syrup odor and/or go into a metabolic crisis.

- **Thiamine-responsive maple syrup urine disease** is so named because large doses of thiamine given to these individuals will result in an increase in the enzyme activity which breaks down leucine, isoleucine, and valine. Only moderate protein restriction is needed to manage this type of MSUD.

Is It Possible for an Adult to Develop Maple Syrup Urine Disease?

At times a peculiar maple syrup smell in the urine or sweat can occur in older, healthy children or adults who are nonsymptomatic. The reason for this is unknown. However, these individuals should be checked for a milder form of MSUD, especially if there are other symptoms suggestive of MSUD.

How Can You Get Tested for Maple Syrup Urine Disease?

GeneTests lists laboratories offering clinical genetic testing for MSUD. Clinical genetic tests are ordered to help diagnose a person or family and to aid in decisions regarding medical care or reproductive issues. Talk to your healthcare provider or a genetic professional to learn more about your testing options.

Section 23.7

Medium-Chain Acyl-Coenzyme A Dehydrogenase Deficiency

This section includes text excerpted from "Medium-Chain Acyl-Coenzyme A Dehydrogenase Deficiency," Genetic and Rare Diseases Information Center (GARD), National Center for Advancing Translational Sciences (NCATS), August 29, 2017.

What Is Medium-Chain Acyl-Coenzyme A Dehydrogenase Deficiency?

Medium-chain acyl-coenzyme A dehydrogenase deficiency (MCADD) is an inherited metabolic disorder that prevents the body from converting certain fats to energy, particularly during periods without food (fasting). People with MCADD do not have enough of an enzyme needed to metabolize a group of fats called "medium-chain fatty acids." Signs and symptoms usually begin by early childhood and may include vomiting, lack of energy, and low blood sugar (hypoglycemia). Symptoms can be triggered by periods of fasting or by illnesses.

MCADD is caused by mutations in the *ACADM* gene and inheritance is autosomal recessive. Treatment includes strict avoidance of fasting and avoidance of medium-chain triglycerides in the diet. If not treated, people with MCADD are at risk of serious complications including sudden death.

What Are the Signs and Symptoms of Medium-Chain Acyl-Coenzyme A Dehydrogenase Deficiency?

The initial signs and symptoms of MCADD typically occur during infancy or early childhood and can include vomiting, lack of energy (lethargy), and low blood sugar (hypoglycemia). In rare cases, the first episode of problems related to MCADD occurs during adulthood. The signs and symptoms of MCADD can be triggered by periods of fasting, or during illnesses, such as viral infections, particularly when eating is reduced. People with MCADD are also at risk of serious complications, such as seizures, breathing difficulties, liver problems, brain damage, coma, and sudden, unexpected death.

What Causes Medium-Chain Acyl-Coenzyme A Dehydrogenase Deficiency

MCADD is caused by mutations in the *ACADM* gene. This gene gives the body instructions for making an enzyme called "medium-chain acyl-CoA dehydrogenase," needed to break down fats called "medium-chain fatty acids." These fatty acids are found in foods and the body's tissues, and are an important source of energy for the heart, muscles, liver, and other tissues. Mutations in this gene lead to low levels of the enzyme, which means that medium-chain fatty acids are not broken down properly. They cannot be converted to energy, leading to the symptoms of MCADD.

How Is Medium-Chain Acyl-Coenzyme A Dehydrogenase Deficiency Diagnosed?

A diagnosis of MCADD requires an evaluation of a person's symptoms as well as the interpretation of several tests. Initial testing may include:

- Plasma acylcarnitine

- Urine organic acid

- Urine acylglycine

Further testing to confirm the diagnosis may include molecular genetic testing of the *ACADM* gene or biochemical genetic testing.

MCADD is included in many newborn screening programs, so a newborn with MCADD who does not yet exhibit symptoms may be diagnosed early. If a newborn screening result for MCADD is not in the normal range ("positive"), additional testing can then be ordered.

How Is Medium-Chain Acyl-Coenzyme A Dehydrogenase Deficiency Inherited?

MCADD is inherited in an autosomal recessive manner. This means that to have MCADD, a person must have a mutation in both copies of the responsible gene in each cell. There is nothing either parent can do, before or during a pregnancy, to cause a child to have this condition.

People with MCADD inherit one mutation from each of their parents. The parents, who each have one mutation, are known as "carriers." Carriers of an autosomal recessive condition typically do not have any signs or symptoms (they are unaffected). When two carriers of an autosomal recessive condition have children, each child has a:

- 25 percent chance to have the condition

- 50 percent chance to be an unaffected carrier like each parent

- 25 percent chance to be unaffected and not a carrier

What Risks Are Posed to Other Members of an Affected Individual's Family?

The risk to other family members depends on the status of the individuals most closely related to the affected individual. At conception, the siblings of an affected individual have a 25 percent risk of being affected, a 50 percent risk of being asymptomatic carriers, and a 25 percent risk of being unaffected and not carriers. The risk could be 50 percent if one of the parents is also affected. Because asymptomatic parents and siblings may have MCAD deficiency, biochemical evaluation and/or molecular genetic testing should be offered to both parents and all siblings.

Section 23.8

Methylmalonic Acidemia

This section includes text excerpted from "Methylmalonic Acidemia," Genetic and Rare Diseases Information Center (GARD), National Center for Advancing Translational Sciences (NCATS), May 5, 2016.

Methylmalonic acidemia (MMA) is an inherited condition in which the body is unable to process certain proteins and fats properly. Signs and symptoms usually appear in early infancy and vary from mild to life-threatening. Affected infants can experience vomiting, dehydration, weak muscle tone (hypotonia), developmental delay, lethargy, hepatomegaly, and failure to thrive. Long-term complications can include feeding problems, intellectual disability, chronic kidney disease, and pancreatitis. Without treatment, this condition can lead to coma and death in some cases. Mutations in the *MUT, MMAA, MMAB, MMADHC,* and *MCEE* genes cause MMA. It is inherited in an autosomal recessive fashion. MMA is treated with a low-protein, high-calorie diet, certain medications, antibiotics and, in some cases, organ transplantation.

Treatment of Methylmalonic Acidemia

No consensus exists regarding the treatment of acute MMA or the chronic complications of this condition. In 2014, professionals across 12 European countries and the United States developed guidelines based on rigorous literature evaluation and expert group meetings that outline the current management recommendations and areas for further research.

In general, MMA is treated with a low-protein, high-calorie diet, certain medications, antibiotics and, in some cases, organ transplantation. Medication treatment consists of cobalamin (vitamin B_{12}) given as an injection, carnitine, and antibiotics. The diet is protein-restricted to limit the intake of isoleucine, threonine, methionine, and valine because these substances can turn into methylmalonic acid in an affected patient. Most patients also need to take a special formula created without certain amino acids but containing others to make sure they are getting enough protein for growth. Each patient's diet and medication regimen should be individually adjusted to meet their specific needs.

Prognosis for Methylmalonic Acidemia

The effects of MMA vary from mild to life-threatening, and therefore, the prognosis and life expectancy may differ significantly among affected individuals.

Affected individuals can die in the newborn period or during a later episode of metabolic decompensation. Despite therapeutic improvements over the past 20 years, several long-term complications remain a threat to affected individuals. Those who survive often have a significant neurodevelopmental disability, although normal cognitive development can occur. Other complications that may occur include renal disease which may result in chronic renal failure (CRF), pancreatitis, cardiomyopathy, recurrent infections, and hypoglycemia.

Survival of individuals with MMA has improved over time. In individuals with methylmalonyl-CoA mutase (MCM) deficiency with no enzyme activity, survival at 1 year of age was over 90 percent, and at 5 years of age was over 80 percent in the 1990s. Studies looking at the median age of death of those with this subtype reported that 20 percent died at a median age of 2.2 years, and overall mortality was about 50 percent (median age of death 2 years). Overall mortality was reported to be 50 percent for the cobalamin B (CblB) subtype (median age of death 2.9 years); 40 percent for those with detectable but decreased MCM activity (median age of death 4.5 years); and about 5 percent for the cobalamin A (CblA) subtype (1 death at 14 days).

Section 23.9

Phenylketonuria

This section includes text excerpted from "Learning about Phenylketonuria (PKU)," National Human Genome Research Institute (NHGRI), January 2, 2019.

What Is Phenylketonuria?

Phenylketonuria (PKU) is an inherited disorder of metabolism that causes an increase in the blood of a chemical known as "phenylalanine." Phenylalanine comes from a person's diet and is used by the body to make proteins. Phenylalanine is found in all food proteins and in some artificial sweeteners. Without dietary treatment, phenylalanine can build up to harmful levels in the body, causing mental retardation and other serious problems.

Women who have high levels of phenylalanine during pregnancy are at high risk for having babies born with mental retardation, heart problems, small head size (microcephaly) and developmental delay. This is because the babies are exposed to their mother's very high levels of phenylalanine before they are born.

In the United States, PKU occurs in 1 in 10,000 to 1 in 15,000 newborn babies. Newborn screening has been used to detect PKU since the 1960's. As a result, the severe signs and symptoms of PKU are rarely seen.

What Are the Symptoms of Phenylketonuria?

Symptoms of PKU range from mild to severe. Severe PKU is called "classic PKU." Infants born with classic PKU appear normal for the first few months after birth. However, without treatment with a low-phenylalanine diet, these infants will develop mental retardation and behavioral problems. Other common symptoms of untreated classic PKU include seizures, developmental delay, and autism. Boys and girls who have classic PKU may also have eczema of the skin and lighter skin and hair than their family members who do not have PKU.

Babies born with less severe forms of PKU (moderate or mild PKU) may have a milder degree of mental retardation unless treated with the special diet. If the baby has only a very slight degree of PKU, often called "mild hyperphenylalaninemia (HPA)," there may be no problems and the special dietary treatment may not be needed.

How Is Phenylketonuria Diagnosed?

PKU is usually diagnosed through newborn screening testing that is done shortly after birth on a blood sample (heel stick). However, PKU should be considered at any age in a person who has developmental delays or mental retardation. This is because, rarely, infants are missed by newborn screening programs.

What Is the Treatment for Phenylketonuria?

PKU is treated by limiting the amount of protein (that contains phenylalanine) in the diet. Treatment also includes using special medical foods as well as special low-protein foods and taking vitamins and minerals. People who have PKU need to follow this diet for their lifetime. It is especially important for women who have PKU to follow the diet throughout their childbearing years.

Is Phenylketonuria Inherited?

PKU is inherited in families in an autosomal recessive pattern. Autosomal recessive inheritance means that a person has two copies of the gene that is altered. Usually, each parent of an individual who has PKU carries one copy of the altered gene. Since each parent also has a normal gene, they do not show signs or symptoms of PKU.

Gene alterations (mutations) in the *PAH* gene cause PKU. Mutations in the *PAH* gene cause low levels of an enzyme called "phenylalanine hydroxylase." These low levels mean that phenylalanine from a person's diet cannot be metabolized (changed), so it builds up to toxic levels in the bloodstream and body. Having too much phenylalanine can cause brain damage unless diet treatment is started.

Section 23.10

Tyrosinemia

This section includes text excerpted from "Tyrosinemia," Genetics Home Reference (GHR), National Institutes of Health (NIH), February 5, 2019.

Tyrosinemia is a genetic disorder characterized by disruptions in the multistep process that breaks down the amino acid tyrosine, a building block of most proteins. If untreated, tyrosine and its byproducts build up in tissues and organs, which can lead to serious health problems.

Types of Tyrosinemia

There are three types of tyrosinemia, which are each distinguished by their symptoms and genetic cause.

Tyrosinemia type I, the most severe form of this disorder, is characterized by signs and symptoms that begin in the first few months of life. Affected infants fail to gain weight and grow at the expected rate (failure to thrive) due to poor food tolerance because high-protein foods lead to diarrhea and vomiting. Affected infants may also have yellowing of the skin and whites of the eyes (jaundice), a cabbage-like odor, and an increased tendency to bleed (particularly nosebleeds).

Tyrosinemia type I can lead to liver and kidney failure, softening and weakening of the bones (rickets), and an increased risk of liver cancer (hepatocellular carcinoma (HCC)). Some affected children have repeated neurologic crises that consist of changes in mental state, reduced sensation in the arms and legs (peripheral neuropathy), abdominal pain, and respiratory failure. These crises can last from one to seven days. Untreated, children with tyrosinemia type I often do not survive past the age of 10.

Tyrosinemia type II can affect the eyes, skin, and mental development. Signs and symptoms often begin in early childhood and include eye pain and redness, excessive tearing, abnormal sensitivity to light (photophobia), and thick, painful skin on the palms of their hands and soles of their feet (palmoplantar hyperkeratosis). About 50 percent of individuals with tyrosinemia type II have some degree of intellectual disability.

Tyrosinemia type III is the rarest of the three types. The characteristic features of this type include intellectual disability, seizures, and periodic loss of balance and coordination (intermittent ataxia).

About 10 percent of newborns have temporarily elevated levels of tyrosine (transient tyrosinemia). In these cases, the cause is not genetic. The most likely causes are vitamin C deficiency or immature liver enzymes due to premature birth.

Frequency and Causes of Tyrosinemia

Worldwide, tyrosinemia type I affects about 1 in 100,000 individuals. This type is more common in Norway where 1 in 60,000 to 74,000 individuals are affected. Tyrosinemia type I is even more common in Quebec, Canada where it occurs in about 1 in 16,000 individuals. In the Saguenay-Lac St. Jean region of Quebec, tyrosinemia type I affects 1 in 1,846 people.

Tyrosinemia type II occurs in fewer than 1 in 250,000 individuals worldwide. Tyrosinemia type III is very rare; only a few cases have been reported.

Mutations in the *FAH*, *TAT*, and *HPD* genes can cause tyrosinemia types I, II, and III, respectively.

In the liver, enzymes break down tyrosine in a five step process, resulting in molecules that are either excreted by the kidneys or used to produce energy or make other substances in the body. The *FAH* gene provides instructions for the fumarylacetoacetate hydrolase (FAH) enzyme, which is responsible for the final step of tyrosine breakdown. The enzyme produced from the *TAT* gene, called "tyrosine aminotransferase" (TAT) enzyme, is involved at the first step in the process. The *HPD* gene provides instructions for making the 4-hydroxyphenylpyruvate dioxygenase (HPPD) enzyme, which is responsible for the second step.

Mutations in the *FAH*, *TAT*, or *HPD* gene cause a decrease in the activity of one of the enzymes in the breakdown of tyrosine. As a result, tyrosine and its byproducts accumulate to toxic levels, which can cause damage and death to cells in the liver, kidneys, nervous system, and other organs.

Section 23.11

Urea Cycle Defect

This section includes text excerpted from "Urea Cycle Disorders," Genetic and Rare Diseases Information Center (GARD), National Center for Advancing Translational Sciences (NCATS), September 10, 2013. Reviewed March 2019.

A urea cycle disorder (UCD) is a genetic disorder that results in a deficiency of one of the six enzymes in the urea cycle. These enzymes are responsible for removing ammonia from the bloodstream. The urea cycle involves a series of biochemical steps in which nitrogen, a waste product of protein metabolism, is changed to a compound called "urea" and removed from the blood. Normally, the urea is removed from the body through the urine. In UCDs, nitrogen builds up in the blood in the form of ammonia, a highly toxic substance, resulting in hyperammonemia (elevated blood ammonia). Ammonia then reaches the brain through the blood, where it can cause irreversible brain damage, coma, and/or death. The onset and severity of UCDs is highly variable. The severity correlates with the amount of urea-cycle enzyme function.

Treatment of Urea Cycle Defects

The U.S. Food and Drug Administration (FDA)-approved treatments for UCDs include:

- **Orphan products.** Benzoate and phenylacetate (Brand name: mmonul®)—Manufactured by Ucyclyd Pharma, Inc.

- **Sodium phenylbutyrate** (Brand name: Buphenyl®)— Manufactured by Ucyclyd Pharma, Inc.

- **Glycerol phenylbutyrate** (Brand name: Ravicti)—
  Manufactured by Horizon Pharma, Inc.

- **Benzoate and phenylacetate** (Brand name: Ucephan)—
  Manufactured by Immunex

Chapter 24

Kidney and Urinary System Disorders

Chapter Contents

Section 24.1

Cystinuria

This section includes text excerpted from "Cystinuria,"
Genetic and Rare Diseases Information Center (GARD), National
Center for Advancing Translational Sciences (NCATS),
May 12, 2015. Reviewed March 2019;

Cystinuria is an inherited condition characterized by a buildup of the amino acid, cystine, in the kidneys and bladder. This leads to the formation of cystine crystals and/or stones which may block the urinary tract. Signs and symptoms of the condition are related to the presence of stones and may include nausea, hematuria, flank pain, and/or frequent urinary tract infections. Cystinuria is caused by changes (mutations) in the *SLC3A1* and *SLC7A9* genes and is inherited in an autosomal recessive manner.

Symptoms of Cystinuria

Signs and symptoms of cystinuria are a consequence of stone formation and may include:

- Nausea

- Blood in the urine (hematuria)

- Flank pain

- Frequent urinary tract infections

- Chronic or acute renal failure (rare)

Cause of Cystinuria

Cystinuria is caused by changes (mutations) in the *SLC3A1* and *SLC7A9* genes. These genes encode a protein complex that helps control the reabsorption of amino acids (such as cystine) in the kidneys. Mutations in these genes disrupt the function of the protein complex, causing cystine to become more concentrated in the urine. As the concentration of cystine increases, cystine crystals and/or stones begin to form in the urinary tract leading to the many signs and symptoms associated with cystinuria.

Inheritance of Cystinuria

Cystinuria is inherited in an autosomal recessive manner. This means that to be affected, a person must have a mutation in both copies of the responsible gene in each cell. The parents of an affected person usually each carry one mutated copy of the gene and are referred to as carriers. Carriers typically do not show signs or symptoms of the condition. When two carriers of an autosomal recessive condition have children, each child has a 25 percent (1 in 4) risk to have the condition, a 50 percent (1 in 2) risk to be a carrier like each of the parents, and a 25 percent chance to not have the condition and not be a carrier.

Diagnosis of Cystinuria

Screening for cystinuria should be considered in people with recurrent or bilateral (i.e., affecting both kidneys) stones; those who develop stones at an early age (before age 30); and people who have a family history of cystinuria. A diagnosis is typically made after an episode of kidney stones when testing reveals that the stones are made of cystine.

The following tests may be recommended to detect kidney stones and diagnose cystinuria:

- 24-hour urine collection
- Abdominal imaging (computed tomography (CT) scan, magnetic resonance imaging (MRI), or ultrasound)
- Intravenous pyelogram (IVP)
- Urinalysis
- Genetic testing

Treatment of Cystinuria

Treatment of cystinuria is focused on relieving symptoms and preventing the formation of additional stones. A more conservative approach is typically tried first. This may include increasing fluid intake, regular monitoring of urinary pH, dietary restrictions (i.e., eating less salt), and increasing the pH of urine with potassium citrate supplements. If these strategies do not prevent the formation of stones, medications may be added to help dissolve the cystine crystals.

Treatment for cystinuria-related stones varies depending on the size and location of the stone, but may include:

- Extracorporeal shock wave lithotripsy (ESWL)
- Ureteroscopy
- Percutaneous nephrolithotomy (PNL)
- Open surgery (in rare cases)

U.S. Food and Drug Administration Approved Treatments

The medication(s) listed below have been approved by the U.S. Food and Drug Administration (FDA) as orphan products for the treatment of this condition.

- Tiopronin (brand name: Thiola®)—manufactured by Retrophin, Inc.

FDA-approved indication: Prevention of cystine nephrolithiasis in patients with homozygous cystinuria.

Prognosis for Cystinuria

Cystinuria is a chronic condition, and many affected people experience recurrent cystine stones in the urinary tract (kidneys, bladder, and ureters). In rare cases, frequent kidney stones can lead to tissue damage or even kidney failure.

Section 24.2

Polycystic Kidney Disease

This section includes text excerpted from "What Is Polycystic Kidney Disease?" National Institute of Diabetes and Digestive and Kidney Diseases (NIDDK), January 2017.

What Is Polycystic Kidney Disease?

Polycystic kidney disease (PKD) is a genetic disorder that causes many fluid-filled cysts to grow in your kidneys. Unlike the usually harmless simple kidney cysts that can form in the kidneys later in life, PKD cysts can change the shape of your kidneys, including making them much larger.

PKD is a form of chronic kidney disease (CKD) that reduces kidney function and may lead to kidney failure. PKD also can cause other complications, or problems, such as high blood pressure, cysts in the liver, and problems with blood vessels in your brain and heart.

What Are the Types of Polycystic Kidney Disease?

The two main types of PKD are:

- Autosomal dominant PKD (ADPKD), which is usually diagnosed in adulthood

- Autosomal recessive PKD (ARPKD), which can be diagnosed in the womb or shortly after a baby is born

How Common Is Polycystic Kidney Disease?

PKD is one of the most common genetic disorders. PKD affects about 500,000 people in the United States.

ADPKD affects 1 in every 400 to 1,000 people in the world, and ARPKD affects 1 in 20,000 children.

Who Is More Likely to Have Polycystic Kidney Disease?

PKD affects people of all ages, races, and ethnicities worldwide. The disorder occurs equally in women and men.

What Causes Polycystic Kidney Disease

A gene mutation, or defect, causes PKD. In most PKD cases, a child got the gene mutation from a parent. In a small number of PKD cases, the gene mutation developed on its own, without either parent carrying a copy of the mutated gene. This type of mutation is called "spontaneous."

What Are the Signs and Symptoms of Polycystic Kidney Disease?

The signs and symptoms of ADPKD, such as pain, high blood pressure, and kidney failure, are also PKD complications. In many cases,

ADPKD does not cause signs or symptoms until your kidney cysts are a half inch or larger in size.

Early signs of ARPKD in the womb are larger-than-normal kidneys and a smaller-than-average size baby, a condition called "growth failure." The early signs of ARPKD are also complications. However, some people with ARPKD do not develop signs or symptoms until later in childhood or even adulthood.

Can I Prevent Polycystic Kidney Disease?

Researchers have not yet found a way to prevent PKD. However, you may be able to slow PKD problems caused by high blood pressure, such as kidney damage. Aim for a blood pressure goal of less than 120/80. Work with a healthcare team to help manage your or your child's PKD. The healthcare team will probably include a general practitioner and a nephrologist, a healthcare provider specializing in kidney health.

What Can I Do to Slow Down Polycystic Kidney Disease?

The sooner you know you or your child has PKD, the sooner you can keep the condition from getting worse. Getting tested if you or your child are at risk for PKD can help you take early action.

You also can take steps to help delay or prevent kidney failure. Healthy lifestyle practices, such as being active, reducing stress, and quitting smoking can help.

Make Lifestyle Changes

Be active for 30 minutes or more on most days. Regular physical activity can help you reduce stress, manage your weight, and control your blood pressure. If you are not active now, ask your healthcare provider about how much and what type of physical activity is right for you.

If you play contact sports, such as football or hockey, a healthcare provider should do a magnetic resonance imaging (MRI) test to see whether these sports are safe for you. Trauma to your body, especially to your back and sides, may cause kidney cysts to burst.

Lose weight. Being overweight makes your kidneys work harder. Losing weight helps protect your kidneys.

Aim for 7 to 8 hours of sleep each night. Getting enough sleep is important to your overall physical and mental health and can help you manage your blood pressure and blood glucose, or blood sugar.

Reduce stress. Long-term stress can raise your blood pressure and even lead to depression. Some of the steps you take to manage your PKD are also healthy ways to cope with stress. For example, getting enough physical activity and sleep helps reduce stress.

Quit smoking. Cigarette smoking can raise your blood pressure, making your kidney damage worse. Quitting smoking may help you meet your blood pressure goals, which is good for your kidneys and can lower your chances of having a heart attack or stroke. Quitting smoking is even more important for people with PKD who have aneurysms. An aneurysm is a bulge in the wall of a blood vessel. For tips on quitting, go to Smokefree.gov.

Change What You Eat and Drink

You may need to change what you eat and drink to help control your blood pressure and protect your kidneys. People with any kind of kidney disease, including PKD, should talk with a dietitian about which foods and drinks to include in their healthy eating plan and which may be harmful. Staying hydrated by drinking the right amount of fluid may help slow PKD's progress toward kidney failure.

Take Blood Pressure Medicines

If lifestyle and diet changes do not help control your blood pressure, a healthcare provider may prescribe one or more blood pressure medicines. Two types of blood pressure medicines, angiotensin-converting enzyme (ACE) inhibitors and angiotensin receptor blockers (ARBs), may slow kidney disease and delay kidney failure. The names of these medicines end in –pril or –sartan.

What Is Autosomal Dominant Polycystic Kidney Disease?

Autosomal dominant polycystic kidney disease (ADPKD) is the most common form of PKD. ADPKD affects 1 in every 400 to 1,000 people and is the most common kidney disorder passed down through family members. Healthcare providers usually diagnose ADPKD between the ages of 30 and 50, when signs and symptoms start to appear, which is why it is sometimes called "adult PKD."

"Autosomal dominant" means you can get the *PKD* gene mutation, or defect, from only one parent. Researchers have found two different gene mutations that cause ADPKD. Most people with ADPKD have defects in the PKD1 gene, and one out of six or one out of seven people with ADPKD have a defective *PKD2* gene.

Healthcare providers can diagnose people with PKD1 sooner because their symptoms appear sooner. People with PKD1 also usually progress more quickly to kidney failure than people with *PKD2*. How quickly ADPKD progresses also differs from person to person.

What Are the Most Common Complications of Autosomal Dominant Polycystic Kidney Disease?

Most people with ADPKD have pain, high blood pressure, and kidney failure at some point in their lives.

Pain

Pain is a common complication of ADPKD and is usually due to kidney or liver cysts. Pain also can be caused by:

- Kidney cyst infection
- Bleeding or burst kidney cysts
- Urinary tract infection (UTI)
- Kidney stones
- Tissue stretching around the kidney due to cyst growth

High Blood Pressure

Almost all people with ADPKD who have kidney failure have high blood pressure. High blood pressure increases your chances of heart disease and stroke. High blood pressure can also damage your kidneys even more. Keep your blood pressure under control to help delay kidney damage.

Kidney Failure

Kidney failure means your kidneys no longer work well enough to stay healthy. Untreated kidney failure can lead to coma and death.

More than half of people with ADPKD progress to kidney failure by 70 years of age.

What Are Other Complications of Autosomal Dominant Polycystic Kidney Disease?

ADPKD complications, or problems, can affect many systems in your body besides your kidneys. Researchers have not found a link between PKD and kidney cancer.

You may see some ADPKD complications right away. Other complications may not appear for many years, depending on whether you have the *PKD1* or *PKD2* gene. Also, ADPKD complications can vary from person to person, so you may not have all of these problems.

Vascular System Problems

Abnormal heart valves. Abnormal heart valves can occur in some people with ADPKD. Abnormal heart valves can cause too little blood to flow into the aorta, the large artery that carries blood from the heart to the rest of your body. Abnormal heart valves in people with ADPKD rarely need to be replaced. However, you may need more tests if your healthcare provider detects a heart murmur.

Brain aneurysms. An aneurysm is a bulge in the wall of a blood vessel. Aneurysms in the brain might cause headaches that are severe or feel different from other headaches. See a healthcare provider even before you take over-the-counter (OTC) pain medicines for severe headaches or headaches that would not go away. Brain aneurysms can break open and cause bleeding inside the skull. Large brain aneurysms are life-threatening and need immediate medical treatment. If you have an aneurysm, stop smoking and control your blood pressure and lipids.

Digestive System Problems

Liver cysts. Liver cysts, which are fluid-filled cysts on the liver, are the most common non-kidney complication of ADPKD. Liver cysts do not usually cause symptoms in people under the age of 30, because liver cysts are normally small and few in number in the early stages of ADPKD. In rare cases, liver cysts can eventually reduce liver function. In the most severe cases, you may need a liver transplant. Because the hormone estrogen may affect liver cyst growth, women are more likely to have liver cysts than men. The more pregnancies a woman with ADPKD has had, the more likely she will have liver cysts.

Pancreatic cysts. PKD can also cause cysts in your pancreas. Pancreatic cysts rarely cause pancreatitis, which is inflammation, or swelling, of the pancreas.

Diverticula. Diverticula are small pouches, or sacs, that push through weak spots in your colon wall. Diverticula can cause diverticulosis. Diverticulosis can cause changes in your bowel movement patterns or pain in your abdomen.

Urinary Tract Problems

Urinary tract infections (UTIs). Kidney cysts can block urine flow through the kidneys so that urine stays in your urinary tract too long. When urine stays in your urinary tract too long, bacteria in your urine can cause a bladder infection or a kidney infection. A kidney infection can cause further damage to your kidneys by causing cysts to become infected.

Kidney stones. People with ADPKD sometimes have kidney stones. Kidney stones can block urine flow and cause infection and pain.

Reproductive Problems

Although most women with PKD have normal pregnancies, women with PKD who have high blood pressure and decreased kidney function are more likely to have preeclampsia, or high blood pressure during pregnancy.

With preeclampsia, the fetus gets less oxygen and fewer nutrients. Women with preeclampsia should be followed closely by their healthcare provider during and after pregnancy. After delivery, preeclampsia goes away.

Many men with ADPKD have cysts on their seminal vesicles, which are glands in the male reproductive system that help produce semen. Seminal vesicle cysts rarely cause infertility.

People with PKD who are considering having children may want to discuss family planning concerns with a genetics counselor.

What Are the Signs and Symptoms of Autosomal Dominant Polycystic Kidney Disease?

In many cases, ADPKD does not cause signs or symptoms until cysts are a half inch or larger in size. For this reason, you should meet with a healthcare provider if you are at risk for PKD before your symptoms start.

The most common symptoms are pain in the back and sides, between the ribs and hips, and headaches. The pain can be short term or ongoing, mild or severe.

Hematuria, or blood in the urine, may be a sign of ADPKD. If you have hematuria, see a healthcare provider right away.

How Do Healthcare Providers Diagnose Autosomal Dominant Polycystic Kidney Disease?

Healthcare providers diagnose ADPKD using imaging tests and genetic testing. A healthcare provider can make a diagnosis based on these tests and your age, family history of PKD, and how many cysts you have.

The sooner a healthcare provider can diagnose ADPKD, the better your chances of delaying complications.

Imaging Tests

A specially trained technician performs imaging tests in a healthcare provider's office, an outpatient center, or a hospital. A radiologist reads the images. Adults usually do not need anesthesia for these tests. However, a healthcare provider may give infants or children a sedative to help them fall asleep during the test.

Ultrasound. Ultrasound uses a device called a "transducer" that bounces safe, painless sound waves off your organs to create an image of their structure. An abdominal ultrasound can create images of your entire urinary tract or focus specifically on the kidneys. The images can show cysts in the kidneys.

Computed tomography (CT) scans. CT scans use a combination of X-rays and computer technology to create images of your urinary tract. For a CT scan of your urinary tract, a healthcare provider may give you an injection of contrast medium. Contrast medium is a dye or other substance that makes structures inside your body easier to see during imaging tests. You lie on a table that slides into a tunnel-shaped device that takes the X-rays. CT scans can show more detailed images of kidney cysts than ultrasound.

Magnetic resonance imaging (MRI). MRI machines use radio waves and magnets to produce detailed pictures of your body's internal organs and soft tissues without using X-rays. An MRI may include an injection of contrast medium. With most MRI machines, you lie on a table that slides into a tunnel-shaped machine that may be open on each end or closed at one end. Some newer machines allow you to lie in a more open space. Healthcare providers use MRIs to measure kidney and cyst size and monitor kidney and cyst growth. Measuring kidney and cyst size and growth can help track the progress of PKD.

Genetic Testing

Your healthcare provider may refer you to a geneticist if you are at risk for ADPKD. A geneticist is an expert in genes and diseases that are passed down through families. You will provide the geneticist with a blood or saliva sample, which will be tested in a special lab for the gene mutations that cause ADPKD. The genetic testing may take many days or weeks to complete.

A healthcare provider may also use genetic testing results to find out whether someone with a family history of PKD is likely to develop PKD in the future.

When to Consider Genetic Counseling

If you are considering genetic testing, you and your family may want to talk with a genetic counselor as part of your healthcare team. Genetic counseling may be useful when you're deciding whether to have genetic testing and again later when test results are available. Genetic counseling can help you and your family understand how test results may affect your lives.

How Does My Healthcare Team Treat the Most Common Complications of Autosomal Dominant Polycystic Kidney Disease?

Although a cure does not exist yet for ADPKD, treatment can help reduce your complications, which can help you live longer.

Manage Pain

A healthcare provider needs to find the source of your pain before he or she can treat it. For example, if growing cysts are causing pain, the healthcare provider may first suggest OTC pain medicines, such as aspirin or acetaminophen.

Always talk with a healthcare provider before taking any OTC medicines because some may be harmful to your kidneys. People with ADPKD have a higher risk for acute kidney injury (AKI), which is the sudden and temporary loss of kidney function. Sometimes AKI is caused by using OTC painkillers for a long time.

Depending on the size and number of cysts and whether medicine helps your pain, a healthcare provider may suggest surgery. Surgery to shrink cysts can help the pain in your back and sides for a while. However, surgery does not slow PKD's progress toward kidney failure.

Control Your Blood Pressure

Controlling your blood pressure can slow the effects of ADPKD. Lifestyle changes and medicines can lower high blood pressure. Sometimes you can control blood pressure with healthy eating and regular physical activity alone.

Some healthcare providers will recommend blood pressure medicines called "angiotensin-converting enzyme" (ACE) inhibitors or "angiotensin receptor blockers" (ARBs).

Treat Kidney Failure

ADPKD can eventually cause your kidneys to fail. People with kidney failure must have dialysis or a kidney transplant to replace their kidney function.

The two forms of dialysis are hemodialysis and peritoneal dialysis. Hemodialysis uses a machine to circulate your blood through a filter outside the body. Peritoneal dialysis uses the lining of your abdomen to filter the blood inside the body.

A kidney transplant is a surgery to place a healthy kidney from a donor into your body.

How Does Autosomal Dominant Polycystic Kidney Disease Affect My Day-to-Day Life?

Managing PKD successfully will probably include several lifestyle changes, such as changes in your physical activity level and what you eat. Visiting with a healthcare team on a regular basis is an important part of your routine as you work to limit your kidney problems.

PKD is a costly disease to manage and treat, especially if health insurance does not cover some or any of your costs. Financial help may be available from the Federal Government and other sources.

Many people with PKD may find it hard, but not impossible, to get life insurance. Contact an insurance company that specializes in "impaired risk life insurance."

Chapter 25

Leukodystrophies

Leukodystrophy refers to progressive degeneration of the white matter of the brain due to imperfect growth or development of the myelin sheath, the fatty covering that acts as an insulator around nerve fiber. Myelin, which lends its color to the white matter of the brain, is a complex substance made up of at least ten different chemicals.

Types of Leukodystrophy

The leukodystrophies are a group of disorders that are caused by genetic defects in how myelin produces or metabolizes these chemicals. Each of the leukodystrophies is the result of a defect in the gene that controls one (and only one) of the chemicals.

Specific leukodystrophies include:

- Metachromatic leukodystrophy (MLD)

- Krabbé disease (KD)

- Adrenoleukodystrophy (ALD)

- Pelizaeus-Merzbacher disease (PMD)

- Canavan disease

- Childhood ataxia with central nervous system hypomyelination or CACH (also known as "Vanishing White Matter Disease")

This chapter includes text excerpted from "Leukodystrophy Information Page," National Institute of Neurological Disorders and Stroke (NINDS), June 13, 2018.

- Alexander disease
- Refsum disease (RD)
- Cerebrotendinous xanthomatosis (CTX)

Symptoms of Leukodystrophy

The most common symptom of a leukodystrophy disease is a gradual decline in an infant or child who previously appeared well. Progressive loss may appear in body tone, movements, gait, speech, ability to eat, vision, hearing, and behavior. There is often a slowdown in mental and physical development. Symptoms vary according to the specific type of leukodystrophy and may be difficult to recognize in the early stages of the disease.

Treatment of Leukodystrophy

Treatment for most of the leukodystrophies is symptomatic and supportive and may include medications; physical, occupational, and speech therapies; and nutritional, educational, and recreational programs. Bone marrow transplantation (BMT) is showing promise for a few of the leukodystrophies.

Prognosis for Leukodystrophy

The prognosis for the leukodystrophies varies according to the specific type of leukodystrophy.

Chapter 26

Lipid Storage Diseases

What Are Lipid Storage Diseases?

Lipid storage diseases, or the lipidoses, are a group of inherited metabolic disorders in which harmful amounts of fatty materials (lipids) accumulate in various cells and tissues in the body. People with these disorders either do not produce enough of one of the enzymes needed to break down (metabolize) lipids, or they produce enzymes that do not work properly. Over time, this excessive storage of fats can cause permanent cellular and tissue damage, particularly in the brain, peripheral nervous system (the nerves from the spinal cord to the rest of the body), liver, spleen, and bone marrow.

What Are Lipids?

Lipids are fat-like substances that are important parts of the membranes found within and between cells and in the myelin sheath that coats and protects the nerves. Lipids include oils, fatty acids, waxes, steroids (such as cholesterol and estrogen), and other related compounds.

These fatty materials are stored naturally in the body's cells, organs, and tissues. Tiny bodies within cells called "lysosomes" regularly convert, or metabolize, the lipids and proteins into smaller components to provide energy for the body. Disorders in which intercellular material

This chapter includes text excerpted from "Lipid Storage Diseases Fact Sheet," National Institute of Neurological Disorders and Stroke (NINDS), August 14, 2018.

that cannot be metabolized is stored in the lysosomes are called "lyso-somal storage diseases (LSDs)." In addition to lipid storage diseases, other LSDs include the mucolipidoses, in which excessive amounts of lipids with attached sugar molecules are stored in the cells and tissues, and the mucopolysaccharidoses, in which excessive amounts of large, complicated sugar molecules are stored.

How Are Lipid Storage Diseases Inherited?

Lipid storage diseases are inherited from one or both parents who carry a defective gene that regulates a particular lipid-metabolizing enzyme in a class of the body's cells. They can be inherited in two ways:

- **Autosomal recessive inheritance** occurs when both parents carry and pass on a copy of the faulty gene, but neither parent is affected by the disorder. Each child born to these parents has a 25 percent chance of inheriting both copies of the defective gene, a 50 percent chance of being a carrier like the parents, and a 25 percent chance of not inheriting either copy of the defective gene. Children of either gender can be affected by an autosomal recessive pattern of inheritance.

- **X-linked (or sex-linked) recessive inheritance** occurs when the mother carries the affected gene on the X chromosome. The X and Y chromosomes are involved in gender determination. Females have two X chromosomes, and males have one X chromosome and one Y chromosome. Sons of female carriers have a 50 percent chance of inheriting and being affected with the disorder, as the sons receive one X chromosome from the mother and a Y chromosome from the father. Daughters have a 50 percent chance of inheriting the affected X chromosome from the mother and are carriers or mildly affected. Affected men do not pass the disorder to their sons, but their daughters will be carriers for the disorder.

What Are the Types of Lipid Storage Disease?

The various types of lipid storage diseases are discussed below.

Gaucher Disease

Gaucher disease is caused by a deficiency of the enzyme gluco-cerebrosidase. Fatty material can collect in the brain, spleen, liver, kidneys, lungs, and bone marrow. Symptoms may include brain damage, enlarged spleen and liver, liver malfunction, skeletal disorders and bone lesions that may cause pain and fractures, swelling of lymph nodes and (occasionally) adjacent joints, distended abdomen, a brownish tint to the skin, anemia, low blood platelets, and yellow spots in the eyes. Individuals affected most seriously may also be more susceptible to infection. The disease affects males and females equally.

Gaucher disease has three common clinical subtypes:

- **Type 1 (or nonneuronopathic type)** is the most common form of the disease in the United States and Europe. The brain is not affected, but there may be lung and, rarely, kidney impairment. Symptoms may begin early in life or in adulthood and include enlarged liver and grossly enlarged spleen, which can rupture and cause additional complications. Skeletal weakness and bone disease may be extensive. People in this group usually bruise easily due to low blood platelet count. They may also experience fatigue due to anemia. Depending on disease onset and severity, individuals with type 1 may live well into adulthood. Many affected individuals have a mild form of the disease or may not show any symptoms. Although Gaucher type 1 occurs often among persons of Ashkenazi Jewish heritage, it can affect individuals of any ethnic background.

- **Type 2 (or acute infantile neuropathic Gaucher disease)** typically begins within three months of birth. Symptoms include extensive and progressive brain damage, spasticity, seizures, limb rigidity, enlarged liver and spleen, abnormal eye movement, and a poor ability to suck and swallow. Affected children usually die before age two.

- **Type 3 (the chronic neuronopathic form)** can begin at any time in childhood or even in adulthood. It is characterized by slowly progressive but milder neurologic symptoms compared to the acute or type 2 Gaucher disease. Major symptoms include eye movement disorders, cognitive deficit, poor coordination, seizures, an enlarged spleen and/or liver, skeletal irregularities, blood disorders including anemia, and respiratory problems. Nearly everyone with type 3 Gaucher disease who receives enzyme replacement therapy will reach adulthood.

For type 1 and most type 3 individuals, enzyme replacement treatment given intravenously every two weeks can dramatically decrease liver and spleen size, reduce skeletal abnormalities, and reverse other manifestations. Successful bone marrow transplantation cures the non-neurological manifestations of the disease. However, this procedure carries significant risk and is rarely performed in individuals with Gaucher disease. Surgery to remove all or part of the spleen may be required on rare occasions (if the person has very low platelet counts or when the enlarged organ severely affects the person's comfort). Blood transfusion may benefit some anemic individuals. Others may require joint replacement surgery to improve mobility and quality of life (QOL). There is no effective treatment for the brain damage that may occur in people with types 2 and 3 Gaucher disease.

Niemann-Pick Disease

Niemann-Pick disease is a group of autosomal recessive disorders caused by an accumulation of fat and cholesterol in cells of the liver, spleen, bone marrow, lungs, and, in some instances, brain. Neurological complications may include ataxia (lack of muscle coordination that can affect walking steadily, writing, and eating, among other functions), eye paralysis, brain degeneration, learning problems, spasticity, feeding and swallowing difficulties, slurred speech, loss of muscle tone, hypersensitivity to touch, and some clouding of the cornea due to excess buildup of materials. A characteristic cherry-red halo that can be seen by a physician using a special tool develops around the center of the retina in 50 percent of affected individuals.

Niemann-Pick disease is subdivided into three categories:

- Type A, the most severe form, begins in early infancy. Infants appear normal at birth but develop profound brain damage by 6 months of age, an enlarged liver and spleen, swollen lymph nodes, and nodes under the skin (xanthomas). The spleen may enlarge to as great as 10 times its normal size and can rupture, causing bleeding. These children become progressively weaker, lose motor function, may become anemic, and are susceptible to recurring infection. They rarely live beyond 18 months. This form of the disease occurs most often in Jewish families.

- Type B (or juvenile onset) does not generally affect the brain but most children develop ataxia, damage to nerves exiting from the spinal cord (peripheral neuropathy), and pulmonary difficulties that progress with age. Enlargement of the liver and spleen characteristically occurs in the preteen years. Individuals with type B may live a comparatively long time but may require supplemental oxygen because of lung involvement.

Niemann-Pick types A and B result from an accumulation of the fatty substance called "sphingomyelin," due to deficiency of an enzyme called "sphingomyelinase."

* Type C may appear early in life or develop in the teen or even adult years. Niemann-Pick disease type C is not caused by a deficiency of sphingomyelinase but by a lack of the NPC1 or NPC2 proteins. As a result, various lipids and cholesterol accumulate inside nerve cells and cause them to malfunction. Brain involvement may be extensive, leading to an inability to look up and down, difficulty in walking and swallowing, progressive loss of hearing, and progressive dementia. People with type C have only moderate enlargement of their spleens and livers. Those individuals with Niemann-Pick type C who share a common ancestral background in Nova Scotia were previously referred to as type D. The life expectencies of people with type C vary considerably. Some individuals die in childhood while others who appear to be less severely affected can live into adulthood.

Fabry Disease

Fabry disease, also known as "alpha-galactosidase-A deficiency," causes a buildup of fatty material in the autonomic nervous system (the part of the nervous system that controls involuntary functions such as breathing and heartbeat), eyes, kidneys, and the cardio-vascular system. Fabry disease is the only X-linked lipid storage disease. Males are primarily affected, although a milder and more variable form is common in females. Occasionally, affected females have severe manifestations similar to those seen in males with the disorder. The onset of symptoms is usually during childhood or ado-lescence. Neurological signs include burning pain in the arms and legs, which worsens in hot weather or following exercise, and the buildup of excess material in the clear layers of the cornea (resulting in clouding but no change in vision). Fatty storage in blood vessel walls may impair circulation, putting the person at risk for stroke or heart attack. Other symptoms include heart enlargement, pro-gressive kidney impairment leading to renal failure, gastrointes-tinal difficulties, decreased sweating, and fever. Angiokeratomas (small, non-cancerous, reddish-purple elevated spots on the skin) may develop on the lower part of the trunk of the body and become more numerous with age.

313

People with Fabry disease often die prematurely of complications from heart disease, renal failure, or stroke. Drugs such as phenytoin and carbamazepine are often prescribed to treat pain that accompanies Fabry disease but do not treat the disease. Metoclopramide or Lipisorb (a nutritional supplement) can ease gastrointestinal distress that often occurs in people with Fabry disease, and some individuals may require a kidney transplant or dialysis. Enzyme replacement can reduce storage, ease the pain, and preserve organ function in some people with Fabry disease.

Farber Disease

Farber disease, also known as "Farber's lipogranulomatosis," describes a group of rare autosomal recessive disorders that cause an accumulation of fatty material in the joints, tissues, and central nervous system. It affects both males and females. Disease onset is typically in early infancy but may occur later in life. Children who have the classic form of Farber disease develop neurological symptoms within the first few weeks of life that may include increased lethargy and sleepiness, and problems with swallowing. The liver, heart, and kidneys may also be affected. Other symptoms may include joint contractures (chronic shortening of muscles or tendons around joints), vomiting, arthritis, swollen lymph nodes, swollen joints, hoarseness, and nodes under the skin which thicken around joints as the disease progresses. Affected individuals with breathing difficulty may require a breathing tube. Most children with the disease die by the age of two, usually from lung disease. In one of the most severe forms of the disease, an enlarged liver and spleen can be diagnosed soon after birth. Children born with this form of the disease usually die within six months.

Farber disease is caused by a deficiency of the enzyme called "ceramidase." There is no specific treatment for Farber disease. Corticosteroids may be prescribed to relieve pain. Bone marrow transplants may improve granulomas (small masses of inflamed tissue) on people with little or no lung or nervous system complications. Older persons may have granulomas surgically reduced or removed.

Gangliosidosis

The gangliosidoses are comprised of two distinct groups of genetic diseases. Both are autosomal recessive and affect females and males equally.

GM1 Gangliosidoses

The GM1 gangliosidoses are caused by a deficiency of the enzyme beta-galactosidase, resulting in abnormal storage of acidic lipid materials particularly in the nerve cells in the central and peripheral nervous systems. GM1 gangliosidosis has three clinical presentations:

- GM1 (the most severe subtype, with onset shortly after birth) may include neurodegeneration, seizures, liver and spleen enlargement, coarsening of facial features, skeletal irregularities, joint stiffness, distended abdomen, muscle weakness, exaggerated startle response, and problems with gait. About half of affected individuals develop cherry-red spots in the eye. Children may be deaf and blind by the age of one and often die by the age of three from either cardiac complications or pneumonia.

- Late infantile GM1 gangliosidosis typically begins between one and three years of age. Neurological symptoms include ataxia, seizures, dementia, and difficulties with speech.

- GM1 gangliosidosis develops between the ages of 3 and 30. Symptoms include decreased muscle mass (muscle atrophy), neurological complications that are less severe and progress at a slower rate than in other forms of the disorder, corneal clouding in some people, and sustained muscle contractions that cause twisting and repetitive movements or abnormal postures (dystonia). Angiokeratomas may develop on the lower part of the trunk of the body. The size of the liver and spleen in most affected individuals is normal.

GM2 Gangliosidoses

The GM2 gangliosidoses also cause the body to store excess acidic fatty materials in tissues and cells, most notably in nerve cells. These disorders result from a deficiency of the enzyme beta-hexosaminidase. GM2 disorders include:

- **Tay-Sachs disease** (also known as "GM2 gangliosidosis-variant B") and its variant forms are caused by a deficiency in the enzyme hexosaminidase A. The incidence has been particularly high among Eastern European and Ashkenazi Jewish populations, as well as certain French Canadians and Louisianan Cajuns. Affected children appear to develop normally for the first few months of life. Symptoms begin by six months of age and include progressive loss of mental ability, dementia, decreased eye contact, increased startle response to noise, progressive loss of hearing leading to deafness, difficulty in swallowing, blindness, cherry-red spots in the retina, and some paralysis. Seizures may begin in the child's second year. Children may eventually need a feeding tube and they often die by the age of four from recurring infection. No specific treatment is available. Anticonvulsant medications may initially control seizures. Other supportive treatment includes proper nutrition and hydration and techniques to keep the airway open. A rare form of the disorder, called "late-onset Tay-Sachs disease," occurs in people in their twenties and early thirties and is characterized by unsteadiness of gait and progressive neurological deterioration.

- **Sandhoff disease** (variant AB) is a severe form of Tay-Sachs disease. Onset usually occurs at the age of six months and is not limited to any ethnic group. Neurological signs may include progressive deterioration of the central nervous system, motor weakness, early blindness, marked startle response to sound, spasticity, shock-like or jerking of a muscle (myoclonus), seizures, abnormally enlarged head (macrocephaly), and cherry-red spots in the eye. Other symptoms may include frequent respiratory infections, heart murmurs, doll-like facial features, and an enlarged liver and spleen. There is no specific treatment for Sandhoff disease. As with Tay-Sachs disease, supportive treatment includes keeping the airway open and proper nutrition and hydration. Anti-seizure medications may initially control seizures. Children generally die by the age of three from respiratory infections.

Krabbe Disease

Krabbe disease (also known as "globoid cell leukodystrophy" and "galactosylceramide lipidosis") is an autosomal recessive disorder caused by a deficiency of the enzyme galactocerebrosidase. The disease most often affects infants, with onset before the age of six months, but can occur in adolescence or adulthood. The buildup of undigested fats affects the growth of the nerve's protective insulating sheath (myelin sheath) and causes severe deterioration of mental and motor skills. Other symptoms include muscle weakness, reduced ability of stretching a muscle (hypertonia), muscle stiffening (spasticity), sudden shock-like or jerking of the limbs (myoclonic seizures), irritability, unexplained fever, deafness, blindness, paralysis, and difficulty when swallowing. Prolonged weight loss may also occur. The disease may be diagnosed by enzyme testing and by identification of its characteristic grouping of cells into globoid bodies in the white matter of the brain, demyelination of nerves and degeneration, and destruction of brain cells. In infants, the disease is generally fatal before the age of two. Individuals with a later onset form of the disease have a milder course of the disease and live significantly longer. No specific treatment for Krabbe disease has been developed, although early bone marrow transplantation may help some people.

Metachromatic Leukodystrophy

Metachromatic leukodystrophy, or MLD, is a group of disorders marked by storage buildup in the white matter of the central nervous system and in the peripheral nerves and, to some extent, in the kidneys. Similar to Krabbe disease, MLD affects the myelin that covers and protects the nerves. This autosomal recessive disorder is caused by a deficiency of the enzyme arylsulfatase A. Both males and females are affected by this disorder.

MLD has three characteristic forms: late infantile, juvenile, and adult.

- Late infantile MLD typically begins between 12 and 20 months following birth. Infants may appear normal at first but develop difficulty in walking and a tendency to fall, followed by intermittent pain in the arms and legs, progressive loss of vision leading to blindness, developmental delays and loss of previously acquired milestones, impaired swallowing, convulsions, and dementia before the age of 2. Children also develop gradual muscle wasting and weakness and eventually lose the ability to walk. Most children with this form of the disorder die by the age of 5.

- Juvenile MLD typically begins between 3 and 10 years of age. Symptoms include impaired school performance, mental deterioration, ataxia, seizures, and dementia. Symptoms are progressive with death occurring 10 to 20 years following onset.

- Adult symptoms begin after the age of 16 and may include ataxia, seizures, abnormal shaking of the limbs (tremor), impaired concentration, depression, psychiatric disturbances, and dementia. Death generally occurs within 6 to 14 years after onset of symptoms.

There is no cure for MLD. Treatment is symptomatic and supportive. Bone marrow transplantation may delay progression of the disease in some cases. Considerable progress has been made with regard to gene therapies in animal models of MLD and in clinical trials.

Wolman Disease

Wolman disease, also known as "acid lipase deficiency," is a severe lipid storage disorder that is usually fatal by the age of one. This autosomal recessive disorder is marked by accumulation of cholesteryl esters (normally a transport form of cholesterol) and triglycerides (a chemical form in which fats exist in the body) that can build up significantly and cause damage in the cells and tissues. Both males and females are affected by this disorder. Infants are normal and active at birth but quickly develop progressive mental deterioration, enlarged liver and grossly enlarged spleen, distended abdomen, gastrointestinal problems, jaundice, anemia, vomiting, and calcium deposits in the adrenal glands, causing them to harden.

Another type of acid lipase deficiency is **cholesteryl ester storage disease**. This extremely rare disorder results from storage of cholesteryl esters and triglycerides in cells in the blood and lymph and lymphoid tissue. Children develop an enlarged liver, leading to cirrhosis and chronic liver failure before adulthood. Children may also have calcium deposits in the adrenal glands and may develop jaundice late in the disorder.

Enzyme replacement for both Wolman's disease and cholesteryl ester storage disease is under active investigation.

How Are Lipid Storage Diseases Diagnosed?

In some states, some of these disorders (most notably and controversially Krabbe disease) are screened for at birth.

In older children, diagnosis is made through clinical examination, enzyme assays (laboratory tests that measure enzyme activity), genetic testing, biopsy, and molecular analysis of cells or tissues. In some forms of the disorder, urine analysis can identify the presence of stored material. In others, the abnormality in enzyme activity can be detected in white blood cells without a tissue biopsy. Some tests can also determine if a person carries the defective gene that can be passed on to her or his children. This process is known as "genotyping."

Biopsy for lipid storage disease involves removing a small sample of the liver or other tissue and studying it under a microscope. In this procedure, a physician will administer a local anesthetic and then remove a small piece of tissue either surgically or by needle biopsy (a small piece of tissue is removed by inserting a thin, hollow needle through the skin).

Genetic testing can help individuals who have a family history of lipid storage disease determine if they are carrying a mutated gene that causes the disorder. Other genetic tests can determine if a fetus has the disorder or is a carrier of the defective gene. Prenatal testing is usually done by chorionic villus sampling, in which a very small sample of the placenta is removed and tested during early pregnancy. The sample, which contains the same deoxyribonucleic acid (DNA) as the fetus, is removed by a catheter inserted through the cervix or by a fine needle inserted through the abdomen. Results are usually available within two to four weeks.

How Are Lipid Storage Diseases Treated?

There is no specific treatment available for most of the lipid storage disorders but highly effective enzyme-replacement therapy is available for type 1 and type 3 Gaucher disease. Enzyme replacement therapy is also available for Fabry disease, although it is not as effective as for Gaucher disease. However, anti-platelet medications can help prevent strokes and medications that lower blood pressure can slow the decline of kidney function in people with Fabry disease. The U.S. Food and Drug Administration (FDA) has approved the drug migalastat (Gala-fold) as an oral medication for adults with Fabry disease who have a certain genetic mutation. Eliglustat tartrate, an oral drug approved for Gaucher treatment, works by administering small molecules that reduce the action of the enzyme that catalyzes glucose to ceramide. Medications, such as gabapentin and carbamazepine, may be pre-scribed to help treat pain (including bone pain). Restricting one's diet does not prevent lipid buildup in cells and tissues.

Chapter 27

Mitochondrial Diseases

Chapter Contents

Section 27.1

What Are Mitochondrial Diseases?

This section contains text excerpted from the following sources: Text beginning with the heading "What Is Metabolism?" is excerpted from "Mitochondrial Diseases," MedlinePlus, National Institutes of Health (NIH), August 23, 2016; Text under the heading "Inheritance" is excerpted from "Mitochondrial Genetic Disorders," Genetic and Rare Diseases Information Center (GARD), National Center for Advancing Translational Sciences (NCATS), January 26, 2015. Reviewed March 2019.

What Is Metabolism?

Metabolism is the process your body uses to make energy from the food you eat. Food is made up of proteins, carbohydrates, and fats. Chemicals in your digestive system (enzymes) break the food parts down into sugars and acids, which is your body's fuel. Your body can use this fuel right away, or it can store the energy in your body tissues. If you have a metabolic disorder, something goes wrong with this process. Mitochondrial diseases are a group of metabolic disorders.

Mitochondria and Mitochondrial Diseases

Mitochondria are small structures that produce energy in almost all of your cells. They make it by combining oxygen with the fuel molecules (sugars and fats) that come from your food. When the mitochondria are defective, the cells do not have enough energy. The unused oxygen and fuel molecules build up in the cells and cause damage.

Symptoms of Mitochondrial Diseases

The symptoms of the mitochondrial disease can vary. It depends on how many mitochondria are defective, and where they are in the body. Sometimes only one organ, tissue, or cell type is affected. But often the problem affects many of them. Muscle and nerve cells have especially high energy needs, so muscular and neurological problems are common. The diseases range from mild to severe. Some types can be fatal.

Causes of Mitochondrial Diseases?

Genetic mutations cause these diseases. They usually happen before the age of 20, and some are more common in infants. There are no cures for these diseases, but treatments may help with symptoms and slow down the disease. They may include physical therapy, vitamins and supplements, special diets, and medicines.

Inheritance

Mitochondrial genetic disorder can be inherited in a variety of manners, depending on the type of condition and the location of the disease-causing change (mutation). Those caused by mutations in mitochondrial DNA are transmitted by maternal inheritance. Only egg cells (not sperm cells) contribute mitochondria to the next generation, so only females can pass on mitochondrial mutations to their children. Conditions resulting from mutations in mitochondrial DNA can appear in every generation of a family and can affect both males and females. In some cases, the condition results from a new (de novo) mutation in a mitochondrial gene and occurs in a person with no history of the condition in the family.

Mitochondrial genetic disorders caused by mutations in nuclear DNA may follow an autosomal dominant, autosomal recessive, or X-linked pattern of inheritance. In autosomal dominant conditions, one mutated copy of the responsible gene in each cell is enough to cause signs or symptoms of the condition. In some cases, an affected person inherits the mutation from an affected parent. Other cases may result from new mutations in the gene. These cases occur in people with no history of the disorder in their family. A person with an autosomal dominant condition has a 50 percent chance of passing along the altered gene to his or her child.

When a condition is inherited in an autosomal recessive manner, a person must have a change in both copies of the responsible gene in each cell. The parents of an affected person usually each carry one mutated copy of the gene and are referred to as carriers. Carriers typically do not show signs or symptoms of the condition. When 2 carriers of an autosomal recessive condition have children, each child has a 25 percent (1 in 4) risk to have the condition, a 50 percent (1 in 2) risk to be a carrier like each of the parents, and a 25 percent chance to not have the condition and not be a carrier.

A condition is considered X-linked if the mutated gene that causes the condition is located on the X chromosome, one of the two sex chromosomes (the Y chromosome is the other sex chromosome). Women have two X chromosomes and men have an X and a Y chromosome. X-linked conditions can be X-linked dominant or X-linked recessive. The inheritance is X-linked dominant if one copy of the altered gene in each cell is sufficient to cause the condition. Women with an X-linked dominant condition have a 50 percent chance of passing the condition on to a son or a daughter with each pregnancy. Men with an X-linked dominant condition will pass the condition on to all of their daughters and none of their sons. The inheritance is X-linked recessive if a gene on the X chromosome causes the condition in men with one gene mutation (they have only one X chromosome) and in females with two gene mutations (they have two X chromosomes). A woman with an X-linked condition will pass the mutation on to all of her sons and daughters. This means that all of her sons will have the condition and all of her daughters will be carriers. A man with an X-linked recessive condition will pass the mutation to all of his daughters (carriers) and none of his sons.

Section 27.2

Multiple Mitochondrial Dysfunctions Syndrome

This section includes text excerpted from "Multiple Mitochondrial Dysfunctions Syndrome," Genetics Home Reference (GHR), National Institutes of Health (NIH), June 15, 2018.

Multiple mitochondrial dysfunctions syndrome (MMDS) is characterized by impairment of cellular structures called "mitochondria," which are the energy-producing centers of cells. While certain mitochondrial disorders are caused by impairment of a single stage of energy production, individuals with multiple mitochondrial dysfunctions syndrome have reduced function of more than one stage. The signs and symptoms of this severe condition begin early in life, and affected individuals usually do not live past infancy.

Affected infants typically have severe brain dysfunction (encephalopathy), which can contribute to weak muscle tone (hypotonia), seizures, and delayed development of mental and movement abilities (psychomotor delay). These infants often have difficulty growing and gaining weight at the expected rate (failure to thrive). Most affected babies have a buildup of a chemical called "lactic acid" in the body (lactic acidosis), which can be life-threatening. They may also have high levels of a molecule called "glycine" (hyperglycinemia) or elevated levels of sugar (hyperglycemia) in the blood. Some babies with multiple mitochondrial dysfunctions syndrome have high blood pressure (HBP) in the blood vessels that connect to the lungs (pulmonary hypertension (PH) or weakening of the heart muscle (cardiomyopathy).

Signs and Symptoms of Multiple Mitochondrial Dysfunctions Syndrome

The signs and symptoms of this severe condition begin early in life, and affected individuals usually do not live past infancy. Affected infants typically have severe brain dysfunction (encephalopathy), which can contribute to weak muscle tone (hypotonia), seizures, and delayed development of mental and movement abilities (psychomotor delay). These infants often have difficulty growing and gaining weight at the expected rate (failure to thrive). Most affected babies have a buildup of a chemical called "lactic acid" in the body (lactic acidosis), which can be life-threatening. They may also have high levels of a molecule called "glycine" (hyperglycinemia) or elevated levels of sugar (hyperglycemia) in the blood. Some babies with multiple mitochondrial dysfunctions syndrome have high blood pressure (HBP) in the blood vessels that connect to the lungs (pulmonary hypertension (PH)) or weakening of the heart muscle (cardiomyopathy).

Frequency and Causes of Multiple Mitochondrial Dysfunctions Syndrome

Multiple mitochondrial dysfunctions syndrome is a rare condition; its prevalence is unknown. It is one of several conditions classified as mitochondrial disorders, which affect an estimated 1 in 5,000 people worldwide.

Multiple mitochondrial dysfunctions syndrome can be caused by mutations in the *NFU1* or *BOLA3* gene. The proteins produced from each of these genes appear to be involved in the formation of molecules called "iron-sulfur (Fe-S) clusters" or in the attachment of these clusters to other proteins. Certain proteins require attachment of Fe-S clusters to function properly.

The NFU-1 and BOLA3 proteins play an important role in mitochondria. In these structures, several proteins carry out a series of chemical steps to convert the energy in food into a form that cells can use. Many of the proteins involved in these steps require Fe-S clusters to function, including protein complexes called "complex I," "complex II," and "complex III."

Fe-S clusters are also required for another mitochondrial protein to function; this protein is involved in the modification of additional proteins that aid in energy production in mitochondria, including the pyruvate dehydrogenase complex (PDC) and the alpha-ketoglutarate dehydrogenase complex (KGDHC) (also known as the "oxoglutarate dehydrogenase complex" (OGDC)). This modification is also critical to the function of the glycine cleavage system, a set of proteins that breaks down a protein building block (amino acid) called "glycine" when levels become too high.

Mutations in the *NFU1* or *BOLA3* gene reduce or eliminate production of the respective protein, which impairs Fe-S cluster formation. Consequently, proteins affected by the presence of Fe-S clusters, including those involved in energy production and glycine breakdown, cannot function normally. Reduced activity of complex I, II, or III, pyruvate dehydrogenase, or alpha-ketoglutarate dehydrogenase leads to potentially fatal lactic acidosis, encephalopathy, and other signs and symptoms of multiple mitochondrial dysfunctions syndrome. In some affected individuals, impairment of the glycine cleavage system leads to a buildup of glycine.

Section 27.3

Mitochondrial Myopathy

This section includes text excerpted from "Mitochondrial Myopathy Fact Sheet," National Institute of Neurological Disorders and Stroke (NINDS), July 6, 2018.

What Are Mitochondrial Myopathies?

Mitochondrial diseases are caused by defects in mitochondria, which are energy factories found inside almost all the cells in the body. Mitochondrial diseases that cause prominent muscular problems are called "mitochondrial myopathies" (*myo* means muscle and *pathos* means disease), while mitochondrial diseases that causes both prominent muscular and neurological problems are called "mitochondrial encephalomyopathies" (*encephalo* refers to the brain).

A typical human cell relies on hundreds of mitochondria to meet its energy needs. The symptoms of mitochondrial disease vary, because a person can have a unique mixture of healthy and defective mitochondria, with a unique distribution in the body. In most cases, mitochondrial disease is a multisystem disorder affecting more than one type of cell, tissue, or organ.

Because muscle and nerve cells have especially high energy needs, muscular and neurological problems are common features of mitochondrial disease. Other frequent complications include impaired vision, cardiac arrhythmia (abnormal heartbeat), diabetes, and stunted growth. Usually, a person with a mitochondrial disease has two or more of these conditions, some of which occur together so regularly that they are grouped into syndromes.

What Causes Mitochondrial Myopathies

Mitochondrial diseases are caused by genetic mutations. Genes provide the instructions for making proteins, and the genes involved in mitochondrial disease normally make proteins that work inside mitochondria. Within each mitochondrion, these proteins make up part of an assembly line that uses fuel molecules (sugars and fats) derived from food combined with oxygen to manufacture the energy molecule adenosine triphosphate (ATP).

Proteins at the beginning of the assembly line import sugars and fats into the mitochondrion and then break them down to provide energy. Proteins toward the end of the line—organized into five groups called "complexes I, II, III, IV, and V"—harness that energy to make ATP. This highly efficient part of the ATP manufacturing process requires oxygen, and is called the "respiratory chain." Some mitochondrial diseases are named for the part of the respiratory chain that is affected, such as complex I deficiency.

A cell filled with defective mitochondria becomes deprived of ATP and can accumulate a backlog of unused fuel molecules and destructive forms of oxygen called "free radicals" or "reactive oxygen species." These are the targets of antioxidant compounds (found in many foods and nutritional supplements) that appear to offer general defenses against aging and disease.

In such cases, excess fuel molecules are used to make ATP by inefficient means, which can generate potentially harmful byproducts, such as lactic acid. (This also occurs when a cell has an inadequate oxygen supply, which can happen to muscle cells during strenuous exercise.) The buildup of lactic acid in the blood—called "lactic acidosis"—is associated with muscle fatigue, and might damage muscle and nerve tissue.

Muscle and nerve cells use the ATP derived from mitochondria as their main source of energy. The combined effects of energy deprivation and toxin accumulation in these cells can lead to many muscular and neurological symptoms.

What Are the Symptoms of Mitochondrial Myopathy?
Myopathy

The main symptoms of mitochondrial myopathy are muscle fatigue, weakness, and exercise intolerance. The severity of any of these symptoms varies greatly from one person to the next, even in the same family.

In some individuals, weakness is most prominent in muscles that control movements of the eyes and eyelids. Two common consequences are the gradual paralysis of eye movements, called "progressive external ophthalmoplegia (PEO)," and drooping of the upper eyelids, called "ptosis." Often, people automatically compensate for PEO by moving their head to look in different directions, and might not notice any visual problems. Ptosis can impair vision and cause a listless expression but can be corrected by surgery.

Mitochondrial myopathies also can cause weakness and wasting in other muscles of the face and neck, which can lead to difficulty with swallowing and, more rarely, slurred speech. People with mitochondrial myopathies also may experience muscle weakness in their arms and legs.

Exercise intolerance, also called "exertional fatigue," refers to unusual feelings of exhaustion brought on by physical exertion. The degree of exercise intolerance varies greatly among individuals. Some people might have trouble only with athletic activities, such as jogging, while others might experience problems with everyday activities, such as walking to the mailbox or lifting a milk carton.

Sometimes, mitochondrial disease is associated with muscle cramps. In rare instances, it can lead to muscle breakdown and pain after exercise. This breakdown causes leakage of a protein called "myoglobin" from the muscles into the urine (myoglobinuria). Cramps or myoglobinuria usually occur when someone with exercise intolerance "overdoes it," and can happen during the overexertion or several hours afterward.

While overexertion should be avoided, moderate exercise appears to help people with mitochondrial myopathy maintain strength.

Encephalomyopathy

A mitochondrial encephalomyopathy typically includes some of the symptoms of myopathy plus one or more neurological symptoms. Again, these symptoms vary greatly among individuals in both type and severity.

In addition to affecting eye muscles, a mitochondrial encephalomyopathy can affect the eye itself and parts of the brain involved in vision. For instance, vision loss, due to optic atrophy (shrinkage of the optic nerve) or retinopathy (degeneration of some of the cells that line the back of the eye), is a common symptom of mitochondrial encephalomyopathy.

Sensorineural hearing loss is a common symptom of mitochondrial diseases. It is caused by damage to the inner ear (the cochlea) or to the auditory nerve, which connects the inner ear to the brain. Sensorineural hearing loss is permanent but it can be managed through alternative forms of communication, hearing aids, or cochlear implants. Hearing aids amplify sounds before they reach the inner ear. Cochlear implants bypass damaged parts of the inner ear and stimulate the auditory nerve.

Mitochondrial diseases can cause ataxia, which refers to trouble with balance and coordination. People with ataxia are prone to falls, and may need to use supportive aids, such as railings, a walker, or a wheelchair. Physical and occupational therapy also may help.

Other common symptoms of mitochondrial encephalomyopathy include migraine headaches and seizures. There are many effective medications for treating and helping to prevent migraines and seizures, including anticonvulsants and other drugs developed to treat epilepsy.

Special Issues in Mitochondrial Diseases
Respiratory Care

Mitochondrial diseases can affect the muscles or parts of the brain that support breathing. A person with mild respiratory problems might require occasional respiratory support, such as pressurized air. Someone with more severe problems might require permanent support from a ventilator. People should watch for signs of respiratory problems (such as shortness of breath or morning headaches) and have regular checkups with a respiratory specialist.

Cardiac Care

Some mitochondrial diseases can cause cardiomyopathy (heart muscle weakness) or arrhythmia (irregular heart beat). Although dangerous, cardiac arrhythmia is treatable with a pacemaker, which stimulates a normal heartbeat. People with mitochondrial disorders may need to have regular examinations by a cardiologist.

Other Potential Health Issues

People with a mitochondrial disease may experience gastrointestinal (GI) problems, diabetes, and/or kidney problems. Some of these problems are direct effects of mitochondrial defects in the digestive system, pancreas (in diabetes), or kidneys, and others are indirect effects of mitochondrial defects in other tissues. For example, myoglobinuria stresses the kidneys' ability to filter waste from the blood and can cause kidney damage.

What Issues Are of Special Concern in Children
Vision

Although gradual paralysis of eye movements (PEO) and ptosis typically cause only mild visual impairment in adults, they are potentially more harmful in children with mitochondrial myopathies.

Because the development of the brain is sensitive to childhood experiences, either PEO or ptosis during childhood can cause permanent damage to the brain's visual system. It is important for children with signs of PEO or ptosis to have their vision checked by a specialist.

Developmental Delays

Due to muscle weakness, brain abnormalities, or a combination of both, children with mitochondrial diseases may have difficulty developing certain skills. For example, they might take an unusually long time to reach motor milestones, such as sitting, crawling, and walking. As they get older, they may be unable to get around as easily as other children their age and may have speech problems and/or learning disabilities. Children affected by these problems may benefit from early intervention and services, such as physical and speech therapy, and possibly an individualized education program at school.

Are There Specific Treatments for the Mitochondrial Myopathies?

Instead of focusing on specific complications of mitochondrial disease, some treatments under investigation aim at fixing or bypassing the defective mitochondria. These treatments are nutritional supplements based on three natural substances involved in ATP production in our cells.

One substance, **creatine,** normally acts as a reserve for ATP by forming a compound called "creatine phosphate" (also called "phosphocreatine"). When a cell's demand for ATP exceeds the amount its mitochondria can produce, creatine can release phosphate (the "P" in ATP) to rapidly enhance the ATP supply. In fact, creatine phosphate typically provides the initial burst of ATP required for strenuous muscle activity.

Another substance, **carnitine**, generally improves the efficiency of ATP production by helping import certain fuel molecules into mitochondria and cleaning up some of the toxic byproducts of ATP production. Carnitine is available as an over-the-counter (OTC) supplement called "L-carnitine."

Finally, **coenzyme Q_{10},** also called "CoQ_{10}" or "ubiquinone," is a component of the mitochondrial respiratory chain (which uses oxygen to manufacture ATP). CoQ_{10} is also an antioxidant. Some mitochondrial diseases are caused by CoQ_{10} deficiency, and CoQ_{10} supplementation is clearly beneficial in these cases. It might provide some relief from other mitochondrial diseases.

Creatine, L-carnitine, and CoQ_{10} supplements often are combined into a "cocktail" for treating mitochondrial disease. Although there is a need for careful studies to confirm the value of this treatment, some people with mitochondrial disease have reported modest benefits.

How Are Mitochondrial Myopathies Inherited?

The inheritance of mitochondrial diseases is complex, and often a mitochondrial myopathy can be difficult to trace through a family tree. In fact, many cases of mitochondrial disease are sporadic, meaning that they occur without any family history.

To understand how mitochondrial diseases are inherited, it is important to know that there are two types of genes essential to mitochondria. The first type is housed within the nucleus—a compartment within our cells that contains most of our genetic material, or DNA. The second type resides exclusively within the DNA contained inside the mitochondria.

Mutations in either nuclear DNA (nDNA) or mitochondrial DNA (mtDNA) can cause mitochondrial disease.

Nuclear DNA is packaged into structures called "chromosomes"—22 pairs of sex-related chromosomes (called "autosomes") and a single pair of sex chromosomes (XX in females and XY in males). This means that except for genes on the X chromosome, everyone has two copies of the genes in nDNA, with one copy inherited from each parent. There are three inheritance patterns seen for diseases caused by nDNA mutations:

- Autosomal recessive means that it takes two mutant copies of a gene—one inherited from each parent—to cause the disease.

- Autosomal dominant means it takes just one mutant copy of a gene—inherited from one parent—to cause the disease.

Usually, X-linked diseases appear only in males. An affected male's mother and any daughters he has will carry the gene for the disease but typically will not have symptoms.

Unlike nDNA, mtDNA passes only from mother to child. This is because during conception, when the sperm fuses with the egg, the sperm's mitochondria and its mtDNA are destroyed. Mitochondrial diseases caused by mtDNA mutations are unique because they are inherited in a maternal pattern. A mother can pass defective mtDNA to any of her children, but only her daughters—and not her sons—will pass it to the next generation.

Another unique feature of mtDNA diseases arises from the fact that a typical human cell contains only one nucleus but hundreds of mitochondria. A single cell can contain both mutant and normal mitochondria, and the balance between the two will determine the cell's health, which can also explain the range of symptoms in mtDNA diseases.

The risk of passing on a mitochondrial disease to a child depends on many factors, including whether the disease is caused by mutations in nDNA or mtDNA.

What Syndromes Occur with Mitochondrial Diseases

Some syndromes associated with mitochondrial disease are:

Barth Syndrome

Onset. Infancy

Features. Typical symptoms include cardiomyopathy, general muscle weakness, and a low white blood cell (WBC) count, which leads to an increased risk of infection. This syndrome was once considered uniformly fatal in infancy, but some individuals are now living much longer.

Inheritance pattern. X-linked

Chronic Progressive External Ophthalmoplegia (cPEO)

Onset. Usually in adolescence or early adulthood

Features. PEO is often a symptom of mitochondrial disease. In some people, it is a chronic, slowly progressive condition associated with instability to move the eyes and general weakness and exercise intolerance.

Inheritance pattern. Autosomal, but may occur sporadically

Kearns-Sayre Syndrome (KSS)

Onset. Before the age of 20

Features. PEO (usually as the initial symptom) and pigmentary retinopathy, a "salt-and-pepper" pigmentation in the retina that can affect vision. Other common symptoms include cardiomyopathy, conduction block (a type of cardiac arrhythmia), ataxia, short stature, neuropathy, and deafness.

Inheritance pattern. Autosomal (mostly sporadic)

Leigh Syndrome (MILS, or Maternally Inherited Leigh Syndrome)

Onset. Infancy or early childhood

Features. Brain abnormalities that can result in abnormal muscle tone, ataxia, seizures, impaired vision and hearing, developmental delays, and respiratory problems. Infants with the disease have a poor prognosis.

Inheritance pattern. Maternal, autosomal recessive, X-linked

Mitochondrial DNA Depletion Syndromes (MDDS)

Onset. Infancy

Features. A myopathic form of mitochondrial DNA depletion syndrome (MDS or MDDS) is characterized by weakness that eventually affects the respiratory muscles. Some forms of MDDS, such as Alpers syndrome, are marked by brain abnormalities and progressive liver disease. The anticonvulsant sodium valproate should be used with caution in children with Alpers syndrome because it can increase the risk of liver failure.

Inheritance pattern. Autosomal

Mitochondrial Encephalomyopathy, Lactic Acidosis, and Stroke-like Episodes (MELAS)

Onset. Childhood to early adulthood

Features. The hallmarks of MELAS are encephalomyopathy with seizures and/or dementia, lactic acidosis, and recurrent stroke-like episodes. These episodes are not typical strokes, which are interruptions in the brain's blood supply that cause sudden neurological symptoms. However, the episodes can produce stroke-like symptoms in the short term (such as temporary vision loss, difficulty speaking, or difficulty understanding speech) and lead to progressive brain injury. The cause of the stroke-like episodes is unclear.

Inheritance pattern. Maternal

Mitochondrial Neurogastrointestinal Encephalomyopathy (MNGIE)

Onset. Usually before the age of 20

Features. This disorder is characterized by PEO, ptosis, limb weakness, and gastrointestinal (digestive) problems, including vomiting, chronic diarrhea, and abdominal pain. Another common symptom is peripheral neuropathy (a malfunction of the nerves that can lead to sensory impairment and muscle weakness).

Inheritance pattern. Autosomal recessive

Myoclonus Epilepsy with Ragged Red Fibers (MERRF)

Onset. Late childhood to adolescence

Features. The most prominent symptoms of MERRF are myoclonus (muscle jerks), seizures, ataxia, and muscle weakness. The disease also can cause hearing impairment and short stature.

Inheritance pattern. Maternal

Neuropathy, Ataxia, and Retinitis Pigmentosa (NARP)

Onset. Infancy to adulthood

Features. NARP is caused by an mtDNA mutation that is also linked to maternally inherited Leigh syndrome (MILS) for which it is named. NARP can involve developmental delay, seizures, and dementia. (Retinitis pigmentosa refers to a degeneration of the retina in the eye, with resulting loss of vision).

Inheritance pattern. Maternal

Pearson Syndrome

Onset. Infancy

Features. This syndrome involves severe anemia and malfunction of the pancreas. Children who have the disease usually go on to develop Kearns-Sayre syndrome.

Inheritance pattern. Autosomal (often sporadic)

How Are Mitochondrial Diseases Diagnosed?

The hallmark symptoms of mitochondrial myopathy include muscle weakness, exercise intolerance, impaired hearing and vision, ataxia, seizures, learning disabilities, heart defects, diabetes, and poor growth—none of which are unique to mitochondrial disease. However, a combination of three or more of these symptoms in one person strongly points to mitochondrial disease, especially when the symptoms involve more than one organ system.

To evaluate the extent of these symptoms, a physician usually begins by taking the individual's medical history. Because mitochondrial diseases are genetic, a family history also is an important part of the diagnosis. Physical and neurological exams also will be part of the evaluation.

The physical exam typically includes tests of strength and endurance, such as an exercise test (which can involve activities like repeatedly making a fist). The neurological exam can include tests of reflexes, vision, speech, and basic cognitive (thinking) skills.

Typically, the doctor will order laboratory tests to look for diabetes and liver and kidney problems. The doctor is likely to order an electrocardiogram (EKG) to check the heart for signs of arrhythmia and cardiomyopathy.

Tests may be ordered to look for abnormalities in the brain and muscles. Diagnostic imaging that produces detailed pictures of organs, bones, and tissues, such as computed tomography (CT) or magnetic resonance imaging (MRI), might be used to inspect the brain for developmental abnormalities or signs of damage. In an individual who has seizures, the doctor might order an electroencephalogram (EEG), which involves placing electrodes on the scalp to record brain activity.

Since lactic acidosis is a common feature of mitochondrial disease, it is routine to test for elevated lactic acid in the blood and urine. Some cases might warrant measuring lactic acid in the cerebral spinal fluid (CSF) that fills spaces within the brain and spinal cord. The measurement can be made by collecting CSF through a spinal tap, or estimated by magnetic resonance (MR) spectroscopy—a technique that uses an MRI signal to detect changes in the level of lactic acid and other chemicals in the brain.

One of the most important tests for mitochondrial disease is the muscle biopsy, which involves removing and examining a small sample of muscle tissue. When treated with a dye that stains mitochondria red, muscles affected by mitochondrial disease often show ragged red fibers—muscle cells (fibers) that have excessive mitochondria. Other stains can detect the absence of essential mitochondrial enzymes in the muscle. It also is possible to extract mitochondrial proteins from the muscle and measure their activity.

Noninvasive techniques can be used to examine muscle without taking a tissue sample. For instance, MR spectroscopy can be used to measure levels of the organic molecule phosphocreatine and ATP (which are often depleted in muscles affected by mitochondrial disease).

Finally, genetic testing can determine whether someone has a genetic mutation that causes mitochondrial disease. These tests use genetic material extracted from blood or from a muscle biopsy. Although a positive test result can confirm diagnosis of a mitochondrial disorder, a negative test result can be harder to interpret. It could mean a person has a genetic mutation that the test was not able to detect.

Chapter 28

Neurofibromatosis

What Is Neurofibromatosis?

Neurofibromatosis (NF) is a genetic neurological disorder that can affect the brain, spinal cord, nerves, and skin. Tumors, or neurofibromas, grow along the body's nerves or on or underneath the skin. Scientists have classified NF into two distinct types: neurofibromatosis type 1 (NF1) and NF2. NF1, formerly known as "von Recklinghausen's NF," is the more common of the two types. It occurs in approximately 1 in 4,000 births. NF2, also referred to as "bilateral acoustic NF," "central NF" or "vestibular NF," occurs less frequently—1 in 40,000 births. Occurrences of NF1 and NF2 are present among all racial groups and affect both sexes equally. The tumors arise from changes in the nerve cells and skin cells. Tumors also may press on the body's vital areas as their size increases. NF may lead to developmental abnormalities and/or increased chances of having learning disabilities. Other forms of NF, where the symptoms are not consistent with that of NF1 or NF2, have been observed. A rare form of NF is schwannomatosis. However, the genetic cause of this form of NF has not been found.

What Are the Symptoms of Neurofibromatosis?

Symptoms for neurofibromatosis type 1 include:

- Presence of light brown sports (café-au-lait) on the skin

This chapter includes text excerpted from "Learning about Neurofibromatosis," National Human Genome Research Institute (NHGRI), August 16, 2016.

- Appearance of two or more neurofibromas (pea-sized bumps) that can grow either on the nerve tissue, under the skin or on many nerve tissues

- Manifestation of freckles under the armpits or in the groin areas

- Appearance of tiny tan clumps of pigment in the iris of the eyes (Lisch nodules)

- Tumors along the optic nerve of the eye (optic glioma)

- Severe curvature of the spine (scoliosis)

- Enlargement or malformation of other bones in the skeletal system

Symptoms for NF1 vary for each individual. Those that are skin-related are often present at birth, during infancy, and by a child's tenth birthday. From 10 to 15 years of age, neurofibromas may become apparent. Symptoms—such as café-au-lait spots, freckling, and Lisch nodules—pose minimal or no health risk to a person. Though neurofibromas are generally a cosmetic concern for those with NF1, they can sometimes be psychologically distressing. For 15 percent of individuals with NF1, the symptoms can be severely debilitating. Neurofibromas can grow inside the body and may affect organ systems. Hormonal changes at puberty and/or even pregnancy may increase the size of neurofibromas. Nearly 50 percent of children with NF1 have speech problems, learning disabilities, seizures, and hyperactivity. Less than 1 percent of those affected with NF1 may have malignant tumors and may require treatment.

Symptoms for neurofibromatosis type 2 include:

- Tumors along the eighth cranial nerve (schwannomas)

- Meningiomas and other brain tumors

- Ringing noises inside the ear (tinnitus), hearing loss and/or deafness

- Cataracts at a young age

- Spinal tumors

- Balance problems

- Wasting of muscles (atrophy)

Individuals with NF2 develop tumors that grow on the eighth cranial nerves and on the vestibular nerves. These tumors often cause pressure on the acoustic nerves, which result in hearing loss. Hearing loss may begin as early as an individual's teenage years. Tinnitus, dizziness, facial numbness, balance problems, and chronic headaches may also surface during the teenage years. Numbness may also occur in other parts of the body, due to spinal cord tumors.

The rare form of NF, schwannomatosis, which was identified, does not develop on the eighth cranial nerves and does not cause hearing loss. It causes pain primarily, and in any part of the body. Though schwannomatosis may also lead to numbness, weakness or balance problems, such as NF1 or NF2, the symptoms are less severe.

How Is Neurofibromatosis Diagnosed?

Neurofibromatosis is diagnosed from a combination of findings. For children to be diagnosed with NF1, they must show at least two of the aforementioned symptoms associated with NF1. A physical examination by a doctor familiar with the disorder is usually performed. Doctors may use special lamps to examine the skin for café-au-lait spots. Doctors may also rely on magnetic resonance imaging (MRI), X-rays, computerized tomography (CT scan) and blood tests to detect defects in the *NF1* gene.

For NF2, doctors will pay close attention to hearing loss. Hearing tests, as well as imaging tests, are used to look for tumors in and around the auditory nerves, the spinal cord, or the brain. Audiometry and brainstem auditory evoked response tests can help determine whether the eighth cranial nerve is functioning properly. Family history of NF2 is also a key focal area for diagnosis.

Genetic testing is also used to diagnose NF1 and NF2. Testing conducted before birth (prenatal) is helpful to identify individuals who have a family history of the disorder but do not yet have the symptoms. Still, gene tests have no way of predicting the severity of NF1 or NF2. Genetic testing is performed by either direct gene mutation analysis and/or linkage analysis. Mutation analysis looks to identify the particular gene changes that cause NF. Linkage analysis is useful if the mutation analysis does not provide enough conclusive information. With a linkage analysis, blood tests from multiple family members are taken to track the chromosome that carries the disease-causing gene through two or more generations. Linkage testing is around 90 percent accurate in determining whether individuals have NF. Mutation analysis is 95 percent accurate in finding a mutation for NF1, and 65 percent accurate for NF2.

How Is Neurofibromatosis Treated?

Though there is no cure for either NF1 or NF2, there are ways to treat the effects of the disease. Surgery may be helpful in removing tumors, though there is a risk of the tumors regenerating. For optic gliomas, treatment may include surgery and/or radiation. For scoliosis, treatment may include surgery or back braces. For symptoms associated with NF2, surgery may be a viable option, however not without complications that could result in additional loss of hearing or deafness. Hearing aids are ineffective when parts of the auditory nerve are removed. A breakthrough in treatment became available recently to NF2 patients when the U.S. Food and Drug Administration (FDA) approved an Auditory Brainstem Implant (ABI) for those who have parts of their auditory nerve removed and have suffered from subsequent hearing loss. The implant transmits sound signals to the brain directly and allows people to hear certain sounds and speech. Radiation treatment may also help relieve symptoms associated with NF2.

What Do We Know about Heredity and Neurofibromatosis?

Neurofibromatosis can either be an inherited disorder or the product of a gene mutation. Both NF1 and NF2 are caused by two separate abnormal genes and may be inherited from parents who have NF or may be the result of a mutation in the sperm or egg cells. NF is considered an autosomal dominant disorder because the gene is located on one of the 22 chromosome pairs, called "autosomes." The gene for NF1 is located on chromosome 17. The gene for NF2 is located on chromosome 22. Children have a 50 percent chance of inheriting the genes that cause NF if the parent has NF. The type of NF the child inherits will be the same as that of the parent. Therefore, if the parent has NF1, there will be a 50 percent chance the child will have NF1. If the parent has NF2, there will be a 50 percent chance the child will have NF2. The only difference between the child and the parent in these circumstances is the severity of NF and the appearance of symptoms. The presence of only one changed or affected gene can cause the disorder to appear. However, the action of the unaffected gene that is paired with the dominant gene does not prevent the disorder from appearing. People with NF can make two different kinds of reproductive cells: one that can cause a child to have NF and the other that will produce an unaffected child if that is the gene that happens to be used. When an unaffected individual conceives a child with a person with NF, there are four possible cell combinations—two combinations that will yield a child with NF and the other two that will yield an unaffected child.

Chapter 29

Neuromuscular Disorders

Chapter Contents

Section 29.1

What Are Neuromuscular Disorders?

This section includes text excerpted from "Neuromuscular Disorders," MedlinePlus, National Institutes of Health (NIH), December 11, 2018.

Neuromuscular disorders affect your neuromuscular system. They can cause problems with:

- The nerves that control your muscles

- Your muscles

- Communication between your nerves and muscles

These disorders can cause your muscles to become weak and waste away. You may also have symptoms such as spasms, twitching, and pain.

Examples of neuromuscular disorders include:

- Amyotrophic lateral sclerosis (ALS)

- Muscular dystrophy (MD)

- Myasthenia gravis

- Spinal muscular atrophy (SMA)

There can be different causes for these diseases. Many of them are genetic. This means they are inherited (run in families) or are caused by a new mutation in your genes. Some neuromuscular disorders are autoimmune diseases. Sometimes the cause is not known.

Many neuromuscular diseases have no cure. But treatments may improve symptoms, increase mobility, and lengthen life.

Section 29.2

Charcot-Marie-Tooth Disease

This section includes text excerpted from "Charcot-Marie-Tooth Disease Fact Sheet," National Institute of Neurological Disorders and Stroke (NINDS), July 6, 2018.

What Is Charcot-Marie-Tooth Disease?

Charcot-Marie-Tooth disease (CMT) is one of the most common inherited neurological disorders, affecting approximately 1 in 2,500 people in the United States. The disease is named for the three physicians who first identified it in 1886—Jean-Martin Charcot and Pierre Marie in Paris, France, and Howard Henry Tooth in Cambridge, England. CMT, also known as "hereditary motor and sensory neuropathy" (HMSN) or peroneal muscular atrophy, comprises a group of disorders that affect peripheral nerves. The peripheral nerves lie outside the brain and spinal cord and supply the muscles and sensory organs in the limbs. Disorders that affect the peripheral nerves are called "peripheral neuropathies."

What Are the Symptoms of Charcot-Marie-Tooth Disease?

The neuropathy of CMT affects both motor and sensory nerves. (Motor nerves cause muscles to contract and control voluntary muscle activity, such as speaking, walking, breathing, and swallowing.) A typical feature includes weakness of the foot and lower leg muscles, which may result in foot drop and a high-stepped gait with frequent tripping or falls. Foot deformities, such as high arches and hammertoes (a condition in which the middle joint of a toe bends upwards) are also characteristic due to weakness of the small muscles in the feet. In addition, the lower legs may take on an "inverted champagne bottle" appearance due to the loss of muscle bulk. Later in the disease, weakness and muscle atrophy may occur in the hands, resulting in difficulty with carrying out fine motor skills (the coordination of small movements usually in the fingers, hands, wrists, feet, and tongue).

Onset of symptoms is most often in adolescence or early adulthood, but some individuals develop symptoms in mid-adulthood. The severity of symptoms varies greatly among individuals and even among family members with the disease. Progression of symptoms is gradual. Pain can range from mild to severe, and some people may need to rely on foot or leg braces or other orthopedic devices to maintain mobility. Although in rare cases, individuals may have respiratory muscle weakness. CMT is not considered a fatal disease and people with most forms of CMT have a normal life expectancy.

What Causes Charcot-Marie-Tooth Disease

A nerve cell communicates information to distant targets by sending electrical signals down a long, thin part of the cell called the "axon." In order to increase the speed at which these electrical signals travel, the axon is insulated by myelin, which is produced by another type of cell called the "Schwann cell." Myelin twists around the axon like a jelly roll cake and prevents the loss of electrical signals. Without an intact axon and myelin sheath, peripheral nerve cells are unable to activate target muscles or relay sensory information from the limbs back to the brain.

CMT is caused by mutations in genes that produce proteins involved in the structure and function of either the peripheral nerve axon or the myelin sheath. Although different proteins are abnormal in different forms of CMT disease, all of the mutations affect the normal function of the peripheral nerves. Consequently, these nerves slowly degenerate and lose the ability to communicate with their distant targets. The degeneration of motor nerves results in muscle weakness and atrophy in the extremities (arms, legs, hands, or feet), and in some cases, the degeneration of sensory nerves results in a reduced ability to feel heat, cold, and pain.

The gene mutations in CMT disease are usually inherited. Each of us normally possesses two copies of every gene, one inherited from each parent. Some forms of CMT are inherited in an autosomal dominant fashion, which means that only one copy of the abnormal gene is needed to cause the disease. Other forms of CMT are inherited in an autosomal recessive fashion, which means that both copies of the abnormal gene must be present to cause the disease. Still, other forms of CMT are inherited in an X-linked fashion, which means that the abnormal gene is located on the X chromosome. The X and Y chromosomes determine an individual's sex. Individuals with two X chromosomes are female and individuals with one X and one Y chromosome are male.

In rare cases, the gene mutation causing CMT disease is a new mutation which occurs spontaneously in the individual's genetic material and has not been passed down through the family.

What Are the Types of Charcot-Marie-Tooth Disease?

There are many forms of CMT disease, including CMT1, CMT2, CMT3, CMT4, and CMTX. CMT1, caused by abnormalities in the myelin sheath, has three main types. CMT1A is an autosomal dominant disease that results from a duplication of the gene on chromosome 17 that carries the instructions for producing the peripheral myelin protein-22 (PMP-22). The PMP-22 protein is a critical component of the myelin sheath. Overexpression of this gene causes the structure and function of the myelin sheath to be abnormal. Patients experience weakness and atrophy of the muscles of the lower legs beginning in adolescence; later they experience hand weakness and sensory loss. Interestingly, a different neuropathy distinct from CMT1A called "hereditary neuropathy" with predisposition to pressure palsy (HNPP) is caused by a deletion of one of the *PMP-22* genes. In this case, abnormally low levels of the *PMP-22* gene result in episodic, recurrent demyelinating neuropathy. CMT1B is an autosomal dominant disease caused by mutations in the gene that carries the instructions for manufacturing the myelin protein zero (P0), which is another critical component of the myelin sheath. Most of these mutations are point mutations, meaning a mistake occurs in only one letter of the DNA genetic code. To date, scientists have identified more than 120 different point mutations in the *P0* gene. As a result of abnormalities in P0, CMT1B produces symptoms similar to those found in CMT1A. The less common CMT1C, CMT1D, and CMT1E, which also have symptoms similar to those found in CMT1A, are caused by mutations in the *LITAF*, *EGR2*, and *NEFL* genes, respectively.

CMT2 results from abnormalities in the axon of the peripheral nerve cell rather than the myelin sheath. It is less common than CMT1. CMT2A, the most common axonal form of CMT, is caused by mutations in Mitofusin 2, a protein associated with mitochondrial fusion. CMT2A has also been linked to mutations in the gene that codes for the kinesin family member 1B-beta protein, but this has not been replicated in other cases. Kinesins are proteins that act as motors to help power the transport of materials along the cell. Other less common forms of CMT2 have been recently identified and are associated with various genes: CMT2B (associated with RAB7), CMT2D (*GARS*), CMT2E (*NEFL*), CMT2H (HSP27), and CMT2l (HSP22).

CMT3 or Dejerine-Sottas disease is a severe demyelinating neuropathy that begins in infancy. Infants have severe muscle atrophy, weakness, and sensory problems. This rare disorder can be caused by a specific point mutation in the *P0* gene or a point mutation in the *PMP-22* gene.

CMT4 comprises several different subtypes of autosomal recessive demyelinating motor and sensory neuropathies. Each neuropathy subtype is caused by a different genetic mutation, may affect a particular ethnic population, and produces distinct physiologic or clinical characteristics. Individuals with CMT4 generally develop symptoms of leg weakness in childhood and by adolescence, they may not be able to walk. Several genes have been identified as causing CMT4, including *GDAP1* (CMT4A), *MTMR13* (CMT4B1), *MTMR2* (CMT4B2), *SH3TC2* (CMT4C), *NDG1* (CMT4D), *EGR2* (CMT4E), *PRX* (CMT4F), *FDG4* (CMT4H), and *FIG4* (CMT4J).

CMTX is caused by a point mutation in the *connexin-32* gene on the X chromosome. The connexin-32 protein is expressed in Schwann cells—cells that wrap around nerve axons, making up a single segment of the myelin sheath. This protein may be involved in Schwann cell communication with the axon. Males who inherit one mutated gene from their mothers show moderate to severe symptoms of the disease, beginning in late childhood or adolescence (the Y chromosome that males inherit from their fathers does not have the *connexin-32* gene). Females who inherit one mutated gene from one parent and one normal gene from the other parent may develop mild symptoms in adolescence or later, or may not develop symptoms of the disease at all.

How Is Charcot-Marie-Tooth Disease Diagnosed?

Diagnosis of CMT begins with a standard medical history, family history, and neurological examination. Individuals will be asked about the nature and duration of their symptoms and whether other family members have the disease. During the neurological examination, a physician will look for evidence of muscle weakness in the individual's arms, legs, hands, and feet, decreased muscle bulk, reduced tendon reflexes, and sensory loss. Doctors look for evidence of foot deformities, such as high arches, hammertoes, inverted heel, or flat feet. Other orthopedic problems, such as mild scoliosis or hip dysplasia, may also be present. A specific sign that may be found in people with CMT1 is nerve enlargement that may be felt or even seen through the skin. These enlarged nerves, called "hypertrophic nerves," are caused by abnormally thickened myelin sheaths.

If CMT is suspected, the physician may order electrodiagnostic tests. This testing consists of two parts: nerve conduction studies and electromyography (EMG). During nerve conduction studies, electrodes are placed on the skin over a peripheral motor or sensory nerve. These electrodes produce a small electric shock that may cause mild discomfort. This electrical impulse stimulates sensory and motor nerves and provides quantifiable information that the doctor can use to arrive at a diagnosis. EMG involves inserting a needle electrode through the skin to measure the bioelectrical activity of muscles. Specific abnormalities in the readings signify axon degeneration. EMG may be useful in further characterizing the distribution and severity of peripheral nerve involvement.

Genetic testing is available for some types of CMT and results are usually enough to confirm a diagnosis. In addition, genetic counseling is available to assist individuals in understanding their condition and plan for the future.

If all the diagnostic workup is inconclusive or genetic testing comes back negative, a neurologist may perform a nerve biopsy to confirm the diagnosis. A nerve biopsy involves removing a small piece of peripheral nerve through an incision in the skin. This is most often done by removing a piece of the nerve that runs down the calf of the leg. The nerve is then examined under a microscope. Individuals with CMT1 typically show signs of abnormal myelination. Specifically, "onion bulb" formations may be seen, which represent axons surrounded by layers of demyelinating and remyelinating Schwann cells. Individuals with CMT1 usually show signs of axon degeneration. Skin biopsy has been used to study unmyelinated and myelinated nerve fibers in a minimally invasive way, but their clinical use in CMT has not yet been established.

How Is Charcot-Marie-Tooth Disease Treated?

There is no cure for CMT, but physical therapy, occupational therapy, braces, and other orthopedic devices, and even orthopedic surgery can help individuals cope with the disabling symptoms of the disease. In addition, pain-killing drugs can be prescribed for individuals who have severe pain.

Physical and occupational therapy, the preferred treatment for CMT, involves muscle-strength training, muscle and ligament stretching, stamina training, and moderate aerobic exercise. Most therapists recommend a specialized treatment program designed with the approval of the person's physician to fit individual abilities and needs. Therapists also suggest entering into a treatment program early; muscle strengthening may delay or reduce muscle atrophy, so strength training is most useful if it begins before nerve degeneration and muscle weakness progress to the point of disability.

Stretching may prevent or reduce joint deformities that result from uneven muscle pull on bones. Exercises to help build stamina or increase endurance will help prevent the fatigue that results from performing everyday activities that require strength and mobility. Moderate aerobic activity can help to maintain cardiovascular fitness and overall health. Most therapists recommend low-impact or no-impact exercises, such as biking or swimming, rather than activities such as walking or jogging, which may put stress on fragile muscles and joints.

Many CMT patients require ankle braces and other orthopedic devices to maintain everyday mobility and prevent injury. Ankle braces can help prevent ankle sprains by providing support and stability during activities, such as walking or climbing stairs. High-top shoes or boots can also provide support for weak ankles. Thumb splints can help with hand weakness and loss of fine motor skills. Assistive devices should be used before disability sets in because the devices may prevent muscle strain and reduce muscle weakening. Some individuals with CMT may decide to have orthopedic surgery to reverse foot and joint deformities.

Section 29.3

Early-Onset Primary Dystonia

This section includes text excerpted from "DYT-TOR1A," Genetic and Rare Diseases Information Center (GARD), National Center for Advancing Translational Sciences (NCATS), October 31, 2016.

Early-onset generalized dystonia is a neurologic movement disorder that usually begins in childhood or adolescence. This is the most common hereditary form of dystonia. Symptoms start in one part of the body (usually an arm, foot, or leg) and are usually first apparent with actions such as writing or walking. With time, the contractions may spread to other parts of the body, causing the muscles to twist the body into unnatural positions. Symptoms can vary greatly, even among members of the same family. For some, the disorder can cause significant disability, while others may experience only isolated writer's cramp. A small deletion in the *DYT1* gene is the major cause of early-onset dystonia. The genetic change responsible for early-onset generalized dystonia is inherited in an autosomal dominant manner, though not everyone who inherits the genetic change will develop the condition. It is thought that only 30 percent of individuals who inherit the mutation will develop *DYT1* dystonia. This is known as "reduced penetrance." Treatments include oral medications such as trihexyphenidyl, baclofen, and clonazepam. Botulinum toxin injections may be used in conjunction with oral medications when symptoms are focused in a certain area. In some cases, deep brain stimulation may be indicated.

Treatment
U.S. Food and Drug Administration Approved Treatments

The medication listed below has been approved by the U.S. Food and Drug Administration (FDA) as an orphan product for treatment of this condition.

- Botulinum toxin type A (Brand name: Botox). Manufactured by Allergan, Inc.

FDA-approved indication: Treatment of cervical dystonia in adults is to decrease the severity of abnormal head position and neck pain associated with cervical dystonia. Treatment of blepharospasm or strabismus associated with dystonia in adults (patients 12 years of age and above).

Section 29.4

Friedreich Ataxia

This section includes text excerpted from "Friedreich Ataxia Fact Sheet," National Institute of Neurological Disorders and Stroke (NINDS), August 15, 2018.

Friedreich ataxia (FA) is a rare inherited disease that causes progressive nervous system damage and movement problems. It usually begins in childhood and leads to impaired muscle coordination (ataxia) that worsens over time.

In FA, nerve fibers in the spinal cord and peripheral nerves degenerate, becoming thinner. Peripheral nerves carry information from the brain to the body and from the body back to the brain, such as a message that the feet are cold or a signal to the muscles to generate movement. The cerebellum, part of the brain that coordinates balance and movement, also degenerates to a lesser extent. This damage results in awkward, unsteady movements and impaired sensory functions. The disorder also causes problems in the heart (in as many as one-third of affected individuals) and spine, and some people with the condition will also develop diabetes. The disorder does not affect thinking and reasoning abilities (cognitive functions).

FA is caused by a defect (mutation) in a gene labeled *FXN*, which carries the genetic code for a protein called "frataxin." Individuals who inherit 2 defective copies of the gene, 1 from each parent, will develop the disease. Although rare, FA is the most common form of hereditary ataxia in the United States, affecting about 1 in every 50,000 people. Both male and female children can inherit the disorder.

The rate of progression varies from person to person. Generally, within 10 to 20 years after the appearance of the first symptoms, the person is confined to a wheelchair. Individuals may become completely incapacitated in later stages of the disease. FA can shorten life expectancy, and heart disease is the most common cause of death. However, some people with less severe features of FA live into their sixties or older.

The disorder is named after Nikolaus Friedreich, a German doctor who described the condition in the 1860s.

What Are the Signs and Symptoms?

Symptoms typically begin between the ages of 5 and 15, although they sometimes appear in adulthood. Approximately 15 percent of people with FA have onset after the age of 25. The first neurological symptom to appear is usually difficulty walking and poor balance (gait ataxia, often described as appearing dizzy or even drunk). Another early sign of the disease is slowness and slurring of speech (dysarthria). With time, speech becomes hesitant and jerky (often referred to as "scanning of speech"). The difficulty coordinating movement (ataxia) can affect all of the muscles. It gradually worsens and slowly spreads to the arms and the trunk (torso). As the muscle weakness progresses, most affected individuals develop increased muscle tone (spasticity). Up to two-thirds of people with FA also develop scoliosis (a curving of the spine to one side) that often requires surgical intervention for treatment. Most affected individuals also develop difficulty swallowing, due to difficulty coordinating the muscles of the tongue and throat.

In addition to the movement impairments, there is often a loss of sensation in the arms and legs, which may spread to other parts of the body. Other features include loss of normal reflexes, especially in the knees and ankles, and muscle weakness. Many individuals with later stages of FA also develop hearing and vision loss.

Other symptoms that may occur include heart palpitations and shortness of breath. These symptoms are the result of various forms of heart disease that often accompany FA, such as enlargement of the heart (hypertrophic cardiomyopathy), formation of fiber-like material in the muscles of the heart (myocardial fibrosis), and heart failure. Heart-rhythm abnormalities, such as a fast heart rate (tachycardia) and impaired conduction of cardiac impulses within the heart (heart block), are also common.

About 50 percent of people with FA develop carbohydrate intolerance and 30 percent develop diabetes. Most individuals with the disease tire very easily and find that they require more rest and take a longer time to recover from common illnesses, such as colds and the flu.

How Is Friedreich Ataxia Diagnosed?

A diagnosis of FA requires a careful clinical examination, which includes a medical history and a thorough physical exam, in particular looking for balance difficulty, loss of joint sensation (proprioception), absence of reflexes, and signs of neurological problems. Genetic testing now provides a conclusive diagnosis. Other tests that may aid in the diagnosis or management of the disorder include:

- Electromyogram (EMG), which measures the electrical activity of muscle cells

- Nerve conduction studies, which measure the speed with which nerves transmit impulses

- Electrocardiogram (EKG or ECG), which gives a graphic presentation of the electrical activity or beat pattern of the heart

- Echocardiogram, which records the position and motion of the heart muscle

- Blood tests to check for elevated glucose levels and vitamin E levels

- Magnetic resonance imaging (MRI) or computed tomography (CT) scans, tests which provide brain and spinal cord images that are useful for ruling out other neurological conditions

How Is Friedreich Ataxia Inherited?

People have two copies of every gene, with one copy being inherited from each parent. In FA, a person needs to inherit two copies of the defective *FXN* gene to develop the disease. A person who inherits only one abnormal copy of the gene is called a "carrier." A carrier will not develop the disease but could pass the gene mutation on to her or his children. About 1 in 90 Americans of European ancestry carries an abnormal *FXN* gene.

How Is the Protein Frataxin Affected?

The *FXN* gene provides instructions for the production of a protein called "frataxin." In the normal version of the gene, a triplet sequence of DNA (labeled guanine-adenine-adenine, or GAA) is repeated between 7 and 22 times. In the defective *FXN* gene, the GAA repeat occurs over and over again—hundreds, even up to a thousand times. The GAA repeat sequence greatly reduces the amount of frataxin produced by the cell. Earlier disease onset and severity of progression may be related to the number of GAA copies in the individual genetic code.

This abnormal pattern, called a "triplet repeat expansion," has been implicated as the cause of several diseases in which the individual needs to inherit only one abnormal gene. FA is the only known genetic disorder that requires inheriting two copies of the abnormal *FXN* gene to cause the disease. Almost all people with FA (98%) have two copies of this mutant form of *FXN*, but it is not found in all cases of the disease. About two percent of affected individuals have other defects in the *FXN* gene that are responsible for causing the disease.

The triplet repeat expansion greatly disrupts the normal production of frataxin. Frataxin is found in the energy-producing parts of the cell called "mitochondria." Research suggests that without a normal level of frataxin, certain cells in the body (especially peripheral nerve, spinal cord, brain, and heart muscle cells) produce energy less effectively and have been hypothesized to have a buildup of toxic byproducts leading to what is called "oxidative stress." Lack of normal levels of frataxin also may lead to increased levels of iron in the mitochondria. When the excess iron reacts with oxygen, free radicals can be produced. Although free radicals are essential molecules in the body metabolism, they can also destroy cells and harm the body.

Can Friedreich Ataxia Be Cured or Treated?

As with many degenerative diseases of the nervous system, there is currently no cure or effective treatment for FA. However, many of the symptoms and accompanying complications can be treated to help individuals maintain optimal functioning as long as possible. A multi-specialty team approach is essential to the treatment of the individual with FA. Doctors can prescribe treatments for diabetes if present; some of the heart problems can be treated with medication as well. Orthopedic problems, such as foot deformities and scoliosis, can be corrected with braces or surgery. Physical therapy may prolong use of the arms and legs. Swallowing and speech issues should be followed closely. Hearing impairment can be helped with hearing aids.

What Services Are Useful to Friedreich Ataxia Patients and Their Families

Genetic testing is essential for proper clinical diagnosis and can aid in prenatal diagnosis and determining a person's carrier status. Genetic counselors can help explain how FA is inherited.

A primary-care physician can screen people for complications, such as heart disease, diabetes, and scoliosis, and can refer individuals to specialists, such as cardiologists, physical therapists, and speech therapists, to help deal with some of the other associated problems.

Support and information for families is also available through a number of private organizations. These groups can offer ways to network and communicate with others affected by FA. They can also provide access to patient registries, clinical trials information, and other useful resources.

Section 29.5

Hereditary Spastic Paraplegia

This section includes text excerpted from "Hereditary
Spastic Paraplegia," Genetic and Rare Diseases Information
Center (GARD), National Center for Advancing Translational
Sciences (NCATS), April 24, 2016.

What Is Hereditary Spastic Paraplegia?

Hereditary spastic paraplegia (HSP) is a group of hereditary, degenerative, neurological disorders that primarily affect the upper motor neurons. Upper motor neurons in the brain and spinal cord deliver signals to the lower motor neurons, which in turn, carry messages to the muscles. In HSP, upper motor neurons slowly degenerate so the muscles do not receive the correct messages, causing progressive spasticity (increased muscle tone/stiffness) and weakness of the legs. This leads to difficulty walking. As degeneration continues, symptoms worsen. If only the lower body is affected, HSP is classified as uncomplicated or pure. HSP is classified as complicated or complex if other systems are involved. In these cases, additional symptoms, including impaired vision, ataxia, epilepsy, cognitive impairment, peripheral neuropathy, and/or deafness, occur. The different forms of HSP are caused by mutations in different genes. Inheritance varies. There are no specific treatments to prevent, slow, or reverse HSP. Individual symptoms may be treated with medications and/or physical therapy.

How Is Hereditary Spastic Paraplegia Inherited?

At this point, over 70 different types of HSP have been described. The different patterns of inheritance are autosomal dominant, autosomal recessive, and X-linked recessive.

My Family History of Hereditary Spastic Paraplegia Includes My Mother and Her Brother. Is There a 50 Percent Chance That I Will Also Be Affected?

HSP can be inherited in different ways in different families. Consult with a genetics professional to discuss how this condition is inherited in your family and your risk of developing HSP. In general, when HSP is inherited in an autosomal dominant pattern, there is a 50 percent chance that the child of an affected individual will also be affected. When only two siblings are affected, it typically cannot be determined if the condition is autosomal dominant. The condition may also be inherited in an autosomal recessive manner.

What Is Autosomal Recessive Inheritance?

Autosomal recessive inheritance refers to the inheritance pattern in which two mutated copies of the gene that causes a disorder are present in each cell. An affected person usually has unaffected parents who each carry a single copy of the mutated gene (and are referred to as carriers). Autosomal-recessive disorders are typically not seen in every generation of an affected family. When two people who are carriers of an autosomal recessive condition have a child, there is a 25 percent (one in four) chance that the child will be affected.

What Is Autosomal Dominant Inheritance?

Autosomal dominant inheritance is when one mutated copy of the gene that causes a disorder in each cell is needed for a person to be affected. Autosomal dominant conditions may occur for the first time in a person in a family due to a spontaneous gene mutation, or these conditions may be inherited from an affected parent. When a person with an autosomal-dominant disorder has a child, there is a 50 percent chance that their child will inherit the condition.

Since My Family Members' Cases of Hereditary Spastic Paraplegia Are Severe, Does This Mean I Could Also Have Severe Hereditary Spastic Paraplegia?

It is difficult to predict the severity of HSP without a diagnosis of a specific subtype. In some types, there is variation in the severity of symptoms among family members. Family members in subsequent generations may be more or less severely affected. In some types, a person can inherit the genetic change that causes HSP but not show any symptoms. This phenomenon is called "reduced" or "incomplete penetrance." Even though these individuals show no symptoms of the disorder, they can still have affected children.

Section 29.6

Muscular Dystrophy

This section includes text excerpted from "Muscular Dystrophy: Condition Information," *Eunice Kennedy Shriver* National Institute of Child Health and Human Development (NICHD), December 1, 2016.

What Is Muscular Dystrophy?

Muscular dystrophy (MD) refers to a group of more than 30 inherited diseases that cause muscle weakness and muscle loss. Some forms of MD appear in infancy or childhood, while others may not appear until middle age or even later. In addition, the types of MD differ in the areas of the body they affect and in the severity of the symptoms. All forms of MD grow worse as the person's muscles get weaker. Most people with MD eventually lose their ability to walk.

What Causes Muscular Dystrophy

MD is generally an inherited disease caused by gene mutations (changes in the deoxyribonucleic acid (DNA) sequence) that affect proteins in muscles. In some cases, the mutation was not inherited from a person's parents but instead happened spontaneously. Such a mutation can then be inherited by the affected person's offspring.

Hundreds of genes are involved in making the proteins that affect muscles. Each type of MD is caused by a genetic mutation that is specific to that type. Some of the forms, such as limb-girdle and distal, are caused by defects in the same gene.

MD is not contagious and cannot be caused by injury or activity.

What Are Common Symptoms of Muscular Dystrophy?

Muscle weakness that worsens over time is a common symptom of all forms of MD. Each form of MD varies in the order in which symptoms occur and in the parts of the body that are affected.

What Are the Types of Muscular Dystrophy?

There are more than 30 forms of muscular dystrophy (MD), with information on the primary types included in the table below.

Table 29.1. Types of Muscular Dystrophy

Type of Muscular Dystrophy	What It Is	Common Symptoms	How It Develops
Duchenne (DMD)	The most common and severe form of MD among children, DMD accounts for more than 50 percent of all cases. DMD is caused by a deficiency of dystrophin, a protein that helps strengthen muscle fibers and protect them from injury.	"Weakness begins in the upper legs and pelvis. People with DMD may also: Fall down a lot Have trouble rising from a lying or sitting position Waddle when walking Have difficulty running and jumping Have calf muscles that appear large because of fat accumulation"	DMD appears typically in boys between ages 3 and 5 and progresses rapidly. Most people with DMD are unable to walk by age 12 and may later need a respirator to breathe. They usually die in their late teens or early 20s from heart trouble, respiratory complications, or infection.
Becker	Also caused by a deficiency of dystrophin, and with symptoms similar to those of DMD, Becker can progress slowly or quickly.	Patients with Becker MD may: Walk on their tiptoes Fall down a lot Have difficulty rising from the floor Have cramping in their muscles	Becker MD appears primarily in males between ages 11 and 25. Some people may never need to use a wheelchair, while others lose the ability to walk during their teens, mid-30s, or later.
Myotonic	The most common adult form of MD, myotonic MD appears in two forms, type 1 and type 2. Type 1 is more common and is caused by an abnormally large number of repeats of a three-letter "word" (CTG) in genetic code. While most people have up to 37 repeats of CTG, people with myotonic can have up to 4,000. The number of repeats may reflect the severity of symptoms.	Myotonic MD causes an inability to relax muscles following a sudden contraction. Other symptoms include: Long, thin face and neck Swallowing difficulties Drooping eyelids, cataracts, and other vision problems Baldness at the front of the scalp Weight loss Increased sweating Drowsiness Heart problems that may lead to death during the 30s or 40s Irregular menstrual periods Infertility Impotence	Myotonic MD affects both men and women between ages 20 and 30.

Table 29.1. Continued

Type of Muscular Dystrophy	What It Is	Common Symptoms	How It Develops
Congenital	About half of all U.S. cases with congenital MD are caused by a defect in the protein merosin, which surrounds muscle fibers. When caused by defects in other proteins, this type of MD may also affect the central nervous system.	People with congenital MD may: Have problems with motor function and muscle control that appear at birth or during infancy Develop chronic shortening of muscles or tendons around joints, which prevents joints from moving freely Develop scoliosis (curvature of the spine) Have trouble breathing and swallowing Have foot deformities have intellectual disabilities	This form of MD appears at birth or by age 2. Congenital means "present from birth." Congenital MD affects both boys and girls, who often require support to sit or stand and may never learn to walk. Some patients die in infancy, but others live into adulthood with only mild disability.
Emery-Dreifuss	Affecting boys primarily, the two forms of Emery-Dreifuss MD are caused by defects in the proteins that surround the nucleus in cells.	Weakness begins in the upper arm and lower leg muscles. People with this form may also Develop chronic shortening of muscles around joints (preventing them from moving freely), in the spine, ankles, knees, elbows, and back of the neck Have elbows locked in a flexed position Develop shoulder deterioration Have a rigid spine Walk on their toes Experience mild weakness in their facial muscles	Symptoms usually begin by age 10 but can appear in patients up to their mid-20s. People with this form often develop heart problems by age 30, and they may die in mid-adulthood from progressive pulmonary or cardiac failure.

Table 29.1. Continued

Type of Muscular Dystrophy	What It Is	Common Symptoms	How It Develops
Facioscapulohumeral (FSHD)	FSHD refers to the areas affected: the face (facio), the shoulders (scapulo), and the upper arms (humeral). Researchers don't know what gene causes FSHD. They do know where the defect occurs and that it affects specific muscle groups.	FSHD MD often appears first in the eyes (difficulty in opening and shutting) and mouth (inability to smile or pucker). Other symptoms may include: Muscle wasting that causes shoulders to appear slanted and shoulder blades to appear "winged" Impaired reflexes only at the biceps and triceps Trouble swallowing, chewing, or speaking Hearing problems Swayback curve in the spine, called lordosis	FSHD affects teen boys and girls typically but may occur as late as age 40. Most individuals have a normal life span, but symptoms can vary from mild to severely disabling.
Limb-girdle	Affecting both males and females, different types of limb-girdle are caused by different gene mutations. Patients with limb-girdle inherit a defective gene from either parent, or, in the more severe form, the same defective gene from both parents.	Patients with limb-girdle MD may: First develop weakness around the hips, which then spreads to the shoulders, legs, and neck Have trouble rising from chairs, climbing stairs, or carrying things Waddle when they walk Have a rigid spine Fall down a lot	This form of MD can appear in childhood but most often appears in adolescence or young adulthood. Limb-girdle can progress quickly or slowly, but most patients become severely disabled (with muscle damage and inability to walk) within 20 years of developing the disease.

Table 29.1. Continued

Type of Muscular Dystrophy	What It Is	Common Symptoms	How It Develops
Distal	Distal MDs refer to a group of diseases that affect the muscles of the forearms, hands, lower legs, and feet. They are caused by defects in the protein dysferlin5 and can occur in both men and women.	Distal MD may cause: Inability to perform hand movements Difficulty extending fingers Trouble walking and climbing stairs Inability to hop or stand on the heels	This form typically appears between ages 40 and 60. Distal MD is less severe and progresses more slowly than other forms of MD, but it can spread to other muscles. Patients may eventually need a ventilator.
Oculopharyngeal	This form occurs in both men and women, and it can be mild or severe. It is caused by a defect in a protein that binds to molecules that help make other proteins. It is common among Americans of French-Canadian descent, Jewish Ashkenazi, and Hispanics from the Southwest region.	Oculopharyngeal MD may cause: Drooping eyelids and other vision problems Swallowing problems Muscle wasting and weakness in the neck, shoulders, and sometimes limbs Heart problems	This form of MD typically appears in a person's 40s or 50s. Some people will eventually lose their ability to walk.

How Many People Are Affected by or Are at Risk of Muscular Dystrophy?

The incidence of MD in the United States varies because different kinds of MD are rarer than others. The most common forms in children—Duchenne and Becker—affect approximately 1 in every 5,600 to 7,700 males between the ages of 5 and 24. The most common adult form, type 1 myotonic MD, affects 1 in 8,000 worldwide.

How Is Muscular Dystrophy Diagnosed?

The first step in diagnosing MD is a visit with a healthcare provider for a physical exam. The healthcare provider will ask a series of questions about the patient's family history and medical history, including any problems affecting the muscles that the patient may be experiencing.

The healthcare provider may order tests to determine whether the problems are a result of MD and, if so, what form of this disorder. The tests may also rule out other problems that could cause muscle weakness, such as surgery, toxic exposure, medications, or other muscle diseases. These tests may include:

- **Blood tests** to measure levels of serum creatine kinase, an enzyme that is released into the bloodstream when muscle fibers are deteriorating, and serum aldolase, an enzyme that helps break down sugars into energy. Elevated levels of either of these enzymes can signal muscle weakness and indicate a need for additional testing.

- **Muscle biopsies**, which involve the removal of muscle tissue using a biopsy needle. The tissue is then examined under a microscope to provide information on the amount and level of the genes that may cause MD. Patients diagnosed by muscle biopsy typically require genetic testing as well to determine any mutations in their genes.

- **Genetic testing** to evaluate missing or repeated mutations in the *dystrophin* gene. A lack of the *dystrophin* gene can lead to a diagnosis of Duchenne or Becker MD. The test is important not only to confirm the MD diagnosis in males, but also to determine whether women with a family history of Duchenne or Becker MD may be carriers.

- **Neurological tests** to rule out other nervous system disorders, to identify patterns of muscle weakness and wasting, to test reflexes and coordination, and to detect contractions.

- **Heart testing**, such as an electrocardiogram (ECG), to measure the rate and frequency of heartbeats. Some forms of MD cause heart problems, such as an irregular heartbeat.

- **Exercise assessments** to evaluate the patient's level of strength and respiratory function and to detect any increased rates of certain chemicals, such as nitric oxide, following exercise.

- **Imaging tests** such as magnetic resonance imaging (MRI) and ultrasound imaging. These painless tests use radio waves and sound waves (ultrasound) to obtain pictures of the inside of the body and to examine muscle quality and bulk, as well as the fatty replacement of muscle tissue.

What Are the Treatments for Muscular Dystrophy?

No treatment is available to stop or reverse any form of MD. Instead, certain therapies and medications aim to treat the various problems that result from MD and improve the quality of life (QOL) for patients. They include the following:

Physical Therapy

Beginning physical therapy early can help keep muscles flexible and strong. A combination of physical activity and stretching exercises may be recommended.

Respiratory Therapy

Many people with MD do not realize they have little respiratory strength until they have difficulty coughing or an infection leads to pneumonia. Regular visits to a specialist early in the diagnosis of MD can help guide treatment before a respiratory problem occurs. Eventually, many MD patients require assisted ventilation.

Speech Therapy

MD patients who experience weakness in the facial and throat muscles may benefit from learning to slow the pace of their speech by pausing more between breaths and by using special communication equipment.

Occupational Therapy

As physical abilities change, occupational therapy can help patients with MD relearn these movements and abilities. Occupational therapy also teaches patients to use assistive devices such as wheelchairs and utensils.

Corrective Surgery

At various times and depending on the form of MD, many patients require surgery to treat the conditions that result from MD. People with myotonic MD may need a pacemaker to treat heart problems or surgery to remove cataracts, a clouding of the lens of the eye that blocks light from entering the eye.

Drug Therapy

Certain medications can help slow or control the symptoms of MD. These include the following:

- **Glucocorticoids, such as prednisone.** Studies show that daily treatment with prednisone can increase muscle strength, ability, and respiratory function and slow the progression of weakness. Side effects may include weight gain. Long-term use may result in brittle bones, cataracts, and high blood pressure. The National Institutes of Health's (NIH) Therapeutics for Rare and Neglected Diseases (TRND) Program is collaborating on a new glucocorticoid treatment called "VBP15." Early clinical trial results show that the treatment may have the same positive results as prednisone but without the side effects.

- **Anticonvulsants.** Typically taken for epilepsy, these drugs may help control seizures and some muscle spasms.

- **Immunosuppressants.** Commonly given to treat autoimmune diseases, such as lupus and eczema, immunosuppressant drugs may help delay some damage to dying muscle cells.

- **Antibiotics** to treat respiratory infections.

Muscular Dystrophy: Other FAQs
How Do People Cope with Muscular Dystrophy (MD)?

Although MD presents many challenges in many different aspects of daily life, those with MD enjoy full lives. Advances in drug therapies, physical therapies, and assistive technologies can help to make some daily activities easier to further improve health and QOL.

Almost all people with any form of MD experience a worsening of symptoms over time. Typically, muscles weaken over the life course, and patients may have greater difficulty performing tasks as they age.

Several factors also can influence how well those with MD and their families can overcome the challenges of the disorder, including:

- **Making the environment accessible.** This may include adding ramps, widening doorways, moving bedrooms to the ground level, and making other changes to ensure access for devices, such as wheelchairs, that aid with mobility.

- **Improving mobility.** Braces, crutches, wheelchairs, and electric scooters can help people move within their environments independently.

- **Maintaining a healthy weight.** Reaching and maintaining a healthy weight is an important way to reduce added stress on muscles and to prevent certain health conditions, such as respiratory problems.

- **Getting physical activity.** Low-impact physical activity, such as swimming, can help improve muscle strength and overall well-being.

- **Getting restful sleep.** As muscles weaken, it can be more difficult to find a comfortable sleeping position. Certain beds, pads, and mattresses can help improve comfort, which can improve the quality of sleep.

Those with MD and their families may also benefit from getting involved with support groups and local organizations so they can meet others who are dealing with similar challenges and learn possible solutions.

Section 29.7

Spinal Muscular Atrophy

This section includes text excerpted from "Spinal Muscular Atrophy," Genetic and Rare Diseases Information Center (GARD), National Center for Advancing Translational Sciences (NCATS), September 4, 2018.

Spinal muscular atrophy (SMA) is a group of genetic neuromuscular disorders that affect the nerve cells that control voluntary muscles (motor neurons). The loss of motor neurons causes progressive muscle weakness and loss of movement due to muscle wasting (atrophy). The severity of the symptoms, the age at which symptoms begin, and the genetic cause varies by type. Many types of SMA mainly affect the muscles involved in walking, sitting, arm movement, and head control. Breathing and swallowing may also become difficult as the disease progresses in many types of SMA. In some types of SMA, the loss of motor neurons makes it hard to control the movement of the hands and feet.

SMA type 1, 2, 3, and 4 are caused by changes (pathogenic variants, also known as "mutations") in the *SMN1* gene and are inherited in an autosomal recessive manner. Extra copies of the nearby related gene, *SMN2*, modify the severity of SMA. There are other rarer types of SMA caused by changes in different genes. Other autosomal recessive forms include SMA with progressive myoclonic epilepsy (SMA-PME), caused by changes in the *ASAH1* gene, and SMA with respiratory distress 1 (SMARD1), caused by changes in the *IGHMBP2* gene. Autosomal dominant forms include distal MSA type V (DSMA-V) caused by changes in *BSCL2* and *GARS*, SMA with lower extremity predominance (SMA-LED) caused by changes in *DYNC1H1* or *BICD2*, and adult-onset form of SMA caused changes by *VAPB*. X-linked forms include X-linked infantile SMA caused by changes in *UBA1*.

A diagnosis of SMA is suspected by symptoms and confirmed by genetic testing. Treatments are, in general, supportive aiming to increase quality of life (QOL) and avoid complications. Treatments may include physical therapy, nutrition support, chest physiotherapy, and, in severe cases, breathing machines (ventilators). In December 2016, nusinersen (Spinraza) became the first U.S. Food and Drug Administration (FDA)-approved treatment for SMA types 1, 2, 3, and 4. Continued treatment with nusinersen has been shown to slow the progression of the disease and even improve muscle function, but individual response to the treatment does vary. Due to the success of nusinersen as well as other promising treatments presently in clinical trials, SMA caused by changes in the *SMN1* gene has been added to the list of recommended newborn screening tests in the United States, so that treatment may begin before symptoms develop. However, as of July 2018, not all states have added the test to their newborn screening panel.

Symptoms

SMA is primarily characterized by progressive muscle weakness and atrophy. Depending on the type, onset may range from before birth to adolescence or young adulthood.

SMA type 0 (the prenatal form) is the most severe form and begins before birth. Usually, the first symptom of type 0 is reduced movement of the fetus that is first seen between 30 and 36 weeks of the pregnancy. After birth, these newborns have little movement and have difficulties with swallowing and breathing. Life span is approximately 2 to 6 months.

There are 3 types of SMA that tend to affect children before the age of 1 (SMA type I, SMA type II, and X-linked SMA). SMA type I is a severe form that may be apparent at birth or the first few months of life. Features may include difficulty swallowing or breathing and inability to sit without support. The life span is usually less than 2 years. SMA type II typically becomes apparent between 6 and 12 months of age; affected children may sit without support, although they cannot stand or walk unaided. About 70 percent of people with this type live to be at least 25 years of age. X-linked infantile SMA is similar to SMA type I; additional features may include joint deformities (contractures) or even broken bones at birth in very severe cases.

Three other types of SMA can affect people in early childhood and adulthood. SMA type III (also called "Kugelberg-Welander disease" or "juvenile type") is a milder form of SMA with symptoms that generally appear between early childhood (older than 1 year of age) and early adulthood. People with type III are able to stand and walk without help, although they usually lose this ability later in life. SMA type IV and Finkel type occur in adulthood, usually after the age of 30. Symptoms of adult-onset SMA are usually mild to moderate and include muscle weakness, tremor, and twitching.

Inheritance

Most forms of SMA (types I, II, III, and IV, specifically) are inherited in an autosomal recessive pattern. This means that to be affected, a person must have a mutation in both copies of the responsible gene in each cell. The parents of an affected person usually each carry one mutated copy of the gene and are referred to as carriers. Carriers typically do not show signs or symptoms of the condition. When two carriers of an autosomal recessive condition have children, each child has a 25 percent (1 in 4) risk to have the condition, a 50 percent (1 in 2) risk to be a carrier like each of the parents, and a 25 percent chance to not have the condition and not be a carrier.

Finkel type spinal muscular atrophy is inherited in an autosomal dominant pattern, which means an affected person only needs a mutation in one copy of the responsible gene in each cell.

X-linked infantile SMA is inherited in an X-linked pattern. The gene associated with this condition is located on the X chromosome, which is 1 of the 2 sex chromosomes. In males (who have only 1 X chromosome), one altered copy of the gene in each cell is sufficient to cause the condition. In females (who have 2 X chromosomes), a mutation would have to occur in both copies of the gene to cause the disorder. Because it is unlikely that females will have 2 altered copies of this gene, males are affected by X-linked disorders much more frequently than females. A striking characteristic of X-linked inheritance is that fathers cannot pass X-linked traits to their sons.

Treatment

Treatment for SMA may vary depending on the subtype of SMA and severity of symptoms but generally focuses on supportive care to increase the person's quality of life. In general, treatment may include physical therapy and assistive equipment to increase mobility, such as leg braces, walkers, and wheelchairs. Back braces may be used to assist sitting and prevent scoliosis and other complications affecting the backbone. Special breathing exercises, cough machines, and chest physiotherapy can help maintain the function of the lungs and keep the airways clear of mucus, especially in times of illness. A dietitian may help support nutrition if eating or swallowing becomes difficult.

For SMA types I, II, III, and IV, nusinersen (Spinraza) is the first and only FDA-approved treatment. Continued treatment with nusinersen has been found to increase motor function and slow the progression of symptoms. Many babies and young children with types I and II are able to reach developmental milestones and maintain those milestones over time. In general, breathing problems, nutrition problems, and hospital admissions also decrease. Older children with type III and adults with type IV have also been shown to benefit from continuous treatment with nusinersen, including, for some, regaining the ability to walk longer distances, improving arm movement, and slowing or stopping the progression of the disorder. Ongoing, long-term medical studies continue to report improvements. However, response to treatment does vary and some people with SMA types I, II, III, and IV may not respond to the drug at all or may have medical complications that prevent the use of the treatment.

Cure SMA has more detailed information about the management of medical issues associated with SMA. Their webpage includes hyperlinks to the latest published consensus medical guidelines (2018) for SMA treatment to share with the doctors involved in the care of the person with SMA.

U.S. Food and Drug Administration-Approved Treatments

The medication listed below has been approved by the U.S. Food and Drug Administration (FDA) as an orphan product for the treatment of this condition.

- Nusinersen (Brand name: Spinraza). Manufactured by Biogen, Inc.

FDA-approved indication: December 2016, nusinersen (Spinraza) was approved for the treatment of spinal muscular atrophy in pediatric and adult patients.

Chapter 30

Noonan Syndrome

Noonan syndrome (NS) is a genetic disorder that causes abnormal development of multiple parts of the body. Features of NS may include a distinctive facial appearance, short stature, a broad or webbed neck, congenital heart defects, bleeding problems, problems with bone structure (skeletal malformations), and developmental delay. NS may be caused by a mutation in any of several genes and can be classified into subtypes based on the responsible gene. It is typically inherited in an autosomal dominant manner, but many cases are due to a new mutation and are not inherited from either parent. Treatment depends on the symptoms present in each person.

NS belongs to a group of related conditions called the "RASopathies." These conditions have some overlapping features and are all caused by genetic changes that disrupt the body's RAS pathway, affecting growth and development. Other conditions in this group include:

- Neurofibromatosis type 1 (NF1)

- LEOPARD syndrome (LS), also called "NS with multiple lentigines"

- Costello syndrome (CS)

- Cardiofaciocutaneous syndrome (CFS)

This chapter includes text excerpted from "Noonan Syndrome," Genetic and Rare Diseases Information Center (GARD), National Center for Advancing Translational Sciences (NCATS), October 2, 2017.

- Legius syndrome (LS)
- Capillary malformation-arteriovenous malformation syndrome (CM-AVM)

Symptoms of Noonan Syndrome

Some of the signs and symptoms seen in people with NS are listed below. Please note that the list below does not include all possible symptoms of NS, and that not all people with NS will have all of these signs and symptoms. In general, the signs and symptoms of NS are more obvious early in life and become less obvious as individuals get older.

- Head/neck:
  - Widely spaced eyes (hypertelorism)
  - Large ears rotated back
  - Short webbed neck
  - Droopy eyelids (ptosis)
  - Low hairline
  - Multiple giant cell lesions (MGCL): painless, benign growths in the jaw that can lead to dental or orthodontic issues
- Heart:
  - Pulmonary stenosis (PS)
  - Aortic regurgitation (AR)
  - Atrial septal defect (ASD)
- Skeletal:
  - Short stature
  - Concave chest (pectus excavatum)
  - Bending or curvature of the finger (clinodactyly)
  - Weak bones (generalized osteopenia)
- Skin:
  - Café au lait spots
  - Hemangioma (raised red birthmark)

- Neurological:
  - Delayed milestones due to low muscle tone
  - Developmental delay
  - Learning disabilities or intellectual impairment
  - Bleeding disorder
  - Undescended testicles (cryptorchidism)

A syndrome named "Noonan-like/multiple giant cell lesion syndrome" used to be considered a separate condition from NS. It is now known that multiple giant cell lesions are one of the possible symptoms that can occur in people with NS.

Inheritance of Noonan Syndrome

NS is inherited in an autosomal dominant manner. This means that having one changed or mutated copy of the responsible gene in each cell is enough to cause the condition. Each child of a person with NS has a 50 percent (1 in 2) chance to inherit the condition.

In other cases, the change in one of the genes that can cause NS is new and not found in either parent. This means that the genetic change was not passed down from either the mother or the father, but instead occurred for the first time (de novo) in the child who has the syndrome. New changes or mutations in a gene can happen by mistake during the making of the egg or the sperm.

Treatment of Noonan Syndrome

Management of NS, generally, focuses on the specific signs and symptoms present in each person. Treatments for the complications of NS (such as cardiovascular problems) are generally standard and do not differ from treatment in the general population.

Developmental disabilities are addressed by early intervention programs. Some children with NS may need special help in school, including, for example, an individualized educational program (IEP).

Treatment for bleeding problems depends on the cause. Growth hormone (GH) therapy can increase the rate at which a child with NS grows in most cases. GH therapy during childhood and teen years may also increase final adult height slightly, often enough to reach the low normal range of average height.

Chapter 31

Porphyria

What Is Porphyria?

The porphyrias are a group of different diseases, each caused by a specific abnormality in the heme production process. Heme is a chemical compound that contains iron and gives blood its red color. The essential functions of heme depend on its ability to bind oxygen. Heme is incorporated into hemoglobin, a protein that enables red blood cells (RBCs) to carry oxygen from the lungs to all parts of the body. Heme also plays a role in the liver where it assists in breaking down chemicals (including some drugs and hormones) so that they are easily removed from the body.

Heme is produced in the bone marrow and liver through a complex process controlled by eight different enzymes. As this production process of heme progresses, several different intermediate compounds (heme precursors) are created and modified. If one of the essential enzymes in heme production is deficient, certain precursors may accumulate in tissues (especially in the bone marrow or liver), appear in excess in the blood, and get excreted in the urine or stool. The specific precursors that accumulate depend on which enzyme is deficient. Porphyria results in a deficiency or inactivity of a specific enzyme in the heme production process, with resulting accumulation of heme precursors.

This chapter includes text excerpted from "Learning about Porphyria," National Human Genome Research Institute (NHGRI), April 18, 2013. Reviewed March 2019.

What Are the Signs and Symptoms of Porphyria?

The signs and symptoms of porphyria vary among types. Some types of porphyria (called "cutaneous porphyria") cause the skin to become overly sensitive to sunlight. Areas of the skin exposed to the sun develop redness, blistering and often scarring.

The symptoms of other types of porphyria (called "acute porphyrias") affect the nervous system (NS). These symptoms include chest and abdominal pain, emotional and mental disorders, seizures, and muscle weakness. These symptoms often appear quickly and last from days to weeks. Some porphyrias have a combination of acute symptoms and symptoms that affect the skin.

Environmental factors can trigger the signs and symptoms of porphyria. These include:

- Alcohol
- Smoking
- Certain drugs, hormones
- Exposure to sunlight
- Stress
- Dieting and fasting

How Is Porphyria Diagnosed?

Porphyria is diagnosed through blood, urine, and stool tests, especially at or near the time of symptoms. Diagnosis may be difficult because the range of symptoms is common to many disorders and interpretation of the tests may be complex. A large number of tests are available, however, but results among laboratories are not always reliable.

How Is Porphyria Treated?

Each form of porphyria is treated differently. Treatment may involve treating with heme, giving medicines to relieve the symptoms, or drawing blood. People who have severe attacks may need to be hospitalized.

What Do We Know about Porphyria and Heredity?

Most of the porphyrias are inherited conditions. The genes for all the enzymes in the heme pathway have been identified. Some forms of porphyria result from inheriting one altered gene from one parent (autosomal dominant). Other forms result from inheriting two altered genes, one from each parent (autosomal recessive). Each type of porphyria carries a different risk that individuals in an affected family will have the disease or transmit it to their children.

Porphyria cutanea tarda (PCT) is a type of porphyria that is most often not inherited. Eighty percent of individuals with PCT have an acquired disease that becomes active when factors, such as iron, alcohol, hepatitis C virus (HCV), human immunodeficiency virus (HIV), estrogens (ER) (such as those used in oral contraceptives and prostate cancer treatment), and possibly smoking, combine to cause an enzyme deficiency in the liver. Hemochromatosis, an iron overload disorder, can also predispose individuals to PCT. Twenty percent of individuals with PCT have an inherited form of the disease. Many individuals with the inherited form of PCT never develop symptoms.

What Triggers a Porphyria Attack

Porphyria can be triggered by drugs (barbiturates, tranquilizers, birth control pills, sedatives), chemicals, fasting, smoking, drinking alcohol, infections, emotional and physical stress, menstrual hormones, and exposure to the sun. Attacks of porphyria can develop over hours or days and last for days or weeks.

How Is Porphyria Classified?

The porphyrias have several different classification systems. The most accurate classification is by the specific enzyme deficiency. Another classification system distinguishes porphyrias that cause neurologic symptoms (acute porphyrias) from those that cause photosensitivity (cutaneous porphyrias). A third classification system is based on whether the excess precursors originate primarily in the liver (hepatic porphyrias) or primarily in the bone marrow (erythropoietic porphyrias). Some porphyrias are classified as more than one of these categories.

What Are the Cutaneous Porphyrias?

The cutaneous porphyrias affect the skin. People with cutaneous porphyria develop blisters, itching, and swelling of their skin when it is exposed to sunlight. The cutaneous porphyrias include the following types:

Congenital erythropoietic porphyria, also called "congenital porphyria," is a rare disorder that mainly affects the skin. It results from low levels of the enzyme responsible for the fourth step in heme production. It is inherited in an autosomal recessive pattern.

Erythropoietic protoporphyria is an uncommon disorder that mainly affects the skin. It results from reduced levels of the enzyme responsible for the eighth and final step in heme production. The inheritance of this condition is not fully understood. Most cases are probably inherited in an autosomal dominant pattern, however, it shows autosomal recessive inheritance in a small number of families.

Hepatoerythropoietic porphyria is a rare disorder that mainly affects the skin. It results from very low levels of the enzyme responsible for the fifth step in heme production. It is inherited in an autosomal recessive pattern.

Hereditary coproporphyria is a rare disorder that can have symptoms of acute porphyria and symptoms that affect the skin. It results from low levels of the enzyme responsible for the sixth step in heme production. It is inherited in an autosomal dominant pattern.

Porphyria cutanea tarda (PCT) is the most common type of porphyria. It occurs in an estimated 1 in 25,000 people, including both inherited and sporadic (noninherited) cases. An estimated 80 percent of PCT cases are sporadic. It results from low levels of the enzyme responsible for the fifth step in heme production. When this condition is inherited, it occurs in an autosomal dominant pattern.

A disorder that can have symptoms of acute porphyria and symptoms that affect the skin. It results from low levels of the enzyme responsible for the seventh step in heme production. It is inherited in an autosomal dominant pattern.

What Are the Acute Porphyrias?

The acute porphyrias affect the nervous system. Symptoms of acute porphyria include pain in the chest, abdomen, limbs, or back; muscle numbness, tingling, paralysis, or cramping; vomiting; constipation;

and personality changes or mental disorders. These symptoms appear intermittently. The acute porphyrias include the following types:

Acute intermittent porphyria. This is probably the most common porphyria with acute (severe but usually not long-lasting) symptoms. It results from low levels of the enzyme responsible for the third step in heme production. It is inherited in an autosomal dominant pattern.

ALAD deficiency porphyria is a very rare disorder that results from low levels of the enzyme responsible for the second step in heme production. It is inherited in an autosomal recessive pattern.

Chapter 32

Retinoblastoma

Retinoblastoma Is a Disease in Which Malignant (Cancer) Cells Form in the Tissues of the Retina

The retina is the nerve tissue that lines the inside of the back of the eye. The retina senses light and sends images to the brain by way of the optic nerve.

Although retinoblastoma may occur at any age, it occurs most often in children younger than two years of age. Cancer may be in one eye (unilateral) or in both eyes (bilateral). Retinoblastoma rarely spreads from the eye to nearby tissue or other parts of the body.

Cavitary retinoblastoma is a rare type of retinoblastoma in which cavities (hollow spaces) form within the tumor.

Retinoblastoma Occurs in Heritable and Nonheritable Forms

A child is thought to have the heritable form of retinoblastoma when one of the following is true:

- There is a family history of retinoblastoma.

- There is a certain mutation (change) in the *RB1* gene. The mutation in the *RB1* gene may be passed from the parent to the

---

This chapter includes text excerpted from "Retinoblastoma Treatment (PDQ®)—Patient Version," National Cancer Institute (NCI), January 29, 2018.

child or it may occur in the egg or sperm before conception or soon after conception.

- There is more than one tumor in the eye or there is a tumor in both eyes.

- There is a tumor in one eye and the child is younger than one year of age.

After heritable retinoblastoma has been diagnosed and treated, new tumors may continue to form for a few years. Regular eye exams to check for new tumors are usually done every 2 to 4 months for at least 28 months.

Nonheritable retinoblastoma is retinoblastoma that is not the heritable form. Most cases of retinoblastoma are the nonheritable form.

Treatment for Both Forms of Retinoblastoma Should Include Genetic Counseling

Parents should receive genetic counseling (a discussion with a trained professional about the risk of genetic diseases) to discuss genetic testing to check for a mutation (change) in the *RB1* gene. Genetic counseling also includes a discussion of the risk of retinoblastoma for the child and the child's brothers or sisters.

Children with a Family History of Retinoblastoma Should Have Eye Exams to Check for Retinoblastoma

A child with a family history of retinoblastoma should have regular eye exams beginning early in life to check for retinoblastoma unless it is known that the child does not have the *RB1* gene change. Early diagnosis of retinoblastoma may mean the child will need less intense treatment.

Brothers or sisters of a child with retinoblastoma should have regular eye exams by an ophthalmologist until three to five years of age unless it is known that the brother or sister does not have the *RB1* gene change.

A Child Who Has Heritable Retinoblastoma Has an Increased Risk of Trilateral Retinoblastoma and Other Cancers

A child with heritable retinoblastoma has an increased risk of a pineal tumor in the brain. When retinoblastoma and a brain tumor occur at the same time, it is called "trilateral retinoblastoma" (TRb). The brain tumor is usually diagnosed between 20 and 36 months of age. Regular screening using magnetic resonance imaging (MRI) may be done for a child thought to have heritable retinoblastoma or for a child with retinoblastoma in one eye and a family history of the disease. Computerized tomography (CT) scans are usually not used for routine screening in order to avoid exposing the child to ionizing radiation.

Heritable retinoblastoma also increases the child's risk of other types of cancer, such as lung cancer, bladder cancer, or melanoma, in later years. Regular follow-up exams are important.

Signs and Symptoms of Retinoblastoma Include "White Pupil" and Eye Pain or Redness

These and other signs and symptoms may be caused by retinoblastoma or by other conditions. Check with a doctor if your child has any of the following:

- Pupil of the eye appears white instead of red when light shines into it. This may be seen in flash photographs of the child

- Eyes appear to be looking in different directions (lazy eye)

- Pain or redness in the eye

- Infection around the eye

- Eyeball is larger than normal

- Colored part of the eye and pupil look cloudy

Tests That Examine the Retina Are Used to Detect (Find) and Diagnose Retinoblastoma

The following tests and procedures may be used:

- **Physical exam and history:** An exam of the body to check general signs of health, including checking for signs of disease, such as lumps or anything else that seems unusual. A history of the patient's health habits and past illnesses and treatments will also be taken. The doctor will ask if there is a family history of retinoblastoma.

- **Eye exam with dilated pupil:** An exam of the eye in which the pupil is dilated (opened wider) with medicated eye drops to allow the doctor to look through the lens and pupil to the retina. The inside of the eye, including the retina and the optic nerve, is examined with a light. Depending on the age of the child, this exam may be done under anesthesia.

- There are several types of eye exams that are done with the pupil dilated:

  - **Ophthalmoscopy:** An exam of the inside of the back of the eye to check the retina and optic nerve using a small magnifying lens and a light.

  - **Slit-lamp biomicroscopy:** An exam of the inside of the eye to check the retina, optic nerve, and other parts of the eye using a strong beam of light and a microscope.

  - **Fluorescein angiography:** A procedure to look at blood vessels and the flow of blood inside the eye. An orange fluorescent dye called "fluorescein" is injected into a blood vessel in the arm and goes into the bloodstream. As the dye travels through blood vessels of the eye, a special camera takes pictures of the retina and choroid to find any blood vessels that are blocked or leaking.

- *RB1* **gene test:** A laboratory test in which a sample of blood or tissue is tested for a change in the *RB1* gene.

- **Ultrasound exam of the eye:** A procedure in which high-energy sound waves (ultrasound) are bounced off the internal tissues of the eye to make echoes. Eye drops are used to numb the eye and a small probe that sends and receives sound waves is placed gently on the surface of the eye. The echoes make a picture of the inside of the eye and the distance from the cornea to the retina is measured. The picture, called a "sonogram," shows on the screen of the ultrasound monitor. The picture can be printed to be looked at later.

- **Magnetic resonance imaging (MRI):** A procedure that uses a magnet, radio waves, and a computer to make a series of detailed pictures of areas inside the body, such as the eye. This procedure is also called "nuclear magnetic resonance imaging" (NMRI).

- **Computed tomography (CT or CAT)** A procedure that makes a series of detailed pictures of areas inside the body, such as the eye, taken from different angles. The pictures are made by a computer linked to an X-ray machine. A dye may be injected into a vein or swallowed to help the organs or tissues show up more clearly.

Retinoblastoma can usually be diagnosed without a biopsy.

When retinoblastoma is in one eye, it sometimes forms in the other eye. Exams of the unaffected eye are done until it is known if the retinoblastoma is the heritable form.

Certain Factors Affect Prognosis (Chance of Recovery) and Treatment Options

The prognosis (chance of recovery) and treatment options depend on the following:

- Whether the cancer is in one or both eyes
- The size and number of tumors
- Whether the tumor has spread to the area around the eye, to the brain, or to other parts of the body
- Whether there are symptoms at the time of diagnosis, for trilateral retinoblastoma
- The age of the child
- How likely it is that vision can be saved in one or both eyes
- Whether the second type of cancer has formed

Treatment Option Overview
There Are Different Types of Treatment for Patients with Retinoblastoma

Different types of treatment are available for patients with retinoblastoma. Some treatments are standard (the currently used treatment), and some are being tested in clinical trials. A treatment clinical trial is a research study meant to help improve current treatments or obtain information on new treatments for patients with cancer. When clinical trials show that a new treatment is better than the standard treatment, the new treatment may become the standard treatment.

Because cancer in children is rare, taking part in a clinical trial should be considered. Some clinical trials are open only to patients who have not started treatment.

Children with Retinoblastoma Should Have Their Treatment Planned by a Team of Healthcare Providers Who Are Experts in Treating Cancer in Children

The goals of treatment are to save the child's life, to save vision and the eye, and to prevent serious side effects. Treatment will be overseen by a pediatric oncologist, a doctor who specializes in treating children with cancer. The pediatric oncologist works with other healthcare providers who are experts in treating children with eye cancer and who specialize in certain areas of medicine. These may include a pediatric ophthalmologist (children's eye doctor) who has a lot of experience in treating retinoblastoma and the following specialists:

- Pediatric surgeon
- Radiation oncologist
- Pediatrician
- Pediatric nurse specialist
- Rehabilitation specialist
- Social worker
- Geneticist or genetic counselor

Treatment for Retinoblastoma May Cause Side Effects

Side effects from cancer treatment that begin after treatment and continue for months or years are called "late effects." Late effects of treatment for retinoblastoma may include the following:

- Physical problems, such as seeing or hearing problems, or if the eye is removed, a change in the shape and size of the bone around the eye
- Changes in mood, feelings, thinking, learning, or memory
- Second cancers (new types of cancer), such as lung and bladder cancers, osteosarcoma, soft tissue sarcoma, or melanoma

The following risk factors may increase the risk of having another cancer:

- Having the heritable form of retinoblastoma
- Past treatment with radiation therapy, especially before the age of one
- Having already had a previous second cancer

It is important to talk with your child's doctors about the effects cancer treatment can have on your child. Regular follow-up by health professionals who are experts in diagnosing and treating late effects is important.

Six Types of Standard Treatment Are Used
Cryotherapy

Cryotherapy is a treatment that uses an instrument to freeze and destroy abnormal tissue. This type of treatment is also called "cryosurgery."

Thermotherapy

Thermotherapy is the use of heat to destroy cancer cells. Thermotherapy may be given using a laser beam aimed through the dilated pupil or onto the outside of the eyeball. Thermotherapy may be used alone for small tumors or combined with chemotherapy for larger tumors. This treatment is a type of laser therapy.

Chemotherapy

Chemotherapy is a cancer treatment that uses drugs to stop the growth of cancer cells, either by killing the cells or by stopping them from dividing. The way the chemotherapy is given depends on the stage of cancer and where the cancer is in the body.

There are different types of chemotherapy:

- Systemic chemotherapy: When chemotherapy is taken by mouth or injected into a vein or muscle, the drugs enter the bloodstream and can reach cancer cells throughout the body. Systemic chemotherapy is given to shrink the tumor (chemoreduction) and avoid surgery to remove the eye. After chemoreduction, other treatments may include radiation therapy, cryotherapy, laser therapy, or regional chemotherapy.

  Systemic chemotherapy may also be given to kill any cancer cells that are left after the initial treatment or to patients with retinoblastoma that occurs outside the eye. Treatment given after the initial treatment, to lower the risk that cancer will come back, is called "adjuvant therapy."

- Regional chemotherapy: When chemotherapy is placed directly into the cerebrospinal fluid (CSF) (intrathecal chemotherapy),

389

an organ (such as the eye), or a body cavity, the drugs mainly affect cancer cells in those areas. Several types of regional chemotherapy are used to treat retinoblastoma.

- Ophthalmic artery infusion chemotherapy (OAIC): Ophthalmic artery infusion chemotherapy carries anticancer drugs directly to the eye. A catheter is put into an artery that leads to the eye and the anticancer drug is given through the catheter. After the drug is given, a small balloon may be inserted into the artery to block it and keep most of the anticancer drug trapped near the tumor. This type of chemotherapy may be given as the initial treatment when the tumor is in the eye only or when the tumor has not responded to other types of treatment. Ophthalmic artery infusion chemotherapy is given at special retinoblastoma treatment centers.

- Intravitreal chemotherapy (IVitC): Intravitreal chemotherapy is the injection of anticancer drugs directly into the vitreous humor (jelly-like substance) inside of the eye. It is used to treat cancer that has spread to the vitreous humor and has not responded to treatment or has come back after treatment.

Radiation Therapy

Radiation therapy is a cancer treatment that uses high-energy X-rays or other types of radiation to kill cancer cells or keep them from growing. There are two types of radiation therapy:

- **External-beam radiation therapy (EBRT)** uses a machine outside the body to send radiation toward cancer. Certain ways of giving radiation therapy can help keep radiation from damaging nearby healthy tissue. These types of radiation therapy include the following:

  - **Intensity-modulated radiation therapy (IMRT):** IMRT is a type of 3-dimensional (3-D) external radiation therapy that uses a computer to make pictures of the size and shape of the tumor. Thin beams of radiation of different intensities (strengths) are aimed at the tumor from many angles.

  - **Proton-beam radiation therapy:** Proton-beam therapy is a type of high-energy, external radiation therapy. A radiation therapy machine aims streams of protons (tiny, invisible, positively-charged particles) at the cancer cells to kill them.

- **Internal radiation therapy** uses a radioactive substance sealed in needles, seeds, wires, or catheters that are placed directly into or near cancer. Certain ways of giving radiation therapy can help keep radiation from damaging nearby healthy tissue. This type of internal radiation therapy may include the following:

    - **Plaque radiotherapy:** Radioactive seeds are attached to one side of a disk, called a "plaque" and placed directly on the outside wall of the eye near the tumor. The side of the plaque with the seeds on it faces the eyeball, aiming radiation at the tumor. The plaque helps protect other nearby tissue from the radiation.

The way radiation therapy is given depends on the type and stage of the cancer being treated and how cancer responded to other treatments. External and internal radiation therapy is used to treat retinoblastoma.

High-Dose Chemotherapy with Stem Cell Rescue

High-dose chemotherapy with stem cell rescue is a way of giving high doses of chemotherapy and replacing blood-forming cells destroyed by the cancer treatment. Stem cells (immature blood cells) are removed from the blood or bone marrow of the patient and are frozen and stored. After the chemotherapy is completed, the stored stem cells are thawed and given back to the patient through an infusion. These reinfused stem cells grow into (and restore) the body's blood cells.

Surgery (Enucleation)

Enucleation is surgery to remove the eye and part of the optic nerve. A sample of the eye tissue that is removed will be checked under a microscope to see if there are any signs that the cancer is likely to spread to other parts of the body. This should be done by an experienced pathologist, who is familiar with retinoblastoma and other diseases of the eye. Enucleation is done if there is little or no chance that vision can be saved and when the tumor is large, did not respond to treatment, or comes back after treatment. The patient will be fitted for an artificial eye.

Close follow-up is needed for two years or more to check for signs of recurrence in the area around the affected eye and to check the other eye.

New Types of Treatment Are Being Tested in Clinical Trials

This section describes treatments that are being studied in clinical trials. It may not mention every new treatment being studied.

Targeted Therapy

Targeted therapy is a type of treatment that uses drugs or other substances to attack cancer cells. Targeted therapies usually cause less harm to normal cells than chemotherapy or radiation therapy do.

Targeted therapy is being studied for the treatment of retinoblastoma that has recurred (come back).

Patients May Want to Think about Taking Part in a Clinical Trial

For some patients, taking part in a clinical trial may be the best treatment choice. Clinical trials are part of the cancer research process. Clinical trials are done to find out if new cancer treatments are safe and effective or better than the standard treatment.

Many of nowadays standard treatments for cancer are based on earlier clinical trials. Patients who take part in a clinical trial may receive the standard treatment or be among the first to receive a new treatment.

Patients who take part in clinical trials also help improve the way cancer will be treated in the future. Even when clinical trials do not lead to effective new treatments, they often answer important questions and help move research forward.

Patients Can Enter Clinical Trials before, during, or after Starting Their Cancer Treatment

Some clinical trials only include patients who have not yet received treatment. Other trials test treatments for patients whose cancer has not gotten better. There are also clinical trials that test new ways to stop cancer from recurring (coming back) or reduce the side effects of cancer treatment.

Clinical trials are taking place in many parts of the country.

Follow-Up Tests May Be Needed

Some of the tests that were done to diagnose cancer or to find out the stage of cancer may be repeated. Some tests will be repeated in order to see how well the treatment is working. Decisions about whether to continue, change, or stop treatment may be based on the results of these tests.

Some of the tests will continue to be done from time to time after treatment has ended. The results of these tests can show if your child's condition has changed or if cancer has recurred (come back). These tests are sometimes called "follow-up tests" or "check-ups."

Chapter 33

Rett Syndrome

What Is Rett Syndrome?

Rett syndrome was first reported by Dr. Andreas Rett in 1966. Rett syndrome is a complex neurological and developmental disorder in which early growth and development appear normal at first, but then the infant stops developing and affected children even lose skills and abilities. Rett syndrome occurs mostly in females.

Over time, the effects of Rett syndrome can lead to cognitive, sensory, emotional, motor, cardiac, and such autonomic nervous system problems, such as difficulties with digestion or breathing.

What Are the Types and Phases of Rett Syndrome?

There are two main types of Rett syndrome: classic and atypical. The two types may differ by their symptoms or by the specific gene mutation.

The majority of Rett syndrome patients have the classic form, which typically develops in four phases. Healthcare providers and researchers, relying on consensus criteria, view the progression of classic Rett syndrome as the following phases

- **Early onset phase**. In this phase, development stalls or stops completely. Sometimes, the syndrome takes hold at such a subtle

This chapter includes text excerpted from "Rett Syndrome: Condition Information," *Eunice Kennedy Shriver* National Institute of Child Health and Human Development (NICHD), December 1, 2016.

pace that parents and healthcare providers do not notice it at first. Researchers once thought that this phase began around 6 months of age. However, after analyzing videotapes of Rett individuals taken from birth, they now know that some infants with Rett syndrome only seem to develop normally. In fact, these infants show problems with very early development. In one study, all of the infants with Rett syndrome showed problems with body movements from birth through age 6 months. Another 42 percent showed stereotyped hand movements during this time period.

- **Rapid destructive phase**. The child loses skills (regresses) quickly. Purposeful hand movements and speech are usually the first skills lost. Breathing problems and stereotypic hand movements, such as wringing (clasping or squeezing), washing (a movement that resembles washing the hands), and clapping or tapping also tend to start during this stage.

- **Plateau phase.** The child's regression slows and other problems may seem to lessen, or there may even be improvement in some areas. Seizures and movement problems are common at this stage. Many people with Rett syndrome spend most of their lives in this stage.

- **Late motor deterioration phase**. Individuals in this stage may become stiff or lose muscle tone; some become immobile. Scoliosis (an abnormal curvature of the spine) may be present and even become severe enough to require bracing or surgery. Stereotypic hand movements and breathing problems seem to become less common.

There are five known variants of atypical Rett syndrome and are defined by characteristic symptoms, age at which the symptoms are present, or genetic makeup.

Forms of atypical Rett syndrome that have been identified to date include:

- Congenital Rett syndrome (Rolando variant)

- Early-Onset Rett syndrome (Hanefeld variant)

- Late-Childhood Rett syndrome

- Forme Fruste Rett syndrome

- Preserved-Speech variant of Rett syndrome (Zappella variant)

What Are the Symptoms of Rett Syndrome?

The first symptom of Rett syndrome is usually the loss of muscle tone, called "hypotonia." With hypotonia, an infant's arms and legs will appear "floppy."

Although hypotonia and other symptoms of Rett syndrome often present themselves in stages, some typical symptoms can occur at any stage. Symptoms may vary among patients and range from mild to severe.

Typical symptoms (may occur at any stage) and can include:

- Loss of ability to grasp and intentionally touch things

- Loss of ability to speak. (Initially, a child may stop saying words or phrases that he or she once said; later, the child may make sounds, but not say any purposeful words.)

- Severe problems with balance or coordination, leading to loss of the ability to walk. (These problems may start out as clumsiness and trouble walking. Although a majority of those with Rett Syndrome are still able to walk later in life, others may become unable to sit up or walk or may become immobile.)

- Mechanical, repetitive hand movements, such as hand wringing, hand washing, or grasping

- Complications with breathing, including hyperventilation and breath holding when awake

- Anxiety and social-behavioral problems

- Intellectual disability

In addition, a person with Rett syndrome may experience one or more of the following associated problems:

- Scoliosis is a problem for the majority of girls with Rett syndrome. In some cases, the curving of the spine can become so severe that the girls require surgery. For some, bracing relieves the problem, prevents it from getting worse, or delays or eliminates the need for surgery.

- Seizures. (These may involve the whole body, or they may be staring spells with no movement.)

- Constipation and gastroesophageal reflux

- Discomfort in the abdomen or gallbladder problems, such as gallstones

- Cardiac or heart problems, usually problems with heart rhythm. (Some persons with Rett syndrome may have abnormally long pauses between heartbeats, as measured by an electrocardiogram, or they may experience other types of arrhythmia.)

- Trouble feeding oneself, swallowing, and chewing food. (In some cases, too, in spite of healthy appetites, girls with Rett syndrome do not gain weight or have trouble maintaining a healthy weight. As a result, some girls with Rett syndrome rely on feeding tubes.)

- Disrupted sleep patterns at night (during childhood) and increased sleep (after the age of 5). (Some researchers suggest that problems with sleep are among the earliest symptoms of Rett syndrome and can appear between 1 and 2 months of age. Such problems can lead to sudden death during sleep.)

  - Excessive saliva and drooling

  - Poor circulation in hands and legs

  - Walking on toes or the balls of feet

  - Walking with a wide gait (ataxia)

  - Grinding the teeth (bruxism)

Symptoms can vary from person to person and from one stage to the next. Symptoms may also improve in the "plateau phase."

What Causes Rett Syndrome

Most cases of Rett syndrome are caused by a change (also called a "mutation") in a single gene. In 1999, *Eunice Kennedy Shriver* National Institute of Child Health and Human Development (NICHD)-supported scientists discovered that most classic Rett syndrome cases are caused by a mutation within the Methylcytosine-binding protein 2 (*MECP2*) gene. The *MECP2* gene is located on the X chromosome. Between 90 and 95 percent of girls with Rett syndrome have a mutation in the *MECP2* gene. Among families with a child affected by Rett syndrome the chance of having a second child with the syndrome is very low.

Eight mutations in the *MECP2* gene represent the most prevalent causes of Rett syndrome. The development and severity of Rett syndrome symptoms depend on the location and type of the mutation on the *MECP2* gene.

The *MECP2* gene makes a protein that is necessary for the development of the nervous system, especially the brain. The mutation causes the gene to either make insufficient amounts of this protein or to make a damaged protein that the body cannot use. In either case, if there is not enough of the working protein for the brain to develop normally, Rett syndrome develops.

Researchers are still trying to understand exactly how the brain uses this protein, called "MeCP2," and how problems with this protein cause the typical features of Rett syndrome.

Mutations on two other genes can cause some of the atypical variants of Rett syndrome: Congenital Rett syndrome (Rolando variant) is associated with mutations of the *FOXG1* gene, and *CDKL5* mutations are linked with the early-onset, or Hanefeld, variant. Males affected by these types of mutations can survive infancy. Males can also have a duplication of a normal *MECP2* gene and survive, but are severely affected. Too much MeCP2 protein is as bad for development as too little.

Is Rett Syndrome Passed from One Generation to the Next?

In nearly all cases, the genetic change that causes Rett syndrome is spontaneous, meaning it happens randomly. Such random mutations are usually not inherited or passed from one generation to the next. However, in a very small percentage of families, Rett mutations are inherited and passed on by female carriers.

Why Do Mostly Females and so Few Boys Have Rett Syndrome?

Two types of chromosomes determine the sex of an embryo: the X and the Y chromosomes. Girls have two X chromosomes, and boys have one X and one Y chromosome.

Because the mutated gene that causes Rett syndrome is located on the X chromosome, females have twice the opportunity to develop a mutation in one of their X chromosomes. Females with Rett syndrome usually have one mutated X chromosome and one normal X chromosome. Only one X chromosome in a given cell remains active throughout life and cells randomly determine which X chromosome will remain active. If the cells have an active mutated gene more often than the normal gene, the symptoms of Rett syndrome will be more severe. This random process allows most females with Rett syndrome to survive infancy.

Because most boys have only one X chromosome, when this gene is mutated to cause Rett syndrome, the detrimental effects are not softened by the presence of a second, normal X chromosome. As a result, many males with Rett syndrome are stillborn or do not live past infancy.

Some boys with Rett syndrome, however, do live past infancy, likely for one of three reasons:

- Mosaicism, a condition in which individual cells within the same person have a different genetic makeup. This means that some of the X chromosome genes in a boy's body have the Rett mutation, and some genes do not have the mutation. When a lower percentage of genes have the Rett syndrome mutation, the symptoms are not as severe.

- A boy may have two X chromosomes and one Y chromosome (Klinefelter syndrome). Only one X chromosome will be active in each cell, so if one X carries a mutation in MECP2, the severity of symptoms will depend on how many cells have that the mutant X active in the body.

- The genetic mutation is less severe than that of other forms of Rett syndrome mutations.

Duplication of the *MECP2* gene can occur in boys and affects intellectual and physical function.

How Do Healthcare Providers Diagnose Rett Syndrome?
Blood Test

Genetic evaluation of a blood sample can identify whether a child has one of the known mutations that cause Rett syndrome. Even if a child has a mutation of the Methylcytosine-binding protein 2 (*MECP2*) gene (which also occurs in other conditions), the symptoms of Rett syndrome may not always be present, so healthcare providers also need to evaluate the child's symptoms to confirm a diagnosis.

Clinical Symptoms

A child must meet the following five necessary criteria to be diagnosed with classic Rett syndrome:

Main Diagnostic Criteria

- A pattern of development, regression, then recovery or stabilization

- Partial or complete loss of purposeful hand skills, such as grasping with fingers, reaching for things, or touching things on purpose

- Partial or complete loss of spoken language

- Repetitive hand movements, such as wringing the hands, washing, squeezing, clapping, or rubbing

- Gait abnormalities, including walking on toes or with an unsteady, wide-based, stiff-legged gait

A slowing of head growth between three months and four years of age, leading to acquired microcephaly, is also characteristic of Rett syndrome and calls for a diagnosis to be considered.

Healthcare providers will also consider whether any of the following conditions are present. The presence of any of the symptoms below would rule out a Rett syndrome diagnosis.

Atypical Rett Syndrome

Genetic mutations causing some atypical variants of Rett syndrome have been identified. After a blood test to confirm a child's genetic makeup, a healthcare provider may diagnose the child with atypical Rett syndrome if the child demonstrates development, followed by regression, and then recovery or stabilization. In addition, the healthcare provider will confirm at least 2 of the other 4 main criteria, and 5 of the 11 supportive criteria before making a diagnosis.

Other Possible Diagnoses

Sometimes Rett syndrome is misdiagnosed as regressive autism, cerebral palsy, or nonspecific developmental delays.

For some males, the features of Rett syndrome occur with another genetic condition called "Klinefelter syndrome," in which a boy has two X chromosomes and one Y chromosome. This means that the boy may have one mutated *MECP2* gene and one normal *MECP2* gene, reducing the effects of the mutated gene.

What Are the Treatments for Rett Syndrome?

Most people with Rett syndrome benefit from well-designed interventions no matter what their age, but the earlier that treatment begins, the better. With therapy and assistance, people with Rett syndrome can participate in school and community activities.

These treatments, forms of assistance, and options for medication generally aim to slow the loss of abilities, improve or preserve movement, and encourage communication and social contact. A list of treatment options is presented below; the need for these treatments depends on the severity of different symptoms.

Physical Therapy / Hydrotherapy

- Improves or maintains mobility and balance
- Reduces misshapen back and limbs
- Provides weight-bearing training for patients with scoliosis

Occupational Therapy

- Improves or maintains use of hands
- Reduces stereotypic hand movements, such as wringing, washing, clapping, rubbing, or tapping
- Teaches self-directed activities, such as dressing and feeding

Speech-Language Therapy

- Teaches nonverbal communication
- Improves social interaction

Feeding Assistance

- Supplements for calcium and minerals to strengthen bones and slow scoliosis
- High-calorie, high-fat diet to increase height and weight
- Insertion of a feeding tube, if patients accidentally swallow their food into their lungs (aspiration)

Physical Assistance

- Braces or surgery to correct scoliosis
- Splints to adjust hand movements

Medication

- To reduce breathing problems
- To eliminate problems with abnormal heart rhythm
- To relieve indigestion and constipation
- To control seizures

Chapter 34

Tuberous Sclerosis

What Is Tuberous Sclerosis?

Tuberous sclerosis—also called "tuberous sclerosis complex" (TSC)—is a rare, multi-system genetic disease that causes benign tumors to grow in the brain and on other vital organs, such as the kidneys, heart, eyes, lungs, and skin. It usually affects the central nervous system and results in a combination of symptoms including seizures, developmental delay, behavioral problems, skin abnormalities, and kidney disease.

The disorder affects as many as 25,000 to 40,000 individuals in the United States and about 1 to 2 million individuals worldwide, with an estimated prevalence of 1 in 6,000 newborns. TSC occurs in all races and ethnic groups, and in both genders.

The name tuberous sclerosis comes from the characteristic tuber or potato-like nodules in the brain, which calcify with age and become hard or sclerotic. The disorder—once known as "epiloia" or "Bourneville's disease"—was first identified by a French physician more than 100 years ago.

Many TSC patients show evidence of the disorder in the first year of life. However, clinical features can be subtle initially, and many signs and symptoms take years to develop. As a result, TSC can be unrecognized or misdiagnosed for years.

This chapter includes text excerpted from "Tuberous Sclerosis Fact Sheet," National Institute of Neurological Disorders and Stroke (NINDS), July 6, 2018.

What Causes Tuberous Sclerosis

TSC is caused by defects, or mutations, on two genes—*TSC1* and *TSC2*. Only one of the genes needs to be affected for TSC to be present. The *TSC1* gene, discovered in 1997, is on chromosome 9 and produces a protein called "hamartin." The *TSC2* gene, discovered in 1993, is on chromosome 16 and produces the protein tuberin. Scientists believe these proteins act in a complex as growth suppressors by inhibiting the activation of a master, evolutionarily conserved kinase called "mTOR." Loss of regulation of mTOR occurs in cells lacking either hamartin or tuberin, and this leads to abnormal differentiation and development, and to the generation of enlarged cells, as seen in TSC brain lesions.

Is Tuberous Sclerosis Inherited?

Although some individuals inherit the disorder from a parent with TSC, most cases occur as sporadic cases due to new, spontaneous mutations in TSC1 or TSC2. In this situation, neither parent has the disorder or the faulty gene(s). Instead, a faulty gene first occurs in the affected individual.

In familial cases, TSC is an autosomal dominant disorder, which means that the disorder can be transmitted directly from parent to child. In those cases, only one parent needs to have the faulty gene in order to pass it on to a child. If a parent has TSC, each offspring has a 50 percent chance of developing the disorder. Children who inherit TSC may not have the same symptoms as their parent and they may have either a milder or a more severe form of the disorder.

Rarely, individuals acquire TSC through a process called "gonadal mosaicism." These patients have parents with no apparent defects in the two genes that cause the disorder. Yet these parents can have a child with TSC because a portion of one of the parent's reproductive cells (sperm or eggs) can contain the genetic mutation without the other cells of the body being involved. In cases of gonadal mosaicism, genetic testing of a blood sample might not reveal the potential for passing the disease to offspring.

What Are the Signs and Symptoms of Tuberous Sclerosis?

TSC can affect many different systems of the body, causing a variety of signs and symptoms. Signs of the disorder vary depending on which system and which organs are involved. The natural course of TSC varies from individual to individual, with symptoms ranging from very mild to quite severe. In addition to the benign tumors that frequently occur in TSC, other common symptoms include seizures, cognitive impairment, behavior problems, and skin abnormalities. Tumors can grow in nearly any organ, but they most commonly occur in the brain, kidneys, heart, lungs, and skin. Malignant tumors are rare in TSC. Those that do occur primarily affect the kidneys.

Brain involvement in TSC. Three types of brain lesions are seen in TSC: cortical tubers, for which the disease is named, generally form on the surface of the brain but may also appear in the deep areas of the brain: subependymal nodules (SEN), which form in the walls of the ventricles—the fluid-filled cavities of the brain; and subependymal giant-cell astrocytomas (SEGA), which develop from SEN and grow such that they may block the flow of fluid within the brain, causing a buildup of fluid and pressure and leading to headaches and blurred vision.

TSC usually causes the greatest problems for those affected and their family members through effects on brain function. Most individuals with TSC will have seizures at some point during their life. Seizures of all types may occur, including infantile spasms; tonic-clonic seizures (also known as "grand mal seizures"); or tonic, akinetic, atypical absence, myoclonic, complex partial or generalized squires. Infantile spasms can occur as soon as the day of birth and are often difficult to recognize. Seizures can also be difficult to control by medication, and sometimes surgery or other measures are used.

About one-half to two-thirds of individuals with TSC have developmental delays ranging from mild learning disabilities to severe impairment. Behavior problems, including aggression, sudden rage, attention deficit hyperactivity disorder, acting out, obsessive-compulsive disorder (OCD), and repetitive, destructive, or self-harming behavior occur in children with TSC and can be difficult to manage. About one-third of children with TSC meet criteria for autism spectrum disorder.

Kidney problems, such as cysts and angiomyolipomas, occur in an estimated 70 to 80 percent of individuals with TSC, usually occurring between the ages of 15 and 30. Cysts are usually small, appear in limited numbers, and cause no serious problems. Approximately 2 percent of individuals with TSC develop large numbers of cysts in a pattern similar to polycystic kidney disease during childhood. In these cases, kidney function is compromised and kidney failure occurs. In rare instances, the cysts may bleed, leading to blood loss and anemia.

Angiomyolipomas—benign growths consisting of fatty tissue and muscle cells—are the most common kidney lesions in TSC. These growths are seen in the majority of individuals with TSC, but are also found in about 1 of every 300 people without TSC. Angiomyolipomas caused by TSC are usually found in both kidneys and in most cases they produce no symptoms. However, they can sometimes grow so large that they cause pain or kidney failure. Bleeding from angiomyolipomas may also occur, causing both pain and weakness. If severe bleeding does not stop naturally, there may severe blood loss, resulting in profound anemia and a life-threatening drop in blood pressure, and warrants urgent medical attention.

Other rare kidney problems include renal cell carcinoma, developing from an angiomyolipoma, and oncocytomas, benign tumors unique to individuals with TSC.

Tumors called "cardiac rhabdomyomas" are often found in the hearts of infants and young children with TSC, and they are often seen on prenatal fetus ultrasound exams. If the tumors are large or there are multiple tumors, they can block circulation and cause death. However, if they do not cause problems at birth—when in most cases they are at their largest size—they usually become smaller with time and do not affect the individual in later life.

Benign tumors called "phakomas" are sometimes found in the eyes of individuals with TSC, appearing as white patches on the retina. Generally they do not cause vision loss or other vision problems, but they can be used to help diagnose the disease.

Additional tumors and cysts may be found in other areas of the body, including the liver, lung, and pancreas. Bone cysts, rectal polyps, gum fibromas, and dental pits may also occur.

A wide variety of skin abnormalities may occur in individuals with TSC. Most cause no problems but are helpful in diagnosis. Some cases may cause disfigurement, necessitating treatment. The most common skin abnormalities include:

- Hypomelanotic macules ("ash leaf spots"), which are white or lighter patches of skin that may appear anywhere on the body and are caused by a lack of skin pigment or melanin—the substance that gives skin its color.

- Reddish spots or bumps called "facial angiofibromas" (also called "adenoma sebaceum"), which appear on the face (sometimes resembling acne) and consist of blood vessels and fibrous tissue.

- Raised, discolored areas on the forehead called "forehead plaques," which are common and unique to TSC and may help doctors diagnose the disorder.

- Areas of thick leathery, pebbly skin called "shagreen patches," usually found on the lower back or nape of the neck.

- Small fleshy tumors called "ungual" or "subungual fibromas" that grow around and under the toenails or fingernails and may need to be surgically removed if they enlarge or cause bleeding. These usually appear later in life between the ages of 20 and 50.

- Other skin features that are not unique to individuals with TSC, including molluscum fibrosum or skin tags, which typically occur across the back of the neck and shoulders, café au lait spots or flat brown marks, and poliosis, a tuft or patch of white hair that may appear on the scalp or eyelids.

Lung lesions are present in about one-third of adult women with TSC and are much less commonly seen in men. Lung lesions include lymphangioleiomyomatosis (LAM) and multinodular multifocal pneumocyte hyperplasia (MMPH). LAM is a tumor-like disorder in which cells proliferate in the lungs, and there is lung destruction with cyst formation. There is a range of symptoms with LAM, with many TSC individuals having no symptoms, while others suffer with breathlessness, which can progress and be severe. MMPH is a more benign tumor that occurs in men and women equally.

How Is Tuberous Sclerosis Diagnosed?

The diagnosis of TSC is based upon clinical criteria. In many cases the first clue to recognizing TSC is the presence of seizures or delayed development. In other cases, the first sign may be white patches on the skin (hypomelanotic macules) or the identification of cardiac tumor rhabdomyoma.

Diagnosis of the disorder is based on a careful clinical exam in combination with computed tomography (CT) or magnetic resonance imaging (MRI) of the brain, which may show tubers in the brain, and an ultrasound of the heart, liver, and kidneys, which may show tumors in those organs. Doctors should carefully examine the skin for the wide variety of skin features, the fingernails and toenails for ungual fibromas, the teeth and gums for dental pits and/or gum fibromas, and the eyes for retinal lesions. A Wood's lamp or ultraviolet light may be used to locate the hypomelantic macules which are sometimes hard to see on infants and individuals with pale or fair skin. Because of the wide variety of signs of TSC, it is best if a doctor experienced in the diagnosis of TSC evaluates a potential patient.

In infants, TSC may be suspected if the child has cardiac rhabdomyomas or seizures (infantile spasms) at birth. With a careful examination of the skin and brain, it may be possible to diagnose TSC in a very young infant. However, many children are not diagnosed until later in life when their seizures begin and other symptoms, such as facial angiofibromas, appear.

How Is Tuberous Sclerosis Treated?

There is no cure for TSC, although treatment is available for a number of the symptoms. Antiepileptic drugs may be used to control seizures. Vigabatrin is a particularly useful medication in TSC, and has been approved by the U.S. Food and Drug Administration (FDA) for treatment of infantile spasms in TSC, although it has significant side effects. The FDA has approved the drug everolimus (Afinitor®) to treat subependymal giant cell astrocytomas (SEGA brain tumors) and angiomyolipoma kidney tumors. Specific medications may be prescribed for behavior problems. Intervention programs, including special schooling and occupational therapy, may benefit individuals with special needs and developmental issues. Surgery may be needed in case of complications connected to tubers, SEN or SEGA, as well as in risk of hemorrhage from kidney tumors. Respiratory insufficiency due to LAM can be treated with supplemental oxygen therapy or lung transplantation if severe.

Because TSC is a lifelong condition, individuals need to be regularly monitored by a doctor to make sure they are receiving the best possible treatments. Due to the many varied symptoms of TSC, care by a clinician experienced with the disorder is recommended.

Basic laboratory studies have revealed insight into the function of the TSC genes and has led to recent use of rapamycin and related drugs for treating some manifestations of TSC. Rapamycin has been shown to be effective in treating SEGA, the brain tumor seen in TSC. However, its benefit for a variety of other aspects of and tumors seen in people with TSC is less certain, and clinical trials looking at the benefit carefully are continuing. Rapamycin and related drugs are not yet approved by the FDA for any purpose in individuals with TSC.

What Is the Prognosis for Tuberous Sclerosis?

The prognosis for individuals with TSC is highly variable and depends on the severity of symptoms. Those individuals with mild symptoms usually do well and have a normal life expectancy, while paying attention to TSC-specific issues. Individuals who are severely affected can suffer from severe developmental delays and persistent epilepsy.

All individuals with TSC are at risk for life-threatening conditions related to the brain tumors, kidney lesions, or LAM. Continued monitoring by a physician experienced with TSC is important. With appropriate medical care, most individuals with the disorder can look forward to normal life expectancy.

Chapter 35

Vision Disorders

Chapter Contents

Section 35.1

Color Vision Deficiency

This section includes text excerpted from "Facts about
Color Blindness," National Eye Institute (NEI), February 2015.
Reviewed March 2019.

What Is Color Blindness?

Most of us share a common color vision sensory experience. Some people, however, have a color vision deficiency, which means their perception of colors is different from what most of us see. The most severe forms of these deficiencies are referred to as "color blindness." People with color blindness aren't aware of differences among colors that are obvious to the rest of us. People who don't have the more severe types of color blindness may not even be aware of their condition unless they're tested in a clinic or laboratory.

Inherited color blindness is caused by abnormal photopigments. These color-detecting molecules are located in cone-shaped cells within the retina, called "cone cells." In humans, several genes are needed for the body to make photopigments, and defects in these genes can lead to color blindness.

There are three main kinds of color blindness, based on photopigment defects in the three different kinds of cones that respond to blue, green, and red light. Red-green color blindness is the most common, followed by blue-yellow color blindness. A complete absence of color vision—total color blindness—is rare.

Sometimes color blindness can be caused by physical or chemical damage to the eye, the optic nerve, or parts of the brain that process color information. Color vision can also decline with age, most often because of cataract—a clouding and yellowing of the eye's lens.

Who Gets Color Blindness

As many as eight percent of men and 0.5 percent of women with Northern European ancestry have the common form of red-green color blindness.

Men are much more likely to be colorblind than women because the genes responsible for the most common, inherited color blindness are on the X chromosome. Males only have one X chromosome, while females have two X chromosomes. In females, a functional gene on only one of the X chromosomes is enough to compensate for the loss on the other. This kind of inheritance pattern is called "X-linked" and primarily affects males. Inherited color blindness can be present at birth, begin in childhood, or not appear until the adult years.

How Genes Are Inherited

Genes are bundled together on structures called "chromosomes." One copy of each chromosome is passed by a parent at conception through egg and sperm cells. The X and Y chromosomes, known as "sex chromosomes," determine whether a person is born female (XX) or male (XY) and also carry other traits not related to gender.

In X-linked inheritance, the mother carries the mutated gene on 1 of her X chromosomes and will pass on the mutated gene to 50 percent of her children. Because females have 2 X chromosomes, the effect of a mutation on one X chromosome is offset by the normal gene on the other X chromosome. In this case, the mother will not have the disease, but she can pass on the mutated gene and so is called a "carrier." If a mother is a carrier of an X-linked disease (and the father is not affected), there is a:

- One in two chance that a son will have the disease

- One in two chance that a daughter will be a carrier of the disease

- No chance that a daughter will have the disease

In autosomal recessive inheritance, it takes two copies of the mutant gene to give rise to the disease. An individual who has one copy of a recessive gene mutation is known as a "carrier." When two carriers have a child, there is a:

- One in four chance of having a child with the disease

- One in two chance of having a child who is a carrier

- One in four chance of having a child who neither has the disease nor is a carrier

In autosomal dominant inheritance, it takes just one copy of the mutant gene to bring about the disease. When an affected parent with one dominant gene mutation has a child, there is a one in two chance that a child will inherit the disease.

How Do We See Color?

What color is a strawberry? Most of us would say red, but do we all see the same red? Color vision depends on our eyes and brain working together to perceive different properties of light.

We see the natural and artificial light that illuminates our world as white, although it is actually a mixture of colors that, perceived on their own, would span the visual spectrum from deep blue to deep red. You can see this when rain separates sunlight into a rainbow or a glass prism separates white light into a multi-color band. The color of light is determined by its wavelength. A longer wavelength corresponds to a red light, and a shorter wavelength corresponds to blue light.

Strawberries and other objects reflect some wavelengths of light and absorb others. The reflected light we perceive as color. So, a strawberry is red because its surface is only reflecting the long wavelengths we see as red and absorbing the others. An object appears white when it reflects all wavelengths and black when it absorbs all wavelengths.

Vision begins when light enters the eye, and the cornea and lens focus it onto the retina, a thin layer of tissue at the back of the eye that contains millions of light-sensitive cells called "photoreceptors." Some photoreceptors are shaped like rods, and some are shaped like cones. In each eye, there are many more rods than cones—approximately 120 million rods compared to only 6 million cones. Rods and cones both contain photopigment molecules that undergo a chemical change when they absorb light. This chemical change acts like an on-switch, triggering electrical signals that are then passed from the retina to the visual parts of the brain.

Rods and cones are different in how they respond to light. Rods are more responsive to the dim light, which makes them useful for night vision. Cones are more responsive to bright light, such as in the daytime when the light is plentiful.

Another important difference is that all rods contain only one photopigment, while cones contain one of three different photopigments. This makes cones sensitive to long (red), medium (green), or short (blue) wavelengths of light. The presence of three types of photopigments, each sensitive to a different part of the visual spectrum, is what gives us our rich color vision.

Humans are unusual among mammals for our trichromatic vision— named for the three different types of photopigments we have. Most mammals, including dogs, have just two photopigment types. Other creatures, such as butterflies, have more than three. They may be able to see colors we can only imagine.

Most of us have a full set of the three different cone photopigments, and so we share a very similar color vision experience, but because the human eye and brain together translate light into color, each of us sees colors differently. The differences may be slight. Your blue may be bluer than someone else's, or in the case of color blindness, your red and green may be someone else's brown.

What Are the Different Types of Color Blindness?

The most common types of color blindness are inherited. They are the result of defects in the genes that contain the instructions for making the photopigments found in cones. Some defects alter the photopigment's sensitivity to color; for example, it might be slightly more sensitive to a deeper red and less sensitive to green. Other defects can result in the total loss of a photopigment. Depending on the type of defect and the cone that is affected, problems can arise with red, green, or blue color vision.

Red-Green Color Blindness

The most common types of hereditary color blindness are due to the loss or limited function of the red cone (known as "protan") or green cone (deutran) photopigments. This kind of color blindness is commonly referred to as "red-green color blindness."

- **Protanomaly:** In males with protanomaly, the red cone photopigment is abnormal. Red, orange, and yellow appear greener, and colors are not as bright. This condition is mild and doesn't usually interfere with daily living. Protanomaly is an X-linked disorder estimated to affect one percent of males.

- **Protanopia:** In males with protanopia, there are no working red cone cells. Red appears as black. Certain shades of orange, yellow, and green all appear as yellow. Protanopia is an X-linked disorder that is estimated to affect one percent of males.

- **Deuteranomaly:** In males with deuteranomaly, the green cone photopigment is abnormal. Yellow and green appear redder, and it is difficult to tell violet from blue. This condition is mild and doesn't interfere with daily living. Deuteranomaly is the most common form of color blindness and is an X-linked disorder, affecting 5 percent of males.

- **Deuteranopia:** In males with deuteranopia, there are no working green cone cells. They tend to see reds as brownish-yellow and greens as beige. Deuteranopia is an X-linked disorder that affects about one percent of males.

Blue-Yellow Color Blindness

Blue-yellow color blindness is rarer than red-green color blindness. Blue-cone (tritan) photopigments are either missing or have limited function.

- **Tritanomaly:** People with tritanomaly have functionally limited blue cone cells. Blue appears greener, and it can be difficult to tell yellow and red from pink. Tritanomaly is extremely rare. It is an autosomal dominant disorder affecting males and females equally.

- **Tritanopia:** People with tritanopia, also known as "blue-yellow color blindness," lack blue cone cells. Blue appears green, and yellow appears violet or light grey. Tritanopia is an extremely rare autosomal recessive disorder affecting males and females equally.

Complete Color Blindness

People with complete color blindness (monochromacy) don't experience color at all, and the clearness of their vision (visual acuity) may also be affected.

There are two types of monochromacy:

- **Cone monochromacy:** This rare form of color blindness results from a failure of two of the three cone cell photopigments to work. There is red cone monochromacy, green cone monochromacy, and blue cone monochromacy. People with cone monochromacy have trouble distinguishing colors because the brain needs to compare the signals from different types of cones in order to see color. When only one type of cone works, this comparison isn't possible. People with blue cone monochromacy may also have reduced visual acuity, near-sightedness, and uncontrollable eye movements, a condition known as "nystagmus." Cone monochromacy is an autosomal recessive disorder.

- **Rod monochromacy or achromatopsia:** This type of monochromacy is rare and is the most severe form of color blindness. It is present at birth. None of the cone cells have functional photopigments. Lacking all cone vision, people with rod monochromacy see the world in black, white, and gray. And since rods respond to dim light, people with rod monochromacy tend to be photophobic—very uncomfortable in bright environments. They also experience nystagmus. Rod monochromacy is an autosomal recessive disorder.

How Is Color Blindness Diagnosed?

Eye-care professionals use a variety of tests to diagnose color blindness. These tests can quickly diagnose specific types of color blindness.

The Ishihara Color Test is the most common test for red-green color blindness. The test consists of a series of colored circles, called "Ishihara plates," each of which contains a collection of dots in different colors and sizes. Within the circle are dots that form a shape clearly visible to those with normal color vision, but invisible or difficult to see for those with red-green color blindness.

The newer Cambridge Color Test uses a visual array similar to the Ishihara plates, except displayed on a computer monitor. The goal is to identify a C shape that is different in color from the background. The "C" is presented randomly in one of four orientations. When test-takers see the "C," they are asked to press one of four keys that correspond to the orientation.

The anomaloscope uses a test in which two different light sources have to be matched in color. Looking through the eyepiece, the viewer sees a circle. The upper half is a yellow light that can be adjusted in brightness. The lower half is a combination of red and green lights that can be mixed in variable proportions. The viewer uses one knob to adjust the brightness of the top half, and another to adjust the color of the lower half. The goal is to make the upper and lower halves the same brightness and color.

The HRR Pseudoisochromatic Color Test is another red-green color blindness test that uses color plates to test for color blindness.

The Farnsworth-Munsell 100 Hue Test uses a set of blocks or pegs that are roughly the same color but in different hues (shades of the color). The goal is to arrange them in a line in order of hue. This test measures the ability to discriminate subtle color changes. It is used by industries that depend on the accurate color perception of its employees, such as graphic design, photography, and food quality inspection.

The Farnsworth Lantern Test is used by the U.S. military to determine the severity of color blindness. Those with mild forms pass the test and are allowed to serve in the armed forces.

Are There Treatments for Color Blindness?

There is no cure for color blindness. However, people with red-green color blindness may be able to use a special set of lenses to help them perceive colors more accurately. These lenses can only be used outdoors under bright lighting conditions. Visual aids have also been developed to help people cope with color blindness. There are iPhone and iPad apps, for example, that help people with color blindness differentiate colors. Some of these apps allow users to snap a photo and tap it anywhere on the image to see the color of that area. More sophisticated apps allow users to find out both color and shades of color. These kinds of apps can be helpful in selecting ripe fruits, such as bananas, or finding complementary colors when picking out clothing.

How Does Color Blindness Affect Daily Life?

Color blindness can make it difficult to read color-coded information, such as bar graphs and pie charts. This can be particularly troubling for children who aren't yet diagnosed with color blindness, since educational materials are often color-coded. Children with red-green color blindness may also have difficulty reading a green chalkboard when yellow chalk is used. Art classes, which require selecting appropriate colors of paint or crayons, may be challenging.

Color blindness can go undetected for some time since children will often try to hide their disorder. It's important to have children tested, particularly boys, if there is a family history of color blindness. Many school systems offer vision screening tests that include color blindness testing. Once a child is diagnosed, he or she can learn to ask for help with tasks that require color recognition.

Simple everyday tasks, such as cooking meat to the desired color or selecting ripe produce, can be a challenge for adults. Children might find food without bright color as less appetizing. Traffic lights pose challenges, since they have to be read by the position of the light. Since most lights are vertical, with green on bottom and red on top, if a light is positioned horizontally, a color blind person has to do a quick mental rotation to read it. Reading maps or buying clothes that match colors can also be difficult. However, these are relatively minor inconveniences, and most people with color blindness learn to adapt.

Section 35.2

Early-Onset Glaucoma

This section includes text excerpted from "Early-Onset Glaucoma," Genetics Home Reference (GHR), National Institutes of Health (NIH), February 5, 2019.

Glaucoma is a group of eye disorders in which the optic nerves connecting the eyes and the brain are progressively damaged. This damage can lead to a reduction in side (peripheral) vision and eventual blindness. Other signs and symptoms may include bulging eyes, excessive tearing, and abnormal sensitivity to light (photophobia). The term "early-onset glaucoma" may be used when the disorder appears before the age of 40.

In most people with glaucoma, the damage to the optic nerves is caused by increased pressure within the eyes (intraocular pressure). Intraocular pressure depends on a balance between fluid entering and leaving the eyes.

Usually, glaucoma develops in older adults, in whom the risk of developing the disorder may be affected by a variety of medical conditions including high blood pressure (hypertension) and diabetes mellitus, as well as family history. The risk of early-onset glaucoma depends, mainly, on heredity.

Structural abnormalities that impede fluid drainage in the eye may be present at birth and usually become apparent during the first year of life. Such abnormalities may be part of a genetic disorder that affects many body systems, called a "syndrome." If glaucoma appears before the age of five without other associated abnormalities, it is called "primary congenital glaucoma" (PCG).

Other individuals experience early onset of primary open-angle glaucoma, the most common adult form of glaucoma. If primary open-angle glaucoma develops during childhood or early adulthood, it is called "juvenile open-angle glaucoma."

Frequency of Early-Onset Glaucoma

Primary congenital glaucoma affects approximately 1 in 10,000 people. Its frequency is higher in the Middle East. Juvenile open-angle glaucoma affects about 1 in 50,000 people. Primary open-angle glaucoma is much more common after the age of 40, affecting about 1 percent of the population worldwide.

Causes of Early-Onset Glaucoma

Approximately 10 to 33 percent of people with juvenile open-angle glaucoma have mutations in the *MYOC* gene. *MYOC* gene mutations have also been detected in some people with primary congenital glaucoma. The *MYOC* gene provides instructions for producing a protein called "myocilin." Myocilin is found in certain structures of the eye, called the "trabecular meshwork" and the ciliary body, that regulate the intraocular pressure.

Researchers believe that myocilin functions together with other proteins as part of a protein complex. Mutations may alter the protein in such a way that the complex cannot be formed. Defective myocilin that is not incorporated into functional complexes may accumulate in the trabecular meshwork and ciliary body. The excess protein may prevent sufficient flow of fluid from the eye, resulting in increased intraocular pressure and causing the signs and symptoms of early-onset glaucoma.

Between 20 percent and 40 percent of people with primary congenital glaucoma have mutations in the *CYP1B1* gene. *CYP1B1* gene mutations have also been detected in some people with juvenile open-angle glaucoma. The *CYP1B1* gene provides instructions for producing a form of the cytochrome P450 protein. Like myocilin, this protein is found in the trabecular meshwork, ciliary body, and other structures of the eye.

It is not well understood how defects in the CYP1B1 protein cause signs and symptoms of glaucoma. Recent studies suggest that the defects may interfere with the early development of the trabecular meshwork. In the clear covering of the eye (the cornea), the CYP1B1 protein may also be involved in a process that regulates the secretion of fluid inside the eye. If this fluid is produced in excess, the high intraocular pressure, characteristic of glaucoma, may develop.

The CYP1B1 protein may interact with myocilin. Individuals with mutations in both the MYOC and *CYP1B1* genes may develop glaucoma at an earlier age and have more severe symptoms than those with mutations in only one of the genes. Mutations in other genes may also be involved in early-onset glaucoma.

Section 35.3

Retinitis Pigmentosa

This section contains text excerpted from the following sources: Text in this section begins with excerpts from "Retinitis Pigmentosa," Genetic and Rare Diseases Information Center (GARD), National Center for Advancing Translational Sciences (NCATS), October 18, 2016; Text beginning with the heading "What Are Photoreceptors?" is excerpted from "Facts about Retinitis Pigmentosa," National Eye Institute (NEI), December 2015. Reviewed March 2019.

Retinitis pigmentosa (RP) is a group of inherited eye diseases that affect the light-sensitive part of the eye (retina). RP causes cells in the retina to die, causing progressive vision loss. The first sign of RP usually is night blindness. As the condition progresses, affected individuals develop tunnel vision (loss of peripheral vision) and eventually loss of central vision. RP may be caused by mutations in any of at least 50 genes. Inheritance can be autosomal dominant, autosomal recessive, or X-linked. Treatment options to slow the progression of vision loss include light avoidance, use of low-vision aids, and vitamin A supplementation. Researchers are working to develop new treatment options for the future, such as gene therapy, stem cell transplantation, and prosthetic implants.

Inheritance of Retinitis Pigmentosa

RP can be inherited in an autosomal dominant, autosomal recessive, or X-linked manner. The mode of inheritance in a particular family is determined by evaluating the family history and, in some instances, by molecular genetic testing. There are many potential complications in interpreting the family history, so in some cases, identifying the responsible gene with genetic testing is needed.

- Autosomal dominant inheritance means that having a change (mutation) in only one copy of the responsible gene in each cell is enough to cause features of the condition. In some cases, an affected person inherits the mutated gene from an affected parent. In other cases, the mutation occurs for the first time in a person with no family history of the condition. When a person with a mutation that causes an autosomal dominant condition has children, each child has a 50 percent chance to inherit that mutation.

- Autosomal recessive inheritance means that, to be affected, a person must have a mutation in both copies of the responsible gene in each cell. Affected people inherit one mutated copy of the gene from each parent, who is referred to as a carrier. Carriers of an autosomal recessive condition typically are unaffected. When two carriers of an autosomal recessive condition have children, each child has a:

  - 25 percent chance to be affected

  - 50 percent chance to be an unaffected carrier, like each parent

  - 25 percent chance to be unaffected and not a carrier

- X-linked inheritance means that the responsible gene is located on the X chromosome. Males have one X chromosome (and one Y chromosome), while females have two X chromosomes. Males who have a mutation on their X chromosome will be affected, while female carriers of the mutation may be affected or unaffected, because they have another X chromosome with a normal copy of the gene.

  - All the daughters of an affected male will inherit the mutation; none of his sons will inherit the mutation.

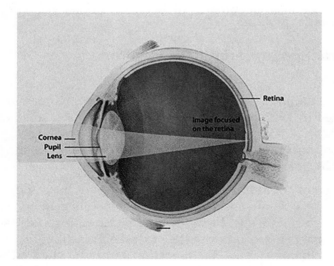

Figure 35.1. *Retinitis Pigmentosa*

The retina is the light-sensitive tissue at the back of the eye that contains photoreceptors and other cell types.

- The sons of a female with a mutation have a 50 percent chance to inherit the mutation and be affected; the daughters have a 50 percent chance to inherit the mutation (and be affected or unaffected).

What are Photoreceptors?

Photoreceptors are cells in the retina that begin the process of seeing. They absorb and convert light into electrical signals. These signals are sent to other cells in the retina and through the optic nerve to the brain, where they are processed into the images we see. There are two general types of photoreceptors, called "rods" and "cones." Rods are in the outer regions of the retina, and allow us to see in dim and dark light. Cones reside mostly in the central portion of the retina, and allow us to perceive fine visual detail and color.

How Does Retinitis Pigmentosa Affect Vision?

In the early stages of RP, rods are more severely affected than cones. As the rods die, people experience night blindness and a progressive loss of the visual field, the area of space that is visible at a given instant without moving the eyes. The loss of rods eventually leads to a breakdown and loss of cones. In the late stages of RP, as cones die, people tend to lose more of the visual field, developing itunnel vision. They may have difficulty performing essential tasks of daily living, such as reading, driving, walking without assistance, or recognizing faces and objects.

How Is Retinitis Pigmentosa Inherited?

To understand how RP is inherited, it's important to know a little more about genes and how they are passed from parent to child. Genes are bundled together on structures called "chromosomes." Each cell in your body contains 23 pairs of chromosomes. One copy of each chromosome is passed by a parent at conception through egg and sperm cells. The X and Y chromosomes, known as "sex chromosomes," determine whether a person is born female (XX) or male (XY). The 22 other paired chromosomes, called "autosomes," contain the vast majority of genes that determine non-sex traits. RP can be inherited in one of three ways:

Autosomal Recessive Inheritance

In autosomal recessive inheritance, it takes two copies of the mutant gene to give rise to the disorder. An individual with a recessive gene mutation is known as a "carrier." When two carriers have a child, there is a:

- One in four chance the child will have the disorder

- One in two chance the child will be a carrier

- One in four chance the child will neither have the disorder nor be a carrier

Autosomal Dominant Inheritance

In this inheritance pattern, it takes just one copy of the gene with a disorder-causing mutation to bring about the disorder. When a parent has a dominant gene mutation, there is a one in two chance that any children will inherit this mutation and the disorder.

X-Linked Inheritance

In this form of inheritance, mothers carry the mutated gene on one of their X chromosomes and pass it to their sons. Because females have two X chromosomes, the effect of a mutation on one X chromosome is offset by the normal gene on the other X chromosome. If a mother is a carrier of an X-linked disorder there is a:

- One in two chance of having a son with the disorder

- One in two chance of having a daughter who is a carrier

How Common Is Retinitis Pigmentosa?

RP is considered a rare disorder. Although current statistics are not available, it is generally estimated that the disorder affects roughly 1 in 4,000 people, both in the United States and worldwide.

How Does Retinitis Pigmentosa Progress?

The symptoms of RP typically appear in childhood. Children often have difficulty getting around in the dark. It can also take abnormally long periods of time to adjust to changes in lighting. As their visual field becomes restricted, patients often trip over things and appear clumsy. People with RP often find bright lights uncomfortable, a condition known as "photophobia." Because there are many gene mutations that cause the disorder, its progression can differ greatly from person to person. Some people retain central vision and a restricted visual field into their fifties, while others experience significant vision loss in early adulthood. Eventually, most individuals with RP will lose most of their sight.

How Is Retinitis Pigmentosa Diagnosed?

RP is diagnosed, in part, through an examination of the retina. An eye-care professional will use an ophthalmoscope, a tool that allows for a wider, clear view of the retina. This typically reveals abnormal, dark pigment deposits that streak the retina. These pigment deposits are in part why the disorder was named "retinitis pigmentosa." Other tests for RP include:

- **Electroretinogram (ERG)**. An ERG measures the electrical activity of photoreceptor cells. This test uses gold foil or a contact lens with electrodes attached. A flash of light is sent to the retina, and the electrodes measure rod and cone cell responses. People with RP have a decreased electrical activity, reflecting the declining function of photoreceptors.

- **Visual field testing**. To determine the extent of vision loss, a clinician will give a visual field test. The person watches as a dot of light moves around the half-circle (180 degrees) of space directly in front of the head and to either side. The patient pushes a button to indicate that he or she can see the light. This process results in a map of their visual field and their central vision.

- **Genetic testing**. In some cases, a clinician takes a DNA sample from the person to give a genetic diagnosis. In this way, a person can learn about the progression of their particular form of the disorder.

Are There Treatments for Retinitis Pigmentosa?
Living with Vision Loss

A number of services and devices are available to help people with vision loss carry out daily activities and maintain their independence. In addition to an eye care professional, it's important to have help from a team of experts, which may include occupational therapists, orientation and mobility specialists, certified low-vision therapists, and others. NEI has more information on living with low vision.

Children with RP may benefit from low vision aids that maximize existing vision. For example, there are special lenses that magnify the central vision to expand the visual field and eliminate glare. Computer programs that read text are readily available. Closed circuit televisions with a camera can adjust the text to suit one's vision. Portable lighting devices can adjust a dark or dim environment. Mobility training can teach people to use a cane or a guide dog, and eye scanning techniques can help people to optimize remaining vision. Once a child is diagnosed, he or she will be referred to a low-vision specialist for a comprehensive evaluation. Parents may also want to meet with the child's school administrators and teachers to make sure that necessary accommodations are put in place.

For parents of children with RP, one challenge is to determine when a child might need to learn to use a cane or a guide dog. Having regular eye examinations to measure the progress of the disorder will help parents make informed decisions regarding low-vision services and rehabilitation.

Targeted Therapies for Retinitis Pigmentosa

An NEI-sponsored clinical trial found that a daily dose of 15,000 international units of vitamin A palmitate modestly slowed the progression of the disorder in adults. Because there are so many forms of RP, it is difficult to predict how any one patient will respond to this treatment. Talk to an eye-care professional to determine if taking vitamin A is right for you or your child.

An artificial vision device called the "Argus II" has also shown promise for restoring some vision to people with late-stage RP. The Argus II, developed by Second Sight with NEI support, is a prosthetic device, which functions in place of lost photoreceptor cells. It consists of a light-sensitive electrode that is surgically implanted on the retina. A pair of glasses with a camera wirelessly transmits signals to the electrode, which are then relayed to the brain. Although it does not restore normal vision, in clinical studies, the Argus II enabled people with RP to read large letters and navigate environments without the use of a cane or guide dog. In 2012, the U.S. Food and Drug Administration (FDA) granted a humanitarian device exemption for use of the Argus II to treat late-stage RP. This means the device has not proven effective, but the FDA has determined that its probable benefits outweigh its risks to health. The Argus II is eligible for Medicare payment.

Section 35.4

X-Linked Juvenile Retinoschisis

This section includes text excerpted from "Juvenile
Retinoschisis," Genetic and Rare Diseases Information
Center (GARD), National Center for Advancing Translational
Sciences (NCATS), February 27, 2016.

What Is Juvenile Retinoschisis?

Juvenile retinoschisis is an eye condition characterized by impaired vision that begins in childhood and occurs almost exclusively in males. The condition affects the retina, which is a specialized light-sensitive tissue that lines the back of the eye. This affects the sharpness of vision. Central vision is more commonly affected. Vision often deteriorates early in life, but then usually becomes stable until late adulthood. A second decline in vision typically occurs in a man's fifties or sixties. Sometimes, severe complications occur, including separation of the retinal layers (retinal detachment) or leakage of blood vessels in the retina (vitreous hemorrhage). These can lead to blindness. Juvenile retinoschisis is caused by mutations in the *RS1* gene. It is inherited in an X-linked recessive pattern. Low-vision aids can be helpful. Surgery may be needed for some complications.

How Does Juvenile Retinoschisis Affect Vision?

People with juvenile retinoschisis begin to experience vision loss during childhood and, in some cases, as early as three months of age. At first, affected males have a vision of 20/60 to 20/120. Their vision declines with age, but generally stabilizes after the age of 20. Visual sharpness remains unchanged in most people until their forties or fifties, when a significant decline in visual acuity typically occurs.

What Causes Juvenile Retinoschisis

Mutations in the *RS1* gene cause most cases of juvenile retinoschisis. The *RS1* gene provides instructions for producing a protein called "retinoschisin," which is found in the retina. Studies suggest that retinoschisin plays a role in the development and maintenance of the retina, perhaps playing a role in cell adhesion (the attachment of cells together).

429

RS1 gene mutations lead to a reduced amount or complete absence of retinoschisin, which can cause tiny splits (schisis) or tears to form in the retina. This damage often forms a "spoke-wheel" pattern in the macula, which can be seen during an eye examination. In about half of individuals, these abnormalities are seen in the area of the macula, affecting visual acuity. In the other half, the sides of the retina are affected, resulting in impaired peripheral vision.

Some individuals with juvenile retinoschisis do not have a mutation in the *RS1* gene. In these individuals, the cause of the disorder is unknown.

What Treatment Is Available for Juvenile Retinoschisis?

There is no specific treatment for juvenile retinoschisis. Low-vision services are designed to benefit those whose ability to function is compromised by impaired vision. Public school systems are mandated by federal law to provide an appropriate education for children who have vision impairment. Surgery may be required to address the infrequent complications of vitreous hemorrhage and retinal detachment. Affected individuals should avoid high-contact sports and other activities that can cause head trauma to reduce the risk of retinal detachment and vitreous hemorrhage.

Chapter 36

Wilson Disease

What Is Wilson Disease?

Wilson disease is a genetic disorder that prevents the body from removing extra copper, causing copper to build up in the liver, brain, eyes, and other organs.

Your body needs a small amount of copper from food to stay healthy, but too much copper is harmful. Without treatment, Wilson disease can lead to high copper levels that cause life-threatening organ damage.

How Common Is Wilson Disease?

Experts are still studying how common Wilson disease is. Older studies suggested that about 1 in 30,000 people have Wilson disease. These studies were conducted before researchers discovered the gene mutations that cause Wilson disease.

Newer studies of people's genes suggest that Wilson disease may be more common. A study in the United Kingdom found that about 1 in 7,000 people have gene mutations that cause Wilson disease.

Experts aren't sure why gene studies suggest that Wilson disease is more common than previously thought. One reason might be that some people with Wilson disease are not diagnosed. Another reason

This chapter includes text excerpted from "Wilson Disease," National Institute of Diabetes and Digestive and Kidney Diseases (NIDDK), May 14, 2018.

might be that some people have gene mutations for Wilson disease but don't develop the disease.

Who Is Most Likely to Have Wilson Disease?

People have a higher chance of having Wilson disease if they have a family history of Wilson disease, especially if a first-degree relative—a parent, sibling, or child—has the disease.

People who have Wilson disease typically develop symptoms when they are between the ages of 5 and 40. However, some people develop symptoms at younger or older ages. Doctors have found the first symptoms of Wilson disease in infants as young as 9 months and in adults older than 70 years of age.

What Are the Complications of Wilson Disease?

Wilson disease may lead to complications, but early diagnosis and treatment can lower your chances of developing them.

Acute Liver Failure

Wilson disease can cause acute liver failure, a condition in which your liver fails rapidly without warning. About five percent of people with Wilson disease have acute liver failure when they are first diagnosed. Acute liver failure most often requires a liver transplant.

Acute kidney failure and a type of anemia called "hemolytic anemia" often occur in people who have an acute liver failure due to Wilson disease.

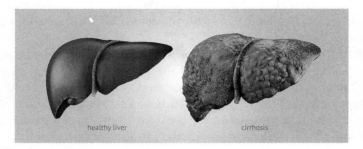

Figure 36.1. *Cirrhosis*

In cirrhosis, scar tissue replaces healthy liver tissue and prevents your liver from working normally.

Cirrhosis

In cirrhosis, scar tissue replaces healthy liver tissue and prevents your liver from working normally. Scar tissue also partially blocks the flow of blood through the liver. As cirrhosis gets worse, the liver begins to fail.

Among people who are diagnosed with Wilson disease, 35 to 45 percent already have cirrhosis at the time of diagnosis.

Cirrhosis increases your chance of getting liver cancer. However, doctors have found that liver cancer is less common in people who have cirrhosis due to Wilson disease than in people who have cirrhosis due to other causes.

Liver Failure

Cirrhosis may eventually lead to liver failure. With liver failure, your liver is badly damaged and stops working. Liver failure is also called "end-stage liver disease." This condition may require a liver transplant.

Symptoms and Causes of Wilson Disease
What Are the Symptoms of Wilson Disease?

The symptoms of Wilson disease vary. Wilson disease is present at birth, but the symptoms don't appear until the copper builds up in the liver, the brain, or other organs.

Some people do not have symptoms of Wilson disease before they are diagnosed with the disease and treated. If you do have symptoms, the symptoms may be related to your liver, nervous system, and mental health, eyes, or other organs.

Liver Symptoms

People with Wilson disease may develop symptoms of hepatitis, or inflammation of the liver. In some cases, people develop these symptoms when they have acute liver failure. These symptoms may include:

- Feeling tired
- Nausea and vomiting
- Poor appetite
- Pain over the liver, in the upper part of the abdomen
- Darkening of the color of urine

- Lightening of the color of stool
- Yellowish tint to the whites of the eyes and skin called "jaundice"

Some people with Wilson disease have symptoms only if they develop chronic liver disease and complications from cirrhosis. These symptoms may include:

- Feeling tired or weak
- Losing weight without trying
- Bloating from a buildup of fluid in the abdomen, called "ascites"
- Swelling of the lower legs, ankles, or feet, called "edema"
- Itchy skin
- Jaundice

Nervous System and Mental-Health Symptoms

People with Wilson disease may develop nervous system and mental health symptoms after copper builds up in their body. These symptoms are more common in adults but sometimes occur in children. Nervous system symptoms may include:

- Problems with speech, swallowing, or physical coordination
- Stiff muscles
- Tremors or uncontrolled movements

Mental health symptoms may include:

- Anxiety
- Changes in mood, personality, or behavior
- Depression
- Psychosis

Eye Symptoms

Many people with Wilson disease have Kayser-Fleischer rings, which are greenish, gold, or brownish rings around the edge of the corneas. A buildup of copper in the eyes causes Kayser-Fleischer rings. A doctor can see these rings during a special eye exam called a "slit-lamp exam."

Among people who have nervous system symptoms of Wilson disease, more than 9 out of 10 have Kayser-Fleischer rings. However, among people who have only liver symptoms, 5 or 6 out of 10 have Kayser-Fleischer rings.

Other Symptoms and Health Problems

Wilson disease can affect other parts of your body and cause symptoms or health problems, including:

- A type of anemia called "hemolytic anemia"
- Bone and joint problems, such as arthritis or osteoporosis
- Heart problems, such as cardiomyopathy
- Kidney problems, such as renal tubular acidosis and kidney stones

What Causes Wilson Disease

Mutations of a gene called "*ATP7B*" cause Wilson disease. These gene mutations prevent the body from removing extra copper. Normally, the liver releases extra copper into bile. Bile carries the copper, along with other toxins and waste products, out of the body through the digestive tract. In Wilson disease, the liver releases less copper into bile, and extra copper stays in the body.

The *ATP7B* mutations that cause Wilson disease are inherited, meaning they are passed from parent to child. These mutations are autosomal recessive, meaning that a person must inherit two *ATP7B* genes with mutations, one from each parent, to have Wilson disease. People who have one *ATP7B* gene without a mutation and one *ATP7B* gene with a mutation do not have Wilson disease, but they are carriers of the disease.

People can inherent Wilson disease if both parents are carriers who don't have the disease.

Diagnosis of Wilson Disease
How Do Doctors Diagnose Wilson Disease?

Doctors diagnose Wilson disease based on your medical and family history, a physical exam, an eye exam, and tests.

Medical and Family History

Your doctor will ask about your family and personal-medical history of Wilson disease and other conditions that could be causing your symptoms.

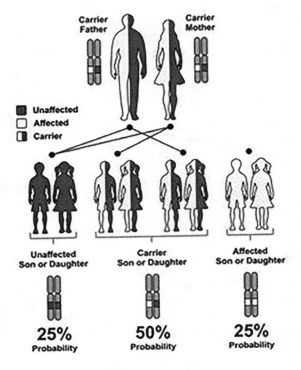

Figure 36.2. *Autosomal Recessive*

The mutations that cause Wilson disease are autosomal recessive, meaning that a person must inherit two genes with mutations to have Wilson disease.

Physical Exam

During a physical exam, your doctor will check for signs of liver damage such as:

- Changes in the skin
- Enlargement of the liver or spleen
- Tenderness or swelling in the abdomen
- Swelling in the lower legs, feet, or ankles, called "edema"
- Yellowish color of the whites of the eyes

Eye Exam

During a slit-lamp exam, a doctor will use a special light to look for Kayser-Fleischer rings in your eyes.

What Tests Do Doctors Use to Diagnose Wilson Disease?

Doctors typically use blood tests and a 24-hour urine collection test to diagnose Wilson disease. Doctors may also use a liver biopsy and imaging tests.

Blood Tests

For a blood test, a healthcare professional will take a blood sample from you and send the sample to a lab.

Your doctor may order one or more blood tests, including tests that check amounts of:

- Ceruloplasmin, a protein that carries copper in the bloodstream. People with Wilson disease often have low ceruloplasmin levels, but not always.

- Copper. People with Wilson disease may have lower than normal blood-copper levels. Acute liver failure due to Wilson disease may cause high blood copper levels.

- Liver enzymes alanine transaminase (ALT) and aspartate transaminase (AST). People with Wilson disease may have abnormal ALT and AST levels.

- Red blood cells (RBC) to look for signs of anemia.

Doctors may order a blood test to check for the gene mutations that cause Wilson disease if other medical tests don't confirm or rule out a diagnosis of the disease.

24-Hour Urine Collection Test

For 24 hours, you will collect your urine at home in a special container that is copper-free, provided by a healthcare professional. A healthcare professional will send the urine to a lab, which will check the amount of copper in your urine. Copper levels in the urine are often higher than normal in people who have Wilson disease.

Liver Biopsy

If the results of blood and urine tests don't confirm or rule out a diagnosis of Wilson disease, your doctor may order a liver biopsy. During a liver biopsy, a doctor will take small pieces of tissue from your liver. A pathologist will examine the tissue under a microscope to look for features of specific liver diseases, such as Wilson disease, and check for liver damage and cirrhosis. A piece of liver tissue will be sent to a lab, which will check the amount of copper in the tissue.

Imaging Tests

In people who have nervous system symptoms, doctors may use imaging tests to check for signs of Wilson disease or other conditions in the brain. Doctors may use:

- Magnetic resonance imaging (MRI), which uses radio waves and magnets to produce detailed images of organs and soft tissues without using X-rays

- Computed tomography (CT) scan, which uses a combination of X-rays and computer technology to create images

Treatment of Wilson Disease
How Do Doctors Treat Wilson Disease?

Doctors treat Wilson disease with:

- Medicines that remove copper from the body, called "chelating agents"

- Zinc, which prevents the intestines from absorbing copper

In many cases, treatment can improve or prevent symptoms and organ damage. Doctors may also recommend changing your diet to avoid foods that are high in copper.

People who have Wilson disease need lifelong treatment. Stopping treatment may cause acute liver failure. Doctors regularly perform blood and urine tests to check how the treatment is working.

Chelating Agents

Penicillamine (Cupramine, Depen) and trientine (Syprine) are two chelating agents used to treat Wilson disease. These medicines remove copper from the body.

Penicillamine is more likely to cause side effects than trientine. Side effects of penicillamine may include fever, rash, kidney problems, or bone marrow problems. Penicillamine may also reduce the activity of vitamin B_6, and doctors may recommend taking a vitamin B_6 supplement along with penicillamine. In some cases, when people with nervous system symptoms begin taking chelating agents, their symptoms get worse.

When treatment begins, doctors gradually increase the dose of chelating agents. People take higher doses of chelating agents until the extra copper in the body has been removed. When Wilson disease symptoms have improved and tests show that copper is at safe levels, doctors may prescribe lower doses of chelating agents as maintenance treatment. Lifelong maintenance treatment prevents copper from building up again.

Chelating agents may interfere with wound healing, and doctors may prescribe a lower dose of chelating agents for people who are planning to have surgery.

Zinc

Zinc prevents the intestines from absorbing copper. Doctors may prescribe zinc as a maintenance treatment, after chelating agents have removed extra copper from the body. Doctors may also prescribe zinc for people who have Wilson disease but do not yet have symptoms. The most common side effect of zinc is stomach upset.

Eating, Diet, and Nutrition
What Should I Avoid Eating If I Have Wilson Disease?

When you start treatment for Wilson disease, your doctor may recommend avoiding foods that are high in copper, such as:

- Chocolate
- Liver
- Mushrooms
- Nuts
- Shellfish

After treatments have lowered your copper levels and you begin maintenance treatment, talk with your doctor about whether you can safely eat moderate amounts of these foods.

If your tap water comes from a well or runs through copper pipes, have the copper levels in your water checked. Water sitting in copper pipes may pick up copper. Run the water to flush the pipes before you drink the water or use it for cooking. You may need to use a water filter to remove copper from your tap water.

For safety reasons, talk with your doctor before using dietary supplements, such as vitamins, or any complementary or alternative medicines or medical practices. Some dietary supplements may contain copper.

Part Three

Chromosome Abnormalities

Chapter 37

An Overview of Chromosome Abnormalities

What Are Chromosomes?

Chromosomes are the structures that hold genes. Genes are the individual instructions that tell our bodies how to develop and function; they govern physical and medical characteristics, such as hair color, blood type and susceptibility to disease.

Many chromosomes have two segments, called "arms," separated by a pinched region known as the centromere. The shorter arm is called the "p" arm. The longer arm is called the "q" arm.

Where Are Chromosomes Found in the Body?

The body is made up of individual units called cells. Your body has many different kinds of cells, such as skin cells, liver cells, and blood cells. In the center of most cells is a structure called the "nucleus." This is where chromosomes are located.

How Many Chromosomes Do Humans Have?

The typical number of chromosomes in a human cell is 46, which creates 23 pairs, holding an estimated total of 20,000 to 25,000 genes.

This chapter includes text excerpted from "Chromosome Abnormalities," National Human Genome Research Institute (NHGRI), January 6, 2016.

One set of 23 chromosomes is inherited from the biological mother (from the egg), and the other set is inherited from the biological father (from the sperm).

Of the 23 pairs of chromosomes, the first 22 pairs are called "autosomes." The final pair is called the "sex chromosomes." Sex chromosomes determine an individual's sex: females have two X chromosomes (XX), and males have an X and a Y chromosome (XY). The mother and father each contribute one set of 22 autosomes and one sex chromosome.

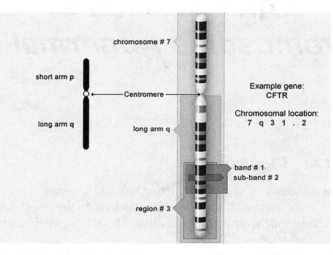

Figure 37.1. *Chromosome Allocation* (Source: "How Do Geneticists Indicate the Location of a Gene?" Genetics Home Reference (GHR), National Institutes of Health (NIH).)

How Do Scientists Study Chromosomes?

For a century, scientists studied chromosomes by looking at them under a microscope. In order for chromosomes to be seen this way, they need to be stained. Once stained, the chromosomes look like strings with light and dark "bands," and their picture can be taken. A picture, or chromosome map, of all 46 chromosomes is called "a karyotype." The karyotype can help identify abnormalities in the structure or the number of chromosomes.

To help identify chromosomes, the pairs have been numbered from 1 to 22, with the 23rd pair labeled "X" and "Y." In addition, the bands that appear after staining are numbered; the higher the number, the farther that area is from the centromere.

In the past decade, newer techniques have been developed that allow scientists and doctors to screen for chromosomal abnormalities without using a microscope. These newer methods compare the patient's deoxyribonucleic acid (DNA) to a normal DNA sample. The comparison can be used to find chromosomal abnormalities where the two samples differ.

One such method is called "noninvasive prenatal testing." This is a test to screen a pregnancy to determine whether a baby has an increased chance of having specific chromosome disorders. The test examines the fetus's DNA in the mother's blood.

What Are Chromosome Abnormalities?

There are many types of chromosome abnormalities. However, they can be organized into two basic groups: numerical abnormalities and structural abnormalities.

- **Numerical abnormalities**: When an individual is missing one of the chromosomes from a pair, the condition is called "monosomy." When an individual has more than two chromosomes instead of a pair, the condition is called "trisomy."

An example of a condition caused by numerical abnormalities is Down syndrome, which is marked by mental retardation, learning difficulties, a characteristic facial appearance, and poor muscle tone (hypotonia) in infancy. An individual with Down syndrome has three copies of chromosome 21 rather than two; for that reason, the condition is also known as "Trisomy 21." An example of monosomy, in which an individual lacks a chromosome, is Turner syndrome. In Turner syndrome, a female is born with only one sex chromosome, an X, and is usually shorter than average and unable to have children, among other difficulties.

- **Structural abnormalities**: A chromosome's structure can be altered in several ways.

  - **Deletions**: A portion of the chromosome is missing or deleted.

  - **Duplications**: A portion of the chromosome is duplicated, resulting in extra genetic material.

  - **Translocations**: A portion of one chromosome is transferred to another chromosome. There are two main types of translocation. In a reciprocal translocation, segments from two different chromosomes have been exchanged. In a Robertsonian translocation, an entire chromosome has attached to another at the centromere.

- **Inversions**: A portion of the chromosome has broken off, turned upside down, and reattached. As a result, the genetic material is inverted.

- **Rings**: A portion of a chromosome has broken off and formed a circle or ring. This can happen with or without loss of genetic material.

Most chromosome abnormalities occur as an accident in the egg or sperm. In these cases, the abnormality is present in every cell of the body. Some abnormalities, however, happen after conception; then some cells have the abnormality and some do not.

Chromosome abnormalities can be inherited from a parent (such as translocation) or be "de novo" (new to the individual). This is why, when a child is found to have an abnormality, chromosome studies are often performed on the parents.

How Do Chromosome Abnormalities Happen?

Chromosome abnormalities usually occur when there is an error in cell division. There are two kinds of cell division: mitosis and meiosis.

- **Mitosis** results in two cells that are duplicates of the original cell. One cell with 46 chromosomes divides and becomes two cells with 46 chromosomes each. This kind of cell division occurs throughout the body, except in the reproductive organs. This is the way most of the cells that make up our body are made and replaced.

- **Meiosis** results in cells with half the number of chromosomes, 23, instead of the normal 46. This is the type of cell division that occurs in the reproductive organs, resulting in the eggs and sperm.

In both processes, the correct number of chromosomes is supposed to end up in the resulting cells. However, errors in cell division can result in cells with too few or too many copies of a chromosome. Errors can also occur when the chromosomes are being duplicated.

Other factors that can increase the risk of chromosome abnormalities are:

- **Maternal age**: Women are born with all the eggs they will ever have. Some researchers believe that errors can crop up in the eggs' genetic material as they age. Older women are at higher risk of giving birth to babies with chromosome abnormalities than younger women. Because men produce new sperm throughout their lives, paternal age does not increase the risk of chromosome abnormalities.

- **Environment**: Although there is no conclusive evidence that specific environmental factors cause chromosome abnormalities, it is still possible that the environment may play a role in the occurrence of genetic errors.

Chapter 38

Angelman Syndrome

What Is Angelman Syndrome?

Angelman syndrome (AS) is a genetic disorder that primarily affects the nervous system. Characteristic features of this condition include developmental delay, intellectual disability, severe speech impairment, problems with movement and balance (ataxia), epilepsy, and a small head size. Individuals with Angelman syndrome typically have a happy, excitable demeanor with frequent smiling, laughter, and hand-flapping movements. Many of the characteristic features of Angelman syndrome result from the loss of function of a gene called *"UBE3A."* Most cases of Angelman syndrome are not inherited; although in rare cases, a genetic change responsible for Angelman syndrome can be inherited from a parent. Treatment is aimed at addressing each individual's symptoms and may include antiepileptics for seizures; physical, occupational, and speech therapy; and special education services.

This chapter contains text excerpted from the following sources: Text beginning with the heading "What Is Angelman Syndrome?" is excerpted from "Angelman Syndrome," Genetic and Rare Diseases Information Center (GARD), National Center for Advancing Translational Sciences (NCATS), March 31, 2016. Text beginning with the heading "Treatment" is excerpted from "Angelman Syndrome Information Page," National Institute of Neurological Disorders and Stroke (NINDS), January 2, 2019.

What Causes Angelman Syndrome

Angelman syndrome is caused by a loss of function of a gene called "*UBE3A*" on chromosome 15. The exact mechanism that causes this loss of function is complex. People normally inherit one copy of the *UBE3A* gene from each parent. Both copies of this gene are turned on (active) in many of the body's tissues. In certain areas of the brain, however, only the copy inherited from a person's mother is active. This parent-specific gene activation is known as "genomic imprinting." If the maternal copy of the *UBE3A* gene is lost because of a chromosomal change or a gene mutation, a person will have no active copies of the gene in some parts of the brain.

Several different genetic mechanisms can inactivate or delete the maternal copy of the *UBE3A* gene. Most cases of Angelman syndrome occur when a segment of the maternal chromosome 15 containing this gene is deleted. In other cases, Angelman syndrome is caused by a mutation in the maternal copy of the *UBE3A* gene.

In a small percentage of cases, a person with Angelman syndrome inherits two copies of chromosome 15 from her or his father, instead of one copy from each parent. This is called "paternal uniparental disomy." Rarely, Angelman syndrome can also be caused by a chromosomal rearrangement called a "translocation," or by a mutation or other defect in the region of deoxyribonucleic acid (DNA) that controls activation of the *UBE3A* gene. These genetic changes can abnormally turn off (inactivate) *UBE3A* or other genes on the maternal copy of chromosome 15.

The cause of Angelman syndrome is unknown in 10 to 15 percent of affected individuals. Changes involving other genes or chromosomes may be responsible for the condition in these individuals.

How Might Angelman Syndrome Be Inherited?

Most cases of Angelman syndrome are not inherited, particularly those caused by a deletion in the maternal chromosome 15 or by paternal uniparental disomy. These genetic changes occur as random events during the formation of reproductive cells (eggs and sperm) or in early embryonic development. In these instances, people typically have no history of the disorder in their family.

Rarely, a genetic change responsible for Angelman syndrome can be inherited. For example, it is possible for a mutation in the *UBE3A* gene or in the nearby region of DNA that controls gene activation to be passed from one generation to the next.

After Having One Child with Angelman Syndrome, What Is the Chance That Future Children Will Inherit It as Well?

Although most cases of Angelman syndrome are not inherited, particularly those caused by a deletion in the maternal chromosome 15, the risk of having another child with Angelman syndrome depends on the specific cause. You will need to speak with a genetics professional to understand the risk in future pregnancies that are specific to your situation.

Is There Any Way to Avoid Having a Child with Angelman Syndrome in a Future Pregnancy?

There are a number of genetic tests that can be used to inform a couple about the possible outcomes of a current or future pregnancy. Examples of two such tests are prenatal diagnosis and preimplantation genetic diagnosis (PGD).

Prenatal diagnosis can be used to diagnose a condition in a developing fetus. If the underlying genetic cause of a disorder in a family is known, testing can be completed to analyze the genetic material of the fetus. This is typically completed around 10 to 13 weeks' gestation via chorionic villus sampling or around 15+ weeks' gestation via amniocentesis. Prenatal diagnosis may help parents prepare emotionally for birth and to plan the delivery with their healthcare providers. Parents can also use this information to make decisions regarding whether or not to continue the pregnancy.

PGD is an alternative to prenatal diagnosis. It is used following in vitro fertilization to diagnose a genetic disease or condition in embryos. Only embryos that do not carry the disease-causing mutation are implanted in the mother's womb. PGD allows testing to occur before pregnancy begins. In many cases, the disease-causing mutation must be identified in an affected parent before PGD or prenatal diagnosis can be performed.

Treatment for Angelman syndrome

There is no specific therapy for Angelman syndrome at this time. The best treatment is to minimize seizures, anxiety, and gastrointestinal issues and maximize sleep. Seizures are treated with medications and dietary therapies, while sleep issues are treated with medications and sleep training. It is also important to test for and treat any

451

problems with vision, hearing, and mobility. Intensive therapies, such as physical, occupational, and speech therapies, are critical to begin early and continue as long as necessary. Applied behavior analysis and/or behavior therapy also are important for many individuals.

Prognosis for Angelman syndrome

Most individuals with Angelman syndrome will have significant developmental delays, speech limitations, and motor difficulties, but they understand much of what is said and often learn to communicate nonverbally and by using communication devices. Those with gene deletions are more severely affected, whereas those with nondeletions typically make more developmental progress with better communications skills. Individuals with AS appear to have normal life spans and generally do not show developmental regression as they age.

As individuals move into adolescence and adulthood, seizures improve or resolve for most people, sleep tends to improve but is still an issue for many, and gastrointestinal symptoms do not change much over time. Anxiety tends to worsen after puberty and can lead to difficult behaviors. Many teens and adults with AS also have frequent twitching in their hands, called "myoclonus," which can spread to their arms and the rest of the body. Myoclonus is not seizure activity but can interfere with quality of life (QOL) and may be treated with medication.

Chapter 39

Cri-du-Chat Syndrome

What Is Cri-du-Chat Syndrome?

Cri-du-chat syndrome—also known as "5p-syndrome" and "cat cry syndrome"—is a rare genetic condition that is caused by the deletion (a missing piece) of genetic material on the small arm (the p arm) of chromosome 5. The cause of this rare chromosomal deletion is unknown.

What Are the Symptoms of Cri-du-Chat Syndrome?

The symptoms of cri-du-chat syndrome vary among individuals. The variability of the clinical symptoms and developmental delays may be related to the size of the deletion on the 5p arm.

The clinical symptoms of cri-du-chat syndrome usually include a high-pitched cat-like cry, mental retardation, delayed development, distinctive facial features, small head size (microcephaly), widely-spaced eyes (hypertelorism), low birth weight, and weak muscle tone (hypotonia) in infancy. The cat-like cry typically becomes less apparent with time.

Most individuals who have cri-du-chat syndrome have difficulty with language. Half of children with the syndrome learn sufficient verbal skills to communicate. Some individuals learn to use short sentences, while others express themselves with a few basic words, gestures, or sign language.

This chapter includes text excerpted from "Learning about Cri Du Chat Syndrome," National Human Genome Research Institute (NHGRI), June 29, 2017.

Other characteristics may include feeding difficulties, delays in walking, hyperactivity, scoliosis, and significant retardation. A small number of children are born with serious organ defects and other life-threatening medical conditions, although most individuals with cri-du-chat syndrome have a normal life expectancy.

Both children and adults with this syndrome are usually friendly and happy, and enjoy social interaction.

How Is Cri-du-Chat Syndrome Diagnosed?

The diagnosis of cri-du-chat syndrome is generally made in the hospital at birth. A healthcare provider may note the clinical symptoms associated with the condition. The cat-like cry is the most prominent clinical feature in newborn children and is usually diagnostic for the cri-du-chat syndrome.

Additionally, analysis of the individual's chromosomes may be performed. The missing portion (deletion) of the short arm of chromosome 5 may be seen on a chromosome analysis. If not, a more detailed type of genetic test called "fluorescence in situ hybridization (FISH)" analysis may be needed to reveal the deletion.

What Is the Treatment for Cri-du-Chat Syndrome?

No specific treatment is available for this syndrome. Children born with this genetic condition will most likely require ongoing support from a team made up of the parents, therapists, and medical and educational professionals to help the child achieve her or his maximum potential. With early and consistent educational intervention, as well as physical and language therapy, children with cri-du-chat syndrome are capable of reaching their fullest potential and can lead full and meaningful lives.

Is Cri-du-Chat Syndrome Inherited?

Most cases of cri-du-chat syndrome are not inherited. The chromosomal deletion usually occurs as a random event during the formation of reproductive cells (eggs or sperm) or in early fetal development. People with cri-du-chat typically have no history of the condition in their family.

About 10 percent of people with cri-du-chat syndrome inherit the chromosome with a deleted segment from an unaffected parent. In these cases, the parent carries a chromosomal rearrangement called a "balanced translocation," in which no genetic material is gained or lost. Balanced translocations usually do not cause any medical problems; however, they can become unbalanced as they are passed to the next generation. A deletion in the short arm of chromosome 5 is an example of an unbalanced translocation, which is a chromosomal rearrangement with extra or missing genetic material. Unbalanced translocations can cause birth defects and other health problems such as those seen in cri-du-chat syndrome.

Chapter 40

Down Syndrome and Other Trisomy Disorders

Chapter Contents

Section 40.1

Down Syndrome

This section includes text excerpted from "Facts about
Down Syndrome," Centers for Disease Control
and Prevention (CDC), February 15, 2018.

What Is Down Syndrome?

Down syndrome is a condition in which a person has an extra chromosome. Chromosomes are small "packages" of genes in the body. They determine how a fetus's body forms during pregnancy and how the body functions as it grows in the womb and after birth. Typically, a baby is born with 46 chromosomes. Babies with Down syndrome have an extra copy of one of these chromosomes, chromosome 21. A medical term for having an extra copy of a chromosome is "trisomy." Down syndrome is also referred to as "Trisomy 21." This extra copy changes how the baby's body and brain develop, which can cause both mental and physical challenges for the baby.

Even though people with Down syndrome might act and look similar, each person has different abilities. People with Down syndrome usually have an intelligence quotient (IQ) (a measure of intelligence) in the mildly-to-moderately low range and are slower to speak than other children.

Some common physical features of Down syndrome include:

- A flattened face, especially the bridge of the nose

- Almond-shaped eyes that slant up

- A short neck

- Small ears

- A tongue that tends to stick out of the mouth

- Tiny white spots on the iris (colored part) of the eye

- Small hands and feet

- A single line across the palm of the hand (palmar crease)

- Small pinky fingers that sometimes curve toward the thumb

- Poor muscle tone or loose joints

- Shorter in height as children and adults

Occurrence

- Down syndrome remains the most common chromosomal condition diagnosed in the United States. Each year, about 6,000 babies born in the United States have Down syndrome. This means that Down syndrome occurs in about 1 out of every 700 babies.

Types of Down Syndrome

There are three types of Down syndrome. People often can't tell the difference between each type without looking at the chromosomes because the physical features and behaviors are similar.

- **Trisomy 21**: About 95 percent of people with Down syndrome have Trisomy 21. With this type of Down syndrome, each cell in the body has three separate copies of chromosome 21 instead of the usual two copies.

- **Translocation Down syndrome**: This type accounts for a small percentage of people with Down syndrome (about 3%). This occurs when an extra part or a whole extra chromosome 21 is present, but it is attached or "trans-located" to a different chromosome rather than being a separate chromosome 21.

- **Mosaic Down syndrome**: This type affects about 2 percent of the people with Down syndrome. Mosaic means mixture or combination. For children with mosaic Down syndrome, some of their cells have three copies of chromosome 21, but other cells have the typical two copies of chromosome 21. Children with mosaic Down syndrome may have the same features as other children with Down syndrome. However, they may have fewer features of the condition due to the presence of some (or many) cells with a typical number of chromosomes.

Causes and Risk Factors

- The extra chromosome 21 leads to the physical features and developmental challenges that can occur among people with Down syndrome. Researchers know that Down syndrome is caused by an extra chromosome, but no one knows for sure why Down syndrome occurs or how many different factors play a role.

- One factor that increases the risk for having a baby with Down syndrome is the mother's age. Women who are 35 years of age or older when they become pregnant are more likely to have a pregnancy affected by Down syndrome than women who become pregnant at a younger age. However, the majority of babies with Down syndrome are born to mothers less than 35 years of age, because there are many more births among younger women.

Diagnosis

There are two basic types of tests available to detect Down syndrome during pregnancy: screening tests and diagnostic tests. A screening test can tell a woman and her healthcare provider whether her pregnancy has a lower or higher chance of having Down syndrome. Screening tests do not provide an absolute diagnosis, but they are safer for the mother and the fetus. Diagnostic tests can typically detect whether or not a fetus will have Down syndrome, but they can be more risky for the mother and the fetus. Neither screening nor diagnostic tests can predict the full impact of Down syndrome on a fetus; no one can predict this.

Screening Tests

Screening tests often include a combination of a blood test, which measures the amount of various substances in the mother's blood (e.g., maternal serum alpha-fetoprotein screening (MS-AFP), triple screen, quad-screen), and an ultrasound, which creates a picture of the fetus. During an ultrasound, one of the things the technician looks at is the fluid behind the fetus's neck. Extra fluid in this region could indicate a genetic problem. These screening tests can help determine the fetus's risk of Down syndrome. Rarely, screening tests can give an abnormal result even when there is nothing wrong with the fetus. Sometimes, the test results are normal and yet they miss a problem that does exist.

Diagnostic Tests

Diagnostic tests are usually performed after a positive screening test in order to confirm a Down syndrome diagnosis. Types of diagnostic tests include:

- Chorionic villus sampling (CVS)—examines material from the placenta

- Amniocentesis—examines the amniotic fluid (the fluid from the sac surrounding the fetus)

- Percutaneous umbilical blood sampling (PUBS)—examines blood from the umbilical cord

These tests look for changes in the chromosomes that would indicate a Down syndrome diagnosis.

Other Health Problems

Many people with Down syndrome have the common facial features and no other major birth defects. However, some people with Down syndrome might have one or more major birth defects or other medical problems. Some of the more common health problems among children with Down syndrome are listed below.

- Hearing loss

- Obstructive sleep apnea, which is a condition where the person's breathing temporarily stops while asleep

- Ear infections

- Eye diseases

- Heart defects present at birth

Healthcare providers routinely monitor children with Down syndrome for these conditions.

Treatments

Down syndrome is a lifelong condition. Services early in life will often help babies and children with Down syndrome to improve their physical and intellectual abilities. Most of these services focus on helping children with Down syndrome develop to their full potential. These services include speech, occupational, and physical therapy, and they are typically offered through early intervention programs in each state. Children with Down syndrome may also need extra help or attention in school, although many children are included in regular classes.

Section 40.2

Edwards Syndrome (Trisomy 18)

This section includes text excerpted from "Trisomy 18," Genetic and
Rare Diseases Information Center (GARD), National Center for
Advancing Translational Sciences (NCATS), July 7, 2015.
Reviewed March 2019.

Trisomy 18 is a chromosome disorder characterized by having three
copies of chromosome 18 instead of the usual two copies. Signs and
symptoms include severe intellectual disability; low birth weight; a
small, abnormally shaped head; a small jaw and mouth; clenched fists
with overlapping fingers; congenital heart defects; and various abnormalities of other organs. Trisomy 18 is a life-threatening condition;
many affected people die before birth or within the first month of life.
Some children have survived to their teenage years, but with serious
medical and developmental problems. Most cases are not inherited
and occur sporadically (by chance).

Cause

In most cases, trisomy 18 is caused by having three copies of chromosome 18 in each cell in the body, instead of the usual two copies.
The extra genetic material from the third copy of the chromosome
disrupts development, causing the characteristic signs and symptoms
of the condition.

About 5 percent of people with trisomy 18 have "mosaic trisomy 18"
(when there is an extra copy of the chromosome in only some of the
body's cells). The severity of mosaic trisomy 18 depends on the number
and locations of cells with the extra copy.

Very rarely, an extra piece of chromosome 18 is attached to another
chromosome; this is called "translocation trisomy 18," or partial trisomy 18. If only part of the long (q) arm of chromosome 18 is present
in three copies, the features may be less severe than in people with
full trisomy 18.

Inheritance

Most cases of trisomy 18 are not inherited and occur randomly due
to errors in the formation of eggs or sperm. If an egg or sperm gains
an extra copy of chromosome 18 during cell division and contributes to

a pregnancy, the embryo will have an extra chromosome 18 (trisomy) in each cell of the body.

Mosaic trisomy 18 is also typically not inherited. Mosaic trisomy 18 is also due to an error in cell division, but the error occurs early in embryonic development. About 5 percent of affected people have a mosaic form of trisomy 18.

Partial trisomy 18 (when only part of chromosome 18 is present in three copies) can be inherited. An unaffected parent can carry a rearrangement of genetic material between chromosome 18 and another chromosome. This rearrangement is called a "balanced translocation" because there is no extra or missing genetic material. However, a person with a balanced translocation has an increased risk with each pregnancy to have a child with trisomy 18.

Section 40.3

Patau Syndrome (Trisomy 13)

This section includes text excerpted from "Trisomy 13," Genetic and Rare Diseases Information Center (GARD), National Center for Advancing Translational Sciences (NCATS), September 3, 2015. Reviewed March 2019.

What Is Trisomy 13?

Trisomy 13 is a type of chromosome disorder characterized by having three copies of chromosome 13 in cells of the body, instead of the usual two copies. In some affected people, only a portion of cells contains the extra chromosome 13 (called "mosaic trisomy 13"), whereas other cells contain the normal chromosome pair. Trisomy 13 causes severe intellectual disability and many physical abnormalities, such as congenital heart defects; brain or spinal cord abnormalities; very small or poorly developed eyes (microphthalmia); extra fingers or toes; cleft lip with or without cleft palate; and weak muscle tone (hypotonia). Most cases are not inherited and result from a random error during the formation of eggs or sperm in healthy parents. Due to various life-threatening medical problems, many infants with trisomy 13 do not survive past the first days or weeks of life.

What Are the Signs and Symptoms of Trisomy 13?

Trisomy 13 is associated with severe intellectual disability and physical abnormalities in many parts of the body. People with this condition often have congenital heart defects, brain or spinal cord abnormalities, very small or poorly developed eyes (microphthalmia), extra fingers and/or toes (polydactyly), cleft lip or palate, and decreased muscle tone (hypotonia). Many infants with trisomy 13 fail to grow and gain weight at the expected rate (failure to thrive), have severe feeding difficulties, and episodes in which there is a temporary cessation of spontaneous breathing (apnea).

Other features or trisomy 13 may include:

- Clenched hands (with outer fingers on top of the inner fingers)
- Close-set eyes
- Hernias: umbilical hernia, inguinal hernia
- A hole, split, or cleft in the iris of the eye (coloboma)
- Low-set ears
- Scalp defects, such as missing skin
- Seizures
- Single palmar crease
- Skeletal (limb) abnormalities
- Small head (microcephaly)
- Small lower jaw (micrognathia)
- Undescended testicle (cryptorchidism)

What Are the Genetic Changes Related to Trisomy 13?

Most cases of trisomy 13 results from having three copies of chromosome 13 in each cell in the body instead of the usual two copies. The extra genetic material disrupts the normal course of development, causing the characteristic features of trisomy 13.

Trisomy 13 can also occur when part of chromosome 13 becomes attached (translocated) to another chromosome during the formation of reproductive cells (eggs and sperm) or very early in fetal development. Affected people have two normal copies of chromosome 13, plus an extra copy of chromosome 13 attached to another chromosome. In rare cases, only part of chromosome 13 is present in three copies. The physical signs and symptoms in these cases may be different than those found in full trisomy 13.

A small percentage of people with trisomy 13 have an extra copy of chromosome 13 in only some of the body's cells. In these people, the condition is called "mosaic trisomy 13." The severity of mosaic trisomy 13 depends on the type and number of cells that have the extra chromosome. The physical features of mosaic trisomy 13 are often milder than those of full trisomy 13.

How Might Trisomy 13 Be Treated?

Treatment for trisomy 13 depends on the affected person's signs and symptoms, and is generally symptomatic and supportive. Surgeries are generally withheld for the first few months of life because of the high mortality rate associated with trisomy 13. Parents and medical personnel must carefully weigh decisions about extraordinary life-prolonging measures against the severity of the neurological and physical defects that are present and the likelihood of postsurgical recovery or prolonged survival.

What Is the Long-Term Outlook for People with Trisomy 13?

Trisomy 13 involves multiple abnormalities, many of which are life-threatening. More than 80 percent of children with trisomy 13 do not survive past the first month of life. For those that do survive, complications are common and may include:

- Breathing difficulty or lack of breathing (apnea)
- Deafness
- Feeding problems
- Heart failure
- Seizures
- Vision problems

People with trisomy 13 who survive infancy have severe intellectual disability and developmental delays, and are at increased risk for cancers.

Section 40.4

Triple X Syndrome

This section includes text excerpted from "47 XXX Syndrome,"
Genetic and Rare Diseases Information Center (GARD),
National Center for Advancing Translational Sciences (NCATS),
December 7, 2016

47 XXX syndrome, also called "trisomy X" or "triple X syndrome," is characterized by the presence of an additional (third) X chromosome in each of a female's cells (which normally have two X chromosomes). An extra copy of the X chromosome is associated with tall stature, learning problems, and other features in some girls and women. Seizures or kidney abnormalities occur in about 10 percent of affected females. 47 XXX syndrome is usually caused by a random event during the formation of reproductive cells. An error in cell division called "nondisjunction" can result in reproductive cells with an abnormal number of chromosomes. Treatment typically focuses on specific symptoms, if present. Some females with 47 XXX syndrome have an extra X chromosome in only some of their cells; this is called "46,XX/47,XXX mosaicism."

Symptoms

Many women with 47 XXX syndrome have no symptoms or only mild symptoms. In other cases, symptoms may be more pronounced. Females with 47 XXX syndrome may be taller than average, but the condition usually does not cause unusual physical features. Minor physical findings can be present in some individuals and may include epicanthal folds, hypertelorism (widely spaced eyes), upslanting palpebral fissures, clinodactyly, overlapping digits (fingers or toes), pes planus (flat foot), and pectus excavatum. The condition is associated with an increased risk of learning disabilities and delayed development of speech and language skills. Delayed development of motor skills (such as sitting and walking), weak muscle tone (hypotonia), and behavioral and emotional difficulties are also possible, but these characteristics vary widely among affected girls and women. Seizures or kidney abnormalities occur in about 10 percent of affected females. Most females with the condition have normal sexual development and are able to conceive children.

Inheritance

Most cases of 47 XXX syndrome are not inherited. The chromosomal change usually occurs as a random event during the formation of reproductive cells (eggs and sperm). An error in cell division called "nondisjunction" can result in reproductive cells with an abnormal number of chromosomes. For example, an egg or sperm cell may gain an extra copy of the X chromosome as a result of nondisjunction. If one of these reproductive cells contributes to the genetic makeup of a child, the child will have an extra X chromosome in each of the body's cells. 46,XX/47,XXX mosaicism is also not inherited. It occurs as a random event during cell division in the early development of an embryo. As a result, some of an affected person's cells have two X chromosomes (46,XX), and other cells have three X chromosomes (47,XXX).

Transmission of an abnormal number of X chromosomes from women with 47 XXX syndrome is rare, although it has been reported. Some reports suggest a less than 5 percent increased risk for a chromosomally abnormal pregnancy, and other more recent reports suggest that less than one percent may be more accurate. These risks are separate from the risks of having a chromosomally abnormal pregnancy due to maternal age or any other factors. Furthermore, these risks generally apply only to women with nonmosaic 47 XXX syndrome, as mosaicism may increase the risk of passing on an abnormal number of X chromosomes and potential outcomes. Each individual with 47 XXX syndrome who is interested in learning about their own risks to have a child with a chromosome abnormality or other genetic abnormality should speak with their healthcare provider or a genetics professional.

Diagnosis

47 XXX syndrome may first be suspected based on the presence of certain developmental, behavioral, or learning disabilities in an individual. The diagnosis can be confirmed with chromosomal analysis (karyotyping), which can be performed on a blood sample. This test would reveal the presence of an extra X chromosome in body cells. 47 XXX syndrome may also be identified before birth (prenatally), based on chromosomal analysis performed on a sample taken during an amniocentesis or by a chorionic villus sampling (CVS) procedure. However, in these cases, confirmation testing with a test called "fluorescence in situ hybridization (FISH)," which gives more details of

the chromosomes, is recommended in order to evaluate the fetus for mosaicism.

Treatment

There is no cure for 47 XXX syndrome, and there is no way to remove the extra X chromosome that is present in an affected individual's cells. Management of the condition varies and depends on several factors including the age at diagnosis, the specific symptoms that are present, and the overall severity of the disorder in the affected individual. Recommendations include:

- Early intervention services for infants and children that are diagnosed with the condition. Evidence suggests that children with 47 XXX syndrome are very responsive to early intervention services and treatment. These services may include speech, occupational, physical, or developmental therapy, starting in the early months of life or as soon as needs are identified.

- Periodic screenings throughout childhood. Specific recommendations include a developmental assessment by 4 months of age to evaluate muscle tone and strength; language and speech assessment by 12 months of age; prereading assessment during preschool years; and an assessment of additional learning disabilities as well as social and emotional problems.

- Educational assistance. Receiving educational help to learn techniques and strategies to be successful in school and daily life.

- Supportive environment and counseling. Girls with triple X syndrome may be more prone to anxiety, as well as behavior and emotional problems. It is important to have a supportive environment and psychological counseling which may help to teach the family how to demonstrate love and encouragement, and discourage behaviors that might negatively impact learning and social functioning.

- Assistance and support in daily functioning. If there is developmental delays, this assistance and support may include help with activities of daily living, social opportunities, and employment.

It is also recommended that infants and children with 47 XXX syndrome receive kidney and heart evaluations to detect possible abnormalities. Adolescent and adult women who have late periods, menstrual abnormalities, or fertility issues should be evaluated for primary ovarian failure (POF). Additional treatment for this disorder depends on the specific signs and symptoms present in the affected individual.

Chapter 41

Fragile X Syndrome

What Is Fragile X Syndrome?

Fragile X syndrome is the most common form of inherited intellectual disability in males and is also a significant cause of intellectual disability in females. It affects about 1 in 4,000 males and 1 in 8,000 females and occurs in all racial and ethnic groups.

Nearly all cases of fragile X syndrome are caused by an alteration (mutation) in the *FMR1* gene where a deoxyribonucleic acid (DNA) segment, known as the CGG triplet repeat, is expanded. Normally, this DNA segment is repeated from 5 to about 40 times. In people with fragile X syndrome, however, the CGG segment is repeated more than 200 times. The abnormally expanded CGG segment inactivates (silences) the *FMR1* gene, which prevents the gene from producing a protein called "fragile X mental retardation protein (FMRP)." Loss of this protein leads to the signs and symptoms of fragile X syndrome. Both boys and girls can be affected, but because boys have only one X chromosome, a single fragile X is likely to affect them more severely.

What Are the Symptoms of Fragile X Syndrome?

A boy who has the full FMR1 mutation has fragile X syndrome and will have a moderate intellectual disability. They have a particular

This chapter includes text excerpted from "Learning about Fragile X Syndrome," National Human Genome Research Institute (NHGRI), June 27, 2016.

facial appearance, characterized by large head size, a long face, prominent forehead and chin, and protruding ears. In addition, males who have fragile X syndrome have loose joints (joint laxity), and large testes (after puberty).

Affected boys may have behavioral problems, such as hyperactivity, hand flapping, hand biting, temper tantrums, and autism. Other behaviors in boys after they have reached puberty include poor eye contact, perseverative speech, problems in impulse control and distractibility. Physical problems that have been seen include eye, orthopedic, heart, and skin problems.

Girls who have the full FMR1 mutation have a mild intellectual disability.

Family members who have fewer repeats in the *FMR1* gene may not have an intellectual disability but may have other problems. Women with less severe changes may have premature menopause or difficulty becoming pregnant.

Both men and women may have problems with tremors and poor coordination.

What Does It Mean to Have a Fragile X Premutation?

People with about 55 to 200 repeats of the CGG segment are said to have an FMR1 premutation (an intermediate variation of the gene). In women, the premutation is liable to expand to more than 200 repeats in cells that develop into eggs. This means that women with the FMR1 premutation have an increased risk of having a child with fragile X syndrome. By contrast, the premutation CGG repeat in men remains at the same size or shortens as it is passed to the next generation.

Males and females who have a fragile X premutation have normal intellect and appearance. A few individuals with a premutation have subtle intellectual or behavioral symptoms, such as learning difficulties or social anxiety. The difficulties are usually not socially debilitating, and these individuals may still marry and have children.

Males who have a premutation with 59 to 200 CGG trinucleotide repeats are usually unaffected and are at risk for fragile X-associated tremor/ataxia syndrome (FXTAS). The FXTAS is characterized by late-onset, progressive cerebellar ataxia, and intention tremor in males who have a premutation. Other neurologic findings include short-term memory loss, executive function deficits, cognitive decline, parkinsonism, peripheral neuropathy, lower-limb proximal muscle weakness, and autonomic dysfunction.

The degree to which clinical symptoms of fragile X are present (penetrance) is age-related; symptoms are seen in 17 percent of males aged 50 to 59 years, in 38 percent of males aged 60 to 69 years, in 47 percent of males aged 70 to 79 years, and in 75 percent or males aged 80 years or older. Some female premutation carriers may also develop tremor and ataxia.

Females who have a premutation usually are unaffected but may be at risk for premature ovarian failure (POF) and FXTAS. Premature ovarian failure is defined as cessation of menses before the age of 40 years, has been observed in carriers of premutation alleles. A review by Sherman (2005) concluded that the risk for POF was 21 percent in premutation carriers compared to 1 percent for the general population.

How Is Fragile X Syndrome Diagnosed?

There are very few outward signs of fragile X syndrome in babies, but one is a tendency to have a large head circumference. An experienced geneticist may note subtle differences in facial characteristics. Intellectual disability is the hallmark of this condition and, in females, this may be the only sign of the problem.

A specific genetic test (polymerase chain reaction (PCR) can now be performed to diagnose fragile X syndrome. This test looks for an expanded mutation (called a "triplet repeat") in the *FMR1* gene.

How Is Fragile X Syndrome Treated?

There is no specific treatment available for fragile X syndrome. Supportive therapy for children who have fragile X syndrome includes:

- Special education and anticipatory management, including avoidance of excessive stimulation to decrease behavioral problems

- Medication to manage behavioral issues, although no specific medication has been shown to be beneficial

- Early intervention, special education, and vocational training

- Vision, hearing, connective tissue problems, and heart problems when present are treated in the usual manner

Is Fragile X Syndrome Inherited?

This condition is inherited in an X-linked dominant pattern. A condition is considered X-linked if the mutated gene that causes the disorder is located on the X chromosome, one of the two sex chromosomes. The inheritance is dominant if one copy of the altered gene in each cell is sufficient to cause the condition. In most cases, males experience more severe symptoms of the disorder than females. A striking characteristic of X-linked inheritance is that fathers cannot pass X-linked traits to their sons.

Chapter 42

Klinefelter Syndrome

What Is Klinefelter Syndrome?

The term "Klinefelter syndrome," or KS, describes a set of features that can occur in a male who is born with an extra X chromosome in his cells. It is named after Dr. Henry Klinefelter, who identified the condition in the 1940s.

Usually, every cell in a male's body, except sperm and red blood cells (RBC), contains 46 chromosomes. The 45th and 46th chromosomes—the X and Y chromosomes—are sometimes called "sex chromosomes" because they determine a person's sex. Normally, males have one X and one Y chromosome, making them XY. Males with KS have an extra X chromosome, making them XXY.

KS is sometimes called "47, XXY" (47 refers to total chromosomes) or the "XXY condition." Those with KS are sometimes called "XXY males."

Some males with KS may have both XY cells and XXY cells in their bodies. This is called "mosaic." Mosaic males may have fewer symptoms of KS depending on the number of XY cells they have in their bodies and where these cells are located. For example, males who have normal XY cells in their testes may be fertile.

In very rare cases, males might have two or more extra X chromosomes in their cells, for instance, XXXY or XXXXY, or an extra Y, such

---

This chapter includes text excerpted from "Klinefelter Syndrome (KS): Condition Information," *Eunice Kennedy Shriver* National Institute of Child Health and Human Development (NICHD), December 1, 2016.

as XXYY. This is called "poly-X Klinefelter syndrome," and it causes more severe symptoms.

What Causes Klinefelter Syndrome

The extra chromosome results from a random error that occurs when a sperm or egg is formed; this error causes an extra X cell to be included each time the cell divides to form new cells. In very rare cases, more than one extra X or an extra Y is included.

How Many People Are Affected by or at Risk for Klinefelter Syndrome?

Researchers estimate that 1 male in about 500 newborn males has an extra X chromosome, making KS among the most common chromosomal disorders seen in all newborns. The likelihood of a third or fourth X is much rarer:

Table 42.1. Prevalence of Klinefelter Syndrome Variants

Number of Extra X Chromosomes	One (XXY)	Two (XXXY)	Three (XXXXY)
Number of newborn males with the condition	1 in 500	1 in 50,000	1 in 85,000 to 100,000

Scientists are not sure what factors increase the risk of KS. The error that produces the extra chromosome occurs at random, meaning the error is not hereditary or passed down from parent to child. Research suggests that older mothers might be slightly more likely to have a son with KS. However, the extra X chromosome in KS comes from the father about one-half of the time.

What Are Common Symptoms of Klinefelter Syndrome?

Because XXY males do not really appear different from other males and because they may not have any or have mild symptoms, XXY males often don't know they have KS.

In other cases, males with KS may have mild or severe symptoms. Whether or not a male with KS has visible symptoms depends on many factors, including how much testosterone his body makes, if he is mosaic, and his age when the condition is diagnosed and treated.

KS symptoms fall into these main categories:

Physical Symptoms

Many physical symptoms of KS result from low testosterone levels in the body. The degree of symptoms differs based on the amount of testosterone needed for a specific age or developmental stage and the amount of testosterone the body makes or has available.

During the first few years of life, when the need for testosterone is low, most XXY males do not show any obvious differences from typical male infants and young boys. Some may have slightly weaker muscles, meaning they might sit up, crawl, and walk slightly later than average. For example, on average, baby boys with KS do not start walking until the age of 18 months.

After age five years of age, when compared to typically developing boys, boys with KS may be slightly:

- Taller

- Fatter around the abdomen

- Clumsier

- Slower in developing motor skills, coordination, speed, and muscle strength

Puberty for boys with KS usually starts normally. But because their bodies make less testosterone than non-KS boys, their pubertal development may be disrupted or slow. In addition to being tall, KS boys may have:

- Smaller testes and penis

- Breast growth (about one-third of teens with KS have breast growth)

- Less facial and body hair

- Reduced muscle tone

- Narrower shoulders and wider hips

- Weaker bones, greater risk for bone fractures

- Decreased sexual interest

- Lower energy

- Reduced sperm production

An adult male with KS may have these features:

- Infertility. Nearly all men with KS are unable to father a biologically-related child without help from a fertility specialist.

- Small testes, with the possibility of testes shrinking slightly after the teen years

- Lower testosterone levels, which lead to less muscle, hair, and sexual interest and function

- Breasts or breast growth (called "gynecomastia").

In some cases, breast growth can be permanent, and about 10 percent of XXY males need breast-reduction surgery.

Language and Learning Symptoms

Most males with KS have normal intelligence quotients (IQ) and successfully complete education at all levels. (IQ is a frequently used intelligence measure, but does not include emotional, creative, or other types of intelligence.) Between 25 and 85 percent of all males with KS have some kind of learning or language-related problem, which makes it more likely that they will need some extra help in school. Without this help or intervention, KS males might fall behind their classmates as schoolwork becomes harder.

KS males may experience some of the following learning and language-related challenges:

- **A delay in learning to talk.** Infants with KS tend to make only a few different vocal sounds. As they grow older, they may have difficulty saying words clearly. It might be hard for them to distinguish differences between similar sounds.

- **Trouble using language to express their thoughts and needs.** Boys with KS might have problems putting their thoughts, ideas, and emotions into words. Some may find it hard to learn and remember some words, such as the names of common objects.

- **Trouble processing what they hear.** Although most boys with KS can understand what is being said to them, they might take longer to process multiple or complex sentences. In some cases, they might fidget or "tune out" because they take longer to process the information. It might also be difficult for KS males to concentrate in noisy settings. They might also be less able to understand a speaker's feelings from just speech alone.

- **Reading difficulties.** Many boys with KS have difficulty understanding what they read (called "poor reading comprehension"). They might also read more slowly than other boys.

By adulthood, most males with KS learn to speak and converse normally, although they may have a harder time doing work that involves extensive reading and writing.

Social and Behavioral Symptoms

Many of the social and behavioral symptoms in KS may result from the language and learning difficulties. For instance, boys with KS who have language difficulties might hold back socially and could use help building social relationships.

Boys with KS, compared to typically developing boys, tend to be:

- Quieter

- Less assertive or self-confident

- More anxious or restless

- Less physically active

- More helpful and eager to please

- More obedient or more ready to follow directions

In the teenage years, boys with KS may feel their differences more strongly. As a result, these teen boys are at higher risk of depression, substance abuse, and behavioral disorders. Some teens might withdraw, feel sad, or act out their frustration and anger.

As adults, most men with KS have lives similar to those of men without KS. They successfully complete high school, college, and other levels of education. They have successful and meaningful careers and professions. They have friends and families.

Contrary to research findings published several decades ago, males with KS are no more likely to have serious psychiatric disorders or to get into trouble with the law.

Symptoms of Poly-X Klinefelter Syndrome

Males with poly-X KS have more than one extra X chromosome, so their symptoms might be more pronounced than in males with KS. In childhood, they may also have seizures, crossed eyes, constipation, and recurrent ear infections. Poly-KS males might also show slight differences in other physical features.

Some common additional symptoms for several poly-X KS are listed below.

48, XXYY

- Long legs
- Little body hair
- Lower IQ, an average of 60 to 80 (normal IQ is 90 to 110)
- Leg ulcers and other vascular disease symptoms
- Extreme shyness, but also sometimes aggression and impulsiveness

48, XXXY (Or Tetrasomy)

- Eyes set further apart
- Flat nose bridge
- Arm bones connected to each other in an unusual way
- Short
- Fifth (smallest) fingers curve inward (clinodactyly)
- Lower IQ, average 40 to 60
- Immature behavior

49, XXXXY (Or Pentasomy)

- Low IQ, usually between 20 and 60
- Small head
- Short
- Upward-slanted eyes
- Heart defects, such as when the chambers do not form properly
- High feet arches
- Shy, but friendly
- Difficulty with changing routines

What Are the Treatments for Symptoms in Klinefelter Syndrome?

It's important to remember that because symptoms can be mild, many males with KS are never diagnosed are treated.

The earlier in life that KS symptoms are recognized and treated, the more likely it is that the symptoms can be reduced or eliminated. It is especially helpful to begin treatment by early puberty. Puberty is a time of rapid physical and psychological change, and treatment can successfully limit symptoms. However, treatment can bring benefits at any age.

The type of treatment needed depends on the type of symptoms being treated.

Treating Physical Symptoms

Treatment for Low Testosterone

About one-half of XXY males' chromosomes have low testosterone levels. These levels can be raised by taking supplemental testosterone. Testosterone treatment can:

- Improve muscle mass

- Deepen the voice

- Promote the growth of facial and body hair

- Help the reproductive organs to mature

- Build and maintain bone strength and help prevent osteoporosis in later years

- Produce a more masculine appearance, which can also help relieve anxiety and depression

- Increase focus and attention

There are various ways to take testosterone:

- Injections or shots, every two to three weeks

- Pills

- Through the skin, also called "transdermal;" current methods include wearing a testosterone patch or rubbing testosterone gel on the skin

Males taking testosterone treatment should work closely with an endocrinologist, a doctor who specializes in hormones and their functions, to ensure the best outcome from testosterone therapy.

Is Testosterone Therapy Right for Every XXY Male?

Not all males with XXY condition benefit from testosterone therapy.

For males whose testosterone level is low to normal, the benefits of taking testosterone are less clear than for when testosterone is very low. Side effects, although generally mild, can include acne, skin rashes from patches or gels, breathing problems (especially during sleep), and a higher risk of an enlarged prostate gland or prostate cancer in older age. In addition, testosterone supplementation will not increase testicular size, decrease breast growth, or correct infertility.

Although the majority of boys with KS grow up to live as males, some develop atypical gender identities. For these males, supplemental testosterone may not be suitable. Gender identity should be discussed with healthcare specialists before starting treatment.

Treatment for Enlarged Breasts

No approved drug treatment exists for this condition of over-developed breast tissue, termed "gynecomastia." Some healthcare providers recommend surgery—called "mastectomy"—to remove or reduce the breasts of XXY males.

When adult men have breasts, they are at higher risk for breast cancer than other men and need to be checked for this condition regularly. The mastectomy lowers the risk of cancer and can reduce the social stress associated with XXY males having enlarged breasts.

Because it is a surgical procedure, mastectomy carries a variety of risks. XXY males who are thinking about mastectomy should discuss all the risks and benefits with their healthcare provider.

Treatment for Infertility

Between 95 and 99 percent of XXY men are infertile because they do not produce enough sperm to fertilize an egg naturally. But, sperms are found in more than 50 percent of men with KS.

Advances in assistive-reproductive technology (ART) have made it possible for some men with KS to conceive. One type of ART, called "testicular sperm extraction with intracytoplasmic sperm injection" (TESE-ICSI), has shown success for XXY males. For this procedure, a surgeon removes sperm from the testes and places one sperm into an egg.

Like all ART, TESE-ICSI carries both risks and benefits. For instance, it is possible that the resulting child might have the XXY condition. In addition, the procedure is expensive and is often is not covered by health insurance plans. Importantly, there is no guarantee the procedure will work.

Recent studies suggest that collecting sperm from adolescent XXY males and freezing the sperm until later might result in more pregnancies during subsequent fertility treatments. This is because although XXY males may make some healthy sperm during puberty, this becomes more difficult as they leave adolescence and enter adulthood.

Treating Language and Learning Symptoms

Some, but not all, children with KS have language development and learning delays. They might be slow to learn to talk, read, and write, and they might have difficulty processing what they hear. But various interventions, such as speech therapy and educational assistance, can help to reduce and even eliminate these difficulties. The earlier treatment begins, the better the outcomes.

Parents might need to bring these types of problems to the teacher's attention. Because these boys can be quiet and cooperative in the classroom, teachers may not notice the need for help.

Boys and men with KS can benefit by visiting therapists who are experts in areas such as coordination, social skills, and coping. XXY males might benefit from any or all of the following:

- **Physical therapists** design activities and exercises to build motor skills and strength and to improve muscle control, posture, and balance.

- **Occupational therapists** help build skills needed for daily functioning, such as social and play skills, interaction and conversation skills, and job or career skills that match interests and abilities.

- **Behavioral therapists** help with specific social skills, such as asking other kids to play and starting conversations. They can also teach productive ways of handling frustration, shyness, anger, and other emotions that can arise from feeling "different."

- **Mental-health therapists or counselors** help males with KS find ways to cope with feelings of sadness, depression, self-doubt, and low self-esteem. They can also help with substance-abuse problems. These professionals can also help families deal with the emotions of having a son with KS.

- **Family therapists** provide counseling to a man with KS, his spouse, partner, or family. They can help identify relationship problems and help patients develop communication skills and understand other people's needs.

Parents of XXY males have also mentioned that taking part in physical activities at low-key levels, such as karate, swimming, tennis, and golf, were helpful in improving motor skills, coordination, and confidence.

With regard to education, some boys with KS will qualify to receive state-sponsored special needs services to address their developmental and learning symptoms. But, because these symptoms may be mild, many XXY males will not be eligible for these services. Families can contact a local school district official or special education coordinator to learn more about whether XXY males can receive the following free services:

- The Early Intervention Program for Infants and Toddlers with Disabilities is required by two national laws: the Individuals with Disabilities and Education Improvement Act (IDEIA) and the Individuals with Disabilities Education Act (IDEA). Every state operates special programs for children from birth to three years of age, helping them develop in areas such as behavior, development, communication, and social play.

- An Individualized Education Plan (IEP) for school is created and administered by a team of people, starting with parents and including teachers and school psychologists. The team works together to design an IEP with specific academic, communication, motor, learning, functional, and socialization goals, based on the child's educational needs and specific symptoms.

Treating Social and Behavioral Symptoms

Many of the professionals and methods for treating learning and language symptoms of the XXY condition are similar to or the same as the ones used to address social and behavioral symptoms.

For instance, boys with KS may need help with social skills and interacting in groups. Occupational or behavioral therapists might be able to assist with these skills. Some school districts and health centers might also offer these types of skill-building programs or classes.

In adolescence, symptoms—such as lack of body hair—could make XXY males uncomfortable in school or other social settings, and this discomfort can lead to depression, substance abuse, and behavioral problems or "acting out." They might also have questions about their masculinity or gender identity. In these instances, consulting a psychologist, counselor, or psychiatrist may be helpful.

How Do Healthcare Providers Diagnose Klinefelter Syndrome?

The only way to confirm the presence of an extra chromosome is by a karyotype test. A healthcare provider will take a small blood or skin sample and send it to a laboratory, where a technician inspects the cells under a microscope to find the extra chromosome. A karyotype test shows the same results at any time in a person's life.

Tests for chromosome disorders, including KS, may be done before birth. To obtain tissue or liquid for this test, a pregnant woman undergoes chorionic villus sampling or amniocentesis. These types of prenatal testing carry a small risk for miscarriage and are not routinely conducted unless the woman has a family history of chromosomal disorders, has other medical problems, or is above 35 years of age.

Factors That Influence When Klinefelter Syndrome Is Diagnosed

Because symptoms can be mild, some males with KS are never diagnosed.

Several factors affect whether and when diagnosis occurs:

- Few newborns and boys are tested for or diagnosed with KS.

- Although newborns in the United States are screened for some conditions, they are not screened for XXY or other sex-chromosome differences.

- In childhood, symptoms can be subtle and overlooked easily. Only about 1 in 10 males with KS is diagnosed before puberty.

- Sometimes, visiting a healthcare provider will not produce a diagnosis. Some symptoms, such as delayed early speech, might be treated successfully without further testing for KS.

- Most XXY diagnoses occur at puberty or in adulthood.

- Puberty brings a surge in diagnoses as some males (or their parents) become concerned about slow testes growth or breast development and consult a healthcare provider.

- Many men are diagnosed for the first time in fertility clinics. Among men seeking help for infertility, about 15 percent have KS.

Is There a Cure for Klinefelter Syndrome?

Currently, there is no way to remove chromosomes from cells to cure the XXY condition.

But many symptoms can be successfully treated, minimizing the impact the condition has on length and quality of life (QOL). Most adult XXY men have full independence and have friends, families, and normal social relationships. They live about as long as other men, on average.

Other Frequently Asked Questions

Are There Disorders or Conditions Associated with Klinefelter Syndrome?

Males with KS are at higher risk for some other health conditions, for reasons that are not fully understood. But these risks can be minimized by paying attention to symptoms and treating them appropriately.

Associated conditions include:

- **Autoimmune disorders**, such as type 1 diabetes, rheumatoid arthritis, hypothyroidism, and lupus. In these disorders, the immune cells attack parts of the body instead of protecting them.

- **Breast cancer**. Males with KS have a higher risk of developing this cancer, although still a lower risk than females'. XXY males should pay attention to any changes in their breasts, such as lumps or any leakage from the nipple, and should see their healthcare provider right away if they have any concerns.

- **Venous disease**, or diseases of the arteries and veins. Some of these include:

  - Varicose veins

  - Deep vein thrombosis, a blood clot in a deep vein

- Pulmonary embolism, a blockage of an artery in the lungs

- To reduce their risk, males can keep a normal body weight; get regular, moderate physical activity; quit smoking; avoid sitting or standing in the same position for long periods of time. If venous diseases develop, they can be treated in different ways, depending on their severity. For instance, some treatments include wearing compression socks and others require taking blood-thinner medications.

- **Tooth decay.** Almost one-half of men with KS have taurodontism, a dental problem in which the teeth have larger-than-normal chambers for holding pulp (the soft tissue that contains nerve endings and blood vessels) and shorter-than-normal tooth roots, both of which make it easier for tooth decay to develop. Regular dental check-ups and good oral hygiene habits will help prevent, catch, and treat problems.

- **Osteoporosis,** in which bones lose calcium, become brittle, and break more easily, may develop over time in KS males who have low testosterone levels for long periods of time. Testosterone treatment; regular, moderate physical activity; and eating a healthy diet can decrease the risk of osteoporosis. If the disease develops, medications can help limit its severity.

Can Klinefelter Syndrome Lead to Cancer?

Compared with the general male population, men with KS may have a higher chance over time of getting breast cancer, non-Hodgkin lymphoma, and lung cancer. There are ways to reduce this risk, such as removing the breasts and avoiding the use of tobacco products. In general, XXY males are also at lower risk for prostate cancer.

If I Have Klinefelter Syndrome, Will I Be Able to Get a Woman Pregnant?

It is possible that an XXY male could get a woman pregnant naturally. Although sperm is found in more than 50 percent of men with KS, low sperm production could make conception very difficult.

A few men with KS have recently been able to father a biologically-related child by undergoing assisted fertility services, specifically, a procedure called "TESE-ICSI." TESE-ICSI carries a slightly higher risk of chromosomal disorders in the child, including having an extra X.

If My Son, Family Member, Partner, or Spouse Is Diagnosed with XXY Condition, How Can I Help Him and the Family?

If someone you know is diagnosed with KS:

- **Recognize your feelings**. It is natural for parents or family members to feel that they have done something to cause KS. But, remember it is a genetic disorder that occurs at random— there is nothing you could have done or not done to prevent it from happening. Allow yourself and your family time to deal with your feelings. Talk with your healthcare provider about your concerns.

- **Educate yourself about the disorder**. It is common to fear the unknown. Educate yourself about the XXY condition and its symptoms so you know how you can help your son, family member, or partner/spouse.

- **Support your son, family member, or partner/spouse**. Provide appropriate education about KS, and give him the emotional support and encouragement he needs. Remember, most XXY males go through life with few problems, and many never find out they have the condition.

- **Be actively involved in your son's, family member's, or partner's/spouse's care**. Talk with your healthcare provider and his healthcare provider about his treatment. If counseling for behavioral problems is needed, or if special learning environments or methods are needed, get help from qualified professionals who have experience working with XXY males.

- **Encourage your son, family member, partner/spouse to do activities** to improve his physical motor skills, such as karate or swimming.

- **Work with your teachers/educators and supervisors/ coworkers.**

  - Contact these people regularly to compare how he is doing at home and at school/work.

  - When appropriate, encourage him to talk with his teachers, educators, supervisor, and coworkers. Suggest using brief notes, telephone calls, and meetings to identify problems and propose solutions.

- **Encourage your son's, family member's, partner's/ spouse's independence.** Although it is important to be supportive, realize that watching over too much can send the message that you think he is not able to do things on his own.

- **Share the following information with healthcare providers about XXY problems:**

Table 42.2. Information about XXY Problems

XXY Males May Have	Consider Recommending
Delayed early expressive language and speech milestones	Early speech therapy and language evaluation
Difficulty during transition from elementary school to middle school or high school	Re-testing to identify learning areas that require extra attention at or before entrance to middle/high school
Difficulty with math at all ages	Testing to identify problem areas and remediation for math disabilities
Difficulty with complex language processing, specifically with understanding and creating spoken language	Language evaluation, increased opportunities to communicate through written language, possibly getting written notes from lectures/discussions
Decreased running speed, agility, and overall strength in childhood	Physical therapy, occupational therapy, activities that build strength

What Is the Best Way to Teach or Communicate with Males Who Have Klinefelter Syndrome?

Research has identified some ways in which educators and parents can improve learning and communication among XXY males, including:

- Using images and visual clues
- Teaching them new words
- Encouraging conversation
- Using examples in the language
- Minimizing distractions
- Breaking tasks into small steps
- Creating opportunities for social interaction and understanding
- Reminding them to stay focused

Chapter 43

Prader-Willi Syndrome

What Is Prader-Willi Syndrome?

The term Prader-Willi syndrome (PWS) refers to a genetic disorder that affects many parts of the body. Genetic testing can successfully diagnose nearly all infants with PWS.

The syndrome usually results from deletions or partial deletions on chromosome 15 that affect the regulation of gene expression, or how genes turn on and off. Andrea Prader and Heinrich Willi first described the syndrome in the 1950s.

One of the main symptoms of PWS is the inability to control eating. In fact, PWS is the leading genetic cause of life-threatening obesity. Other symptoms include low muscle tone and poor feeding as an infant, delays in intellectual development, and difficulty controlling emotions.

There is no cure for PWS, but people with the disorder can benefit from a variety of treatments to improve their symptoms. These treatments depend on the individual's needs, but they often include strict dietary supervision, physical therapy, behavioral therapy, and treatment with growth hormone, among others. As adults, people with PWS usually do best in special group homes for people with this disorder. Some can work in sheltered environments.

Scientists do not know what increases the risk of Prader-Willi syndrome. The genetic error that leads to Prader-Willi syndrome occurs

This chapter includes text excerpted from "Prader-Willi Syndrome (PWS): Condition Information," *Eunice Kennedy Shriver* National Institute of Child Health and Human Development (NICHD), December 1, 2016.

randomly, usually very early in fetal development. The syndrome is usually not hereditary.

What Are Common Symptoms?
What Are the Symptoms of Prader-Willi Syndrome?

Scientists think that the symptoms of PWS may be caused by a problem in a portion of the brain called the "hypothalamus." The hypothalamus lies in the base of the brain. When it works normally, it controls hunger or thirst, body temperature, pain, and when it is time to awaken and to sleep. Problems with hypothalamus can affect various body functions and pathways, leading to a variety of symptoms.

Individuals with PWS may have mild to severe symptoms, which often include:

- Feeding and metabolic symptoms

- Physical symptoms

- Intellectual symptoms

- Behavioral and psychiatric symptoms

- Stages of PWS symptoms

Feeding and Metabolic Symptoms

An important early symptom of PWS is an infant's inability to suck, which affects the ability to feed. Nearly all infants with PWS need help with feeding. Infants may require feeding support for several months. Without assistance, they will not grow. Nursing systems with one-way valves and manual sucking assistive devices, similar to those used with cleft palate (such as bottles with special nipples for babies who do not have the sucking reflex), often are needed. Occasionally, feeding tubes are required, but generally for no more than the first six months after birth. The infants may need fewer calories because of the reduced metabolism associated with PWS and may not demand to feed on their own. Frequent weight checks will help in adjusting the infant's diet to maintain a suitable weight gain.

As the infants grow into toddlers and children, compulsive over-eating replaces the need for feeding support. Because the metabolic rate of individuals with PWS is lower than normal, their caloric intake must be restricted to maintain a healthy weight, often to 60 percent of the caloric requirement of comparably-sized children without the syndrome.

Feeding and metabolic symptoms persist into adulthood. Unless individuals with PWS live in environments that limit access to food (such as locked cabinets and a locked refrigerator), they will eat uncontrollably, even food that is rotten or sitting in the garbage. Uncontrollable eating can cause choking, a ruptured esophagus, and blockages in the digestive system. It can also lead to extreme weight gain and morbid obesity. Because of their inability to stop eating, people with PWS are at increased risk for diabetes, trouble breathing during sleep, and other health risks. For these reasons, people with PWS need to be monitored by a healthcare professional their entire lives.

Physical Symptoms

Many physical symptoms of PWS arise from poor regulation of various hormones, including growth hormone, thyroid hormone, and possibly adrenalin. Individuals with PWS grow slowly and experience delays in reaching physical activity milestones (e.g., standing, walking).

Children with PWS tend to be substantially shorter than other children of similar age. They may have small hands and feet and a curvature of the back called scoliosis. In addition, they frequently have difficulty making their eyes work together to focus, a condition called strabismus.

Infants with PWS are often born with underdeveloped sex organs, including a small penis and scrotum or a small clitoris and vaginal lips. Most individuals with PWS are infertile.

Intellectual Symptoms

Individuals with PWS have varying levels of intellectual disabilities. Learning disabilities are common, as are delays in starting to talk and in the development of language.

Behavioral and Psychiatric Symptoms

Imbalances in hormone levels may contribute to behavioral and psychiatric problems. Behavioral problems may include temper tantrums, extreme stubbornness, obsessive-compulsive symptoms (OCD), picking the skin, and general trouble in controlling emotions. The individual will often repeat questions or statements. Sleep disturbances may include excessive daytime sleepiness and disruptions of sleep. Many individuals with PWS have a high pain threshold.

Stages of Prader-Willi Syndrome Symptoms

The appearance of PWS symptoms occurs in two recognized stages:

Stage 1 (Infancy to Two Years of Age)

- "Floppiness" and poor muscle tone
- Weak cries and a weak sucking reflex
- Inability to breastfeed, which may require feeding support, such as tube feeding
- Developmental delays
- Small genital organs

Stage 2 (Ages 2 to 8)

- Unable to feel satisfied with the normal intake of food
- Inability to control eating, which can lead to overeating if not monitored
- Food-seeking behaviors
- Low metabolism
- Weight gain and obesity
- Daytime sleepiness and sleep problems
- Intellectual disabilities
- Small hands and feet
- Short Stature
- Curvature of the spine (scoliosis)
- High pain threshold
- Behavioral problems, including the display of obsessive-compulsive symptoms, picking the skin, and difficulty controlling emotions
- Small genitals, often resulting in infertility in later life

What Causes It

Prader-Willi syndrome is caused by genetic changes on an "unstable" region of chromosome 15 that affects the regulation of gene expression, or how genes turn on and off. This part of the chromosome is called unstable because it is prone to be shuffled around by the cell's genetic machinery before the chromosome is passed on from parent to child.

The genetic changes that cause Prader-Willi syndrome occur in a portion of the chromosome, referred to as the Prader-Willi critical region (PWCR), around the time of conception or during early fetal development. This region was identified in 1990 using genetic DNA probes. Although Prader-Willi syndrome is genetic, it usually is not inherited and generally develops due to deletions or partial deletions on chromosome 15.

Specific changes to the chromosome can include the following:

- **Deletions.** A section of a chromosome may be lost or deleted, along with the functions that this section supported. A majority of PWS cases result from a deletion in one region of the father's chromosome 15 that leads to a loss of function of several genes. The corresponding mother's genes on chromosome 15 are always inactive and thus cannot make up for the deletion on the father's chromosome 15. The missing paternal genes normally play a fundamental role in regulating hunger and fullness.

- **Maternal uniparental disomy**. A cell usually contains one set of chromosomes from the father and another set from the mother. In ordinary cases, a child has two chromosome 15s, one from each parent. In around one-fourth of PWS cases, the child has two copies of chromosome 15 from the mother and none from the father. Because genes located in the PWCR are normally inactive in the chromosome that comes from the mother, the child's lack of active genes in this region leads to PWS.

- **An imprinting center defect.** Genes in the PWCR on the chromosome that came from the mother are normally inactivated, due to a process known as "imprinting" that affects whether the cell is able to "read" a gene or not. In a small percentage of PWS cases, chromosome 15 inherited from the father is imprinted in the same way as the mother's. This can be caused by a small deletion in a region of the father's chromosome that controls the imprinting process, called the imprinting center. In these cases, both of the child's copies of chromosome 15 have inactive PWCRs, leading to Prader-Willi syndrome.

How Is It Diagnosed?

How Do Healthcare Providers Diagnose Prader-Willi Syndrome?

In many cases of Prader-Willi syndrome, diagnosis is prompted by physical symptoms in the newborn.

If a newborn is unable to suck or feed for a few days and has a "floppy" body and weak muscle tone, a healthcare provider may conduct genetic testing for Prader-Willi syndrome. Formal diagnostic criteria for recognizing Prader-Willi syndrome depend on the age of the individual-specifically, whether the third birthday has been reached. Before age three, the most important symptom is extremely poor muscle tone, called hypotonia, which makes infants feel floppy. In affected children three years of age and older, other symptoms become apparent, such as obesity, intellectual delays, learning disabilities, or behavior problems, especially connected with food and eating.

- Children younger than three years of age must have at least four major criteria and at least one minor criterion for a Prader-Willi syndrome diagnosis.

- Those older than three years of age must have at least five major criteria and at least three minor criteria for a diagnosis of Prader-Willi syndrome.

Major Clinical Criteria of Prader-Willi Syndrome

- Extremely weak muscles in the body's torso

- Difficulty sucking, which improves after the first few months

- Feeding difficulties and/or failure to grow, requiring feeding assistance, such as feeding tubes or special nipples to aid in sucking

- Beginning of rapid weight gain, between ages one and six, resulting in severe obesity

- Excessive, uncontrollable overeating

- Specific facial features, including narrow forehead and downturned mouth

- Reduced development of the genital organs, including small genitalia (vaginal lips and clitoris in females and small scrotum and penis in males); incomplete and delayed puberty; infertility

- Developmental delays, mild-to-moderate intellectual disability, multiple learning disabilities

Minor Clinical Criteria of Prader-Willi Syndrome

- Decreased movement and noticeable fatigue during infancy

- Behavioral problems—specifically temper tantrums, obsessive-compulsive behavior, stubbornness, rigidity, stealing, and lying (especially related to food)

- Sleep problems, including daytime sleepiness and sleep disruption

- Short stature, compared with other members of the family noticeable by the age of 15

- Light color of skin, eyes, and hair

- Small hands and feet in comparison to standards for height and age

- Narrow hands

- Nearsightedness and/or difficulty focusing both eyes at the same time

- Thick saliva

- Poor pronunciation

- Picking of the skin

Additional Findings

- High pain threshold

- Inability to vomit

- Curvature of the spine (scoliosis)

- Earlier-than-usual activity in the adrenal glands, which can lead to early puberty

- Especially brittle bones

Genetic testing must confirm the Prader-Willi syndrome diagnosis. Almost all individuals with Prader-Willi syndrome have an abnormality within a specific area of chromosome 15. Early diagnosis is best because it enables affected individuals to begin early intervention/ special needs programs and treatment specifically for Prader-Willi symptoms.

Genetic testing can confirm the chance that a sibling might be born with Prader-Willi syndrome. Prenatal diagnosis also is available for at-risk pregnancies—that is pregnancies among women with a family history of Prader-Willi syndrome abnormalities.

Genetic Counseling and Testing of At-Risk Relatives

Genetic counseling and testing provide individuals and families with information about the nature, inheritance, and implications of genetic disorders so that they can make informed medical and personal decisions about having children. Genetic counseling helps people understand their risks. The risk of occurrence in siblings of patients with Prader-Willi syndrome depends on what caused the disorder to occur.

Is There a Cure?

Prader-Willi syndrome has no cure. However, early diagnosis and treatment may help prevent or reduce the number of challenges that individuals with Prader-Willi syndrome may experience, and which may be more of a problem if diagnosis or treatment is delayed.

What Are the Treatments?

Parents can enroll infants with PWS in early intervention programs. However, even if a PWS diagnosis is delayed, treatments are valuable at any age.

The types of treatment depend on the individual's symptoms. The healthcare provider may recommend the following:

- **Use of special nipples or tubes for feeding difficulties**. Difficulty in sucking is one of the most common symptoms of newborns with Prader-Willi syndrome. Special nipples or tubes are used for several months to feed newborns and infants who are unable to suck properly, to make sure that the infant is fed adequately and grows. To ensure that the child is growing properly, the healthcare provider will monitor height, weight, and body mass index (BMI) monthly during infancy.

- **Strict supervision of daily food intake**. Once overeating starts between ages 2 and 4 years, supervision will help to minimize food hoarding and stealing and prevent rapid weight gain and severe obesity. Parents should lock refrigerators and all cabinets containing food. No medications have proven beneficial in reducing food-seeking behavior.

A well-balanced, low-calorie diet and regular exercise are essential and must be maintained for the rest of the individual's life. People with PWS rarely need more than 1,000 to 1,200 calories per day. Height, weight, and BMI should be monitored every 6 months during the first 10 years of life after infancy and once a year after age 10 for the rest of the person's life to make sure he or she is maintaining a healthy weight. Ongoing consultation with a dietitian to guarantee adequate vitamin and mineral intake, including calcium and vitamin D, might be needed.

- **Growth hormone (GH) therapy.** GH therapy has been demonstrated to increase height, lean body mass, and mobility; decrease fat mass; and improve movement and flexibility in individuals with PWS from infancy through adulthood. When given early in life, it also may prevent or reduce behavioral difficulties. Additionally, GH therapy can help improve speech, improve abstract reasoning, and often allow information to be processed more quickly. It also has been shown to improve sleep quality and resting energy expenditure. GH therapy usually is started during infancy or at diagnosis with PWS. This therapy often continues during adulthood at 20 percent to 25 percent of the recommended dose for children.

- **Treatment of eye problems by a pediatric ophthalmologist.** Many infants have trouble getting their eyes to focus together. These infants should be referred to a pediatric ophthalmologist who has expertise in working with infants with disabilities.

- **Treatment of curvature of the spine by an orthopedist.** An orthopedist should evaluate and treat, if necessary, curvature of the spine (scoliosis). Treatment will be the same as that for people with scoliosis who do not have PWS.

- **Sleep studies and treatment.** Sleep disorders are common with PWS. Treating a sleep disorder can help improve the quality of sleep. The same treatments that healthcare providers use with the general population can apply to individuals with PWS.

- **Physical therapy.** Muscle weakness is a serious problem among individuals with PWS. For children younger than age three, physical therapy may increase muscular strength and help such children achieve developmental milestones. For older children, daily exercise will help build lean body mass.

- **Behavioral therapy.** People with PWS have difficulty controlling their emotions. Using behavioral therapy can help. Stubbornness, anger, and obsessive-compulsive behavior, including obsession with food, should be handled with behavioral management programs using firm limit-setting strategies. Structure and routines also are advised.

- **Medications.** Medications, especially serotonin reuptake inhibitors (SRIs), may reduce obsessive-compulsive symptoms. SRIs also may help manage psychosis.

- **Early interventions/special needs programs**. Individuals with PWS have varying degrees of intellectual difficulty and learning disabilities. Early intervention programs, including speech therapy for delays in acquiring language and for difficulties with pronunciation, should begin as early as possible and continue throughout childhood.

Special education is almost always necessary for school-age children. Groups that offer training in social skills may also prove beneficial. An individual aide is often useful in helping PWS children focus on schoolwork.

- **Sex hormone treatments and/or corrective surgery.** These treatments are used to treat small genitals (penis, scrotum, clitoris).

- **Replacement of sex hormones.** Replacement of sex hormones during puberty may result in the development of adequate secondary sex characteristics (e.g., breasts, pubic hair, a deeper voice).

- **Placement in group homes during adulthood.** Group homes offer necessary structure and supervision for adults with PWS, helping them avoid compulsive eating, severe obesity, and other health problems.

Other Frequently Asked Questions
Does Prader-Willi Syndrome Affect Pregnancy?

Until recently, experts believed that people with PWS were infertile. However, because several pregnancies have occurred in women with PWS, birth control should be considered.

Inheritance of Prader-Willi Syndrome and Angelman Syndrome

PWS could affect the offspring of someone with the syndrome, depending on how the individual developed the disorder and the individual's sex. The offspring could be at risk of being born with PWS or with Angelman syndrome (AS). Angelman syndrome, like PWS, results from defects in one region of chromosome 15. The two syndromes both involve missing or silenced genes in this region, called the "Prader-Willi critical region" (PWCR). This section of the chromosome is "imprinted," and the genes involved in Angelman syndrome and PWS have different sex-specific imprinting patterns. This is the reason why the sex of the parent with PWS affects which disorder the offspring are at risk to inherit.

Deletion

- If a mother with PWS developed the syndrome because of the deletion of a section of one of her two copies of chromosome 15, her child will have a 50 percent risk of being born with Angelman syndrome. That is, if the mother with PWS passes on her chromosome 15 with the deletion, the child will have Angelman syndrome. This is because the father's genes in this region that are linked to Angelman syndrome are normally inactivated; thus, the child will have no active copies of these genes, causing Angelman syndrome. If the mother passes on her normal copy of chromosome 15, the child will not be born with Angelman syndrome or PWS.

- In the case of a father with PWS who has a deletion in chromosome 15, there is a 50 percent chance that he will pass on the affected chromosome to his child, leading to PWS. This is because a mother's genes that are linked to PWS are normally inactivated; thus, the child will have no active copies of these genes.

Because fertility is so rare in individuals with PWS, only one case of a mother with a deletion passing on Angelman syndrome to her child has been reported. No cases have been reported of a father who had PWS because of a deletion passing on PWS to his child, but it is possible.

Uniparental Disomy

No case of either syndrome in the child of an individual with PWS through uniparental disomy (two copies of chromosome 15 from the mother and none from the father) has ever been reported, but they are theoretically possible. Inheritance could happen in three different ways, but all require the parent with PWS passing on both copies of his or her chromosome 15, which is unlikely.

- If the offspring also receives a copy of chromosome 15 from the other parent and none of these three copies is lost, this condition will be fatal before birth.

- If the parent with PWS is the mother and the offspring end up with only two copies of chromosome 15 during development, the child will probably be born with PWS because he or she has inherited two inactivated copies of the genes in the PWCR.

- If the parent with PWS is the father and the offspring ends up with only two copies of chromosome 15 during development, the child will probably be born with Angelman syndrome. This is because the genes related to Angelman syndrome in the chromosome inherited from the mother are inactivated, and thus the child does not have any working copies of these genes, causing Angelman syndrome

Imprinting Center Defect

No cases have been reported of a parent who has PWS because of an imprinting-center defect passing on PWS to his or her child. However, there is a theoretical possibility of this happening.

Are There Disorders or Conditions Associated with Prader-Willi Syndrome?

Several other disorders and conditions are associated with PWS:

- Obesity and secondary problems due to extreme obesity

- Diabetes
- Sleep apnea
- Obsessive-compulsive disorder (OCD)
- Infertility
- Autism spectrum disorders (ASD)

Chapter 44

Smith-Magenis Syndrome

What Is Smith-Magenis Syndrome?

Smith-Magenis syndrome (SMS) is a developmental disorder that affects many parts of the body. The major features of this condition include mild to moderate intellectual disability, delayed speech and language skills, distinctive facial features, sleep disturbances, and behavioral problems. Most people with SMS have a deletion of genetic material in each cell from a specific region of chromosome 17. Although this region contains multiple genes, researchers believe that the loss of one particular gene, *RAI1*, is responsible for most of the features of the condition. In most of these cases, the deletion is not inherited, occurring randomly during the formation of eggs or sperm, or in early fetal development. In rare cases, the deletion is due to a chromosomal-balanced translocation in one of the parents. In about 10 percent of cases, SMS is caused by a mutation in the *RAI1* gene. These mutations may occur randomly, or may be inherited from a parent in an autosomal dominant manner. Treatment for SMS depends on the symptoms present in each person.

This chapter includes text excerpted from "Smith-Magenis Syndrome," Genetic and Rare Diseases Information Center (GARD), National Center for Advancing Translational Sciences (NCATS), August 28, 2017.

505

What Are the Signs and Symptoms of Smith-Magenis Syndrome?

The major features of SMS includes mild to moderate intellectual disability, delayed speech, and motor skills, distinctive facial features, sleep disturbances, skeletal and dental abnormalities, and behavioral problems.

Facial features in people with SMS may be subtle in early childhood but usually, become more apparent with age. They may include:

- A broad, square-shaped face with deep-set eyes, full cheeks, and a prominent lower jaw

- A "flattened" appearance to the middle of the face and the bridge of the nose

- A downward-turned mouth with a full, outward-curving upper lip

While people with SMS often have affectionate, engaging personalities, most also have behavioral problems. These may include:

- Frequent temper tantrums and outbursts

- Aggression

- Anxiety

- Impulsiveness

- Difficulty paying attention

- Self-injury, including biting, hitting, head-banging, and skin picking

- Repetitive self-hugging (a trait that may be unique to SMS)

- Compulsively licking the fingers and flipping pages of books (a behavior is known as "lick and flip")

Additional features of SMS may include short stature, scoliosis, reduced sensitivity to pain and temperature, chronic ear infections, obesity, and a hoarse voice.

Can Children with Smith-Magenis Syndrome Be Potty-Trained?

Many children with SMS have toileting difficulties. These may include delayed potty training and/or persistence of nighttime bed-wetting (enuresis).

Can Children with Smith-Magenis Syndrome Learn to Talk?

Many children with SMS experience early speech delays, particularly with expressive language. However, with appropriate intervention and a total communication program that includes sign language, gestures, or a picture system, verbal speech generally develops by school age. In some, articulation problems may persist.

What Are the Educational Capabilities of Children with Smith-Magenis Syndrome?

Developmental delays are frequently evident in early childhood and the majority of older children and adults with SMS function within the mild-to-moderate range of retardation. A cognitive profile has been described with relative weaknesses observed in sequential processing and short-term memory; relative strengths were found in long-term memory and perceptual closure (i.e., a process whereby an incomplete visual stimulus is perceived to be complete: 'parts of a whole').

Chapter 45

Turner Syndrome

What Is Turner Syndrome?

Turner syndrome (TS) is a disorder caused by a partially or completely missing X chromosome. This condition affects only females.

Most people have 46 chromosomes in each cell—23 from their mother and 23 from their father. The 23rd pair of chromosomes are called the "sex chromosomes"—X and Y—because they determine whether a person is male or female. Females have two X chromosomes (XX) in most of their cells, and males have one X chromosome and one Y chromosome (XY) in most of their cells. A female with all of her chromosomes is referred to as "46, XX." A male is "46, XY."

Turner syndrome most often occurs when a female has one normal X chromosome, but the other X chromosome is missing (45, X). Other forms of Turner syndrome result when one of the two chromosomes is partially missing or altered in some way.

What Are Common Symptoms?

Turner syndrome causes a variety of symptoms in girls and women. For some people, symptoms are mild, but for others, Turner syndrome can cause serious health problems. In general, women with Turner syndrome have female sex characteristics, but these characteristics

This chapter includes text excerpted from "Turner Syndrome: Condition Information," *Eunice Kennedy Shriver* National Institute of Child Health and Human Development (NICHD), December 1, 2016.

are underdeveloped compared to the typical female. Turner syndrome can affect:

- **Appearance.** Features of Turner syndrome may include a short neck with a webbed appearance, low hairline at the back of the neck, low-set ears, hands, and feet that are swollen or puffy at birth, and soft nails that turn upward.

- **Stature.** Girls with Turner syndrome grow more slowly than other children. Without treatment, they tend to have short stature (around 4 feet, 8 inches) as adults.

- **Puberty.** Most girls with Turner syndrome do not start puberty naturally.

- **Reproduction.** In most girls with Turner syndrome, the ovaries are missing or do not function properly. Without the estrogen (ER) made by their ovaries, girls with Turner syndrome will not develop breasts. Most women with Turner syndrome cannot become pregnant without assistive technology.

- **Cardiovascular.** Turner syndrome can cause problems with the heart or major blood vessels. In addition, some women and girls with Turner syndrome have high blood pressure (HBP).

- **Kidney.** Kidney function is usually normal in Turner syndrome, but some people with this condition have kidneys that look abnormal.

- **Osteoporosis.** Women with Turner syndrome often have low levels of the hormone estrogen, which can put them at risk for osteoporosis. Osteoporosis can cause height loss and bone fractures.

- **Diabetes.** People with Turner syndrome are at higher risk for type 2 diabetes.

- **Thyroid.** Many people with Turner syndrome have thyroid problems. The most common one is hypothyroidism, an underactive thyroid gland.

- **Cognitive.** People with Turner syndrome have normal intelligence. Some, however, have problems learning mathematics and can have trouble with visual-spatial coordination (such as determining the relative positions of objects in space).

How Many People Are Affected?

Turner syndrome affects about 1 of every 2,500 female live births worldwide.

This disorder affects all races and regions of the world equally. There are no known environmental risks for Turner syndrome. Parents who have had many unaffected children can still have a child with Turner syndrome later on.

Generally, Turner syndrome is not passed on from mother to child. In most cases, women with Turner syndrome are infertile.

What Causes It

Turner syndrome occurs when part or all of an X chromosome is missing from most or all of the cells in a girl's body. A girl normally receives one X chromosome from each parent. The error that leads to the missing chromosome appears to happen during the formation of the egg or sperm.

Most commonly, a girl with Turner syndrome has only one X chromosome. Occasionally, she may have a partial second X chromosome. Because she is missing part or all of a chromosome, certain genes are missing. The loss of these genes leads to the symptoms of Turner syndrome.

Sometimes, girls with Turner syndrome have some cells that are missing one X chromosome (45, X) and some that are normal. This is because not every cell in the body is exactly the same, so some cells might have the chromosome, while others might not. This condition is called "mosaicism." If the second sex chromosome is lost from most of a girl's cells, then it's likely that she will have symptoms of Turner syndrome. If the chromosome is missing from only some of her cells, she may have no symptoms or only mild symptoms.

How Is It Diagnosed?

Healthcare providers use a combination of physical symptoms and the results of a genetic blood test, called a "karyotype," to determine the chromosomal characteristics of the cells in a female's body. The test will show if one of the X chromosomes is partially or completely missing.

Turner syndrome also can be diagnosed during pregnancy by testing the cells in the amniotic fluid. Newborns may be diagnosed after heart problems are detected or after certain physical features, such as swollen hands and feet or webbed skin on the neck, are noticed. Other characteristics, such as widely spaced nipples or low-set ears, also may lead to a suspicion of Turner syndrome. Some girls may be diagnosed as teenagers because of a slow growth rate or a lack of puberty-related changes. Still, others may be diagnosed as adults when they have difficulty becoming pregnant.

What Are Common Treatments?

Although there is no cure for Turner syndrome, some treatments can help minimize its symptoms. These include:

- **Human growth hormone (HGH)**. If given in early childhood, hormone injections can often increase adult height by a few inches.

- **Estrogen replacement therapy (ERT)**. ERT can help start the secondary sexual development that normally begins at puberty (around the age of 12). This includes breast development and the development of wider hips. Healthcare providers may prescribe a combination of estrogen and progesterone to girls who haven't started menstruating by the age of 15. ERT also provides protection against bone loss.

Regular health checks and access to a wide variety of specialists are important to care for the various health problems that can result from Turner syndrome. These include ear infections, high blood pressure, and thyroid problems.

Other Frequently Asked Questions
Is Turner Syndrome Inherited?

Turner syndrome is usually not inherited, but it is genetic. It is caused by a random error that leads to a missing X chromosome in the sperm or egg of a parent.

Very few pregnancies in which the fetus has Turner Syndrome result in live births. Most end in early pregnancy loss.

Most women with Turner syndrome cannot get pregnant naturally. In one study, as many as 40 percent of women with Turner syndrome got pregnant using donated eggs. However, pregnant women with Turner syndrome are at increased risk for high blood pressure during pregnancy, which can result in complications, including preterm birth and fetal growth restriction.

Women with Turner syndrome also are at risk for aortic dissection during pregnancy. This happens about two percent of the time. An aortic dissection is a tear in or damage to the inner wall of the aorta, the major artery carrying blood to the heart. Damage to the aorta's inner wall causes blood to flow rapidly into the lining of the aorta. This can restrict the main flow of blood through the aorta or cause the aorta to balloon—a condition called an "aneurysm." An aneurysm can rupture, which can be life-threatening.

Can Turner Syndrome Be Prevented?

Turner syndrome cannot be prevented. It is a genetic problem that is caused by a random error that leads to a missing X chromosome in the sperm or egg of a parent. There is nothing the father or mother can do to prevent the error from occurring. However, there are many options for treatment.

What Health Complications Can Occur with Turner Syndrome?

Hearing Problems

Ear malformations and hearing problems are common in people with Turner syndrome. They may need hearing aids as children or adults. Girls with Turner syndrome may be prone to ear infections.

Heart

Some girls with Turner syndrome have a constriction, or narrowing, of the aorta. Many girls with Turner syndrome have an abnormal valve between the heart and the aorta. The abnormal valve usually does not cause symptoms, but it can lead to infection of the valve or damage to the aorta. Heart defects are the major cause of premature death in people with Turner syndrome.

Kidneys

Many people with Turner syndrome have abnormalities in their kidneys. However, these usually do not cause problems. The only reported effect has been an increased risk for urinary tract infections (UTIs).

Diabetes

People with Turner syndrome are at high risk for type 2 diabetes. Researchers are not sure why this is so, but because diabetes can cause many medical complications, women with Turner syndrome should be checked regularly for diabetes.

Osteoporosis

Many women with Turner syndrome have osteoporosis. Women with Turner syndrome are at higher risk for osteoporosis because their bodies do not make enough estrogen. Estrogen is a hormone that helps to maintain bone density. Women who are given estrogen can lower their risk of osteoporosis.

Thyroid Conditions

Many women with Turner syndrome also have a thyroid disorder. The most common is hypothyroidism. Symptoms include decreased energy, intolerance to cold, and dry skin. This condition is easily treated with medication.

Gluten Intolerance

Some people with Turner syndrome have gluten intolerance, also called "celiac disease."

Is Turner Syndrome Considered a Disability?

Turner syndrome is not considered a disability, although it can cause certain learning challenges, including problems learning mathematics and with memory. Most girls and women with Turner syndrome lead a normal, healthy, productive life with proper medical care.

My Daughter Has Been Diagnosed with Turner Syndrome. Now What?

If your daughter has been diagnosed with Turner syndrome, you may be wondering what to expect as she grows up. A few of these questions, with answers, are listed here.

- Will she mature normally?

- Most girls with Turner syndrome do not mature typically. They may not develop breasts or start getting a period. Estrogen treatment can replace hormones that the body doesn't naturally produce, spurring development and preventing osteoporosis.

- Will she have problems in school?

- Some girls with Turner syndrome have difficulty with arithmetic, visual memory, and visio-spatial skills (such as determining the relative positions of objects in space). They may also have some trouble understanding nonverbal communication (body language, facial expression) and interacting with peers.

- What care will she need as she grows up?

- Girls and women with Turner syndrome usually require care from a variety of specialists throughout their lives.

- Will she be able to have a normal sex life as an adult?

- Women with Turner syndrome can enjoy normal sex lives.

- Will she be able to have children?

- Most women with Turner syndrome cannot get pregnant naturally. Those who can are at risk for blood pressure-related complications, which can lead to premature birth or fetal growth restriction. Pregnancy also is associated with increased risk for maternal complications, including aortic dissection and rupture.

Chapter 46

Velocardiofacial Syndrome

What Is Velocardiofacial Syndrome?

Velocardiofacial syndrome (VCFS) is a genetic condition that is sometimes hereditary. VCFS is characterized by a combination of medical problems that vary from child to child. These medical problems include: cleft palate, or an opening in the roof of the mouth, and other differences in the palate; heart defects; problems fighting infection; low calcium levels; differences in the way the kidneys are formed or work; a characteristic facial appearance; learning problems; and speech and feeding problems.

The name VCFS comes from the Latin words "velum" meaning palate, "cardio" meaning heart, and "facies" having to do with the face. Not all of these identifying features are found in each child who is born with VCFS. The most common features are palatal differences (~75%), heart defects (75%), problems fighting infection (77%), low calcium levels (50%), differences in the kidney (35%), characteristic facial appearance (numbers vary depending on the individual's ethnic and racial background), learning problems (~90%), and speech (~75%) and feeding problems (35%).

Two genes—*COMT* and *TBX1*—are associated with VCFS. However, not all of the genes that cause VCFS have been identified. Most children who have been diagnosed with this syndrome are missing a small part of chromosome 22. Chromosomes are thread-like structures

This chapter includes text excerpted from "Learning about Velocardiofacial Syndrome," National Human Genome Research Institute (NHGRI), June 29, 2017.

found in every cell of the body. Each chromosome contains hundreds of genes. A human cell normally contains 46 chromosomes (23 from each parent). The specific location or address of the missing segment in individuals with VCFS is 22q11.2.

VCFS is also called the "22q11.2 deletion syndrome." It also has other clinical names, such as "DiGeorge syndrome." As a result of this deletion, about 30 genes are generally absent from this chromosome.

VCFS affects about 1 in 4,000 newborns. VCFS may affect more individuals, however, because some people who have the 22q11.2 deletion may not be diagnosed as they have very few signs and symptoms.

What Are the Symptoms of Velocardiofacial Syndrome?

Despite the involvement of a very specific portion of chromosome 22, there is great variation in the symptoms of this syndrome. At least 30 different symptoms have been associated with the 22q11 deletion. Most of these symptoms are not present in all individuals who have VCFS.

Symptoms include: Cleft palate, usually of the soft palate (the roof of the mouth nearest the throat which is behind the bony palate); heart problems; similar faces (elongated face, almond-shaped eyes, wide nose, small ears); eye problems; feeding problems that include food coming through the nose (nasal regurgitation) because of the palatal differences; middle-ear infections (otitis media); low calcium due to hypoparathyroidism (low levels of the parathyroid hormone that can result in seizures); immune-system problems which make it difficult for the body to fight infections; differences in the way the kidneys are formed or how they work; weak muscles; differences in the spine, such as curvature of the spine (scoliosis) or bony abnormalities in the neck or upper back; and tapered fingers. Children are born with these features.

Children who have VCFS also often have learning difficulties and developmental delays. About 65 percent of individuals with the 22q11.2 deletion are found to have a nonverbal learning disability. When tested, their verbal intelligence quotient (IQ) scores are greater than 10 points higher than their performance IQ scores. This combination of test scores brings down the full-scale IQ scores, but they won't represent the abilities of the individual accurately. As a result of this type of learning disability, students will have relative strengths in reading and rote memorization but will struggle with math and abstract reasoning. These individuals may also have communication and social interaction problems, such as autism. As adults, these individuals have an increased risk for developing mental illness, such as depression, anxiety, and schizophrenia.

How Is Velocardiofacial Syndrome Diagnosed?

VCFS is suspected as a diagnosis based on clinical examination and the presence of the signs and symptoms of the syndrome.

A special blood test called "fluorescence in situ hybridization" (FISH) is then done to look for the deletion in chromosome 22q11.2. More than 95 percent of individuals who have VCFS have a deletion in chromosome 22q11.2.

Those individuals who do not have the 22q11.2 deletion by standard FISH testing may have a smaller deletion that may only be found using more sophisticated lab studies, such as comparative genomic hybridization, Multiplex ligation-dependent probe amplification (MLPA), additional FISH studies performed in a research laboratory, or using specific gene studies to look for mutations in the genes known to be in this region. Again, these studies may only be available through a research lab.

What Is the Treatment for Velocardiofacial Syndrome?

Treatment is based on the type of symptoms that are present. For example, heart defects are treated as they would normally be via surgical interventions in the newborn period. Individuals who have low calcium levels are given calcium supplements and, frequently, vitamin D to help them absorb the calcium. Palate problems are treated by a team of specialists called a "cleft palate team" or "craniofacial team" and again often require surgical interventions and intensive speech therapy. Infections are generally treated aggressively with antibiotics in infants and children with immune problems.

Early intervention and speech therapies are started when possible at one year of age to assess and treat developmental delays.

Is Velocardiofacial Syndrome Inherited?

VCFS is due to a 22q11.2 deletion. Most often neither parent has the deletion, meaning that is new in the child (93%), and the chance for the couple to have another child with VCFS is quite low (close to zero). However, once the deletion is present in a person she or he has a 50 percent chance for having children who also have the deletion. The

22q11 deletion happens as an accident when either the egg or sperm are being formed or early in fetal development.

In less than 10 percent of cases, a person with VCFS inherits the deletion in chromosome 22 from a parent. When the VCFS is inherited in families, this means that other family members may be affected as well.

Since some people with the 22q11.2 deletion are very mildly affected, it is suggested that all parents of children with the deletion have testing. Furthermore, some people with the deletion have no symptoms but they have the deletion in some of their cells but not all. This is called "mosaicism." Even other people have the deletion only in their egg cells or sperm cells but not in their blood cells. It is recommended that all parents of a child with a 22q11.2 deletion seek genetic counseling before or during a subsequent pregnancy to learn more about their chances of having another child with VCFS.

Chapter 47

Williams Syndrome

Williams syndrome (WS) is a genetic condition that affects many parts of the body. Signs and symptoms include mild to moderate intellectual disability (MID), unique personality traits, distinctive facial features, and heart and blood vessel problems. Williams syndrome is caused by a person missing more than 25 genes from a specific area of chromosome 7 (a "deletion"). The loss of these genes contributes to the characteristic features. Although Williams syndrome is an autosomal dominant condition, most cases are not inherited and occur sporadically in people with no family history of Williams syndrome. Treatments are based on each person's signs and symptoms, as there is no cure at this time.

What Are the Signs and Symptoms of Williams Syndrome?

The signs and symptoms of Williams syndrome can vary, but generally, include:

- Mild to moderate intellectual disability

- A distinctive facial appearance

- A unique personality that combines overfriendliness and high levels of empathy with anxiety

This chapter includes text excerpted from "Williams Syndrome," Genetic and Rare Diseases Information Center (GARD), National Center for Advancing Translational Sciences (NCATS), September 21, 2018.

People with Williams syndrome typically have difficulty with tasks, such as drawing and assembling puzzles. They tend to do well on tasks that involve spoken language, music, and learning by repetition.

Facial features common in young children with Williams syndrome include a broad forehead; a short nose with a broad tip; full cheeks; and a wide mouth with full lips. In older children and adults, the face appears longer and gaunter. Dental problems are common and may include small, widely spaced teeth and teeth that are crooked or missing.

People with Williams syndrome often have outgoing, engaging personalities and tend to take an extreme interest in other people. Attention deficit disorder (ADD), problems with anxiety, and phobias are common.

The most significant medical problem associated with Williams syndrome is a form of heart disease called "supravalvular aortic stenosis (SVAS)." SVAS is a narrowing of the large blood vessel that carries blood from the heart to the rest of the body (the aorta). If this condition is not treated, it can lead to shortness of breath, chest pain, and heart failure. The presence of other heart and blood vessel problems has also been reported.

Additional signs and symptoms of Williams syndrome may include:

- Abnormalities of connective tissue (tissue that supports the body's joints and organs), such as joint problems, and soft, loose skin

- Increased calcium levels in the blood (hypercalcemia) in infancy

- Developmental delays

- Problems with coordination

- Short stature

- Vision and eye problems

- Digestive problems

- Urinary problems

What Causes Williams Syndrome

Williams syndrome is caused by a missing piece (deletion) of genetic material from a specific region of chromosome 7. The deleted region includes more than 25 genes.

CLIP2, ELN, GTF2I, GTF2IRD1, and *LIMK1* are among the genes that are typically deleted in people with Williams syndrome.

Researchers have found that the loss of the *ELN* gene is associated with the connective tissue abnormalities and heart disease in many people with this condition. Studies suggest that deletions of *CLIP2, GTF2I, GTF2IRD1, LIMK1*, and perhaps other genes, may help explain many of the unique behavioral characteristics and cognitive difficulties. Loss of the *GTF2IRD1* gene may also contribute to the distinctive facial features often present. The relationship between some of the other deleted genes and the features of Williams syndrome is not yet known.

Is Williams Syndrome Inherited?

Most cases of Williams syndrome are not inherited. The condition typically occurs due to random events during the formation of an egg or sperm cells in a parent. Therefore, it most often occurs in people with no family history of Williams syndrome.

In a small portion of cases, people with Williams syndrome inherit the chromosome deletion from a parent with the condition. In these cases, it is inherited in an autosomal dominant manner. This is because having only one changed copy of chromosome 7 in each cell is enough to cause signs and symptoms.

Regardless of whether Williams syndrome occurs randomly or is inherited from a parent, each child of a person with Williams syndrome has a 50 percent chance of inheriting the condition.

If My Sibling Has Williams Syndrome, What Are the Chances That I Could Have a Child with This Condition?

It is recommended to seek the advice of a genetics professional for further information regarding your specific risks to have a child affected by Williams syndrome. Visit the living with a section for guidance on how to locate a genetics professional in your area.

The risk posed to the siblings of an individual with Williams syndrome (proband) depends on the status of the proband's parents. If a proband's parent is affected, the risk is 50 percent to all siblings. If neither parent is clinically affected, the risk to the siblings of a proband appears to be low because few familial cases have been reported. The clinically unaffected sibling of an individual with Williams syndrome who has clinically unaffected parents likely has no greater risk to have a child with Williams syndrome than does the average person.

Can Williams Syndrome Be Prevented?

There is no known way to prevent the genetic problem that causes Williams syndrome. Prenatal testing is available for couples with a family history of Williams syndrome who wish to conceive. For instance, for pregnancies at 50 percent risk of Williams syndrome, fluorescence in situ hybridization, or FISH testing, may be used to detect the microdeletion of the Williams-Beuren syndrome chromosome region (WBSCR) critical region in fetal cells obtained by chorionic villus sampling (CVS) at about 10 to 12 weeks gestation or amniocentesis usually performed at about 15 to 18 weeks gestation. Prenatal testing may also be offered to unaffected parents who have had a child with Williams syndrome (and perhaps other family members) because of the recurrence risk associated with the possibility of germline mosaicism or inversion polymorphism, or in cases of parental anxiety. Prenatal testing for pregnancies not known to be at increased risk for Williams syndrome is available but is rarely used because most cases are a single occurrence in a family.

Part Four

Complex Disorders with Genetic and Environmental Components

Chapter 48

Genes, Behavior, the Environment, and Health

Gene–Environment Interaction

Nearly all diseases result from a complex interaction between an individual's genetic makeup and the environmental agents that he or she is exposed to.

Examples of environmental agents:

- Mold

- Ozone

- Pesticides

- Air pollution

- Cleaning solutions

- Dust mites

- Some foods and medications

This chapter contains text excerpted from the following sources: Text under the heading "Gene-Environment Interaction" is excerpted from "Gene-Environment Interaction," National Institute of Environmental Health Sciences (NIEHS), December 28, 2018; Text beginning with the heading "Yesterday" is excerpted from "Genes, Behavior, the Environment, and Health," Research Portfolio Online Reporting Tools (RePORT), National Institutes of Health (NIH), June 30, 2018.

Subtle differences in genetic factors cause people to respond differently when exposed to the same environmental agent. As a result, some possess a low risk for developing a disease through an environmental insult, while others are much more vulnerable.

As scientists learn more about the connection between genetics and environmental factors and how that connection may influence human disease, they'll begin to develop new strategies for the treatment and prevention of many illnesses.

Yesterday

- People observed for thousands of years that diseases run in families, but it was only with 20th-century genetic discoveries that we began to understand how specific genes affect health.

- Research showed that some diseases, including cystic fibrosis (CF), Duchenne muscular dystrophy (DMD), and sickle cell disease (SCD), are caused by changes in a single gene. However, it became apparent that multiple genes, acting in concert, confer risk for other complex diseases including diabetes and hypertension, psychiatric disorders, such as schizophrenia and depression, and alcohol and drug dependence.

- Genes alone were not the whole story. Identical twins who had exactly the same genetic makeup but who were raised in different families sometimes developed different diseases or health outcomes. These types of findings suggested that our living conditions or environments were also very important contributors to health and disease.

Today

- The now-completed mapping of the entire human genome gives researchers powerful tools to identify genetic contributions to health and disease.

- We know that genes alone do not cause many common diseases, such as heart disease, diabetes, cancer, and depression, as well as alcohol, tobacco, and other drug addictions. Rather, many genes influence our risk of developing diseases, and whether or not that risk actually leads to disease depends on a lifetime of complex interactions between our genes and our environments. Similarly, certain environments or experiences that are known to increase our chances of physical or mental health problems are especially risky for people who also have a particularly vulnerable genetic makeup.

- Major stressful events, such as job loss, divorce, abuse, or caring for a seriously ill family member, may lead to depression. Research on gene-environment interactions shows that children experiencing highly stressful environments are more likely to become depressed as adults if they also have a particular version of a gene that influences the level of the brain chemical serotonin. Individuals experiencing high levels of stress as children but devoid of this genetic variation are not as likely to become depressed.

- This same serotonin-related gene may be involved in alcohol consumption. National Institutes of Health (NIH) researchers revealed that female monkeys with a particular version of the gene prefer to drink alcohol more than monkeys with a different version of the gene. If the monkeys with the version of the gene that prefer alcohol are reared in groups of other young monkeys rather than by their mothers, they show an even greater preference for alcohol and drink more of it when they are young adults. This is an example of how a genetic risk is made worse by specific conditions during the early stages of development. These monkey studies, in which researchers can better control the environment, allow us to pinpoint more specifically how gene-environment interactions lead to disorders and diseases in an animal model that closely resembles humans.

- Scientists doing research on rats discovered that the behavior of rat moms toward their newborn pups—how they nurse, lick, and groom the pups—changes the lifelong responses of those offspring to stress. The mothers' behaviors change the activity of genes in their offspring's brains—specifically, genes that are involved in the response to stress hormones.

- Toxic environments also contribute to influencing our behavior. Studies with children have shown that cumulative exposure to lead contributes to risk for delinquent behavior. Exposures to certain pesticides and industrial chemicals increase the risk of developing attention deficit hyperactivity disorder (ADHD) in children. Animals similarly exposed also show abnormal patterns in the developing brain. Moreover, different strains of rodents show different outcomes from similar chemical exposures, indicating that genetic differences can influence the response to environmental exposure.

- More and more studies are showing that gene-environment interactions during early development may have long-lasting effects on health that do not show up until adulthood.

- In order to develop successful treatments for the many disorders caused by gene-environment interactions, the NIH launched the Genes and Environment Initiative (GEI) and the Genetic Association Information Network (GAIN) to explore and catalog how genes and environment interact to influence the occurrence of common diseases.

Tomorrow

- The identification of subsets of individuals with high disease risks due to particular combinations of genetic variations and environmental exposures or stressors will allow development of more targeted screening, interventions, and preventative strategies, as well as more effective maintenance of health.

- Prevention of neurological disease and behavioral dysfunction caused by chemical exposures can be implemented by identifying and eliminating exposures to chemicals that cause risk, especially for those with known genetic susceptibility.

- We can develop more personalized, and therefore, more effective, behavioral treatments, such as changing social support, improving diet and exercise habits, or helping to cope with stress, to counteract higher risks for disease among those with certain genetic vulnerabilities or to enhance the effects of other genetic factors that offer protection against health problems.

- Knowledge gained from research on gene-environment interactions can also be used by policymakers to design more user-friendly living conditions that delay or prevent the genetic risks of disease from being realized.

Chapter 49

The Genetics of Addiction

Why do some people have addictions while others do not? Family studies that include identical twins, fraternal twins, adoptees, and siblings suggest that as much as half of a person's risk of becoming addicted to nicotine, alcohol, or other drugs depends on her or his genetic makeup. Pinning down the biological basis for this risk is an important avenue of research for scientists trying to solve the problem of drug addiction.

Genes—functional units of deoxyribonucleic acid (DNA) that make up the human genome—provide the information that directs a body's basic cellular activities. Research on the human genome has shown that, on average, the DNA sequences of any 2 people are 99.9 percent the same. However, that 0.1 percent variation is profoundly important; it is still 3 million differences in the nearly 3 billion base pairs of DNA sequence. These differences contribute to visible variations, such as height and hair color, and invisible traits, such as increased risk for or protection from certain diseases, such as heart attack, stroke, diabetes, and addiction.

Some diseases, such as sickle cell anemia (SCA) or cystic fibrosis (CF), are caused by an error, known as a "mutation," in a single gene. Some mutations, such as the BRCA 1 and 2 mutations that are linked to a much higher risk of breast and ovarian cancer, have become critical medical tools in evaluating a patient's risk for serious

This chapter includes text excerpted from "Genetics and Epigenetics of Addiction," National Institute on Drug Abuse (NIDA), February 2016.

diseases. Medical researchers have had striking success at unraveling the genetics of these single-gene disorders, though finding treatments or cures have not been as simple. Most diseases, including addiction, are complex, and variations in many different genes contribute to a person's overall level of risk or protection. The good news is that scientists are actively pursuing many more paths to the treatment and prevention of these more complex illnesses.

Linking Genes to Health: Genome-Wide Association Studies

Advances in DNA analysis are helping researchers untangle complex genetic interactions by examining a person's entire genome all at once. Technologies, such as genome-wide association studies (GWAS), whole genome sequencing, and exome sequencing (looking at just the protein-coding genes), identify subtle variations in DNA sequence called "single-nucleotide polymorphisms (SNPs)." SNPs are differences in just a single letter of the genetic code from one person to another. If an SNP appears more often in people with a disease than those without, it is thought to either directly affect susceptibility to that disease or be a marker for another variation that does.

GWAS and sequencing are extremely powerful tools because they can find a connection between a known gene or genes and a disorder, and they can identify genes that may have been overlooked or were previously unknown.

Through these methods, scientists can gather more evidence from affected families or use animal models and biochemical experiments to verify and understand the link between a gene and the risk of addiction. These findings would then be the basis for developing new treatment and intervention approaches.

Research Advance: Genetic Variation May Increase Risk for Nicotine Addiction and Lung Cancer

National Institute on Drug Abuse (NIDA)-sponsored research has led to an understanding of how certain gene variants are linked to nicotine dependence. This major breakthrough has paved the way for analysis in animal models, revealing the importance of these variants in the brain's response to nicotine, including withdrawal and nicotine aversion (the body's resistance to nicotine addiction). In addition, some genetic variants are associated with a two- to threefold increase in risk for lung cancer, which may be even higher among those who smoke fewer than 20 cigarettes a day. These discoveries have inspired investigators to develop new medications and other ways that affect how agents bind to brain receptors. Gene variants in these nicotinic receptors, as well as enzymes that metabolize nicotine, are also beginning to provide clinically useful markers to guide treatment decisions.

The Role of the Environment in Diseases Such as Addiction

That old saying "nature or nurture" might be better phrased "nature and nurture" because research shows that a person's health is the result of dynamic interactions between genes and the environment. For example, both genetics and lifestyle factors—such as diet, physical activity, and stress—affect high blood pressure (HBP) risk. NIDA research has led to discoveries about how a person's surroundings affect drug use in particular.

For example, a community that provides healthy after-school activities has been shown to reduce vulnerability to drug addiction, and data show that access to exercise can discourage drug-seeking behavior, an effect that is more pronounced in males than in females.

In addition, studies suggest that an animal's drug use can be affected by that of its cage mate, showing that some social influences can enhance risk or protection. In addition, exposure to drugs or stress in a person's social or cultural environment can alter both gene expression and gene function, which, in some cases, may persist throughout a person's life. Research also suggests that genes can play a part in how a person responds to her or his environment, placing some people at higher risk for disease than others.

Epigenetics: Where Genes Meet the Environment

Epigenetics is the study of functional, and sometimes inherited, changes in the regulation of gene activity and expression that are not dependent on gene sequence. "Epi-" itself means "above" or "in addition to." Environmental exposures or choices people make can actually remodel the structure of DNA at the cell level or even at the level of the whole organism. So, although each cell type in the human body effectively contains the same genetic information, epigenetic-regulatory systems enable the development of different cell types (e.g., skin, liver, or nerve cells) in response to the environment. These epigenetic marks can affect health and even the expression of the traits passed to children. For example, when a person uses cocaine, it can mark the DNA, increasing the production of proteins common in addiction. Increased levels of these altered proteins correspond with drug-seeking behaviors in animals.

Histones, as another example, are like protein spools that provide an organizational structure for genes. Genes coil around histones, tightening or loosening to control gene expression. Drug exposure can affect specific histones, modifying gene expression in localized brain regions. Science has shown that manipulation of histone-modifying enzymes and binding proteins may have promise in treating substance use disorders (SUD).

The development of multidimensional data sets that include and integrate genetic and epigenetic information provides unique insights into the molecular genetic processes underlying the causes and consequences of drug addiction. Studying and using these data types to identify biological factors involved in substance abuse is increasingly important, because technologic advances have improved the ability of researchers to single out individual genes or brain processes that may inform new prevention and treatment interventions.

Genetics and Precision Medicine

Clinicians often find substantial variability in how individual patients respond to treatment. Part of that variability is due to genetics. Genes influence the numbers and types of receptors in peoples' brains, how quickly their bodies metabolize drugs, and how well they respond to different medications.

Scientists will be able to translate this knowledge into new treatments directed at specific targets in the brain or to treatment approaches that can be customized for each patient—called "pharmacogenomics." This emerging science, often called "precision medicine," promises to harness the power of genomic information to improve treatments for addiction by tailoring the treatment to the person's specific genetic makeup. By knowing a person's genomic information, healthcare providers will be better equipped to match patients with the most suitable treatments and medication dosages and to avoid or minimize adverse reactions.

Chapter 50

Alzheimer Disease and Genetics

Chapter Contents

Section 50.1

Genes Related to Alzheimer Disease

This section includes text excerpted from "Alzheimer's Disease Genetics Fact Sheet," National Institute on Aging (NIA), National Institutes of Health (NIH), August 30, 2015. Reviewed March 2019.

The Genetics of Disease

Some diseases are caused by a genetic mutation, or permanent change in one or more specific genes. If a person inherits a genetic mutation that causes a certain disease, then she or he will usually get the disease. Sickle cell anemia (SCA), cystic fibrosis (CF), and early-onset familial Alzheimer disease (eFAD) are examples of inherited genetic disorders.

In other diseases, a genetic variant may occur. A single gene can have many variants. Sometimes, this difference in a gene can cause disease directly. More often, a variant plays a role in increasing or decreasing a person's risk of developing a disease or condition. When a genetic variant increases disease risk but does not directly cause a disease, it is called a "genetic risk factor."

Identifying genetic variants may help researchers find the most effective ways to treat or prevent diseases, such as Alzheimer, in an individual. This approach, called "precision medicine," takes into account individual variability in genes, environment, and lifestyle for each person.

Alzheimer Disease Genetics

Alzheimer disease (AD) is an irreversible, progressive brain disease. It is characterized by the development of amyloid plaques and neurofibrillary, or tau, tangles (NFTs); the loss of connections between nerve cells (neurons) in the brain; and the death of these nerve cells. There are two types of Alzheimer—early-onset and late-onset. Both types have a genetic component.

What Are Deoxyribonucleic Acid, Chromosomes, and Genes?

The nucleus of almost every human cell contains a "blueprint" that carries the instructions a cell needs to do its job. The blueprint is made up of deoxyribonucleic acid (DNA), which is present in long strands that would stretch to nearly 6 feet in length if attached end to end. The DNA is packed tightly together with proteins into compact structures called "chromosomes." Normally, each cell has 46 chromosomes in 23 pairs, which are inherited equally from a person's biological parents. The DNA in nearly all cells of an individual is identical.

Each chromosome contains many thousands of segments, called "genes." People inherit two copies of each gene from their parents, except for genes on the X and Y chromosomes, which, among other functions, determine a person's sex. The genes "instruct" the cell to make unique proteins that, in turn, dictate the types of cells made. Genes also direct almost every aspect of the cell's construction, operation, and repair.

Even slight changes in a gene can produce a protein that functions abnormally, which may lead to disease. Other changes in genes may increase or decrease a person's risk of developing a particular disease.

Early-Onset Alzheimer Disease

Early-onset Alzheimer disease (EOAD) occurs between a person's thirties to mid-sixties and represents less than 10 percent of all people with Alzheimer. Some cases are caused by an inherited change in 1 of 3 genes, resulting in a type known as "early-onset familial Alzheimer disease (EOFAD)," or "FAD."

A child whose biological mother or father carries a genetic mutation for early-onset FAD has a 50/50 chance of inheriting that mutation. If the mutation is in fact inherited, the child has a very strong probability of developing early-onset FAD.

Early-onset FAD is caused by any one of a number of different single-gene mutations on chromosomes 21, 14, and 1. Each of these mutations causes abnormal proteins to be formed. Mutations on chromosome 21 cause the formation of the abnormal amyloid precursor protein (APP). A mutation on chromosome 14 causes abnormal presenilin 1 to be made, and a mutation on chromosome 1 leads to abnormal presenilin 2.

Each of these mutations plays a role in the breakdown of APP, a protein whose precise function is not yet fully understood. This breakdown is part of a process that generates harmful forms of amyloid plaques, a hallmark of the disease.

Critical research findings about early-onset Alzheimer have helped identify key steps in the formation of brain abnormalities typical of the more common late-onset form of Alzheimer. Genetic studies have helped explain why the disease develops in people at various ages.

National Institute on Aging (NIA)-supported scientists are continuing research into early-onset disease through the Dominantly Inherited Alzheimer Network (DIAN), an international partnership to study families with early-onset FAD. By observing the Alzheimer-related brain changes that occur in these families long before symptoms of memory loss or cognitive issues appear, scientists hope to gain insight into how and why the disease develops in both its early- and late-onset forms.

In addition, an NIA-supported clinical trial in Colombia, South America, is testing the effectiveness of an amyloid-clearing drug in symptom-free volunteers at high risk of developing early-onset FAD.

Late-Onset Alzheimer Disease

Most people with Alzheimer have the late-onset form of the disease, in which symptoms become apparent in the mid-60s and later. The causes of late-onset Alzheimer are not yet completely understood, but they likely include a combination of genetic, environmental, and lifestyle factors that affect a person's risk for developing the disease.

Researchers have not found a specific gene that directly causes the late-onset form of the disease. However, one genetic risk factor—having one form of the apolipoprotein E (*APOE*) gene on chromosome 19—does increase a person's risk. *APOE* comes in several different forms, or alleles:

- *APOE* ε2 is relatively rare and may provide some protection against the disease. If Alzheimer disease occurs in a person with this allele, it usually develops later in life than it would in someone with the *APOE* ε4 gene.

- *APOE* ε3, the most common allele, is believed to play a neutral role in the disease—neither decreasing nor increasing risk.

- *APOE* ε4 increases the risk for Alzheimer disease and is also associated with an earlier age of disease onset. A person has zero, one, or two *APOE* ε4 alleles. Having more *APOE* ε4 alleles increases the risk of developing Alzheimer.

- *APOE* ε4 is called a "risk-factor gene" because it increases a person's risk of developing the disease. However, inheriting an *APOE* ε4 allele does not mean that a person will definitely develop Alzheimer. Some people with an *APOE* ε4 allele never get the disease, and others who develop Alzheimer do not have any *APOE* ε4 alleles.

Using a relatively new approach called "genome-wide association study" (GWAS), researchers have identified a number of regions of interest in the genome (an organism's complete set of DNA, including all of its genes) that may increase a person's risk for late-onset Alzheimer to varying degrees. By 2015, they had confirmed 33 regions of interest in the Alzheimer genome.

A method called "whole genome sequencing" determines the complete DNA sequence of a person's genome at a single time. Another method called "whole exome sequencing" looks at the parts of the genome that directly code for the proteins. Using these two approaches, researchers can identify new genes that contribute to or protect against disease risk. Discoveries have led to new insights about biological pathways involved in Alzheimer and may one day lead to effective interventions.

Genetic Testing

A blood test can identify which *APOE* alleles a person has, but results cannot predict who will or will not develop Alzheimer disease. It is unlikely that genetic testing will ever be able to predict the disease with 100 percent accuracy, researchers believe, because too many other factors may influence its development and progression.

APOE testing is used in research settings to identify study participants who may have an increased risk of developing Alzheimer. This knowledge helps scientists look for early brain changes in participants and compare the effectiveness of treatments for people with different *APOE* profiles. Most researchers believe that *APOE* testing is useful for studying Alzheimer disease risk in large groups of people but not for determining any one person's risk.

Genetic testing is used by researchers conducting clinical trials and by physicians to help diagnose early-onset Alzheimer disease. However, genetic testing is not otherwise recommended.

Epigenetics: Nature Meets Nurture

Scientists have long thought that genetic and environmental factors interact to influence a person's biological makeup, including the predisposition to different diseases. They have discovered the biological mechanisms for those interactions. The expression of genes (when particular genes are "switched" on or off) can be affected—positively and negatively—by environmental factors at any time in life. These factors include exercise, diet, chemicals, or smoking, to which an individual may be exposed, even in the womb.

Epigenetics is an emerging science focused on how and when particular genes are turned on or off. Diet and exposure to chemicals in the environment, among other factors, can alter a cell's DNA in ways that affect the activity of genes. That can make people more or less susceptible to developing a disease.

There is emerging evidence that epigenetic mechanisms contribute to Alzheimer disease. Epigenetic changes, whether protective, benign, or harmful, may help explain, for example, why one family member develops the disease and another does not. Scientists are learning more about Alzheimer-related epigenetics, with the hope of developing individualized treatments based on epigenetic markers and their function.

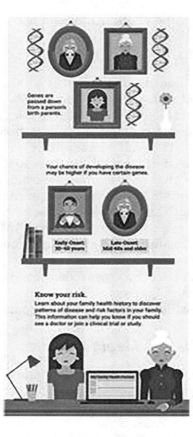

Figure 50.1. *Alzheimer Disease Genetic Infographic*

Section 50.2

People at Genetic Risk for Alzheimer Disease to Test Prevention Drugs

This section includes text excerpted from "People at Genetic Risk for Alzheimer's Disease to Test Prevention Drugs," National Institute on Aging (NIA), National Institutes of Health (NIH), August 23, 2016.

The two biggest risk factors for late-onset Alzheimer disease (AD)—age and carrying a risk gene—cannot be changed. But what if people could do something to counteract those risks and possibly tip the balance in their favor? A groundbreaking clinical trial aims to find out if two experimental drugs can prevent or delay dementia in people at high genetic risk for developing the disorder.

The Alzheimer Prevention Initiatives (APIs) Generation Study is studying cognitively normal older adults with two copies of the *APOE ε4* gene. People with two copies of this risk-factor gene are more likely than not to develop late-onset Alzheimer, the most common form of the brain disorder, which so far has no cure.

A growing number of trials are testing promising therapies that may prevent or delay memory loss and other symptoms of Alzheimer in the most vulnerable people. The drugs being tested in A4, DIAN, API's autosomal dominant Alzheimer disease trial and now Generation are designed to attack beta-amyloid, a protein that plays a key role in the brain changes that lead to Alzheimer dementia.

Supported by a public-private partnership, with $33.2 million from the National Institute on Aging (NIA), part of the National Institutes of Health (NIH), the Generation Study will be conducted at about 90 sites in North America, Europe, and Australia, about half of them in the United States. The research team plans to enroll 1,340 cognitively normal adults, between the ages of 60 and 75, who will be randomly assigned to take either a test drug or a placebo for at least 5 years.

The NIA-supported Banner Alzheimer Institute (BAI), based in Phoenix, AZ, is running the trial with Novartis Pharmaceuticals, which is providing the drugs to be tested, CAD106, CNP520, and Amgen, which helped develop CNP520.

Attacking an Early Alzheimer Culprit

The failure of past antiamyloid drugs to stop Alzheimer in people with mild to moderate dementia has led researchers to test some of the same drugs, and new ones, earlier in the disease process, when therapies might be most effective at altering the course of the disease.

In a handful of prevention trials, experimental therapies are being tested in symptom-free people who, because of their age, genes, or amyloid levels in the brain, are most likely to develop Alzheimer disease—sooner rather than later.

"The results of this and our other prevention trials will help us learn whether and how antiamyloid therapies can slow or perhaps prevent cognitive decline in individuals who are most likely to develop Alzheimer disease," said Laurie Ryan, Ph.D., chief of the Dementias of Aging branch at NIA's Division of Neuroscience.

"We will also gain valuable biomarker data that will be shared with the wider scientific community."

She added, "The ultimate goal is to find a way to block Alzheimer damage in the brain at the earliest possible point, long before symptoms appear, and to prevent a disease that burdens more than five million Americans and many more around the world."

Zeroing in on Uncommon Genetic Risk Factors

The Generation Study seeks people who have inherited two copies of a specific form of the apolipoprotein E (*APOE*) gene, called "*APOE* ε4*.*" *APOE*, which helps transport cholesterol and other fats in the bloodstream, has three forms. About 25 percent of people carry one copy of the *APOE* ε4 gene, which increases the likelihood of developing late-onset Alzheimer and is associated with an earlier age of onset.

About 2 to 3 percent of the world's population has 2 copies of *APOE* ε4. Studies show that up to 60 percent of them will develop Alzheimer dementia by age 85, compared with 10 to 15 percent of the general population. However, some people with an *APOE* ε4 allele never get the disease, and others who develop Alzheimer do not have any *APOE* ε4 alleles.

API's prevention trial in Colombia involves a different genetic risk. It is studying 300 cognitively normal adults who are at high risk of developing a rare, inherited type of early-onset Alzheimer that can begin in people in their thirties.

The Generation and Colombia trials share an ambitious goal: to determine whether data collected from brain scans and cerebrospinal fluid (CSF) measurements can predict clinical benefit. The hope is that these measurements could be used to quickly test prevention therapies in a much larger segment of the population.

"We have to find that sweet spot between starting early enough before Alzheimer pathology develops and yet late enough so that there is enough decline over the next few years to see if the treatments actually work," said Eric Reiman, M.D., executive director of BAI and one of API's leaders.

"Our goal is to help individuals at the highest imminent risk in a way that helps everyone at risk for Alzheimer, and to do so as soon as possible," he added.

Thousands of Volunteers Needed

Banner scientists expect to screen about 80,000 people to find enough participants for the Generation Study. "People with a family history of Alzheimer are good potential volunteers for this study because they may carry the *APOE ε4* gene," said Jessica Langbaum, Ph.D., a BAI scientist and associate director of API. "We need more people to join to fight this devastating disease."

To speed the process for this and other studies, Banner started GeneMatch, a registry that will collect genetic information from adults between the ages of 55 to 75 living in the United States. GeneMatch's genetic testing will allow researchers to match potential volunteers with and without the *APOE ε4* gene for this and other studies.

Testing CAD106 and CNP520

The two drugs being tested in Generation, CAD106 and CNP520, attack beta-amyloid in different ways. If the brain produces too much beta-amyloid or does not clear it fast enough, it clumps together into the plaques found in Alzheimer. Over time, these plaques damage and destroy nerve cells throughout the brain, leading to problems with memory, reasoning, and other cognitive functions.

CAD106 is an active immunotherapy designed to trigger the body's immune system to produce antibodies that attack different forms of amyloid. This second-generation drug does not have the brain-inflammation side effect found with some first-generation immunotherapies, said Dr. Pierre Tariot, M.D., one of API's leaders and director of BAI.

CNP520 inhibits beta-secretase, an enzyme that helps turn a normal protein into harmful beta-amyloid. "The idea is to block the production of pathological amyloid," Dr. Tariot said.

Researchers will determine if either of the drugs leads to changes in overall cognition and how long it takes participants to be diagnosed with mild cognitive impairment (MCI) (a condition that often precedes Alzheimer) or dementia. The drugs' safety and side effects will also be assessed.

In addition, investigators will gather biomarker data to compare to results of cognitive tests. Participants will undergo brain scans to measure the accumulation of amyloid plaques and tau tangles, as well as declines in brain size and energy utilization that are associated with Alzheimer. They will also have lumbar punctures to measure Alzheimer-related proteins in cerebrospinal fluid.

Chapter 51

Asthma and Genetics

Chapter Contents

Section 51.1

Basic Facts about Allergic Asthma

This section includes text excerpted from "Allergic Asthma," Genetic
and Rare Diseases Information Center (GARD), National Center for
Advancing Translational Sciences (NCATS), March 5, 2019.

Asthma is a breathing disorder characterized by inflammation of
the airways and recurrent episodes of breathing difficulty. These episodes, sometimes referred to as "asthma attacks," are triggered by
irritation of the inflamed airways. In allergic asthma, the attacks occur
when substances known as "allergens" are inhaled, causing an allergic
reaction. Allergens are harmless substances that the body's immune
system mistakenly reacts to as though they are harmful. Common
allergens include pollen, dust, animal dander, and mold. The immune
response leads to the symptoms of asthma. Allergic asthma is the most
common form of the disorder.

A hallmark of asthma is bronchial hyperresponsiveness, which means
the airways are especially sensitive to irritants and respond excessively.
Because of this hyperresponsiveness, attacks can be triggered by irritants other than allergens, such as physical activity, respiratory infections, or exposure to tobacco smoke, in people with allergic asthma.

An asthma attack is characterized by tightening of the muscles around
the airways (bronchoconstriction), which narrows the airway and makes
breathing difficult. Additionally, the immune reaction can lead to swelling of the airways and overproduction of mucus. During an attack, an
affected individual can experience chest tightness, wheezing, shortness
of breath, and coughing. Over time, the muscles around the airways can
become enlarged (hypertrophied), further narrowing the airways.

Some people with allergic asthma have another allergic disorder,
such as hay fever (allergic rhinitis) or food allergies. Asthma is sometimes part of a series of allergic disorders, referred to as the "atopic
march." Development of these conditions typically follows a pattern,
beginning with eczema (atopic dermatitis), followed by food allergies,
then hay fever, and finally asthma. However, not all individuals with
asthma have progressed through the atopic march, and not all individuals with one allergic disease will develop others.

Frequency

Approximately 235 million people worldwide have asthma. In the
United States, the condition affects an estimated 8 percent of the

population. In nearly 90 percent of children and 50 percent of adults with asthma, the condition is classified as allergic asthma.

Causes

The cause of allergic asthma is complex. It is likely that a combination of multiple genetic and environmental factors contribute to the development of the condition. Doctors believe genes are involved because having a family member with allergic asthma or another allergic disorder increases a person's risk of developing asthma.

Studies suggest that more than 100 genes may be associated with allergic asthma, but each seems to be a factor in only one or a few populations. Many of the associated genes are involved in the body's immune response. Others play a role in lung and airway function.

There is evidence that an unbalanced immune response underlies allergic asthma. While there is normally a balance between type 1 (or Th1) and type 2 (or Th2) immune reactions in the body, many individuals with allergic asthma predominantly have type 2 reactions. Type 2 reactions lead to the production of immune proteins called "IgE antibodies" and the generation of other factors that predispose to bronchial hyperresponsiveness. Normally, the body produces IgE antibodies in response to foreign invaders, particularly parasitic worms. For unknown reasons, in susceptible individuals, the body reacts to an allergen as if it is harmful, producing IgE antibodies specific to it. Upon later encounters with the allergen, IgE antibodies recognize it, which stimulates an immune response, causing bronchoconstriction, airway swelling, and mucus production.

Not everyone with a variation in one of the allergic asthma-associated genes develops the condition; exposure to certain environmental factors also contributes to its development. Studies suggest that these exposures trigger epigenetic changes to the DNA. Epigenetic changes modify DNA without changing the DNA sequence. They can affect gene activity and regulate the production of proteins, which may influence the development of allergies in susceptible individuals.

Section 51.2

Genetics and Pollution Drive Severity of Asthma Symptoms

This section includes text excerpted from "Genetics and
Pollution Drive Severity of Asthma Symptoms," National
Institutes of Health (NIH), August 31, 2018.

Asthma patients, with a specific genetic profile, exhibit more intense
symptoms following exposure to traffic pollution, according to researchers at the National Institutes of Health (NIH) and collaborators. The
study appeared online in Scientific Reports.

The research team made up of scientists from the National Institute
of Environmental Health Sciences (NIEHS), part of NIH, and Rice University, Houston, also found that asthma patients that lack this genetic
profile do not have the same sensitivity to traffic pollution and do not
experience worse asthma symptoms. The work brings scientists closer
to being able to use precision medicine, an emerging field that intends
to prevent and treat disease based on factors specific to an individual.

Co-lead author Shepherd Schurman, M.D., associate medical director of the NIEHS Clinical Research Unit, stated the results are based
on genetic variation, the subtle differences in DNA that make each
person unique. He further added that to understand the concept, one
should think of human genes, which are made up of DNA base pairs
A, C, G, and T, as written instructions for making proteins.

"All humans have the same genes, in other words, the same basic
instructions, but in some people, one DNA base pair has been changed,"
Schurman said. "This common type of genetic variation is called a 'single nucleotide polymorphism' or SNP, and it can alter the way proteins
are made and make individuals more or less prone to illness."

Schurman is also head of the Environmental Polymorphisms Registry (EPR), the DNA bank in North Carolina that provided volunteers
for the study. The EPR studies how SNPs impact disease risk in combination with environmental exposures.

Together with NIEHS colleague and lung disease expert Stavros
Garantziotis, M.D., medical director of the NIEHS Clinical Research
Unit, the two scientists examined four SNPs that are involved in a
biochemical pathway that leads to inflammatory responses in the body.
They explained that SNPs are usually studied one at a time, but they
wanted to learn if different combinations of these SNPs, along with

pollution exposure, could worsen symptoms in a person with an inflammatory disease like asthma.

Schurman and Garantziotis gathered information about the SNPs, severity of asthma symptoms, and residential addresses of 2,704 EPR participants with asthma. Using the SNPs data, they divided the participants into three groups: hyper-responders, or those very sensitive to air pollution and likely to develop inflammation; hypo-responders, or those insensitive to air pollution and less likely to develop inflammation; and those in between. With the help of collaborators at Rice University, the team used the participants' addresses to calculate their distance from a major road. Participants were categorized depending on whether they lived more or less than 275 yards from a major roadway. Data suggest that air pollution levels are elevated closer to major roads.

The researchers found that asthma sufferers who were hyper-responders and lived closer to heavily traveled roads had the worst asthma symptoms, such as difficulty breathing, chest pain, cough, and wheezing, compared to the other groups. In contrast, asthma patients who were hypo-responders and lived further away from busy roads had milder symptoms. Garantziotis concluded the work could greatly enhance the quality of life (QOL) for people with asthma.

"Based on this research, we could propose that hyper-responders, who are exposed to traffic pollution, receive air purification intervention, such as HEPA filters, for their home," Garantziotis said.

NIEHS Clinical Director Janet Hall, M.D., said the results emphasize the importance of gene-environment interactions in the progression of a disease.

"This research is a great example of how we can approach disease prevention on a personal level, and tailor our treatments to suit individual patients," she said. "That way we can be more efficient with our treatments and preventative measures, while at the same time cutting healthcare costs."

Chapter 52

Cancer and Genetics

Chapter Contents

Section 52.1

The Genetics of Cancer

This section includes text excerpted from "The Genetics of Cancer,"
National Cancer Institute (NCI), October 12, 2017.

Genetic Changes and Cancer

Cancer is a genetic disease—that is, cancer is caused by certain changes to genes that control the way our cells function, especially how they grow and divide.

Genes carry the instructions to make proteins, which do much of the work in our cells. Certain gene changes can cause cells to evade normal growth controls and become cancer. For example, some cancer-causing gene changes increase production of a protein that makes cells grow. Others result in the production of a misshapen, and therefore, non-functional, form of a protein that normally repairs cellular damage.

Genetic changes that promote cancer can be inherited from our parents if the changes are present in germ cells, which are the reproductive cells of the body (eggs and sperm). Such changes, called "germline changes," are found in every cell of the offspring.

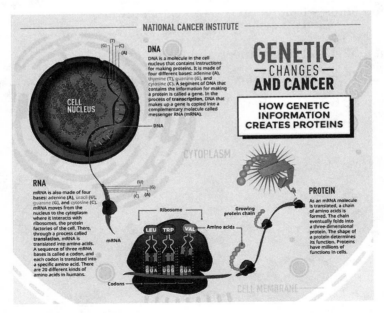

Figure 52.1. *How Genetic Information Creates Proteins*

Cancer-causing genetic changes can also be acquired during one's lifetime, as the result of errors that occur as cells divide or from exposure to carcinogenic substances that damage deoxyribonucleic acid (DNA), such as certain chemicals in tobacco smoke and radiation, such as ultraviolet (UV) rays from the sun. Genetic changes that occur after conception are called "somatic" (or acquired) changes.

There are many different kinds of DNA changes. Some changes affect just one unit of DNA, called a "nucleotide." One nucleotide may be replaced by another, or it may be missing entirely. Other changes involve larger stretches of DNA and may include rearrangements, deletions, or duplications of long stretches of DNA.

Sometimes the changes are not in the actual sequence of DNA. For example, the addition or removal of chemical marks, called "epigenetic modifications," on DNA can influence whether the gene is "expressed"—that is, whether and how much messenger ribonucleic acid (RNA) is produced. (Messenger RNA, in turn, is translated to produce the proteins encoded by the DNA.)

In general, cancer cells have more genetic changes than normal cells. But each person's cancer has a unique combination of genetic alterations. Some of these changes may be the result of cancer, rather than the cause. As the cancer continues to grow, additional changes will occur. Even within the same tumor, cancer cells may have different genetic changes.

Hereditary Cancer Syndromes

Inherited genetic mutations play a major role in about 5 to 10 percent of all cancers. Researchers have associated mutations in specific genes with more than 50 hereditary cancer syndromes, which are disorders that may predispose individuals to develop certain cancers.

Genetic tests for hereditary cancer syndromes can tell whether a person from a family that shows signs of such a syndrome has one of these mutations. These tests can also show whether family members without obvious disease have inherited the same mutation as a family member who carries a cancer-associated mutation.

Many experts recommend that genetic testing for cancer risk be considered when someone has a personal or family history that suggests an inherited cancer risk condition, as long as the test results can be adequately interpreted (that is, they can clearly tell whether a specific genetic change is present or absent) and when the results provide information that will help guide a person's future medical care.

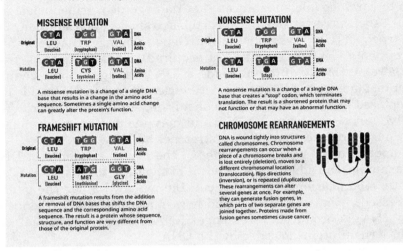

DNA alterations can affect the structure, function, and amount of the corresponding proteins. All of these effects can change a cell's behavior from normal to cancerous. For example, a genetic alteration can intensify or eliminate the protein's function, which could make cells divide uncontrollably. Many different kinds of genetic mutations are found in cancer cells, including missense, nonsense, and frameshift mutations and chromosome rearrangements.

MISSENSE MUTATION

A missense mutation is a change of a single DNA base that results in a change in the amino acid sequence. Sometimes a single amino acid change can greatly alter the protein's function.

NONSENSE MUTATION

A nonsense mutation is a change of a single DNA base that creates a "stop" codon, which terminates translation. The result is a shortened protein that may not function or that may have an abnormal function.

FRAMESHIFT MUTATION

A frameshift mutation results from the addition or removal of DNA bases that shifts the DNA sequence and the corresponding amino acid sequence. The result is a protein whose sequence, structure, and function are very different from those of the original protein.

CHROMOSOME REARRANGEMENTS

DNA is wound tightly into structures called chromosomes. Chromosome rearrangements can occur when a piece of a chromosome breaks and is lost entirely (deletion), moves to a different chromosomal location (translocation), flips directions (inversion), or is repeated (duplication). These rearrangements can alter several genes at once. For example, they can generate fusion genes, in which parts of two separate genes are joined together. Proteins made from fusion genes sometimes cause cancer.

Figure 52.2. *Types of Genetic Mutations in Cancer*

Cancers that are not caused by inherited genetic mutations can sometimes appear to "run in families." For example, a shared environment or lifestyle, such as tobacco use, can cause similar cancers to develop among family members. However, certain patterns in a family—such as the types of cancer that develop, other noncancer conditions that are seen, and the ages at which cancer develops—may suggest the presence of a hereditary cancer syndrome.

Even if a cancer-predisposing mutation is present in a family, not everyone who inherits the mutation will necessarily develop cancer. Several factors influence the outcome in a given person with the mutation, including the pattern of inheritance of the cancer syndrome.

Here are examples of genes that can play a role in hereditary cancer syndromes.

- The most commonly mutated gene in all cancers is *TP53*, which produces a protein that suppresses the growth of tumors. In addition, germline mutations in this gene can cause Li-Fraumeni syndrome (LFS), a rare, inherited disorder that leads to a higher risk of developing certain cancers.

- Inherited mutations in the *BRCA1* and *BRCA2* genes are associated with hereditary breast and ovarian cancer syndrome, which is a disorder marked by an increased lifetime risk of breast and ovarian cancers in women. Several other cancers have been associated with this syndrome, including pancreatic and prostate cancers, as well as male breast cancer.

- Another gene that produces a protein that suppresses the growth of tumors is *PTEN*. Mutations in this gene are associated with Cowden syndrome, an inherited disorder that increases the risk of breast, thyroid, endometrial, and other types of cancer.

Genetic Tests for Hereditary Cancer Syndromes

Genetic tests for mutations that cause hereditary cancer syndromes are usually requested by a person's doctor or other healthcare providers. Genetic counseling can help people consider the risks, benefits, and limitations of genetic testing in their particular situations.

A genetic counselor, doctor, or other healthcare professional trained in genetics can help an individual or family understand their test results and explain the possible implications of test results for other family members.

People considering genetic testing should understand that their results may become known to other people or organizations that have legitimate legal access to their medical records, such as their insurance company or employer, if their employer provides the patient's health insurance as a benefit. Legal protections are in place to prevent genetic discrimination, including the Genetic Information Nondiscrimination Act (GINA) of 2008 and the Privacy Rule of the Health Information Portability and Accountability Act (HIPAA) of 1996.

Identifying Genetic Changes in Cancer

Lab tests called "DNA sequencing tests" can read DNA. By comparing the sequence of DNA in cancer cells with that in normal cells, such as blood or saliva, scientists can identify genetic changes in cancer cells that may be driving the growth of an individual's cancer. This information may help doctors sort out which therapies might work best against a particular tumor.

Tumor DNA sequencing can also reveal the presence of inherited mutations. Indeed, in some cases, the genetic testing of tumors has shown that a patient's cancer could be associated with a hereditary cancer syndrome that the family was not aware of.

As with testing for specific mutations in hereditary cancer syndromes, clinical DNA sequencing has implications that patients need to consider. For example, they may learn incidentally about the presence of inherited mutations that may cause other diseases, in them or in their family members.

Section 52.2

Breast and Ovarian Cancer and Heredity

This section includes text excerpted from "Does Breast or Ovarian Cancer Run in Your Family?" Centers for Disease Control and Prevention (CDC), October 16, 2018.

If you have close relatives with breast or ovarian cancer, you may be at higher risk for developing these diseases. Does your family health history put you at higher risk? Would you benefit from cancer genetic counseling and testing?

Each year, about 242,000 women in the United States are diagnosed with breast cancer and more than 21,000 are diagnosed with ovarian cancer. About 3 percent of breast cancers (about 7,300 women per year) and 10 percent of ovarian cancers (about 2,100 women per year) result from inherited mutations (changes) in the *BRCA1* and *BRCA2* genes that are passed on in families. Inherited mutations in other genes can also cause breast and ovarian cancer, but *BRCA1* and *BRCA2* are the genes most commonly affected. Although breast cancer is much more common in women, men with *BRCA1* or *BRCA2* mutations are more likely to get breast cancer than other men. *BRCA* mutations also increase the likelihood of getting pancreatic cancer and, in men, high-grade prostate cancer. Knowing your family health history can help you find out if you could be more likely to develop breast, ovarian, and other cancers. If so, you can take steps to prevent cancer or to detect it earlier when it may be more treatable.

Does Your Family Health History Put You at Risk?

Collect your family health history of breast, ovarian, and other cancers and share this information with your doctor. You can inherit *BRCA* and other mutations from your mother or your father, so be sure to include information from both sides of your family. Include your close relatives: parents, sisters, brothers, children, grandparents, aunts, uncles, nieces, nephews, and grandchildren. If you have had breast, ovarian, or other cancers, make sure that your family members know about your diagnosis.

Tell your doctor if you have a personal or family health history of any of the following:

- Breast cancer, especially at a younger age (50 years of age or younger)

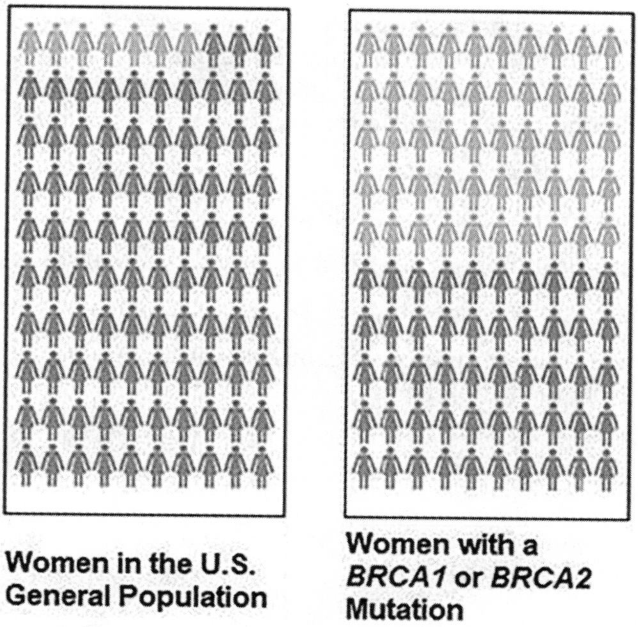

**Women in the U.S.
General Population**

**Women with a
BRCA1 or *BRCA2*
Mutation**

Figure 52.3. *Breast Cancer Risk*

Figure 52.4. *Ovarian Cancer Risk*

- Triple-negative breast cancer at the age of 60 or younger in women (Triple-negative cancers are a type of breast cancer that lack estrogen receptors, progesterone receptors and human epidermal growth factor receptor 2.)

- Cancer in both breasts

- Breast cancer in a male relative

- Ovarian, fallopian tube, or primary peritoneal cancer

- Pancreatic cancer or high-grade prostate cancer

- Breast, ovarian, pancreatic, or high-grade prostate cancer among multiple blood relatives

- Ashkenazi (Eastern European) Jewish ancestry

- A known *BRCA* mutation in the family

Update your family health history on a regular basis and let your doctor know if any new cases of breast or ovarian cancer occur.

Cancer Risks for Women with BRCA1/BRCA2 Mutations

Women who inherit a mutation in the *BRCA1* or *BRCA2* gene have a much higher risk of developing breast and ovarian cancer. But, important steps can be taken to help lower the risk for cancer in these women. It is important to know that not everyone who inherits a *BRCA1* or *BRCA2* mutation will get breast or ovarian cancer and that not all inherited forms of breast or ovarian cancer are due to mutations in *BRCA1* and *BRCA2*.

What Can You Do If You Are Concerned about Your Risk?

If your doctor decides that your family health history makes you more likely to get breast, ovarian, and other cancers, he or she may refer you for genetic counseling. Even if your doctor does not recommend genetic testing and counseling, your family health history of breast cancer can affect when you start mammography screening. If you are a woman with a parent, sibling, or child with breast cancer, you are at higher risk for breast cancer. Based on current recommendations, you should consider talking to your doctor about starting mammography screening in your forties.

The genetic counselor can use your family health history information to determine your possible cancer risks and whether you might consider *BRCA* genetic testing to find out if you have a *BRCA1* or *BRCA2* mutation. Genetic testing is most useful if first performed on someone in your family who has had breast or ovarian cancer. If this relative has a *BRCA1* or *BRCA2* mutation, then her close relatives can be offered testing for that mutation. If she does not have a *BRCA1* or *BRCA2* mutation, then her relatives may not need to be tested. Remember that most breast and ovarian cancer is not caused by *BRCA* mutations so most women do not need *BRCA* genetic testing.

The genetic counselor can discuss the pros and cons of testing and what possible test results could mean for you and your family. It is important to note that genetic testing for *BRCA* mutations will not find all causes of hereditary breast or ovarian cancer. In some cases, the genetic counselor might recommend genetic testing using a panel that looks for mutations in several genes in addition to *BRCA1* and *BRCA2*. *BRCA* genetic counseling and testing is often, but not always, covered without cost sharing by many health plans under the Affordable Care Act (ACA).

Table 52.1. Breast Cancer Risk

Women in the U.S. General Population	Women with a *BRCA1* or *BRCA2* Mutation
About 7 out of 100 women in the U.S. general population will get breast cancer by age 70.	About 50 out of 100 women with a *BRCA1* or *BRCA2* mutation will get breast cancer by age 70.
About 93 out of 100 of these women will NOT get breast cancer by age 70.	About 50 out of 100 of these women will NOT get breast cancer by age 70.

Table 52.2. Ovarian Cancer Risk

Women in the U.S. General Population	Women with a *BRCA1* or *BRCA2* Mutation
About 1 out of 100 women in the U.S. general population will get ovarian cancer by age 70.	About 30 out of 100 women with a *BRCA1* or *BRCA2* mutation will get ovarian cancer by age 70.
About 99 out of 100 of these women will NOT get ovarian cancer by age 70.	About 70 out of 100 of these women will NOT get ovarian cancer by age 70.

Section 52.3

Colorectal (Colon) Cancer and Heredity

This section includes text excerpted from "Have You or a Family
Member Had Colorectal (Colon) Cancer?" Centers for Disease
Control and Prevention (CDC), March 19, 2018.

Have You or a Family Member Had Colorectal (Colon) Cancer?

Having a family health history of colorectal (colon) cancer can
make you more likely to get colorectal cancer yourself. If you have
close family members with colorectal cancer, collect your family health
history of colorectal and other cancers, and share this information
with your doctor. Be sure to have any screening tests that your doctor
recommends. If you have had colorectal cancer, make sure that your
family members know about your diagnosis, especially if you have
Lynch syndrome.

Why Is It Important to Know Your Family Health History?

If you have a family health history of colorectal cancer, your doctor
may consider your family health history when deciding which colorectal cancer screening might be right for you. For example, if you have a
close family member who had colorectal cancer at a young age or have
multiple close family members with colorectal cancer, your doctor may
recommend the following:

- Start screening at a younger age

- Get screened more frequently

- Use colonoscopy only instead of other tests

- In some cases, have genetic counseling

The genetic counselor may recommend genetic testing based on your
family health history. When collecting your family health history, be
sure to include your close relatives: parents, brothers, sisters, children,
grandparents, aunts, uncles, nieces, and nephews. List any cancers
that each relative had and at what age he or she was diagnosed. For
relatives who have died, list age and cause of death.

What Is Lynch Syndrome and Why Is It Important to Know If You Have It?

In some cases, colorectal cancer is caused by an inherited genetic condition called "Lynch syndrome," also known as "hereditary nonpolyposis colorectal cancer (HNPCC)." About three percent (1 in 30) of colorectal cancer cases are due to Lynch syndrome. People with Lynch syndrome are much more likely to develop colorectal cancer, especially at a younger age (before the age of 50), and women with Lynch syndrome are much more likely to get endometrial (uterine) cancer. People with Lynch syndrome also have an increased chance of getting other cancers, including ovarian, stomach, liver, kidney, brain, and skin cancer. If you or your family members are found to have Lynch syndrome, your doctor can help you take steps to reduce your risk of getting cancer in the future or to find it early if you get it.

Lynch syndrome is hereditary, meaning that it is caused by inherited genetic changes or mutations, that can be passed from parents to children. If you have Lynch syndrome, your parents, children, sisters, and brothers have a 50 percent (1 in 2) chance of having this condition. Your other close relatives are also at increased risk of having Lynch syndrome.

After surgery to remove colorectal cancer, tumor-tissue samples are often screened to see if the tumor could have been caused by Lynch syndrome. In some cases, additional testing is needed to know for sure if the tumor was caused by Lynch syndrome. If you have had colorectal cancer in the last few years, your tumor may have been checked for Lynch syndrome. In some cases, endometrial (uterine) tumors are checked. Genetic counseling and testing for Lynch syndrome also might be recommended for you if:

- You were diagnosed with colorectal cancer in the past

- You have been diagnosed with endometrial cancer (especially before the age of 50)

- You have several family members with colorectal or other cancers associated with Lynch syndrome

- You have a family member with Lynch syndrome

If you have been diagnosed with Lynch syndrome, talk to your doctor about your increased chances of getting the other cancers caused by Lynch syndrome. Your doctor might recommend additional regular screening to check for these cancers or other actions you can take to prevent cancer. Be sure to let your family members know if you have

Lynch syndrome. Once a mutation that causes Lynch syndrome is found in one person in a family, other family members can then be tested for that mutation to find out if they have Lynch syndrome.

If you are concerned about your personal or family health history of colorectal cancer, talk to your healthcare provider.

Section 52.4

Lung Cancer and Genetics

This section includes text excerpted from "Lung Cancer," Genetics Home Reference (GHR), National Institutes of Health (NIH), December 2017.

Lung cancer is a disease in which certain cells in the lungs become abnormal and multiply uncontrollably to form a tumor. Lung cancer may not cause signs or symptoms in its early stages. Some people with lung cancer have chest pain, frequent coughing, blood in the mucus, breathing problems, trouble swallowing or speaking, loss of appetite and weight loss, fatigue, or swelling in the face or neck. Additional symptoms can develop if the cancer spreads (metastasizes) into other tissues. Lung cancer occurs most often in adults in their sixties or seventies. Most people who develop lung cancer have a history of long-term tobacco smoking; however, the condition can occur in people who have never smoked.

Lung cancer is generally divided into two types, small cell lung cancer, and nonsmall cell lung cancer, based on the size of the affected cells when viewed under a microscope. Nonsmall cell lung cancer accounts for 85 percent of lung cancer, while small cell lung cancer accounts for the remaining 15 percent.

Small cell lung cancer grows quickly and in more than half of cases, the cancer has spread beyond the lung by the time the condition is diagnosed. Small cell lung cancer often metastasizes, most commonly to the liver, brain, bones, and adrenal glands (small hormone-producing glands located on top of each kidney). After diagnosis, most people with small cell lung cancer survive for about one year; less than seven percent survive five years.

Nonsmall cell lung cancer is divided into three main subtypes: adenocarcinoma, squamous cell carcinoma, and large cell lung carcinoma. Adenocarcinoma arises from the cells that line the small air sacs (alveoli) located throughout the lungs. Squamous cell carcinoma arises from squamous cells that line the passages leading from the windpipe (trachea) to the lungs (bronchi). Large cell carcinoma arises from epithelial cells that line the lungs. Large cell carcinoma encompasses nonsmall cell lung cancers that do not appear to be adenocarcinomas or squamous cell carcinomas. The five-year survival rate for people with nonsmall cell lung cancer is usually between 11 and 17 percent; it can be lower or higher depending on the subtype and stage of the cancer.

Frequency

In the United States, lung cancer is the second most commonly diagnosed cancer, after breast cancer, accounting for about one-quarter of all cancer diagnoses. It is estimated that more than 222,500 people develop lung cancer each year. Approximately 6.6 percent of individuals will develop lung cancer during their lifetime. An estimated 72 to 80 percent of lung cancer cases occur in tobacco smokers. Lung cancer is the leading cause of cancer deaths, accounting for an estimated 27 percent of all cancer deaths in the United States.

Causes

Cancers occur when genetic mutations build up in critical genes, specifically those that control cell growth and division (proliferation) or the repair of damaged deoxyribonucleic acid (DNA). These changes allow cells to grow and divide uncontrollably to form a tumor. In nearly all cases of lung cancer, these genetic changes are acquired during a person's lifetime and are present only in certain cells in the lung. These changes, which are called "somatic mutations," are not inherited. Somatic mutations in many different genes have been found in lung cancer cells. In rare cases, the genetic change is inherited and is present in all the body's cells (germline mutations).

Somatic mutations in the *TP53*, *EGFR*, and *KRAS* genes are common in lung cancers. The *TP53* gene provides instructions for making a protein, called "p53," that is located in the nucleus of cells throughout the body, where it attaches (binds) directly to DNA. The protein regulates cell growth and division by monitoring DNA damage. When DNA becomes damaged, p53 helps determine whether the DNA will be repaired or the cell will self-destruct (undergo apoptosis). The *EGFR* and *KRAS* genes each provide instructions for making a protein that is embedded within the cell membrane. When these proteins are turned on (activated) by binding to other molecules, signaling pathways are triggered within cells that promote cell proliferation.

TP53 gene mutations result in the production of an altered p53 protein that cannot bind to DNA. The altered protein cannot regulate cell proliferation effectively and allows DNA damage to accumulate in cells. Such cells may continue to divide in an uncontrolled way, leading to tumor growth. Mutations in the *EGFR* or *KRAS* gene lead to the production of a protein that is constantly turned on (constitutively activated). As a result, cells constantly receive signals to proliferate, leading to tumor formation. When these genetic changes occur in cells in the lungs, lung cancer develops.

Mutations in many other genes have been found to recur in lung cancer cases. Most of these genes are involved in the regulation of gene activity (expression), cell proliferation, the process by which cells mature to carry out specific functions (differentiation), and apoptosis.

Researchers have identified many lifestyle and environmental factors that expose individuals to cancer-causing compounds (carcinogens) and increase the rate at which somatic mutations occur, contributing to a person's risk of developing lung cancer. The greatest risk factor is long-term tobacco smoking, which increases a person's risk of developing lung cancer 25-fold. Other risk factors include exposure to air pollution, radon, asbestos, certain metals, and chemicals, or secondhand smoke; long-term use of hormone replacement therapy for menopause; and a history of lung diseases, such as tuberculosis, emphysema, or chronic bronchitis. A history of lung cancer in closely related family members is also an important risk factor; however, because relatives with lung cancer are frequent smokers, it is unclear whether the increased risk is the result of genetic factors or exposure to secondhand smoke.

Section 52.5

Skin Cancer and Heredity

This section includes text excerpted from "Learning about Skin Cancer," National Human Genome Research Institute (NHGRI), October 30, 2012. Reviewed March 2019.

Skin cancer is the most common type of cancer in the United States. An estimated 40 to 50 percent of Americans who live to the age of 65 will have skin cancer at least once. The most common skin cancer is basal cell carcinoma, which accounts for more than 90 percent of all skin cancers in the United States.

The most virulent form of skin cancer is melanoma. In some parts of the world, especially in Western countries, the number of people who develop melanoma is increasing faster than any other cancer. In the United States, for example, the number of new cases of melanoma has more than doubled in the past 20 years.

What Are the Most Common Forms of Skin Cancer?

Three types of skin cancer are the most common:

- **Basal cell carcinoma** is a slow-growing cancer that seldom spreads to other parts of the body. Basal cells, which are round, form the layer just underneath the epidermis, or outer layer of the skin.

- **Squamous cell carcinoma** spreads more often than basal cell carcinoma but still is considered rare. Squamous cells, which are flat, make up most of the epidermis.

- **Melanoma** is the most serious type of skin cancer. It occurs when melanocytes, the pigment cells in the lower part of the epidermis, become malignant, meaning that they start dividing uncontrollably. If melanoma spreads to the lymph nodes it may also reach other parts of the body, such as the liver, lungs, or brain. In such cases, the disease is called "metastatic melanoma."

What Are the Symptoms of Skin Cancer?

The most commonly noticed symptom of skin cancer is a change on the skin, especially a new growth or a sore that doesn't heal. Both basal and squamous cell cancers are found mainly on areas of the skin that are exposed to the sun—the head, face, neck, hands, and arms. However, skin cancer can occur anywhere.

For melanoma, the first sign often is a change in the size, shape, color or feel of an existing mole. Melanomas can vary greatly in the way they look, but generally, show one or more of the "ABCD" features:

- Their shape may be **A**symmetrical.

- Their **B**orders may be ragged or otherwise irregular.

- Their **C**olor may be uneven, with shades of black and brown.

- Their **D**iameter may change in size.

What Do We Know about the Causes and Heredity of Skin Cancer?

Ultraviolet (UV) radiation from the sun is the main cause of skin cancer, although artificial sources of UV radiation, such as sunlamps and tanning booths, also play a role. UV radiation can damage the deoxyribonucleic acid (DNA), or genetic information, in skin cells, creating "misspellings" in their genetic code and, as a result, alter the function of those cells.

Cancers generally are caused by a combination of environmental and genetic factors. With skin cancer, the environment plays a greater role, but individuals can be born with a genetic disposition toward or vulnerability to getting cancer. The risk is greatest for people who have light-colored skin that freckles easily—often those who also have red or blond hair and blue or light-colored eyes—although anyone can get skin cancer.

Skin cancer is related to lifetime exposure to UV radiation; therefore, most skin cancers appear after the age of 50. However, the sun's damaging effects begin at an early age. People who live in areas that get high levels of UV radiation from the sun are more likely to get skin cancer. For example, the highest rates of skin cancer are found in South Africa and Australia, areas that receive high amounts of UV radiation.

About 10 percent of all patients with melanoma have family members who also have had the disease. Research suggests that a mutation in the *CDKN2* gene on chromosome 9 plays a role in this form of melanoma. Studies have also implicated genes on chromosomes 1 and 12 in cases of familial melanoma.

Can I Do Anything to Prevent or Test for Skin Cancer?

When it comes to skin cancer, prevention is your best line of defense. Protection should start early in childhood and continue throughout life. Suggested protections include:

- Whenever possible, avoid exposure to the midday sun.

- Wear protective clothing—for example, long sleeves and broad-rimmed hats.

- Use sunscreen lotions with a sun protection factor (SPF) of at least 15.

- If a family member has had melanoma, have your doctor check for early warning signs regularly.

How Is Skin Cancer Treated?

Melanoma can be cured if it is diagnosed and treated when the tumor has not deeply invaded the skin. However, if a melanoma is not removed in its early stages, cancer cells may grow downward from the skin surface. When a melanoma becomes thick and deep, the disease often spreads to other parts of the body and is difficult to control.

Surgery is the standard treatment for melanoma, as well as other skin cancers. However, if the cancer has spread to other parts of the body, doctors may use other treatments, such as chemotherapy, immunotherapy, radiation therapy, or a combination of these methods.

Section 52.6

Genetic Risks for Prostate Cancer

This section includes text excerpted from "Genetics of Prostate Cancer (PDQ®)—Health Professional Version," National Cancer Institute (NCI), December 18, 2018.

The risk of developing and dying from prostate cancer is dramatically higher among Blacks, is of intermediate levels among Whites, and is lowest among Native Japanese. Conflicting data have been published regarding the etiology of these outcomes, but some evidence is available that access to healthcare may play a role in disease outcomes.

Family History of Prostate Cancer

Prostate cancer is highly heritable; the inherited risk of prostate cancer has been estimated to be as high as 60 percent. As with breast and colon cancer, familial clustering of prostate cancer has been reported frequently. From 5 to 10 percent of prostate cancer cases are believed to be primarily caused by high-risk inherited genetic factors or prostate cancer susceptibility genes. Results from several large case-control studies and cohort studies representing various populations suggest that family history is a major risk factor in prostate cancer. A family history of a brother or father with prostate cancer increases the risk of prostate cancer, and the risk is inversely related to the age of the affected relative. However, at least some familial aggregation is due to increased prostate cancer screening in families thought to be at high risk.

Although some of the prostate cancer studies examining risks associated with family history have used hospital-based series, several studies described population-based series. The latter are thought to provide information that is more generalizable. A meta-analysis of 33 epidemiologic case-control and cohort-based studies has provided more detailed information regarding risk ratios related to family history of prostate cancer. Risk appeared to be greater for men with affected brothers than for men with affected fathers in this meta-analysis. Although the reason for this difference in risk is unknown, possible hypotheses have included X-linked or recessive inheritance. In addition, risk increased with increasing numbers of affected close relatives. Risk also increased when a first-degree relative (FDR) was diagnosed with prostate cancer before 65 years of age.

Among the many data sources included in this meta-analysis, those from the Swedish population-based Family-Cancer Database warrant special comment. These data were derived from a resource that contained more than 11.8 million individuals, among whom there were 26,651 men with medically verified prostate cancer, of which 5,623 were familial cases. The size of this data set, with its nearly complete ascertainment of the entire Swedish population and objective verification of cancer diagnoses, should yield risk estimates that are both accurate and free of bias. When the familial age-specific hazard ratios (HRs) for prostate cancer diagnosis and mortality were computed, as expected, the HR for prostate cancer diagnosis increased with more family history. Specifically, HRs for prostate cancer were 2.12 (95% CI, 2.05–2.20) with an affected father only, 2.96 (95% CI, 2.80–3.13) with an affected brother only, and 8.51 (95% CI, 6.13–11.80) with a father and two brothers affected. The highest HR, 17.74 (95% CI, 12.26–25.67), was seen in men with 3 brothers diagnosed with prostate cancer. The HRs were even higher when the affected relative was diagnosed with prostate cancer before 55 years of age.

A separate analysis of this Swedish database reported that the cumulative (absolute) risks of prostate cancer among men in families with 2 or more affected cases were 5 percent by age 60 years, 15 percent by age 70 years, and 30 percent by age 80 years, compared with 0.45 percent, 3 percent, and 10 percent, respectively, by the same ages in the general population. The risks were even higher when the affected father was diagnosed before age 70 years. The corresponding familial population attributable fractions (PAFs) were 8.9 percent, 1.8 percent, and 1.0 percent for the same 3 age groups, respectively, yielding a total PAF of 11.6 percent (i.e., approximately 11.6 percent of all prostate cancers in Sweden can be accounted for on the basis of familial history of the disease).

The risk of prostate cancer may also increase in men who have a family history of breast cancer. Approximately 9.6 percent of the Iowa cohort had a family history of breast and/or ovarian cancer in a mother or sister at baseline, and this was positively associated with prostate cancer risk (age-adjusted RR, 1.7; 95% CI, 1.0–3.0; multivariate RR, 1.7; 95% CI, 0.9–3.2). Men with a family history of both prostate and breast/ovarian cancer were also at increased risk of prostate cancer (RR, 5.8; 95% CI, 2.4–14.0). Analysis of data from the Women's Health Initiative also showed that a family history of prostate cancer was associated with an increase in the risk of postmenopausal breast cancer (adjusted HR, 1.14; 95% CI, 1.02–1.26). Further analyses showed that breast cancer risk was associated with a family history of both breast and prostate cancers; the risk was higher in Black women than in White women. Other studies, however, did not find an association between family history of female breast cancer and risk of prostate cancer. A family history of prostate cancer also increases the risk of breast cancer among female relatives. The association between prostate cancer and breast cancer in the same family may be explained, in part, by the increased risk of prostate cancer among men with *BRCA1/BRCA2* pathogenic variants in the setting of hereditary breast/ovarian cancer or early-onset prostate cancer.

Prostate cancer clusters with particular intensity in some families. Highly penetrant genetic variants are thought to be associated with prostate cancer risk in these families. Members of such families may benefit from genetic counseling. Emerging recommendations and guidelines for genetic counseling referrals are based on prostate cancer age at diagnosis and specific family cancer history patterns. Individuals meeting the following criteria may warrant referral for genetic consultation:

- Multiple affected FDRs with prostate cancer

- Early-onset prostate cancer (less than 55 years of age)

- Metastatic prostate cancer

- Prostate cancer with a family history of other cancers (e.g., breast, ovarian, pancreatic)

Family history has been shown to be a risk factor for men of different races and ethnicities. In a population-based case-control study of prostate cancer among African Americans, Whites, and Asian Americans in the United States (Los Angeles, San Francisco, and Hawaii) and Canada (Vancouver and Toronto), 5 percent of controls and 13 percent of all cases reported a father, brother, or son with prostate cancer. These prevalence estimates were somewhat lower among Asian Americans than among African Americans or Whites. A positive family history was associated with a twofold to threefold increase in RR in each of the three ethnic groups. The overall odds ratio associated with a family history of prostate cancer was 2.5 (95% CI, 1.9–3.3) with adjustment for age and ethnicity.

There is little evidence that family history alone is associated with inferior clinical outcomes. In a cohort of 7,690 men in Germany who were undergoing radical prostatectomy for localized prostate cancer, family history had no bearing on prostate cancer-specific survival.

Chapter 53

Crohn Disease and Genetics

What Is Crohn Disease?

Crohn disease (CD) is a type of inflammatory bowel disease (IBD), and is the general name for conditions that cause inflammation in the gastrointestinal (GI) tract. Common signs and symptoms include abdominal pain and cramping, diarrhea, and weight loss. Other general symptoms include feeling tired, nausea, and loss of appetite, fever, and anemia. Complications of Crohn disease may include intestinal blockage, fistulas, anal fissures, ulcers, malnutrition, and inflammation in other areas of the body. Crohn disease can occur in people of all age groups but is most often diagnosed in young adults. The exact cause is unknown but is thought to be due from a combination of certain genetic variations, changes in the immune system, and the presence of bacteria in the digestive tract. Many of the major genes related to Crohn disease, including *NOD2, ATG16L1, IL23R,* and *IRGM,* are involved in immune system function. The disease is not inherited, but it appears to run in some families because in about 15 percent of the cases the disease is present in more than 1 relative.

Treatment is aimed at relieving symptoms and reducing inflammation and may include diet and medication, but some people require surgery. Surgery often involves removal of the diseased segment of bowel (resection), the two ends of healthy bowel are then joined together

This chapter includes text excerpted from "Crohn's Disease," Genetic and Rare Diseases Information Center (GARD), National Center for Advancing Translational Sciences (NCATS), May 11, 2018.

571

(anastomosis). About 30 percent of people who have surgery for Crohn disease symptoms may come back within 3 years, and up to 60 percent will have a recurrence within 10 years.

How Many People in the United States Have Crohn Disease?

Crohn disease may affect as many as 700,000 people in the United States. Men and women are affected in equal numbers. While the condition can occur at any age, it is more common among adolescents and young adults between the ages of 15 and 35.

What Are the Signs and Symptoms of Crohn Disease?

Crohn disease causes inflammation of the digestive or gastrointestinal tract. It usually occurs in the lower part of the small intestine, called the "ileum," but it can affect any part of the digestive tract, from the mouth to the anus. The inflammation extends deep into the lining of the affected organ, which can cause abdominal pain and diarrhea. Affected individuals may also have loss of appetite, weight loss, and fever.

About one-third of individuals with Crohn disease have symptoms outside of the intestines, which may include arthritis, uveitis (inflammation of the covering of the eye), skin lesions, and sacroiliitis (inflammation of the large joints of the tail bone and pelvis).

Symptoms of Crohn disease may range from mild to severe. Most people will go through periods in which the disease flares up and causes symptoms, alternating with periods when symptoms disappear or decrease. People with Crohn disease who smoke tend to have more severe symptoms and more complications. In general, people with Crohn disease lead active and productive lives.

What Causes Crohn Disease

The exact cause of Crohn disease is not known, but it appears to be a multifactorial condition. This means that both genetic and environmental factors likely interact to predispose an individual to be affected. Studies suggest that Crohn disease may result from a combination of certain genetic variations, changes in the immune system, and the presence of bacteria in the digestive tract.

Recent studies have found that variations in specific genes, including the *ATG16L1, IL23R, IRGM,* and *NOD2* genes, influence the risk of developing Crohn disease. These genes provide instructions for making proteins that are involved in immune system function. Variations in any of these genes may disrupt the ability of intestinal cells to respond to bacteria, leading to chronic inflammation and thus the signs and symptoms of the condition. There may also be genetic variations in regions of chromosome 5 and chromosome 10 that contribute to an increased risk to develop Crohn disease.

Is Crohn Disease Inherited?

Crohn disease, like most other autoimmune diseases, is thought to be a multifactorial condition. This means it is likely associated with the effects of multiple genes, in combination with lifestyle and environmental factors. Once an autoimmune disease is present in a family, other relatives may be at risk to develop the same autoimmune disease or a different autoimmune disease. However, if an autoimmune disease, such as Crohn disease, occurs in a family, it does not necessarily mean that relatives will develop an autoimmune disease. Having an affected family member means that there may be a genetic predisposition in the family that could increase an individual's chance of developing an autoimmune disease. Thus, having an affected family member is considered a risk factor for Crohn disease.

What Genes Are Currently Known to Be Associated with Crohn Disease?

More than 30 distinct genes, or presumed locations of genes (loci), have been suggested to be related to CD, including those related to susceptibility, the age of onset, disease location, diagnosis, and prognosis. So far, the strongest associations with CD have been found with the *NOD2* (also called "*CARD15*"), *IL23R,* and *ATG16L1* genes.

The search for specific susceptibility genes (genes in which variations may increase a person's risk) has been difficult due to complex genetics, including factors, such as the lack of simple inheritance patterns and involvement of several genes. Studies have already led to the identification of a number of susceptibility genes: *NOD2, DLG5, OCTN1* (also called "*SLC22A4*"), *OCTN2* (*SLC22A5*), *NOD1, IL23R, PTGER4, ATG16L1,* and *IRGM.* The *NOD2* gene is currently the most replicated and understood.

With respect to age of CD onset and, more specifically, to childhood or early-onset Crohn disease, the following genes/loci have been implicated: *TNFRSF6B, CXCL9, IL23R, NOD2, ATG16L1 rs2241880, CNR1, IL-10,* and *MDR1* (also called "*ABCB1*").

In terms of genes related to CD location, studies have suggested that upper-GI Crohn disease has been related to *NOD2* and *MIF* variants. Ileal CD has been related to the *IL-10, CRP, NOD2, ZNF365,* and *STAT3* genes. Genes/loci associated with ileocolonic CD are *3p21, ATG16L1,* and *TCF-4 (TCF7L2).*

Variations in a number of genes have also been found to be associated with other aspects of CD, such as disease behavior, risk for cancer, and the presence of extraintestinal manifestations.

How Is Crohn Disease Diagnosed?

A variety of tests are used to diagnose and monitor Crohn disease. A combination of tests is often needed because some symptoms of the condition are similar to other intestinal disorders, such as irritable bowel syndrome (IBS) and to another type of inflammatory bowel disease (IBD) called "ulcerative colitis" (UC). Tests used to narrow down the diagnosis may include blood tests, tissue tests, ultrasound, X-rays, computed tomography (CT) scan, and/or endoscopy. A proper diagnosis also involves identifying the extent and severity of disease, as well as any related complications.

Chapter 54

Mental Illness and Genetics

Chapter Contents

Section 54.1

Looking at My Genes: What Can They Tell Me about My Mental Health?

This section includes text excerpted from "Looking at My Genes:
What Can They Tell Me about My Mental Health?" National
Institute of Mental Health (NIMH), 2017.

Mental disorders are health conditions that affect how a person thinks, feels, and acts. These disorders can impact a person's life in significant ways, including how she or he copes with life, earns a living, and relates to others.

"Why did this happen?" That is a common question that patients and their families have following a psychotic episode, suicide attempt, or the diagnosis of any serious mental disorder.

Research conducted and funded by the National Institute of Mental Health (NIMH) has found that many mental disorders are caused by a combination of biological, environmental, psychological, and genetic factors. In fact, a growing body of research has found that certain genes and gene variations are associated with mental disorders. So what is the best way to look at your genes and determine your own personal risk?

Your Family Health History

Your family history is one of your best clues about your risk of developing mental disorders and many other common illnesses. Certain mental illnesses tend to run in families, and having a close relative with a mental disorder could mean you are at a higher risk.

If a family member has a mental disorder, it does not necessarily mean you will develop one. Many other factors also play a role. But knowing your family mental-health history can help you determine whether you are at a higher risk for certain disorders, help your doctor recommend actions for reducing your risk, and enable both you and your doctor to look for early warning signs.

To gain a better understanding of your family health history, it may help to:

Talk to Your Blood Relatives

The first step in creating a family health history is to talk to your blood relatives. The most helpful information comes from "first-degree" relatives—parents, brothers, and sisters, and children. Information from "second-degree" relatives, such as nieces, nephews, half-brothers, half-sisters, grandparents, aunts, and uncles, can also be helpful.

Do not worry if you cannot get complete information on every relative. Some people may not want to talk. Others may be unable to remember information accurately. That is okay. Whatever information you can collect will be helpful.

Keep a Record

Free print and online tools can help you create a family health history. One tool is "My Family Health Portrait" from the United States Surgeon General. It helps organize your family health history information. The following instructions describe how to use the print and online versions of this tool.

You can download and print out "My Family Health Portrait" and use it to record information about your family's health. Once you fill in the information, you can keep it for your records, share the completed form with your doctor or healthcare provider, or share it with family members.

As a family grows or family members are diagnosed with health conditions, new or updated information can be added. It may take a little time and effort, but this lasting legacy can improve the health of your family for generations to come.

Talk to a Mental-Health Professional

If you have mental illness in your family, you may want to consult with a mental-health professional who can help you understand risk factors and preventive factors. The NIMH Help for Mental Illness webpage provides a number of resources for finding immediate help, locating a healthcare provider or treatment, and participating in clinical trials.

Your Genes

Genes are segments of deoxyribonucleic acid (DNA) found in every cell and are passed down from parents to children at conception. Some diseases, such as sickle cell anemia (SCA) or cystic fibrosis (CF), are caused by genetic mutation(s), or a permanent change in one or more specific genes.

In other diseases, including many brain disorders, gene variants play a role in increasing or decreasing a person's risk of developing a disease or condition. Research is advancing the understanding of the role of genetics in mental health. Although there are common genetic variants associated with rare disorders, such as Fragile X or Rett syndrome (RTT), no gene variants can predict with certainty that a person will develop a mental disorder. In most cases, even the genetic variant with the most supporting research raise a person's risk by only very small amounts. Knowing that you have one of these gene variants would not tell you nearly as much about your risk as your family history can.

What about Genetic Testing or Genome Scans? Can They Help Predict My Risk of Developing a Mental Disorder?

The short answer to this question is no—not yet.

One day, genetic research may make it possible to provide a more complete picture of a person's risk of getting a particular mental disorder or to diagnose it, based on her or his genes. For example, recent NIMH-funded research has identified five major mental disorders— autism spectrum disorders (ASD), attention deficit hyperactivity disorder (ADHD), bipolar disease, schizophrenia, and major depression— that can share common genetic components. Studies have also found that specific gene variants are associated with a higher risk of certain disorders, such as ASD or schizophrenia.

Although studies have begun to identify the genetic markers associated with certain mental disorders and may eventually lead to better screening and more personalized treatment, it is still too early to use genetic tests or genome scans to accurately diagnose or treat mental illness.

Genetic Testing versus Genome Scans
Traditional Genetic Testing

Doctors order traditional genetic testing for people they think are at high risk of one of the rare diseases for which specific genes are known to be the cause. The results enable patients and their doctors to make informed healthcare decisions together. There are many different types of genetic tests. Genetic tests can help to:

- Identify gene changes that may increase the risk of developing a disease

- Diagnose disease
- Identify gene changes that are implicated in an already-diagnosed disease
- Determine the severity of a disease
- Guide doctors in deciding on the best medicine or treatment to use for certain individuals
- Screen newborn babies for certain treatable conditions

Genetic testing cannot accurately predict your risk of developing a mental-health disorder. If a disease runs in your family, your health-care professional can tell you if it is the kind of illness that can be detected through genetic testing. Your healthcare professional can help you make decisions about whether to be tested and can help you understand test results and their implications.

Genome Scans

Genome scans are different from traditional genetic testing. For a fee, anyone can mail a saliva sample to companies that sell the scan—without a prescription or a healthcare provider's advice. Advertisements say that the company can provide information about a person's risks of developing specific diseases, based on gene variations.

But here is one thing genome scans have in common with genetic testing: it is too early for genome scans to give people a complete picture of their risk of mental illnesses or to be used to diagnose a disorder. Although research is underway, scientists do not yet know all of the gene variations that contribute to mental illnesses, and those that are known, so far, raise the risk by very small amounts.

Section 54.2

Genetic Links in Bipolar Disorder

This section includes text excerpted from "Bipolar
Disorder," Genetics Home Reference (GHR), National
Institutes of Health (NIH), February 5, 2019.

Bipolar disorder is a mental-health condition that causes extreme
shifts in mood, energy, and behavior. This disorder most often appears
in late adolescence or early adulthood, although symptoms can begin
at any time of life.

People with bipolar disorder experience both dramatic "highs,"
called "manic episodes," and "lows," called "depressive episodes." These
episodes can last from hours to weeks, and many people have no symptoms between episodes. Manic episodes are characterized by increased
energy and activity, irritability, restlessness, an inability to sleep, and
reckless behavior. Depressive episodes are marked by low energy and
activity, a feeling of hopelessness, and an inability to perform everyday tasks. People with bipolar disorder often have repeated thoughts
of death and suicide, and they have a much greater risk of dying by
suicide than the general population.

Manic and depressive episodes can include psychotic symptoms,
such as false perceptions (hallucinations) or strongly held false beliefs
(delusions). Mixed episodes, which have features of manic and depressive episodes at the same time, also occur in some affected individuals.

Bipolar disorder often occurs with other mental-health conditions,
including anxiety disorders (such as panic attacks), behavioral disorders (such as attention deficit hyperactivity disorder (ADHD)), and
substance abuse.

Frequency

Bipolar disorder is a common form of mental illness. At some point
during their lifetime, 2.4 percent of people worldwide and 4.4 percent
of people in the United States are diagnosed with this condition.

Causes

Very little is known for certain about the genetics of bipolar disorder. Studies suggest that variations in many genes, each with a small
effect, may combine to increase the risk of developing the condition.
However, most of these genetic variations have been identified in single

studies, and subsequent research has not verified them. It is unclear what contribution each of these changes makes to disease risk. Some of the genetic changes associated with bipolar disorder have also been found in people with other common mental-health disorders, such as schizophrenia. Understanding the genetics of bipolar disorder and other forms of mental illness is an active area of research.

Studies suggest that nongenetic (environmental) factors also contribute to a person's risk of developing bipolar disorder. Stressful events in a person's life, such as a death in the family, can trigger disease symptoms. Substance abuse and traumatic head injuries have also been associated with bipolar disorder. It seems likely that environmental conditions interact with genetic factors to determine the overall risk of developing this disease.

Section 54.3

Genetic Links in Obsessive-Compulsive Disorder

This section includes text excerpted from "Obsessive-Compulsive Disorder," Genetics Home Reference (GHR), National Institutes of Health (NIH), February 5, 2019.

Obsessive-compulsive disorder (OCD) is a mental-health condition characterized by features called "obsessions" and "compulsions." Obsessions are intrusive thoughts, mental images, or urges to perform specific actions. While the particular obsessions vary widely, they often include fear of illness or contamination; a desire for symmetry or getting things "just right;" or intrusive thoughts involving religion, sex, or aggression. Compulsions consist of the repetitive performance of certain actions, such as checking or verifying, washing, counting, arranging, acting out specific routines, or seeking assurance. These behaviors are performed to relieve anxiety, rather than to seek pleasure as in other compulsive behaviors like gambling, eating, or sex.

While almost everyone experiences obsessive feelings and compulsive behaviors occasionally or in particular contexts, in OCD they take up more than an hour a day and cause problems with work, school, or social life. People with OCD generally experience anxiety and other distress around their need to accommodate their obsessions or compulsions.

About half the time, OCD becomes evident in childhood or adolescence, and most other cases appear in early adulthood. It is unusual for OCD to start after 40 years of age. It tends to appear earlier in males, but by adulthood it is slightly more common in females. Affected individuals can experience periods when their symptoms increase or decrease in severity, but the condition usually does not go away completely.

Some people with OCD have additional mental-health disorders, such as generalized anxiety, depression, phobias, panic disorders, or schizophrenia. OCD can also occur in people with other neurological conditions, such as Tourette syndrome (TS) and similar disorders, traumatic brain injury (TBI), stroke, or dementia.

Frequency

OCD is a common condition, occurring in about two percent of the population.

Causes

The cause of OCD is unknown. Researchers are investigating whether the condition might involve changes in the brain's response to chemical messengers (neurotransmitters), such as serotonin or dopamine. Problems with regulating the activity and interaction between various parts of the brain are also thought to contribute to the condition.

Variations in certain genes that provide instructions for proteins that react to or transport serotonin have been associated with an increased risk of OCD. Variations in other genes involved in communication in the brain may also be associated with the condition. However, not all people with OCD have an associated variation, and not all people with the variations will develop OCD.

In addition to genetic factors, researchers are studying environmental factors that might contribute to OCD, including complications during pregnancy or childbirth and stressful life events. However, none have been conclusively associated with this disorder. It seems likely that environmental conditions interact with genetic factors to determine the overall risk of developing OCD.

Section 54.4

Genetic Links in Schizophrenia

This section includes text excerpted from "Schizophrenia,"
Genetics Home Reference (GHR), National Institutes
of Health (NIH), February 5, 2019.

Schizophrenia is a brain disorder classified as a psychosis, which means that it affects a person's thinking, sense of self, and perceptions. The disorder typically becomes evident during late adolescence or early adulthood.

Signs and symptoms of schizophrenia include false perceptions called "hallucinations." Auditory hallucinations of voices are the most common hallucinations in schizophrenia, but affected individuals can also experience hallucinations of visions, smells, or touch (tactile) sensations. Strongly held false beliefs (delusions) are also characteristic of schizophrenia. For example, affected individuals may be certain that they are a particular historical figure or that they are being plotted against or controlled by others.

People with schizophrenia often have decreased ability to function at school, at work, and in social settings. Disordered thinking and concentration, inappropriate emotional responses, erratic speech and behavior, and difficulty with personal hygiene and everyday tasks can also occur. People with schizophrenia may have diminished facial expression and animation (flat affect), and in some cases become unresponsive (catatonic). Substance abuse and suicidal thoughts and actions are common in people with schizophrenia.

Certain movement problems, such as tremors, facial tics, rigidity, and unusually slow movement (bradykinesia) or an inability to move (akinesia) are common in people with schizophrenia. In most cases, these are side effects of medicines prescribed to help control the disorder. However, some affected individuals exhibit movement abnormalities before beginning treatment with medication.

Some people with schizophrenia have mild impairment of intellectual function, but schizophrenia is not associated with the same types of physical changes in the brain that occur in people with dementias, such as Alzheimer disease (AD).

Psychotic disorders, such as schizophrenia, are different from mood disorders, including depression and bipolar disorder, which primarily affect emotions. However, these disorders often occur together.

Individuals who exhibit strong features of both schizophrenia and mood disorders are often given the diagnosis of schizoaffective disorder.

Frequency

Schizophrenia is a common disorder that occurs all over the world. It affects almost one percent of the population, with slightly more males than females developing the disorder.

Causes

Variations in many genes likely contribute to the risk of developing schizophrenia. In most cases, multiple genetic changes, each with a small effect, combine to increase the risk of developing the disorder. The ways that these genetic changes are related to schizophrenia are not well understood, and the genetics of this disease is an active area of research. The genetic changes can also interact with environmental factors that are associated with increased schizophrenia risk, such as exposure to infections before birth or severe stress during childhood.

Deletions or duplications of genetic material in any of several chromosomes, which can affect multiple genes, are also thought to increase schizophrenia risk. In particular, a small deletion (microdeletion) in a region of chromosome 22 called "22q11" may be involved in a small percentage of cases of schizophrenia. Some individuals with this deletion have other features in addition to schizophrenia, such as heart abnormalities, immune system problems, and an opening in the roof of the mouth (cleft palate), and are diagnosed with a condition called "22q11.2 deletion syndrome."

Chapter 55

Diabetes and Genetics

Chapter Contents

Section 55.1

Type 1 Diabetes

This section includes text excerpted from "Type 1 Diabetes,"
Genetics Home Reference (GHR), National Institutes of Health
(NIH), March 2013. Reviewed March 2019.

Type 1 diabetes is a disorder characterized by abnormally high blood-sugar levels. In this form of diabetes, specialized cells in the pancreas called "beta cells" stop producing insulin. Insulin controls how much glucose (a type of sugar) is passed from the blood into cells for conversion to energy. Lack of insulin results in the inability to use glucose for energy or to control the amount of sugar in the blood.

Type 1 diabetes can occur at any age; however, it usually develops by early adulthood, most often starting in adolescence. The first signs and symptoms of the disorder are caused by high blood sugar and may include frequent urination (polyuria), excessive thirst (polydipsia), fatigue, blurred vision, tingling or loss of feeling in the hands and feet, and weight loss. These symptoms may recur during the course of the disorder if blood sugar is not well controlled by insulin-replacement therapy. Improper control can also cause blood-sugar levels to become too low (hypoglycemia). This may occur when the body's needs change, such as during exercise or if eating is delayed. Hypoglycemia can cause headache, dizziness, hunger, shaking, sweating, weakness, and agitation.

Uncontrolled type 1 diabetes can lead to a life-threatening complication called "diabetic ketoacidosis." Without insulin, cells cannot take in glucose. A lack of glucose in cells prompts the liver to try to compensate by releasing more glucose into the blood, and blood sugar can become extremely high. The cells, unable to use the glucose in the blood for energy, respond by using fats instead. Breaking down fats to obtain energy produces waste products called "ketones," which can build up to toxic levels in people with type 1 diabetes, resulting in diabetic ketoacidosis. Affected individuals may begin breathing rapidly; develop a fruity odor in the breath; and experience nausea, vomiting, facial flushing, stomach pain, and dryness of the mouth (xerostomia). In severe cases, diabetic ketoacidosis can lead to coma and death.

Over many years, the chronic high blood sugar associated with diabetes may cause damage to blood vessels and nerves, leading to complications affecting many organs and tissues. The retina, which is the light-sensitive tissue at the back of the eye, can be damaged (diabetic retinopathy), leading to vision loss and eventual blindness. Kidney damage (diabetic nephropathy) may also occur and can lead to kidney failure and end-stage renal disease (ESRD). Pain, tingling, and loss of normal sensation (diabetic neuropathy) often occur, especially in the feet. Impaired circulation and absence of the normal sensations that prompt reaction to injury can result in permanent damage to the feet; in severe cases, the damage can lead to amputation. People with type 1 diabetes are also at increased risk of heart attacks, strokes, and problems with urinary and sexual function.

Frequency

Type 1 diabetes occurs in 10 to 20 per 100,000 people per year in the United States. By the age of 18, approximately 1 in 300 people in the United States develop type 1 diabetes. The disorder occurs with similar frequencies in Europe, the United Kingdom, Canada, and New Zealand. Type 1 diabetes occurs much less frequently in Asia and South America, with reported incidences as low as 1 in 1 million per year. For unknown reasons, during the past 20 years, the worldwide incidence of type 1 diabetes has been increasing by 2 to 5 percent each year.

Type 1 diabetes accounts for 5 to 10 percent of cases of diabetes worldwide. Most people with diabetes have type 2 diabetes, in which the body continues to produce insulin but becomes less able to use it.

Causes

The causes of type 1 diabetes are unknown, although several risk factors have been identified. The risk of developing type 1 diabetes is increased by certain variants of the *HLA-DQA1*, *HLA-DQB1*, and *HLA-DRB1* genes. These genes provide instructions for making proteins that play a critical role in the immune system. The *HLA-DQA1*, *HLA-DQB1*, and *HLA-DRB1* genes belong to a family of genes called the "human leukocyte antigen (HLA) complex." The HLA complex helps the immune system distinguish the body's own proteins from proteins made by foreign invaders, such as viruses and bacteria.

Type 1 diabetes is generally considered to be an autoimmune disorder. Autoimmune disorders occur when the immune system attacks the body's own tissues and organs. For unknown reasons, in people with type 1 diabetes, the immune system damages the insulin-producing beta cells in the pancreas. Damage to these cells impairs insulin production and leads to the signs and symptoms of type 1 diabetes.

HLA genes, including *HLA-DQA1, HLA-DQB1,* and *HLA-DRB1*, have many variations, and individuals have a certain combination of these variations, called a "haplotype." Certain HLA haplotypes are associated with a higher risk of developing type 1 diabetes, with particular combinations of *HLA-DQA1, HLA-DQB1,* and *HLA-DRB1* gene variations resulting in the highest risk. These haplotypes seem to increase the risk of an inappropriate immune response to beta cells. However, these variants are also found in the general population, and only about 5 percent of individuals with the gene variants develop type 1 diabetes. HLA variations account for approximately 40 percent of the genetic risk for the condition. Other HLA variations appear to be protective against the disease. Additional contributors, such as environmental factors and variations in other genes, are also thought to influence the development of this complex disorder.

Section 55.2

Type 2 Diabetes

This section includes text excerpted from "Type 2 Diabetes,"
Genetics Home Reference (GHR), National Institutes
of Health (NIH), November 2017.

Type 2 diabetes is a disorder characterized by abnormally high blood-sugar levels. In this form of diabetes, the body stops using and making insulin properly. Insulin is a hormone produced in the pancreas that helps regulate blood-sugar levels. Specifically, insulin controls how much glucose (a type of sugar) is passed from the blood into cells, where it is used as an energy source. When blood-sugar levels are high (such as after a meal), the pancreas releases insulin to move the excess glucose into cells, which reduces the amount of glucose in the blood.

Most people who develop type 2 diabetes first have insulin resistance, a condition in which the body's cells use insulin less efficiently than normal. As insulin resistance develops, more and more insulin is needed to keep blood-sugar levels in the normal range. To keep up with the increasing need, insulin-producing cells in the pancreas (called "beta cells") make larger amounts of insulin. Over time, the beta cells become less able to respond to blood sugar changes, leading to an insulin shortage that prevents the body from reducing blood-sugar levels effectively. Most people have some insulin resistance as they age, but inadequate exercise and excessive weight gain make it worse, greatly increasing the likelihood of developing type 2 diabetes.

Type 2 diabetes can occur at any age, but it most commonly begins in middle age or later. Signs and symptoms develop slowly over years. They include frequent urination (polyuria), excessive thirst (polydipsia), fatigue, blurred vision, tingling or loss of feeling in the hands and feet (diabetic neuropathy), sores that do not heal well, and weight loss. If blood-sugar levels are not controlled through medication or diet, type 2 diabetes can cause long-lasting (chronic) health problems including heart disease and stroke; nerve damage; and damage to the kidneys, eyes, and other parts of the body.

Frequency

Type 2 diabetes is the most common type of diabetes, accounting for 90 to 95 percent of all cases. In 2015, more than 23 million people in the United States had diagnosed diabetes, and an additional 7 million people likely had undiagnosed diabetes. The prevalence of diabetes increases with age, and the disease currently affects more than 20 percent of Americans over the age of 65. It is the seventh leading cause of death in the United States.

The risk of diabetes varies by ethnic and geographic background. In the United States, the disease is most common in Native Americans and Alaska Natives. It also has a higher prevalence among people of African American or Hispanic ancestry than those of non-Hispanic white or Asian ancestry. Geographically, diabetes is most prevalent in the southern and Appalachian regions of the United States.

The prevalence of diabetes is rapidly increasing worldwide. Due to an increase in inactive (sedentary) lifestyles, obesity, and other risk factors, the frequency of this disease has more than quadrupled in the past 35 years.

Causes

The causes of type 2 diabetes are complex. This condition results from a combination of genetic and lifestyle factors, some of which have not been identified.

Studies have identified at least 150 deoxyribonucleic acid (DNA) variations that are associated with the risk of developing type 2 diabetes. Most of these changes are common and are present both in people with diabetes and in those without. Each person has some variations that increase risk and others that reduce risk. It is the combination of these changes that help determine a person's likelihood of developing the disease.

The majority of genetic variations associated with type 2 diabetes are thought to act by subtly changing the amount, timing, and location of gene activity (expression). These changes in expression affect genes involved in many aspects of type 2 diabetes, including the development and function of beta cells in the pancreas, the release, and processing of insulin, and cells' sensitivity to the effects of insulin. However, for many of the variations that have been associated with type 2 diabetes, the mechanism by which they contribute to disease risk is unknown.

Genetic variations likely act together with health and lifestyle factors to influence an individual's overall risk of type 2 diabetes. All of these factors are related, directly or indirectly, to the body's ability to produce and respond to insulin. Health conditions that predispose to the disease include being overweight or obese, insulin resistance, prediabetes (higher-than-normal blood-sugar levels that do not reach the cutoff for diabetes), and a form of diabetes called "gestational diabetes" that occurs during pregnancy. Lifestyle factors including smoking, a poor diet, and physical inactivity also increase the risk of type 2 diabetes.

Chapter 56

Cardiovascular Disease and Heredity

Chapter Contents

Section 56.1

Family History and Your Risk for Heart Disease

This section includes text excerpted from "Heart Disease,"
Centers for Disease Control and Prevention (CDC),
August 10, 2015. Reviewed March 2019.

About Heart Disease

The term "heart disease" refers to several types of heart conditions. The most common type of heart disease in the United States is coronary artery disease (CAD), which affects the blood flow to the heart. Decreased blood flow can cause a heart attack.

Family History and Other Characteristics That Increase Risk for Heart Disease

Family members share genes, behaviors, lifestyles, and environments that can influence their health and their risk for the disease. Heart disease can run in a family, and your risk for heart disease can increase based on your age and your race, or ethnicity.

Genetics and Family History

When members of a family pass traits from one generation to another through genes, that process is called "heredity."

Genetic factors likely play some role in high blood pressure (HBP), heart disease, and other related conditions. However, it is also likely that people with a family history of heart disease share common environments and other potential factors that increase their risk.

The risk for heart disease can increase even more when heredity combines with unhealthy lifestyle choices, such as smoking cigarettes and eating an unhealthy diet.

Other Characteristics

Both men and women can have heart disease. Some other characteristics that you cannot control, such as your age, sex, and race or ethnicity, can affect your risk for heart disease.

- **Age.** Your risk for heart disease increases as you get older.

- **Sex**. Heart disease was the number one killer of both men and women in 2013.

- **Race or ethnicity.** In 2013 heart disease was the leading cause of death in the United States for non-Hispanic Whites, non-Hispanic Blacks, and American Indians. For Hispanics, and Asian Americans, and Pacific Islanders, heart disease is second only to cancer as a cause of death.

Section 56.2

Genetics of Hypertension

This section includes text excerpted from "Hypertension," Genetics Home Reference (GHR), National Institutes of Health (NIH), February 5, 2019.

Hypertension is abnormally high blood pressure (HBP) in the arteries, which are the blood vessels that carry blood from the heart to the rest of the body. As the heart beats, it forces blood through the arteries to deliver nutrients and oxygen to the rest of the body. The strength of the blood pushing against the artery walls is blood pressure, which is measured in units called "millimeters of mercury" (mmHg). The top number in a blood pressure reading is the pressure when the heart pumps (systolic blood pressure), and the bottom number is the pressure between heartbeats (diastolic blood pressure). In adults, a normal blood pressure measurement is about 120/80 mmHg. Blood pressure is considered high when the measurement is 130/80 mmHg or greater.

Hypertension usually has no symptoms, and many affected individuals do not know they have the condition. However, hypertension is a major risk factor for heart disease, stroke, kidney failure, and eye problems. When blood pressure is elevated, the heart and arteries have to work harder than normal to pump blood through the body. The extra work thickens the muscles of the heart and arteries and hardens or damages artery walls. As a result, the flow of blood and oxygen to the heart and other organs is reduced. Damage to the heart caused by the extra work and a lack of oxygen causes heart disease.

In addition, damage to the arteries increases the risk of blood clots that block the flow of blood to the heart, causing a heart attack, or to the brain, causing a type of stroke known as an "ischemic stroke." Another type of stroke, called a "hemorrhagic stroke," can occur when a weakened blood vessel in the brain bursts. Damage to blood vessels in the kidneys impairs their ability to filter waste and remove fluid, leading to kidney failure. Problems with blood flow in the arteries of the eyes can lead to vision loss.

In rare cases, dangerously high blood pressure can cause severe headaches, confusion, shortness of breath, chest pain, or nosebleeds.

In about 95 percent of cases, the cause of hypertension is unknown. These cases are classified as essential hypertension. When hypertension results from an underlying condition, such as blood vessel defects that reduce blood flow; kidney disorders, which alter the amount of fluids and salts in the body; or problems with hormone-producing glands called the "adrenal glands" or the "thyroid gland," it is classified as secondary hypertension. Hypertension is a key feature of some rare genetic disorders, including familial hyperaldosteronism, pseudohypoaldosteronism type 2 (PHA2), Liddle syndrome (LS), Bartter syndrome (BS), Gitelman syndrome (GS), and tumors known as "paragangliomas."

Frequency

Hypertension affects an estimated 29 percent of adults in the United States. Prevalence of the condition increases with age, and approximately 63 percent of people over the age of 60 are affected. In African Americans, the condition is more common, starts at a younger age, and is more severe than in other populations.

Causes

Hypertension can have a variety of causes. Secondary hypertension results from other disorders that raise blood pressure, in addition to other problems. Rare, genetic forms of hypertension are caused by mutations in particular genes, many of which help control the balance of fluids and salts in the body and affect blood pressure. The causes of essential hypertension, however, are not well understood. Essential hypertension is a complex condition with a variety of factors, both genetic and environmental, contribute to its development.

More than 100 genetic variations have been associated with essential hypertension. While these variations have been found more commonly in people with essential hypertension than in unaffected individuals, none are common causes of the condition.

The most-studied genetic association in essential hypertension is with genes involved in the renin-angiotensin-aldosterone system (RAAS). The renin-angiotensin-aldosterone system is a step-wise process that produces hormones to regulate blood pressure and the balance of fluids and salts in the body. Because these genes play an integral role in normal blood pressure control, researchers suspect that variations in them might impair blood pressure control and contribute to hypertension.

Other genes associated with essential hypertension are important for the normal function of the lining of blood vessels (the vascular endothelium). Changes in these genes are thought to impair this cell layer (endothelial dysfunction). Such changes may result in vessels that are abnormally constricted or narrowed, which raises blood pressure. Still, other genes have been linked to hypertension risk, although the roles most of them play in the development of the condition are still unclear.

Environmental factors also contribute to hypertension. In addition to race and age, activity level, alcohol consumption, and salt intake influence blood pressure. Other disorders, such as obesity, diabetes, and obstructive sleep apnea also increase the risk of developing hypertension.

Researchers suspect epigenetic changes to deoxyribonucleic acid (DNA) also play a role in the development of essential hypertension. Epigenetic changes modify DNA without changing the DNA sequence. They can affect gene activity and the production of proteins, which may influence blood pressure.

Section 56.3

Familial Hypercholesterolemia

This chapter includes text excerpted from "Learning about Familial Hypercholesterolemia," National Human Genome Research Institute (NHGRI), December 26, 2013. Reviewed March 2019.

What Is Familial Hypercholesterolemia?

Familial hypercholesterolemia (FH) is an inherited condition that causes high levels of low-density lipoprotein (LDL) cholesterol beginning at birth and heart attacks at an early age. Cholesterol is a fat-like substance that is found in the cells of the body. Cholesterol is also found in some foods. The body needs some cholesterol to work properly and uses cholesterol to make hormones, vitamin D, and substances that help with food digestion. However, if too much cholesterol is present in the bloodstream, it builds up in the wall of the arteries and increases the risk of heart disease.

Cholesterol is carried in the bloodstream in small packages called "lipoproteins." These small packages are made up of fat (lipid) on the inside and proteins on the outside. There are two main kinds of lipoprotein that carry cholesterol throughout the body. These are: low-density lipoprotein (LDL) and high-density lipoprotein (HDL).

The cholesterol carried by LDL is sometimes called the "bad cholesterol." People who have familial hypercholesterolemia have high levels of LDL cholesterol because they cannot remove the LDL from the bloodstream properly. The organ responsible for the removal of the LDL is the liver. High levels of LDL cholesterol in the blood increase the risk for heart attacks and heart disease.

The cholesterol carried by HDL is sometimes called the "good cholesterol." HDL carries cholesterol from other parts of the body to the liver. The liver removes cholesterol from the body. Higher levels of HDL cholesterol lower a person's chance for getting heart disease.

Men who have familial hypercholesterolemia have heart attacks in their forties to fifties, and 85 percent of men with the disorder have a heart attack by the age of 60. Women who have familial hypercholesterolemia also have an increased risk for heart attack, but it happens 10 years later than in men (so in their fifties and sixties).

Familial hypercholesterolemia is inherited in families in an autosomal dominant manner. In autosomal-dominant inherited conditions, a parent who carries an altered gene that causes the condition has a

1 in 2 (50%) chance to pass on that altered gene to each of her or his children.

The altered gene (gene mutation) that causes familial hypercholesterolemia is located on chromosome number 19. It contains the information for a protein called "LDL receptor" that is responsible to clear up LDL from the bloodstream. 1 in 500 individuals carries one altered gene causing familial hypercholesterolemia. These individuals are called "heterozygotes." More rarely, a person inherits the gene mutation from both parents, making them genetically homozygous. Individuals who are homozygous have a much more severe form of hypercholesterolemia, with heart attack and death often occurring before the age of 30.

What Are the Symptoms of Familial Hypercholesterolemia?

The major symptoms and signs of familial hypercholesterolemia are:

- High levels of total cholesterol and LDL cholesterol
- A strong family history of high levels of total and LDL cholesterol and/or early heart attack
- Elevated and therapy-resistant levels of LDL in either or both parents
- Xanthomas (waxy deposits of cholesterol in the skin or tendons)
- Xanthelasmas (cholesterol deposits in the eyelids)
- Corneal arcus (cholesterol deposit around the cornea of the eye)
- If angina (chest pain) is present, it may be sign that heart disease is present

Individuals who have homozygous familial hypercholesterolemia (HoFH) develop xanthomas beneath the skin over their elbows, knees, and buttocks as well as in the tendons at a very early age, sometime in infancy. Heart attacks and death may occur before 30 years of age.

How Is Familial Hypercholesterolemia Diagnosed?

Diagnosis of familial hypercholesterolemia is based on physical examination and laboratory testing. Physical examination may find xanthomas and xanthelasmas (skin lesions caused by cholesterol-rich lipoprotein deposits), and cholesterol deposits in the eye called "corneal arcus."

Laboratory testing includes blood testing of cholesterol levels, studies of heart function, and genetic testing. Blood testing of cholesterol levels may show: increased total cholesterol usually above 300 mg/dl (total cholesterol of more than 250 mg/dl in children) and LDL levels usually above 200 mg/dl. Studies of heart function, such as a stress test, may be abnormal. Genetic testing may show an alteration (mutation) in the LDL receptor gene.

What Is the Treatment for Familial Hypercholesterolemia?

The overall goal of treatment is to lower the risk for atherosclerotic heart disease by lowering the LDL cholesterol levels in the bloodstream. Atherosclerosis is a condition in which fatty material collects along the walls of arteries. This fatty material thickens, hardens, and may eventually block the arteries. Atherosclerosis happens when fat and cholesterol and other substances build up in the arteries and form a hardened material called "plaque." The plaque deposits make the arteries less flexible and more difficult for blood to flow leading to heart attack and stroke.

The first step in treatment for an individual who has heterozygous familial hypercholesterolemia (HeFH) is changing the diet to reduce the total amount of fat eaten to 30 percent of the total daily calories. This can be done by limiting the amount of beef, pork, and lamb in the diet; cutting out butter, whole milk, and fatty cheeses as well as some oils like coconut and palm oils; and eliminating egg yolks, organ meats and other sources of saturated fat from animals. Dietary counseling is often recommended to help people to make these changes in their eating habits.

Exercise, especially to lose weight, may also help in lowering cholesterol levels.

Drug therapy is usually necessary in combination with diet, weight loss, and exercise, as these interventions may not be able to lower cholesterol levels alone. There are a number of cholesterol-lowering medications that are currently used. The first and more effective choice are drugs called "statins." Other drugs that may be used in combination with or instead of the statins are: bile acid sequestrant resins (for example, cholestyramine), ezetimibe, nicotinic acid (niacin), gemfibrozil, and fenofibrate.

Individuals who have homozygous familial hypercholesterolemia need more aggressive therapies to treat their significantly elevated levels of cholesterol. Often drug therapies are not sufficient to lower LDL cholesterol levels at the desiderated goal, and these individuals may require periodical LDL apheresis, a procedure to "clean up" LDL from the bloodstream, or highly invasive surgery, such as a liver transplant.

Is Familial Hypercholesterolemia Inherited?

Familial hypercholesterolemia is inherited in an autosomal dominant manner. This means that to have this condition, it is sufficient that the altered (mutated) gene is present on only one of the person's two number 19 chromosomes. A person who inherits one copy of the gene mutation causing familial hypercholesterolemia from one of his/her parents is said to have heterozygous familial hypercholesterolemia. This person has a 1 in 2 (50%) chance to pass on the mutated gene to each of his/her children.

A person who inherits a mutated copy of the gene causing familial hypercholesterolemia from both parents is said to have homozygous familial hypercholesterolemia. This is a much more severe form of familial hypercholesterolemia than heterozygous familial hypercholesterolemia. Each of this person's children will inherit one copy of the mutated gene and will have heterozygous familial hypercholesterolemia.

Chapter 57

Heredity and Movement Disorders

Chapter Contents

Section 57.1

Genetics of Essential Tremor

This section includes text excerpted from "Essential Tremor,"
Genetic and Rare Diseases Information Center (GARD),
National Center for Advancing Translational Sciences (NCATS),
September 12, 2014. Reviewed March 2019.

What Is Essential Tremor?

Essential tremor (ET) is the most common movement disorder. It is characterized by involuntary and rhythmic shaking (tremor), especially in the hands, without any other signs or symptoms. It is distinguished from tremor that results from other disorders or known causes, such as tremors seen with Parkinson disease (PD) or head trauma. Most cases of essential tremor are hereditary. There are five forms of essential tremors that are based on different genetic causes. Several genes, as well as lifestyle and environmental factors, likely play a role in a person's risk of developing this complex condition. In mild cases, treatment may not be necessary. In cases where symptoms interfere with daily living, medications may help to relieve symptoms.

What Causes Essential Tremor

The causes of essential tremor are unknown. Researchers are studying several areas (loci) on particular chromosomes that may be linked to essential tremor, but no specific genetic associations have been confirmed. Several genes, as well as environmental factors, are likely involved in an individual's risk of developing this complex condition.

Can the Symptoms of Essential Tremor Interfere with the Activities of Daily Life?

Although essential tremor is not life-threatening, it can make it harder to perform daily tasks and is embarrassing to some people. Hand tremor is most common, but the head, arms, voice, tongue, legs, and trunk may also be involved. Although it may be mild and nonprogressive in some people, in others the tremor is slowly progressive, starting on one side of the body but eventually affecting both sides. Tremor frequency may decrease as a person ages, but the severity may increase, affecting the person's ability to perform certain tasks or activities of daily living. In many people, the tremor may be mild throughout life.

If severe, essential tremor may interfere with fine motor skills used to do simple tasks, such as holding eating utensils, drinking a glass of water, tying shoelaces, writing, sewing, shaving, or applying makeup. Sometimes the tremors affect the voice box, which occasionally leads to speech problems.

The symptoms of essential tremor may be aggravated by emotional stress, fever, fatigue, hunger (low blood sugar), caffeine, cigarette smoking, or extremes of temperature.

How Might Essential Tremor Be Treated?

Treatment for essential tremor may not be necessary unless the tremors interfere with daily activities or cause embarrassment. Although there is no definitive cure for essential tremor, medicines may help relieve symptoms. How well medicines work depends on the individual patient. Two medications used to treat tremors include:

- Propranolol, a drug that blocks the action of stimulating substances called "neurotransmitters," particularly those related to adrenaline

- Primidone, an antiseizure drug that also controls the function of some neurotransmitters

These drugs can have significant side effects.

Eliminating tremor "triggers," such as caffeine and other stimulants, from the diet is often recommended. Physical therapy may help to reduce tremor and improve coordination and muscle control for some patients.

Section 57.2

Parkinson Disease: Genetic Links

This section includes text excerpted from "Parkinson Disease,"
Genetic and Rare Diseases Information Center (GARD),
National Center for Advancing Translational
Sciences (NCATS), November 16, 2017.

What Is Parkinson Disease?

Parkinson disease (PD) is a neurologic disease that affects movement. The four main symptoms are tremors of the hands, arms, legs, jaw, or head (especially at rest); rigidity, or stiffness; bradykinesia, or slow movement; and postural instability or inability to find balance. The symptoms start slowly, but progress over time, impairing everyday activities, such as walking, talking, or completing simple tasks. Other symptoms may include emotional problems, trouble swallowing and speaking, urinary problems or constipation, skin problems, sleep problems, low blood pressure when standing up from sitting or lying down (postural hypotension), and inexpressive face. Some people will lose their mental abilities (dementia).

Parkinson disease affects several regions of the brain, especially a region known as "substantia nigra" that helps controlling balance and movement. Most cases of PD are sporadic (with no family history), and with onset around 60 years of age; onset before the 20 years of age is considered to be juvenile-onset Parkinson disease, and after 50 years of age is considered late-onset Parkinson disease (LOPD). However, in some families, there are several cases of Parkinson disease. Familial cases of Parkinson disease, and maybe some sporadic cases, can be caused by changes (mutations) in several genes, such as:

- Mutations in the *SNCA (PARK1), LRRK2 (PARK8),* and *VPS35 (PARK17)* genes are inherited in an autosomal dominant manner.

- Mutations in genes *PARK2, PARK7*, and *PINK1 (PARK6)* appear to be inherited in a recessive manner.

- Very rare mutations in the *TAF1* gene cause Parkinson disease with X-linked inheritance.

- Mutations in some genes, including *GBA* and *UCHL1 (PARK 5)*, do not seem to cause Parkinson disease, but to increase the risk of developing the disease in some families.

Autosomal recessive PD has an earlier onset than autosomal dominant PD. Some studies suggest that these genes are also involved in early-onset or juvenile PD. However, inheriting a mutation does not always mean that a person will have Parkinson disease, because there may be other genes and environmental factors determining who will develop Parkinson disease.

Treatment is usually based on a medication known as "levodopa." Other medication includes bromocriptine, pramipexole, ropinirole, amantadine, rasagiline, and safinamide. Deep brain stimulation (DBS), a surgical procedure where electrodes are implanted into the brain, may be useful for some people. Prognosis varies, and while some people become disabled, others will have only minor movement problems. Studies have shown that people with PD who have cognitive impairment, postural hypotension, and sleep problems may have a more rapid progression of the disease.

What Causes Parkinson Disease

Parkinson disease occurs when the nerve cells in the brain that make dopamine, a chemical messenger which transmits signals within the brain to produce smooth physical movements, are slowly destroyed. Without dopamine, the nerve cells in the substantia nigra cannot properly send messages. This leads to progressive loss of muscle function. Exactly why these brain cells waste away is unknown. Studies have shown that people with Parkinson disease also experience damage to the nerve endings that produce the neurotransmitter norepinephrine (NE). Norepinephrine, which is closely related to dopamine, is the main chemical messenger of the sympathetic nervous system (SNS), the part of the nervous system that controls the automatic functions of the body, including pulse and blood pressure. The loss of norepinephrine may explain some of the nonmotor features seen in Parkinson disease, including fatigue and problems with blood pressure regulation.

Is Parkinson Disease Inherited?

Most cases of Parkinson disease are classified as sporadic and occur in people with no apparent history of the disorder in their family. Although the cause of these cases remains unclear, sporadic cases probably result from a complex interaction of environmental and genetic factors. Additionally, certain drugs may cause Parkinson-like symptoms.

Approximately 15 percent of people with Parkinson disease have a family history of the disorder. These familial cases are caused by mutations in the *LRRK2, PARK2, PARK7, PINK1,* or *SNCA* gene, or by alterations in genes that have not yet been identified. Mutations in some of these genes may also play a role in cases that appear to be sporadic.

It is not fully understood how mutations in the *LRRK2, PARK2, PARK7, PINK1,* or *SNCA* gene cause Parkinson disease. Some mutations appear to disturb the cell machinery that breaks down (degrades) unwanted proteins. As a result, un-degraded proteins accumulate, leading to the impairment or death of dopamine-producing neurons. Other mutations may involve mitochondria, the energy-producing structures within cells. As a byproduct of energy production, mitochondria make unstable molecules, called "free radicals," that can damage the cell. Normally, the cell neutralizes free radicals, but some gene mutations may disrupt this neutralization process. As a result, free radicals may accumulate and impair or kill dopamine-producing neurons.

In some families, alterations in the *GBA, SNCAIP,* or *UCHL1* gene appear to modify the risk of developing Parkinson disease. Researchers have identified some genetic changes that may reduce the risk of developing the disease, while other gene alterations seem to increase the risk.

How Do People Inherit Parkinson Disease?

Most cases of Parkinson disease occur in people with no family history of the disorder. The inheritance pattern in these cases is unknown. Among familial cases of Parkinson disease, the inheritance pattern differs depending on the gene that is altered. If the *LRRK2* or *SNCA* gene is involved, the disorder is inherited in an autosomal dominant pattern, which means one copy of an altered gene in each cell is sufficient to cause the disorder. Parkinson disease is inherited in an autosomal recessive pattern if the *PARK2, PARK7,* or *PINK1* gene is involved. This type of inheritance means that two copies of the gene in each cell are altered. Most often, the parents of an individual with autosomal recessive Parkinson disease each carry one copy of the altered gene but do not show signs and symptoms of the disorder.

The inheritance pattern is unclear when an increased risk of Parkinson disease or parkinsonism is associated with mutations in the *GBA* gene. SNCAIP and UCHL1 mutations have been identified in just a few individuals. It is unclear how these mutations are related to Parkinson disease, and the inheritance pattern remains unknown.

How Is Parkinson Disease Diagnosed?

There are currently no blood or laboratory tests that have been proven to help diagnose sporadic cases of Parkinson disease. The diagnosis is generally made after careful evaluation of medical history, current symptoms, and exclusion of other conditions. The clinical findings of tremor, rigidity, and bradykinesia are highly suggestive of Parkinson disease. The genetic cause of some forms of Parkinson disease has been identified. In those cases, genetic testing may be utilized to identify affected family members.

Is Genetic Testing Available for Parkinson Disease?

GeneTests lists laboratories offering clinical genetic testing for the *HTRA2*-related, *LRRK2*-related, *PARK7*-related, *PINK1*-related, Parkin, and *SCNA*-related types of Parkinson disease. Clinical genetic tests are ordered to help diagnose a person or family and to aid in decisions regarding medical care or reproductive issues. Individuals and families who are interested in having genetic testing can learn more about their risk for Parkinson disease and the availability and accuracy of genetic testing for this disease by setting up an appointment with a genetics professional.

Chapter 58

Genetic Factors in Obesity

Obesity results from the energy imbalance that occurs when a person consumes more calories than their body burns. Obesity is a serious public-health problem because it is associated with some of the leading causes of death in the United States and worldwide, including diabetes, heart disease, stroke, and some types of cancer.

Do Genes Have a Role in Obesity?

In recent decades, obesity has reached epidemic proportions in populations whose environments promote physical inactivity and increased consumption of high-calorie foods. However, not all people living in such environments will become obese, nor will all obese people have the same body fat distribution or suffer the same health problems. These differences can be seen in groups of people with the same racial or ethnic background and even within families. Genetic changes in human populations occur too slowly to be responsible for the obesity epidemic. Nevertheless, the variation in how people respond to the same environment suggests that genes do play a role in the development of obesity.

This chapter includes text excerpted from "Behavior, Environment, and Genetic Factors All Have a Role in Causing People to Be Overweight and Obese," Centers for Disease Control and Prevention (CDC), January 19, 2018.

How Could Genes Influence Obesity?

Genes give the body instructions for responding to changes in their environment. Studies of resemblances and differences among family members, twins, and adoptees offer indirect scientific evidence that a sizable portion of the variation in weight among adults is due to genetic factors. Other studies have compared obese and nonobese people for variation in genes that could influence behaviors (such as a drive to overeat or a tendency to be sedentary) or metabolism (such as a diminished capacity to use dietary fats as fuel or an increased tendency to store body fat). These studies have identified variants in several genes that may contribute to obesity by increasing hunger and food intake.

Rarely, a clear pattern of inherited obesity within a family is caused by a specific variant of a single gene (monogenic obesity). Most obesity, however, probably results from complex interactions among multiple genes and environmental factors that remain poorly understood (multifactorial obesity).

Any explanation of the obesity epidemic has to consider both genetics and the environment. One explanation that is often cited is the mismatch between the environment and "energy-thrifty genes" that multiplied in the distant past when food sources were unpredictable. In other words, according to the "thrifty genotype" hypothesis, the same genes that helped our ancestors survive occasional famines are now being challenged by environments in which food is plentiful year round. Other hypotheses have been proposed including a role for the gut microbiome, as well as, early life exposures associated with epigenetic changes.

Can Public Health Genomics Help?

With the exception of rare genetic conditions associated with extreme obesity, currently, genetic tests are not useful for guiding personal diet or physical activity plans. Research on genetic variation that affects response to changes in diet and physical activity is still at an early stage. Doing a better job of explaining obesity in terms of genes and environmental factors could help encourage people who are trying to reach and maintain a healthy weight.

What about Family History

Healthcare practitioners routinely collect family health history to help identify people at high risk of obesity-related diseases, such as diabetes, cardiovascular diseases, and some forms of cancer. Family health history reflects the effects of shared genetics and the environment among close relatives. Families cannot change their genes but they can change the family environment to encourage healthy eating habits and physical activity. Those changes can improve the health of family members and improve the family health history of the next generation.

How Can You Tell If You or Your Family Members Are Overweight?

Most healthcare practitioners use the body mass index (BMI) to determine whether a person is overweight. Check your body mass index with a BMI calculator.

Chapter 59

Family History and Risk for Stroke

A stroke, sometimes called a "brain attack," occurs when something blocks blood supply to part of the brain or when a blood vessel in the brain bursts. In either case, parts of the brain become damaged or die. A stroke can cause lasting brain damage, long-term disability, or even death.

Understanding Stroke

To understand stroke, it helps to understand the brain. The brain controls our movements, stores our memories, and is the source of our thoughts, emotions, and language. The brain also controls many functions of the body, such as breathing and digestion.

To work properly, your brain needs oxygen. Although your brain makes up only 2 percent of your body weight, it uses 20 percent of the oxygen you breathe. Your arteries deliver oxygen-rich blood to all parts of your brain.

What Happens during a Stroke

If something happens to block the flow of blood, brain cells start to die within minutes because they cannot get oxygen. This causes a stroke.

This chapter includes text excerpted from "About Stroke," Centers for Disease Control and Prevention (CDC), May 3, 2018.

There are two types of stroke:

- An ischemic stroke occurs when blood clots or other particles block the blood vessels to the brain. Fatty deposits called "plaque" can also cause blockages by building up in the blood vessels.

- A hemorrhagic stroke occurs when a blood vessel bursts in the brain. Blood builds up and damages the surrounding brain tissue.

Both types of stroke damage brain cells. Symptoms of that damage start to show in the parts of the body controlled by those brain cells.

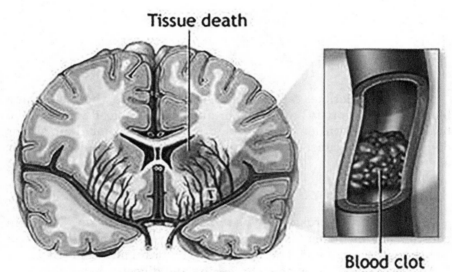

Figure 59.1. *Stroke*

A stroke happens when a blood clot blocks blood flow to the brain. This causes brain tissue to become damaged or die

Quick Treatment Is Critical for Stroke

A stroke is a serious medical condition that requires emergency care. Act F.A.S.T.

- F—Face: Ask the person to smile. Does one side of the face droop?

- A—Arms: Ask the person to raise both arms. Does one arm drift downward?

- S—Speech: Ask the person to repeat a simple phrase. Is the speech slurred or strange?

- T—Time: If you see any of these signs, call 911 right away.

Call 911 right away if you or someone you are with shows any signs of a stroke. Time lost is brain lost. Every minute counts.

Family History and Other Characteristics That Increase Risk for Stroke

Family members share genes, behaviors, lifestyles, and environments that can influence their health and their risk for the disease. Stroke risk can be higher in some families than in others, and your chances of having a stroke can go up or down depending on your age, sex, and race or ethnicity.

The good news is you can take steps to prevent stroke. Work with your healthcare team to lower your risk for stroke.

Genetics and Family History

When members of a family pass traits from one generation to another through genes, that process is called "heredity."

Genetic factors likely play some role in high blood pressure (HBP), stroke, and other related conditions. Several genetic disorders can cause a stroke, including sickle cell disease (SCD). People with a family history of stroke are also likely to share common environments and other potential factors that increase their risk.

The chances for stroke can increase even more when heredity combines with unhealthy lifestyle choices, such as smoking cigarettes and eating an unhealthy diet.

Age

The older you are, the more likely you are to have a stroke. The chance of having a stroke doubles about every 10 years after 55 years of age. Although stroke is common among older adults, many people younger than 65 years of age also have strokes.

In fact, about 1 in 7 strokes occur in adolescents and young adults between the ages of 15 to 49. Experts think younger people are having more strokes because more young people are obese and have high blood pressure and diabetes.

Sex

Stroke is more common in women than men, and women of all ages are more likely than men to die from stroke. Pregnancy and use of birth control pills (BCP) pose special stroke risks for women.

Race or Ethnicity

Blacks, Hispanics, American Indians, and Alaska Natives may be more likely to have a stroke than non-Hispanic Whites or Asians. The risk of having a first stroke is nearly twice as high for Blacks as for Whites.

Chapter 60

Genetics and Tourette Syndrome

What Is Tourette Syndrome?

Tourette syndrome (TS) is a complex neurological disorder that is characterized by repetitive, sudden, uncontrolled (involuntary) movements and sounds (vocalizations) called "tics." Tourette syndrome is named for Georges Gilles de la Tourette, who first described this disorder in 1885. A variety of genetic and environmental factors likely play a role in causing Tourette syndrome. A small number of people with Tourette syndrome have been found to have mutations involving the *SLITRK1* gene. The syndrome is believed to be linked to problems in certain areas of the brain and the chemical substances (dopamine, serotonin, and norepinephrine) that help nerve cells talk to one another. It is estimated that about one percent of the population has Tourette syndrome. Many people with very mild tics may not be aware of them and never seek medical help. Tourette syndrome is four times as likely to occur in boys as in girls. Although Tourette syndrome can be a chronic condition with symptoms lasting a lifetime, most people with the condition experience their worst symptoms in their early teens, with improvement occurring in the late teens and continuing into adulthood.

This chapter includes text excerpted from "Tourette Syndrome," Genetic and Rare Diseases Information Center (GARD), National Center for Advancing Translational Sciences (NCATS), March 6, 2016.

What Are the Signs and Symptoms of Tourette Syndrome?

The early symptoms of Tourette syndrome are almost always noticed first in childhood, with the average onset between the ages of three and nine. Although the symptoms of Tourette syndrome vary from person to person and range from very mild to severe, the majority of cases fall into the mild category.

The repetitive, stereotyped, involuntary movements and vocalizations called "tics" are classified as either simple or complex. Simple motor tics are sudden, brief, repetitive movements that involve a limited number of muscle groups. Some of the more common simple tics include eye blinking and other eye movements, facial grimacing, shoulder shrugging, and head or shoulder jerking. Simple vocalizations might include repetitive throat-clearing, sniffing/snorting, grunting, or barking sounds.

Complex tics are distinct, coordinated patterns of movements involving several muscle groups. Complex motor tics might include facial grimacing combined with a head twist and a shoulder shrug. Other complex motor tics may actually appear purposeful, including sniffing or touching objects, hopping, jumping, bending, or twisting. Complex vocal tics include words or phrases. Perhaps the most dramatic and disabling tics include motor movements that result in self-harm, such as punching oneself in the face or vocal tics including coprolalia (uttering swear words) or echolalia (repeating the words or phrases of others). Some tics are preceded by an urge or sensation in the affected muscle group, commonly called a "premonitory urge." Some individuals with Tourette syndrome will describe a need to complete a tic in a certain way or a certain number of times in order to relieve the urge or decrease the sensation.

Tics are often worse with excitement or anxiety and better during calm, focused activities. Certain physical experiences can trigger or worsen tics, for example, tight collars may trigger neck tics, or hearing another person sniff or throat-clear may trigger similar sounds. Tics do not go away during sleep but are often significantly diminished.

What Causes Tourette Syndrome

Although the cause of Tourette Syndrome is unknown, current research points to abnormalities in certain brain regions (including the basal ganglia, frontal lobes, and cortex), the circuits that interconnect these regions, and the neurotransmitters (dopamine, serotonin, and norepinephrine) responsible for communication among nerve cells. Given the often complex presentation of Tourette syndrome, the cause of the disorder is likely to be equally complex. In many cases, there is a family history of tics, Tourette Syndrome, attention deficit hyperactivity disorder (ADHD), obsessive-compulsive disorder (OCD).

In 2005, scientists discovered the first gene mutation that may cause some cases of Tourette syndrome. This gene, named *SLITRK1*, is normally involved with the growth of nerve cells and how they connect with other neurons. The mutated gene is located in regions of the brain (basal ganglia, cortex, and frontal lobes) previously identified as being associated with Tourette syndrome.

Is Tourette Syndrome Inherited?

Evidence from twin and family studies suggests that Tourette syndrome is an inherited disorder. Although early family studies suggested an autosomal dominant mode of inheritance (an autosomal dominant disorder is one in which only one copy of the defective gene, inherited from one parent, is necessary to produce the disorder), more recent studies suggest that the pattern of inheritance is much more complex. Although there may be a few genes with substantial effects, it is also possible that many genes with smaller effects and environmental factors may play a role in the development of Tourette syndrome. Genetic studies also suggest that some forms of ADHD and OCD are genetically related to Tourette syndrome, but there is less evidence for a genetic relationship between Tourette syndrome and other neurobehavioral problems that commonly co-occur with Tourette syndrome.

Due to the complex nature of Tourette syndrome inheritance, affected families and those at risk may benefit from consulting with a genetics professional.

How Might Tourette Syndrome Be Treated?

Many individuals with Tourette syndrome have mild symptoms and do not require medication. However, effective medications are available for those whose symptoms interfere with functioning. Neuroleptics are the most consistently useful medications for tic suppression; a number are available but some are more effective than others (for example, haloperidol and pimozide). Unfortunately, there is no one medication that is helpful to all people with Tourette syndrome, nor does any medication completely eliminate symptoms. In addition, all medications have side effects. Additional medications with demonstrated efficacy include alpha-adrenergic agonists, such as clonidine and guanfacine. These medications are used primarily for hypertension but are also used in the treatment of tics.

Effective medications are also available to treat some of the associated neurobehavioral disorders that can occur in patients with Tourette syndrome. Recent research shows that stimulant medications, such as methylphenidate and dextroamphetamine, can lessen ADHD symptoms in people with Tourette syndrome without causing tics to become more severe. However, the product labeling for stimulants currently contraindicates the use of these drugs in children with tics/Tourette syndrome and those with a family history of tics.

For obsessive-compulsive symptoms that significantly disrupt daily functioning, the serotonin reuptake inhibitors (clomipramine, fluoxetine, fluvoxamine, paroxetine, and sertraline) have been proven effective in some individuals.

Behavioral treatment, such as awareness training and competing response training, can also be used to reduce tics. Psychotherapy may be helpful as well. It can help with accompanying problems, such as ADHD, obsessions, depression, and anxiety. Therapy can also help people cope with Tourette syndrome. For debilitating tics that do not respond to other treatment, deep brain stimulation (DBS) may help. DBS consists of implanting a battery-operated medical device (neurostimulator) in the brain to deliver electrical stimulation to targeted areas that control movement. Further research is needed to determine whether DBS is beneficial for people with Tourette syndrome.

Can Tourette Syndrome Be Cured?

Although there is no cure for Tourette syndrome, the condition in many individuals improves in the late teens and early twenties. As a result, some may actually become symptom-free or no longer need medication for tic suppression.

What Is the Prognosis for Individuals with Tourette Syndrome?

Many individuals with Tourette syndrome notice improvement of their symptoms in their late teens and early twenties. As a result, some may actually become symptom-free or no longer need medication for tic suppression. Although the disorder is generally lifelong and chronic, it is not a degenerative condition. Individuals with Tourette syndrome have a normal life expectancy. Tourette syndrome does not impair intelligence. Although tic symptoms tend to decrease with age, it is possible that neurobehavioral disorders, such as ADHD, OCD, depression, generalized anxiety, panic attacks, and mood swings can persist and cause impairment in adult life.

What Other Disorders Are Associated with Tourette Syndrome?

Many individuals with Tourette syndrome experience additional neurobehavioral problems including inattention; hyperactivity and impulsivity ADHD and related problems with reading, writing, and arithmetic; and obsessive-compulsive symptoms, such as intrusive thoughts/worries and repetitive behaviors. For example, worries about dirt and germs may be associated with repetitive handwashing, and concerns about bad things happening may be associated with ritualistic behaviors, such as counting, repeating, or ordering and arranging. People with Tourette syndrome have also reported problems with depression or anxiety disorders, as well as other difficulties with living, that may or may not be directly related to Tourette syndrome.

Part Five

Genetic Research

Chapter 61

The Human Genome Project

What Is a Genome?

A genome is an organism's complete set of deoxyribonucleic acid (DNA), including all of its genes. Each genome contains all of the information needed to build and maintain that organism. In humans, a copy of the entire genome—more than three billion DNA base pairs—is contained in all cells that have a nucleus.

What Was the Human Genome Project and Why Has It Been Important?

The Human Genome Project (HGP) was an international research effort to determine the sequence of the human genome and identify the genes that it contains. The project was coordinated by the National Institutes of Health (NIH) and the U.S. Department of Energy (DOE). Additional contributors included universities across the United States and international partners in the United Kingdom, France, Germany, Japan, and China. The HGP formally began in 1990 and was completed in 2003, two years ahead of its original schedule.

The work of the HGP has allowed researchers to begin to understand the blueprint for building a person. As researchers learn more about the functions of genes and proteins, this knowledge will have a major impact in the fields of medicine, biotechnology, and the life sciences.

This chapter includes text excerpted from "What Is a Genome?" Genetics Home Reference (GHR), National Institutes of Health (NIH), February 5, 2019.

What Were the Goals of the Human Genome Project?

The main goals of the HGP were to provide a complete and accurate sequence of the 3 billion DNA base pairs that make up the human genome and to find all of the estimated 20,000 to 25,000 human genes. The project also aimed to sequence the genomes of several other organisms that are important to medical research, such as the mouse and the fruit fly.

In addition to sequencing DNA, the HGP sought to develop new tools to obtain and analyze the data and to make this information widely available. Also, because advances in genetics have consequences for individuals and society, the HGP committed to exploring the consequences of genomic research through its Ethical, Legal, and Social Implications (ELSI) program.

What Did the Human Genome Project Accomplish?

In April 2003, researchers announced that the HGP had completed a high-quality sequence of essentially the entire human genome. This sequence closed the gaps from a working draft of the genome, which was published in 2001. It also identified the locations of many human genes and provided information about their structure and organization. The project made the sequence of the human genome and tools to analyze the data freely available via the Internet.

In addition to the human genome, the HGP sequenced the genomes of several other organisms, including brewers' yeast, the roundworm, and the fruit fly. In 2002, researchers announced that they had also completed a working draft of the mouse genome. By studying the similarities and differences between human genes and those of other organisms, researchers can discover the functions of particular genes and identify which genes are critical for life.

The project's ELSI program became the world's largest bioethics program and a model for other ELSI programs worldwide.

What Were Some of the Ethical, Legal, and Social Implications Addressed by the Human Genome Project?

The ELSI program was founded in 1990 as an integral part of the HGP. The mission of the ELSI program was to identify and address issues raised by genomic research that would affect individuals, families, and society. A percentage of the HGP budget at the NIH and DOE was devoted to ELSI research.

The ELSI program focused on the possible consequences of genomic research in four main areas:

- Privacy and fairness in the use of genetic information, including the potential for genetic discrimination in employment and insurance

- The integration of new genetic technologies, such as genetic testing, into the practice of clinical medicine

- Ethical issues surrounding the design and conduct of genetic research with people, including the process of informed consent

- The education of healthcare professionals, policymakers, students, and the public about genetics and the complex issues that result from genomic research

Chapter 62

Genomic Medicine

What Is Genomic Medicine?

NHGRI defines genomic medicine as "an emerging medical discipline that involves using genomic information about an individual as part of their clinical care (e.g., for diagnostic or therapeutic decision-making) and the health outcomes and policy implications of that clinical use." Already, genomic medicine is making an impact in the fields of oncology, pharmacology, rare and undiagnosed diseases, and infectious disease.

The nation's investment in the Human Genome Project (HGP) was grounded in the expectation that knowledge generated as a result of that extraordinary research effort would be used to advance our understanding of biology and disease and to improve health. In the years since the HGP's completion, there has been much excitement about the potential for so-called "personalized medicine" to reach the clinic. More recently, a report from the National Academy of Sciences has called for the adoption of "precision medicine," where genomics, epigenomics, environmental exposure, and other data would be used to more accurately guide individual diagnosis. Genomic medicine, as defined above, can be considered a subset of precision medicine.

The translation of new discoveries to use in patient care takes many years. Based on discoveries over the past 5 to 10 years, genomic

This chapter includes text excerpted from "Genomic Medicine," National Human Genome Research Institute (NHGRI), March 31, 2015. Reviewed March 2019.

medicine is beginning to fuel new approaches in certain medical specialties. Oncology, in particular, is at the leading edge of incorporating genomics, as diagnostics for genetic and genomic markers are increasingly included in cancer screening and the guidance of tailored treatment strategies.

How Do We Get There?

It has often been estimated that it takes, on average, 17 years to translate a novel research finding into routine clinical practice. This time lag is due to a combination of factors, including the need to validate research findings, the fact that clinical trials are complex and take time to conduct and then analyze, and because disseminating information and educating healthcare workers about a new advance is not an overnight process.

Once sufficient evidence has been generated to demonstrate a benefit to patients, or "clinical utility," professional societies and clinical standards groups will use that evidence to determine whether to incorporate the new test into clinical practice guidelines. This determination will also factor in any potential ethical and legal issues, as well as economic factors, such as cost-benefit ratios.

The NHGRI Genomic Medicine Working Group (GMWG) has been gathering expert stakeholders in a series of Genomic Medicine meetings to discuss issues surrounding the adoption of genomic medicine. Particularly, the GMWG draws expertise from researchers at the cutting edge of this new medical specialty, with the aim of better informing future translational research at NHGRI. Additionally, the working group provides guidance to the National Advisory Council on Human Genome Research (NACHGR) and NHGRI in other areas of genomic medicine implementation, such as outlining infrastructural needs for the adoption of genomic medicine, identifying related efforts for future collaborations, and reviewing progress overall in genomic medicine implementation.

Examples of Genomic Medicines
Translational

- The causes of intellectual disability are often unknown, but a team in the Netherlands has used diagnostic exome sequencing of 100 affected individuals and their unaffected parents in order to uncover novel candidate genes and mutations that cause severe intellectual disability.

- Colorectal cancers with a particular mutation can benefit from treatment with aspirin postdiagnosis. Aspirin (and other nonsteroidal anti-inflammatory drugs) decrease the activity of a signaling pathway called "PI3K." Between 15 and 20 percent of colorectal cancer patients have a mutation in a gene called *"PIK3CA,"* which makes a protein that's part of the PI3K pathway, and it has been discovered that regular aspirin treatment is associated with increased survival compared to colorectal cancer patients who have the nonmutated version of *PIK3CA*.

- Currently, every baby born in the United States is tested at birth for between 29 and 50 severe, inherited, treatable genetic diseases through a public health program called "newborn screening." Whole-genome sequencing would enable clinicians to look for mutations across the entire genome simultaneously for a much larger number of diseases or conditions. Rapid whole-genome sequencing has been shown to provide a useful differential diagnosis within 50 hours for children in the neonatal intensive care unit.

- Researchers at Stanford University in California have been developing a new test to detect when a transplanted heart may be rejected by the recipient. Currently, the only way to detect the onset of rejection is by performing an invasive tissue biopsy. This novel approach only requires blood samples and detects the levels of cell-free circulating DNA from the donor organ in the recipient's bloodstream. This circulating DNA from the donor can be elevated for up to five months before rejection can be detected by biopsy, and the level of DNA correlates with the severity of the rejection event (i.e., more circulating DNA signals a more severe event).

- Cell-free circulating DNA is also being explored as a biomarker for cancers. As tumor cells die, they release fragments of their mutated DNA into the bloodstream. Sequencing this DNA can give insights into the tumor and possible treatments, and even be used to monitor tumor progression (as an alternative to invasive biopsies).

Clinical

- Pharmacogenomics involves using an individual's genome to determine whether or not a particular therapy, or dose of therapy, will be effective. Currently, more than 100 FDA-approved drugs have pharmacogenomics information in their labels, in diverse fields, such as analgesics, antivirals, cardiovascular drugs, and anti-cancer therapeutics.

- The FDA has also cleared or approved 45 human genetic tests and more than 100 nucleic acid-based tests for microbial pathogens.

- DNA sequencing is being used to investigate infectious disease outbreaks, including Ebola virus, drug-resistant strains of *Staphylococcus aureas and Klebsiella pneumoniae,* as well as food poisoning following contamination with Escherichia coli. Sequencing has also recently been used to diagnose bacterial meningoencephalitis, rapidly identifying the correct therapeutic agent for the patient.

- Cystic fibrosis is one of the most common genetic diseases, caused by mutations in a gene called "*CTFR*." More than 900 different *CTFR* mutations that cause cystic fibrosis have been identified to date. Approximately 4 percent of cases are caused by a mutation known as "G551D," and now a drug called "ivacaftor" has been developed that is extraordinarily effective at treating this disease in individuals with this particular mutation.

- Whole genome sequencing or whole exome sequencing (where only the protein-coding exons within genes, rather than the entire genome, are sequenced), has been used to help doctors diagnose and, in some extraordinary cases, to identify available treatments-in rare disease cases. For example, Alexis and Noah Beery, a pair of Californian twins, were misdiagnosed with cerebral palsy, but DNA sequencing pointed to a new diagnosis, as well as a treatment, to which both children are responding well. Another patient who was misdiagnosed (for 30 years) with cerebral palsy was also found to have treatable dopa-responsive dystonia thanks to whole exome sequencing. In another case, a young boy in Wisconsin, Nic Volker, was able to be cured of an extreme form of inflammatory bowel disease after his genome sequence revealed that a bone marrow transplant would likely be life-saving.

- The translation of new genomic medicine discoveries is already making a difference in patient care.

Chapter 63

Gene Therapy

What Is Gene Therapy?

Gene therapy is an experimental technique that uses genes to treat or prevent disease. In the future, this technique may allow doctors to treat a disorder by inserting a gene into a patient's cells instead of using drugs or surgery. Researchers are testing several approaches to gene therapy, including:

- Replacing a mutated gene that causes disease with a healthy copy of the gene

- Inactivating, or "knocking out," a mutated gene that is functioning improperly

- Introducing a new gene into the body to help fight disease

Although gene therapy is a promising treatment option for a number of diseases (including inherited disorders, some types of cancer, and certain viral infections), the technique remains risky and is still under study to make sure that it will be safe and effective. Gene therapy is currently being tested only for diseases that have no other cures.

This chapter includes text excerpted from "What Is Gene Therapy?" Genetics Home Reference (GHR), National Institutes of Health (NIH), February 5, 2019.

How Does Gene Therapy Work?

Gene therapy is designed to introduce genetic material into cells to compensate for abnormal genes or to make a beneficial protein. If a mutated gene causes a necessary protein to be faulty or missing, gene therapy may be able to introduce a normal copy of the gene to restore the function of the protein.

A gene that is inserted directly into a cell usually does not function. Instead, a carrier called a "vector" is genetically engineered to deliver the gene. Certain viruses are often used as vectors because they can deliver the new gene by infecting the cell. The viruses are modified so they can not cause disease when used in people. Some types of virus, such as retroviruses, integrate their genetic material (including the new gene) into a chromosome in the human cell. Other viruses, such as adenoviruses, introduce their deoxyribonucleic acid (DNA) into the nucleus of the cell, but the DNA is not integrated into a chromosome.

The vector can be injected or given intravenously (by IV) directly into a specific tissue in the body, where it is taken up by individual cells. Alternately, a sample of the patient's cells can be removed and exposed to the vector in a laboratory setting. The cells containing the vector are then returned to the patient. If the treatment is successful, the new gene delivered by the vector will make a functioning protein.

Researchers must overcome many technical challenges before gene therapy will be a practical approach to treating disease. For example, scientists must find better ways to deliver genes and target them to particular cells. They must also ensure that new genes are precisely controlled by the body.

Is Gene Therapy Safe?

Gene therapy is under study to determine whether it could be used to treat disease. Current research is evaluating the safety of gene therapy; future studies will test whether it is an effective treatment option. Several studies have already shown that this approach can have very serious health risks, such as toxicity, inflammation, and cancer. Because the techniques are relatively new, some of the risks may be unpredictable; however, medical researchers, institutions, and regulatory agencies are working to ensure that gene therapy research is as safe as possible.

Comprehensive federal laws, regulations, and guidelines help protect people who participate in research studies (called "clinical trials"). The U.S. Food and Drug Administration (FDA) regulates all gene therapy products in the United States and oversees research in this area. Researchers who wish to test an approach in a clinical trial must first obtain permission from the FDA. The FDA has the authority to reject or suspend clinical trials that are suspected of being unsafe for participants.

The National Institutes of Health (NIH) also plays an important role in ensuring the safety of gene therapy research. NIH provides guidelines for investigators and institutions (such as universities and hospitals) to follow when conducting clinical trials with gene therapy. These guidelines state that clinical trials at institutions receiving NIH funding for this type of research must be registered with the NIH Office of Biotechnology Activities. The protocol, or plan, for each clinical trial, is then reviewed by the NIH Recombinant DNA Advisory Committee (RAC) to determine whether it raises medical, ethical, or safety issues that warrant further discussion at one of the RAC's public meetings.

An Institutional Review Board (IRB) and an Institutional Biosafety Committee (IBC) must approve each gene therapy clinical trial before it can be carried out. An IRB is a committee of scientific and medical advisors and consumers that reviews all research within an institution. An IBC is a group that reviews and approves an institution's potentially hazardous research studies. Multiple levels of evaluation and oversight ensure that safety concerns are a top priority in the planning and carrying out of gene therapy research.

What Are the Ethical Issues Surrounding Gene Therapy?

Because gene therapy involves making changes to the body's set of basic instructions, it raises many unique ethical concerns. The ethical questions surrounding gene therapy include:

- How can "good" and "bad" uses of gene therapy be distinguished?

- Who decides which traits are normal and which constitute a disability or disorder?

- Will the high costs of gene therapy make it available only to the wealthy?

- Could the widespread use of gene therapy make society less accepting of people who are different?

- Should people be allowed to use gene therapy to enhance basic human traits, such as height, intelligence, or athletic ability?

Current gene therapy research has focused on treating individuals by targeting the therapy to body cells, such as bone marrow or blood cells. This type of gene therapy cannot be passed to a person's children. Gene therapy could be targeted to egg and sperm cells (germ cells), however, which would allow the inserted gene to be passed to future generations. This approach is known as "germline gene therapy."

The idea of germline gene therapy is controversial. While it could spare future generations in a family from having a particular genetic disorder, it might affect the development of a fetus in unexpected ways or have long-term side effects that are not yet known. Because people who would be affected by germline gene therapy are not yet born, they cannot choose whether to have the treatment. Because of these ethical concerns, the U.S. Government does not allow federal funds to be used for research on germline gene therapy in people.

Is Gene Therapy Available to Treat My Disorder?

Gene therapy is currently available primarily in a research setting. The FDA has approved only a limited number of gene therapy products for sale in the United States.

Hundreds of research studies (clinical trials) are underway to test gene therapy as a treatment for genetic conditions, cancer, and human immunodeficiency virus (HIV)/acquired immunodeficiency syndrome (AIDS). If you are interested in participating in a clinical trial, talk with your doctor or genetics professional about how to participate.

Chapter 64

Pharmacogenomics

What Is Pharmacogenomics?

Pharmacogenomics (sometimes called "pharmacogenetics") is a field of research that studies how a person's genes affect how she or he responds to medications. Its long-term goal is to help doctors select the drugs and doses best suited for each person. It is part of the field of precision medicine, which aims to treat each patient individually.

What Role Do Genes Play in How Medicines Work?

Just as our genes determine our hair and eye color, they partly affect how our bodies respond to medicine.

Genes are instructions, written in deoxyribonucleic acid (DNA), for building protein molecules. Different people can have different versions of the same gene. Each version has a slightly different DNA sequence. Some of these variants are common, and some are rare. And some affect health, such as those gene variants linked to certain diseases.

Scientists know that certain proteins affect how drugs work. Pharmacogenomics looks at variations in genes for these proteins. Such proteins include liver enzymes that chemically change drugs. Sometimes chemical changes can make the drugs more—or less—active in the body. Even small differences in the genes for these liver enzymes can have a big impact on a drug's safety or effectiveness.

This chapter includes text excerpted from "Pharmacogenomics," National Institute of General Medical Sciences (NIGMS), October 2017.

One liver enzyme, known as "CYP2D6," acts on a quarter of all prescription drugs. For example, it converts the painkiller codeine into its active form, morphine. There are more than 160 versions of the *CYP2D6* gene. Many vary by only a single difference in their DNA sequence. Others have larger changes. Most of these variants do not affect how people respond to the drug.

Typically, people have two copies of each gene. However, some people have hundreds or even thousands of copies of the *CYP2D6* gene. Those with extra copies produce too much of the CYP2D6 enzyme and process the drug very fast. As a result, their bodies may convert codeine to morphine so quickly and completely that a standard dose can be an overdose. In contrast, some variants of CYP2D6 create an enzyme that does not work. People with these variants process codeine slowly, if at all, leading to little, if any, pain relief. For them, doctors can prescribe a different drug.

How Is Pharmacogenomics Affecting Drug Design, Development, and Prescribing Guidelines?

The U.S. Food and Drug Administration (FDA) monitors drug safety in the United States. It now includes pharmacogenomic information on the labels of around 200 medications. This information can help doctors tailor drug prescriptions for individual patients by providing guidance on dose, possible side effects, or differences in effectiveness for people with certain gene variants.

Drug companies are also using pharmacogenomics to develop and market medicines for people with specific genetic profiles. By studying a drug only in people likely to benefit from it, drug companies might be able to speed up the drug's development and maximize its therapeutic benefit.

In addition, if scientists can identify genes that cause serious side effects, doctors could prescribe those drugs only to people who do not have those genes. This would allow some individuals to receive potentially lifesaving medicines that otherwise might be banned because they pose a risk for other people.

How Is Pharmacogenomics Affecting Medical Treatment?

Currently, doctors prescribe drugs based mostly on factors such as a patient's age, weight, sex, and liver and kidney function. For a few drugs, researchers have identified gene variants that affect how people respond. In these cases, doctors can select the best medication and dose for each patient.

Additionally, learning how patients respond to medications helps to discern the different forms of their diseases.

Chapter 65

Next Steps in Genomic Research

What Are the Next Steps in Genomic Research?

Discovering the sequence of the human genome was only the first step in understanding how the instructions coded in deoxyribonucleic acid (DNA) lead to a functioning human being. The next stage of genomic research will begin to derive meaningful knowledge from the DNA sequence. Research studies that build on the work of the Human Genome Project (HGP) are underway worldwide.

The objectives of continued genomic research include the following:

- Determine the function of genes and the elements that regulate genes throughout the genome

- Find variations in the DNA sequence among people and determine their significance. The most common type of genetic variation is known as a "single nucleotide polymorphism" or SNP. These small differences may help predict a person's risk of particular diseases and response to certain medications.

- Discover the 3-dimensional structures of proteins and identify their functions

This chapter includes text excerpted from "What Are the Next Steps in Genomic Research?" Genetics Home Reference (GHR), National Institutes of Health (NIH), February 5, 2019.

- Explore how DNA and proteins interact with one another and with the environment to create complex living systems

- Develop and apply genome-based strategies for the early detection, diagnosis, and treatment of disease

- Sequence the genomes of other organisms, such as the rat, cow, and chimpanzee, in order to compare similar genes between species

- Develop new technologies to study genes and DNA on a large scale and store genomic data efficiently

- Continue to explore the ethical, legal, and social issues raised by genomic research

What Are Single Nucleotide Polymorphisms?

Single nucleotide polymorphisms, are the most common type of genetic variation among people. Each SNP represents a difference in a single DNA building block, called a "nucleotide." For example, a SNP may replace the nucleotide cytosine (C) with the nucleotide thymine (T) in a certain stretch of DNA.

SNPs occur normally throughout a person's DNA. They occur almost once in every 1,000 nucleotides on average, which means there are roughly 4 to 5 million SNPs in a person's genome. These variations may be unique or occur in many individuals; scientists have found more than 100 million SNPs in populations around the world. Most commonly, these variations are found in the DNA between genes. They can act as biological markers, helping scientists locate genes that are associated with the disease. When SNPs occur within a gene or in a regulatory region near a gene, they may play a more direct role in disease by affecting the gene's function.

Most SNPs have no effect on health or development. Some of these genetic differences, however, have proven to be very important in the study of human health. Researchers have found SNPs that may help predict an individual's response to certain drugs, susceptibility to environmental factors such as toxins, and risk of developing particular diseases. SNPs can also be used to track the inheritance of disease genes within families. Future studies will work to identify SNPs associated with complex diseases, such as heart disease, diabetes, and cancer.

What Are Genome-Wide Association Studies?

Genome-wide association studies are a relatively new way for scientists to identify genes involved in human disease. This method searches the genome for SNPs, that occur more frequently in people with a particular disease than in people without the disease. Each study can look at hundreds or thousands of SNPs at the same time. Researchers use data from this type of study to pinpoint genes that may contribute to a person's risk of developing a certain disease.

Because genome-wide association studies examine SNPs across the genome, they represent a promising way to study complex, common diseases in which many genetic variations contribute to a person's risk. This approach has already identified SNPs related to several complex conditions including diabetes, heart abnormalities, Parkinson disease (PD), and Crohn disease (CD). Researchers hope that future genome-wide association studies will identify more SNPs associated with chronic diseases, as well as variations that affect a person's response to certain drugs and influence interactions between a person's genes and the environment.

What Is the International HapMap Project?

The International HapMap Project is a scientific effort to identify common genetic variations among people. This project represents a collaboration of scientists from public and private organizations in six countries. Data from the project is freely available to researchers worldwide. Researchers can use the data to learn more about the relationship between genetic differences and human disease.

The haplotype map (HapMap) is a catalog of common SNPs. These variations occur normally throughout a person's DNA. When several SNPs cluster together on a chromosome, they are inherited as a block known as a "haplotype." The HapMap describes haplotypes, including their locations in the genome and how common they are in different populations throughout the world.

The human genome contains roughly 10 million SNPs. It would be difficult, time-consuming, and expensive to look at each of these changes and determine whether it plays a role in human disease. Using haplotypes, researchers can sample a selection of these variants instead of studying each one. The HapMap will make carrying out genome-wide association studies cheaper, faster, and less complicated.

The main goal of the International HapMap Project is to describe common patterns of human genetic variation that are involved in human health and disease. Additionally, data from the project will help researchers find genetic differences that can help predict an individual's response to particular medicines or environmental factors (such as toxins.)

What Is the Encyclopedia of Deoxyribonucleic Acid Elements Project?

The Encyclopedia of Deoxyribonucleic Acid Elements (ENCODE) Project was planned as a follow-up to the HGP. The HGP sequenced the DNA that makes up the human genome; the ENCODE Project seeks to interpret this sequence. Coinciding with the completion of the HGP in 2003, the ENCODE Project began as a worldwide effort involving more than 30 research groups and more than 400 scientists.

The approximately 20,000 genes that provide instructions for making proteins account for only about 1 percent of the human genome. Researchers embarked on the ENCODE Project to figure out the purpose of the remaining 99 percent of the genome. Scientists discovered that more than 80 percent of this nongene component of the genome, which was once considered "junk DNA," actually has a role in regulating the activity of particular genes (gene expression).

Researchers think that changes in the regulation of gene activity may disrupt protein production and cell processes and result in disease. A goal of the ENCODE Project is to link variations in the expression of certain genes to the development of the disease.

The ENCODE Project has given researchers insight into how the human genome functions. As researchers learn more about the regulation of gene activity and how genes are expressed, the scientific community will be able to better understand how the entire genome can affect human health.

What Are Genome Editing and CRISPR-Cas9?

Genome editing (also called "gene editing") is a group of technologies that give scientists the ability to change an organism's DNA. These technologies allow genetic material to be added, removed, or altered at particular locations in the genome. Several approaches to genome editing have been developed. A recent one is known as "CRISPR-Cas9," which is short for clustered regularly interspaced short palindromic repeats and CRISPR-associated protein 9. The CRISPR-Cas9 system has generated a lot of excitement in the scientific community because it is faster, cheaper, more accurate, and more efficient than other existing genome editing methods.

CRISPR-Cas9 was adapted from a naturally occurring genome editing system in bacteria. The bacteria capture snippets of DNA from invading viruses and use them to create DNA segments known as "CRISPR arrays." The CRISPR arrays allow the bacteria to "remember" the viruses (or closely related ones). If the viruses attack again, the bacteria produce ribonucleic acid (RNA) segments from the CRISPR arrays to target the viruses' DNA. The bacteria then use Cas9 or a similar enzyme to cut the DNA apart, which disables the virus.

The CRISPR-Cas9 system works similarly in the lab. Researchers create a small piece of RNA with a short "guide" sequence that attaches (binds) to a specific target sequence of DNA in a genome. The RNA also binds to the Cas9 enzyme. As in bacteria, the modified RNA is used to recognize the DNA sequence, and the Cas9 enzyme cuts the DNA at the targeted location. Although Cas9 is the enzyme that is used most often, other enzymes (for example Cpf1) can also be used. Once the DNA is cut, researchers use the cell's own DNA-repair machinery to add or delete pieces of genetic material or to make changes to the DNA by replacing an existing segment with a customized DNA sequence.

Genome editing is of great interest in the prevention and treatment of human diseases. Most research on genome editing is done to understand diseases using cells and animal models. Scientists are still working to determine whether this approach is safe and effective for use in people. It is being explored in research on a wide variety of diseases, including single-gene disorders, such as cystic fibrosis (CF), hemophilia, and sickle cell disease (SCD). It also holds promise for the treatment and prevention of more complex diseases, such as cancer, heart disease, mental illness, and human immunodeficiency virus (HIV) infection.

Ethical concerns arise when genome editing, using technologies such as CRISPR-Cas9, is used to alter human genomes. Most of the changes introduced with genome editing are limited to somatic cells, which are cells other than egg and sperm cells. These changes affect only certain tissues and are not passed from one generation to the next. However, changes made to genes in egg or sperm cells (germline cells) or in the genes of an embryo could be passed to future generations. Germline cell and embryo genome editing bring up a number of ethical challenges, including whether it would be permissible to use this technology to enhance normal human traits (such as height or intelligence). Based on concerns about ethics and safety, germline cell and embryo genome editing are currently illegal in many countries.

Chapter 66

DNA Sequencing

What Is Deoxyribonucleic Acid Sequencing?

Sequencing deoxyribonucleic acid (DNA) means determining the order of the four chemical building blocks—called "bases"—that make up the DNA molecule. The sequence tells scientists the kind of genetic information that is carried in a particular DNA segment. For example, scientists can use sequence information to determine which stretches of DNA contain genes and which stretches carry regulatory instructions, turning genes on or off. In addition, and importantly, sequence data can highlight changes in a gene that may cause disease.

In the DNA double helix, the four chemical bases always bond with the same partner to form "base pairs." Adenine (A) always pairs with thymine (T); cytosine (C) always pairs with guanine (G). This pairing is the basis for the mechanism by which DNA molecules are copied when cells divide, and the pairing also underlies the methods by which most DNA sequencing experiments are done. The human genome contains about three billion base pairs that spell out the instructions for making and maintaining a human being.

How New Is Deoxyribonucleic Acid Sequencing?

Since the completion of the Human Genome Project (HGP), technological improvements and automation have increased speed and

This chapter includes text excerpted from "DNA Sequencing," National Human Genome Research Institute (NHGRI), December 18, 2015. Reviewed March 2019.

lowered costs to the point where individual genes can be sequenced routinely, and some labs can sequence well over 100,000 billion bases per year, and an entire genome can be sequenced for just a few thousand dollars.

Many of these new technologies were developed with support from the National Human Genome Research Institute (NHGRI) Genome Technology Program and its Advanced DNA Sequencing Technology awards. One of NHGRI's goals is to promote new technologies that could eventually reduce the cost of sequencing a human genome of even higher quality than is possible nowadays and for less than one thousand dollars.

Are Newer Sequencing Technologies under Development?

One new sequencing technology involves watching DNA polymerase molecules—the same molecules that make new copies of DNA in our cells—as they copy DNA with a very fast movie camera and microscope, and incorporate different colors of bright dyes, one each for the letters A, T, C and G. This method provides different and very valuable information than what is provided by the instrument systems that are in most common use.

Another new technology in development entails the use of nanopores to sequence DNA. Nanopore-based DNA sequencing involves threading single DNA strands through extremely tiny pores in a membrane. DNA bases are read one at a time as they squeeze through the nanopore. The bases are identified by measuring differences in their effect on ions and electrical current flowing through the pore.

Using nanopores to sequence DNA offers many potential advantages over current methods. The goal is for sequencing to cost less and be done faster. Unlike sequencing methods currently in use, nanopore DNA sequencing means researchers can study the same molecule over and over again.

What Do Improvements in Deoxyribonucleic Acid Sequencing Mean for Human Health?

Researchers now are able to compare large stretches of DNA—one million bases or more—from different individuals quickly and cheaply. Such comparisons can yield an enormous amount of information about the role of inheritance in susceptibility to disease and in response to environmental influences. In addition, the ability to sequence the genome more rapidly and cost-effectively creates a vast potential for diagnostics and therapies.

Although routine DNA sequencing in the doctor's office is still many years away, some large medical centers have begun to use sequencing to detect and treat some diseases. In cancer, for example, physicians are increasingly able to use sequence data to identify the particular type of cancer a patient has. This enables the physician to make better choices for treatments.

Researchers in the NHGRI-supported Undiagnosed Diseases Program (UDN) use DNA sequencing to try to identify the genetic causes of rare diseases. Other researchers are studying its use in screening newborns for disease and disease risk.

Moreover, The Cancer Genome Atlas (TCGA) project, which is supported by NHGRI and the National Cancer Institute (NCI), is using DNA sequencing to unravel the genomic details of some 30 cancer types. Another National Institutes of Health (NIH) program examines how gene activity is controlled in different tissues and the role of gene regulation in disease. Ongoing and planned large-scale projects use DNA sequencing to examine the development of common and complex diseases, such as heart disease and diabetes, and in inherited diseases that cause physical malformations, developmental delay, and metabolic diseases.

Comparing the genome sequences of different types of animals and organisms, such as chimpanzees and yeast, can also provide insights into the biology of development and evolution.

Part Six

Information for Parents of Children with Genetic Disorders

Chapter 67

What Are Birth Defects?

Birth defects are structural or functional abnormalities present at birth that can cause physical disability, intellectual and developmental disability (IDD), and other health problems. Some may be fatal, especially if not detected and treated early.

There are two main categories of birth defects: structural birth defects and functional/developmental birth defects. Some birth defects affect many parts or processes in the body, leading to both structural and functional problems. Researchers have identified thousands of different birth defects. According to the Centers for Disease Control and Prevention (CDC), birth defects are the leading cause of death for infants in the United States during the first year of life.

What Are the Types of Birth Defects?

There are two main categories of birth defects.

Structural Birth Defects

Structural birth defects are related to a problem with the structure of body parts. These can include:

- Cleft lip or cleft palate

This chapter includes text excerpted from "About Birth Defects," *Eunice Kennedy Shriver* National Institute of Child Health and Human Development (NICHD), September 1, 2017.

- Heart defects, such as missing or misshaped valves

- Abnormal limbs, such as a clubfoot

- Neural-tube defects, such as spina bifida, and problems related to the growth and development of the brain and spinal cord

Functional or Developmental Birth Defects

Functional or developmental birth defects are related to a problem with how a body part or body system works or functions. These problems can include:

- **Nervous system or brain problems.** These include intellectual and developmental disabilities, behavioral disorders, speech or language difficulties, seizures, and movement trouble. Some examples of birth defects that affect the nervous system include Down syndrome (DS), Prader-Willi syndrome (PWS), and fragile X syndrome (FXS).

- **Sensory problems.** Examples include hearing loss, such as deafness, and visual problems, such as blindness.

- **Metabolic disorders.** These involve problems with certain chemical reactions in the body, such as conditions that limit the body's ability to rid itself of waste materials or harmful chemicals. Two common metabolic disorders are phenylketonuria and hypothyroidism.

- **Degenerative disorders.** These are conditions that might not be obvious at birth but cause one or more aspects of health to steadily get worse. Examples of degenerative disorders are muscular dystrophy (MD) and X-linked adrenoleukodystrophy, which leads to problems of the nervous system and the adrenal glands and was the subject of the movie "Lorenzo's Oil."

Some birth defects affect many parts or processes in the body, leading to both structural and functional problems.

How Many People Are Affected by/at Risk for Birth Defects?

The CDC estimates that birth defects occur in about 1 in every 33 infants born in the United States each year.

Birth defects can occur during any pregnancy, but some factors increase the risk for birth defects. The following situations place pregnant women at higher risk of having a child with a birth defect:

- **Lack of folic acid.** Women who are pregnant or who could become pregnant should take 400 micrograms of folic acid every day to prevent neural-tube defects (NTDs). However, according to the CDC, only 2 out of every 5 women of childbearing age take folic acid every day.

- **Drinking alcohol.** Drinking alcohol during pregnancy can lead to a variety of problems, including birth defects. For example, using alcohol can lead to fetal alcohol syndrome (FAS), which is characterized by IDDs, physical challenges, and behavioral problems. There is no safe level of alcohol consumption during pregnancy.

- **Smoking cigarettes.** Smoking cigarettes during pregnancy can lead to a variety of problems, including lung problems such as asthma. Evidence also strongly suggests that certain birth defects, such as problems with the heart and intestines, are caused by smoking during pregnancy.

- **Using drugs.** Using drugs during pregnancy can increase the risk of various birth defects, including IDDs and behavioral problems, as well as pregnancy loss and stillbirth.

- **Medication use.** Certain medications are known to cause birth defects if taken during pregnancy. Thalidomide, which is currently used to treat certain cancers and other serious conditions, was once sold as a treatment for morning sickness until it was discovered that it caused severe birth defects. Infants whose mothers took thalidomide had a range of structural and functional problems, including misshapen ears and shortened limbs. Although the thalidomide situation led to much stricter controls on drugs used during pregnancy, the majority of medications currently used by pregnant women have not been tested for safety or efficacy in pregnant women. Addressing this issue is the primary focus of *Eunice Kennedy Shriver* National Institute of Child Health and Human Development's (NICHD) Obstetric-Fetal Pharmacology Research (OPRU) Units Network. Women who are pregnant or who might become pregnant should discuss all medications, both prescription and over-the-counter (OTC), and supplements they take with their healthcare providers.

- **Infections.** Women who get certain infections during pregnancy are at higher risk for having a child with birth defects. Some of the more common infections that are linked to birth defects are cytomegalovirus, a common virus that spreads through body fluids and usually causes no symptoms in healthy people, and toxoplasmosis, a parasitic infection that spreads through contact with cat feces, raw meat, and contaminated food and water. Zika virus infection is linked to microcephaly in newborn babies—a condition in which the brain and skull are smaller than normal.

- **Obesity or uncontrolled diabetes.** NICHD research found that the risk of newborn heart defects and neural-tube defects increased with maternal obesity. Additional NICHD research suggests that children of obese parents may be at risk for developmental delays. Obesity is also associated with other health problems and long-term health issues. Poorly controlled blood sugar places women at higher risk of having a baby who is too large, has breathing problems, or has other poor health outcomes. These outcomes are likely regardless of whether the woman had diabetes before she got pregnant (type 1 or 2 diabetes) or whether she developed diabetes during pregnancy (gestational diabetes).

- **Exposure to things in the environment.** Pregnant women who breathe in, eat, drink, or get things into their bodies in other ways may also be at increased risk of birth defects. For example, pregnant women who are exposed to high levels of radiation, such as cancer treatments, are at higher risk for birth defects in their infants. Handling or breathing in certain chemicals can also increase the risk of birth defects.

What Causes Birth Defects

Different birth defects have different causes, and the causes of many birth defects remain unknown.

A specific condition might be caused by one or more of the following primary problems:

- **Genetic problems.** One or more genes might have a change or mutation that results in them not working properly, such as in FXS. Similarly, a gene or part of the gene might be missing.

- **Chromosomal problems.** In some cases, a chromosome or part of a chromosome might be missing, such as in Turner syndrome, when a female is missing an X chromosome. Other birth defects result from having an extra chromosome, such as in Klinefelter syndrome and Down syndrome.

- **Infections.** Women who get certain infections during pregnancy are at higher risk for having a child with birth defects. For example, infection with Zika virus during pregnancy is linked with the birth defect called "microcephaly," in which the brain and skull are smaller than normal. Zika infection in pregnancy is linked to other structural problems with the brain as well.

- **Exposure to medications, chemicals, or other agents during pregnancy.** The infants whose mothers took thalidomide are examples of an exposure leading to birth defects. Other examples include exposure to rubella (also called "German measles") and toxic chemicals, such as hydrocarbons.

Chapter 68

Tips for Parenting a Child with a Disability

What Is Happening?

Children develop in many ways and at different rates. While each child is unique, there are developmental milestones or skills that children are expected to develop by certain ages. Parents expect these age-specific tasks to occur naturally. Children do not necessarily learn skills at the same pace, but when milestones do not develop within the expected broad timeframe or do not appear at all, parents and caregivers may become concerned.

What You Might Be Seeing

Parents and primary caregivers are in the best position to note any ongoing concerns about their child's development that may require action. Although children develop at their own rate, some differences may be signs of developmental delays or disabilities. You may want to observe your child in the following areas to decide if your child is on a typical developmental path:

This chapter includes text excerpted from "Parenting Your Child with Developmental Delays and Disabilities," Child Welfare Information Gateway, U.S. Department of Health and Human Services (HHS), February 14, 2011. Reviewed March 2019.

- **Gross motor skills:** Using large groups of muscles to sit, stand, walk, run, etc.; keeping balance; and changing positions

- **Fine motor skills:** Using hands to eat, draw, dress, play, write, and do many other things

- **Language:** Speaking, using body language, and gestures, communicating, and understanding what others say

- **Cognitive:** Thinking skills including learning, understanding, problem-solving, reasoning, and remembering

- **Social:** Interacting with others; having relationships with family, friends, and teachers; and cooperating and responding to the feelings of others.

What You Can Do
First Steps

- If your child's development worries you, share your concerns with someone who can and will help you get clear answers about your child's development. Do not accept others dismissing your concerns by saying "You worry too much," or "That will go away in a few months." You know your child and are her or his best advocate.

- If your child seems to be losing ground—in other words, starts to not be able to do things they could do in the past—you should request an evaluation right away. Get professional input for your concerns.

- If you think your child may be delayed or have a disability, take her or him to a primary healthcare provider or pediatrician and request a developmental screening. If you do not understand the words used to assess or describe your child, be sure to ask questions such as, "What does that mean?"

Next Steps

- If your child is diagnosed with a developmental delay or disability, remember that you are not alone. Meet and interact with other families of children with special needs, including those with your child's identified disability. You may have many questions about how your child's diagnosis affects your whole family.

- Seek information. Learn the specifics about your child's special needs. When your child is diagnosed with a delay or a disability, you should begin interventions as early as possible so your child can make the best possible progress.

- Find resources for your child. Seek referrals from your physician or other advisors. Do not let your child's delay or disability label become the entire focus. Your child has special challenges but is also a member of your family. Seeing your child grow and develop as an individual and part of the family is one of the great pleasures of being a parent.

- Find professionals and agencies that will help your child. Keep in mind that some services that assist your child may also provide programs to benefit your entire family.

Ongoing Strategies

- Locate or start a support group. You may appreciate the opportunity to give and receive assistance or encouragement from others who can truly identify with your experience.

- Take a break and give yourself the gift of time to regroup, reestablish your relationships with family members, or reconnect with friends. You will be a better champion for your child when you take the time to care for yourself as well.

- Do not let your child's delay or disability label become the entire focus. Your child has special challenges but is also a member of your family. Seeing your child grow and develop as an individual and part of the family is one of the great pleasures of being a parent.

Chapter 69

Early Intervention: An Overview

Why Act Early If You Are Concerned about Development

Act early on developmental concerns to make a real difference for you and your child. If you are concerned about your child's development, do not wait. You know your child best.

Early intervention helps children improve their abilities and learn new skills. Take these steps to help your child:

- Tell your child's doctor or nurse if you notice any signs of possible developmental delay and ask for a developmental screening.

If you or the doctor still feel worried:

- Ask for a referral to a specialist

- Call your state or territory's early intervention program to find out if your child can get services to help

---

This chapter includes text excerpted from "Why Act Early If You Are Concerned about Development?" Centers for Disease Control and Prevention (CDC), June 19, 2018.

What Is Early Intervention?

Early intervention:

- Is the term used to describe services and support that help babies and toddlers (from birth to three years of age in most states/territories) with developmental delays or disabilities and their families

- May include speech therapy, physical therapy, and other types of services based on the needs of the child and family

- Can have a significant impact on a child's ability to learn new skills and increase their success in school and life

- Programs are available in every state and territory. These services are provided for free or at a reduced cost for any child who meets the state's criteria for developmental delay

Why Early Intervention Is Important
Earlier Is Better

Intervention is likely to be more effective when it is provided earlier in life rather than later.

The connections in a baby's brain are most adaptable in the first three years of life. These connections, also called "neural circuits," are the foundation for learning, behavior, and health. Over time, these connections become harder to change.

Intervention Works

Early intervention services can change a child's developmental path and improve outcomes for children, families, and communities.

Help Your Child, Help Your Family

Families benefit from early intervention by being able to better meet their children's needs from an early age and throughout their lives.

How to Talk to the Doctor about Developmental Concerns

The following tips will help you talk with your child's doctor's office and the evaluation centers.

Doctor's Office

When you call your child's doctor's office, say, "I would like to make an appointment to see the doctor because I am concerned about my child's development."

Be ready to share your specific concerns about your child when you call. If you wrote down your concerns, keep them. Your notes will be helpful during your visit with the doctor.

Early Intervention Services Office

When you call your state's early intervention services office (if your child is not yet three years old), say, "I am concerned about my child's development and would like to request an evaluation. Can you help me or let me speak with someone who can?"

- Be ready to share your specific concerns about your child. You will also be asked for some general information about yourself and your child (your name, your child's name and age, where you live, and more).

- Write down who you speak to, the date, and what was said; you might need this information later.

Elementary School or Board of Education

When you call your local elementary school or board of education (if your child is three or older), say, "I am concerned about my child's development and would like to talk with someone about having my child evaluated. Can you help me or let me speak with someone who can?"

- Be ready to share your specific concerns about your child. You will also be asked for some general information about yourself and your child (your name, your child's name and age, where you live, and more).

- Write down who you speak to, the date, and what was said; you might need this information later.

While You Wait

If you have to wait to get an appointment, to see a specialist, or start intervention services, know that there are some simple things you can do today and every day to help your child's development.

What to Do While You Wait to See a Developmental Specialist

Unfortunately, families may have to wait many weeks or sometimes months before they are able to get an appointment to see a specialist or start intervention services for their child's developmental problem. This can be a frustrating time for parents who want answers and help now.

If you find yourself in this situation, know that there are some simple things you can do today and every day to help your child's development.

Make the Most of Playtime

Interact with your child as much as possible. Read books, sing songs, play with toys, make crafts, do household chores, and play outside together. Talk to your child: label items, point out interesting things, tell stories, comment about what you see and how you feel, and explain how things work and why things happen. Your child may not always seem to be listening, but she or he may be hearing more than you think.

Find Support

Reach out. You are not alone. To find support and information for your family, visit the Family Voices website (familyvoices.org) or call 888-835-5669.

Chapter 70

Rehabilitative and Assistive Technology

Rehabilitative and assistive technologies are tools, equipment, or products that can help people with disabilities function successfully at school, home, work, and in the community.

Assistive technology can be as simple as a magnifying glass or as complex as a digital communication system. An assistive device can be as large as a power wheelchair lift for a van or as small as a handheld hook that assists with buttoning a shirt.

Tools to help people recover or improve their functioning after injury or illness are sometimes called "rehabilitative technology." But the term is often used interchangeably with the term "assistive technology."

Eunice Kennedy Shriver National Institute of Child Health and Human Development (NICHD) supports research on developing and evaluating technologies, devices, instruments, and other aids to help people with disabilities achieve their full potential.

Rehabilitative engineers use scientific principles to study how people with disabilities function in society. They study barriers to optimal function and design solutions so that people with disabilities can interact successfully in their environments.

This chapter includes text excerpted from "About Rehabilitative and Assistive Technology," *Eunice Kennedy Shriver* National Institute of Child Health and Human Development (NICHD), October 24, 2018.

What Are Some Types of Assistive Devices and How Are They Used?

Some examples of assistive technologies are:

- Mobility aids, such as wheelchairs, scooters, walkers, canes, crutches1, prosthetic devices, and orthotic devices.

- Hearing aids to help people hear or hear more clearly.

- Cognitive aids, including computer or electrical assistive devices, to help people with memory, attention, or other challenges in their thinking skills.

- Computer software and hardware, such as voice recognition programs, screen readers, and screen enlargement applications, to help people with mobility and sensory impairments use computers and mobile devices.

- Tools, such as automatic page turners, book holders, and adapted pencil grips to help learners with disabilities participate in educational activities

- Closed captioning to allow people with hearing problems to watch movies, television programs, and other digital media.

- Physical modifications in the built environment, including ramps, grab bars, and wider doorways to enable access to buildings, businesses, and workplaces.

- Lightweight, high-performance mobility devices that enable persons with disabilities to play sports and be physically active.

- Adaptive switches and utensils to allow those with limited motor skills to eat, play games, and accomplish other activities.

- Devices and features of devices to help perform tasks, such as cooking, dressing, and grooming; specialized handles and grips, devices that extend reach, and lights on telephones and doorbells are a few examples.

What Are Some Types of Rehabilitative Technologies?

Rehabilitative technologies and techniques help people recover or improve function after injury or illness. Examples include the following:

- **Robotics.** Specialized robots help people regain and improve function in arms or legs after a stroke.

- **Virtual reality.** People who are recovering from injury can retrain themselves to perform motions within a virtual environment.

- **Musculoskeletal modeling and simulations.** These computer simulations of the human body can pinpoint underlying mechanical problems in a person with a movement-related disability. This technique can help improve assistive aids or physical therapies.

- **Transcranial magnetic stimulation (TMS).** TMS sends magnetic impulses through the skull to stimulate the brain. This system can help people who have had a stroke recover movement and brain function.

- **Transcranial direct current stimulation (tDCS).** In tDCS, a mild electrical current travels through the skull and stimulates the brain. This can help recover movement in patients recovering from stroke or other conditions.

- **Motion analysis.** Motion analysis captures video of human motion with specialized computer software that analyzes the motion in detail. The technique gives healthcare providers a detailed picture of a person's specific movement challenges to guide proper therapy.

Some devices incorporate multiple types of technologies and techniques to help users regain or improve function. For example, the BrainGate project, which was partially funded by NICHD through the National Center for Medical Rehabilitation Research (NCMRR), relied on tiny sensors being implanted in the brain. The user could then think about moving their arm, and a robotic arm would carry out the thought.

How Does Rehabilitative Technology Benefit People with Disabilities?

Rehabilitative technology can help restore or improve function in people who have developed a disability due to disease, injury, or aging. Appropriate assistive technology often helps people with disabilities compensate, at least in part, for a limitation.

For example, assistive technology enables students with disabilities to compensate for certain impairments. This specialized technology promotes independence and decreases the need for other support.

Rehabilitative and assistive technology can enable individuals to:

- Care for themselves and their families

- Work

- Learn in typical school environments and other educational institutions

- Access information through computers and reading

- Enjoy music, sports, travel, and the arts

- Participate fully in community life

Assistive technology also benefits employers, teachers, family members, and everyone who interacts with people who use the technology.

As assistive technologies become more commonplace, people without disabilities are benefiting from them. For example, people for whom English is a second language are taking advantage of screen readers. Older individuals are using screen enlargers and magnifiers.

The person with a disability, along with her or his caregivers and a team of professionals and consultants, usually decide which type of rehabilitative or assistive technology would be most helpful. The team is trained to match particular technologies to specific needs to help the person function better or more independently. The team may include family doctors, regular and special education teachers, speech-language pathologists, rehabilitation engineers, occupational therapists, and other specialists, including representatives from companies that manufacture assistive technology.

What Conditions May Benefit from Assistive Devices?

Some disabilities are quite visible, while others are "hidden." Most disabilities can be grouped into the following categories:

- **Cognitive disability**, such as intellectual and learning disabilities/disorders, distractibility, reading disorders, and inability to remember or focus on large amounts of information

- **Hearing disability**, such as hearing loss or impaired hearing

- **Physical disability**, such as paralysis, difficulties with walking or other movements, inability to use a computer mouse, slow response time, and difficulty in controlling movement

- **Visual disability**, such as blindness, low vision, and color blindness

- **Mental conditions**, such as posttraumatic stress disorder (PTSD), anxiety disorders, mood disorders, eating disorders, and psychosis

Hidden disabilities are those that might not be immediately apparent when you look at someone. They can include visual impairments, movement problems, hearing impairments, and mental-health conditions.

Some medical conditions may also contribute to disabilities or may be categorized as hidden disabilities under the Americans with Disabilities Act (ADA). For example, epilepsy; diabetes; sickle cell conditions; human immunodeficiency virus (HIV)/acquired immunodeficiency syndrome (AIDS); cystic fibrosis (CF); cancer; and heart, liver, or kidney problems may lead to problems with mobility or daily function and may be viewed as disabilities under the law. The conditions may be short term or long term; stable or progressive; constant or unpredictable; and changing, treatable, or untreatable. Many people with hidden disabilities can benefit from assistive technologies for certain activities or during certain stages of their diseases or conditions.

People who have spinal cord injuries (SCIs), traumatic brain injury (TBI), cerebral palsy (CP), muscular dystrophy (MD), spina bifida, osteogenesis imperfecta (OI), multiple sclerosis (MS), demyelinating diseases, myelopathy, progressive muscular atrophy, amputations, or paralysis often benefit from complex rehabilitative technology. The assistive devices are individually configured to help each person with her or his own unique disability.

Chapter 71

Education of Children with Special Needs

An Individualized Education Program (IEP) is a written statement of the educational program designed to meet a child's individual needs. Every child who receives special education services must have an IEP. That is why the process of developing this vital document is of great interest and importance to educators, administrators, and families alike. Here is a crash course on the IEP.

What Is the Individualized Education Program's Purpose?

The IEP has two general purposes:

- To set reasonable learning goals for a child

- To state the services that the school district will provide for the child

Who Develops the Individualized Education Program?

The IEP is developed by a team of individuals that includes key school staff and the child's parents. The team meets, reviews the

This chapter includes text excerpted from "The Short-and-Sweet IEP Overview," Center for Parent Information and Resources (CPIR), U.S. Department of Education (ED), August 1, 2017.

assessment information available about the child, and designs an educational program to address the child's educational needs that result from her or his disability.

When Is the Individualized Education Program Developed?

An IEP meeting must be held within 30 calendar days after it is determined, through a full and individual evaluation, that a child has one of the disabilities listed in The Individuals with Disabilities Education Act (IDEA) and needs special education and related services. A child's IEP must also be reviewed at least annually thereafter to determine whether the annual goals are being achieved and must be revised as appropriate.

What Is in an Individualized Education Program?

Each child's IEP must contain specific information, as listed within IDEA, our nation's special education law. This includes (but is not limited to):

- The child's present levels of academic achievement and functional performance, describing how the child is currently doing in school and how the child's disability affects her or his involvement and progress in the general curriculum

- Annual goals for the child, meaning what parents and the school team think she or he can reasonably accomplish in a year

- The special education and related services to be provided to the child, including supplementary aids and services (such as a communication device) and changes to the program or supports for school personnel

- How much of the school day the child will be educated separately from nondisabled children or not participate in extracurricular or other nonacademic activities, such as lunch or clubs

- How (and if) the child is to participate in state and district-wide assessments, including what modifications to tests the child needs

- When services and modifications will begin, how often they will be provided, where they will be provided, and how long they will last

- How school personnel will measure the child's progress toward the annual goals

Can Students Be Involved in Developing Their Own Individualized Education Programs?

Yes, they certainly can be. IDEA actually requires that the student is invited to any IEP meeting where transition services will be discussed. These are services designed to help the student plan for his or her transition to adulthood and life after high school.

Chapter 72

Transition Planning for Children with Special Needs

Transition Planning: Opportunities and Programs to Prepare Students with Disabilities for Success

As a student approaches the time to leave high school, it is important that preparations for adult life are well underway. For early transition planning and active participation in decision making to occur for students with disabilities, members of the planning team need to be well-informed about the student's abilities, needs, and available services. This chapter highlights educational opportunities, credentials, and employment strategies designed to assist students with disabilities while in school to prepare for meaningful postsecondary education and a thriving career.

Transition Planning

A truly successful transition process is the result of comprehensive team planning that is driven by the dreams, desires, and abilities of youth. A transition plan provides the basic structure for preparing an individual to live, work and play in the community, as fully and independently as possible.

This chapter includes text excerpted from "A Transition Guide: To Postsecondary Education and Employment for Students and Youth with Disabilities," U.S. Department of Education (ED), May 2017.

Local educational agencies (LEAs) and state vocational rehabilitation (VR) agencies participate in planning meetings to assist students and family members to make critical decisions about this stage of the student's life and her or his future postschool goals. During the planning process, schools and VR agencies work together to identify the transition needs of students with disabilities, such as the need for assistive or rehabilitation technology, orientation and mobility services or travel training, and career exploration through vocational assessments or work experience opportunities.

The individualized education program (IEP), developed under the Individuals with Disabilities Education Act (IDEA), for each student with a disability must address transition services requirements beginning not later than the first IEP to be in effect when the child turns 16 years of age, or younger if determined appropriate by the IEP Team, and must be updated annually thereafter. The IEP must include:

- Appropriate measurable postsecondary goals based upon age-appropriate transition assessments related to training, education, employment, and, where appropriate, independent living skills

- The transition services (including courses of study) needed to assist the student with a disability in reaching those goals)

While the IDEA statute and regulations refer to courses of study, they are but one example of appropriate transition services. Examples of independent living skills to consider when developing postsecondary goals include self-advocacy, management of the home and personal finances, and the use of public information.

Education and Training Opportunities

There are a number of opportunities and programs available for students preparing to exit secondary school. Many of these education and training opportunities involve formal or informal connections between educational, VR, employment, training, social services, and health services agencies. Specifically, high schools, career centers, community colleges, four-year colleges and universities, and state technical colleges are key partners. These partners offer federal, state, and local funds to assist a student in preparing for postsecondary education.

Further, research suggests that enrollment in more rigorous, academically intense programs (e.g., Advanced Placement (AP), International Baccalaureate (IB), or dual enrollment) in high school prepares students, including those with low achievement levels, to enroll and persist in postsecondary education at higher rates than similar students who pursue less challenging courses of study.

The following are examples of exiting options, programs, and activities that may be available as IEP Teams develop IEPs to prepare the student for the transition to adult life:

Regular High School Diploma

The term "regular high school diploma means:

- The standard high school diploma awarded to the preponderance of students in the state that is fully aligned with state standards, or a higher diploma, except that a regular high school diploma shall not be aligned to the alternate academic-achievement standards

- Does not include a recognized equivalent of a diploma, such as a general equivalency diploma, certificate of completion, certificate of attendance, or similar lesser credential, such as a diploma based on meeting IEP goals

The vast majority of students with disabilities should have access to the same high-quality academic coursework as all other students in the state that reflects grade-level content for the grade in which the student is enrolled and that provides for assessment against grade-level achievement standards.

Alternate High School Diploma

Some students with the most significant cognitive disabilities may be awarded a state-defined alternate high school diploma based on alternate academic-achievement standards, but that diploma must be standards-based.

Working towards an alternate diploma sometimes causes delay or keeps the student from completing the requirements for a regular high school diploma. However, students with the most significant cognitive disabilities who are working towards an alternate diploma must receive instruction that promotes their involvement and progress in the general education curriculum, consistent with the IDEA.

Further, states must continue to make a free appropriate public education (FAPE) available to any student with a disability who graduates from high school with a credential other than a regular high school diploma, such as an alternate diploma, GED, or certificate of completion, or a diploma based on meeting IEP goals. While FAPE under the IDEA does not include education beyond grade 12, states and school districts are required to continue to offer to develop and implement an IEP for a student with a disability who graduates from high school with a credential other than a regular high school diploma, until the student has exceeded the age of eligibility for FAPE under state law, or has been evaluated and determined to no longer be a child with a disability under IDEA. Depending on state law, which sets the state's upper age limit of FAPE, the entitlement to FAPE of a student with a disability who has not graduated high school with a regular high school diploma could last until the student's twenty-second birthday. IEPs could include transition services in the form of coursework at a community college or other postsecondary institution, provided that the state recognizes the coursework as secondary school education under state law. Secondary school education does not include education that is beyond grade 12 and must meet state education standards.

Dual or Concurrent Enrollment Program

Increasingly, states and school districts are permitting students to participate in dual or concurrent enrollment programs while still in high school. The term "dual or concurrent enrollment program" refers to a partnership between at least one college or university and at least one local school district in which the student who has not yet graduated from high school with a regular high school diploma is able to enroll in one or more postsecondary courses and earn postsecondary credit. The credit(s) can be transferred to the college or university in the partnership and applied toward completion of a degree or recognized educational credential, which the student would earn after leaving high school. Programs are offered both on campuses of colleges or universities, or in high school classrooms. Examples of dual or concurrent enrollment programs include institution-specific dual enrollment programs, AP, IB, and statewide dual enrollment programs with an emphasis on implementation at one site. The Office of Special Education Programs (OSEP) has stated in prior policy guidance that, if under state law, attending classes at a postsecondary institution, whether auditing or for credit, is considered secondary school education for students in grade 12 or below and the education provided meets applicable state standards, those services can be designated as transition services on a student's IEP and paid for with IDEA Part B funds, consistent with the student's entitlement to FAPE.

Early College High School

The term "early college high school" refers to a partnership between at least one school district and at least one college or university that allows a student to simultaneously complete requirements toward earning a regular high school diploma and earn not less than 12 credits that are transferable to the college or university within the partnership as part of her or his course of study toward a postsecondary degree or credential at no cost to the student or student's family.

Summary of Performance

A summary of performance (SOP) is required for each student with an IEP whose eligibility for services under IDEA terminates due to graduation from secondary school with a regular high school diploma or due to exceeding the age of eligibility for FAPE under state law. The school district must provide the student with a summary of the student's academic achievement and functional performance that includes recommendations on how to assist the student in meeting the student's postsecondary goals. This summary of the student's achievement and performance can be used to assist the student in accessing postsecondary education and/or employment services.

Employment Opportunities
Community-Based Work Experiences

Whether the student's next step is employment or entering a postsecondary training or an educational program, it is important for students with disabilities to obtain as much work experience as possible to prepare for adult life. The National Collaborative on Workforce and Disability for Youth (NCWD) reports that the value of work experience, whether paid or unpaid work:

- Helps students acquire jobs at higher wages after they graduate

- Promotes students who participate in occupational education and special education in integrated settings to be competitively employed more than students who have not participated in such activities

The NCWD also recommends that a student with a disability participate in multiple work-based learning experiences and those experiences be directly related to the student's education program. Community-based work experiences, such as internships,

681

apprenticeships, and other on-the-job training experiences, provide increased opportunities for students to learn a specific job, task, or skill at an integrated employment site, and to transfer the knowledge gained to real-time work experiences.

VR agencies provide a variety of community-based work experiences and on-the-job training services to students and youth with disabilities on a case-by-case basis under the VR program. The VR counselor and the student or youth with a disability will identify a specific vocational goal to determine whether community-based work experience is a necessary service for the individual with a disability to achieve an employment outcome in competitive integrated employment or supported employment. "Competitive integrated employment" is employment with earnings comparable to those paid to individuals without disabilities in a setting that allows them to interact with individuals who do not have disabilities. "Supported employment" is competitive integrated employment or employment in an integrated work setting in which individuals with the most significant disabilities are working on a short-term basis toward competitive integrated employment while receiving ongoing support services in order to support and maintain those individuals in employment.

Community-based work experiences allow the student or youth with a disability to explore potential careers related to the specific vocational goal, potential workplace environments and demands, and other aspects of the work. These experiences offer the student opportunities to gain first-hand knowledge of a particular job skill or to learn the culture of day-to-day employment. These experiences can be offered in lieu of, or to supplement, vocational training or educational programs, or as a stand-alone service. To ensure the success of community-based work experiences, VR agencies are encouraged to develop agreements with employers and the student or youth with a disability that describe the training objectives, services to be provided, timelines, and financial responsibilities necessary for successful community-based work experience.

The following list describes work-based strategies used to enhance competitive integrated employment opportunities for students and youth with disabilities:

Internships

Internships are formal agreements whereby a student or youth is assigned specific tasks in a workplace over a predetermined period of time. Internships can be paid or unpaid, depending on the nature of the agreement with the company and the nature of the tasks.

Internships are usually temporary on-the-job work experiences. They not only provide individuals, including students and youth with disabilities, actual work experience and the opportunity to develop skills, but also the opportunity to determine if the type of work involved is in keeping with the individuals' career interests, abilities, and goals. There is no guarantee that an internship will lead to a permanent employment offer. However, VR counselors refer students or youth with a disability to an internship to increase their employment opportunities. The internship experience is frequently enriched by the provision of services or supports, such as transportation and vocational counseling, as described in an approved individualized plan for employment (IPE) under the VR program.

Mentorships

A young person with or without a disability may participate in a mentoring relationship to hone her or his occupational skills and work habits. The business community describes mentoring as an employee training system under which a senior or more experienced individual (the mentor) is assigned as an advisor, counselor, or guide to a junior or trainee (mentee). The mentor is responsible for providing support to, and feedback on, the individual in her or her charge. The mentor's area of experience is sought based on her or his career, disability, and history or life experience similar to the mentee or a host of other possibilities.

Many schools, or existing community organizations, such as the Young Men's Christian Association (YMCA), Boys and Girls Clubs, and Centers for Independent Living (CILs), introduce students and youth to older peer or adult mentors who have achieved success in a particular area that is important for the student and youth (for example, employers, college students, recovering substance abusers). Interaction with successful role models with disabilities enhances the disability-related knowledge and self-confidence of students and youth with disabilities, as well as parents' perceptions of the knowledge and capabilities of their students and youth with disabilities.

Apprenticeships

Apprenticeships are formal, sanctioned work experiences of extended duration in which an apprentice, frequently known as a "trainee," learns specific occupational skills related to a standardized trade, such as carpentry, plumbing, or drafting. Many apprenticeships also include paid work components.

In an apprenticeship program, an individual has the opportunity to learn a trade through on-the-job training as well as through related academic knowledge. Often, these programs involve an employer and a community college or university and a trade union. An individual applies for specific training and, once accepted, is able to participate in the apprenticeship program. Employment opportunities are usually offered to an individual who successfully completes the program. VR counselors assist individuals with disabilities to prepare for the apprenticeship application process, develop a plan to gain the prerequisite knowledge and skills for the trade, and identify support services needed to be successful in the apprenticeship program.

Paid Employment

Paid employment involves existing standard jobs in a company or customized employment positions that are negotiated with an employer. These jobs always feature a wage paid directly to the student or youth. Such work is scheduled during or after the school day. Paid employment is frequently an integral part of a student's course of study or simply a separate adjunctive experience. Often times, these employment experiences are the first steps towards building a meaningful career for students and youth with disabilities.

Career Pathways

As students and youth with disabilities prepare for their careers, they are counseled to consider and explore a specific career to determine if it meets their career interests, abilities, and goals. The career pathways model is designed to facilitate an individual's career interest and advancement with multiple entrances and exit points in the individual's career over her or his lifetime. Key program design features of the career pathways model include contextualized curricula, integrated basic education, and occupational training, career counseling, support services, assessments and credit transfer agreements that ease entry and exit points towards credential attainment.

Career pathways are also designed as a systematic strategy for integrating educational instruction, workforce development, and human services and linking these service delivery systems to labor market trends and employer needs. Career pathways systems use real-time labor market information and active employer involvement to ensure that training and education programs meet the skill and competency needs of local employers. The more the systems are aligned at the state and local levels, the easier it may be to create a level of integration necessary to develop comprehensive programs and ensure an individual's success.

Conclusion: Connections Help Achieve Desired Careers

Many of the opportunities, programs, and strategies discussed in this section involve partnerships between high schools, colleges, VR agencies, employers, American Jobs Centers, workforce development boards, social service agencies, students, and their families to identify and secure a career uniquely suited to the student or youth with a disability. It is essential that students and youth with disabilities, along with family members and professional support staff, examine numerous and challenging programs to prepare students and youth with disabilities for their desired postschool goals.

Chapter 73

Government Benefits for Children and Adults with Disabilities

Both the school system and virtual reality (VR) program provide opportunities designed to prepare students and youth with disabilities for careers in the twenty-first-century workforce.

This chapter describes services and key requirements of the Individuals with Disabilities Education Act (IDEA) and the Rehabilitation Act that facilitate the transition from school to postschool activities, including postsecondary education and competitive integrated employment (CIE). These requirements are in place for students and youth with disabilities to seamlessly access services and support to achieve their career goals.

Transition Services

Transition services are integral to free appropriate public education (FAPE) under IDEA. A primary purpose of IDEA is to ensure that all children with disabilities have available to them a FAPE that emphasizes special education and related services designed to meet

This chapter includes text excerpted from "A Transition Guide: To Postsecondary Education and Employment for Students and Youth with Disabilities," U.S. Department of Education (ED), May 2017.

their unique needs and prepare them for further education, employment, and independent living. As noted earlier in this guide, IDEA contains transition services requirements for students with disabilities, which must be addressed in the first Individualized Education Program (IEP) to be in effect when the student turns 16, or younger, if determined appropriate by the IEP Team. The Rehabilitation Act authorizes a continuum of services, such as preemployment transition services (Pre-ETS), transition services, job placement services, other VR services, and supported employment services for students and youth with disabilities, as appropriate, to secure meaningful careers. Implementing regulations for both the schools and the state VR Services program define transition services similarly.

Providing transition services is a shared responsibility between the school and the VR agency.

Transition Services for Students under Individuals with Disabilities Education Act

Schools provide an array of supports and services for IDEA-eligible students designed to enable them to be prepared for college or careers. Under IDEA, states and school districts must make FAPE available to all eligible children with disabilities in mandatory age ranges. FAPE includes the provision of special education and related services at no cost to the parents in conformity with a properly developed IEP. Each child with a disability must receive FAPE in the least restrictive environment (LRE), and, to the maximum extent appropriate, must be educated with children who do not have disabilities. The LRE requirements apply to transition services, including employment-related transition services, and apply equally to the employment portion of the student's program and placement.

The Individualized Education Program: Postsecondary Goals and Transition Services
The Individualized Education Program

Each student with a disability served under IDEA must have an IEP developed by a team that includes:

- The parents of a child with a disability

- Not less than one regular education teacher of such child (if the child is, or may be, participating in the regular education environment)

- Not less than one special education teacher or, where appropriate, not less than one special education provider of such child

- A representative of the local educational agency (LEA) who is: qualified to provide, or supervise the provision of, specially designed instruction to meet the unique needs of children with disabilities; knowledgeable about the general education curriculum; and knowledgeable about the availability of resources of the LEA

- An individual who can interpret the instructional implications of evaluation results, who may be a member of the team described above;

- At the discretion of the parent or the agency, other individuals who have the knowledge or special expertise regarding the child, including related services personnel as appropriate

- Whenever appropriate, the child with a disability. Parents are an essential source of information in IEP development and play an important role in the IEP Team to establish the student's goals. There are many resources to assist parents through the IEP and transition process.

Other Agency Representatives at Individualized Education Program Team Meetings

Representatives of other agencies, such as the VR agency, can be invited to participate at IEP Team meetings in which transition services and postsecondary goals are discussed, if that agency is likely to be responsible for providing or paying for the transition services to be included in the student's IEP. However, IDEA requires the consent of the parents or the student who has reached the age of majority under state law to invite other agency representatives to participate in the meeting. If a participating agency, other than a public agency, fails to provide the transition services described in the student's IEP, the public agency must reconvene the IEP Team to identify alternative strategies to meet the transition objectives for the student.

To meet IDEA's transition services provisions, the IEP must contain the services and supports needed to assist the student to gain the skills and experiences to achieve her or his desired postschool goals. By the time the student turns 16, or younger, if determined appropriate by the IEP Team, the student's IEP must include:

- Appropriate measurable postsecondary goals based upon age-appropriate transition assessments related to training, education, employment, and where appropriate, independent living skills

- The transition services (including courses of study) needed to assist the student in reaching those goals

- Age-appropriate transition assessments based on the individual needs of the student to be used to determine appropriate measurable postsecondary goals

States and school districts are in the best position, along with the student and the student's family member or representative, to determine the most appropriate types of transition assessments based upon a student's needs.

As a student gets older, the IEP Team must consider whether the student's needs have changed, taking into account the student's strengths, preferences, and interests; and develop measurable goals that are focused on the student's life after high school, specifying the transition services needed to help her or him reach those goals. Parents have to recognize that decisions about the specific content of postsecondary goals and transition services are the responsibility of the IEP Team. These decisions are made at IEP Team meetings, which sometimes include additional school personnel with specific knowledge related to the identified goals and services. Nothing in IDEA requires a specific service, placement, or course of study to be included in the student's IEP as a transition service. Rather, IDEA leaves such decisions to the IEP Team.

School districts, which are responsible for conducting IEP Team meetings, must:

- Invite the student to an IEP Team meeting if the purpose of the meeting is to discuss the student's postsecondary goals and the transition services needed to assist the student in reaching those goals

- Take steps to ensure that the student's preferences and interests are considered if the student does not attend the meeting

- Take steps to ensure that the parents are present at IEP Team meetings or are afforded the opportunity to participate

- Notify parents of the meeting early enough to ensure that parents have an opportunity to attend, and specifically inform them if a purpose of the meeting is consideration of postsecondary goals and transition services for the student

- Schedule the meeting at a mutually convenient time and place

- Use other methods to ensure parental participation, including individual or conference telephone calls, if neither parent can attend the meeting

- Use alternative means of meeting participation, such as video conferences and conference calls, if agreed to by the parent and the school district.

Parental and student input is also vital in determining postsecondary goals related to needed postsecondary education and training services for postschool activities, including independent living and employment. Students with disabilities and their parents should be knowledgeable about the range of transition services available, and how to access those services at the local level. School districts should encourage both the student and their parents to be fully engaged in discussions regarding the need for and availability of other services, including application and eligibility for VR services and supports to ensure formal connections with agencies and adult services, as appropriate.

Transition Services for Students and Youth with Disabilities under the Rehabilitation Act
A Continuum of Services

One of the primary roles of state VR agencies is to empower individuals with disabilities, including students and youth with disabilities, to make informed choices about their careers by providing a continuum of services to achieve employment outcomes in competitive integrated employment or supported employment. Students and youth with disabilities receive a broad range of services under the VR program, in group settings or on an individual basis, as appropriate. The services available will differ from person to person because they are customized for each individual's needs. Furthermore, certain VR services (e.g., preemployment transition services) are available to students with disabilities, regardless of whether they have applied for VR services, but are not available to youth with disabilities who do not meet the definition of a "student with a disability" under the Rehabilitation Act.

Eligibility Requirements for Services Provided under the Virtual Reality Program

To be eligible for VR services, an individual must meet the following criteria:

- Have a physical or mental impairment that constitutes or results in a substantial impediment to employment

- Requires VR services to prepare for, secure, retain, advance in, or regain employment

However, individuals who receive Supplemental Security Income (SSI) and/or Social Security Disability Insurance (SSDI) benefits are presumed to be eligible for VR services, unless there is clear and convincing evidence that they are unable to benefit from VR services. These individuals, including students and youth with disabilities, are determined to be eligible for VR services based on existing documentation indicating that the individual is a recipient of SSI and/or SSDI benefits.

Most notably, Section 113 of the Rehabilitation Act references "potentially eligible" students with disabilities with respect to the provision of preemployment transition services. In this regard, all students with disabilities, regardless of whether they have applied for or been determined eligible for VR services are considered "potentially eligible" for purposes of receiving preemployment transition services. The term "potentially eligible" is applicable only with respect to the requirements related to preemployment transition services.

Students with disabilities who need individualized transition services or other VR services beyond the scope of preemployment transition services must apply and be determined eligible for the VR program, and develop an approved IPE with their VR counselor. Students with disabilities who receive preemployment transition services before applying for VR services, and are likely to need other VR services, are encouraged to submit an application as early as possible in the transition planning process. A VR agency is required to implement an order of selection for services when it cannot provide the full range of VR services to all eligible individuals with disabilities who apply for services under the state VR services program. If a state has implemented an order of selection due to limited fiscal or staff resources, the assignment to a priority category under the order of selection to be served is based on the date of application for VR services, not the date of referral or receipt of preemployment transition services.

In other words, a student's position on a VR agency's waitlist for services is dependent upon applying for VR services. VR agencies that have implemented an order of selection may continue to provide preemployment transition services to students with disabilities who were receiving these services prior to the determination of eligibility and assignment to a closed priority category.

Distinctions between New Terms
"Student with a Disability" and "Youth with a Disability"

The Rehabilitation Act, as amended by Title IV of the Workforce Innovation and Opportunity Act (WIOA), created distinct definitions for the terms "student with a disability" and "youth with a disability." In general, a "student with a disability" is an individual with a disability who is enrolled in an education program; meets certain age requirements; and is eligible for and receiving special education or related services under IDEA or is an individual with a disability for purposes of Section 504. Educational programs include secondary education programs; nontraditional or alternative secondary education programs, including homeschooling; postsecondary education programs; and other recognized educational programs, such as those offered through the juvenile justice system. Age requirements for a student with a disability include minimum and maximum age requirements. A student cannot be younger than the earliest age to receive transition services under IDEA unless a state elects to provide preemployment transition services at an earlier age. A student cannot be older than 21, unless state law for the state provides for a higher maximum age for the receipt of services under IDEA, then the student cannot be older than that maximum age. A "youth with a disability" is an individual with a disability who is between the ages of 14 and 24 years of age. There is no requirement that a "youth with a disability" be participating in an educational program. The age range for a "youth with a disability" is broader than that for a "student with a disability" under the Rehabilitation Act.

As previously discussed, the continuum of services available through the VR program includes: preemployment transition services that are available only to VR eligible or potentially eligible students with disabilities; transition services that are available to groups of students or youth with disabilities, or on an individual basis under an approved IPE; and other VR services that are provided to eligible students and youth with disabilities under an approved IPE.

"Preemployment Transition Services" and Individualized Transition Services

"Preemployment transition services" are offered as an early start at job exploration and are designed to help students with disabilities that are eligible or potentially eligible for VR services identify their career interests. These services include:

- Job exploration counseling

- Work-based learning experiences, which may include in-school or after school opportunities, or experience outside the traditional school setting (including internships) provided in an integrated environment to the maximum extent possible

- Counseling on opportunities for enrollment in comprehensive transition or postsecondary educational programs at institutions of higher education

- Workplace readiness training to develop social skills and independent living

- Instruction in self-advocacy, (including instruction in person-centered planning), which may include peer mentoring

As noted earlier, preemployment transition services are only available to students with disabilities. For students with disabilities who are not enrolled in an education program administered by an LEA, but who are enrolled in other public programs, VR agencies may coordinate the provision of preemployment transition services for these students with disabilities with the public entities administering those educational programs. Services arranged or provided by the VR agency should be based upon an individual's need and should enrich, not delay, the transition planning process, application to the VR program, and the continuum of services necessary for movement from school to postschool activities.

Although the five distinct preemployment transition services discussed above are only available to students with disabilities at the earliest stage of this continuum, either in a group setting or on an individual basis, VR agencies may provide transition services—another set of VR services in the continuum of services—to students and youth with disabilities. Some transition services are provided to groups of students and youth with disabilities prior to or after submitting an application for VR services. While these group services are not individualized or specifically related to the individual needs of the student or an approved IPE, they are beneficial and increase the student's opportunities to participate in activities, such as group tours of universities and vocational training programs, employer site visits to learn about career opportunities, and career fairs coordinated with workforce development and employers.

Individualized transition services or other individualized VR services must be provided to students and youth who have been determined eligible for VR services, and the services are described in an approved IPE. Examples of transition services provided in accordance with an approved IPE include travel expenses, vocational and other training services, employment-development activities, job search and placement services, and job coaching.

Transition services are outcome-oriented services designed to facilitate the movement from the receipt of services from schools to the receipt of services from VR agencies, and/or as appropriate, other state agencies. Transition services are also designed to facilitate movement towards postschool activities, including postsecondary education and vocational training that lead to employment outcomes in competitive integrated employment or supported employment.

Individualized Virtual Reality Services

As noted earlier, if a student or youth with a disability needs individualized VR services, the student or youth must apply and be determined eligible for such services and have an approved IPE in place to receive those services. Individualized VR services are any services described in the IPE necessary to assist an individual with a disability in preparing for, securing, advancing in, retaining, or regaining an employment outcome that is consistent with the strengths, resources, priorities, concerns, abilities, capabilities, interests, and informed choice of the individual.

The VR services provided depend on the student's or youth's individual needs and include, but are not limited to:

- An assessment for determining eligibility and VR needs by qualified personnel, including, if appropriate, an assessment by personnel skilled in rehabilitation technology

- Counseling and guidance, including information and support services to assist an individual in exercising informed choice consistent with the provisions of Section 102(d) of the Rehabilitation Act

- Referral and other services to secure needed services from other agencies through agreements developed if such services are not available under the VR program

- Job-related services, including job search and placement assistance, job retention services, follow-up services, and follow-along services

- Transition services for students with disabilities, that facilitate the achievement of the employment outcome identified in the IPE

- Supported employment services for individuals with the most significant disabilities

- Services to the family of an individual with a disability necessary to assist the individual to achieve an employment outcome

The Individualized Plan for Employment Procedures

Once a student or youth is determined eligible for VR services, the student or youth, or her or his representative, develops an IPE. The student or youth, or her or his representative, may seek assistance in the development of the IPE from a qualified VR counselor or another advocate. However, only a qualified VR counselor employed by the VR agency may approve and sign the IPE.

The following IPE requirements facilitate a seamless transition process:

- The IPE is a written document that is agreed to and signed by the eligible individual or the individual's representative

- The IPE is approved and signed by a qualified VR counselor employed by the VR agency

- The individual with a disability, including a student or youth, must be given the opportunity to make an informed choice in selecting an employment outcome, needed VR services, providers of those VR services, and related components of the IPE

- A copy of the IPE must be provided to the individual or individual's representative in writing or appropriate mode of communication

- The IPE must be reviewed annually by the VR counselor, and amended, as necessary if there are substantive changes in the components of the IPE

- The IPE must be developed no later than 90 days after the date of eligibility determination

For students with disabilities who receive special education and related services under IDEA, the IPE must be developed and approved (i.e., agreed to and signed by the student, or the student's representative, and the VR agency counselor) no later than the time each VR-eligible student leaves the school setting. Also, the IPE for a student with a disability who receives special education and related services under Part B of IDEA or educational services under Section 504 must be developed so that it is consistent with and complementary to the student's IEP or plan for Section 504 services.

Coordination and Collaboration between State Educational Agency and Virtual Reality Agency

Transition planning and services begin while students are in school. According to the fiscal year (FY) 2015 RSA data, of all the individuals with disabilities whose service records were closed and who applied for VR services between the ages of 14 and 24, 52 percent were referred to VR agencies from elementary and secondary schools. Schools and VR agencies have maintained a longstanding relationship to meet the transition needs of students with disabilities.

A VR agency is required to describe in its VR services portion of the Unified or Combined state Plan, its plans, policies, and procedures for the coordination between VR and education officials to facilitate the transition of students with disabilities from the receipt of educational services in school to the receipt of VR services, including preemployment transition services. Under IDEA, services are provided at no cost to the student or her or his family. Under the Rehabilitation Act, VR-eligible individuals may be required to provide financial support towards VR services, such as training and postsecondary education, as outlined in their approved IPE. To ensure effective collaboration and coordination for service delivery, VR agencies and the schools are required to plan and coordinate preemployment transition services and transition services for students with disabilities, as agreed upon in the state's formal interagency agreement.

The interagency agreements meet the requirement for collaboration between the state education and VR agencies at the state-level and are important because the agreements provide the basis for determining which agency pays for certain services. It is important for students with disabilities and family members to be aware of these agreements because they serve as the foundation for coordinated services for students with disabilities exiting school and pursuing VR services. In this way, students, family members, and representatives can be more informed participants during the transition planning process and service delivery.

Formal Interagency Agreement

In each state, a formal interagency agreement or other mechanisms must be developed between the SEA, as appropriate, the LEA, and the VR agency. This agreement is intended to facilitate a seamless delivery system of services from school to postschool activities. The formal interagency agreement required under the VR program regulations must include provisions that address, at a minimum, the following:

- Consultation and technical assistance by the state VR agency to assist educational agencies in planning for the transition of students with disabilities from school to postschool activities, including VR services

- Transition planning by state VR agency and school personnel for students with disabilities that facilitates the development and implementation of their IEPs

- The roles and responsibilities, including financial responsibilities, of each agency, including provisions for determining state lead agencies and qualified personnel responsible for preemployment transition services and transition services

- Procedures for outreach to and identification of students with disabilities who need transition services

- Coordination necessary to satisfy documentation requirements with regard to students and youth with disabilities who are seeking subminimum wage employment

- Assurance that neither the SEA nor the LEA will enter into an agreement with an employer holding a Section 14(c) certificate under the Fair Labor Standards Act for the purpose of operating a program in which students or youth with disabilities are paid subminimum wage

- An understanding that nothing in the formal interagency agreement will be construed to reduce the obligation under

IDEA or any other agency to provide or pay for preemployment transition services or transition services that are also considered special education or related services and necessary for FAPE

Additionally, under IDEA, these interagency agreements must include:

- An identification of, or method for defining, the financial responsibility of each agency in order to ensure that all services that are needed to ensure a FAPE are provided, provided that the financial responsibility of each public agency, including the state Medicaid agency and other public insurers of youth with disabilities, shall precede the financial responsibility of the LEA (or state agency responsible for developing the child's IEP). The services that are needed to ensure FAPE include, but are not limited to, services described in IDEA relating to assistive technology devices and services, related services, supplementary aids and services, and transition services

- The conditions, terms, and procedures under which an LEA shall be reimbursed by other agencies

- Procedures for resolving interagency disputes (including procedures under which LEAs may initiate proceedings) under the agreement or other mechanisms to secure reimbursement from other agencies or otherwise implement the provisions of the agreement or mechanism

It is expected that SEAs, LEAs, and VR agencies will work together to implement the provisions of their respective interagency agreements. Decisions about whether the service is related to an employment outcome or education attainment, or if it is considered a special education or related service, as well as whether the service is one customarily provided under IDEA or the Rehabilitation Act are ones that are made at the state and local level by SEA, VR, and LEA personnel. For example, work-based learning experiences, such as internships, short-term employment, or on-the-job training located in the community, may be appropriate preemployment transition services under the Rehabilitation Act or transition services under IDEA, as determined by the IEP Team and depending on the student's individualized needs. The mere fact that those services are now authorized under the Rehabilitation Act as preemployment transition services do not mean the school should cease providing them and refer those students to the VR program. If these work-based learning experiences are not customary services provided by an LEA, the VR agencies and LEA are urged to collaborate and coordinate the provision of such services.

Youth with Disabilities No Longer in School

Transition planning is critical for any youth with a disability, whether they are in school or not. A VR counselor can assist youth with disabilities in exploring careers, identifying a career path leading to their vocational goal, and identifying the services and steps to reach that goal. With the exception of preemployment transition services and transition services provided to groups of individuals with disabilities, VR services are provided only to those individuals with disabilities, including youth with disabilities, who have been determined eligible for services and the services are described in an approved IPE. Although youth with disabilities who do not meet the definition of a "student with a disability" may not receive pre-employment transition services, they may receive transition services as group transition services, prior to or after applying for VR services, as well as individualized transition or other VR services, after being determined eligible for the VR program and under an approved IPE. Individualized transition services provided under an approved IPE to a youth with a disability eligible for the VR program may consist of, among other things: job exploration counseling, including assessments and vocational guidance and counseling; work adjustment training, vocational/occupational training, or postsecondary education; and job development services, including job search, job placement, and job coaching services.

Coordination of Services

Often, youth with disabilities are not familiar with the community programs and services that are available to them as young adults, especially if they are no longer in school. The VR program is designed to assess, plan, develop, and provide VR services to eligible individuals with disabilities, consistent with their strengths, resources, priorities, concerns, abilities, capabilities, interests, and informed choice. The VR agency assigns a VR counselor to each eligible individual, and the VR counselor can help the youth develop the IPE.

A VR counselor can assist youth in finding and applying for essential daily living services and resources, such as health and housing referrals needed to successfully implement their employment plans. Each community agency sets its criteria for services and, once the youth meets the eligibility criteria, service delivery begins. The VR counselor is available to coordinate VR services with services provided by employment-related programs, such as youth programs funded by the U.S. Department of Labor (DOL) and provided at American job centers.

United States Department of Labor Youth Programs

Youth programs funded under Title I of WIOA include five new program elements: financial literacy instruction; entrepreneurial skills training; provision of local labor market and employment information; activities that help youth transition to postsecondary education and training; and education offered concurrently with workforce preparation activities and training for a specific occupation or occupational cluster.

Two well-known youth programs funded by DOL are the Job Corps and YouthBuild. Each of these programs integrates vocational (including classroom and practical experiences), academic and employability skills training designed to prepare youth for stable, long-term, high-paying employment. Job Corps programs offer career technical training in over 100 career areas. YouthBuild programs focus on construction trades. Some students are eligible to receive youth services from DOL programs. These youth must be between the ages of 14 and 21, attending school, from a low-income family, and they must meet one or more additional conditions, such as being an English language learner, homeless, an offender, or others.

Social Security Administration Work Program

The Social Security Administration (SSA) funds the Ticket to Work program to provide career development services to beneficiaries between the ages of 18 and 64 to assist these individuals to become financially independent. SSA issues a letter, referred to as the "ticket," to eligible beneficiaries that can be used to obtain free employment services from a provider of their choice that is registered with SSA. Both a single agency and a group of providers are comprised of a consortium of employers referred to as the "employment network." While pursuing employment, the individual continues to receive SSA benefits and employment-related services to become employed and to maintain that employment. Services include, but are not limited to, vocational counseling, training, education, and job coaching, and are provided based on the individual's needs.

Examples to Consider: States Are Coordinating Transition Services

Vocational Rehabilitation Supporting Students with Disabilities

In one state, a community rehabilitation program provides supported employment services and intensive case management services for youth with significant emotional and behavioral disabilities who dropped out of high school or are at risk of dropping out. The program uses work as a means to reach individuals with significant employment challenges. The state VR program works in partnership with the state Department of Justice (DOJ), Department of Health/Division of Mental Health (DMH), and the Department of Children and Families (DCF) in various sites around this state. Program data report that more than 90 percent of these students were not working when they entered the program; however, after receiving career preparation services and related employment supports and services, approximately three-quarters of the students had paid employment and more than a third of the students achieved an employment outcome.

State Educational Agency and State Vocational Rehabilitation Agency Collaboration

A VR agency partnered with a school district to co-locate a dedicated transition VR Counselor and technician in an office with school district transition personnel. Full-time VR agency and school district personnel worked together to secure employment opportunities for eligible students with disabilities. The office space was funded by the school district. The VR agency and school district operated under a signed agreement in which the VR agency provided its own office equipment, clerical supplies, computer, phones, and staff. This collaboration provided an opportunity for VR staff to work side-by-side with school district transition personnel to facilitate improved outcomes.

Conclusion: Coordination Is Required

Transition services are best delivered within a framework of structured planning, meaningful youth, and family engagement, and state agency coordination and accountability.

Part Seven

Additional Help and Information

Chapter 74

Glossary of Terms Related to Human Genetics

akinesia: Trouble initiating or carrying out movements.

allele: A form of a gene. Each person receives two alleles of a gene, one from each biological parent. This combination is one factor among many that influence a variety of processes in the body. On chromosome 19, the *apolipoprotein E (APOE)* gene has three common alleles ε2, ε3, and ε4.

amino acids: A set of twenty different molecules used to build proteins. Proteins consist of one or more chains of amino acids called polypeptides. The sequence of the amino acid chain causes the polypeptide to fold into a shape that is biologically active. The amino acid sequences of proteins are encoded in the genes.

***apolipoprotein E (APOE)* gene:** A gene on chromosome 19 involved in making a protein that helps carry cholesterol and other types of fat in the bloodstream. The APOE ε4 allele is the major known risk-factor gene for late-onset Alzheimer disease.

apoptosis: The process of programmed cell death. It is used during early development to eliminate unwanted cells. In adults, apoptosis is used to rid the body of cells that have been damaged beyond repair.

This glossary contains terms excerpted from documents produced by several sources deemed reliable.

Apoptosis also plays a role in preventing cancer. If apoptosis is for some reason prevented, it can lead to uncontrolled cell division and the subsequent development of a tumor.

atrophy: A decrease in size or wasting away of a body part or tissue.

autosomal dominant: A pattern of inheritance characteristic of some genetic diseases. "Autosomal" means that the gene in question is located on one of the numbered, or nonsex, chromosomes. "Dominant" means that a single copy of the disease-associated mutation is enough to cause the disease.

autosomal recessive: A pattern of inheritance in which both parents carry and pass on a defective gene to their child.

autosome: Any of the numbered chromosomes, as opposed to the sex chromosomes. Humans have 22 pairs of autosomes and one pair of sex chromosomes (the X and Y). Autosomes are numbered roughly in relation to their sizes. That is, Chromosome 1 has approximately 2,800 genes, while chromosome 22 has approximately 750 genes.

base pair: Two chemical bases bonded to one another forming a "rung of the deoxyribonucleic acid (DNA) ladder." The DNA molecule consists of two strands that wind around each other like a twisted ladder. Each strand has a backbone made of alternating sugar (deoxyribose) and phosphate groups. Attached to each sugar is one of four bases—adenine (A), cytosine (C), guanine (G), or thymine (T). The two strands are held together by hydrogen bonds between the bases, with adenine forming a base pair with thymine, and cytosine forming a base pair with guanine.

beta-blockers: A class of medications also known as beta-adrenergic blockers that affect the body's response to certain nerve impulses. This, in turn, decreases the rate and force of the heart's contractions, which lowers blood pressure and reduces the heart's demand for oxygen. In addition to treating high blood pressure, beta-blockers may be used for angina, and to prevent heart attacks, migraine headaches, and glaucoma.

biopsy: A procedure in which tissue or other material is removed from the body and studied for signs of disease.

birth defect: An abnormality present at birth. Also called a congenital defect, it can be caused by a genetic mutation, an unfavorable environment during pregnancy, or a combination of both. The effect of a birth defect can be mild, severe, or incompatible with life.

bradykinesia: Gradual loss of spontaneous movement.

BRCA1 **and** *BRCA2***:** The first two genes found to be associated with inherited forms of breast cancer. Both genes normally act as tumor suppressors, meaning that they help regulate cell division. When these genes are rendered inactive due to mutation, uncontrolled cell growth results, leading to breast cancer. Women with mutations in either gene have a much higher risk for developing breast cancer than women without mutations in the genes.

cancer: A group of diseases characterized by uncontrolled cell growth. Cancer begins when a single cell mutates, resulting in a breakdown of the normal regulatory controls that keep cell division in check.

carrier: A person who carries a gene for a recessive genetic disorder. The person has the potential to pass the disorder on to his or her child, but is not personally affected by the disorder.

cell: The basic building block of living things. An adult human body is estimated to contain between 10 and 100 trillion cells.

centromere: A constricted region of a chromosome that separates it into a short arm (p) and a long arm (q).

chromosome: An organized package of DNA found in the nucleus of the cell. Different organisms have different numbers of chromosomes. Humans have 23 pairs of chromosomes—22 pairs of numbered chromosomes, called autosomes, and one pair of sex chromosomes, X and Y.

codon: A trinucleotide sequence of DNA or RNA that corresponds to a specific amino acid. There are sixty-four different codons sixty-one specify amino acids while the remaining three are used as stop signals.

collagen: The principal protein of the skin, bones, cartilage, tendons, and other connective tissues.

contracture: Chronic shortening of a muscle or tendon that limits movement of a bony joint, such as the elbow.

copy number variation (CNV): When the number of copies of a particular gene varies from one individual to the next. The extent to which copy number variation contributes to human disease is not yet known. It has long been recognized that some cancers are associated with elevated copy numbers of particular genes.

deep brain stimulation (DBS): A treatment that uses an electrode implanted into part of the brain to stimulate it in a way that temporarily inactivates some of the signals it produces.

deletion: A type of mutation involving the loss of genetic material. It can be small, involving a single missing DNA base pair, or large, involving a piece of a chromosome.

deoxyribonucleic acid (DNA): The chemical name for the molecule that carries genetic instructions in all living things. The DNA molecule consists of two strands that wind around one another to form a shape known as a double helix. Each strand has a backbone made of alternating sugar (deoxyribose) and phosphate groups. Attached to each sugar is one of four bases—adenine (A), cytosine (C), guanine (G), and thymine (T). The two strands are held together by bonds between the bases; adenine bonds with thymine, and cytosine bonds with guanine. The sequence of the bases along the backbones serves as instructions for assembling protein and RNA molecules.

DNA sequencing: A laboratory technique used to determine the exact sequence of bases (A, C, G, and T) in a DNA molecule. The DNA base sequence carries the information a cell needs to assemble protein and RNA molecules. DNA sequence information is important to scientists investigating the functions of genes.

dominant: A genetic trait (or genetically transmitted disorder) that is evident when only one copy of the gene for that trait is present. Most dominant traits are due to genes on the autosomes (nonsex chromosomes). They affect males and females equally.

dopamine: A chemical messenger, deficient in the brains of people with Parkinson disease, that transmits impulses from one nerve cell to another.

double helix: The description of the structure of a DNA molecule. A DNA molecule consists of two strands that wind around each other like a twisted ladder.

duplication: A type of mutation that involves the production of one or more copies of a gene or region of a chromosome. Gene duplication is an important mechanism by which evolution occurs.

dystonia: Involuntary muscle contractions that cause slow repetitive movements or abnormal postures.

dystrophin: A protein that helps maintain the shape and structure of muscle fibers.

Ehlers-Danlos syndrome (EDS): A heritable connective tissue disease characterized by easy bruising, joint laxity (the ability to bend beyond normal range of motion), lax skin, and tissue weakness.

electromyography: A recording and study of the electrical properties of skeletal muscle.

epigenetics: An emerging field of science that studies heritable changes caused by the activation and deactivation of genes without any change in the underlying DNA sequence of the organism.

exon: The portion of a gene that codes for amino acids.

first-degree relative: A family member who shares about 50 percent of their genes with a particular individual in a family. This includes parents, offspring, and siblings.

frameshift mutation: A type of mutation involving the insertion or deletion of a nucleotide in which the number of deleted base pairs is not divisible by three. This is important because the cell reads a gene in groups of three bases. Each group of three bases corresponds to one of 20 different amino acids used to build a protein. If a mutation disrupts this reading frame, then the entire DNA sequence following the mutation will be read incorrectly.

gene: A basic unit of heredity. Genes direct a cell to make proteins and guide almost every aspect of a cell's construction, operation, and repair.

gene expression: The process by which the information encoded in a gene is used to direct the assembly of a protein molecule. The cell reads the sequence of the gene in groups of three bases. Each group of three bases (codon) corresponds to one of twenty different amino acids used to build the protein.

gene regulation: The process of turning genes on and off. Gene regulation ensures that the appropriate genes are expressed at the proper times.

gene therapy: An experimental technique for treating disease by altering the patient's genetic material. Most often, gene therapy works by introducing a healthy copy of a defective gene into the patient's cells.

genetic counseling: The professional interaction between a healthcare provider with specialized knowledge of genetics and an individual or family. The genetic counselor determines whether a condition in the family may be genetic and estimates the chances that another relative may be affected.

genetic mutation: A permanent change in a gene that can be passed on to children. The rare, early-onset familial form of Alzheimer disease is associated with mutations in genes on chromosomes 21, 14, and 1.

genetic risk factor: A change in a gene that increases a person's risk of developing a disease.

genetic testing: The use of a laboratory test to look for genetic variations associated with a disease. The results of a genetic test can be used to confirm or rule out a suspected genetic disease or to determine the likelihood of a person passing on a mutation to their offspring.

genetic variant: A change in a gene that may increase or decrease a person's risk of developing a disease or condition.

genome: An organism's complete set of DNA, including all of its genes. Each genome contains all of the information needed to build and maintain that organism.

genomics: The study of the entire genome of an organism.

heritable: Capable of being transmitted from parent to child through genes.

heterozygous: Having inherited different forms of a particular gene from each parent.

homocystinuria: A genetically transmitted disease in which an enzyme deficiency permits the buildup of the amino acid homocysteine. The result, if not treated, can be mental retardation, blood vessel disease, and atherosclerosis (hardening of the arteries).

insertion: A type of mutation involving the addition of genetic material.

karyotype: An individual's collection of chromosomes.

linkage: The close association of genes or other DNA sequences on the same chromosome.

lordosis: An abnormal forward curving of the spine.

Marfan syndrome: A heritable disorder of connective tissue resulting from mutations in the gene that specifies the genetic code for fibrillin-1, a protein important to connective tissue. The disorder is characterized by excessively long leg bones and long "spider-like" fingers. Other problems include skeletal malformations, abnormal position of the lens of the eye, and enlargement at the beginning part of the aorta, the major vessel carrying blood away from the heart. If left untreated, an enlarged aorta can lead to hemorrhage and even death.

marker: A DNA sequence with a known physical location on a chromosome. Markers can help link an inherited disease with the responsible genes.

mitochondrial DNA (mtDNA): The small circular chromosome found inside mitochondria. The mitochondria are organelles found in cells that are the sites of energy production.

mitosis: A cellular process that replicates chromosomes and produces two identical nuclei in preparation for cell division.

monosomy: The state of having a single copy of a chromosome pair instead of the usual two copies found in diploid cells. Monosomy can be partial if a portion of the second chromosome copy is present. Monosomy, or partial monosomy, is the cause of some human diseases such as Turner syndrome and Cri-du-Chat syndrome.

muscle wasting: A decrease in muscle strength and size.

mutations: Changes in genes that can occur randomly or as a result of some factor in the environment.

myopathy: Any disorder of muscle tissue or muscles.

neuropathy: Nervous system disease or dysfunction that may cause symptoms including muscle weakness, loss of muscle bulk, muscle cramps and spasms, and pain.

neurotransmitters: Chemicals which carry messages from one nerve cell, or neuron, to another.

newborn screening: Testing performed on newborn babies to detect a wide variety of disorders. Typically, testing is performed on a blood sample obtained from a heel prick when the baby is two or three days old.

nonsense mutation: The substitution of a single base pair that leads to the appearance of a stop codon where previously there was a codon specifying an amino acid. The presence of this premature stop codon results in the production of a shortened, and likely nonfunctional, protein.

osteogenesis imperfecta: A condition that results from mutation in two genes that make type I collagen, a protein important to bones and teeth. These mutations cause the body to either make too little collagen or poor-quality collagen. The result includes bones that fracture easily, low muscle mass, and joints and ligaments that move beyond their intended range of motion.

parkinsonism: A term referring to a group of conditions that are characterized by four typical symptoms—tremor, rigidity, postural instability, and bradykinesia.

pharmacogenomics: A branch of pharmacology concerned with using DNA and amino acid sequence data to inform drug development and testing. An important application of pharmacogenomics is correlating individual genetic variation with drug responses.

point mutation: When a single base pair is altered. Point mutations can have one of three effects. First, the base substitution can be a silent mutation where the altered codon corresponds to the same amino acid. Second, the base substitution can be a missense mutation where the altered codon corresponds to a different amino acid. Or third, the base substitution can be a nonsense mutation where the altered codon corresponds to a stop signal.

polymorphism: One of two or more variants of a particular DNA sequence. The most common type of polymorphism involves variation at a single base pair. Polymorphisms can also be much larger in size and involve long stretches of DNA. Called a single nucleotide polymorphism, or SNP (pronounced snip), scientists are studying how SNPs in the human genome correlate with disease, drug response, and other phenotypes.

protein: A substance that determines the physical and chemical characteristics of a cell and, therefore, of an organism. Proteins are essential to all cell functions and are created using genetic information.

recessive: A genetic trait or disorder that is usually expressed when only two copies of a gene for that trait, one from each parent, are present.

ribosome: A cellular particle made of RNA and protein that serves as the site for protein synthesis in the cell. The ribosome reads the sequence of the messenger RNA (mRNA) and, using the genetic code, translates the sequence of RNA bases into a sequence of amino acids.

rigidity: A symptom of the disease in which muscles feel stiff and display resistance to movement even when another person tries to move the affected part of the body, such as an arm.

ribonucleic acid (RNA): A molecule similar to DNA. Unlike DNA, RNA is single-stranded. An RNA strand has a backbone made of alternating sugar (ribose) and phosphate groups. Attached to each sugar is one of four bases—adenine (A), uracil (U), cytosine (C), or guanine (G). Different types of RNA exist in the cell messenger RNA (mRNA), ribosomal RNA (rRNA), and transfer RNA (tRNA).

scoliosis: An abnormal lateral, or sideways, curving of the spine.

sex chromosome: A type of chromosome that participates in sex determination. Humans and most other mammals have two sex chromosomes, the X and the Y. Females have two X chromosomes in their cells, while males have both X and a Y chromosomes in their cells.

somatic cell: Any cell of the body except sperm and egg cells. Somatic cells are diploid, meaning that they contain two sets of chromosomes, one inherited from each parent.

stem cell: A cell with the potential to form many of the different cell types found in the body. When stem cells divide, they can form more stem cells or other cells that perform specialized functions.

substantia nigra: Movement-control center in the brain where loss of dopamine-producing nerve cells triggers the symptoms of PD; substantia nigra means "black substance," so called because the cells in this area are dark.

susceptibility: A condition of the body that increases the likelihood that the individual will develop a particular disease. Susceptibility is influenced by a combination of genetic and environmental factors.

syndrome: A collection of recognizable traits or abnormalities that tend to occur together and are associated with a specific disease.

telomere: The end of a chromosome. Telomeres are made of repetitive sequences of noncoding DNA that protect the chromosome from damage. Each time a cell divides, the telomeres become shorter. Eventually, the telomeres become so short that the cell can no longer divide.

trait: A specific characteristic of an organism. Traits can be determined by genes or the environment, or more commonly by interactions between them. The genetic contribution to a trait is called the genotype. The outward expression of the genotype is called the phenotype.

transcription: The process of making an RNA copy of a gene sequence. This copy, called a messenger RNA (mRNA) molecule, leaves the cell nucleus and enters the cytoplasm, where it directs the synthesis of the protein, which it encodes.

transfer RNA (tRNA): small RNA molecule that participates in protein synthesis. Each tRNA molecule has two important areas a trinucleotide region called the anticodon and a region for attaching a specific amino acid. During translation, each time an amino acid is added to the growing chain, a tRNA molecule forms base pairs with its complementary sequence on the messenger RNA (mRNA) molecule, ensuring that the appropriate amino acid is inserted into the protein.

translation: The process of translating the sequence of a messenger RNA (mRNA) molecule to a sequence of amino acids during protein synthesis.

translocation: A type of chromosomal abnormality in which a chromosome breaks and a portion of it reattaches to a different chromosome.

tremor: Shakiness or trembling, often in a hand, which in PD is usually most apparent when the affected part is at rest.

X chromosome: One of two sex chromosomes.

X-linked recessive: A pattern of disease inheritance in which the mother carries the affected gene on the chromosome that determines the child's sex and passes it to her son.

X-ray: A type of high-energy radiation. In low doses, X-rays are used to diagnose diseases by making pictures of the inside of the body.

Y chromosome: One of two sex chromosomes.

Chapter 75

Sources of Further Help and Information Related to Genetic Disorders

General

Eunice Kennedy Shriver
National Institute of
Child Health and Human
Development (NICHD)
P.O. Box 3006
Rockville, MD 20847
Toll-Free: 800-370-2943
Toll-Free TTY: 888-320-6942
Toll-Free Fax: 866-760-5947
Website: www.nichd.nih.gov
E-mail: NICHDInformation
ResourceCenter@mail.nih.gov

Genetics Home Reference
(GHR)
National Institutes of Health
(NIH)
8600 Rockville Pike
Bethesda, MD 20894
Website: ghr.nlm.nih.gov

National Digestive Diseases
Information Clearinghouse
(NDDIC)
Two Information Way
Bethesda, MD 20892-3570
Toll-Free: 800-891-5389
Phone: 301-654-3810
Fax: 703-738-4929
Website: www.ninds.nih.gov
E-mail: nddic@info.niddk.nih.gov

Resources in this chapter were compiled from several sources deemed reliable; all contact information was verified and updated in March 2019.

National Heart, Lung, and Blood Institute (NHLBI)
31 Center Dr.
Bethesda, MD 20892
Website: www.nhlbi.nih.gov
E-mail: nhlbiinfo@nhlbi.nih.gov

National Human Genome Research Institute (NHGRI)
Communications and Public Liaison Branch
Bldg. 31, Rm. 4B09
9000 Rockville Pike
Bethesda, MD 20892-2152
Phone: 301-402-0911
Fax: 301-402-2218
Website: www.genome.gov
E-mail: nhgripressoffice@mail.nih.gov

National Institute of Arthritis and Musculoskeletal and Skin Diseases (NIAMS)
NIAMS Information Clearinghouse
One AMS Cir.
Bethesda, MD 20892-3675
Toll-Free: 877-22-NIAMS (877-226-4267)
Phone: 301-495-4484
TTY: 301-565-2966
Fax: 301-718-6366
Website: www.niams.nih.gov/about/contact-us
E-mail: NIAMSinfo@mail.nih.gov

National Institute of Diabetes and Digestive and Kidney Diseases (NIDDK)
Office of Communications and Public Liaison (OCPL)
Bldg. 31, Rm. 9A06
31 Center Dr., MSC 2560
Bethesda, MD 20892-2560
Toll-Free: 800-472-0424
Phone: 301-496-3583
Website: www.niddk.nih.gov/health-information/endocrine-diseases/national-hormone-pituitary-program/comprehensive-report
E-mail: niddkinquiries@nih.gov

National Institute of General Medical Sciences (NIGMS)
Office of Communications and Public Liaison (OCPL)
45 Center Dr.
MSC 6200
Bethesda, MD 20892-6200
Phone: 301-496-7301
Website: www.nigms.nih.gov
E-mail: info@nigms.nih.gov

National Institute of Neurological Disorders and Stroke (NINDS)
31 Center Dr.
Rm. 8A07, MSC 2540
Bethesda, MD 20892-2540
Toll-Free: 800-352-9424
Phone: 301-496-5751
Fax: 301-402-2186
Website: www.ninds.nih.gov
E-mail: braininfo@ninds.nih.gov

Albinism

National Organization for Albinism and Hypopigmentation (NOAH)
P.O. Box 959
East Hampstead, NH 03826-0959
Toll-Free: 800-473-2310 (United States and Canada)
Phone: 603-887-2310
Fax: 603-887-6049
Website: www.albinism.org
E-mail: info@albinism.org

Angelman Syndrome

Angelman Syndrome Foundation (ASF)
75 Executive Dr.
Ste. 327
Aurora, IL 60504
Toll-Free: 800-432-6435
Phone: 630-978-4245
Fax: 630-978-7408
Website: www.angelman.org
E-mail: info@angelman.org

Canadian Angelman Syndrome Society (CASS)
P.O. Box 68195
Crowfoot P.O.
CALGARY, AB, T3G 3N8
Canada
Website: www.angelmancanada.org

Blood Disorders

American Hemochromatosis Society (AHS)
4044 W. Lake Mary Blvd.
PMB 416
Lake Mary, FL 32746-2012
Toll-Free: 888-655-IRON (888-655-4766)
Phone: 407-829-4488
Fax: 561-266-9038
Website: www.americanhs.org
E-mail: mail@americanhs.org

Canadian Fanconi Anemia Research Fund
P.O. Box 38157
Toronto, ON M5N 3A9
Canada
Phone: 416-489-6393
Fax: 416-489-6393
Website: www.fanconicanada.org
E-mail: admin@fanconicanada.org

Fanconi Anemia Research Fund
1801 Willamette St.
Ste. 200
Eugene, OR 97401
Toll-Free: 888-FANCONI (888-326-2664)
Phone: 541-687-4658
Website: www.fanconi.org
E-mail: info@fanconi.org

Iron Disorders Institute
P.O. Box 4891
Greenville, SC 29608
Website: www.irondisorders.org
E-mail: info@irondisorders.org

National Hemophilia Foundation (NHF)
Seven Penn Plaza.
Ste. 1204
New York, NY 10001
Phone: 212-328-3700
Fax: 212-328-3777
Website: www.hemophilia.org

Sickle Cell Disease Association of America (SCDAA)
3700 Koppers St.
Ste. 570
Baltimore, MD 21227
Toll-Free: 800-421-8453
Phone: 410-528-1555
Fax: 410-528-1495
Website: www.sicklecelldisease.org
E-mail: admin@sicklecelldisease.org

CHARGE Syndrome

The CHARGE Syndrome Foundation
318 Half Day Rd.
Ste. 305
Buffalo Grove, IL 60089
Toll-Free: 800-442-7604
Phone: 516-684-4720
Toll-Free Fax: 888-317-4735
Fax: 516-883-9060
Website: www.chargesyndrome.org
E-mail: info@chargesyndrome.org

Connective Tissue Disorders

Canadian Marfan Association (CMA)
Centre Plaza Postal Outlet
128 Queen St. S.
P.O. Box 42257
Mississauga, ON L5M 4Z0
Canada
Toll-Free: 866-722-1722
Phone: 905-826-3223
Website: www.gadacanada.ca
E-mail: info@gadacanada.ca

Cornelia de Lange Syndrome Foundation (CdLS)
302 W. Main St.
Ste. 100
Avon, CT 06001
Toll-Free: 800-753-2357;
800-223-8355
Phone: 860-676-8166;
860-676-8255
Fax: 860-676-8337
Website: www.cdlsusa.org
E-mail: info@cdlsusa.org

Ehlers-Danlos National Foundation (EDNF)
1760 Old Meadow Rd.
Ste. 500
McLean, VA 22102
Website: www.ednf.org
E-mail: ednfstaff@ednf.org

National Marfan Foundation (NMF)
22 Manhasset Ave.
Port Washington, NY 11050
Toll-Free: 800-862-7326
Phone: 516-883-8712
Fax: 516-883-8040
Website: www.marfan.org
E-mail: staff@marfan.org

Osteogenesis Imperfecta Foundation (OIF)
804 W. Diamond Ave., Ste. 210
Gaithersburg, MD 20878
Toll-Free: 800-981-2663
Phone: 301-947-0083
Fax: 301-947-0456
Website: www.oif.org
E-mail: bonelink@oif.org

Cystic Fibrosis

Cystic Fibrosis Foundation (CFF)
4550 Montgomery Ave.
Ste. 1100 N.
Bethesda, MD 20814
Toll-Free: 800-FIGHT-CF
(800-344-4823)
Phone: 301-951-4422
Fax: 301-951-6378
Website: www.cff.org
E-mail: info@cff.org

Fragile X Syndrome

FRAXA Research Foundation
10 Prince Pl., Ste. 203
Newburyport, MA 01950
Phone: 978-462-1866
Website: www.fraxa.org
E-mail: info@fraxa.org

National Fragile X Foundation (FXS)
1861 International Dr.
Ste. 200
McLean, VA 22102
Toll-Free: 800-688-8765
Fax: 925-938-9315
Website: www.fragilex.org
E-mail: natlfx@fragilex.org

Gene Therapy

American Society of Gene & Cell Therapy (ASGCT)
555 E. Wells St.
Ste. 1100
Milwaukee, WI 53202
Phone: 414-278-1341
Fax: 414-276-3349
Website: www.asgct.org
E-mail: info@asgct.org

Huntington Disease

Huntington's Disease Society of America (HDSA)
505 Eighth Ave.
Ste. 902
New York, NY 10018
Toll-Free: 800-345-HDSA
(800-345-4372)
Phone: 212-242-1968
Fax: 212-239-3430
Website: www.hdsa.org
E-mail: hdsainfo@hdsa.org

Jewish Genetic Disorders

Center for Jewish Genetics (CJG)
30 S. Wells St.
Chicago, IL 60606
Phone: 312-346-6700
Website: www.jewishgenetics.org
E-mail: jewishgeneticsctr@juf.org

Leukodystrophy

United Leukodystrophy Foundation (ULF)
224 N. Second St., Ste. 2
DeKalb, IL 60115
Toll-Free: 800-728-5483
Phone: 815-748-3211
Fax: 815-748-0844
Website: www.ulf.org
E-mail: office@ulf.org

Lipid Storage Diseases

Batten Disease Support and Research Association (BDSRA)
2780 Airport Dr., Ste. 342
Columbus, OH 43219
Toll-Free: 800-448-4570
Toll-Free Fax: 866-648-8718
Website: www.bdsra.org
E-mail: bdsra1@bdsra.org

Canadian Fabry Association (CFA)
748 Kelly St.
Thunder Bay, ON P7E 2A1
Canada
Website: www.fabrycanada.com

Children's Brain Disease Foundation (CBDF)
350 Parnassus Ave.
Ste. 900
San Francisco, CA 94117
Phone: 415-665-3003
Fax: 415-665-3003
Website: rarediseases.org

Children's Gaucher Research Fund (CGRF)
8110 Warren Ct.
Granite Bay, CA 95746
Phone: 916-797-3700
Fax: 916-797-3707
Website: www.childrensgaucher.org
E-mail: research@childrensgaucher.org

Fabry Support & Information Group (FSIG)
108 N.E. Second St.
Ste. C, P.O. Box 510
Concordia, MO 64020-0510
Phone: 660-463-1355
Website: www.fabry.org
E-mail: info@fabry.org

Nathan's Battle Foundation [For Batten Disease Research]
459 State Rd. 135 S.
Greenwood, IN 46142
Phone: 317-888-7396
Fax: 317-888-0504
Website: www.nathansbattle.com
E-mail: pmilto@indy.net

National Fabry Disease Foundation (NFDF)
4301 Connecticut Ave. N.W.
Ste. 404
Washington, DC 20008-2369
Toll-Free: 800-651-9131
Fax: 919-932-7786
Website: www.fabrydisease.org
E-mail: info@fabrydisease.org

National Gaucher Foundation (NGF)
5410 Edson Ln.
Ste. 220
Rockville, MD 20852
Toll-Free: 800-504-3189
Fax: 920-563-0931
Website: www.gaucherdisease.org
E-mail: ngf@gaucherdisease.org

National Niemann-Pick Disease Foundation, Inc. (NNPDF)
401 Madison Ave.
Ste. B, P.O. Box 49
Fort Atkinson, WI 53538
Toll-Free: 877-CURE-NPC
(877-287-3672)
Phone: 920-563-0930
Website: www.nnpdf.org
E-mail: nnpdf@nnpdf.org

National Tay-Sachs and Allied Diseases Association (NTSAD)
2001 Beacon St.
Ste. 204
Boston, MA 02135
Toll-Free: 800-90-NTSAD
(800-906-8723)
Phone: 617-277-4463
Fax: 617-277-0134
Website: www.ntsad.org
E-mail: info@ntsad.org

Mitochondrial Diseases

Children's Tumor Foundation (CTF)
120 Wall St.
16th Fl.
New York, NY 10005-3904
Toll-Free: 800-323-7938
Phone: 212-344-6633
Fax: 212-747-0004
Website: www.ctf.org
E-mail: info@ctf.org

Neurofibromatosis Acoustic Neuroma Association (ANA)
600 Peachtree Pkwy
Ste. 108
Cumming, GA 30041-6899
Toll-Free: 877-200-8211
Phone: 770-205-8211
Toll-Free Fax: 877-202-0239
Fax: 770-205-0239
Website: www.anausa.org
E-mail: info@anausa.org

Neurofibromatosis Network
213 S. Wheaton Ave.
Wheaton, IL 60187
Toll-Free: 800-942-6825
Phone: 630-510-1115
Fax: 630-510-8508
Website: www.nfnetwork.org
E-mail: admin@nfnetwork.org

United Mitochondrial Disease Foundation (UMDF)
8085 Saltsburg Rd.
Ste. 201
Pittsburgh, PA 15239
Toll-Free: 888-317-UMDF
(888-317-8633)
Phone: 412-793-8077
Fax: 412-793-6477
Website: www.umdf.org
E-mail: info@umdf.org

Neuromuscular Disorders

Charcot-Marie-Tooth Association (CMTA)
P.O. Box 105
Glenolden, PA 19036
Toll-Free: 800-606-CMTA
(800-606-2682)
Phone: 610-499-9264
Fax: 610-499-9267
Website: www.cmtausa.org
E-mail: info@cmtausa.org

Coalition to Cure Calpain 3
Website: www.curecalpain3.org
E-mail: info@curecalpain3.org

Cure Congenital Muscular Dystrophy (CMD)
19401 S. Vermont Ave.
Ste. J100
Torrance, CA 90502
Website: www.curecmd.org
E-mail: info@curecmd.com

Facioscapulohumeral Muscular Dystrophy (FSH) Society
450 Bedford St.
Lexington, MA 02420
Phone: 781-301-6060
Fax: 781-862-1116
Website: www.fshsociety.org
E-mail: info@fshsociety.org

Families of Spinal Muscular Atrophy (SMA)
925 Busse Rd.
Elk Grove Village, IL 60007
Toll-Free: 800-886-1762
Phone: 847-367-7620
Fax: 847-367-7623
Website: www.curesma.org
E-mail: info@fsma.org

Friedreich's Ataxia Research Alliance (FARA)
533 W. Uwchlan Ave.
Downingtown, PA 19335
Phone: 484-879-6160
Fax: 484-872-1402
Website: info@curefa.org
E-mail: info@curefa.org

Hereditary Neuropathy Foundation (HNF)
432 Park Ave. S.
Fourth Fl.
New York, NY 10016
Toll-Free: 855-HELPCMT
(855-435-7268)
Phone: 212-722-8396
Fax: 917-591-2758
Website: www.hnf-cure.org
E-mail: info@hnf-cure.org

Jain Foundation
9725 Third Ave. N.E., Ste. 204
Seattle, Washington 98115
Phone: 425-882-1492
Fax: 425-658-1703
Website: www.jain-foundation.
org
E-mail: admin@jain-foundation.
org

Muscular Dystrophy Association (MDA)
National Office
161 N. Clark
Ste. 3550
Chicago, Illinois 60601
Toll-Free: 800-572-1717
Phone: 520-529-2000
Website: www.mda.org
E-mail: mda@mdausa.org

Muscular Dystrophy Family Fund
P.O. Box 776
Carmel, IN 46082
United Kingdom
Phone: 317-249-8488 or
317-615-9140
Fax: 317-853-6743
Website: www.mdff.org

Myotonic Dystrophy Foundation (MDF)
1004-A O'Reilly Ave.
San Francisco, CA 94129
Toll-Free: 866-968-6642
Phone: 415-800-7777
Website: www.myotonic.org
E-mail: info@myotonic.org

National Ataxia Foundation (NAF)
600 Hwy 169 S., Ste. 1725
Minneapolis, MN 55426
Phone: 763-553-0020
Fax: 763-553-0167
Website: www.ataxia.org
E-mail: naf@ataxia.org

Neuropathy Association
60 E. 42nd St.
Ste. 942
New York, NY 10165-0999
Toll-Free: 888-PN-FACTS
(888-763-2287)
Phone: 212-692-0662
Fax: 212-692-0668
Website: www.neuropathy.org
E-mail: info@neuropathy.org

Parent Project Muscular Dystrophy (PPMD)
401 Hackensack Ave.
Ninth Fl.
Hackensack, NJ 07601
Toll-Free: 800-714-KIDS
(800-714-5437)
Phone: 201-250-8440
Fax: 201-250-8435
Website: www.parentprojectmd.
org
E-mail: info@parentprojectmd.
org

Spastic Paraplegia Foundation (SPF)
1605 Goularte Pl.
Fremont, CA 94539-7241
Toll-Free: 877-SPF-GIVE
(877-773-4483)
Website: www.sp-foundation.org
E-mail: information@
sp-foundation.org

Spinal Muscular Atrophy Foundation (SMA)
888 Seventh Ave.
Ste. 400
New York, NY 10019
Toll-Free: 877-FUND-SMA
(877-386-3762)
Phone: 646-253-7100
Fax: 212-247-3079
Website: www.smafoundation.
org
E-mail: info@smafoundation.org

Porphyria

American Porphyria Foundation (APF)
4915 St. Elmo Ave.
Ste. 105
Bethesda, MD 20814
Toll-Free: 866-APF-3635
(866-273-3635)
Phone: 713-266-9617
Fax: 713-840-9552
Website: www.
porphyriafoundation.org
E-mail: porphyrus@
porphyriafoundation.com

Prader-Willi Syndrome

Foundation for Prader-Willi Research (PWS)
340 S. Lemon Ave.
Ste. 3620
Walnut, CA 91789
Toll-Free: 888-322-5487
Website: www.fpwr.org
E-mail: info@fpwr.org

Prader-Willi Syndrome Association (PWSA) (USA)
8588 Potter Park Dr.
Ste. 500
Sarasota, FL 34238
Toll-Free: 800-926-4797
Phone: 941-312-0400
Fax: 941-312-0142
Website: www.pwsausa.org

Retinoblastoma

Retinoblastoma International
18030 Brookhurst St.
P.O. Box 408
Fountain Valley, CA 92708
Website: www.retinoblastoma.
net
E-mail: info@retinoblastoma.net

Rett Syndrome

International Rett Syndrome Foundation (IRSF)
4600 Devitt Dr.
Cincinnati, OH 45246
Toll-Free: 800-818-7388
Website: www.rettsyndrome.org
E-mail: admin@rettsyndrome.
org

Rett Syndrome Research Trust (RSRT)
67 Under Cliff Rd.
Trumbull, CT 06611
Phone: 203-445-0041
Website: www.rsrt.org

Smith-Magenis Syndrome

Parents and Researchers Interested in Smith-Magenis Syndrome (PRISMS)
21800 Town Center Plaza
Ste. 266A-633
Sterling, VA 20164
Phone: 972-231-0035
Fax: 972-499-1832
Website: www.prisms.org
E-mail: hgraf@prisms.org

Smith-Magenis Syndrome (SMS) Research Foundation
P.O. Box 661
Georgetown, CT 06829-0661
Phone: 203-450-9022
Website: www.
smsresearchfoundation.org
E-mail: info@
smsresearchfoundation.org

Trisomy Disorders

National Association for Down Syndrome (NADS)
1460 Renaissance Dr.
Ste. 102
Park Ridge, IL 60068
Phone: 630-325-9112
Website: www.nads.org
E-mail: info@nads.org

National Down Syndrome Congress (NDSC)
30 Mansell Ct.
Ste. 108
Roswell, GA 30076
Toll-Free: 800-232-NDSC
(800-232-6372)
Phone: 770-604-9500
Fax: 770-604-9898
Website: www.ndsccenter.org
E-mail: info@ndsccenter.org

National Down Syndrome Society (NDSS)
8 E. 41st Ste.
Eighth Fl.
New York, NY 10017
Toll-Free: 800-221-4602
Fax: 646-870-9320
Website: www.ndss.org
E-mail: info@ndss.org

Trisomy 18 Foundation
4491 Cheshire Stn Plaza
Ste. 157
Dale City, VA 22193
Phone: 810-867-4211
Website: www.trisomy18.org
E-mail: T18info@trisomy18.org

Tuberous Sclerosis

Tuberous Sclerosis Alliance
801 Roeder Rd.
Ste. 750
Silver Spring, MD 20910-4487
Toll-Free: 800-225-6872
Phone: 301-562-9890
Fax: 301-562-9870
Website: www.tsalliance.org
E-mail: info@tsalliance.org

Tuberous Sclerosis Canada (TSC)
P.O. Box 35057 Essa Rd. RO
Barrie, ON L4N 5Z2
Canada
Website: www.tscanada.ca
E-mail: TSCanadaST@gmail.
com

Urea Cycle Disorders

National Urea Cycle Disorders Foundation (NUCDF)
75 S. Grand Ave.
Pasadena, CA 91105
Toll-Free: 800-38-NUCDF
(800-386-8233)
Phone: 626-578-0833
Fax: 626-578-0823
Website: www.nucdf.org
E-mail: info@nucdf.org

Vision Disorders

Glaucoma Associates of Texas (GAT)
10740 N. Central Expy.
Ste. 300
Dallas, TX 75231
Phone: 214-360-0000
Fax: 214-739-8562
Website: www.
glaucomaassociates.com
E-mail: ablankenship@
glaucomaassociates.com

Glaucoma Research Foundation (GRF)
251 Post St.
Ste. 600
San Francisco, CA 94108
Toll-Free: 800-826-6693
Phone: 415-986-3162
Fax: 415-986-3763
Website: www.glaucoma.org
E-mail: question@glaucoma.org

Williams Syndrome

Williams Syndrome Association (WSA)
570 Kirts Blvd.
Ste. 223
Troy, MI 48084-4156
Toll-Free: 800-806-1871
Phone: 248-244-2229
Fax: 248-244-2230
Website: www.williams-
syndrome.org
E-mail: info@williams-syndrome.
org

Wilson Disease

Wilson Disease Association (WDA)
1732 First Ave.
Ste. 20043
New York, NY 10128
Toll-Free: 866-961-0533
Phone: 414-961-0533
Fax: 414-962-3886
Website: www.wilsonsdisease.
org
E-mail: info@wilsonsdisease.org

Index

Index

Page numbers followed by 'n' indicate a footnote. Page numbers in *italics* indicate a table or illustration.

729